The North Americans

James R. Christopher

Oxford University Press
Toronto

Oxford University Press, 70 Wynford Drive, Don Mills, Ontario, M3C 1J9
Toronto   Oxford   New York   Delhi   Bombay   Calcutta   Madras   Karachi
Petaling Jaya   Singapore   Hong Kong   Tokyo   Nairobi   Dar es Salaam
Cape Town   Melborne   Auckland
and associated companies in
Berlin   Ibadan
Oxford is a trademark of Oxford University Press

Canadian Cataloguing in Publication Data

Christopher, James R., 1951–
    The North Americans

Bibliography: p. 684
Includes index.
ISBN 0-19-540740-7

1. Canada — History. 2. United States — History. I. Title.
E45.C48 1988   970   C88-093380-1

Designer: **Christine Alexiou**
Illustrator: **Christine Alexiou**
Production Manager: **Joanna Gertler**
Project Editor: **Geraldine Kikuta**
Editor: **Loralee Case**
Editorial Assistance: **Elizabeth Long, Deborah Giles**
Photo Researchers: **Sandra Lafortune**
Compositor: **Q Composition Inc.**
Printed and bound in Canada by Gagné Printing Ltd.
1 2 3 4 5 6 7 8 9   96 95 94 93 92 91 89

Contents

Preface

When one of my students asked me what this book is about, I told her that it is a look at the commonality of the North American experience. She laughed and asked how a hard-core Canadian nationalist like myself could ever write such a thing!

It was a legitimate question. For years I had been indoctrinating my students with all of the intimate details of the uniquely Canadian experience. Now, it seemed, I had thrown all that away in favour of a continentalist vision of society. The reality, however, is something quite different.

Canadians and Americans have long shared a common continental experience. This book is a journey from the late fifteenth century to the present in which we examine some of the characteristics of that experience. It is not a study of parallel national histories, nor is it a study of two faces of the same coin. It is a combination of both.

North Americans, from their vantage point across the Atlantic, have little difficulty in identifying the commonalities of the European experience. Few Canadians decry comparing the British experience with that of the German, or the French with that of the Russian. From our perspective the historical parallels of this geographically confined group of nations seem painfully obvious. No Canadian student would say that Britain and Germany industrialized at the same time, or that France and Russia staged coincidental anti-aristocratic revolutions. In the European case we are quite willing to recognize that events do not have to happen in exactly the same fashion or at precisely the same time to be comparable. Are we as open-minded about our own history? Or are we chauvinistic enough to feel that each and every sequence of Canadian events is a sacrosanct and unique development without parallel elsewhere?

Our national history is important to us, but it becomes even more significant when compared with that of the United States. Canada and the United States are North American nations. If the European experience holds true on this continent, then generalizations and parallels on which we draw so effectively in the study of their continent should prove to be effective tools in the study of our own.

The North Americans looks at the evidence. Together we will consider many aspects of our historical past. Using the speeches, diaries, letters, and photographs of the people who took part in events, we will reconstruct that past as they saw and lived it. From the cultural issues surrounding contact; to the political issues of revolution and national identity; through the social and economic problems of industrialization and urbanization; to the foreign policy and domestic concerns of the modern world, we will examine the combined experiences that have made us Canadians. At the same time, the "laboratory" of North America has given us a neighbour to hold up for comparison. The United States has been our alter ego from the days of New France. Reflected in its image we are able to gain greater insights into our own character. Revolution, the frontier, the development of the federal state, imperialism, the Depression, and the affluent society all had their impact on the two neighbours.

Faced with similar problems, Canadians often chose a different path from the

United States. Our "parallel" histories resemble more the congruent spirals of a North American DNA than the twin rails of a transcontinental railway. As our paths have crossed and recrossed, our national and personal lives have never ceased to influence one another.

This book is not a history of Canada, with a few American examples thrown in. Nor is it an American text sprinkled with Canadian crumbs. This book is about North America from a Canadian perspective. We have prospered alongside our powerful neighbour by learning from its successes and its failures. But although we have taken a distinctly Canadian route, it has been a North American journey, and in that journey we have not been alone.

Acknowledgements

In many ways writing *The North Americans* was a bit like writing two books at once. On one side is the narrative account of the history of the North Americans. It presents a commentary on the response of the two nations to a set of common experiences. The other book is a collection of documents. Taken from both Canada and the United States these primary sources provide a "window on the past" from the point of the view of people living at the time.

To write two books at once was something that I never could have done without the advice and support of a wide range of people. On the professional side I owe a debt of thanks to Paul Rutherford and Michael Wayne from the University of Toronto, whose insights helped me to develop an understanding and appreciation of Canada in a North American perspective; Patricia Baker of Leaside High School, who first successfully field-tested the concept behind this book; Bryan Vickers and Bill Atwell for their advice and encouragement; and especially librarian Debbie Chorney who helped bring a clear organizational focus to a seemingly endless number of documents and resources.

Editorially, a strong staff at Oxford helped to bail me out again. Editor Loralee Case smoothed out my prose and second-guessed my interpretation; Elizabeth Long played the role of primary source detective. Working with fragments of information, she traced obscure sources and bartered for permission to print the documents in the book. Deborah Giles and Kim Hall spent hours keyboarding text.

Of course, once again my personal devil, Geraldine Kikuta, coaxed, bullied, and masterfully piloted my work from a random collection of discs and files to become a cohesive and balanced whole. As usual this book is as much a testimony to her organizational genius as it is to my writing.

Finally, this book was once again purchased with the infinite patience of my family. Tennis, swimming, skiing, the Science Centre, the museum, and even the Blue Jays took a back seat to the library, the archives, and the word processor. So to Brett, Brandon, Mary-Kate, and especially Wendy, thank you. By the time you read this I hope that I will have made up for some of our lost time together.

1
CANADA IN A NORTH AMERICAN PERSPECTIVE

> We are building a new society in Canada. It should not be surprising that
> the external manifestations of this society may be somewhat different than
> has been the case in the past. But just as one of the invariable principles of
> that domestic society is the primacy of the individual, so is one of the
> invariables of our foreign policy genuine friendship with the United States.

When Prime Minister Pierre Elliot Trudeau spoke these words to the National
Press Club in Washington almost twenty years ago, he was simply stating the
obvious. For people living in what we call Canada, the past two centuries of history
have been immediately effected by the "twitches and grunts" of our southern
neighbour. To much of the world it is one of the oddities of history that two
nations, sharing a continent, a majority language, a common political and cultural
heritage, and an integrated economic system could actually exist separately. It is
even more astonishing, in fact, when one takes into consideration both the difference in population of the two countries and the concept of Manifest Destiny
taken for granted so often in the past by citizens of the United States. Why might
such a situation develop? Trudeau felt that he had the answer: "Americans should
never underestimate the constant pressure upon Canada which the mere presence
of the United States has produced. We are a different people from you. We are
a different people partly because of you."

Citizens of Canada and the United States think of themselves as North Americans. It is a label which geographically should also apply to the citizens of Mexico,
Central America, and the Caribbean. The fact that it really doesn't is evident in
American racist attitudes at the time of the Mexican War, but it is also in a very
real sense a product of a common colonial experience. When Britain and France
brought the culture of the northern renaissance to the territory east of the Rocky
Mountains they established an intellectual and cultural base that has survived
intact to the present.

Canadians, as implied by Trudeau, have often defined themselves in terms of
their differences from the United States. The inhabitants of the old Province of
Quebec saw a difference at the time of the Revolution, as did the Loyalists and
their collective successors in the Canadas in the first half of the nineteenth century.

In 1865 Sir George Etienne Cartier summed up the case for Confederation this
way: "Either we must obtain British American Confederation or be absorbed in
an American Confederation." One hundred and twenty-two years later, popular
Canadian historian Pierre Berton was still sounding the same tune, this time in
reference to the free trade deal negotiated by the cabinet of Brian Mulroney and
Ronald Reagan's White House: "If this goes through, and it's only the thin wedge,
in a quarter of a century we may as well ask for a vote in congress."

In January 1988 *Maclean's* magazine published the results of a national poll
which, in part, measured Canadian attitudes with regard to the United States. An

overwhelming majority of those polled said that Canadians were different from Americans (33 percent significantly, 46 percent slightly). A majority of the same people also believed that Canadians performed better or at least as well as Americans in such areas as news coverage (82 percent), political leadership (78 percent), literature (77 percent), music (73 percent), business (63 percent), and film production (54 percent). Americans held the edge in areas such as television (78 percent) and science and technology (82 percent). Canadians saw themselves as more concerned about the environment and about the poor than their southern neighbours, more hardworking, more honest and more sophisticated, and they believed themselves to be if less competitive, less violent as well. The survey, although limited in scope, begs some interesting questions. Why do Canadians feel that the two societies are so different? How did such differences come about? To what extent do Canadians define their own identity in the terms of its difference from that of Americans?

No issue in recent times crystallized this basic Canadian wariness with regard to the cultural, political, and economic influence of the United States as did the debate over free trade.

On January 2, 1988, Prime Minister Brian Mulroney and President Ronald Reagan signed a historic agreement to reduce tariff barriers between the two nations. This was actually the fourth such contract drawn up between the two trading partners. The first, the reciprocity treaty of 1854, was abrogated by the United States in protest over British aid to the Confederacy during the Civil War. The next pact, negotiated in 1911 by the Laurier government, disappeared with the defeat of the Liberals in the election of that year. A third attempt was made by the government of Mackenzie King in early 1948. King himself changed his mind in that case, and it became a non-issue over the next thirty-five years. In fact, so strongly did most Canadians oppose the idea of free trade with the United States during this period, that then leadership candidate Brian Mulroney stated emphatically in 1983: "Free trade is terrific until the elephant twitches, and if it rolls over, you're a dead man. We will have none of it."

With this kind of history it is no wonder that the country found itself split down the middle on the deal. According to the *Maclean's* poll, in late 1987 49 percent of the country felt that the agreement was a "good step" for Canada, 44 percent called it a "bad step," and only 7 percent had no opinion. Much of the debate was rhetoric, but much cut to the larger issue of Canada's place in North America. To Mulroney, that place was clear:

> I am confident that . . . Canada will continue to flourish under a free trade agreement. We want a country renowned for its competitive excellence . . . a country capable of creating interesting jobs for its youth . . . a country celebrated for its economic achievements and its social compassion. A country that is united, prosperous, sovereign, and strong. A country called Canada. A model of tolerance and prosperity among the nations of the earth.

His view was countered by two opposition leaders. Former Liberal Prime Minister John Turner said:

This is a 'Sale of Canada Act'! It is the most massive sell-out of Canadian economic sovereignty in our history. Mulroney tells us that in opposing his deal, we are 'timid' and 'fearful' and 'don't have confidence in Canada.' He is dead wrong.

We do have confidence in Canada—a confidence in our future. But it is not a continental future. It is a Canadian future.

Regardless of one's stand on free trade, therefore, it would appear that for the Canadian half of the North Americans, continentalism remains something to be resisted, not embraced.

Canadians and Americans have expounded that cliché of the "undefended border" for decades. Unquestionably an examination of the winter population of Florida, or the summer population of Canadian resort and cottage areas, would attest to the fluidity of population flow between the two nations. Like all neighbours, North Americans feel comfortable in each other's backyards. However, like all neighbours, they don't necessarily feel at home there. Things may look the same, people may share many of the same ideas and values, but the other person's nation will never quite be like home.

In 1988, Canadians are Canadians. The "other" North Americans have survived centuries of the kind of pressure to which Trudeau alluded and have emerged as an interesting alternative to life in the United States. There is no question that North Americans have shared a commonality of experience that goes beyond that of other nations and continents. Canada and the United States, the political descendants of New France and the Thirteen Colonies, began together and have advanced in tandem to the present. The Native cultures that preceded European invasion, varied and complex, spanned the continent with little or no regard to boundaries other than natural ones. The national lines drawn by later settlers established a framework, but unlike other peoples, North Americans were then left alone. The "splendid isolation" of the nineteenth and twentieth centuries has allowed North Americans to determine their own course and pattern of development. On each side of the 49th parallel, (a geographic convenience, not actuality, since the most densely populated parts of Canada lie south of this line), the two nations have had to face a common set of challenges: nature, revolution, the search for national identity, the evolution of new political institutions, industrialization, urbanization, continental and overseas imperialism, social change, cultural differences, and relationships with the larger world.

Each nation met these challenges in its own unique way. Canadians for over a century have often felt inferior to Americans. If the United States tackled problems forcefully and head-on, Canada was often tentative and indirect. If Americans loudly boasted of their nation and its accomplishments, Canadians were self-effacing and quiet. In spite of all that, in the late 1980s Canadians have come to a realization. The American way is not the only way. Canadians, the "other North Americans" as columnist Richard Gwyn describes us (see readings), have come to recognize that their approach to problems might not only be different, it might even be better!

THIRSTY OR HUNGR

BUT SOMEONE JUST SUGGESTED THAT I COULD POSSIBLY BE REMEMBERED AS CANADA'S WORST-EVER PRIME MINISTER...

NOT A CHANCE, SIR—IF OUR HISTORIANS END UP BEING THE AMERICANS!

The open relationship celebrated by Brian Mulrone and Ronald Reagan at the Shamrock Summit receive more critical treatment in the two editorial cartoons.

The Study of the Past

This book is not about Canadian-American relations. Certainly that reality of life is an underlying theme throughout the various problems discussed, but in actual fact such an approach to continental history, while significant to the Canadian side, has little meaning south of the border. It is instead about North America, and the common challenges that living here has meant for citizens on both sides of the border. For if Canadians and Americans have faced similar problems, the solutions have varied widely. Sometimes the difference has been based upon a deliberate rejection by Canadians of the American option, as in 1784 and 1812. At other times Canadians have enjoyed the luxury of "going second" and learning from the mistakes of their powerful neighbour, as was obvious in 1867 and during the process of urban development. Finally, Canada has often taken the lead itself in foreign policy initiatives and in providing social services for its citizens.

You are about to examine the record of the past five centuries, from about the time of initial contact between native North Americans and Europeans to the present day. The focus will always be upon our common experiences and an examination of the ways in which both nations have responded to them. Coupled with this survey of our history will be an opportunity to open a window on our collective past through the use of *primary source* materials. Documents, cartoons, and photographs have been included to provide us with some "first-hand" insight into the issues and time periods to be studied.

It is difficult to travel into the past without taking our contemporary ideas along with us. We tend to examine past events, people, and ideas with the benefit of hindsight rather than from the perspective of the period. As a result, students of history often make the mistake of assuming that the actual outcome was either obvious or inevitable to people living at that time. This is often a critical error.

In all fairness, every historical investigation should begin with an attempt to transplant oneself into the physical and mental setting of the participants. It is only when you come to understand how people thought and acted, and why they did so, that you can begin to apply the more sophisticated tools of historical analysis to events.

It is, therefore, necessary for us to take a candid and unrestricted view of the past. This is often difficult. Frequently, evidence is fragmented and contradictory. Winners tend to preserve the records of their ideas and deeds more completely than losers. The attitudes of men tend to be recorded more often than those of women, and the viewpoints of racial and linguistic minorities are often not heard at all.

As noted above, in this book we have attempted to do two things. Each chapter is divided into two distinct sections. The first half presents you with a historical overview of the issue or concept involved. Information, ideas, and analysis are provided from the perspective of our own twentieth-century Canadian society. The second half of each chapter attempts to allow the participants in the events to speak to you in their own words. These primary sources provide us with a direct window on the past. The ideas expressed are either ones that were currently in fashion at the time or the viewpoints of subsequent generations of historians.

This approach does present the modern student with a problem. Many of the ideas and actions of past societies seem alien and even repugnant to us in the present. Attitudes toward Native peoples, Blacks, immigrant groups, and women often reflect a point of view which is no longer acceptable in our day and age. Why do we include them in the book? We hope the answer is obvious. It does a disservice to homogenize the past.

To fully understand why people acted the way they did, we must first understand how they thought. As a result, many of the primary sources in this book reflect a wide variety of differing points of view or *biases*. Part of your task as a student using this book will be to uncover bias and to deal with it in its historical context. The first half of each chapter is designed to give you the analytical background to do so, but just in case you need a reminder, here are a few questions to ask yourself when you are considering the primary source materials provided.

1. Who is speaking? What is her/his background? What might be her/his point of view?
2. Why is this document being written? Is it a personal diary or does it have an intended audience with certain demands or expectations?
3. Is a contradicting viewpoint presented? Has the document been presented in isolation or is there an opposing opinion for comparison?
4. What is the general historical background surrounding the document? Is it being written in a time of crisis or relative calm?
5. What are the prevailing social, political, and economic attitudes of the time in which the document appears? How might these affect the point of view being expressed?

In summary, what you are considering are the identity of the author, the purpose of the document, historical balance, and historical context. It is important to remember, however, that while these five sets of questions will help you interpret the document, they are not all-inclusive.

It is an easy matter for us to sit in judgment on the past. After years or even decades of further experience even the novice historian may find her/himself in a position to see through the biases of past participants in historical events. It is important, therefore, to not only recognize the bias inherent in each of the documents presented but also to recognize the documents in terms of their historical time and place. The result will be a more complete and intellectually mature understanding of the past.

The North Americans

The early study of the North American experience is not new. Since the American Revolution, the unsuccessful invasion of Quebec, and the subsequent Loyalist migration a great deal has been written about the two alternatives to life on this continent. In this prologue we have discussed briefly current Canadian attitudes toward the United States and its approach to the challenges of the North American experience. While the remainder of this book is going to focus upon the commonality of our experiences and the variety of our responses to them, this chapter concentrates upon our mutual perceptions of one another.

Travels into North America, 1748-49

Peter Kalm was a Swedish observer who travelled extensively throughout eastern North America in the late 1740s. In this excerpt, he outlines the impact of the existence of Canada upon the attitudes of the Thirteen Colonies.

For it is to be observed, that each English colony in North America is independent of the other, and that each has its proper laws and coin, and may be looked upon in several lights as a state by itself. From hence it happens, that in time of war, things go on very slowly and irregularly here: for not only the sense of one province is sometimes directly opposite to that of another; but frequently the views of the governor, and those of the assembly, of the same province are quite different: . . . It has commonly happened, that whilst some provinces have been suffering from their enemies, the neighbouring ones were quiet and inactive, and as if it did not in the least concern them. . . .

The French in Canada, who are but an inconsiderable body, in comparison with the English in America, have, by this position of affairs, been able to obtain great advantages in times of war; for if we judge from the number and power of the English, it would seem very easy for them to get the better of the French in America.

It is however of great advantage to the crown of England, that the North American colonies are near a country, under the government of the French, like Canada. There is reason to believe that the king never was in earnest in his attempts to expel the French from their possessions there; though it might have been done with little difficulty. For the English colonies in this part of the world have increased so much in their number of inhabitants, and in their riches, that they almost vie with Old England. . . .

From Peter Kalm, *Travels into North America*, 1770.

1. What relationship does Kalm perceive among the thirteen British colonies?
2. Logistically, how does New France compare with the Thirteen Colonies?
3. Why does Kalm state that the existence of New France is of advantage to the British?

Why Americans Are Vain, 1831

Alexis de Tocqueville visited the United States during the 1830s to prepare a report on prison reform for the French government. As you will see in a later chapter, in the process he made a number of insightful observations on the state of American democracy. In this excerpt he discusses the American psyche.

All free nations are vainglorious, but national pride is not displayed by all in the same manner. The Americans, in their intercourse with strangers, appear impatient of the smallest censure and insatiable of praise. The most slender eulogy is acceptable to them, the most exalted seldom contents them; they unceasingly harass you to extort praise, and if you resist their entreaties, they fall to praising themselves. It would seem as if, doubting their own merit, they wished to have it constantly exhibited before their eyes. Their vanity is not only greedy, but restless and jealous; it will grant nothing, whilst it demands everything, but is ready to beg and to quarrel at the same time.

If I say to an American that the country he lives in is a fine one, "Ay," he replies, "there is not its fellow in the world." If I applaud the freedom which its inhabitants enjoy, he answers: "Freedom is a fine thing, but few nations are worthy to enjoy it." If I remark on the purity of morals which distinguishes the United States, "I can imagine," says he, "that a stranger, who has been struck by the corruption of all other nations, is astonished at the difference." At length I leave him to the contemplation of himself; but he returns to the charge and does not desist till he has got me to repeat all I had been saying. It is impossible to conceive a more troublesome or more garrulous patriotism; it wearies even those who are disposed to respect it.

. . . Men living in democracies love their country just as they love themselves, and they transfer the habits of their private vanity to their vanity as a nation.

The restless and insatiable vanity of a democratic people originates so entirely in the equality and precariousness of their social condition that the members of the haughtiest nobility display the very same passion in those lesser portions of their existence in which there is anything fluctuating or contested. . . .

From H.H. Quint, *et al*, *Main Problems in American History* (Homewood, Illinois: Dorsey Press, 1978).

1. In what ways does de Tocqueville describe the character of American nationalism?
2. How does the author characterize American moral values?
3. Comment upon de Tocqueville's relation between democracy and vanity.

Canada and the Canadian Question, 1891

Goldwin Smith was the most prominent intellectual in late nineteenth century Canada. Smith, who immigrated to Canada in 1871, was a geographic determinist who argued that union with the United States was inevitable. He stated his case in Canada and the Canadian Question, *which, although subject to much contemporary criticism, poses the basic challenge to Canadian nationalists to the present day.*

A grand idea may be at the same time practical. The idea of a United Continent of North America, securing free trade and intercourse over a vast area, with external safety and internal peace, is no less practical than it is grand. The benefits of such a union would be always present to the mind of the least instructed citizen. The sentiment connected with it would be a foundation on which the political architect could build. Imperial Federation, to the mass of the people comprised in it, would be a mere name conveying with it no definite sense of benefit, on which anything could be built.

Political Union

Annexation is an ugly word; it seems to convey the idea of force or pressure applied to the smaller State, not of free, equal, and honourable union, like that between England and Scotland. Yet there is no reason why the union of the two sections of the English-speaking people on this Continent should not be as free, as equal, and as honourable as the union of England and Scotland. We should rather say their reunion than their union, for before their unhappy schism they were one people. Nothing but the historical accident of a civil war ending in secession, instead of amnesty, has made them two. When the Anglo-Saxons of England and those of Scotland were reunited they had been many centuries apart; those of the United States and Canada have been separated for one century only. The Anglo-Saxons of England and Scotland had the memory of many wars to estrange them: the Anglo-Saxons of Canada and the United States have the memory, since their separation, only of one war.

That union of Canada with the American Commonwealth, like that into which Scotland entered with England, would in itself be attended with great advantages cannot be questioned, whatever may be the considerations on the other side or the reasons for delay. It would give to the inhabitants of the whole Continent as complete a security for peace and immunity from war taxation as is likely to be attained by any community or group of communities on this side of the Millenium.

From Goldwin Smith, *Canada and the Canadian Question* (Toronto: University of Toronto Press, 1971).

1. What appears to be the basis of Smith's argument?
2. In what way does Smith dismiss the concept of the two separate nations?
3. What parallels does he draw with the English-Scottish relationship?

The Americanization of Canada, 1907

Samuel Moffett was an American who saw the world in terms of the Manifest Destiny of the United States. Moffett saw the spread of American ideals, technology, and economic influence as a process which would inevitably lead to a worldwide hegemony. Canada's assimilation would be the result of a natural process.

. . . THE BULK of the North American continent is divided into two almost equal parts.

One of these parts is inhabited by about eighty-five million people, substantially all speaking English, or in the way to do so. The other has about six million people, of whom two thirds speak English and one third French, the French element tending constantly to gain on the other through natural increase, and the English to maintain its lead through immigration.

These two halves of the continent are separated by a boundary line four thousand miles long [6400 km] (not including that of Alaska), corresponding to no natural division either of topography or of nationality. In some parts this line is a parallel of latitude; in others it follows small and hardly identifiable rivers; in others it takes its unmarked way through the middle of inland seas. The question to be considered here is whether this boundary is an actual fence, separating one people from another, or whether there is a tendency on both sides to ignore it, and to merge the six millions and eighty-five millions together.

When the American colonies declared their independence, there was no such division. Canada, then, meant what is now the Province of Quebec, and it was almost purely French. There were a few English settlers in the Maritime Provinces, which were not then considered parts of Canada, but the whole region west of the St. Lawrence Rapids was substantially uninhabited. From this point to the Pacific Ocean the continent was absolutely one. A hunter might have started at the mouth of the Ohio and worked his way to the Arctic Ocean without ever noticing anything but the weather to remind him that he had passed from one country to another. The difference between Canada and the United States then, was the difference between French and English. When the revolting colonists invited the Canadians to join them the Canadians refused, as Frenchmen, unwilling to associate themselves with their hereditary English enemies. . . .

Had matters remained in this condition, the British connection with Canada could hardly have outlasted the War of 1812. But the end of the Revolution brought the first of a long series of American mistakes through which that connection has been maintained to the present time. The oppression of the Tories in the States created two new provinces, inhabited by an energetic English population, and gave the infant commonwealths an anti-American bias that has not been entirely overcome to this day. It was this now hostile United Empire Loyalist population created by American blunders that gave the British generals the backing without which they could have had no success in the War of 1812. . . . The settlement of New Brunswick was almost entirely United Empire Loyalist. The Loyalist refugees reinforced the small English population of Nova Scotia and definitely settled the long-fought issue whether the Acadian peninsula should be English or French. . . . But for their coming the British possessions in North America would have consisted of a wilderness with a little oasis of a hundred thousand French Canadians on the St. Lawrence, and a smaller group of about fifteen thousand people of mixed nationalities, half of them Americans, in Acadia. . . . Canada would then have remained as it always had been before, another name for Quebec, and the idea of a continental Canadian Dominion would never have entered any human mind.

For generations the American stream of migration was diverted from Canada, but a Canadian stream was turned toward the United States. . . .

The conclusion to which all the converging lines of evidence unmistakably point is that the Americans and the English-speaking Canadians have been welded into one people. The French Canadians are of course different from both, but even in their case the international boundary is not a dividing line. There are nearly two-thirds as many persons of pure French Canadian stock in the United States as in all Canada, and the density of the French Canadian population of Massachusetts is over ten times as great as that of Quebec. The

boundary of French Canada runs down the Ottawa and southward to Long
Island Sound, not easterly and westerly along the forty-fifth parallel and the
St. Lawrence. But French Canada is merely a little island in the midst of a sea of
English speaking people, of diverse origins indeed, but unified by a common lan-
guage, common institutions and common habits of life. The English-speaking
Canadians protest that they will never become Americans without knowing it.

From Samuel E. Moffet, *The Americanization of Canada* (Toronto: University of Toronto Press, 1972).

1. How does Moffett account for the historical division between the two nations?
2. Account for Moffett's view of the French Canadian role in North America.
3. Write a rebuttal to, or defence of, Moffett's thesis.

Lament for a Nation, 1965

*Professor George Grant viewed the Canadian experience as a glorious failure by the
mid-1960s. In this first excerpt he examines both the reasons for its failure and what
the future holds in store.*

The impossibility of conservatism in our era is the impossibility of Canada. As
Canadians we attempt a ridiculous task in trying to build a conservative nation
in the age of progress, on a continent we share with the most dynamic nation
on earth. The current of modern history was against us.

A society only articulates itself as a nation through some common intention
among its people. The constitutional arrangements of 1791, and the wider
arrangements of the next century, were only possible because of a widespread
determination not to become part of the great Republic. Among both the
French and the British, this negative intention sprang from widely divergent
traditions. What both peoples had in common was the fact they both recognized, that they could only be preserved outside the United States of America.
The French were willing to co-operate with the English because they had no
alternative but to go along with the endurable arrangements proposed by the
ruling power. Both the French and the British had limited common ground on
their sense of social order—belief that society required a high degree of law,
and respect for a public conception of virtue. Both would grant the state much
wider rights to control the individual than was recognized in the libertarian
ideas of the American constitution. If their different conservatisms could have
become a conscious bond, this nation might have preserved itself. An indigenous society might have continued to exist on the northern half of this
continent.

. . . The inherited determination not to be Americans allowed these British
people to come to a *modus vivendi* with the more defined desires of the French.
English-speaking Canadians have been called a dull, stodgy, and indeed costive
lot. . . . Yet our stodginess has made us a society of greater simplicity, formal-
ity, and perhaps even innocence than the people to the south. Nothing was
more alien to them than the "emancipation of the passions", desired in American liberalism. . . . The early leaders of British North America identified lack

of public and personal restraint with the democratic Republic. Their conservatism was essentially the social doctrine that public order and tradition, in contrast to freedom and experiment, were central to the good life. Our opening of the West differed from that of the United States, in that the law of the central government was used more extensively, and less reliance was placed on the free settler. Until recently, Canadians have been much more willing than Americans to use governmental control over economic life to protect the public good against private freedom.

English-speaking Canadians had never broken with their origins in Western Europe. Many Canadians saw it as a means of preserving at every level of our life—religious, educational, political, social—certain forms of existence that distinguish us from the United States.

Canada has ceased to be a nation, but its formal political existence will not end quickly. Our social and economic blending into the empire will continue apace, but political union will probably be delayed. Some international catastrophe or great shift of power might speed up this process. Its slowness does not depend only on the fact that large numbers of Canadians do not want it, but also on sheer lethargy. . . . The dominant forces in the Republic do not need to incorporate us. A branch-plant satellite, which has shown in the past that it will not insist on any difficulties in foreign or defence policy, is a pleasant arrangement for one's northern frontier . . . If the negotiations for union include Quebec, there will be strong elements in the United States that will dislike their admission. . . . The formal end of Canada may be prefaced by a period during which the government of the United States has to resist the strong desire of English-speaking Canadians to be annexed.

From George Grant, *Lament for a Nation* (Princeton, 1965).

In this excerpt Grant compares the American intellectual tradition to its present situation (1965).

The old platitude must be repeated once again: the United States is the society with the least history prior to the age of progress. (Other societies rush fast to kill what they have, but they still have something to kill.) The basic moral teachers of the United States from Locke to Franklin and from Jefferson to Dewey have been morally shallow. . . . (The forlorn hope of Canada once was that from earlier European traditions, British and French, we would maintain moral roots which would allow us to deal more deeply with existence.) Indeed, the highest public hope in the United States was the belief in pluralism—that their society would be made of many streams and that as the society matured these streams would deepen beyond the shallowness of the pioneering moment. But the many streams have widened into one great lake, the defining element of which is belief in affluence through technology.

How can this society of affluence and freedom (freedom about any issue which does not question the basic assumptions) be responsible for the monstrous occurrences in Vietnam? . . . the society of affluence and freedom has shown itself capable, not of the maniacal genocide of Auschwitz, but of the bland, impersonal wiping out of an Asian people who could not otherwise be brought to do what American leaders deemed necessary. This is the hardest thing for liberals to understand: how this could arise out of the progressive society they had built. . . .

To think ill of the dominant American tradition must not allow one to forget that which remains straight and clear among Americans themselves. Living next to them Canadians should know better than most how incomplete are the stereotyped gibes of Europeans. The cranes and the starlings still fly high through their skies; sane and wise families grow up; people strive to be good citizens; some men still think. Above all, many Americans have seen with clarity the nature of that which chokes them and seek for ways to live beyond it.

From George Grant, "From Roosevelt to LBJ," from Al Purdy, ed., *The New Romans: Candid Canadian Opinions*, (Edmonton: M.G. Hurtig Pub., 1968).

1. What are the historical roots of Canada's problem identified by Grant?
2. What future does Grant see for Canada?
3. How does Grant equate American problems in the 1960s with their intellectual tradition?

Canada's Great Cliché, 1967

In these two excerpts, historian J.M.S. Careless examines the historical roots of the Canadian-American experience.

The United States is Canada's great cliché. Our reactions to the country and its people have all the hard-worn polish of "it's a nice place to visit" or "some of my best friends." This is inevitably so because Canadians have been worrying over and responding to the United States ever since the American Revolution created both countries by running a political boundary across the mass of North America. Since then we have been obsessed with the far greater magnitude of American power and success: fearing it, resisting it, and leaning on it; criticizing, deploring, and emulating it.

Again this is all but inevitable, since to a very large degree the American presence has shaped Canada. It gave French-Canadians a reason for accepting British imperial rule and then for aligning politically with English-Canadian colonists as the best means to ensure survival in the face of huge American absorptive power. It gave English-Canadians the War of 1812, the one conflict they have fought on their own soil, with its consequent memories of successful national defense to reinforce the original Loyalists' declaration of independence from the United States. And sharp strains during the American Civil War did much to impel the separate British-American colonies to combine in Confederation in 1867 in order to form a political and economic unit big enough to be viable outside of a notably unfriendly republic. In short, through varied impacts with deep historic effect, the United States has served repeatedly, if unwittingly, as the best friend nationalism could have in a country as culturally and sectionally divided as Canada.

The process continued throughout the century after Confederation. American probing into the Northwest, American railroad projects, spurred the building of the C.P.R. The rising wall of the United States tariffs provided sanction for the adoption of Canadian policies of economic nationalism. Then the influx of American capital and techniques, from dry-farming in the West to factory industry in the East, gave increasing breadth and substance to the Canadian continental system. And later improved relations with the United States stimulated a sense of North American defensive security, which had its own consequence in the drive to realize full Canadian nationhood out of the declining British Empire. In striking ways—though certainly not as the only factor—the United States has worked to build the modern Canadian nation.

Obviously, it has no less helped to impair it; for instance, to offer always the seductive charm of giving up: to cease to pay the cost of Canada, either personally through emigration or collectively through annexation by joining the great world of the American union. What country other than Canada exists with the implicit assumption that if we can't go home to Mother anymore, Uncle (supposedly) will always take us in?

From J.M.S. Careless, "Hooray for the Scars and Gripes!," from Al Purdy, ed., *The New Romans: Candid Canadian Opinions*, (Edmonton: M.G. Hurtig Pub., 1968).

The lines now, for Canadians, converge on New York, Chicago and Los Angeles; the roads (for the pursuit of happiness) lead to Florida and California. The consequences for Canadian nationalism have inevitably been great. Despite the growth of an interconnected internal metropolitan pattern, the various highly organized metropolitan regions and sub-regions in this country all find places in continental vassal-chains centred below the border. The question still remains whether this broader metropolitanism will work to produce Canadian absorption in a continental American nationality, or may yet induce some basic reaction beyond impotent fears and frustration—so that another phase of Canadian nationalism may follow, stimulated by resistance to an external metropolitan dominance.

From J.M.S. Careless, "Metropolitanism and Nationalism," from Peter Russell, ed., *Nationalism in Canada*, (Toronto: McGraw-Hill Ryerson, 1966).

1. Outline the historical roots of the relationship.
2. How does Careless relate the Canadian-American relationship to his metropolitan thesis?
3. Respond to Careless' contention with regard to the North American experience.

The New Romans

The New Romans *is a book of Canadian essays about the United States that appeared in the late sixties. In the following excerpts, Farley Mowat and Larry Zolf comment on the Canadian-American relationship.*

Letter to my Son
"What the U.S. wants, it will get," he told me. "And if we don't *give* them

what they want, they'll take it anyway. And what they want—is most of what we've got."

That was about as clear an expression of *Realpolitik* as one can expect from the political animal, even if it was primarily a rationalization intended to excuse our political masters for having *already* given the Yanks almost everything of any value in this country. Nevertheless, Joey's point was well taken since those who rule us (they do not "govern"—that word implies statesmanship combined with honourable intentions) have, for their own reasons, long since sold us out. Or maybe they just saw the light a long way back and, in keeping with their dubious professional practices, took the line of least resistance. Some of them, that is. Others sold out with deliberate intent. . . .

. . . I realized what the politicians, at least, were up to ages ago. My naivety —if such it was—lay in my continuing conviction that the *people* of this land would not forever continue to acquiesce in this piecemeal betrayal of themselves and of their country. I was much influenced by what took place in Cuba and, before that, in Mexico. I believed that if such small, relatively powerless serf states could muster the guts to really kick Big Uncle in the backside, the people of Canada might be goaded into an equivalent demonstration of courage. Alas, Canadians are not Mexicans or Cubans, and I realize now that I miscalculated on a horrendous scale in ever thinking that Canadians would risk cutting off rich Uncle's dole. . . .

This is a fact that I am going to have to learn to live with. We have become a prostrate people—by our own volition. Actually the only time Canadians even raise themselves on their elbows these days is to *defend* their chosen masters and to attack, with the bitter hostility only known to turncoats, those who dare reproach them for their spineless espousal of slave status. . . .

Despite poor old Lester Pearson's recent statement in *Maclean's* that "the Americans are the least imperialistic people in history" . . . the Yanks now control the largest empire the world has ever known. Its citizens have, as Henry R. Luce (founder of Canada's two favourite magazines—*Life* and *Time*) once put it, now risen to the challenge: "to accept wholeheartedly the duty and opportunity as the most powerful and vital nation in the world and in consequence to exert upon the world the full impact of our influence, *for such purposes as we see fit and by such means as we see fit* (italics mine)." In this delightfully frank statement, combined with one by John Foster Dulles—"There are two ways of conquering a foreign nation. One is to gain control of its people by force of arms. The other is to gain control of its economy by financial means."—you have the essential dogma subscribed to by the military-political-economic hegemony that runs the U.S.A.

Farley Mowat, from Al Purdy, ed., *The New Romans: Candid Canadian Opinions*, (Edmonton: M.G. Hurtig, 1968).

Boil me no Melting Pots, Dream me no Dreams

When the Fathers of Confederation built this country in 1867, there was universal agreement among *all* Canadians, English- and French-speaking, that there was no place for the American Dream on the northern half of this continent. In 1776 we embraced the United Empire Loyalists and rejected George Washington's Revolutionary Army by force of arms. We booted Uncle Sam in the pants in 1812 and slapped his wrists in the Fenian Raids of the 1880's. We rejected slavery and provided sanctuary for American Negroes fleeing that "peculiar institution."

We rejected republicanism, the American idea that the people in and of themselves can shape their own ends and destinies. We countered Jacksonian democracy with the responsible government of a constitutional monarchy and made it plain to our southern neighbours that there were higher forces shaping our destinies than the untutored rabble of the untouched West. And while we did agree with the Yankee that life and liberty were inseparable, we differed in our pursuit of happiness. In Canada, that pursuit didn't necessarily entail egalite and fraternite. We flatly rejected the American egalitariansism of the Western frontier and the American fraternity of the melting pot.

Larry Zolf, from Al Purdy, ed., *The New Romans: Candid Canadian Opinions*, (Edmonton: M.G. Hurtig, 1968).

1. Select one of the pieces and write a review.
2. Using one of the literary styles employed by the authors, create your own statement on the Canadian-American experience.
3. To what extent are the sentiments expressed here in the 1960s similar to the response of the artistic community to the free trade deal of the late 1980s?

Nationalism in Canada, 1966

These three excerpts examine the roots of Canadian nationalism. In the first Stephen Clarkson considers Canada as a developing nation and the implications in terms of its relationship with the United States. The second, by George Heimann, considers Canadian nationalism as a product of anti-Americanism. The third, by Cole Harris, considers Canada in terms of the relationship between Canadians and their land.

A Programme for Binational Development

If . . . we look at ourselves as a developing nation, not in the sense of having to overcome a grinding poverty, but as having certain problems in common with the ex-colonies of the "third world," we gain a new perspective from which to look at our own future. Like many developing countries, we have a heterogenous population requiring a sense of national identity strong enough to offset the centrifugal forces of ethnic division. Like the developing nations, too, we can harness that potent force of twentieth century politics, nationalism, to provide the necessary stimulus for Canada's continuing existence as a federal state.

Much of our current nationalism is piously meaningless: we are provided at school with an ambiguous anti-Americanism to counterbalance our underlying sense of inferiority; we are cajoled at elections to vote for *the* party that will preserve national unity. But this is hardly the kind of nationalism which can support the programme of nation-building we must achieve if we are to survive as an integral state. . . . By thinking of Canada not as an old, fading country, but as a new, developing state, Canadian nationalism can acquire a dynamic role as an instrument to inspire and sustain workable policies that can complete the construction of a durable state.

If such a state does not yet exist, what then is the national situation in Canada today? What type of development can realistically be envisaged for it? It is only when we have answered these two basic questions that we can go on to propose examples of practical policies, which, based on the situation of today, can lead us to the state of affairs we desire for tomorrow.

Stephen Clarkson, from Peter Russell, ed., *Nationalism in Canada*, (Toronto: McGraw-Hill Ryerson, 1966).

The 19th Century Legacy: Nationalism or Patriotism?

Patriotism and nationalism, the nation-state and nationality, these basic concepts are dominant when the ultimate thought of social collectivity is considered today. It is quite useless to advocate far-reaching alternatives at the moment. Nor is there any point in lamenting the fact that the historical evolution has taken this direction. To do so would be to express a futile regret over an irreversible development. Not only are nationalism and patriotism, but particularly the latter, deeply-rooted ingredients of human nature but they are also the natural corollaries of the large-scale population growth which accompanied the industrialization of Europe and North America. . . . Whether the nation-state is a liberal, constitutional democracy or a totalitarian democracy is, in this instance, of secondary importance. But all rule today is in the name of the "people," regardless of whether the "people" are really consulted or not. But these "people" do, in most instances, speak a common language, share a common geographical home and possess a more or less accurately recorded history. And their dominant political creed is either patriotism or nationalism.

The numerous difficulties which beset the development of a Canadian national spirit are formidable. The existence of two different major nationalities and religious denominations, the federal political structure of the country, in itself an indication of centrifugalism and not only of geographic necessity, the vastness of the land—all these factors present barriers to the emergence of a widely shared sense of national identity. One could also consider the proximity of a huge, militant and cohesive power such as the United States of America as a hindrance to the evolution of the Canadian national sentiment. But such is not necessarily the case. Patriotisms and particularly nationalisms are often fed by a reaction to that which they are not. They depend to varying degrees on the uniqueness, real or imaginary, of their cultural and political identity. Being "non-American," and at times quite pointlessly anti-American, is part and parcel of the Canadian forms of patriotism and nationalism.

George Heimann, from Peter Russell, ed., *Nationalism in Canada*, (Toronto: McGraw-Hill Ryerson, 1966).

The Myth of the Land in Canadian Nationalism

When people weigh the nature and basis of their nationalism they usually dwell on aspects of their culture, history, or race; but English-speaking Canadians tend to explain themselves in terms of land and location. Some Canadians, . . . considered their countrymen to have been shaped and strengthened by a hard northern realm, while others have envisaged a Canadian nation forged by the development of northern resources. An appeal to our northern destiny was one of the responsive notes struck by Diefenbaker in 1957 and 1958, and that appeal was probably strengthened by the Canadian apprehension that geographically we are North American, a fringe of regions on top of the United States. These two conflicting geographical propositions are central to many discussions about the nature of Canada: Canada exists because it is a distinctive northern land; Canada is North American, its southern boundary is geographically illogical and therefore fragile and probably temporary.

In print these geographical poles are clearest in the historical literature, for Canadian historians, along with some Canadian novelists, have most frequently turned to the land to explain the character of Canada. The Laurentian theme running through the writings of Harold Innis, Donald Creighton, William Morton, and other Canadian historians, is the theme of the fur trade—the transcontinental enterprise based on the resources of the north, and anchored to the towns which provided manpower, capital, and skills for northern development. . . .

At the other pole are the continentalists: A.S. Morton, Fred Landon and, to a degree, A.R.M. Lower, Frank Underhill and A.L. Burt. Their studies have tended to emphasize "the mingling of the Canadian and American People," and have agreed with J.B. Brebner who opened his history of Canada with the sentence, "Perhaps the most striking thing about Canada is that it is not part of the United States."

Cole Harris, from Peter Russell, ed., *Nationalism in Canada*, (Toronto: McGraw-Hill Ryerson, 1966).

1. What case does Clarkson build to show Canada's role as a developing nation?
2. How does Heimann describe the impact of the existence of the United States upon Canadian nationalism?
3. Account for Brebner's remark quoted by Cole that "Perhaps the most striking thing about Canada is that it is not part of the United States."

Some Feelings About the United States

Canadian historian William Kilbourn describes Canada as an "America in the making." In this excerpt he outlines the impact of American culture upon Canadians.

Chiefly, however, I can be angry at "the Americans" because I am so American myself. America is my past: most of my ancestors originally came from the United States where they had lived for many generations. America is my foster parent: I lived and worked and studied there for three years; one of my sons is a Yankee. America, from New York to San Francisco, is our change of air and our other place of business. Above all it is our ultimate metropolis, the one that speaks our North American style and serves as a place of refuge when Canadian smugness and pettiness become too hard to take. America is our cultural asylum, just as Canada has been a *political* asylum for American-way-of-life dodgers ever since the underground railway and the United Empire Loyalists.

America provides us with so many of our heroes, from Jefferson and Lincoln to FDR and Kennedy, from Hawthorne to John Cage, Bob Dylan, and Buckminster Fuller. America gives the Canadian writer a usable major past to nourish both his craft and his way of seeing things, a past perhaps even more accessible to us than it is to contemporary American writers. As for speech, Huckleberry Finn invented the American dialect for Canadians as well as for his countrymen. It was certainly not my English-Canadian schoolmasters who encouraged me to say "who to" instead of "to whom." They never gave me permission to try yawping like Whitman or fooling about with *Moby Dick* as the pattern for a book about steelmaking—or to begin another one with the words "Call me Bill." Juvenalia, perhaps, but then a mature Canadian like Jean Lemoyne can find in Henry James and T.S. Eliot not only the imagination to become and to remain a North American, but also the strength to cope with Europe without descending into colonialism. And finally, it was not Governor Simcoe and Doctor Strachan who taught me freedom from the paralysis of the European class system. It was not my five generations of Ontario farm ancestors, though I owe them much, who made me feel that one of the chief blessings of the human condition is to know the privilege of being a North American.

Canada has long been another America, an America in the making, but one with a difference. We still have the chance, in this open, half-formed, dimly identified society of ours, to make something new, even marvellous, out of our American heritage. Not in the way Emerson had in mind a century ago when he turned his back on the whole western tradition ("the storied cliffs of Salamis and Marathon") and proudly proclaimed "We shall be classic to *ourselves.*" Nor in Lincoln's sense of being a land that is "the last best hope of earth". There is, after all, a foulness that has flowed in the wake of that divine archaic dream, and it has produced Fortress America and John Birch, Jay Gatsby's friends and Senator Joe McCarthy . . . .

An un-Canadian activity, thank God, there is no such thing as; it is like the purple cow—something we need never hope to see. Charles Hanly has pointed out that while a good U.S. citizen may plausibly say "I am an American, therefore I am a man," the Canadian patriot can at best state "I am a man, and I am also grateful that I happened to be a Canadian."

Al Purdy, ed., *The New Romans: Candid Canadian Opinions*, (Edmonton: M.G. Hurtig, 1968).

1. Update Kilbourn's thesis with reference to issues distinguishing the two nations in the 1980s.

Revolution and Counter Revolution: The United States and Canada

American historian Seymour Lipset compares the Canadian and American political traditions. In this excerpt, Lipset accounts for differing values as a product of the historical experience.

Ironically, civil liberties for unpopular groups would seem to be stronger in elitist democracies than in egalitarian ones. The lesser respect for public authorities in the United States than in Canada may also be indicated by the considerable variation in the extent to which the public has insisted on the right to elect officials or to change them with the fortunes of elections. In Canada legal officers tend to have life tenure, and are not directly involved in politics. Judges in Canada at every level are appointed for life by the federal authorities. Crown attorneys are designated by the provincial governments for indefinite terms, and are rarely terminated before retirement. They are not fired when a new party comes to power, and since prohibited from political activity, they are never under pressure to handle cases in a way that might facilitate their re-election or attainment of higher electoral office.

. . . The lesser respect for the law, for the "rules of the game" in the United States, may be viewed as inherent in a system in which egalitarianism is strongly valued and in which diffuse elitism is lacking. Generalized deference is not accorded to those at the top; therefore, in the United States there is a greater propensity to redefine the rules or to ignore them. . . . While Canadians incline toward the use of "lawful" and traditionally institutionalized means for altering regulations which they believe are unjust, Americans seem more disposed to employ informal and often extralegal means to correct what they perceive as wrong.

The greater lawlessness and corruption in the United States may be attributed in part to the greater strength of the achievement and self-orientation values in the more populous nation. . . . Since Americans are more likely than their Canadian neighbors to be concerned with the achievement of ends—particularly pecuniary success—they will be less concerned with the use of the socially appropriate *means*; hence we should expect a high incidence of deviations from conventional norms in politics and other aspects of life south of the forty-ninth parallel.

. . . The variation in the strength of the achievement and self-orientation values in the United States and Canada may account for another political difference—the fact that "free enterprise" ideology, though accepted in Canada, has never been the source of as violent political conflicts there as in the United States. The greater respect for government and political leaders, derived in part from elitism and in part from the need dictated by special historic circumstances requiring that the central government intervene repeatedly in economic and local political matters to assure national survival, has inhibited the development of strong economic individualism as a dominant political virtue.

. . . The significance of the "leftist" egalitarian populist character of core values in the American political tradition may best be perceived from the vantage point of comparative North American history. For although American historians and political philosophers may debate the extent of radicalism, liberalism, leftism, or even conservatism, in Revolutionary and post-colonial American politics, there is little doubt in the mind of most Canadian historians. Looking at the divergent political history of north and south of the border, they see the continued politics of their nation as reflecting the fact that it is a descendant of a counterrevolution, while the United States is a product of a successful revolution. Once these events had formed the structure of the two nations, their institutional characters were set. Subsequent events tended to enforce "leftist" values in the south and "rightist" in the north. The success of the Revolutionary ideology, the defeat of the Tories, and the emigration of many of them north to Canada or across the ocean to Britain—all served to enhance the strength of the forces favoring egalitarian democratic principles in the new nation and to weaken conservative tendencies.

The Canadians, being more prone to identify liberty and democracy with legal traditions and procedures than with populism, the right of the people to rule, or with the freedom of business and enterprise, have given equal juridical rights to minority and ethnic groups, while in the United States debates over the position of minority groups have been at the root of Indian wars and of the Civil War. On the American frontier the quality of law enforcement was often dependent on local policy authority which reflected the values of the frontiersmen, including their prejudices against Indians and their lack of understanding for legal procedures incorporating the guarantee of due process. In Canada, Indian chiefs "were impressed by the fact that, if Indians were punished for crimes against the whites, the whites were equally punished for outrages against the Indians. Their previous experience [with American whites] had taught them to appreciate such impartial justice."

. . . Canadian national identity is clearly not bound up with the ideology of a successful revolution or a dramatic political movement. Rather, as we have seen, Canadian identity is the product of a victorious counterrevolution, and in a sense must justify its *raison d'être* by emphasizing the virtues of being separate from the United States. Frank Underhill has pointed out that Canadians are the world's oldest and continuing anti-Americans. The Canadian sense of nationality has always felt itself threatened by the United States, physically in earlier days, and culturally and economically in more recent years. As S.D. Clark has put it: "Canadian national life can almost be said to take its rise in the negative will to resist absorption in the American Republic. It is largely about the United States as an object that the consciousness of Canadian national unity has grown up. . . ."

From Thomas Ford, ed., *The Revolutionary Theme in Contemporary America*, (Lexington, Kentucky: The University Press of Kentucky, 1965).

1. Outline the differences in attitude toward law and order between the two nations.
2. How does Lipsett describe the difference between the "leftist" and "rightest" attitudes of the two nations?
3. How do the views of liberty and democracy differ between the two countries?

The Canadians

Andrew Malcolm wrote about Canada for the New York Times. In this excerpt from his book The Canadians, *he outlines his views of the country and its people.*

For Americans, perhaps the most surprising discovery about Canada is that a land so rich in so many ways, still so pure in so many places, with a people so obviously intelligent, hardy, warm, and so insistent on who they are not, still suffers such anguish over its national identity. Americans are basically ignorant about most aspects of Canada, but at least they see it as one country. Canadians, instead, mostly see their land in a wide assortment of pieces with large gaps in between.

They are always looking so hard for their identity, perhaps too hard, in monthly magazines, weekly supplements, daily newspapers, on radio and television, and in intellectual discussions. . . . I began to think during my years in Canada, chatting, overhearing, and reading, that for many Canadians perhaps their unfortunate identity was to search forever for an identity, a Sisyphean task guaranteed to insure eternal angst. The search itself had become the identity because Canadians were always staring so hard straight ahead in the dark woods, intensely looking for it. If they ever sat down and relaxed and pretended not to care about it for a moment, they would suddenly find that elusive sense of self-comfort lurking just out of the corners of their eyes, back where the pale light from the campfire merges with the edge of the deep forest. It would be fuzzy and indistinct, to be sure, but nonetheless reassuring.

American schoolchildren and perhaps even their parents might have a tough time identifying exactly what an American is. They might lapse into the past, pulling up names like Paul Revere, George Washington, Abraham Lincoln, Daniel Boone, Davy Crockett, and others from the nation's colorful history. They might talk about the Revolution or the Civil War or Pearl Harbour or how their great-grandparents came from Italy speaking no English and carrying only a suitcase and a burning desire to become an American. And an American child could talk about these things regardless of where he or she grew up or went to school. More important, perhaps, Americans with their peripheral vision assume they know who they are.

Not in Canada, where it seems some Canadians are also uncertain of even where it is. Leo Doucet of New Brunswick tells the not uncommon story of moving to Whitehorse, the capital of the Yukon Territory, a few years ago. He wrote to his Canadian insurance company to change his policy address and was promptly notified that it was cancelling the policy because that company insured only drivers in Canada.

There was no Revolution in Canada, no Civil War, no broad mythology of national heroes for Canadians to share, however subconsciously, across their broad, geographically fragmented land. The first prime minister of Canada, for instance, was Sir John A. Macdonald, a dour Scot and alcoholic whose name is often misspelled and whose birthday (January 11, 1815) is unobserved these days. Canadians do, however, celebrate religiously the May birthday of Queen Victoria, the British sovereign whose birthday passes unnoticed now in her own nation. Possibly the only "hero" of national stature most Canadians might know is Louis Riel, . . . whose late-nineteenth-century western rebellion actually symbolized the bitter French-English linguistic divisions that still plague Canada. He was hanged.

. . . By their official departure in 1867, the British, as they had in their other foreign colonies, had instilled magnificently in Canadians an inferiority mindset from the start. One Canadian comedian, noting how Britain did not always dispatch its finest folk to the people new colonies, described the difference between two such colonies, Australia and Canada. He noted Australia was populated by British convicts. In Canada, he said, they were never caught.

One bright January morning in Toronto I drove to the Moore Park area of the city for a long visit with John Hirsch, one of millions of immigrants to Canada. . . . He shared his analysis of the situation. "Canada's inferiority complex," he said, "stems from a colonial mentality. Successful colonization consists of convincing the natives that whatever they have or can produce is . . . inferior to the culture, skill, and standards of the colonial power. The British were masters at this. They managed with brutal charm and incredible arrogance to walk into many colonies of older culture and convince them they weren't worth anything. . . . The Americans were smart and got out of that. But I can never understand here how a country, even before it starts, accepts that it is not as good as the guy next door. . . . If I had enough money, I'd send Canada to a good shrink for twenty years." Instead, Mr. Hirsch became the artistic director for the famed Stratford Festival, further enhancing, despite considerable frustrations from his countrymen, one of Canada's few internationally recognized symbols of excellence.

"American students have been conditioned from infancy," said Northrop Frye, who has taught many Americans at the University of Toronto, "to think of themselves as citizens of one of the world's great powers. Canadians are conditioned from infancy to think of themselves as citizens of a country of uncertain identity, a confusing past and a hazardous future." And he notes some distinct historical differences. "The pattern of Canadian history has been almost the opposite of the pattern of American history. The United States had a War of Independence against a European power in the 18th Century, and a civil war on its own soil a century later. Canada had a civil war of European powers on its own soil, and a movement of independence against its American partner in the 19th."

. . . It is, of course, impossible to generalize about all immigrants' motives. But the sense one gets is that many immigrants went to the United States with a specific goal to do something they could not do elsewhere—to practice a particular religion, for example, like the Pilgrims. Many of Canada's immigrants were simply fleeing something—the Irish potato famine, the Highland clearances in Scotland, persecution against Indians in Kenya, or, in the case of some English nobility, a somewhat sullied reputation back home. . . .

"Americans," Professor Careless told me over lunch one day, "cannot conceive of losing unless there's a conspiracy somewhere. Canadians, constrained by climate, distance, and history, see no reason to expect victory." . . . Donald Sutherland, a Canadian who left his country to excel elsewhere, once described Canadians as being like the children who press their noses against the window of life, secretly suspecting they are missing all the fun that their rambunctious American neighbors have but too worried to try it themselves lest they fail.

. . . The United States-Canadian border is a unique place. Officially it separates, or rather tries to separate, two distinct political entities. Faced with some 70 million border crossings each year along a line covering more than one-fifth of the world's circumference, agents on both sides grow weary and often-times rude, perhaps because of the nearly complete futility of their jobs. . . .

Unofficially the line has created a unique third country, a special long lineal culture where nationality matters less than personality, where the currency of each country is acceptable in the other, and where bilingual, binational families with American sons and Canadian daughters, paychecks in two currencies, and pensions from two governments are so common that any visitor needs a score-card to keep track of the connections. . . .

But the United States-Canadian border also unites the two countries in a strange way. For in many respects, as a result of geography, climate, and economic and family ties, each region of Canada has much more in common with its American counterpart just beyond the customs booth than it does with any other Canadian region. Manitoba wheat farmers, for instance, are concerned about the price of their grain and fertilizers, the amount of rain, and the possibility of the Red River's flooding again come spring, precisely the same concerns as those of North Dakota's farmers. The same holds true for fishermen in New England and the Maritime Provinces, lumbermen in British Columbia and the Pacific Northwest, cattlemen in Alberta and Montana, and auto workers in Detroit and Windsor.

East-West ties in Canada have been historically weak, while the constant tug of North-South bonds has been so strong at times as to threaten Canada's internal unity; . . . Separatists in western Canada still talk of joining the United States as a realistic alternative, albeit one with an outlook that dims in the face of political realities just outside their meeting rooms.

On the American side there seems little likelihood, either, of a state's secession to join Canada, although in the nation's early days Vermont, geographically coveted by both New York and New Hampshire, once gave the thought consideration. But over the decades millions of Americans themselves have opted to join Canada, and vice versa. More than 6 million immigrants have flowed peacefully between these two contries, one of the largest, and socially smoothest, mass migrations in history.

Each country has provided an accommodating and familiar safety valve for the discontented of the other. The Vietnam era draft dodgers who went to Canadian soil fleeing the reach of distasteful American laws were only following 110 years later in the fleeing footsteps of the South's runaway slaves, whose destination on the Underground Railroad was a British-controlled Canada where slavery had been abolished in 1841. Later nearly 1 million Americans, who had just missed snapping up the free lands on the United States' disappearing western frontier, gushed north at the official invitation of Canada to help populate and farm the less hospitable land of Alberta. . . .

The southbound flow has contained doctors dissatisfied with Canada's national health policies, nurses recruited by staff-starved American hospitals, and Prohibition rumrunners serving a thirsty market of Americans with Canadian hooch. In the late 1930's lack of opportunity and jobs in Canada, where the Depression lingered longer than in the United States, sent thousands of eager, skilled Canadian job seekers, including my father, scrambling south to start careers and families and to finish lives.

. . . Going south to the American sun is important even for Canadians who can't afford to drive the American interstates or fly the American airways south. . . .

Conversely, millions of Americans think as much about crossing the border into Canada for a summer vacation as they do of driving across a state line. American travelers spend more than $2.5 billion a year in Canada. Going fishing or skiing in Canada seems completely normal, as normal as, say, visiting Niagara Falls, which is also mostly in Canada. For baseball fans in Buffalo, the closest place to see the New York Yankees play is Canada, against the Toronto Blue Jays. And each home game weekend, busloads of Buffalonians pour into Toronto's lakefront Exhibition Stadium, which is also the loading site for busloads of National Football League fans from Canada who routinely travel to Buffalo Bills home games. . . .

Like their Canadian counterparts who travel south regularly, thousands of Americans own land in Canada, much of it recreational and much of it now controlled, when sold, by Canadian provincial governments increasingly conscious of the issue of foreign ownership. In Ontario, for instance, an American buyer of land must sign an affidavit that he is a "Canadian resident," which may become technically true if the sale goes through but is rarely so until then. The provision is designed to thwart the kind of real estate speculation by outsiders with big bundles of foreign money that pushed the market value of many properties, such as the tiny outcroppings of rock that pass for vacation islands in Georgian Bay, beyond the reach of average Canadians. . . .

The main struts of the two countries' close relationship are political, economic, and security-oriented. Decisions in Washington on interest rates, for example, have an immediate public and private impact across Canada and in Ottawa, where the currency is also called the dollar and is closely pegged to American money. Yet every day Canadians learn of these foreign decisions directly affecting their own lives only in the news as if they were 10,000 miles away. It breeds within them a deep sense of powerlessness—and resentment . . . .

. . . Many times during my tenure in Canada I was interviewed for articles on how Americans were paying more attention to their northern neighbor. In *The Toronto Star*, Canada's largest circulation daily and one noted for its nationalist themes, one such piece began: "Curse those Americans. They are taking away one of our great Canadian preoccupations. They are not ignoring us anymore." . . .

. . . [There was a] growing awareness of an emerging Canadian presence in the world at large and across North America in particular. Canadian banks, real estate and insurance firms, cable TV concerns, newspaper publishers, oil companies, and high-profile—and tasty—beers added to a widening sense among Americans, even more so than among Canadians themselves, that this once-silent neighbor was developing into a more mature country with its own peculiar set of diverse dynamics. This was interesting in and of itself because it was coming to play a more direct and important role in American life. There could be questions about the country's tactics, perhaps puzzlement over its different responses, but not about its existence or changing character.

. . . Increased and more informed routine American news coverage and expanded Canadian studies programs at American universities offered hope, too, that this change would seep further. Someday perhaps well-meaning Americans, intending a compliment, would notice that now it was only they who kept talking about how alike, how like cousins, these two people were. Nothing could ever change the geographical reality, the similar cultural heritage, the pervasive family and economic ties. But Canadians, not always intending any insult to Americans, were increasingly thinking of the Canadianness of their lives and less of their similarity to the United States. This could, if nurtured properly by leaders on both sides, be a positive sign of growing internal strength and need not be turned into some anti-American threat by opportunistic or ignorant leaders on either side.

. . . As Ambassador Gotlieb put it, "We are, after all, different countries." What other two independent countries in the world require that kind of reminder? And with this comes a recognition that despite ongoing reservoirs of goodwill, the interests of these two countries will not always be the same. "The challenge, in managing this massive bilateral relationship of ours," Mr. Mac-Guigan told a Los Angeles audience, "is to respect our differences as we build on the areas of agreement." Ironically, each country had proved more adept at applying such principles to other more distant and changing lands than to its own next-door neighbor, cousin or not.

"While we would want never to be left alone in the world without America, we would also never want to be left in the world with America alone."
—Dalton Camp, 1980

From Andrew Malcolm, *The Canadians*, (Toronto: Paper Jacks Ltd., 1987).

1. How does Malcolm describe the Canadian experience?
2. What critique does the author offer of the Canadian identity?
3. How do Canadians and Americans view each other?

The 49th Paradox

Columnist Richard Gwyn's insightful analysis of the Canadian-American relationship represents one of the most thoughtful examinations of the subject in recent years. In these excerpts, Gwyn outlines his view of an emergent Canadian nationalism.

This is neither a Lament for a Nation nor a valediction for nationalism. Instead, it is an attempt to begin a search for something new. Since it is different from most books written by political reporters, different indeed from other books of my own, some explanation of its nature and structure may be in order.

. . . Robert Fulford of *Saturday Night* sent me a copy of the introduction he wrote to the 1982 book, *Canada, A Landscape Portrait*. "When they arrive in Canada, political ideas change. The harsh demand and the urgent appeal are dissipated by the size of the country," he wrote. "For this reason, Canada offers an especially frustrating life to intellectuals, whose training is usually based on European or American models. They almost break their swords. They discover that Canadians can't or won't make hard decisions; that every idea approved of in one part of Canada is cancelled out by another part." This warning is entirely sound. Two factors have given me confidence to ignore it. One is that these pages contain no "harsh demand" or "urgent appeal" but only, if the trick is brought off, a kind of insidious temptation. The other is that week in, week out, Fulford waves his own sword around, and when last spotted was still in breath. . . .

. . . Since the Loyalists joined the *Canadiens* in the northern wilderness in 1784, Canadian politics has revolved around just two axes: English-French relations; Canada-U.S. relations. . . .

One discovery in particular was the paradox of the 49th parallel. . . .

The divide that matters is psychic. . . . Through most of its history, Canada has survived despite the odds by consciously aspiring to no higher status than that of being a "not-America." This was a canny, tortoise-like strategy, if scarcely a creative or courageous one. Yet it worked. We hung on, and eventually we grew up. At some time after the Second World War, when Britain ceased to be able to function as a guarantor of Canada's status as a "not-America," we made the rite of passage from semi-nation to full one. The sound barrier was breached. The great dare was taken, and was achieved.

Canadians are no longer "not-Americans." Here, so I believe, truly lies *The 49th Paradox*. We have evolved into a people who are as fully North American as are Americans, and yet who, because of our political culture, are now a quite distinct kind of North American. Conventionally, nations are sorted out from each other by their language, their dress, their customs, their styles of Morris dances. But the worst way to look at North America is in a rearview mirror. Here, as the place where the future always happens first, two nations have evolved that are utterly alike in almost all of their externals and yet are utterly unlike in their political cultures so that they are as distinct from each other as are the Germans from the French, say, even though both are Europeans just as Canadians and Americans are both North Americans. . . .

These personal relationships fix limits to the institutional disagreements and confrontations. Canada and the U.S. are never going to go to war with each other, will always be allies, will always look at the outside world from the same, liberal, democratic premises, will always be, under the skin, good neighbours.

★ ★ ★ ★ ★

The Moose That Roared

This persistence in the popularity of nationalism is almost as much of a puzzle as is the existence of nationalism itself in a nation that is a non-nation in any conventional construct of political science or of anthropology. Nationalism itself is an atavistic urge that arises from a homogenous people who fear that outsiders may change them, let alone press them. With occasional exceptions, the feelings in Canada took the form of nationalism's milder variant–patriotism, a pride of place, a satisfaction in collective accomplishment.

This patriotism, though, came to acquire a sharp edge. By celebrating Canada, Canadians were simultaneously rejecting the United States. Americans personally were never rejected, nor was the best in the U.S., which Canadians copied and envied. What was rejected increasingly over the years was the U.S. as it was seen to have become: violent, polarized, militaristic. In one of Trudeau's first speeches as Prime Minister, he cited as Canada's most considerable threat neither Quebec separatism nor unemployment but that "violence may come to our cities from across the border." At the end of his term, although he himself was hugely unpopular, his peace initiative was enthusiastically applauded. If by the mid-1980s Canadians didn't want their border barricaded, neither did they want if left untended.

★ ★ ★ ★ ★

The Other North Americans
In a long article on Canada for the *New York Times Magazine* published in 1983, the newspaper's Ottawa correspondent, Michael Kaufman, recounted his observations during a coast-to-coast tour. 'There are no slums. There are no graffiti. There is no litter. . . . Parks are used both day and night.' He then expressed his own judgement about what he had seen: 'I have a high regard for the pervasive comfort Canada has bestowed on its citizens. Yet if forced to choose, I would stick to our own messier arrangements, of liberty, pervasive freedom and personal responsibility.'

This was a fair summation of the different ways by which the citizens of the two societies of North America have chosen to order social relationships among themselves. One consequential quarrel can be picked with it though: Kaufman took for granted that "liberty" and "freedom" are constrained on the northern side of the border–so that people don't mug and rape each other in parks–but are unconstrained on its southern side.

Instead, Canadians and Americans interpret the ideals of freedom and liberty differently. Allowing bag ladies the freedom to starve or allowing individuals to be bankrupted for life for lack of medical insurance imposes severe constraints on their freedom. More subtly, since no northern equivalent to the American Dream exists, Canadians possess the freedom not to be Canadians but to be almost anything they choose to be in a bilingual, multicultural, regionalized country. This said, American messiness is unquestionably creative. The homosexual leader, Sister Boom-Boom, roller-skating around the Democratic Convention in San Francisco, would probably, if in Canada, have been ticketed for jaywalking.

From Richard Gwyn, *The 49th Parallel: Canada in North America*, (Toronto: McClelland and Stewart, 1985). Used by permission of the Canadian Publishers, McClelland and Stewart.

1. Account for Gwyn's statement that "Canadians are no longer 'not Americans'."
2. How does the author distinguish nationalism from patriotism?
3. What are the characteristics of the "other North Americans"?

2
NORTH AMERICA BEFORE THE EUROPEANS

On the Eve of Contact

North America, prior to European contact, was a patchwork of Native groups. The continent was divided regionally with like societies emerging under similar geographic conditions. In what is now the United States and Canada, these societies were preliterate. That is they had no written language but rather depended upon an oral tradition. Even so, in each region local nations had developed complex languages, religions, laws, social organizations, and varying levels of technology. There was some conflict, but basically the relatively small numbers of people combined with the vast areas of territory made serious warfare non-existent north of Mexico.

Images of Native peoples in Europe during the first decades of colonization were basically formed from contact with those Natives living on the Eastern Seaboard and the Great Lakes Lowlands. They are known collectively as the "Eastern Woodlands" group. This is obviously a generalization with all of its inherent drawbacks. One might as accurately group Spain, Portugal, France, England, and the Netherlands together during the same period and categorize them as "Western Europeans." Although such a term has its uses, it also encourages many inaccuracies in interpretation.

Two distinct groups dominated the Eastern Woodlands. The first was the Algonkian peoples. The Algonkians were a hunting and gathering people who tended to be nomadic and to depend upon migrating game for food. Similar in language and culture, the Algonkians ranged from the Micmac of New England and the Maritimes to the Cree of the northern prairies. The Algonkians played a major role in the first contacts with Europeans as well as in later interior exploration and settlement. As Europeans penetrated the St. Lawrence Lowlands however they were soon confronted by a second group, the Iroquoians.

The Iroquoians dominated the Great Lakes region. They were a complex and sophisticated people. Controlling one of the major transportation routes on the continent, the Iroquoians became North America's first trading nation. The trading network established by these people resulted in the exchange of such products as citrus fruits from Florida with copper mined north of Lake Superior. To make trade with more northerly groups such as the Algonkians simpler the Iroquoians produced their own trade goods in the form of food. These were the "three sisters" of beans, corn, and squash. Consequently, Iroquoian villages were not only the centres of trade, but farming communities as well.

As with any successful business, the various Iroquoian nations had competitors—each other. The two principal opponents were the League of the Iroquois, sometimes called the Five Nations, who lived in the Finger Lakes region of New York, and the Huron Confederacy, who lived in southern Ontario around Midland. Their competition extended to the occasional raid for captives, but never, in the prehistoric period, to full-scale warfare. As with most early societies, the Natives of North America had certain common values. There was a strong bond of kinship, or loyalty, to family and clan. There was a certain amount of communal living and sharing of resources. And finally there was the land. The land was a resource held in common, used, and then left. It was something which no individual could claim to own or control.

Traditionally, historians and ethnographers have believed that the picture of Native society recorded by European observers at the beginning of the seventeenth century presented a fairly accurate view of pre-contact life. Today, researchers are no longer so certain. While it is clear that the basics of village life and clan organization reflect traditional values, the origins of some other aspects of Native society have been called into question. Many modern historians point to the long period of casual contact between Native North Americans and Europeans prior to the seventeenth century. They claim that the more complex political organization of the League and the Huron Confederacy arose not from local conditions, but out of the need to establish an organized structure for trading with the Europeans. Marxist historians go so far as to claim that the concept of family hunting areas described by early European accounts was a product of the European idea of ownership of property and not a natural development in the New World.

The resolution of this debate between the traditionalists, who contend that early accounts provide a window on pre-contact life, and the revisionists, who at the extreme claim that almost every aspect of Native life was affected by non-recorded early contact, will inevitably depend upon a detailed analysis of the archaeological fragments of the pre- and post-contact periods. Whatever their findings, there is no question but that a complex and developing society existed in North America at the end of the European fifteenth century.

It was into this world that Christopher Columbus sailed in 1492, carrying not just trade goods but a cargo of European values that would change North America forever.

Contact: Tentative Beginnings

In spite of the excitement generated by the voyages of Columbus, European visitors to North America were nothing new. A recent school of research claims that periodic visits from Europe had been taking place for thousands of years. Through an examination of burial pits, petroglyphs, and small megalithic monuments, some historians and linguists assert that North America was probably visited by both Phoenician and Celtic sailors in the first two or three centuries B.C. In addition, manuscripts from the Middle Ages assert that St. Brendan, an Irish monk, sailed to the New World in a leather boat sometime in the fifth century.

Firm archaeological evidence places the Vikings here in the tenth and eleventh centuries. Recent excavations at Anse Aux Meadows in Newfoundland have indicated that attempts at permanent settlement were not uncommon during that period. In addition, Norse sagas from the eleventh century indicate that these Viking colonists did a brisk trade in furs with the local inhabitants. This practice would set a pattern for centuries to come.

It is also probable that Basque fishing fleets visited the Grand Banks long before the "official" discovery. Although so far only wrecks from the sixteenth century have been discovered, evidence would seem to indicate that this was no new pastime.

When early Norse settlers met with Native North Americans, they faced each other on fairly equal terms. Over the intervening five hundred years however, Europe had undergone a technological revolution. The Viking longboats had been replaced by better and more manoeuvrable craft and improved skills in armour and weapons manufacturing, coupled with the introduction of gunpowder, had made the fifteenth century European a far more impressive visitor than that of the eleventh century. The biggest difference in the fifteenth century, however, was not just that the latest visitors were well-armed, but that they had government support and were here to stay!

How did the Native inhabitants view this latest group of visitors? At first, by all accounts, the Europeans were welcomed with open arms. Native leaders offered to share food, shelter, and even their women with the new arrivals. To some extent this is a reflection of a Native belief that the Europeans were in some way connected with the supernatural. There were a number of reasons for this. To begin with, they had come from beyond the oceans where nothing was supposed to exist. Secondly, they appeared to be riding upon "floating islands" with sails that looked like clouds and had cannons that roared and flashed like thunder and lightning. In their chests, they carried items of great power such as polished metal goods and glass beads. Finally, they brought death. Aside from riding fire-breathing animals (as Aztecs described the sight of a man on horseback firing his gun), they brought death just through touch.

Time and time again, European disease spread by simple contact would sweep through an unsuspecting population. The Natives had no immunity to European viruses and epidemics decimated their populations, while their visitors were virtually untouched! Faced with such evidence, it is hardly surprising that Native leaders regarded these visitors with some measure of awe and fear.

During the period of exploration in the late fifteenth and early sixteenth centuries, most trips seemed to have followed one of two routes. Spanish explorers tended to follow the pattern of Columbus arriving in the Caribbean. British and French mariners, on the other hand, took the traditional route toward the Grand Banks finding landfall in Newfoundland. As a result, the Natives in these two areas experienced the first benefits and costs of contact.

One such contact was made on the voyage of Gaspar Corte-Real. A Portuguese expedition under his command made landings in Newfoundland in 1500 and again in 1501. Even at that early date, clear trading patterns had developed. Corte-Real's men reported that some of the Natives already owned a piece of a broken European sword and two silver Venetian rings. The Portuguese described the Natives as being: "most gentle; they laugh considerably, and manifest the greatest pleasure." Fifty of these gentle people, the Beothuk, were taken prisoner back to Portugal. They never returned home.

The Portuguese were not the only explorers engaged in this kidnapping for profit. Spanish businessmen raided the Bahamas for slave labour and, as late as

Engraving showing Champlain taking part in a raid against the League of the Iroquois (top)
This 1635 map reflects the voyages of the Father of New France.

1521, over seventy Natives from South Carolina were taken for use on plantations on Santo Domingo. Native North Americans, however, were soon found to be unsuitable for slave labour. Deprived of their freedom, they tended to die quickly in captivity. Soon interest turned elsewhere and, for the remainder of the colonial period slave labour was imported from Africa.

Native peoples also found themselves being abducted as souvenirs during the early contact period. In 1502, three Natives were presented to King Henry VII of England and in the 1530s, Jacques Cartier repaid Stadaconan hospitality by kidnapping their leader, Donnacona, along with nine of his kinsmen and taking them to France. It is small wonder that the attitudes of Native peoples toward their European visitors began to change.

With increased contact, Europeans began to notice new patterns in Native bargaining for goods. No longer satisfied with low value items such as copper and tin ornaments or glass beads, they began to demand iron cutting tools, knives, and fish-hooks. The volume of trade began to increase as well. In 1583 one observer noted 15 000 livres worth of Canadian furs for sale in Paris, and by the end of the century the St. Lawrence village of Tadoussac had become the most important centre for fur trading on the continent.

This increased trade had a price. As fur became an increasingly valuable "cash crop," more and more time was spent by Native peoples in its acquisition. As a result, by the end of the sixteenth century groups along the coast were actually buying dried foods from European traders. The self-sufficiency of the pre-contact period had been severely undercut by a growing dependency upon the Europeans.

This early period of contact in North America had seen the gradual development of a profitable economic relationship between Native groups and European traders and fishermen. To the south, however, things had happened differently. While British, French, and Dutch traders had been establishing tentative commercial footholds in the North, the Spanish had been carving out an empire.

The Spanish Experience

Christopher Columbus has often been credited with "discovering" America. For the millions of people who already lived here it must have seemed a small accomplishment. As we have seen, the existence of the New World was already a matter of recorded fact in Europe. However, this does not mean that Columbus was just another in a long line. Although sailing for the Orient, and convinced that he was near Japan, the voyages of Columbus opened up the Western Hemisphere to the exploring minds and exploding population of Renaissance Europe.

The Spanish admiral was captivated by the people he first met saying:

I knew that they were a people to be delivered and converted to our holy faith by love than by force . . . [I] gave to some among them . . . things of little value. At this they were greatly pleased and became so entirely our friends that it was a wonder to see.

Although privately commenting that he had found "a very great continent, which until today has been unknown," publicly Columbus went to his death claiming to have landed in Asia. It would be his successors who would build upon his work.

The Spanish crown was quickly convinced that their explorer had stumbled into a vast new territory. So certain were they that, in 1494, they signed the Treaty of Tordesillas with Portugal to divide the unexplored world in half. All lands discovered east of the line would belong to Portugal, and all lands west to Spain. On paper this left Africa to the Portuguese and the Americas to Spain. In reality there were two problems with this agreement.

To begin with, in 1500, the Portuguese laid claim to Brazil which, unknown to everyone six years earlier, actually lay to the east of the line. The second and more significant problem came from the fact that although Spain and Portugal had an agreement, England, France, and the Netherlands paid no attention to it. The race for colonies was in full gear.

The Spanish moved quickly to establish their presence in the Americas. By the end of the century permanent settlements had been established on Hispanola and, in 1508, the first permanent Spanish settlement on the mainland was founded in Panama. During this period, Native populations were virtually enslaved to become forced labourers for the conquerors. And conquerors they were. Spanish expeditions were private affairs paid for and led by Conquistadors, or mercenary soldiers. New territory and its Native population were there to be exploited. So harsh was the treatment of these people that in some cases entire islands were depopulated for use as labourers within one or two generations. It was on the mainland, however, that the great Spanish conquests took place.

In 1519 a young Spanish soldier, Hernando Cortes, walked into Tenochtitlan with about 550 soldiers and took the Aztec ruler Montezuma as a hostage. How was such a thing possible? American historian Barbara Tuchman says that the Aztecs let it happen to them. Through brutal conquest of their neighbours, the Aztecs had built an empire but had also created bitter enemies. The Spanish were only too willing to take advantage of this situation. In addition, Montezuma himself was a fatalist who saw the Spanish soldiers in their shining armour and smoking guns as messengers from the gods coming to end his rule. This belief was strengthened by the nearly total immunity of the Spanish to the devastating epidemics that accompanied their arrival. Clearly they were in closer communion with the gods!

Although after six months of stalemate the Aztecs finally got fed up and drove Cortes and his men out of the city, the damage had been done. The Aztecs had been shown to be weak. Cortes, now allied with the traditional enemies of the Aztecs, laid siege to the city and eventually destroyed it. Within thirty years, the once mighty centre of the Aztec Empire had become Mexico City, prosperous capital of New Spain.

The French Experience

When Francis I, King of France heard of the Treaty of Tordesillas he laughed and said: "The sun shines on me as well as others, I should be very happy to see the clause in Adam's will which excluded me from my share when the world should come to be divided!"

In spite of this attitude, however, French exploration of the New World did not begin until the voyage of Verrazano in 1524. Ten years after this, Jacques Cartier, the Mariner of St. Malo, laid claim to the territory that was to become the base of French power in North America, New France. Cartier's voyages of 1534 and 1535 resulted in the mapping of the Maritime provinces and exploration up the St. Lawrence as far as present-day Montreal. French contact with the Iroquoians living in the area was quite peaceful. They guided him up the river and hosted the French expedition through the winter of 1535-36. Unlike the Spanish experience in the south, Cartier reported that the Natives he met had "not anything above the value of five sous, their canoes and fishing nets excepted." In response to their hospitality, Cartier took a number of Natives back with him to France. He hoped their stories of riches to be had in the new territory would convince the king to finance still another journey to the New World.

In 1541 the project was launched. Unlike Cartier's earlier voyages, this was to be an invasion force. Based upon the Spanish success, a task force of ten ships was organized. It included seven hundred soldiers and sailors, stonemasons and carpenters to build fortifications, and even artillery. Command of the military force was to be under the Sieur de Roberval. Cartier and half of the fleet set out early. They were met with suspicion and hostility, and Cartier himself began to doubt the Native stories about an interior "Kingdom of the Saguenay" which was said to be filled with riches. Roberval, who had been delayed in leaving, did not arrive that year, and by the time the second half of the expedition sailed into the St. Lawrence, Cartier was on his way home. Roberval spent a miserable winter at Cap Rouge, finding little to justify a military campaign the next year. Finally, he, too, set sail for home and France officially "forgot" about North America for the remainder of the century.

The French made a short-lived attempt to establish an outpost at Fort Caroline near the present-day border of Florida and Georgia. The Spanish resented this incursion and levelled the fort, killing all of its inhabitants. As result, when the Spanish empire was at its peak in 1580, with possessions ranging from Mexico to the Philippines, no other European power had been able to establish even one permanent colony in the New World.

French fishing fleets continued to tap the Grand Banks for the next thirty years, but no further permanent outposts were established. Finally, in 1599 exploration began anew. The first permanent French settlement was established on the Bay of Fundy. Port Royal, established in 1603, soon proved to be too far out of the way for the mainstream of trade through the St. Lawrence. Consequently, in 1608 a new settlement was established at "Kebec," where the river narrows. Quebec, under the leadership of its first governor, Samuel de Champlain, was to become the commercial, military, and political centre of an expansive French empire over the next century and a half.

The life-blood of this empire was to be the fur trade. As a result, local Natives became not slave labourers as in New Spain, but rather commercial partners in a growing industry. From the early seventeenth century on, the fate of New France and of its trading allies, the Huron Confederacy would become inexorably linked.

The Algonkians who dominated the trading centre at Tadoussac resisted early French attempts to establish direct contact with Native groups in the interior. Relishing their role as intermediaries in the trading enterprise, they were reticent to allow the Europeans access into the interior. The founding of Quebec placed the Europeans upriver from Tadoussac; however, the St. Lawrence was not considered a safe route to the Great Lakes owing to the presence of the Mohawks, members of the League of the Iroquois, enemies of the Huron Confederacy. Traders were forced to take a much longer overland route to the trading centre.

In 1607 Champlain decided to take action. He and two colleagues joined a Montagnais and Huron raiding party and headed south. This force of about sixty attacked and defeated a group of Mohawk raiders numbering over two hundred. About fifty of the enemy were slain. Three years later, Champlain joined in another similar attack, and by 1610 had managed to secure the trade route. It would be theirs for the next two decades.

This new economic partnership was not a master servant relationship but rather an arrangement between equals. Each side recognized the strengths and weaknesses of the other. Champlain found the Algonkians to be "sensible and intelligent," but felt it necessary to add that they were "also great liars" and that "you shouldn't trust them unless you have good reason to." Still, as they grew to know them, the French could not help but come to respect the skills of their new allies.

For their part, the Algonkians and Hurons saw the French as being of average or below average intelligence. The French seemed unable to learn Native languages, they could not master even the simplest wilderness skills, and to top it all off, they wore beards! Recollet friar, Gabriel Sagard, remarked that: "they have such a horror of a beard . . . they think it makes people more ugly and weakens their intelligence."

In spite of their criticisms of European characteristics of greed and cruelty, however, the Natives did come to recognize the value of their growing economic relationship. They might never be able to adjust to the Europeans, but they could certainly incorporate their trade goods into their lives.

The second major area of contact between the French and Native North Americans was on the missionary frontier. Early attempts had been made by Roman Catholic Recollet friars to convert the Natives, but it was the Jesuits who really took the task in hand. The Society of Jesus or Jesuits had been formally created in 1540 by an order of the Pope. Established in France after 1618, they soon became involved in the expanding missionary work in New France. Although interested in the semi-nomadic Algonkian peoples of the St. Lawrence Valley, the Jesuits saw their real calling in the conversion of the more settled peoples of Huronia. In annual reports filed from 1611 to 1768, the Jesuits opened a window on the developing colony. Of significant interest are those reports or *Relations* as they are called, that deal with the decades of the 1630s and 1640s when the Jesuits had established their first permanent outposts in the interior. The Jesuits reflect an ambivalent attitude toward their "heathen" charges. While the Jesuits saw

Huronia as a "stronghold of Satan," they also recognized the need to isolate their flock from the corrupting influences of other French Christians.

The Hurons had mixed feelings as well. To some extent the Jesuits were feared. It was clear that they brought death. As elsewhere, living together meant the spread of European diseases. This was reinforced by the fact that each time the priests baptised a sick Native the patient tended to die. For the Hurons, Jesuit celibacy soon became respected as a source of great supernatural power. Unlike in Mexico, however, such power did not invoke fear but only resentment.

In the final analysis, however, the presence of the missionaries was a small price to pay for access to French trade goods. The priests themselves recognized the advantages in this bargaining position. After 1641 French traders were only allowed to sell guns to the baptised, and during a famine two years later, only converted Natives were provided with food.

In spite of such incentives for conversion, the relationship between the French and the Native people remained primarily an economic one throughout the colonial period. Unlike the Spanish exploitation, however it remained a relationship between relatively equal partners, and New France would see the greatest integration of European and Native culture.

The English Pattern

The first British attempt to settle in the future United States began with high hopes in 1585. Sir Walter Raleigh founded the Virginia Company and organized an expedition to North America. The colonists, over one hundred men, women, and children, established a base at Roanoke Island. It was further strengthened by another expedition of over one hundred in 1587.

When the ships sailed back to Britain that fall, they left a prosperous settlement behind. However, at this point international politics intervened. Proposals to visit the colony during the next two years were turned down. Spain was planning a major attack upon Britain—the famous attack of the Spanish Armada—and all ships were needed for defense.

As a result, the next expedition to Roanoke did not return until 1590. Expecting to find a healthy welcoming committee the expedition was shocked to find the settlement deserted, the buildings in ruins, and absolutely no sign of the colonists. There was no sign of violence, nor had they starved because the emergency food supply was still intact. They had just disappeared. Raleigh suspected that they had joined forces with a local Indian tribe, but no trace of them was ever found. Some historians point to another possibility. In the early years of the colony, a silver cup had gone missing. Local Natives were blamed and in retaliation a nearby village was burned and the crops destroyed. Perhaps the Natives, finding the small colony was cut off from outside support, decided to repay the incident in kind. Whatever the reason, to this day the mystery of the "lost colony" has never been solved.

The whole story of the early settlement of Virginia is an example of what happens when a good idea goes wrong. For the next thirty years the colony struggled to survive. Wave after wave of immigration came to the new land, but still little progress was made. What stunted the growth of the colony? The answer is simple: tobacco.

By the beginning of the seventeenth century, the smoking of tobacco was becoming a fashionable habit in Europe. Bringing a relatively high return and being easy to transport, many investors in the Virginia Company saw the production of the weed as a means to get a quick return on their investment. It is interesting to note that during these years when the population was starving to death in Virginia, the exports of tobacco were continually going up. In 1616 the colony had exported 2500 lbs. (1100 kg); by 1618 this was up to almost 50 000 lbs. (23 000 kg); and by 1627, tobacco exports had topped 500 000 lbs. (230 000 kg). However, what these figures do not reveal is the incredible human cost.

This was a "boom time" for Virginia. Fortunes were made and lost overnight. As with any high-profit, high-risk venture all sorts of support services appeared. Ships anchored off-shore became casinos and taverns; men who had just sold a large crop were especially vulnerable to those eager to take it away from them. Visitors to the colony during the period noted that the houses were in ruins, the church was in disrepair, and the streets were dug up, yet everywhere you looked someone had planted tobacco! Because all available land was given over to tobacco, all food had to be imported. It was sold at ridiculous prices. Like the gold rushes of California and the Yukon in the nineteenth century, the tobacco rush of the seventeenth century promised great wealth for everyone, but delivered only to a very few.

This increase in tobacco production worried Native leaders as well. As more and more land came under cultivation, greater encroachments were made upon Indian territory. Finally they struck back. In 1622 local Natives launched an all-out attack against the plantations. The results were devastating. In the past five years over four thousand settlers had come to the colony. Many of these people had starved to death in a colony too preoccupied with tobacco to grow food. One-third of the remainder were killed in this conflict. The seven hundred survivors eventually organized and launched their own retaliatory attacks. This "bloody retribution" would cement the growing feelings of fear and hatred on both sides. By 1701 continued expansion had established a pattern of conflict which would not be broken until after the Seven Years' War.

The English colonies in the North soon fell into a similar pattern. The first ongoing contact with Native people in New England was made by the Pilgrims. Arriving in Plymouth on December 25, 1620, their first winter was extremely hard. The Pilgrims had little opportunity to build adequate winter shelters so late in the season. Consequently by spring almost half their number were dead. Burials took place late at night in unmarked graves so that the Indians would not know how small their numbers had become. In the spring, however, conditions improved and local Natives, far from being threatening, became friends and allies. With their help the Pilgrims managed to clear land and plant enough food to see them through their second winter. By their third year in North America they were self-sufficient.

The Pilgrims repaid this openness with wary caution. Indians were not allowed into their villages, and it soon became a crime to sell a gun to a Native. Although sworn to convert the "heathen," the Pilgrims kept their distance, and the first missionary work did not even begin until almost fifteen years after their arrival.

Meanwhile in England, rich Puritan merchants had established the Massachusetts Bay Company in 1629. According to their charter they were given the rights to the area from the Charles to the Merrimac rivers. A Puritan settlement had already been established in the area in 1626, near present-day Salem, and in 1630 John Winthrop, a prominant Puritan lawyer, secured the right to establish an independent commonwealth in the area.

The new colony grew quickly—too quickly as far as some of the settlers were concerned. One such individual was Roger Williams. Williams questioned the right of the colonists to simply take over land that clearly belonged to the Indians. Winthrop, on the other hand, believed that the Indians had forfeited their rights to the land, and had squandered God's "gift" to them. The proof was that they "enclosed no land, neither have they any settled habitations, nor any tame cattle." Williams and his views were recognized as a danger to the stability of the colony, and in 1636 he was expelled.

The following year, continued expansion of the New England settlements brought conflict with the Pequot nation. Settlers declared these Natives "minions of the devil," and brutally slaughtered many of them near Mystic, Connecticut. Native males who survived the battle were executed, while the women and children were sold into slavery in the West Indies.

One last attempt was made to stem the tide of European expansion in New England. It took place in 1676, and began almost by accident. Metacom was the leader of the Wampanoag people. Called "King Philip" by the English, he was an unusual individual who seemed as at home in the salons of Boston as he did in the wilderness. It turned out that Sassaman, a Harvard-educated Native and former secretary to Metacom, had been passing information to the governor of Plymouth. A small band of Natives caught the traitor and killed him. They in turn were captured, tried (by a mixed white/Native jury), and hanged. Retaliatory attacks began two weeks later. What initially began as isolated raids against Puritan villages soon turned into an all-out war. Of the ninety villages in the colony, fifty-two were attacked and twelve were completely destroyed. The fury of the attacks soon burned themselves out. Shortages of supplies, and the lack of an overall strategy coupled with stiffening white resistance eventually brought the war to an end. The damage, however, had been done. It would be twenty years before the destroyed farms and villages would be resettled, and another forty years before the frontier would begin to advance again.

Until 1492, Native peoples had dominated the North American continent. From the Aztec cities of Mexico to the Algonkian villages of the Canadian Shield, a complex tapestry of over four million people lied their lives isolated from Europe.

Over the next two centuries European powers would carve their own empires out of the new world. It is difficult for us to recreate the rich cultures of pre-contact North America. Archaeological evidence and oral histories give us only a glimpse of this lost world. There are some clues in the writings of European chroniclers but they were witnessing a culture in flux. The insights that do survive the natural mistakes and misinterpretations depict Natives who were quickly adapting to the new reality. It is not surprising that European "civilization" was captivated by the natural riches of the new continent. The only obstacle to their exploitations of these vast resources were the Native inhabitants. They would be conquered, assimilated, or merely pushed aside in the process. Contact posed a challenge to the new arrivals. For the original inhabitants, it constituted a disaster.

First Impressions, 1492

Modern contact with the New World began with the voyages of Christopher Columbus. Columbus kept a detailed record of his voyage. Although this original text has not been seen since the late fifteenth century, what we do have is either a paraphrase or a copy of the admiral's diary compiled by the contemporary Spanish historian Bartolome de las Casas. Las Casas was eighteen years old at the time of the first Columbus voyage. His History of the Indies *was based heavily upon interviews and original court documents of the period. The section dealing with the first contact made by Columbus appears to be a verbatim copy of the actual "formal words of the Admiral" and may, therefore, be considered as a first-hand account. Although traditionally thought to have taken place on Watling Island (renamed San Salvador in 1926), current scholarship places this dramatic first contact on the small island of Samana Cay about 100 km to the southeast.*

October 12, 1492

Two hours after midnight land appeared, at a distance of about two leagues from them. . . . Soon many people of the island gathered there. What follows are the actual words of the admiral, in his book of his first voyage and discovery of these Indies.

"I," he says, "in order that they might feel great amity towards us, because I knew that they were a people to be delivered and converted to our holy faith rather by love than by force, gave to some among them some red caps and some glass beads, which they hung round their necks, and many other things of little value. At this time they were greatly pleased and became so entirely our friends that it was a wonder to see. Afterwards they came swimming to the ships' boats, where we were, and brought us parrots and cotton thread in balls, and spears and many other things, such as small glass beads and hawks' bells, which we gave to them. In fact, they took all and gave all, such as they had, with good will, but it seemed to me that they were a people deficient in everything. They all go naked as their mothers bore them, and the women also, although I saw only one very young girl. And all those whom I did see were youths, so that I did not see one who was over thirty years of age; they were very well built, with very handsome bodies and very good faces. Their hair is coarse almost like the hairs of a horse's tail and short; they wear their hair down over their eyebrows, except for a few strands behind, which they wear long and never cut. Some of them are painted black, and they are the colour of people of the Canaries, neither black nor white, and some of them are painted white and some red and some in any colour that they find. Some of them paint their faces, some their whole bodies, some only the eyes, and some only the nose. They do not bear arms or know of them, for I showed to them swords and they took them by the blade and cut themselves through ignorance. They have no iron. Their spears are certain reeds, without iron, and some of these have a fish tooth at the end, while others are pointed in various ways. They are all generally fairly tall, good looking and well proportioned. I saw some who bore marks of wounds on their bodies, and I made signs to them to ask how this came about, and they indicated to me that people came from other islands, which are near, and wished to capture them, and they defended themselves. And I believe and still believe that they come here from the mainland to take them for slaves. They should be good servants and of quick intelligence, since I see that they very soon say all that is said to them, and I believe that they would easily be made Christians, for it appeared to me that they had no creed. Our Lord willing, at the time of my departure I will bring back six of them to Your Highnesses, that they may learn to talk. I saw no beast of any kind in this island, except parrots." All these are the words of the admiral.

From Cecil Jane, trans., revised and annotated by L.A. Vigneras, *The Journal of Christopher Columbus*, (New York: Clarkson N. Potter, 1960).

1. What does Columbus say was his motivation in trading with the natives?
2. Outline the picture painted by the admiral in terms of the physical appearance, character, level of technology, and cultural sophistication of the Native inhabitants.
3. Paralleling Columbus's account, write a description of the Spanish from a Native point of view.

What Nature Gives Them, 1497

The Americas take their name from the Florentine navigator Amerigo Vespucci, whose assertions that a new continent had been discovered gained great attention in Europe. Sailing on behalf of the Spanish crown, he made a number of voyages to the New World in the late fifteenth and early sixteenth centuries. The following excerpt is taken from a letter written by Vespucci to Piero Soderini Gonfaloniere in 1504. In his letter Vespucci describes his first meetings with the Natives in 1497.

The manner of their living is very barbarous, because they do not eat at fixed times, but as often as they please. And it matters little to them that they should be seized with a desire to eat at midnight rather than by day, for at all times they eat. And their eating is done upon the ground, without tablecloth or any other cloth, because they hold their food either in earthen basins which they make or in half gourds. They sleep in certain nets made of cotton, very big, and hung in the air. And although this their way of sleeping may appear uncomfortable, I say that it is a soft way to sleep; [because it was very frequently our lot to sleep] in them, and we slept better in them than in quilts. They are people neat and clean of person, owing to the constant washing they practise. When, begging your pardon, they evacuate the bowels, they do everything to avoid being seen; and just as in this they are clean and modest, the more dirty and shameless are they in making water [both men and women]. Because, even while talking to us, they let fly such filth, without turning around or showing shame, that in this they have no modesty. They do not practise marriage amongst themselves. Each one takes all the wives he pleases; and when he desires to repudiate them, he does repudiate them without it being considered a wrong on his part or a disgrace to the woman; for in this the woman has as much liberty as the man. They are not very jealous, and are libidinous beyond measure, and the woman far more than the men; for I refrain out of decency from telling you the trick which they play to satisfy their immoderate lust. They are very fertile women, and in their pregnancies avoid no toil. Their parturitions are so easy that one day after giving birth they go out everywhere, and especially to bathe in the rivers; and they are sound as fish. They are so heartless and cruel that, if they become angry with their husbands, they immediately resort to a trick whereby they kill the child within the womb, and a miscarriage is brought about, and for this reason they kill a great many babies. They are women of pleasing person, very well proportioned, so that one does not see on their bodies any ill-formed feature or limb . . . . they go about utterly naked, . . . In short they are no more ashamed [of their shameful parts] than we are in displaying the nose and mouth . . . . They showed themselves very desirous of copulating with us Christians. While among these people we did not learn that they had any religion. They can be termed neither Moors nor Jews; and they are worse than heathen; because we did not see that they offered any sacrifice, nor yet did they have [any] house of prayer. I deem their manner of life to be Epicurean. Their dwellings are in common, and their houses built after the fashion of huts, but stoutly wrought and constructed out of very large trees and thatched with palm leaves, safe against tempests and winds, and in some places of such breadth [and length] that in a single house we found there were 600 souls; [and we saw towns of only thirteen houses where there were 4000 souls] . . . . Their wealth consists of feathers of many-hued birds, or of little rosaries which they make out of fish bones, or of white or green stones which they stick through cheeks, lips, and ears, and of many other things to which we attach no value. They engage in no barter [whatsoever]; they neither buy nor sell. In short, they live and are contented with what nature gives them. The wealth which we affect in this our Europe and elsewhere, such as gold, jewels, pearls, and other riches, they hold of no value at all; and altogether they have them in their lands they do not work to get them, nor do they care for them. They are so [liberal] in giving that it is the exception when they deny you anything; and, on the other hand, [they are free] in the begging, when they show themselves to be your friends. But the greatest token of friendship which they show you is that they give you their wives and daughters; and when a father or a mother brings you the daughter, although she be a virgin, and you sleep with her, they esteem themselves highly honored; and in this way they practise the full extreme of hospitality.

From George Tyler Northrup, ed., *Amerigo Vespucci: Letter to Piero Soderini, Gonfaloniere*, (Princeton: Princeton University Press, 1916).

1. Outline those aspects of Native behaviour that Vespucci found to be distasteful from his European point of view.
2. Contrast the Native view of wealth with that of the Spanish. What might account for the difference?
3. Project the probable impact of European contact upon the existing value system of the Natives.

The Land God Gave to Cain, 1534

In 1534 Francis I of France commissioned Jacques Cartier to "discover . . . countries where it is said that he should find a great quantity of gold and other valuable things." Cartier, sailing out of St. Malo in Brittany arrived in the Gulf of the St. Lawrence late in the summer of 1534. A brief reconnaissance of the region gave him little hope of discovering riches, but over the winter of 1534-35, he managed to convince the king to back a subsequent expedition to explore farther up the St. Lawrence. The first excerpt describes Cartier's impressions in 1534 while the second, in the following year, reflects his much more optimistic view.

If the soil were as good as the harbours, it would be a blessing; but the land should not be called New Land, being composed of stones and horrible rugged rocks; . . . In fine I am rather inclined to believe that this is the land God gave to Cain. There are people on this coast whose bodies are fairly well formed but they are wild and savage folk. They wear their hair tied up on the top of their heads like a handful of twisted hay, with a nail of something of the sort passed through the middle, and into it they weave a few bird's feathers. They clothe themselves with the furs of animals, both men as well as women; but the women are wrapped up more closely and snuggly in their furs; and have a belt about their waists. They have canoes made of birchbark in which they go about, and from which they catch many seals. . . .

This island [Magdalen Island] is the best land we have seen; for two acres of it are worth more than the whole of Newfoundland. We found it to be covered with fine trees and meadows, fields of wild oats, and of pease in flower, as thick and as fine as ever I saw in Brittany, which might have been sown by husband-men. There are numerous gooseberry bushes, strawberry vines, Provins roses, as well as parsley and other useful, strong-smelling herbs. Round about this island are many great beasts, like large oxen, which have two tusks in their jaw like elephant's tusks and swim about in the water. There was one asleep on shore near the water's edge, and we set out in our long-boats to try and catch him; but as soon as we drew near, he threw himself into the sea. . . .

From H.P. Biggar, ed., *The Voyages of Jacques Cartier*, Publication of the Public Archives of Canada, No. 11, (Ottawa: Public Archives of Canada, 1924).

After we had cast anchor between this large island and the north shore, we went on land and took with us two Indians we had seized on our former voyages. We came upon several of the people of the country who began to run away and would not come near, until our two Indians had spoken to them and told them that they were Taignoagny and Dom Agaya. And when they knew who it was, they began to welcome them, dancing and going through many ceremonies. . . . The Captain received them all well and treated them to what he had to offer. And to ingratiate himself with them, he gave them some small presents of little value, at which they were much pleased.

On the morrow, the lord of Canada, named Donnacona, . . . came to our ships accompanied by many Indians in twelve canoes . . . . And when he came opposite to the Captain's vessel, on board of which were Taignoagny and Dom Agaya, the chief spoke to them and they to him, telling him what they had seen in France, and the good treatment meted out to them there. At this the chief was much pleased and begged the Captain to stretch out his arms to him that he might hug and kiss them, which is the way they welcome one in that country . . . . Near this spot lives a tribe of which this Donnacona is chief, and he himself resides there. The village is called Stadacona. This region is as fine land as it is possible to see, being very fertile and covered with magnificent trees of the same varieties as in France, such as oaks, elms, ash, walnut, plum-trees, yew-trees, cedars, vines, hawthorns, bearing fruit as large as a damson, and other varieties of trees. Beneath these grows as good hemp as that of France, which comes up without sowing or tilling it . . . . The Captain, seeing their great affection and good-will, ordered the long-boat in which he was seated to go towards them, and gave them some knives and glass-beads, at which they showed wonderful pleasure. And when we were a league or so away, we still heard them singing, dancing and rejoicing over our visit.

From H.P. Biggar, ed., *The Voyages of Jacques Cartier*, Publication of the Public Archives of Canada, No. 11, (Ottawa: Public Archives of Canada, 1924).

Early next morning the Captain donned his armour and ordered his men to be marshalled in order to visit the town and habitation of this tribe, and a mountain which lies close to the town, whither the captain went with the noblemen and twenty mariners, leaving the rest to guard their boats, and taking three men from the town of Hochelaga to be his guides and escort to the spot. And when on the road we found it as well beaten as could be, in a fair country like a park; with as fine oaks as in any forest in France, and the whole ground beneath them thick with acorns. When we had gone about a league and a half, we came upon one of the chiefest lords of the town of Hochelaga, with a large company, who made sign to us to rest there beside a fire which they had lighted in the roadway. And then this chief began to make a sermon and discourse, which, as we have already said, is their mode of showing joy and friendship, welcoming the captain and his company; and our captain gave him two hatchets and two knives, with a cross and a crucifix which he made him kiss, and the hung it around his neck, whereof the chief thanked our captain. This done, we went along, and about half a league farther on began to come upon ploughed fields, and fair large meadows full of their manner of corn, which resembles the millet of Brazil, as large as a pea or larger, whereon they live as we do on wheat. And amid these fields is situated and placed the said town of Hochelaga, stretching up to a mountain which lies beside it, which is well cultivated and most fertile, and from whose top one can see to a great distance. This mountain we called Mount Royal. The town is built in a circle, and surrounded with a wooden palisade in three tiers, like a pyramid; the top row is crosswise, the centre row upright, and the bottom row is laid lengthwise; the whole compactly joined and lashed together after their manner, rising to about twice the height of a lance. The town has but one gate or entry, closed with bars; on it and at several points along the wall are galleries of a kind, with ladders ascending to them, provided with rocks and stones for its guard and defence. In the town are about fifty houses, each broad, built all of wood, with roofs and sides made of strips of bark or of wood as broad as a table, well and cunningly knotted together after their fashion; within these are several rooms, large and small; in the midst of each house, on the ground, is a large hall where they light their fire and live in common, afterwards retiring, the men and their women and children, to their said chambers. They also have garners at the top of their houses, where they store their corn, which they call caraconi, whereof they make their bread in the following manner. They have wooden mortars, like those for beating hemp, and in these wooden beetles they beat the corn to powder, then make paste of it and cakes of the paste, which they put on a hot stone and cover with hot pebbles, and thus they bake their bread, for want of an oven. They also make many stews of this corn, and also of beans and peas, of which they have good store; also of large cucumbers and other fruits. They have also in their houses large vats like tuns, wherein they store their eels and other fish, which they smoke during the summer and live upon in the winter; of these they gather great plenty, as we by experience have seen. None of their viands have any touch of salt; and they sleep on strips of bark laid on the ground, covered with wretched skins, whereof they also make their garments, such as otters, beavers, martens, foxes, wildcats, roes, stags and other wild beasts, though indeed the greater part of them go practically stark naked.

From Marc Lescarbot, *History of New France*, (1610), translated and edited by W.L. Grant and H.P. Biggar, (Toronto: The Champlain Society, 1907).

1. Contrast the life of Natives living in the St. Lawrence Valley with that of the Natives encountered by the Spanish in the Caribbean.
2. To what extent might these differences affect the nature of colonial policy in those two regions?
3. Create a thesis with regard to Cartier's attitude toward the land and its inhabitants. Defend your thesis with evidence from the document.

Tears of the Indies, 1552

Bartolome de las Casas has been criticized by many Spanish historians as exaggerating the brutality of the conquistadors in their conquest and occupation of the New World. In his Brief Relation of the Destruction of the Indies *published in Seville, Spain in 1552, Las Casas makes a strong case against his fellow Spaniards.*

In the year 1492, the *West-Indies* were discovered. The continent is distant from this about Two hundred miles, stretching it self out in length upon the sea side for above Ten thousand miles in length. This is already found out, and more is daily discovered. These Countreys are inhabited by such a number of people, as if God had assembled and called together to this place, the greatest part of Mankinde.

This infinite multitude of people was so created by God, as that they were without fraud, without subtility or malice, to their natural Governours most faithful and obedient. Toward the *Spaniards* whom they serve, patient, meek and peaceful, and who laying all contentions and tumultous thoughts aside, live without any hatred or desire of revenge; the people are most delicate and tender, enjoying such a feeble constitution of body as does not permit them to endure labour, so that the Children of Princes and great persons here, are not more nice and delicate than the Children of the meanest Countrey-man in that place. The Nation is very poor and indigent, possessing little, and by reason that they gape not after temporal goods, neither proud nor ambitious. Their diet is such that the most holy Hermite cannot feed more sparingly in the wildernesse. They go naked, only hiding the undecencies of nature . . . . They are very apprehensive and docible wit, and capable of all good learning, and very apt to receive our Religion, which when they have but once tasted, they are carried on with a very ardent and zealous desire to make a further progress in it; so that I have heard divers *Spaniards* confess that they have had nothing else to hinder them from enjoying heaven, but their ignorance of the true God.

To these quiet Lambs, endued with such blessed qualities, came the *Spaniards* like most cruel Tygres, Wolves and Lions, enrag'd with a sharp and tedious hunger; for these forty years past, minding nothing else but the slaughter of these unfortunate wretches, whom with divers kinds of torments neither seen nor heard of before, they have so cruelly and inhumanely butchered, that of three millions of people which Hispaniola it self did contain, there are left remaining alive scarce three hundred persons. And for the Island of *Cuba*, which contains as much ground in length, as from *Valladolid* to *Rome*; it lies wholly desert, until'd and ruin'd. The islands of *St. John* and *Jamaica* lie waste and desolate. The *Lucayan* Islands neighbouring toward the North upon *Cuba* and *Hispaniola*, being above Sixty or thereabouts with those Islands that are vulgarly called the Islands of the Gyants, of which that which is least fertile is more fruitful then the King of *Spains* Garden at *Sevil*, being situated in a pure and temperate air, are now totally unpeopled and destroyed; the inhabitants thereof amounting to above 5 000 000 souls, partly killed, and partly forced away to work in other places: so that there going a ship to visit those parts and to glean the remainder of these distressed wretches, there could be found no more than eleven men. . . .

Now to come to the Continent, we are confident, and dare to affirm upon our own knowledge, that there were ten Kingdomes of as large an extent as the Kingdome of *Spain*, joyning to it both *Arragon*, and *Portugal*, containing above a thousand miles every one of them in compass, which the unhumane and abominable villanies of the *Spaniards* have made a wilderness of being now as it were stript of all their people, and made bare of all their inhabitants, though it were a place formerly possessed by vast and infinite numbers of men; And we dare confidently aver, that for those Forty years, wherin the *Spaniards* exercised their abominable cruelties, and detestable tyrannies in those parts, that there have innocently perish'd above Twelve millions of souls, women and children being numbered in this sad and fatall list; moreover I do verily believe that I should speak within compass, should I say that above Fifty millions were consumed in this Massacre.

As for those that come out of *Spain*, boasting themselves to be Christians, they took two several waies to extirpate this Nation from the face of the Earth, the first whereof was a bloudy, unjust, and cruel war which they made upon them: a second by cutting off all that so much as sought to recover their liberty, as some of the stouter sort did intend. And as for the Women and Children that were left alive, they laid so heavy and grievous a yoke of servitude upon them that the conditions of beast was much more tolerable.

. . . For the *Spaniards* so condemned them (I now speak what I have seen without the least untruth) that they used them not like beasts, for that would have been tolerable, but looked upon them as if they had been but the dung and filth of the earth, and so little they regarded the health of their souls, that they suffered this great multitude to die without the least light or Religion; neither is this lesse true then what I have said before, and that which those tyrants and hangmen themselves dare not deny, without speaking a notorious falshood, that the *Indians* never gave them the least cause to offer them violence, but received them as *Angels* sent from heaven, till their excessive cruelties, the torments and slaughters of their Countrey-men mov'd them to take Armes against the *Spaniards*.

From Wilcomb E. Washburn, ed., *The Indian and The White Man*, (Garden City, New York: Anchor Books, 1964).

1. How does las Casas describe Spanish treatment of the Natives in the Caribbean?
2. In light of the Aztec description of Spanish behaviour, to what extent do you agree with the Spanish contention that las Casas overstated the case?
3. To what extent were the roots of this behaviour evident in the documents outlining initial Spanish contact?

New France: Commercial Outpost and Religious Frontier

Samuel de Champlain, more than any other colonial official in the first century of contact, established a positive working relationship with Native peoples. During his decades in New France he built a strong bond with these important trading partners and military allies. His first impressions, however, were often less than charitable. Many of the prevalent attitudes of European cultural superiority are evident in his early reports. This selection is taken from Champlain's Voyages. *In this passage he is describing his conversation with an Algonkian "Sagamo," or chief.*

On the ninth of June the savages started feasting and dancing all over again, still celebrating their victory over the Iroquois. . . .

While they were dancing the Algonkin Sagamo, a man named Besonat[1], took up a position before the women and girls between two poles on which they had hung the scalps of their enemies. After a time he got up and moved off to speak to the Montagnais and Etchemins. "You can see that we are celebrating our victory over our enemies," he cried. "Join us and we will be friends." Upon this they all cried ho ho ho. As soon as he had gone back to his place, they threw off their skins until they had nothing on but their loin cloths. Each of them then took what seemed to him appropriate—a matachia perhaps, or a tomahawk, a knife, a kettle or a piece of fat or moose or seal meat—and gave it as a present to the Algonkins. Then they had foot races, in which two of the best runners in each nation took part, with a prize for the winner. When this was over the dance ended and the Algonkins carried the presents off to their lodges.

The savages are cheerful and laugh a lot, but they aren't excitable. They speak deliberately, as if to make sure you understand them, and they often stop to think. This is especially true when they are speaking in council, which is attended only by the chiefs and elders and never by women or children.

Sometimes they are so short of food, on account of the cold and the snow, that they are sorely tempted to eat one another, for the game and fowl they live on migrate in winter to warmer countries. But I feel sure that if anyone showed them how to cultivate the soil they would learn quickly enough, for they are sensible and intelligent and ready to answer any questions you put to them.

One bad thing about them is that they are very given to revenge. They are also great liars. You shouldn't trust them unless you have good reason to do so and even then you have to be on your guard. They make great promises but seldom keep them.

They have no laws, so far as I could make out from what the grand Sagamo told me. He did tell me that they believe in a God who made all things. I asked him where he thought mankind had come from. He said that after God had made the world He took a number of arrows and stuck them in the ground and they turned into men and women. I told him that this was wrong, that there was but one God who made all things in heaven and earth. He saw that all things were good, but since there was no one to govern the world below, He took the slime of the earth and out of it fashioned Adam, our first father. While Adam was sleeping, I went on, God took one of his ribs and out of it fashioned Eve for his companion. This, I assured him, was the truth of the matter. He said nothing, except that he thought better of my account than of his.

I then asked him if he thought there was more than one God and he said they believed there were four—God, his mother, his son and the sun—but that God Himself was the chief of these. The son and the sun were good to his people, he explained, but the mother was wicked and ate them up when she could. The father, he added, wasn't much better. I showed him where he was mistaken, and he seemed interested.

I asked him if he had ever heard that God Himself had come into the world, and he said that he himself had never seen Him but that a long time before five men had gone far toward the setting sun and had met Him. God had asked them where they were going and they had answered that they were looking for a livelihood. To this God had said, "You will find it here." They ignored Him and continued on their way, whereupon God took up a stone and touched two of them with it, and they were both turned into stone. Then He asked the other three where they were going and they gave the same answer as before, whereupon God said, "Go no farther. You will find it here." They could see no reason to stay where they were, so they moved off, whereupon God took two sticks and touched two of the men and they turned into sticks. The fifth man hesitated. God asked him where he was going and he said all he wanted was to make a living. "Stay here," God answered, "and you will find it." He stayed and God gave him some meat and he ate it. When he had finished he rejoined his fellows and told them what had happened.

Then the Sagamo told me that once upon a time there was a man who had a quantity of tobacco, an herb they use for smoking. God came to this man and asked him where his pipe was. The man took his pipe and gave it to God, who smoked a great while. When he had finished smoking, God broke the pipe into a number of pieces. "Why," the man asked, "did you break my pipe, when you could see it was the only one I had?" God then took one of his own and gave it to the man. "Here is a pipe I will give you. Take it to your grand Sagamo and tell him to keep it. If he keeps it safely he will never want for anything, nor will any of his people." The man took the pipe and gave it to his Sagamo and long as he kept it his people lacked for nothing. But eventually the Sagamo lost the pipe and since then his people have suffered for many great famines. I asked him if he believed all this. He said he did and that it was the truth. I think this must be why they think God is evil. I told him that God is good and that it must have been the devil they had seen.

All Christians, I explained, believe in God the Father, God the Son and God the Holy Ghost—three persons in one God, with no first and no second, no greater and no lesser. I told him that the Virgin Mary, Mother of the Son of God, and all the men and women who had lived in the fear of God and suffered martyrdom for His sake and done miracles by the grace of God and who now belong to the company of the blessed, intercede for us with God the Father, beseeching Him to forgive us for our manifold sins and wickedness and for all the wrongs we have committed against His holy law. By virtue of their prayers and ours, I explained, we are given the strength we need to resist the devil. I added that if they believe in God they would have everything they needed and the devil wouldn't be able to do them any harm.

The Sagamo admitted that this made sense. I then asked him how they prayed to their gods, and he said they didn't have any ceremonies, that each man prayed in his own way. This of course is why they have no principles and know nothing of God and behave like animals. My own opinion is that if the country were settled they would readily enough become good Christians and would be the better for it. . . .

. . . This is all I was able to learn about their beliefs. They are a brutish people.

[1]Variations on this name occur often in Champlain's journal. It was probably some sort of title assumed by the Sagamo.

From M. Macklem, *The Voyages of Samuel de Champlain*, (Ottawa: Oberon Books, 1974).

1. Cite some examples of the contradictory evidence presented by Champlain with regard to the character of the Natives.
2. Analyse the discussion of religious beliefs which takes place in the document. To what extent do you agree with Champlain that after the discussion the Sagamo was persuaded by his arguments?
3. Identify examples of bias or value judgments made by Champlain.

The Jesuit Relations

Some of the best first-hand accounts of Native society come from the records of the Society for Jesus or Jesuits. These two selections illustrate the relationship between the missionaries and the Hurons.

This first short selection is part of a letter written by Father Jean de Brebeuf to Father la Jeune in Quebec. It was included in the Relations *for 1635.*

I find in their marriage customs two things that greatly please me; the first, that they have only one wife; the second, that they do not marry their relatives in a direct or collateral line, however distant they may be. There is, on the other hand, sufficient to censure were it only the frequent changes the men make of wives, and the women of their husbands.

They believe in the immortality of the soul, which they believe to be corporeal. The greater part of their Religion consists of this point. We have seen several stripped, or almost so, of all their goods, because several of their friends were dead, to whose souls they had made presents. Moreover, dogs, fish, deer, and other animals have, in their opinion, immortal and reasonable souls. In proof of this, the old men relate certain fables, which they represent as true; they make no mention either of punishment or reward, in the place to which souls go after death. And so they do not make any distinction between the good and the bad, the virtuous and the vicious, and they honour equally the interment of both, even as we have seen in the case of a young man who poisoned himself from the grief he felt because his wife had been taken away from him. Their superstitions are infinite, their feast, their medicines, their fishing, their hunting, their wars,—in short almost their whole life turns upon this pivot; dreams, above all have here great credit.

As regards morals, the Hurons are lascivious, although in two leading points less so than many Christians, who will blush some day in their presence. You will see no kissing nor immodest caressing; and in marriage a man will remain two or three years apart from his wife, while she is nursing. . . . . They are very lazy, are liars, thieves, pertinacious beggars. Some consider them vindictive; but, in my opinion, this vice is more noticeable elsewhere than here.

We see shining among them some rather noble moral virtues. You note, in the first place, a great love and union, which are careful to cultivate by means of their marriages, of their presents, of their feasts, and of their frequent visits. On returning from their fishing, their hunting, and their trading, they exchange many gifts; if they have thus obtained something unusually good, even if they have bought it, or if it has been given to them, they make a feast to the whole village with it. Their hospitality towards all sorts of strangers is remarkable; they present to them, in their feasts, the best of what they have prepared, and, as I have already said, I do not know if anything similar, in this regard, is to be found anywhere. They never close the door upon a Stranger, and, once having received him into their houses, they share with him the best they have; they never send him away, and when he goes away of his own accord, he repays them by a simple "thank you."

What shall I say of their strange patience in poverty, famine, and sickness? . . . They received indeed the news of death with more constancy than those Christian Gentlemen and Ladies to whom one would not dare to mention it. Our Savages hear of it not only without despair, but without troubling themselves, without the slightest pallor or change of countenance. . . .

We resolved to preach publicly to all, and to acquaint them with the reason of our coming to their Country, which is not for their furs, but to declare to them the true God and his son, Jesus Christ, the universal Saviour of our souls. . . .

Two things among others have aided us very much in the little we have been able to do here, by the grace of our Lord; the first is, as I have already said, the good health that God has granted us in the midst of sickness so general and so widespread. The second is the temporal assistance we have rendered to the sick.

YOUR REVERENCE'S:

From our little House of St. Joseph, in the village of Ihonatiria in the Huron country, this 27th of May, 1635, the day on which the Holy Spirit descended visibly upon the Apostles.

    Very humble and obedient
      servant in our Lord,
      JEAN DE BREBEUF

From S.R. Mealing, ed., *The Jesuit Relations and Allied Documents: A Selection*, (Ottawa: Carleton University Press, 1978).

1 Describe the discussion of religious beliefs between the Jesuits and the Hurons.
2. How does Brebeuf describe the characters and social customs of the Hurons?
3. What general point of view is reflected in the reading?

Instructions for the Fathers of Our Society who shall be sent to the Hurons, 1637

In this second excerpt, Brebeuf gently warns incoming Jesuits of the realities of Native life. Although critical in parts, it is clear from this excerpt of the respect and compassion felt by the priest for his Huron "flock."

The Fathers and Brethren whom God shall call to the holy Mission of the Hurons ought to exercise careful foresight in regard to all the hardships, annoyances, and perils that must be encountered in making this journey, in order to be prepared for all emergencies that may arise.

You must have sincere affection for the Savages,—looking upon them as ransomed by the blood of the son of God, and as our Brethren with whom we are to pass the rest of our lives.

To conciliate the Savages, you must be careful never to make them wait for you in embarking.

You must provide yourself with a tinder box or with a burning mirror, or with both, to furnish them fire in the daytime to light their pipes, and in the evening when they have to encamp; these little services win their hearts.

You should try to eat their sagamite or salmagundi in the way they prepare it, although it may be dirty, half-cooked, and very tasteless. As to the other numerous things which may be unpleasant, they must be endured for the love of God, without saying anything or appearing to notice them.

It is well at first to take everything they offer, although you may not be able to eat it all; for, when one becomes somewhat accustomed to it, there is not too much.

 ⌐ You must try and eat at daybreak unless you can take your meal with you in the canoe; for the day is very long, if you have to pass without eating. The Barbarians eat only at Sunrise and Sunset, when they are on their journeys.

You must be prompt in embarking and disembarking; and tuck up your gowns so that they will not get wet, and so that you will not carry either water or sand into the canoe. To be properly dressed, you must have your feet and legs bare; while crossing the rapids, your can wear your shoes, and, in the long portages, even your leggings.

 ⌐ You must conduct yourself as not to be at all troublesome to even one of these Barbarians.

 ⌐ It is not well to ask many questions, nor should you yield to your desire to learn the language and to make observations on the way; this may be carried too far. You must relieve those in your canoe of this annoyance, especially as you cannot profit much by it during the work. Silence is a good equipment at such a time.

You must bear their imperfections without saying a word, yes, even without seeming to notice them. Even if it be necessary to criticise anything, it must be done modestly, and with words and signs which envince love and not aversion.

 ⌐ In short, you must try to be, and to appear, always cheerful.

Each one should be provided with half a gross awls, two or three dozen little knives called jambettes (pocket-knives), a hundred fish-hooks, with some beads of plain and coloured glass, with which to buy fish or other articles when the tribes meet each other, so as to feast the Savages; and it would be well to say to them in the beginning, "Here is something with which to buy fish." Each one will try, at the portages, to carry some little thing, according to his strength; however little one carries, it greatly pleases the savages, if it be only a kettle.

You must not be ceremonious with the Savages, but accept the comforts they offer you, such as a good place in the cabin. The greatest conveniences are attended with very great inconvenience, and these ceremonies offend them.

Be careful not to annoy anyone in the canoe with your hat; it would be better to take your nightcap. There is no impropriety among the Savages.

Do not undertake anything unless you desire to continue it; for example, do not begin to paddle unless you are inclined to continue paddling. Take from the start the place in the canoe that you wish to keep; do not lend them your garments, unless your are willing to surrender them during the whole journey. It is easier to refuse at first than to ask them back, to change, or to desist afterwards.

Finally, understand that the Savages will retain the same opinion of you in their own country that they will have formed on the way; and one who has passed for an irritable troublesome person will have considerable difficulty afterwards in removing this opinion. You have to do not only with those of your canoe, but also (if it must be so stated) with all those of the country; you meet some today and others tomorrow, who do not fail to inquire, from those who brought you, what sort of man you are. It is almost incredible, how they observe and remember even the slightest fault. . . .

This is a lesson which is easy enough to learn, but very difficult to put into practice; for, leaving a highly civilized community, you fall into the hands of barbarous people who care but little for your Philosophy of your Theology. All the fine qualitites which might make you loved and respected in France are like pearls trampled under the feet of swine, or rather mules, which utterly despise you when they see that you are not as good pack animals as they are. If you could go naked, and carry the load of a horse upon your back, as they do, then you would be wise according to their doctrine, and would be recognized as a great man, otherwise not. Jesus Christ is our true greatness; it is He alone and His cross that should be sought in running after these people, for, if you strive for anything else, you will find naught but bodily and spiritual affliction. But having found Jesus Christ in His cross, you have found the roses in the thorns, sweetness in bitterness, all in nothing.

From S.R. Mealing, ed., *The Jesuit Relations and Allied Documents: A Selection*, (Ottawa: Carleton University Press, 1978).

1. What anticipated Jesuit behaviours are discouraged by Brebeuf?
2. Citing evidence from the document, identify Brebeuf's attitude toward his Huron "flock."
3. Account for Brebeuf's final advice to incoming Jesuit priests and the reasons behind his underlying concerns about their behaviour and attitude.

Instructions for the Virginia Colony, 1606

By the beginning of the seventeenth century, colonizing agents had learned a great deal from the mistakes of the past. The instructions from which this excerpt is taken outline in specific detail the problems involved in establishing a new settlement. From the tenor of the text it is clear that previous experiences with Native peoples were not entirely positive.

When it shall please God to send you on the coast of Virginia, you shall do your best endeavour to find out a safe port in the entrance of some navigable river, making choice of such a one as runneth farthest into the land, and if you happen to discover divers portable rivers, and amongst them any one hath two main branches, if the difference be not great, make choice of that which bedeth most towards the North-West for that way you shall soonest find the other sea. . . .

. . . Secondly, you must in no case suffer any of the native people of the country to inhabit between you and the sea coast; for you cannot carry yourselves so towards them, but they will grow discontented with your habitation, and be ready to guide and assist any nation that shall come to invade you; and if you neglect this, you neglect your safety.

In all passages you must have great care not to offend the naturals [natives], if you can eschew it; and imploy some few of your company to trade with them for corn and all other . . . victuals if you have any; and this you must do before that they perceive you mean to plant among them; for not being sure how your own seed corn will prosper the first year, to avoid the danger of famine, use and endeavour to store yourselves of the country corn.

Your discoverers that pass over land with hired guides, must look well to them that they slip not from them: and for more assurance, let them take a compass with them, and write down how far they go upon every point of the compass; for that country having no way or path, if that your guides run from you in the great woods or desert, you shall hardly ever find a passage back.

And how weary soever your soldiers be, let them never trust the country people with the carriage of their weapons; for if they run from you with your shott, which they only fear, they will easily kill them all with their arrows. And whensoever any of yours shoots before them, be sure they may be chosen out of your best marksmen; for if they see your learners miss what they aim at, they will think the weapon not so terrible, and thereby will be bould to assault you.

Above all things, do not advertize the killing of any of your men, that the country people may know it; if they perceive that they are but common men, and that with the loss of many adventures upon you. If the country be populous, you shall do well also, not to let them see or know of your sick men, if you have any; which may also encourage them to many enterprizes.

You must take especial care that you choose a seat for habitation that shall not be over burthened with woods near your town; for all the men you have, shall not be able to cleanse twenty acres a year; besides that it may serve for a covert for your enemies round about.

Lastly and chiefly the way to prosper and achieve good success is to make yourselves all of one mind for the good of your country and your own, and to serve and fear God the Giver of all Goodness, for every plantation which our Heavenly Father hath not planted shall be rooted out.

From Clarence Van Steeg and Richard Hofstadter, eds., *Great Issues in American History: From Settlement to Revolution*, (New York: Vintage Books, 1969).

1. What practical advice is given with regard to the establishment of a settlement? What attitude toward the Native inhabitants is reflected in this advice?

2. How are new settlers advised to deal with Native peoples? Outline the "do's and don'ts" of such a relationship.
3. What bias is reflected by the instructions included in this document?

God's Promise to His Plantation, 1630

As we have seen, John Winthrop felt justified in occupying land which he believed was being underused by its original inhabitants. The justification for this point of view is outlined in a sermon delivered in 1630 by the Reverend John Cotton. Cotton was a friend of Winthrop's who would soon join the Puritan colony in Massachusetts. In this excerpt he outlines the Biblical precedent for Puritan policy.

Now God makes room for people 3 wayes:

First, when he casts out the enemies of a people before them by lawfull warre with the inhabitants, which God cals them unto: as in *Ps.*44.2. *Thou didst drive out the heathen before them.* But this course of warring against others, & driving them out without provocation, depends upon speciall Commission from God, or else it is not imitable.

Secondly, when he gives a forreigne people favour in the eyes of any native people to come and sit downe with them either by way of purchase, as *Abraham* did obtaine the field of *Machpelah;* or else when they give it in courtesie, as *Pharaoh* did the land of *Goshen* unto the sons of *Jacob.*

Thirdly, when hee makes a Countrey though not altogether void of inhabitants, yet voyd in that place where they reside. Where there is a vacant place, there is liberty for the sonne of *Adam* or *Noah* to come and inhabite, though they neither buy it, nor aske their leaves. *Abraham* and *Isaac*, when they sojourned amongst the Philistines, and they did not buy that land to feede their cattle, because they said There is roome enough. And so did *Jacob* pitch his Tent by *Sechem, Gen.*34.21. There was *roome enough* as *Hamor* said, *Let them sit down amongst us.* And in this case if the people who were former inhabitants did disturbe them in their possessions, they complained to the King, as of wrong done unto them: As *Abraham* did because they took away his well, in *Gen.* 21, 15. For his right whereto he pleaded not his immediate calling from God, (for that would have seemed frivolous amongst the Heathen) but his owne industry and culture in digging the well, verse 30. Nor doth the King reject his plea, with what had he to doe to digge wells in their soyle? but admitteth it as a Principle in Nature, That in a vacant soyle, hee that taketh possession of it, and bestoweth culture and husbandry upon it, his Right it is. And the ground of this is from the grand Charter given to *Adam* and his posterity in Paradise, *Gen.* 1.28. *Multiply, and replenish the earth, and subdue it.* If therefore any sonne of *Adam* come and finde a place empty, he hath liberty to come, and fill, and subdue the earth there. This Charter was renewed to *Noah, Gen.* 9.1. *Fulfill the earth and multiply*: So that it is free from that common Grant for any to take possession of vacant Countries. Indeed no Nation is to drive out another without speciall Commission from heaven, such as the Israelites had, unless the Natives do unjustly wrong them, and will not recompence the wrongs done in peaceable sort, & then they may right themselves by lawfull war, and subdue the Countrey unto themselves. . . .

This may teach us all where we doe now dwell, or where after wee may dwell, be sure you looke at every place appointed to you, from the hand of God: wee may not rush into any place and never say to God, By your leave; but we must discerne how God appoints us this place. There is poore comfort in sitting down in any place, that you cannot say, This place is appointed me of God. Canst thou say that god spied out this place for thee, and there hath settled thee above all hindrances? Didst thou finde that God made roome for thee either by lawfull descent, or purchase, or gift, or other warrantable right? Why then this is the place God hath appointed thee; here hee hath made roome for thee, he hath placed thee in *Rehoboth*, in a peaceable place: This we must discerne, or els we are but intruders upon God. And when wee doe withall discerne, that god giveth us these outward blessings from his love in Christ, and maketh comfortable provision as well for our soule as for our bodies, by the meanes of grace, then doe we enjoy our present possession as well by gracious promise, as by the common, and just, and bountifull providence of the Lord. Or if a man doe remove, he must see that God hath espied out such a Countrey for him.

From Wilcomb E. Washburn, ed., *The Indian and The White Man*, (New York: Anchor Books, 1964).

1. What three ways does God "make room for people"?
2. Which of these justifications does Cotton apply to Massachusetts Bay?
3. What response could the Puritans then give to later Native claims to territory?

North America Before the Europeans: Analysis and Application

1. As discussed in the introduction to the book, almost all primary sources reflect a "biased" point of view. It is our task not only to identify and deal with these biases, but also to escape from our own preconceived notions of the nature of people, places, and events.

One area of research that has been the subject of much controversy in the past is the history of Native peoples in North America.

Select two additional sources describing the treatment of Native peoples by European settlers, and analyse them for bias. To do this you should examine the following aspects of the accounts:

(a) clear statement of hypothesis;

(b) historical accuracy;

(c) selection of data presented (including those things that have been left out);

(d) identity and background of the author.

Based upon your work with the documents in this chapter you should be able to identify two sources with clearly different biases.

Suggestions might include:

(i) a primary source account written at the time, or an analysis from the late nineteenth century, compared with;
(ii) a current interpretation written by a Native historian.

2. Based upon the following research question:
Was a viable (complex, sophisticated) Native society destroyed by European contact?, conduct your own investigation of a specific Native group.

Canadian students have the advantage of having access to a number of local museums, library collections, historical sites, and local individuals and organizations focussing on Native culture.

Based upon your research develop a thesis with regard to the impact of contact. If your research is effective and on task your thesis should answer the initial question.

3. "In any historical investigation, the more one generalizes, the more exceptions one finds to the rule."
Account for this statement with respect to the difficulties in generalizing the nature of the relationship between European and Native groups.

4. Create a first-person journal account describing initial contact from the specific point of view of one of the European authors cited in the documents.

5. Create and deliver an oral account that might have been passed down by a Native storyteller recalling an initial contact experience.

6. Some historians claim that the conquest and/or assimilation of Native peoples was an inevitable outcome of the imperial expansion of European powers in the seventeenth and eighteenth centuries. Others feel that real opportunities for accommodation and peaceful coexistence were destroyed by European prejudice and land hunger. Stage your own discussion of this question. Select one side of the argument. Write a one-page defence of the position chosen. Pair yourself off with a classmate who has prepared a position paper for the other side.

Start by reading one paper, while the other person listens carefully and jots down the main points of the argument. Then reverse the roles and consider the second paper.

From your notes, question one another and try to find weaknesses in your opponent's position.

Now take ten minutes or so and write a final summary of your argument. This summary should attempt to restate the main points of your original paper as well as refute the arguments of your opponent.

Present your final summaries to each other. After you have heard both sides, step out of the role you had assumed and discuss the issues involved. At this point the discussion might be extended to the whole class, where other students have been going through the same process.

3
THE PERFECTIBLE SOCIETY

To many Europeans, the New World was a blank slate. They disregarded the culture and even the existence of the Native inhabitants. To them North America was an empty land offering a chance to make a fresh start.

The Europe of the late sixteenth century was a continent in turmoil. The religious controversies that arose from the Protestant Reformation were about to engulf the continent in a half century of warfare. France was enjoying an uneasy peace between the Catholic majority and the Protestant Hugenot minority following the Edict of Nantes. The Elizabethan settlement in England, while papering the cracks between the Roman Catholic and Anglican churches, had not settled matters between the Church of England and its more reform–minded members.

The difficulty of religious reform in corrupt Europe prompted many reformers to look to North America. There, in the untouched wilderness, they could finally establish the "city of God" on earth. What would follow in the first half of the seventeenth century was a series of attempts to create a new perfect order on the virgin continent.

The Massachusetts Experiment

The Elizabethan settlement had failed to please many English protestants. For them, the new Church of England still retained too many of the trappings of Roman Catholicism. They, on the other hand, were attracted by the reforms proposed by John Calvin. Calvin had written his own set of guidelines for salvation in 1534. Calvinism demanded high morals and a strict adherence to religious discipline. His ideas gained quick acceptance and he soon headed up a theocracy (government by the church) in the city of Geneva. This purified or puritan approach to life had by Elizabeth's day become very popular in the Netherlands and England. To show their dissatisfaction with the Elizabethan model, these English Calvinists called themselves Separatists indicating their desire to remain separate from the Anglican church.

When James IV of Scotland became James I of England following the death of Elizabeth in 1603, the Separatists became worried. James had threatened to drive them out of the country. This threat was enough to force many of them to take refuge in the Netherlands. But even there life was not perfect. Finally in 1620, a small group of about thirty-five of these Separatists decided to leave and try their luck in the New World far away from persecuting governments. These Separatists or Pilgrims, as they came to be called, sailed away from Europe as part of a group of 102 passengers in the small ship the *Mayflower*, never to look back.

The nominal destination of the Pilgrims was Virginia. However, driven off course by fall storms, they arrived far north of their mark near Cape Cod on November 11, 1620. (Recent evidence would indicate that this was probably their actual destination. Since they wanted to be far from Royal reach, it is unlikely that they would have chosen an established colony such as Virginia in which to settle.) After their initial landfall, they sailed northward and finally landed on December 25th. They named the site Plymouth after their departure point in England. The first winter cost them the lives of almost half of the colonists. Nonetheless, the Pilgrims soon established a successful and thriving settlement. They were so successful that by their third year in North America the colonists were self-sufficient. It was a far cry from the Virginia experience.

While still at sea, the Pilgrims had signed the Mayflower Compact. It decreed that the colonists would constitute a body politic which would create laws for the equal and just administration of the colony. This experiment in direct democracy was essential for the Separatists who, being only one–third of the total number of the colonists, wanted guarantees of their religious freedom.

In 1626 the inhabitants of Plymouth Plantation bought out the London capitalists who had originally backed their enterprise and then severed all ties with the mother country. They were totally independent and would remain so until they were absorbed by the Massachusetts Bay Colony in 1691.

As famous as the Pilgrims are, they were merely the precursors of a more serious Puritan attempt to create a new society in North America. Following their initial successes, rich Puritan merchants in England had established the Massachusetts Bay Company in 1629. According to their charter they were given the rights to the area from the Charles to the Merrimac rivers. A Puritan settlement had already been established in the area in 1626 near present-day Salem, and in 1630 John Winthrop, a prominent Puritan lawyer, secured the right to establish an independent commonwealth in the area. He felt that English society was so corrupt that it was essential to evacuate as many people as possible before it was too late. He cried out at the inhumanity of society:

> This land grows weary of her inhabitants, so that man, who is the most precious of all creatures, is here more vile and base than the earth we tread upon, and less valued among us than a horse or a sheep: masters are forced by authority to care for their servants and parents to maintain their own children. All towns complain of the burden of the poor, though we have taken up many unnecessary and even unlawful trades to maintain them . . . and thus it has come to pass that children, servants and neighbours, especially if they are poor, are counted the greatest burdens, which if things were right would be the chief earthly blessings.

It was Winthrop's goal to establish a new society free from the corrupting influences of England. The new colony of Massachusetts Bay would give him his chance. Winthrop moved quickly. In the first six months of 1630 he brought over one thousand settlers to the area around Boston. He had learned from the mistakes of the Virginians. The colony was well prepared for these and future settlers. In fact this was only the first stage in the Great Migration that would see twenty-five thousand people arrive in the next ten years. Massachusetts Bay was to be a religious community based upon Puritan principles. Winthrop likened the experiment to the foundation of a "city upon a hill" in plain view of everyone. It was their task to prove that the ideals of the New Testament could work on earth.

Unlike the Pilgrims who had fled religious persecution ten years earlier, the Puritans of the Great Migration left willingly. Why did they decide to pack up and leave a country that was just beginning to accept their point of view? The answer is simple and is reflected in the quotation by Winthrop cited above. For the Puritans of the Massachusetts Bay Company, England was beyond redemption. It was time to start anew.

The founders of the colony set out to establish a government that would exercise full religious and civil authority in the region. Massachusetts Bay would be ruled by the tenets of the New Testament. Heresy would be suppressed, public morality would be enforced, and posterity would be preserved from the corruptions of the evil world. Yet it would not be a community of equals. The system of social classes that the British believed was established by God would be preserved. While at sea, Winthrop had sermonized that it was not the intention of the new colony to level the distinction between rich and poor. He warned those who saw that New World as a chance for personal advancement and prosperity that if they should "fail to embrace this present world and prosecute our carnal intentions, seeking great things for ourselves and our posterity, the Lord will surely break out in wrath against us be revenged of such a perjured people and make us know the price of the breach of such a Covenant."

Future generations would know that price. Violation of this agreement with God would be blamed for such disasters as crop failures, epidemics, insect infestations, extremes of climate, Indian wars, accidents, and even unsatifactory children.

This "new Jerusalem" was to be a male-oriented society. Although Winthrop has been praised for stating that a man could not beat his wife unless acting in self-defence, Puritan attitudes were usually more direct. John Cotton of Boston wrote that "the woman is more subject to error than man. It is not permitted for a woman to speak in the Church . . . but rather it is required that she should ask her husband at home." The response of the people of Salem to non-conformist behaviour by women is legendary.

Massachusetts Bay was a company operation. Government of the new commonwealth was based upon the election of officers. However, only shareholders (freemen) were eligible to vote. As this represented only about 1 percent of the population, the colony tended to be dominated by the Puritan hierarchy. Over the next fifteen years the franchise was gradually extended, but not before a number of dissenters had moved out to found new settlements. Eventually all male members of the Puritan Church were allowed to vote to elect members to the General Court, which was the legislature of the colony. Non-Puritans had little place in Massachusetts Bay. Winthrop wanted to form a religious commonwealth. Those who disagreed left.

A harsh picture of life in the early Puritan colonies has come down to us over the past three–and–a–half centuries. Plymouth has often been depicted as a rigid and harsh community based on the strict moral values of the Puritan faith applied to a small, insular community. Such an image is full of inaccuracies. To begin with, Plymouth was a vital, expansive colony, not restricted to one small settlement. By 1691, the colony boasted twenty-one recognized townships as well as a number of villages. The Puritan community was so expansive that the first governor,

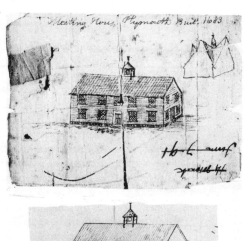

Second meeting house, Plymouth Plantation

Manuscript page from Governor Bradford's History of Plymouth Plantation

Fortified Redoubt of Fort Niagara illustrates the external threats to the Perfectible Society.

William Bradford, lamented that the dispersion of the religious community would be "the ruin of New England."

Nor were these early Puritans as morally restricted as has often been assumed. Premarital sex was severely punished, except when the two people were betrothed. In these cases the punishment was much lighter. The recorded number of "early" births suggests that such relationships happened frequently. Many parishes reported a number of children born after only six months of marriage. Although this was occasionally grounds for condemnation, such births were usually quietly ignored. In spite of such aberrations, however, life in Massachusetts Bay was tightly controlled.

The strict rules enforced in Massachusetts were bound to drive some people out of the colony. One such individual was Roger Williams. Williams disagreed with the appearance of a theocracy in Massachusetts. He accused the Puritan hierarchy of establishing their own state church, the very thing they had left England to escape. He further questioned the right of the colonists to simply take over land that clearly belonged to the Indians.

Unique among colonial leaders of the time, Williams held the Natives in great respect. He actively criticized settlers who dismissed Native customs and culture. In one short verse he wrote:

"If nature's sons both wild and tame
Humane and courteous be,
How ill becomes it sons of God
To want humanity!"

Such attitudes conflicted with the mainstream of Puritan thought in the colony. Williams was identified as a danger to the stability of the colony, and in 1636 he was expelled.

Roger Williams created a new settlement. Providence, as he called it, would become the centre of a new colony, Rhode Island. This move would establish a critical precedent for New England. Williams, by his actions, established the principle of the separation of church and state, and reaffirmed the right of the individual to make personal choices in matters of faith.

Rhode Island also attracted another dissident, Anne Hutchinson, a midwife from Boston. She had questioned the power of the church to decide who received "the Grace of God." Hutchinson felt that an individual might be able to commune with God on a personal level without the approval of the church. The Puritan leaders could not let this go on. Anne Hutchinson was denounced as a servant of Satan. In 1638, therefore, she and her family left Boston and founded the town of Portsmouth. She lived there for four years until, after her husband's death, she moved to the area around New Rochelle, where she was killed in an Indian raid in 1643.

Thomas Hooker left Massachusetts of his own accord. Shut out of the leadership of the colony, he organized settlers in the Connecticut River Valley to form their own commonwealth. Connecticut, which emerged between 1636 and 1639, was based upon a constitution called the "Fundamental Orders of Connecticut." It was written by delegates from the towns of Hartford, Wethersfield, and Windsor, and has been described as the first democratic constitution in the world. Connecticut's constitution still had many of the Puritan restrictions existing in Massachusetts, but it is important to note that in each of these new settlements, the rule of law and the rights of the individual were of prime importance.

Although England was convulsed by civil war from 1640 to 1660, the New England colonies did not side with their English Puritan counterparts, as might be expected. Instead, the colonies declared themselves neutral, and used the two decades of virtual isolation to secure many of the rights and practices outlined in their early years.

New England temporarily lost its independence when James II attempted to assert royal control over the colonies in 1684. After the "glorious revolution" and William of Orange ascended the throne, Massachusetts received a new charter in 1691. It appeared that the Puritan theocracy would be preserved. Soon, however, a new danger arose. Royal threats had not been able to shake the Calvinist principles of the citizens of Massachusetts, but prosperity did. As the New England colonies prospered through trade and commercial ventures in the early years of the eighteenth century, Puritan frugality was gradually replaced by fashionable clothes and elegant houses.

As one contemporary observer commented in 1744:

> There is more hospitality and frankness showed here [Boston] than either New York or Philadelphia . . .
> Assemblies of the gayer sort are frequent here; the gentlemen and ladies meeting almost every week at concerts of music and balls. I . . . saw as fine a ring of ladies, as good dancing, and heard music as elegant as I had been witness to anywhere. I must take notice that this place abounds with pretty women who appear rather more abroad than they do at York and dress elegantly . . . I saw not one prude while I was there.

The Puritan University of Harvard had sunk into this style of life to such an extent that an investigation in 1723 reported that: "There has been a practice of general immoralities, particularly stealing, lying, swearing, idleness, picking of locks and too frequent use of strong drink."

In response purists spearheaded a "Great Awakening" in the 1730s. This revival crusade attempted to return New England to its Puritan roots. Marked at first by thundering sermons and calls for repentance, later the movement became characterized by the devoted writhing around and screaming in righteous ecstasy. Such extremism was bound to burn itself out. On the positive side, there appears to have been a decline in the crime rate and a rise in the level of public morality, but for the most part the Great Awakening was perhaps the last hurrah of the perfectible society in New England.

Church and State in New France

As discussed in chapter 2, the early years of French exploration and settlement in North America were marked by a strong missionary drive to Christianize the Native inhabitants. As a result, the first decades of the French era were dominated by such orders as the Recollets and, of course, the Society of Jesus, or Jesuits.

Father Paul Ragueneau, who would eventually lead the Jesuit retreat from the interior in 1650, was convinced that Native converts could form the core of a new religious community. In one *Relation* he commented that "there are some whose virtue, piety, and remarkable holiness even the most holy Religious might without sin envy."

The strength of the Jesuits as missionaries proved in the long run to be a weakness as they competed for influence in the young colony. Disciplined and dedicated to the conversion of the Natives, these zealous missionaries soon found themselves outside the mainstream of the religious development of New France.

As early as the 1620s the decision had been made that New France should become a model of Roman Catholic Christian society. Priorities established called for the foundation of villages on the traditional French feudal model, the gradual agricultural resettlement of the Native peoples and their assimilation into French society, the construction of a seminary, and the exclusion from the colony of all Huguenots.

These policies tended to favour a more conventional clerical approach to the spiritual leadership of the colony rather than the fanaticism of the Jesuits. Still, for the first half of the century, the superb organization and dedication of the Jesuits kept them in a dominant position in New France. As they pursued their Christianizing goals in Huronia, other religious groups began to appear in the St. Lawrence Valley. Most notable of these was the appearance in 1639 of communities of religious women such as the Ursilines, the Hospitaligeres de la Misericorde de Jesus, and the Sisters of the Congregation. Under their guidance and the leadership of such individuals as Marie de l'Incarnation, Jeanne Mance, and Marguerite Bourgeoys, the colony saw the development of hospitals, social welfare for the needy, kindergarten and nursery facilities, and schools (see readings).

The centre of much of this religious life was Ville Marie, present-day Montreal. This new settlement, on the edge of the wilderness, was to be the centre of a revitalized Christian nation in the New World. In 1639 the *Societe de Notre Dame de Montreal pour la conversion des sauvages* (Society of our Lady of Montreal for the conversion of the savages) was formed. Granted the deed to Montreal Island, they established a community there in 1642. Of all the settlements established in the New World, it could truly be described as the only one established out of purely religious motives. The leader was Paul de Maisonneuve, but much of the leadership came from women.

In 1644 a layperson, Jeanne Mance, established a Hotel-Dieu (hospital), and ten years later Marguerite Bourgeoys opened the first school. Ville Marie was intended to be a privately funded community free from the corrupting control of the government. Slow growth and declining interest, however, took their toll on the financial support for the missionary goals of the town. Eventually the religious community would be diluted by the growth of fur-trading and farming elements in the area, but in the early years the potential for "the perfectible society" seemed great (see readings).

As the settlements grew, so did the need for parish priests and a colonial church hierarchy. By 1640, there was a demand for a bishopric for the colony. The Jesuits, who owed their allegiance directly to the Pope, did not qualify for such a post.

As a result, power began to shift from the missionaries to the established Gallican (French) church. The leader of this new dynamic force in New France, Francois de Laval, would eventually become the bishop. With these changes, the destruction of Sainte-Marie-among-the-Hurons in 1649, and the retreat of the Jesuits from the interior, the leadership of the church in New France passed into new hands.

When Laval became Vicar Apostolic in 1659 (the post of Bishop would not be created until 1674), he complained of the lack of parish organization, the small wooden chapels that passed for churches in major towns such as Trois Rivières and Montreal, and the total absence of churches on the south shore of the St. Lawrence. Laval wanted to start anew. He dreamed of giving the colony the chance to "revitalize the old faith in a New World."

Like Winthrop, Laval tried to establish his own version of a theocracy in New France by securing control of the secular government. By the time of the royal reorganization of the colony in 1663, Laval had already established himself as a powerful and knowledgeable figure in New France. As a result Louis XIV, preoccupied with other matters, deferred to the Vicar with regard to the appointment of a new governor for the colony. Laval chose Augustin Saffray de Mezy, a man he thought he could control. Early events suggested he was right. Within three days of his arrival, the new governor had approved the appointment of a sovereign council comprised entirely of Laval's supporters.

This attempt to control the government, however, soon dissipated. Mezy accused Laval of interfering with his administration of the colony. When the governor had some of Laval's supporters removed from the council, he was attacked from the pulpit. The future bishop went so far as to refuse confession and absolution to the governor, who responded by threatening to withhold funds from the church. It was a stand-off. Meanwhile the day-to-day operations of the government went on as usual. The dispute dragged on, and although Mezy reconciled with Laval on his deathbed in 1665, the damage had been done. The dispute had cost Laval much of his influence both in Quebec and Paris. Never again would a religious leader threaten the secular power of the governor.

The remainder of the century saw a gradual erosion of the political influence of the church. Colbert had mistrusted Laval from the very beginning and had instructed Gaudais (the first Intendant) to make enquiries into the spiritual and temporal conduct of the priest. Over the next few decades Royal policy was clearly designed to check the influence of the clergy. By 1700 it had become a non-issue. The church was clearly subordinate to the state.

Frustrated in the political arena, Laval set out to create a vibrant religious community in the St. Lawrence Valley. Although the church hierarchy took a leadership role in major social issues, the real influence of the church centred upon the parish priest. In addition to normal clerical duties, the priest taught the young, influenced public morality and marital fidelity, and acted as a shining example of Christian life, pious and temperate. Faced with such a task, no wonder most young priests preferred the cloistered life of the seminary. Added to the problem was the question of salary.

In the late seventeenth century, most parish priests estimated that a salary of 800 livres was the minimum needed to survive. Local seigneurs, on the other hand, offered them only about 500 livres for their services. The clerics appealed to Laval who offered a compromise to the king of 600 livres. Louis, however, felt that 400 livres was more than enough and that the difference could be made up through the collection of tithes from the parishioners, the habitants.

As it turned out, this was more easily said than done. Laval, in 1663, asked for a tithe amounting to one-thirteenth of the produce of the land of each habitant. The habitants protested this amount and the Sovereign Council reduced the payment to one-twenty-sixth of the produce, payable in threshed grain. The farmers interpreted this decision to mean that they only had to pay one-twenty-sixth of their wheat crop alone. Laval objected, but to no avail. The church had to be satisfied with a mere fraction of what it felt it needed.

It was an indicator of things to come. In the early seventeenth century, New France had appeared to be a model for a new revitalized Catholicism. Missions such as Sainte-Marie and settlements like Ville Marie were a model of dedication and devotion. Greater immigration and increased prosperity soon began to change the atmosphere in the colony. As early as 1682, Bishop Laval complained about the behaviour of the women. They arrived in church bare shouldered, and dressed more appropriately for a Parisian salon than a parish Sunday mass. By the turn of the century, parish priests were reporting that people came to church drunk and slipped out during the service for a smoke or a drink across the street.

By 1700, then, the dream of the "perfectible society" in New France was only a fleeting memory.

The Legacy of the Ideal

New England and New France would not be the only attempts to establish a new order on the North American continent. Over the ensuing decades and centuries various groups of religious dissenters would come to the continent in search of a new start. The Quakers in Pennsylvania, the Mormons in Utah, the Mennonites in Ontario and Manitoba, and the Hutterites and the Doukhobors in the Prairies all established their own religious communities with varying degrees of success. These later efforts would be different, however.

The perfectible society of the seventeenth century represented an ideal. For leaders like Winthrop, Laval, Raguenault, and Maisonneuve, the communities under their charge were not mere fortresses in a sea of corruption. They saw their efforts as establishing the leading edge of a new social order in North America. Winthrop's "city on the hill" was to be a shining example to all humanity, and one that was to be emulated, not simply tolerated. The eventual failure of these efforts does nothing to tarnish the lustre of the idealism that sparked them.

Establishing the Perfectible Society in New England

Soon after arriving in the New World, the Puritans attempted to legally and morally justify their presence there. In an essay entitled "Reasons and Considerations Touching the Lawfulness of Removing out of England into the Parts of America" states their case. The essay was signed R.C. and has been attributed to Robert Cushman, who emigrated on the Mayflower.

. . . And first, seeing we daily pray for the conversion of the heathens, . . . Now it seemeth unto me that we ought also to endeavor and use the means to convert them, or they come to us. To us they cannot come, our land is full; to them we may go, their land is empty.

This, then, is a sufficient reason to prove our going thither to live lawful. Their land is spacious and void, and they are few, and do but run over the grass, as do also the foxes and wild beasts. They are not industrious, neither have art, science, skill, or faculty to use either the land or the commodities of it, but all spoils, rots, and is marred for want of manuring, gathering, ordering, etc. . . . So is it lawful now to take a land which none useth and make use of it.

. . . For as our faculty that way is small and our strength less, so our warring with them is after another manner, namely by friendly usage, love, peace, honest and just carriages, good counsel, etc., that so we and they may not only live in peace in that land, and they yield subjection to an earthly prince, but that as voluntaries they may be persuaded at length to embrace the Prince of Peace, Christ Jesus, and rest in peace with him forever. . . .

It being, then, first a vast and empty chaos, secondly, acknowledged the right of our sovereign king, thirdly, by a peaceable composition in part possessed of diverse of his loving subjects, I see not who can doubt or call in question the lawfulness of inhabiting or dwelling there. . . . Yea, and as the enterprise is weighty and difficult, so the honor is more worthy, to plant a rude wilderness, to enlarge the honor and fame of our dread sovereign, but chiefly to display the efficacy of power of the gospel, both in zealous preaching, professing, and wise walking under it, before the faces of these poor blind infidels.

. . . For who can show them a place in this world where inequity shall not compass them at the heels, and where they shall have a day without grief, or a lease of life for a moment? And who can tell but God what dangers may lie at our doors, even in our native country, or what plots may be abroad, or when God will cause our sun to go down at noondays, and in the midst of our peace and security lay upon us some lasting scourge for our so long neglect and contempt of His most glorious gospel?

. . . But we have here great peace, plenty of the gospel, and many sweet delights and variety of comforts.

Answer: True indeed; and far be it from us to deny and diminish the last of these mercies. But have we rendered unto God thankful obedience for His long peace, whilst other peoples have been at wars?

. . . Wherein, as God's providence swayeth all, so it is easy to see that the straitness of the place, having in it so many strait hearts, cannot but produce such effects more and more; so as eery indifferent-minded man should be ready to day with father Abraham, "Take thou the right hand, and I will take the left." Let us not thus oppress, straiten, and afflict one another; but seeing there is a spacious land, the way to which is through the sea, we will end this difference in a day . . .

From *Collection of the Massachusetts Historical Society*, (Boston, 1831), from H.H. Quint *et al.*, *Main Problems in American History*, (Homewood, Illinois: Dorsey Press, 1978).

1. Outline Cushman's case for the Puritan "invasion" of New England.
2. (a) What goals in colonization do the Puritans profess to have?
(b) What is your opinion of the author's vision of these goals?

Arbitrary Government Described, 1644

Attacked by some factions in Massachussetts Bay as attempting to run a dictatorial or arbitrary government, John Winthrop fought back by issuing the following declaration.

Arbitrary Government is where a people have men set over them, without their choice or allowance; who have power to govern them, and judge their causes without a rule. God only hath this prerogative; whose sovereignty is absolute, and whose will is a perfect rule, and reason itself; so as for man to usurp such authority, is tyranny, and impiety.

Where the people have liberty to admit or reject their governors, and to require the rule by which they shall be governed and judged, this is not an arbitrary government. . . .

I. The foundation of this Government is the King's Letters Patents: this gave them their form and being, in disposing a certain number of persons into a body politic; whereby they became then (in such a politic respect) as one single person, consisting of several members, and appoint to each its proper place: it regulates their power and motions as might best conduce to the preservation and good of the whole body.

By these it appears, that the officers of this body politic have a rule to walk by in all their administrations, which rule is the Word of God, and such conclusions and deductions as are, or shall be, regularly drawn from thence.

All commonwealths have had some principles, or fundamentals, from which they have framed deductions to particular cases, as occasion hath required. . . .

The fundamentals which God gave to the Commonwealth of Israel were a sufficient rule to them, to guide all their affairs; we having the same, with all the additions, explanations, and deductions, which have followed; it is not possible we should want a rule in any case, if God give wisdom to discern it.

From C.W. Eliot, ed., "Winthrop Arbitrary Government Described (1644)," *American Historical Documents*, 1938.

1. How does Winthrop define arbitrary government?
2. Upon what "fundamentals" does Winthrop say that the government of Massachussetts Bay is founded?

Winthrop and Liberty

Political opponents attempted to have Winthrop impeached in 1645 when he arrested them for anti-government agitation. Winthrop was acquitted of the charges and delivered the following definition of the extent of civic liberty in court.

There is a twofold liberty: natural (I mean as our nature is now corrupt) and civil or federal. The first is common to man with beasts and other creatures. By this, man, as he stands in relation to man simply, hath liberty to do what he lists. It is a liberty to evil as well as to good. This liberty is incompatible and inconsistent with authority, and cannot endure the least restraint of the most just authority. The exercise and maintaining of this liberty makes men grow more evil, and in time to be worse than brute beasts. . . .

The other kind of liberty I call civil or federal. It may also be termed moral, in reference to the covenant between God and man in the moral law, and the politic covenants and constitutions amongst men themselves. . . . Whatsoever crosseth this, is not authority, but a distemper thereof. This liberty is maintained and exercised in a way of subjection to authority. It is of the same kind of liberty wherewith Christ hath made us free.

The woman's own choice makes such a man her husband; yet being so chosen, he is her lord, and she is to be subject to him, yet in a way of liberty, not of bondage. And a true wife accounts her subjection her honor and freedom, and would not think her condition safe and free, but in her subjection to her husband's authority.

Such is the liberty of the church under the authority of Christ, her king and husband. His yoke is so easy and sweet to her as a bride's ornaments: and if through forwardness or wantonness, etc., she shake it off at any time, she is at no rest in her spirit until she take it up again. . . .

Even so, brethren, it will be between you and your magistrates. If you stand for your natural corrupt liberties, and will do what is good in your own eyes, you will not endure the least weight of authority, but will murmur, and oppose, and be always striving to shake off that yoke. But if you will be satisfied to enjoy such civil and lawful liberties, such as Christ allows you, then will you quietly and cheerfully submit unto that authority which is set over you, in all the adminstrations of it, for your good. Wherein if we [magistrates] fail at any time, we hope we shall be willing (by God's assistance) to hearken to good advice from any of you, or in any other way of God. So shall your liberties be preserved, in upholding the honor and power of authority amongst you.

From C.W. Eliot, ed., "Winthrop Arbitary Government Described (1644)," *American Historical Documents*, 1938.

1. (a) How does Winthrop define liberty?
(b) What relationship does he describe as existing between liberty and authority?
2. Based upon the two excerpts you have read, outline Winthrop's view of the "perfectible society."

Establishing the Perfectible Society in New France

After the royal reorganization of New France in 1663, Louis XIV attempted to clarify the nature of the relationship between church and state in the colony.

In the following two excerpts, the first (1665) outlines Talon's instructions to maintain the delicate balance between church and state. The second demonstrates the application of those instructions—the Oath of Fidelity (1672) which Frontenac required the clergy to take.

It is absolutely necessary to hold in just balance the temporal authority, which resides in the person of the King and in those who represent him, and the spiritual authority, which resides there in the person of the said Bishop and the Jesuits, in such a manner nevertheless that the latter always be inferior to the former. The first thing which Sieur Talon will have to observe carefully, and about which it would be good for him to have firm convictions before leaving here [France], is to know perfectly well the state in which these two powers are at present in the colony, and the relationship in which they normally ought to stand.

From the Public Archives of Canada, MG1, Series C11A, Vol. I, Instructions to Talon, 25 March 1665. Translated by Cornelius J. Jaenen in P.W. Bennett, *Emerging Identities*, (Scarborough: Prentice-Hall, 1986).

You swear and promise before God to labour with all your strength for the maintenance of the Catholic, Apostolic and Roman Religion, to promote it as much as you can through your example and care, by the purity of your doctrine and the proclamation of the Gospel, and to be faithful to the King as required under the authority of the charge with which he has honoured you in these provinces. You promise, in addition, that if a matter comes to your knowledge which is contrary to His Majesty's service you will advise us thereof, and in case it were not remedied by us, you will inform his Majesty thereof.

From *Collection de Manuscrits relatifs a la Nouvelle-France*. (Quebec: Cote, 1883), I. Translated by Cornelius J. Jaenen in P.W. Bennett, *Emerging Identities*, (Scarborough: Prentice-Hall, 1986).

1. As outlined by Talon, what relationship existed between church and state in New France at this time?
2. What modifications were placed upon that relationship by the Oath of Fidelity?
3. Compare the relationship of church and state in New France with that of New England.

Nationalism and the Church

Many early French-Canadian nationalists attributed the survival of a distinct Quebecois society to the influence of the Church. Here nationalist historian Abbé Groulx states the case.

To defend the race, there are two bastions, among others, that our bishops fashioned with their hands; the family and the parish. The French-Canadian family is one of the glories of our people, 'one of the greatest marvels of the Catholic Church in the past two centuries,' wrote one historian. The family deserves this great praise for the admirable manner in which it discharged its natural ends. But who created the French-Canadian family? Who gave it its laws, its soul, and those qualities of strength and purity where it found the courage to undertake and the power to accomplish its duty? Here again, let us have the fairness to recognize that the Church played the leading and the most active role . . .

From Abbé Groulx, "Ce que nous devons au catholicisme," *Action Francaise*, November 1933, in P.W. Bennett, *Emerging Identities*, (Scarborough: Prentice-Hall, 1986).

1. Comment upon Groulx's vision of the impact of the search for the perfectible society upon French-Canadian nationalism.

Censorship and the Church, 1703

The clergy in New France exercised considerable control over books and theatrical productions allowed in the colony. One critic of this power, the Baron de Lahontan, launched a scathing criticism of church practice.

When I think of this Tyranny, I cannot but be enrag'd at the impertinent Zeal of the Curate of this City. This inhumane Fellow came one day to my Lodging, and finding the Romance of the Adventures of Petronius upon my table, he fell upon it with an unimaginable fury, and tore out almost all the leaves. This book I valued more than my life, because 'twas not castrated: and indeed I was so provok'd when I saw it all in wrack, that if my Landlord had not held me, I had gone immediately to that turbulent Pator's House, and would have pluck'd out the Hairs of his Beard with as little mercy as he did the Leaves of my book. These animals cannot content themselves with the study of Men's Actions, but they must likewise dive into their Thoughts . . .

From R.G. Thwaites, ed., *New Voyages to North America by the Baron de Lahontan* (Chicago: A.C. McClurg & Co., 1905).

1. According to Lahontan, how did the clergy attempt to control social thought in New France?
2. What does his criticism indicate about the extent of church control during the latter half of the seventeenth century?
3. As you will see in the readings that follow, Lahontan's concerns coincide with the beginning of a decline in church influence in the colony. To what extent do you think such a decline was inevitable?

The Decline of the Perfectible Society

Ordinances, letters, and accounts dating from the first half of the eighteenth century continually identify examples of the neglect, disinterest, or insubordination of parishioners. We have already examined the disputes over the paying of tithes, but there were other concerns as well. One letter written in 1720 to a parish in Detroit chastises the congregation for letting the church fall into disrepair and the cattle to graze in the cemetary. Other accounts were even more direct.

Ordinance concerning refusing absolution to those who do not pay the tithe, April 14, 1717

We have lamented, since we were established as pastor of this diocese, My Dearly Beloved Brethren in Our Lord, the inveterate, and almost irremediable abuses of a large number of our parishioners, who easily persuade themselves that they may approach the Sacraments with surety, and not pay their tithes, or but paying part of them and often with the worst of their wheat, and paying it at the time and in the manner that they judge convenient without any regard for the obligation which they have to pay it all and from the choicest wheat at Easter time as is provided for in the ritual. For this reason, fearing that God may impute to you the negligence of most of the inhabitants of your parishes . . . we continue to assure you that it is our intention that you hold firm to an interrogation of the penitents . . . on the tithes, and to refuse benediction and absolution if they have not satisfied the requirements.
Jean
[Monseigneur de St. Vallier, bishop of New France]

From H. Tetu and C.O. Ganon, *Mandements, lettes pastorales et circularies des eveques de Quebec* (Quebec: A Coté et Cie., 1887-1893), Vol.1.

The trade in brandy and other such liquors is completely contrary to the well-being of the Colony and of the State for four principal reasons. The first reason is that it encourages the laziness and self-interest of the Indians.

When these people are drunk they fly into such rages that they break and shatter everything in their homes. They make terrible cries and shouts and go after their enemies like wild men to stab them. At these times, their friends and relatives do not escape from their rage and they even bite each other's noses and ears.

Father Bruyar, a former missionary, asserted several times that he knew more than one hundred people who had come to settle at Sault St. Louis in the hope of avoiding annoyance from this sort of drunkenness. However, several had gone back seeing that drink and drunkenness were as common and frequent as they had been where they had come from.

Although the Indians love to drink, they are, nevertheless, angry at having done so because in their drunkenness, they lose all they have. They greatly regret this when they have recovered their good sense.

The separation and breaking up of their marriage always follows their drunkenness due to the grief and despair of their wives. They see themselves despoiled by their drunk husbands who take everything from them in order to buy drink. They are frustrated when the catch from the hunt is taken from their husbands by their creditors before their husbands reach the village.

These Indians, encumbered with debt and stripped by their creditors who do not even leave them their rifles, are obliged to leave the country and go to the English because they cannot hope to pay off their debts.

From Archives des Colonies, C A xxxix, in Virginia R. Robeson, ed., *New France 1713-1760*, (Toronto: OISE, 1977).

The extreme distance I am from you, my dearly beloved children, coupled with the very great difficulty wherein I find myself to send you priests to administer the sacraments to you, move me to have you take notice, by means of this Pastoral Letter, of the indispensable obligation you have to live a pure and Christian life, free from all the sins which can separate you from the grace of God and his love. . . . It is right that we exhort you to maintain the material Temple, which we learn is in lamentable state of disrepair, as well as the cemetery which you have allowed to remain open and exposed to all kinds of indignities because of the cattle which enter it, and which by this fact alone deserves to come under interdict. But above all we strongly urge and avise you to show a true obedience to your pastor, when it is so greatly in your interest to keep and accommodate him for we see here none in the regular or secular clergy who might succeed him. . . .

From H.Tetu and Gagnon, *Mandements, lettres pastorales et circularies*, I, in P.W. Bennett, *Emerging Identities*, (Scarborough: Prentice-Hall, 1986).

Memorandum of Instruction from Louis XV to Intendant Dupuy, May 1, 1726

. . . The Bishop of Quebec [Monseigneur de St. Vallier] is aware that the multiplication of taverns in Canada causes much disorder; that young men in Canada drink excessively in front of the churches thus causing a scandal; that in order to provide the money for their debauchery, they take from their Father; and finally, that the success the tavern keepers enjoy stirs up others to try the same business. It is to be feared that eagerness to reap the same profit will persuade several habitants to abandon agriculture. . . .

. . . Besides the disorders the taverns cause, it is to the advantage of the colony that the number of taverns be reduced to the smallest possible number. They should be abolished. It is advisable in a new colony to deprive colonists of anything that could turn them away from agriculture and to accustom them to a lazy life. [Dupuy] will carry out the decision made by the Conseil Superieur of Quebec on August 5, 1715. He will examine and give an account of whether it would not be better to assign to his subdelegated [the task of] giving permission on his orders to have taverns *dans les Costes** by having a yearly fee paid to the vestry of the churches. This would put a stop to a variation in law in Canada concerning this matter and would give some needed money to the churches.

*Refers to areas remote from the shores of the St. Lawrence River and the Gulf of St. Lawrence.

From Archives des Colonies, B, XLIX in Virginia R. Robeson, ed., *New France 1713-1760*, (Toronto: OISE, 1977).

1. Based upon these documents, write a short narrative paper on the state of the perfectible society by 1726.

Declaration from Louis XV concerning religious orders in New France, November 25, 1743
Louis, by the grace of God, King of France and Navarre [sends] greetings to all of those whom these letters concern.

The advancement of religion has always been the main aim of the efforts taken by our former Kings and of the expenses they have undertaken in the establishment of the American colonies. It is having this in mind that prevented them from according too many privileges to those who were destined to carry the light of religion to the colonies. Since our accession to the throne, We have spared nothing to maintain and encourage the zeal of the Ecclesiastical Orders established in the colonies. In addition, We have the satisfaction of seeing that our subjects there find, with respect to religion, all the assistance which they could hope to find in the heart of our kingdom. But, on the other hand, since the communities and religious orders have always known how to make use of their privileges and exemptions which enable them to acquire considerable sums, the King, our very honourable Lord and protector, has judged it necessary to set limits on them. He ruled in the year one thousand seven hundred and three that none of the religious orders established in the islands could extend its land holdings beyond the amount of land that could be worked by 100 Negroes. Since this ruling was not carried out, We ordered by our letters patent of the month of August, one thousand seven hundred and twenty-one that these orders could not in the future make any acquisition, either of land or of buildings without our full and express permission, on penalty of being reclaimed into the King's domain. The present state of all our colonies demands that We make even further arrangements concerning this matter. Whatever favour these establishments founded on religious and charitable motives might merit, it is time for us to take effective precautions to prevent new establishments from being formed in the colonies without our permission. Furthermore, these precautions are necessary to prevent those that are authorized in New France from multiplying their acquisitions and from taking out of circulation a considerable portion of the funds and land in our colonies which could only be considered contrary to the common good of society.

From "Edits, ordonnances royaux, declarations et arrêts du conseil d'Etat du Roi concernant le Canada," (Quebec: P.-E. Débarats, 1803) in Virginia R. Robeson e., *New France 1713-1760*, (Toronto: OISE, 1977).

Memorandum of instruction from Louis XV to La Jonquière, Governor of New France, April 30, 1749
Religion is the first goal proposed by His Majesty in the establishment of colonies. He recommends that La Jonquière give preference to everything within the scope of his government that aids its progress.

He is informed that of all the French colonies, Canada is the only one where a Bishop has been established. Pontbriand [Bishop of Quebec] fills this position, since nothing is more conducive to the well being of religion than mutual understanding between the heads of all the orders in the Colony.

The parishes of the Colony are served by secular priests and by Recollects. The Bishop assigns them to the parishes. The custom followed up until now has been to give the Bishop the freedom of changing the priests from one parish to another. The aim of this custom was to make possible the distribution in each parish of priests from different social levels and also to reward those who had served for a time in parishes of moderate revenue by assigning them to more important parishes.

But the clergy in the Colony and Beauharnois and Hocquart, former Lieutenant-general and Intendant respectively, have stated that it would be better in every respect not to allow this custom to continue any longer. It may have been necessary when the Colony was first established in view of the difficulty the bishops experienced in providing each parish with suitable clergy as was indicated in the report given to His Majesty on the necessity of establishing the parishes. Thus, he entrusted Beauharnois and Hocquart with consulting Pontbriand in order to investigate the matter carefully and give their opinions so that his Majesty could make a definite decision on the matter.

From Archives des Colonies, B, LXXXIX in Virginia R. Robeson, ed., *New France 1713-1760*, (Toronto: OISE, 1977).

1. Why does Louis XV feel that restrictions must be placed upon religious orders in the colony?
2. What actions has the king taken to limit the power of such orders?
3. What constraints does the king propose placing on the bishops?

The Canadiens, 1752

On the eve of the Seven Years' War, the Canadiens bore little resemblence to the ideals envisioned in the early seventeenth century. To a great extent they had become North Americans in dress, habit, and manner. Louis Franquet arrived in Canada in 1750. Here is how he described the inhabitants.

The average Canadian is unruly, obstinate and will do nothing but what he wants or fancies. Those who make their living driving carriages create a scandal and make it a point of honour to flaunt their expertise and their horse's strength by passing the carriages ahead of them without considering the risks and dangers involved.

. . . The habitants generally live in great comfort. They never travel on foot. In summer, they have carriages and in winter they have sleighs. In general, all of the habitants own horses. It is quite common to have as many horses in a household as there are boys. The latter use the horses only when they wish to go out in style and to go courting.

Women there are good looking rather than beautiful. . . . They walk well and carry themselves gracefully. They surpass the men when it comes to wit, for the women generally have a great deal of wit and speak a pure French devoid of the slightest accent. They also like finery and are good looking, kind and even well-mannered. I suspect some coquetry. At least their manner of dress seems to indicate some. Their footwear is generally good, and they wear a very short petticoat. Their waist is drawn in. Instead of a dress, they wear a mantlet of the cleanest kind which reaches only to their waist. It is easy to imagine that under such an outfit all their movements are noticeable and that with only the slightest encouragement from flattering glances, they easily conquer the hearts of men. They are, however, devoted to their husbands and children. They like pleasures and they make a point of heaping compliments on foreigners.

From Louis Franquet, *Voyages et memoires sur le Canada* (Quebec: A. Coté et Cie, 1889).

1. How does Franquet characterize the average Canadian?
2. Comment upon his description of the lifestyle and values of the colonists.
3. Contrast Franquet's image of the Canadiens in 1752 with the vision of the perfectible society.

Character and Social Order in Puritan New England

In this modern analysis, historian John Demos considers historical interpretations of what happened to the perfectible society in New England. In this essay he examines the social forces that worked to undermine the Puritan vision of a religious commonwealth in the New World.

Few aspects of American history have been as widely canvassed as New England Puritanism. Imbued from the start with a sense of divine mission, the Puritan settlers were continually evaluating themselves; and generation after generation of their descendants have returned to the task with monotonous regularity. These investigations have produced some important insights into early American society—and later American character—but they have also fostered serious misconceptions. The subject has evoked the interest of the best of professional scholars and the worst of nonprofessional mythmakers; the result is a maze of history, apologetics, prejudice, legend, and plain bewilderment.

According to one viewpoint, perhaps the most common, Puritanism was a personal style, a character type, based on intense and unswerving moral commitment. This portrayal has been shaded in vastly different ways, depending on the bias of its supporters. In the 19th century the Puritans were hailed as determined exemplars of the nation's destiny. In the early 20th century a reaction set in, and they were increasingly written off as repressed, pleasure-hating bigots. Moral or moralistic, single-minded or narrow-minded, upright or uptight— these impressions of Puritans die hard. And there is certainly some truth in them. The Puritans were remarkably tenacious in holding to their own view of human, and superhuman, activity. They were not, however, so rigidly opposed to pleasure as is sometimes claimed. More particularly, they were not opposed to sexual pleasure. In this regard our own usage of the term "puritanical" is misleading and reflects a larger tendency to confuse Puritans with Victorians. By almost any standard imaginable sex was more problematic in the 19th century than in the 17th.

Puritanism was also, according to a variant interpretation, an "ethic," a pervasive cult of hard work, thrift, and prudent calculation. As such it laid the psychological foundations for "the rise of capitalism." . . . This view contains a different mix of defects and virtues. On the one hand, it explains too much: Members of the "bourgeoisie" have come from a variety of different backgrounds, while some men who most epitomized orthodox Puritanism have looked askance at business pursuits. On the other hand, there is an overlap between Puritan and bourgeois virtues, as well as a rough geographical correlation between "capitalist" development and exposure to the more extreme forms of Protestantism.

It is, indeed, the individual Puritan who has been most neglected under all of the . . . historiographic traditions. He is presented regularly as a kind of vessel; he must always be "filled" with something else—whether moral zeal, or bourgeois virtue, or weighty religious doctrine. In each case he is both larger and smaller than life, and he loses his roots in concrete historical circumstance. He appears in the end as one part abstraction and one part caricature. Thus it seems important to try to relocate the human element in all this—to study Puritan man rather than Puritan"ism" and to evoke the particular drama of time and place in which his life was acted out. This may well be the task of the next generation of Puritan scholarship. . . .

The details of this situation need not detain us here. But we should ask what it was that induced people to become, and remain, Puritans of any stripe. . . .

Central to Walzer's analysis are the concepts of "anxiety" and "discipline." The Puritans were, after all, living through a time of unprecedented social change. The enclosure movement, runaway inflation, a new world of commerce, population growth, the swollen sprawl of the city of London, the disruption of the manorial and parochial systems, a decline in the vitality of local churches: these trends converge to undermine the traditional structure of English life. . . .

A fear of disorder pervaded all their thoughts and organized many of their activities. Yet they found in their religious faith a vital measure of reassurance—strength, hope, the promise of "a new life." For Puritanism enshrined precisely those values that history was destroying. It was rooted, above all, in the principle of control, both inner control of the individual man and outer control among the community of "saints." Intense and unrelenting discipline was the appropriate answer to disorder. . . .

It was no wonder that they chose withdrawal as the best, perhaps the only, solution to their predicament. They were not, however, fully in agreement about the meaning of this decision. Some envisioned a permanent departure; they would leave England and its church to a fate that was long since beyond their power to reverse. This group, usually known as Separatists, included the little band of "Pilgrims" who went first to Holland then across the Atlantic to the spot they named "Plimoth Plantation." John Winthrop and his colleagues in the Massachusetts Bay Company professed a different motive. Their affection for the "mother Church" remained strong—so they declared—and they could yet see much good in her. Their departure for the New World was a strategic retreat, a flanking movement in the struggle for final reform. Theirs would be

a kind of pilot venture that might eventually show the way to a far more perfect
society. For this they deserve recognition as the first in a long line of American
"Utopians." . . .

Yet almost from the beginning there were difficulties, special conditions that
served to frustrate the vision that the Puritans held up to themselves. Time
passed, circumstances changed; the obstacles became more numerous, and the
vision more distant. Still, each new generation produced fresh recruits to carry
on the struggle. In fact, the entire history of early New England can be read as
a kind of dialectical process encompassing the forces of order, harmony, and
permanence on one side, and fluidity, pluralism, and change on the other.
Eventually, it was plain that final success would never come, and some men
yielded to despair. To them New England was set on a path of decline. To
one recent historian of the period, "the story is cast in the form of a tragedy."
To another, it has the shape of an "ironic paradigm." . . .

. . . Expansion did not of itself destroy the Puritan social order. . . .

Much more serious was the prospect of growth and fragmentation within the
individual communities themselves. In time, the original center would come to
seem too confining, and some men would begin to consider moving away. . . .

So much for one side of the argument; the other also deserves its due. Here
the evidence turns more heavily behavioral, stressing the actions of individual
persons, . . .

The bulk of these actions involved only a few individuals at a time, responding to clearly personal grievances. . . .

Another type of conflict—extremely common, and particularly distressing to
all concerned—set ministers against their local congregations. Time and again
both sides squabbled over practical matters like the payment of salary, the
delivery of firewood, the repair and remodeling of the meetinghouse. Sometimes
there was wrangling over doctrine, or simply the clash of discordant personali-
ties. In all such cases arbitration seemed especially appropriate, but it could not
by itself assure an amicable outcome. Some disputes, apparently settled by this
method, simmered for years and eventually required further intervention. When
the strain became too great, the minister might have to look for a new "calling"
in some other town. It is quite astonishing, given the official code of peaceable-
ness, how many New England ministers were sent packing. . . .

But even so a problem remains. There was only a limited range of difference
among the communities in question, and a limited rate of change over time.
It becomes, therefore, our final, inescapable task to face head on the issue of
social stability and social change. . . .

. . . At the very time when their movement was being most sharply persecuted in England, an empty continent beckoned from across the sea. Puritans
were quick to grasp the opportunity to build a new society, with new men, in
a New World.

And yet, as we have seen, they did not find the life they looked for. They
had hoped, as one of them put it, to "be more free here than there from temptation: but I find here a devil to tempt, and a corrupt heart to deceive." Steadily, as the years passed, settlement became dispersed, communities divided and

subdivided, men struggled for personal advantage, and "heart-burning" contentions appeared on all sides. Cohesion and harmony remained the preeminent values, but in trying to practice such values the Puritans constantly disappointed themselves. They were not, of course, the first men to whom this has happened, nor have they been the last. But, more than many, they knew the agonies of the "divided self. "We can now take a longer view of the "contradictions" that seem to have muddled their history. To a very considerable degree, the inner life of Puritanism turned on a kind of axis between the opposite poles of order and chaos, conflict and conciliation, wilfulness and submission. "Tragic" perhaps, "ironic" certainly—their legacy is with us still.

From H.H. Quint *et al.*, "Character and the Social Order in Puritan New England", *Main Problems in American History*, (Homewood, Illinois: Dorsey Press, 1978).

1. What myths about the Puritans does Demos attempt to dispel?
2. What obstacles arose to interfere with the development of the perfectible society in New England?
3. Comment upon the following contention:
"Both the New France and the New England experiences demonstrate the futility of attempting to establish a utopian society in the New World."

The Perfectible Society: Analysis and Application

1. Explain how and why the concept of the "perfectible society" emerged from the religious turmoil of seventeenth-century Europe.

2. Contrast the New France experience with that of Puritan New England. To what extent did the different models of colonial development adopted by France and Britain dictate their relative successes in establishing theocracies in North America?

3. Write a vivid picture of the "perfectible society" as envisioned by John Winthrop.

4. It is 1664. Louis XIV is faced with the reorganization of New France as part of a general restructuring of the entire kingdom. A number of special-interest groups wish to influence the nature of the king's decision. Included among them are: a company hoping for a fur-trade monopoly; representatives of the Society of Jesus; members of the lower nobility wishing to establish a "new feudalism" in North America.

Write a petition to the king from the point of view of one of these groups. Outline your vision of the future of New France and the means by which your goals may be attained.

5. Outline the process through which the relationship between church and state was established in New France.

6. Research the experience of one religious community, for example, Ville Marie, Plymouth Plantation, or Sainte-Marie-Among-the-Hurons. Outline
(i) the principles upon which it was based;

(ii) the success of the venture; and

(iii) its eventual outcome.

7. Select a specific individual such as John Winthrop, Marguerite Bourgeoys, etc., who was living in North America, trying to establish the "perfectible society." Place yourself in his or her position and write a diary or journal entry in which you discuss both your goals for the new society and the frustrations you have encountered.

8. "The Canadiens have often been called the first modern North Americans." Evaluate this statement with respect to the social changes that took place in the New World and the reaction of traditional French authority to them.

9. Account for French-Canadian nationalist Abbé Lionel Groulx's contention that the Church was responsible for maintaining the core of the French identity in Canada.

10. Comment upon John Demos's analysis of Puritan New England. To what extent may his observations be applied to the New France experience? Rework the thesis developed by Demos and apply it to New France. Defend or refute the thesis based upon the evidence.

4
REVOLUTION AND LEGITIMACY

It has often been said that the United States was a product of revolution while Canada was a product of evolution. This makes a nice rhyming couplet, but it obscures the truth. In actual fact, the declaration of American independence and the country's subsequent success represents a pivotal point for both North American nations. What was at stake in the late eighteenth and early nineteenth centuries was the concept of nationhood, identity, and the role of North America in the British world.

To a great extent the citizens of the Thirteen Colonies stumbled onto their path through a combination of dedicated local leadership and imperial bungling. Does this mean that the Canadian route was found by default? Not at all. If the United States was to become heir to the European Enlightenment, then Canada would be the product of the British Parliamentary tradition and the reform movement of the nineteenth century. The societies that would eventually emerge would each take the best that the old world had to offer and apply it to the new continent.

North America on the Eve of Revolution

Victory over the French Empire in the Seven Years' War (1756-63) had left Great Britain as the undisputed master of the eastern half of North America. Settlers of the Thirteen Colonies who had started fighting as early as 1754 finally found the continent open to their dreams and aspirations. In the past, they had always looked to the mother country for support and defence. Now secure, they could turn their attention toward the interior of the continent and the improved possibilities for westward expansion. By the end of the war the colonies had gained not only in military security, but in economic and political strength as well. For the first time in their history, a growing number of colonial leaders were beginning to question the need for British control. Many people in the colonies felt that where Imperial and local interests were in conflict, local "American" concerns should come first.

These were not new sentiments. The attitude of the Puritans in Massachusetts toward the English Civil War had demonstrated this attitude over a century earlier. What was now up for debate was not the desire for new rights, but rather a clear reaffirmation of the existing freedoms expected by any British subject.

What did these people want? Not very much really. At the end of the Seven Years' War the American colonists were far better off than their counterparts in other European colonies. In fact, in many ways life was much better for them than it was for their British cousins. Unlike the English, colonial residents were free from the hereditary class system; they were taxed less (about one twenty-sixth of the average British taxpayer); they did not have to serve in the army or navy; there was no maximum wage; all trades and professions were open; and there was no required contribution to the church. Americans enjoyed a great deal of self-government and had freedom of speech, the press, and assembly. In many ways the British subject who came to live in North America, found her or himself in a remarkably free society. A place where people struggled and fought not to obtain freedom, but to confirm it.

Living in such a free society, the average citizen of the Thirteen Colonies had few complaints with the British government in 1763. Americans were proud to be an important part of the most progressive empire on earth. Conditions were changing. The defeat of France had created the need to reappraise the relationship between colony and mother country. It was clearly the time for relaxed imperial control. This, however, was not to be the case. No sooner had the Treaty of Peace been signed in Paris to the end the Seven Years' War than fighting once again broke out on the frontier. This time it was an Indian uprising.

Deserted by their French allies and fearful of the British, the Native nations formed an alliance and launched an attack on interior military garrisons. The "Pontiac Conspiracy," named after its leader, attacked and destroyed seven out of the nine British-controlled forts. To avoid a war, the government retaliated in another fashion. Through their fur trade connections, the British government distributed thousands of blankets to the Indians. These were not ordinary trade goods, however. Each blanket was infected. The resulting smallpox epidemic spread rapidly and killed thousands. The weakened Indian forces were then offered an "olive branch," the Royal Proclamation of 1763.

The Proclamation dealt mainly with the disposition of the new lands and population acquired with the conquest of New France. Unlike the Quebec Act that would follow a decade later, the Royal Proclamation attempted to lure colonial settlement to Quebec by establishing a system of law and government modelled on the colonies to the south. Had that been the extent of the document it would have been quite acceptable to the Thirteen Colonies; however, there was one more clause.

In order to placate the Indians, the Royal Proclamation closed off the West for settlement. A line was drawn along the crest of the Appalachian Mountains. Settlers were not allowed to homestead west of the line.

Many British were quite pleased with this policy. Not only would it satisfy Native concerns, but it would revive the fur trade, keep colonial industry within reach of the British navy, and perhaps encourage English migration to Quebec, which would assimilate the French habitants already living there. From an imperial point of view it was a far-sighted and practical policy.

Many American colonists were outraged. For years they had been fighting with the French and their Indian allies for control of the rich lands of the Ohio, Missouri, and Mississippi valleys. After finally defeating their enemy, their "friend" was shutting the same door. From a colonial point of view it was short–sighted and ill-conceived.

Although the policy was soon modified, the damage had been done. It became apparent to the colonies that their concerns were not being heard in Westminster. A new system would have to be devised in which North Americans and Britons could sit side by side and discuss policy. The Thirteen Colonies would have to be represented in Parliament.

Britain's problem was fundamental. Throughout the eighteenth century, the Empire had left the colonies pretty much alone. In fact, as they had matured, the

Thirteen Colonies had grown less and less dependent upon the mother country. This alone was not really a concern. The difficulty was that, while the colonies were moving toward economic autonomy from Britain, the British were becoming increasingly dependent upon them. By the early 1770s, 36 percent of British imports came from their North American possessions, and over 37 percent of their exports returned to the colonies. Growing colonial independence therefore spelled economic disaster for Great Britain. It was time to pull in the reins and tie the colonies more tightly to the homeland.

The Seven Years' War had left Britain with a massive public debt. In addition to this, the colonies were now costing the mother country money. By 1763, the cost of maintaining colonial customs offices had risen to £8000, but the officials only managed to collect just over £2000! Clearly something had to be done.

The first move was the passage of the Sugar Act of 1764. This legislation actually cut the tax on molasses by one-half from $.06/gram to $.03. In the past the tax on molasses had rarely been collected. Now this changed. The new "lighter" tax was to be rigorously collected and was to be extended to indigo, coffee, wine, and sugar. This raised a serious question in the colonies.

Most colonists accepted Britain's right to regulate trade. They accepted import restrictions or duties that they saw as control measures. However, duties designed specifically to raise revenue were another thing altogether. This was taxation, and they felt taxation was the right of colonial legislatures, not the British Parliament.

As British subjects, the colonists felt that they had the right to be taxed only with the consent of their representatives, and there were no colonial members of Parliament in London. A whisper was heard "No taxation without representation!"

The Sugar Act was followed by two more "innovations." The Currency Act forbade the colonies to print their own paper money. This move was justifiable. Colonial governments had adopted the practice of repaying their war debts by simply printing their own money and sending it to their creditors. Needless to say, it was practically worthless! Business interests in England put a great deal of pressure upon Parliament to put an end to the practice (much to the dismay of the colonists).

The Currency Act was followed by the Quartering Act, which required colonists to provide food and shelter for any British troops stationed in North America.

The greatest blow was yet to come, however. While the colonies were still adjusting to this barrage of legislation, Parliament gave notice of its intent to pass a Stamp Act the following year. The colonials were given time to submit proposals for alternative ways of raising revenue, but none were accepted. As a result, the legislation went into place in 1764.

The Stamp Act hit everyone. Excise stamps were required on newspapers, pamphlets, playing cards, dice, and every legal document issued in the colonies. The tax increase varied from 33 to 100 percent. Not only were the tax increases high, they were highly visible. Almost every item seemed to be burdened with a stamp. The colonists were incensed. Once again, only louder this time, the question of taxation without representation was raised.

This time the British had an answer. The colonies had representation, they said. According to them, each member of Parliament represented the interests of the

The Boston "massacre" as illustrated in an engraving by Paul Revere

In this painting, habitant defenders barricade a street against American invaders in 1775.

entire empire as well as his own riding. In fact, this theory, known as virtual representation, forms the basis for the parliamentary system in Canada today. The North American colonists, on the other hand, believed in direct representation. Since it was physically impossible to have effective representation in England, then England should leave the matter of taxation to the local colonial legislatures.

Pamphlets and petitions condemning British policy were circulated. Other colonists went further, calling into question the British connection altogether, and laying the foundation for independence. John Dickinson in his "Letters from a Farmer in Pennsylvania to the Inhabitants of the British Colonies" stated:

> Let us consider ourselves as . . . freemen . . . firmly bound together by the same rights, interests and dangers. . . . What have these colonies to ask, while they continue free; or what have they to dread, but insidious attempts to subvert their freedom?

Not all of the protest was merely verbal. Vigilante groups were formed. The Sons of Liberty, as they were called, were young, middle-class men who disguised themselves in "blackface" and sailors' outfits. They stopped and threatened customs officials, and even tarred and feathered some. People today often picture this colonial assault as a humorous prank. Far from it! The victim was dropped into hot tar. Once removed, the person was covered with chicken or goose feathers. Often the mixture was then ignited. Cleaning up was just as unpleasant. Peeling off the tar usually meant taking half the skin along with it. Even after the victim was cleaned up, he usually suffered from infections and scarring.

Often wealthy merchants such as John Weber paid the Sons of Liberty to go after specific targets. Even this was dangerous. In time these gangs took the law into their own hands and began to loot and blackmail. Obviously violence was not the answer.

When the British first announced the tax legislation, a Stamp Act Congress (see readings) was held in October of 1763. Representatives of nine of the thirteen colonies were present. Those missing, for the most part, had been refused permission by their British governors. When the colonists realized the British were unwilling to change their minds, they responded by boycotting English goods. This countermeasure, coupled with the difficulty that the government had had enforcing the duty, led to its repeal in March of 1766.

The next barrage of taxation, the Townsend Duties, took the colonies by surprise. New taxes were imposed on glass, lead paints, paper, and tea. Still suffering from a postwar depression, the new duties left the colonies reeling. In response, the colonists again adopted the strategy that had been so successful a few years before–boycott.

Although only Northern merchants participated in this boycott on imported goods, it decreased overall trade by one-third. In Philadelphia and Boston imports decreased by about 50 percent, while New York saw its business decrease by over 80 percent. To attempt to enforce the duties, the British increased their military presence in the colonies, but it was no use. By the time Lord North became prime minister in March of 1770 it was clear that the Townsend Duties were costing

Britain more than they were bringing in. As a result, the next month all but the taxes on tea were quietly repealed. In response to the British move the colonies gratefully ended their boycott.

With the end of this latest round of trade wars it appeared that the relationship between colony and mother country might improve. Unfortunately fate was not to be so kind. As often happens in history, events took on a life of their own.

Life in the British army was not easy. Most soldiers were poorly paid, and many looked for part-time work to supplement their income. This increased competition for jobs was obviously not popular with local workers. Tempers grew hot and the situation finally boiled over in Boston on the night of March 5, 1770. After the pubs had closed that evening, a group of workers began to harass a lone British sentry. Simply taunting him at first, the mob soon resorted to violence. From insults to snowballs, to stones, and finally to clubs, the abuse continued to escalate. As the mob grew in size, the local British garrison commander called out his twenty men to disperse the mob and restore order. The crowd, now numbering several hundred, would not be intimidated. Finally it happened. After being struck repeatedly by a club one British soldier lost his temper and opened fire. He was quickly joined by his fellow soldiers. When the smoke had cleared, five people were dead and several wounded. Tempers cooled, but the Boston Massacre would not soon disappear from colonial minds.

Most colonial leaders were uncomfortable with the tactics of Sam Adams and his followers. They saw power slipping from the hands of a responsible colonial elite into the clutches of the mob. As a result much of the protest against British policy was softened in the early 1770s. For the most part, these were peaceful years. It could have been a time of negotiation and settlement. Instead they were years of cautious watching and waiting. The explosives were ready; it would take only a spark to set them off.

At first it seemed that the blow–up might come over tea. The East India Company had a monopoly on the export of tea from Britain's Asian colonies. Through corruption and mismanagement, the company found itself, early in 1773, with 8 million kg of surplus tea. As with many powerful commercial interests, the East India Company had a large number of friends in government. The result was the East India (Tea) Act passed by Parliament in May of 1773. The act gave the company the right to sail its surplus tea straight to North America and sell it directly to the colonists, completely by-passing local agents and merchants. Business people in the American ports were furious. After months of futile protest, they decided to act. On the night of December 16th, a group of forty to fifty American patriots, led by Samuel Adams, boarded the British merchant ship *Beaver*. Disguised as Mohawk Indians and Blacks, they proceeded to throw the entire cargo of 342 chests of tea into Boston harbour.

This Boston Tea Party, as it is now called, brought almost immediate retaliation from Britain. The British in fact overreacted. So excessive was their response that it only served to drive more moderate colonists into the radical camp. In an attempt to get the colonies back in line, Parliament quickly passed the Coercive Acts. The inital result was to close the port of Boston, revoke the Massachusetts charter, and impose a military government under General Thomas Gage.

The Boston Port Act, first to be enacted, sparked the most widespread outrage. Instead of dealing with the small group of radicals behind the incident, with one stroke of the pen it declared all citizens of Boston to be equally guilty. This was a far cry from the principles of British justice, and gave proof to the growing cries of "tyranny."

Under the Boston Port Act, the customs houses were moved north to the town of Salem, and all boat and cargo landings in Boston were forbidden. To enforce this move a British naval squadron blockaded the harbour, and eventually five regiments occupied the city.

In the other colonies, the move was like an electric shock. Aid immediately poured in from up and down the seaboard. Virginia, for example, sent corn, wheat, and flour to their fellow colonists. In the House of Burgesses the British move was described as a hostile invasion. In response to this, the British governor, in the name of the king, dissolved the House. Later, the delegates met in a tavern and passed a resolution declaring that "an attack made on one of our sister Colonies, to compel submission to arbitrary taxes, is an attack made on all British America." In other words, colonial leaders were beginning to feel that they had much more in common with their North American neighbours than with their mother country. By 1774 Britain was looking less like a kindly parent and more like a brutal tyrant.

To feed and shelter the increased number of British troops, Parliament revived the Quartering Act, the most hated of all legislation. Finally in a seemingly unrelated move, this flurry of legislation concluded with the declaration of the Quebec Act.

The Quebec Act had an unexpected effect upon the colonies. Designed to secure the loyalty of French-Canadian leaders it was regarded with the utmost suspicion to the south. While the British felt that they were being benevolent in restoring Roman Catholicism, French civil law, and seigneurial land tenure to Quebec, the Thirteen Colonists saw the same actions as denying the rights of British subjects. The greatest shock came with the elimination of an elected assembly in the province and its replacement with an appointed council. If it could be done in Quebec, why not in all of the colonies?

To add insult to injury, the boundaries of the new colony were extended to include the entire Ohio Valley. This was too much. The Thirteen Colonies had fought the Seven Years' War to drive the French from this territory and now the British were handing it back to the French. No wonder the American colonists called this collection of legislation the "Intolerable Acts."

The logical way to protest such actions was for the colonists to unite. However, this was easier said than done. For over a century, the various colonies had been used to local autonomy. In fact the basic dispute with Britain now was that it was restricting that colonial independence. People accustomed to governing their own affairs would be wary about giving up that right to someone else. What was to be gained by simply exchanging one set of masters for another?

In spite of these misgivings, however, there was a still a movement toward unity. By 1774 every colony was informally linked by Committees of Correspondence. Originated two years earlier by Samuel Adams in Massachusetts, these contacts encouraged intercolonial communication and discussion. What they provided was a means of revolutionary planning and implementation outside of the regular colonial channels. In the face of this continued British pressure, the colonists finally decided to meet to discuss their grievances.

This First Continental Congress was held in Philadelphia on September 5, 1774. There were fifty-five delegates representing twelve colonies. Moderates such as John Dickinson and Joseph Galloway of Pennsylvania wanted to strike a compromise. They proposed a union of the colonies under British authority. Although quite popular at first, the Galloway Plan was defeated in a close vote owing mainly to the strong campaign against it led by radicals such as Samuel Adams and Patrick Henry of Virginia. Galloway was so fed up with the way things went at Philadelphia that he later became a Tory supporter of Britain during the Revolution.

With the defeat of the moderate position, more radical voices were heard. A second proposal was brought forward by Thomas Jefferson, among others. They proposed a British imperial system based upon the Dominion principle. The new colonial government would have semi-independence and function under much the same rules as would be adopted in the British North America Act almost a century later.

Jefferson argued that the only link between the colonies and Britain should be a common loyalty to the king. As a result, he reasoned, Parliament would have no power to tax or even legislate for the colonies. These proposals offered a chance for compromise, but they were ignored by the government in England. The Congress finally closed with a formal Declaration of Resolves that called for the repeal of all coercive legislation.

In England, parliamentary opinion was split. Growing numbers of Members of the Houses of Commons and Lords were beginning to question government policy. In February 1775 a private member's bill was introduced to "settle the troubles in America." It proposed that the government accept the Continental Congress as the legitimate voice of the colonies, repeal the Coercive Acts, and bring home the troops. Parliament would only retain its authority over trade and navigation.

Such a move would have been widely accepted in the colonies. In fact it closely resembled Jefferson's position. Unfortunately for history, Parliament was not yet ready to make a deal. The motion was defeated. British policy was in conservative hands.

Policy on the other side of the Atlantic was becoming increasingly radical. A new generation of revolutionary leaders was emerging. Their ideas would help to ignite the flames of revolution against imperial control. As mentioned earlier, the American "revolution" did not necessarily produce any revolutionary ideas. The spokespersons for the Thirteen Colonies owed a great debt to the Englightenment philosophers of Europe.

Colonial pamphleteers and politicians read with great interest the ideas of such writers as John Locke, Jean-Jacques Rousseau, and Charles Secondat, Baron de Montesquieu (see readings). Since the time of the Stamp Act Congress of 1763, a growing faction had been convinced that only through complete independence could the colonies implement these new ideas concerning the nature of humanity, natural rights, and the role of government. During the early 1760s one of these individuals, James Otis of Boston, emerged as a prominent spokesman for colonial rights. When Parliament ordered customs officials to use Writs of Assistance (blanket search warrants that allowed them to enter anyone's home or warehouse without any evidence of wrongdoing) in order to catch potential smugglers, Otis quit his job as a crown attorney, and argued the case on behalf of the local merchants whose rights were being violated. He lost the case, but he gained a great reputation as an orator and defender of colonial rights (see readings). For the next fifteen years his would be an influential voice in the colony. The response of John Dickinson to the Townsend Duties echoed the concerns raised by Otis. It would not be until a decade later, however, that the full impact of these new ideas would be felt.

One of these new generation of radical orators was Patrick Henry of Virginia. Unlike many of the middle-class radicals in the North, Patrick Henry was born and raised in the backwoods of Virginia. With a little formal education he managed to train himself as a lawyer. Once he had established himself as a great courtroom orator, he was elected to the House of Burgesses in 1765 at the age of twenty-nine.

Henry established himself as a constant and vocal opponent of arbitrary government and tyranny wherever he saw it. Such sentiments led him to take the floor in an illegal meeting of the members of the House of Burgesses after its dissolution in 1775. Contemporary observers wrote that when he spoke that day the entire building seemed to sway and every person present sat rigid on the edge of his seat. He had delivered a long and passionate address, pacing about the room while he spoke until suddenly he stopped, turned, and faced the assembly. He "stood in the attitude of a condemned galley slave . . . His form was bowed; his wrists were crossed; his manacles were almost visible." With a deep rumbling voice he spoke:

> It is vain to extenuate the matter. Gentlemen may cry peace, peace, peace, but there is no peace. . . . The next gale that sweeps from the north will bring to our ears the clash of resounding arms. Our brethren are already in the field. Why stand we here idle? What is it these gentlemen wish? What would they have? Is life so dear, or peace so sweet, as to be purchased at the price of chains and slavery?

Suddenly he stood straight up, his hands free of his imaginary chains were extended to the sky:

> Forbid it, Almighty God! I know not what course others may take, but as for me, give me liberty, or give me death!

Henry played an essential role in laying the groundwork for rebellion. With representatives such as these is it any surprise that British belligerence soon resulted in colonial reprisals? Such politicians, however, reached only a limited audience with their ideas. The pamphleteer, Thomas Paine, had a different role to play. For him the real work would begin once the first shots had been fired.

Of all of the prominent revolutionary spokespersons, only Paine was born outside of the colonies. Born in England, Paine had tried his hand at a number of jobs before coming to America. He had started as a corset maker, had run off to sea, tried teaching, had run a tobacco shop, and later a grocery store. He was almost always broke and seldom lucky. Finally when there seemed to be no alternative, he sailed for the colonies. Even then things did not work out well. He took sick at sea and had to be carried ashore in Philadelphia.

It was 1774. Tom Paine had found his place. Within thirteen months he had published *Common Sense*, perhaps the most powerful revolutionary document ever written in English (see readings). Paine's formal education had ended when he was thirteen years old. His words were plain and direct:

I offer nothing more than simple facts, plain arguments, and common sense. Volumes have been written on the subject of the struggle between England and America. Men of all ranks have engaged in the controversy, but all have been ineffectual. The period of debate is over. Arms, as the last resort, must decide the contest. . . .

I have heard some assert that because America has flourished under her connection with Great Britain, that the same connection is necessary for her future happiness. Nothing can be more false than this kind of argument. American would have flourished as much, and probably more, had no European power had anything to do with her. There will always be a market for America's goods, as long as people in Europe continue to eat.. . . .

It is repugnant to reason, to the universal order of things, and to all examples from former ages, to suppose that this continent can longer remain subject to any external power. . . .

Anything short of independence is mere patchwork and it can afford no lasting happiness.

The impact of Paine's words cannot be overestimated. Contemporaries claimed that the success of the revolution owed as much to the "pen of Paine as to the sword of Washington." *Common Sense* was the explanation many colonists had been waiting for. It put their own thoughts into words, and they put the words into action. For people with such "common sense," the world would never be the same again.

Common Sense became an instant best seller, with over one hundred and twenty thousand copies sold in the colonies. For Americans who had been wavering on the issue of independence, *Common Sense* made up their minds.

Momentum had shifted in the colonies. On April 6, 1776, the Continental Congress officially opened up the ports of the United Colonies to the trading nations of the world. Mercantilism was dead! This economic declaration of independence was soon followed by a political one. On June 11th R.H. Lee of Virginia introduced a resolution calling for independence. Four days later the Congress appointed a "committee of five" to draft the resolution. Most of the work was done by Thomas Jefferson of Virginia. On July 1st his draft was submitted to Congress. The next day the Continental Congress voted for independence, and two days later the delegates adopted the formal Declaration of Independence.

Why proclaim independence? To begin with, as long as the Americans were colonists they were British subjects. As a result their fighting was not a war, but an act of treason, and their troops would not be treated as soldiers but as traitors. Secondly, if the United Colonies were going to find any overseas allies, they had to show the world that they meant business.

The Declaration itself is a complex document divided into distinct sections. However, it is structured to be seen as a cohesive whole (see Appendix).

Thomas Jefferson has been credited with the writing of the Declaration. It is, however, a hybrid document. We see in it much of Locke, Otis, Paine, and Franklin, as well as Jefferson. It opens with a firm statement of purpose and then moves into a discussion of the basic principles of natural rights and the social contract. These are the critical sections of the document. They establish the new United States firmly in the Enlightenment tradition. In addition, this portion of the Declaration reaffirms those rights long enjoyed by the colonies and demanded by reformers in Great Britain. The remainder of the Declaration merely shows the attainment of these fundamental rights to be impossible under continued British rule.

The American Revolution is the story of people making a set of choices. While there is no question that in 1776 a small group of individuals in the colonies saw the struggle in terms of the principles outlined in the Declaration, many others identified more closely with the practical grievances and the down-to-earth rhetoric of Thomas Paine. For the dedicated minority of revolutionaries, there was an equally dedicated minority of individuals who remained loyal to Great Britain. Often portrayed as cowardly or treacherous, these individuals actually showed great courage in maintaining their principles in the face of an increasingly hostile population.

We have examined in detail the values and goals of one side in the Revolution, but who were these others? What did they want? Why did some stay markedly neutral during the conflict? Why were others willing to give up home, family, and friends in defence of an ideal?

There were over thirty British colonies in the Western Hemisphere at the time of the Revolution. Those in the Caribbean were closely tied to the imperial trading network. For them separation from the British Empire would have been economic suicide. For others, however, it was a different story.

Certainly the greatest enigma to the American revolutionaries during the period were the colonies to the north. Invited to join in the Continental Congresses, Quebec and Nova Scotia both remained either lukewarm or openly hostile to the goals of the War of Independence.

The Quebec case is relatively straightforward. They saw the revolution as primarily a British affair. With the guarantees provided under the terms of the Quebec Act, the Canadiens had little to gain in siding with the Thirteen Colonies against British rule (see readings). Habitant indifference stiffened into outright resistance with the decision by the Continental Army to invade Quebec in 1775. For them, loyalty to Britain was not the issue; defence of their St. Lawrence homeland was. There would be no francophone fourteenth colony in the new nation to the south.

Nova Scotia was a different case altogether. The "neutral Yankees" of that maritime colony have presented historians with a conundrum. Why would the residents of this region, settled principally by New Englanders since the 1760s, fail to take up arms and join their comrades in the struggle? Traditionally, historians have assumed that the presence of the British military in Halifax, combined with the region's isolation from the rest of the rebellious colonies, encouraged a neutral position. However, recent scholarship has pointed to a number of other possibilities.

To begin with, by the time of the Revolution, only about six out of ten Nova Scotians had emigrated from New England. A growing minority were more recent British immigrants with no ties to the colonies to the south. In addition, American immigrants had left the Thirteen Colonies back in the early 1760s. As a result, they had not taken part in the great protests and the growing discontent of the following decade. The colonies that they had left had been loyal and still basking in the glory of a mutual victory over the French. In addition, Nova Scotia was being swept by a religious revival akin to the Great Awakening of the 1730s. Revolutionary fervour was directed, therefore, along religious rather than political lines. Whatever their reasons, the Nova Scotians stayed out of the action during the war (see readings).

Perhaps the most interesting group of dissenters came from the rebellious colonies themselves. Called Tories by their patriot counterparts, they are better known as the United Empire Loyalists.

It would be easy to simply dismiss these individuals as gamblers who had backed the wrong side. To some extent this was true. However, in most cases the Loyalists were thoughtful individuals who made a painful personal choice to remain loyal to Great Britain. With the formal recognition of the new United States in 1783 there was little choice. The Loyalists, or Tories, had to go. The question was where? The more wealthy could simply return to England, as did former Imperial officials and officers. Most Loyalists, however, could not afford this solution. They looked to the north.

Thirty-thousand Loyalists sailed to Nova Scotia. They settled along the shores of the Bay of Fundy, away from the local inhabitants, whom they felt to be "too neutral" during the Revolution. The Imperial authorities, still hurting from the loss of their colonies to the south, were concerned that the "new" Nova Scotia might become so large and powerful that it too would begin to consider independence. As a result, when the new settlers demanded a government of their own, the British Parliament quickly agreed, and the colony of New Brunswick was created in 1784.

An additional ten thousand loyalists made the overland trek to Quebec. There they found an alien environment with different laws, language, and religion. It was not the British welcome they had expected. As a result, they too agitated for their own colony. In 1791 their wish was granted, and through the Constitutional Act the old province of Quebec was divided in half. East of the Ottawa River, Lower Canada, would continue to be governed under the terms of the Quebec Act of 1774. West of that, the new colony of Upper Canada would be governed under the terms of the Royal Proclamation of 1763.

These people were refugees. They had left prosperous farms and businesses in the United States, and now found themselves starting over in a wilderness. What values and principles had they brought with them to the remaining British colonies in North America? What was the difference between the "loyalists" and the "patriots" whom they had left behind?

Some historians have claimed that the exiles represented the conservative faction of American society, while the liberal elements were left to build the new United States. Most, however, feel this explanation is too simplistic. As we have seen, the basic difference in the two groups was primarily their attitude toward Britain. Where the Loyalists saw British mismanagement and poor judgment, the patriots saw British tyranny and deliberate restrictions on their rights. The Loyalists were the skeptics of the Revolution. They were not convinced that the "new England" that was to be created in North America would necessarily be better than the old. Having voiced this skepticism, they had no option when the war was over but to leave.

This does not necessarily mean that they brought with them a blind faith or unquestioning loyalty to Great Britain. To the contrary, they had fought for British ideals, and now they expected them to be implemented in their new homes. When the first lieutenant-governor of Upper Canada, John Graves Simcoe, promised these newcomers a government that would be "the very image and transcript of the British constitution," they expected him to deliver (see readings).

In the final analysis, the American Revolution was a watershed for the English-speaking peoples of North America. The two schools of thought that existed in the Thirteen Colonies prior to the Revolution would now go their own separate ways. To the south, a nation would slowly be constructed based upon the ideals of the Enlightenment philosophers. On their northern border a sister nation would emerge based not upon revolution but reform. It would find its voice in men such as Lord Grenville who trusted in "the blessings of the English constitution."

Despite the different paths chosen, the end would be basically the same. Out of the British parliamentary and American revolutionary experiences would emerge two dynamic democracies spanning the North American continent.

Of Civil Government, 1690

If Jean-Jacques Rousseau was the spiritual father of the French Revolution, the American Revolution can trace its lineage to the writings of the British political philosopher John Locke. In this excerpt from Two Treatises of Government, *Locke discusses the relationship between society and its government.*

To understand political power aright, we must consider what condition all men are naturally in, and that is a state of perfect freedom to do as they wish and dispose of their possessions and persons as they think fit, within the bounds of the law of nature, without asking leave or depending upon the will of any other man.

A state also of equality, in which no one has more power or authority than another, there being nothing more evident than that creatures of the same species and rank born to all the same advantages of nature, and the use of the same faculties, should also be equal to each other without subordination or subjection. . . .

The state of nature has a law of nature to govern it, and reason, which is that law, teaches all mankind who will but consult it that being all equal and independent, no one ought to harm another in his life, health, liberty, or possessions; . . . All men are naturally in that state, and remain so till, by their own consent, they make themselves members of some political society. . . .

If man in the state of nature is as free as has been said . . . why will he part with his freedom? Why will he give up this empire, and subject himself to the dominion and control of any other power? To which it is obvious to answer, that though in the state of nature he has such a right, yet the enjoyment of it is very uncertain, and constantly exposed to the invasion of others; for all being kings as much as he, every man his equal, and most of them no strict observers of equity and justice, the enjoyment of the property he has in this state is very unsafe, very insecure; and it is not without reason that he seeks out and is willing to join in society with others who are already united, or have a mind to unite for the mutual preservation of their lives, liberties and estates, which I call by the general name—property.

The great and chief end, therefore, of men uniting into commonwealths is the preservation of property. . . .

Since it can never be supposed to be the will of the society that the legislature should be able to destroy that which everyone hopes to secure by entering into society, and for which the people submitted themselves to legislators of their own making; whenever the legislators try to take away and destroy the property of the people, or to reduce them to slavery under arbitrary power, they put themselves into a state of war with the people who are thereupon freed from any further obedience, and are left to the common refuge which God hath provided for all men against force and violence. . . .

But it will be said, this hypothesis may lead to frequent rebellion. To which I answer . . . such revolutions happen not upon every little mismanagement in public affairs, . . . But if a long train of abuses, prevarications and artifices, all tending the same way, make the design visible to the people, they cannot but feel what they lie under, and see whither they are going; it is not to be wondered at that they should then rouse themselves, and endeavor to put the rule into such hands which may secure to them the end for which government was at first erected.

From Edwin Fenton, *32 Problems in World History*, (Glenview, Ill.: Scott, Foresman & Co., 1969).

1. How does Locke describe life in the state of nature?
2. Why does he say people join together into political organizations?
3. Given the concepts expressed above, how does the philosopher define the relationship between a government and society?

The Rights of the British Colonies, 1763

James Otis echoed Locke in this pamphlet outlining colonial concerns about imperial policy in the 1760s.

Is government founded on an agreement between the people and those who govern? Or is government founded on property? It is not altogether founded on either. Then has government any solid foundation that does not change? . . .

Because government is founded on human nature, a supreme power must exist in every society, from whose final decisions there can be no appeal except directly to Heaven. I say this supreme, absolute power is originally and ultimately in the people, and that they can never give this power away since it comes from God.

. . . Hence, it is contrary to reason that supreme, unlimited power should be in the hands of one man.

Since the purpose of government is to promote the welfare of mankind, above all things it should provide for the happy enjoyment of life, liberty, and property. If each individual living by himself could enjoy life, liberty, and property fully there would be no need for government. But the experience of ages has proved that by nature men are weak, imperfect beings. They cannot live independently of each other, and yet they cannot live together without conflict. To settle conflict, men need an arbitrator.

By nature and by right, the individuals of each society may have any form of government they please. The same law of nature and reason applies to a democracy, an aristocracy, or a monarchy.

Whenever the administrators of any government depart from truth, justice, and equity (fairness), they should be opposed. If they prove incorrigible, they should be deposed by the people.

The American colonists, being men, are equally entitled to all the rights of nature. They are also subject to and dependent upon Great Britain. . . .

To say that Parliament is absolute and arbitrary contradicts natural law. Parliament can in all cases declare what it thinks is good for the whole; but the declaration of Parliament alone does not make a thing good. There is in every instance a higher authority, namely God. Should an act of Parliament violate any of His natural laws, the act would be contrary to eternal truth, equity, and justice, and consequently would be void. Parliament would repeal such an act when it became convinced of its mistake.

Summary of "The Rights of the British Colonies Asserted and Proved" by James Otis, 1761. (Unpublished, edited version.)

1. In what way does Otis describe the foundation of government?
2. What rights does he claim on behalf of the colonies?
3. Trace Locke's influence on the writing of Otis.

Letters from a Farmer, 1767-68

John Dickinson was a Philadelphia lawyer who published a series of anonymous letters in the Pennsylvania Chronicle *in 1767. In his "Letters from a Farmer in Pennsylvania to the Inhabitants of the British Colonies," Dickinson outlined the American constitutional argument against imperial taxation. In this excerpt he explains the difference between the use of duties to regulate trade versus using them as a means of taxation.*

There is another late act of parliament, which appears to me to be unconstitutional, and as destructive to the liberty of these colonies, as that mentioned in my last letter; that is, the act for granting the duties on paper, glass, &c. [the Townshend Act].

The parliament unquestionably possesses a legal authority to regulate the trade of Great-Britain and all her colonies. Such an authority is essential to the relation between a mother country and her colonies; and necessary for the common good of all. . . . This power is lodged in the parliament; and we are as much dependent on Great-Britain, as a perfectly free people can be on another.

I have looked over every statute relating to these colonies, from their first settlement to this time; . . . All before, are calculated to regulate trade, and preserve or promote a mutually beneficial intercourse between the several constituent parts of the empire; . . . Never did the British parliament, till the period above mentioned, think of imposing duties in America, FOR THE PURPOSE OF RAISING A REVENUE. . . .

Here then, my dear country men ROUSE yourselves, and behold the ruin hanging over your heads. If you once admit, that Great-Britain may lay duties upon her exportations to us, for the purpose of levying money on us only, she then will have nothing to do, but to lay those duties on the articles which she prohibits us to manufacture–and the tragedy of American liberty is finished. . . . If Great-Britain can order us to come to her for necessaries we want, and can order us to pay what taxes she pleases before we take them away, or when we land them here, we are as abject slaves as France and Poland can shew in wooden shoes, and with uncombed hair.

Richard Hofstadter, ed. *Great Issues in American History: From the Revolution to the Civil War, 1765-1865.* (New York: Vintage Books, 1982, rev. ed.).

1. (a) What legal right does Dickinson maintain that Parliament has?
(b) How does this right differ from the use of tariffs to raise revenues?
2. In what ways does the author claim American liberties are being curtailed by the process?

Resolutions of the Stamp Act Congress, 1763

John Dickinson's influence is evident in the series of resolutions which emerged from an intercolonial congress held in 1763 to protest the passage of the Stamp Act. In the resolutions we can see the emergence of the first clear statement of the concept of "no taxation without representation."

The members of this Congress, sincerely devoted, with the warmest sentiments of affection and duty to His Majesty's Person and Government, inviolably attached to the present happy establishment of the Protestant succession, and with minds deeply impressed by a sense of the present and impending misfortunes of the British colonies on this continent; having considered as maturely as time will permit the circumstances of the said colonies, esteem it our indispensable duty to make the following declarations of our humble opinion, respecting the most essential rights and liberties of the colonists, and of the grievances under which they labour, by reason of several late Acts of Parliament.

I. That His Majesty's subjects in these colonies, owe the same allegiance to the Crown of Great-Britain, that is owing from his subjects born within the realm, . . .

II. That His Majesty's liege subjects in these colonies, are entitled to all the inherent rights and liberties of his natural born subjects within the kingdom of Great-Britain.

III. That it is inseparably essential to the freedom of a people and the undoubted right of Englishmen, that no taxes be imposed on them, but with their own consent given personally, or by their representatives.

IV. That the people of these colonies are not, and from their local circumstances cannot be, represented in the House of Commons in Great-Britain.

V. That the only representatives of the people of these colonies, are persons chose therein by themselves, and that no taxes ever have been or can be constitutionally imposed on them, but by their respective legislatures. . . .

VII. That trial by jury is the inherent and invaluable right of every British subject in these colonies.

VIII. That the late Act of Parliament, [the Stamp Act] . . . and several other Acts, by extending the jurisdiction of the courts of Admiralty beyond its ancient limits, have a manifest tendency to subvert the rights and liberties of the colonists. . . .

XI. That the restrictions imposed by several late Acts of Parliament, on the trade of these colonies, will render them unable to purchase the manufactures of Great-Britain.

XII. That the increase, prosperity, and happiness of these colonies, depend on the full and free enjoyment of their rights and liberties, and an intercourse with Great-Britain mutually affectionate and advantageous. . . .

Lastly, That it is the indispensable duty of these colonies, to the best of sovereigns, to the mother country, and to themselves to endeavour by a loyal and dutiful address to his Majesty, and humble applications to both Houses of Parliament, to procure the repeat of the Act for granting and applying certain stamp duties, of all clauses of any other Acts of Parliament, whereby the jurisdiction of the Admiralty is extended as aforesaid, and of the other late Acts for the restriction of American commerce.

From Hofstadter, *Great Issues in American History: From the Revolution to the Civil War, 1765-1865.*

1. How does the preamble of the document depict the attitude of the colonists toward Great Britain?
2. Outline the arguments presented with regard to the rights of taxation.
3. What demands are put forward in the resolutions?

First Continental Congress 1774, Declaration and Resolves

When colonial leaders met in Philadelphia to protest the passage of the Intolerable Acts, they still saw themselves as good British subjects petitioning for their natural rights. In this excerpt from the "Declaration and Resolves" of the congress the delegates laid out their concerns with British policy and listed their rights as they saw them.

October 14, 1774

Whereas, since the close of the last war, the British parliament, claiming a power of right to bind the people of America, by statute in all cases whatsoever, hath, in some acts expressly imposed taxes on them. . . .

And whereas, in consequence of our statutes, judges, who before held only estates at will in their offices, have been made dependent on the Crown alone for their salaries, and standing armies kept in times of peace. And it has lately been resolved in Parliament, that by force of a statute . . . colonists may be transported to England, and tried there upon accusations for treasons, and misprisons, or concealments of treason committed in the colonies; . . .

And whereas, in the last session of parliament, three statutes were made . . . (the Boston Port Act, the Massachusetts Government Act, and Administration of Justice Act) and another statute was made (the Quebec Act). All which statutes are impolitic, unjust, and cruel, as well as unconstitutional, and most dangerous and destructive of American rights.

And whereas, Assemblies have been frequently dissolved, contrary to the rights of the people, when they attempted to deliberate on grievances; . . .

The good people of the several Colonies . . . justly alarmed at these arbitrary proceedings of parliament and administration, have severally elected, constituted, and appointed deputies to meet and sit in general congress . . . in order to obtain such establishment, as that their religion, laws, and liberties, may not be subverted.

Whereupon, the deputies so appointed . . . declare,

That the inhabitants . . . have the following Rights:

. . . That they are entitled to life, liberty, and property, & they have never ceded to any sovereign power whatever, a right to dispose of either without their consent.

That our ancestors, who first settled these colonies, were at the time of their emigration from the mother country, entitled to all the rights, liberties, and immunities of free and natural-born subjects, within the realm of England. . . .

That the foundation of English liberty, and of all free government, is a right of the people to participate in their legislative council: and as the English colonists are not represented, and from their local and other circumstances, cannot properly be represented in the British parliament, they are entitled to a free and exclusive power of legislation in their several provincial legislatures, where their right of representation can alone be preserved. . . .

That the respective colonies are entitled to the common law of England, and more especially to the great and inestimable privilege of being tried by their peers of the vicinage, according to the course of that law. . . .

That they have a right peaceably to assemble, consider of their grievances, and petition the King; and that all prosecutions, prohibitory proclamations, and commitments for the same, are illegal.

That the keeping of a Standing army in these colonies, in times of peace, without the consent of the legislature of that colony, in which such army is kept, is against law.

It is indispensably necessary to good government, and rendered essential by the English constitution, that the constituent branches of the legislature be independent of each other; that, therefore, the exercise of legislative power in several colonies, by a council appointed, during pleasure, by the crown, is unconstitutional, dangerous, and destructive to the freedom of American legislation.

All and each of which the aforesaid deputies, in behalf of themselves and their constituents, do claim, demand, and insist on, as their indubitable rights and liberties; which cannot be legally taken from them, altered or abridged by any power whatever, without their own consent, by their representatives in their several provincial legislatures.

In the course of our inquiry we find . . . a system formed to enslave America.

Resolved, That the following acts of Parliament are infringements and violations of the rights of the colonists; and that the repeal of them is essentially necessary in order to restore harmony between Great-Britain and the American colonies, . . . viz.:

The several Acts . . . which impose duties for the purpose of raising a revenue in America, extend the powers of the admiralty courts beyond their ancient limits, deprive the American subject of trial by jury, authorize the judges' certificate to indemnify the prosecutor from damages that he might otherwise be liable to, requiring oppressive security from a claimant of ships and goods seized, before he shall be allowed to defend his property, and are subversive of American rights. . . .

To these grievous acts and measures Americans cannot submit, but in hopes that their fellow subjects in Great-Britain will, on a revision of them, restore us to that state in which both countries found happiness and prosperity, ...

From Hofstadter, *Great Issues in American History: From the Revolution to the Civil War, 1765-1865.*

1. What grievances do the colonists have with regard to British policy?
2. Summarize the rights articulated in the declaration.
3. Comment on the degree to which such demands were revolutionary in their scope.

The Loyalist Position, 1774

Daniel Leonard, a lawyer from Taunton, Massachussetts expressed the most articulate defence of the British position of anyone in the colonies. His Tory views resulted in him being driven out of Taunton to Boston where he found refuge with a "patriot" gang. While in Boston he wrote a series of letters outlining his views.

January 9, 1775
Our patriots have been so intent upon building up American rights, that they have overlooked the rights of Great–Britain, and our own interest. Instead of

proving that we are entitled to privileges that our fathers knew our situation would not admit us to enjoy, they have been arguing away our most essential rights. If there be any grievance, it does not consist in our being subject to the authority of parliament, but in our not having an actual representation in it. Were it possible for the colonies to have an equal representation in Parliament, and were refused it upon proper application, I confess I should think it a grievance; but at present it seems to be allowed by all parties, to be impracticable, considering the colonies are distant from Great–Britain and thousand transmarine leagues. If that be the case, the right or privilege, the we complain of being deprived of, is not withheld be Britain, but the first principles of government, and the immutable laws of nature, render it impossible for us to enjoy it. . . . Allegiance and protection are reciprocal. It is our highest interest to continue a part of the British empire; and equally our duty to remain subject to the authority of parliament. Our own internal police may generally be regulated by our provincial legislatures, but in national concerns, or where our own assemblies do not answer the ends of government with respect to ourselves, the ordinance or interposition of the great council of the nation is necessary. In this case, the major must rule the minor. After many more centuries shall have rolled away, long after we, who are now bustling upon the stage of life, shall have been received to the bosom of mother earth, and our names are forgotten, the colonies may be so far increased as to have the balance of wealth, numbers and power, in their favour, the good of the empire make in necessary to fix the seat of government here; and some future George, equally the friend of mankind with him that now sways the British sceptre, may cross the Atlantic, and rule Great–Britain, by an American parliament.

From Hofstadter, *Great Issues in American History: From the Revolution to the Civil War, 1765-1865.*

1. What criticism does Leonard make against the patriot's position?
2. Do you agree with the reasoning behind Leonard's contention that "allegiance and protection" are reciprocal?
3. The excerpt concludes with Leonard's vision of the future. To what extent has this vision become a reality in the late twentieth century?

Novanglus, 1775

John Adams was outraged by Leonard's arguments. In a series of anonymous letters signed "Novanglus," Adams wrote a direct rebuttal to the Loyalist's viewpoints.

February 6, 1775
I agree, that "two supreme and independent authorities cannot exist in the same state," any more than two supreme beings in one universe; And, therefore, I contend, that our provincial legislatures are the only supreme authorities in our colonies. Parliament, notwithstanding this, may be allowed an authority supreme and sovereign over the ocean, which may be limited by the banks of the ocean, or the bounds of our charters; . . .
. . . The British government is still less entitled to the style of *an empire*. It is

a limited monarchy. If Aristotle, Livy, and Harrington knew what a republic was, the British constitution is much more like a republic than an empire. They define a republic to be a *government of laws, and not of men*. If this definition is just, the British constitution is nothing more nor less than a republic, in which the king is first magistrate. This office being hereditary, and being possessed of such ample and splendid prerogatives, is no objection to the government's being a republic, as long as it is bound by fixed laws, which the people have a voice in making, and a right to defend.

From Hofstadter, *Great Issues in American History: From the Revolution to the Civil War, 1765-1865*.

1. What argument does Adams use to support his contention that "two supreme and independent authorities cannot exist in the same state"?
2. Why does Adams argue that Britain is a republic and not an empire?
3. Write the script for a brief face-to-face debate between Adams and Leonard on the issue of the division of powers between Britain and the colonies.

Conciliation: the British View, 1775

Parliamentarian Edmund Burke argued for reconciliation between Britain and the colonies. Ignoring the complex constitutional arguments, Burke used pragmatic reasons. For Burke it was not tax dollars at stake, but the basic nature of the liberty of British subjects.

March 22, 1775
To restore order and repose to an empire so great and so distracted as ours is, merely in the attempt, an undertaking that would ennoble the flights of the highest genius, and obtain pardon for the efforts of the meanest understanding. . . . For, judging of what you are by what you ought to be, I persuaded myself that you would not reject a reasonable proposition because it had nothing but its reason to recommend it. . . .

The proposition is peace. Not peace through the medium of war; not peace to be hunted through the labyrinth of intricate and endless negotiations; not peace to arise out of universal discord, fomented from principle, in all parts of the empire; not peace to depend on the juridical determination of perplexing questions, or the precise marking the shadowy boundaries of a complex government. It is simple peace, sought in its natural course and in its ordinary haunts. . . .

Let the colonies always keep the idea of their civil rights associated with your government—they will cling and grapple to you, and no force under heaven will be of power to tear them from their allegiance. But let it be once understood that your government may be one thing and their privileges another, that these two things may exist without any mutual relation—the cement is gone, the cohesion is loosened, and everything hastens to decay and dissolution. As long as you have the wisdom to keep the sovereign authority of this country as the sanctuary of liberty, the sacred temple consecrated to our common faith, wherever the chosen race and sons of England worship freedom, they will turn their faces towards you. The more they multiply, the more friends you will have, the more ardently they love liberty, the more perfect will be their obedience. . . .

Is it not the same virtue which does every thing for us here in England? Do you imagine, then, that it is the Land–Tax Act which raises your revenue? that it is the annual vote in the Committee of Supply, which gives you your army? or that it is the Mutiny Bill which inspires it with bravery and discipline? No! surely, no! It is the love of the people; it is their attachment to their government, from the sense of the deep stake they have in such a glorious institution, which gives you your army and your navy, and infuses into both that liberal obedience without which your army would be a base rabble and your navy nothing but rotten timber.

. . . By adverting to the dignity of this high calling, our ancestors have turned a savage wilderness into a glorious empire, and have made the most extensive and the only honorable conquests, not by destroying, but by promoting the wealth, the number, the happiness of the human race. Let us get an American revenue as we have got an American empire. English privileges have made it all that it is; English privileges alone will make it all it can be.

From Hofstadter, *Great Issues in American History: From the Revolution to the Civil War, 1765-1865.*

1. Assess Burke's description of the "peace" that he seeks.
2. Burke contends that if the colonies continue to feel that the protection of their civil rights depends on Parliament then "no force under heaven will be of power to tear them from their allegiance." What does he mean? Explain why you agree or disagree with his argument.
3. To what extent do you feel that Burke's arguments presented a possible solution to the crisis?

Forming Republics, 1776

By early 1776 a large number of pamphlets began to appear debating, not whether to take an independent course of action, but what form of government would be most acceptable once the British connection was broken. In the pamphlet excerpted below, by Salus Populi, the author deals with some of the criticisms levelled at republican government.

Pure Monarchy is that form of Government which is framed for the exaltation of the Prince alone, ... The grand monarch is the only being known to the Constitution; who, like the Divinity, (pardon the comparison,) derives every power from himself; from whom the other members of the community derive every privilege they possess, and on whose will they depend for their continuance. . . . Popular Government—sometimes termed Democracy, Republick, or Commonwealth—is the plan of civil society wherein the community at large takes the care of its own representatives elected by the people out of their own body.

Seeing the happiness of the people is the true end of Government; and it appearing by the definition, that the popular form is the only one which has this for its object; it may be worth inquiring into the causes which have prevented its success in the world. . . . Every nation which has hitherto attempted to set up a Republick, entered on the measure too late. They were the convulsed remains of some Government erected upon military principles; and finding too hard to content those with the simple rights of freemen who were once possessed of all power they too easily gave way to claims of a superior nature, whereby they admitted an interest separate and distinct from, and inconsistent with, the general welfare of the people. This interest forever clashing with that of the community, produced continual confusions, until the people, wearied out with the struggle, gave up to the aristocratical party, or blindly following some popular leader, in confidence of his attachment to their interest, gave all power into his hands, which generally ended in tyranny.

The inexperience of mankind was another cause of the decay of popular Governments. Being unacquainted with legislative representation, established on the principles of a free, uninfluenced, and general election, they met in large and, consequently, tumultuous assemblies. This gave ambitious and designing men, to whom such a form of Government is always unfavourable, great opportunities of breeding disturbance, creating factions, which generally terminate in its dissolution. . . .

Political writers, either mistaking the true causes of the uneasinesses which are gound in ancient popular Governments, or willing to make court to Princes, have greatly contributed to bring the Republican forms of Government into discredit. This has been carried to such a length with many, that the mentioning of a Democracy constantly excites in them the idea of anarchy; and few, except such as have emancipated themselves from the shackles of political bigotry and prejudice, can talk of it with patience, and hearken to anything offered in its defence. . . .

Kings and nobles are artificial beings, for whose emolument civil society was never intended; and notwithstanding they have had the good fortune to escape general censure from the world, yet I will boldly affirm that nine–tenths of all the publick calamities which ever befell mankind, were brought on by their means. . . .

Mankind never suffered so much during the existence of a Republick as they have suffered in the short reigns of many Kings. A *Harry* VIII did more mischief to his subjects than any Republick ever did to its members, notwithstanding they were so illy constituted. But the true principles of republicanism are at present so well understood, and the mode of conducting such a Government so simple and easy, as *America* so fit for its reception, that a dozen of wise heads and honest hearts might, in one day, form a plan for the United Colonies which would as much excel any one now existing, as the *British* Constitution does that of *Caffraria*.

When I seriously consider this, and take a survey of the state of civil Government throughout the world, the modes whereby they acquired their present forms, and the causes which gave rise to them, I cannot help cherishing a secret hope that *God* has destined *America* to form the last and best plan that can possibly exist; and that he will gradually carry those who have long been under the galling yoke of tyranny in every other quarter of the globe, into the bosom of perfect liberty and freedom in *America*. . . .

Few opportunities have ever been offered to mankind of framing an entire Constitution of Government, upon equitable principles. All modern authors on this subject agree, that mankind are entitled to freedom by birth, and on a level with, each other when they enter into society. . . .

. . . Perhaps *America* is the only country in the world wholly free from all political impediments, at the very time they are under the necessity of framing a civil Constitution. Having no rank above that of freemen, she has but one interest to consult, and that interest, (blessed be *God* for it,) is the true and only interest of men as members of society.

From Peter Force, ed., *American Archives*, 4th ser. (Washington D.C., 1844), vol. 5, from H.H. Quint, *Main Problems in American History*, (Hammond, Illinois: Dorsey Press, 1978).

1. What defences does the author present for the failure of popular government in the past?
2. What criticisms are levelled at the monarchy?
3. After considering the arguments presented, how effective do you think the pamphlet is in presenting the case for the creation of a democratic republic?

Common Sense, 1776

Fifteen years before he debated Edmund Burke on the merits of the French Revolution, Thomas Paine was living in Philadelphia writing one of the most influential pamphlets in history. An instant best-seller, "Common Sense" helped to lead to the oft-quoted contention that the success of the American Revolution owed as much to the "pen of Paine as to the sword of Washington."

Volumes have been written on the subject of the struggle between England and America. Men of all ranks have embarked in the controversy, from different motives, and with various designs; but all have been ineffectual, and the period of debate is closed. Arms, as the last resource, decide the contest; the appeal was the choice of the king, and the continent hath accepted the challenge. . . .

I have heard it asserted by some, that as America hath flourished under her former connexion with Great–Britain, that the same connexion is necessary towards her future happiness, and will always have the same effect. Nothing can be more fallacious than this kind of argument. We may as well assert that because a child has thrived upon milk, that it is never to have meat, or that the first twenty years of our lives is to become a precedent for the next twenty. But even this is admitting more than is true, for I answer roundly, that America would have flourished as much, and probably much more, had no European power had any thing to do with her. The commerce, by which she hath enriched herself, are the necessaries of like, and will always have a market while eating is the custom of Europe.

But she has protected us, say some. That she has engrossed us is true, and defended the continent at our expense as well as her own is admitted, and she would have defended Turkey from the same motive, viz. the sake of trade and dominion.

Alas, we have been long led away by ancient prejudices, and made large sacrifices to superstition. We have boasted the protection of Great–Britain, without considering, that her motive was *interest* not *attachment*; that she did not protect us from *our enemies* on *our account*, but from *her enemies* on *her own account*, from those who had no quarrel with us on any *other account*, and who will always be our enemies on the *same account*. Let Britain wave her pretensions to the continent, or the continent throw off the dependance, and we should be at peace with France and Spain were they at war with Britain. . . .

But Britain is the parent country, say some. Then the more shame upon her conduct. Even brutes do not devour their young, nor savages make war upon their families; wherefore the assertion, if true, turns to her reproach; but it happens not to be true, or only partly so, and the phrase *parent* or *mother country* hath been jesuitically adopted by the king and his parasites, with a low papistical design of gaining an unfair bias on the credulous weakness of our minds. Europe, and not England, is the parent country of America. This new world hath been the asylum for the persecuted lovers of civil and religious embraces of the mother, but from the cruelty of the monster; and it is so far true of England, that the same tyranny which drove the first emigrants from home, pursues their descendants still. . . .

I challenge the warmest advocate for reconciliation, to shew, a single advantage that this continent can reap, by being connected with Great–Britain. I repeat this challenge, not a single advantage is derived. Our corn will fetch its price in any market in Europe, and our imported goods must be paid for buy them where we will.

But the injuries and disadvantages we sustain by that connection, are without number; and our duty to mankind at large, as well as to ourselves, instruct us to renounce the alliance: Because, any submission to, or dependance on Great–Britain, tends directly to involve this continent in European wars and quarrels; and sets us at variance with nations, who would otherwise seek our friendship, and against whom, we have neither anger not complaint. . . . It is the true interest of America to steer clear of European contentions, which she never can do, while by her dependance on Britain, she is make-weight in the scale of British politics.

Europe is too thickly planted with kingdoms to be long at peace, and whenever a war breaks out between England and any foreign power, the trade of America goes to ruin, *because of her connection with Britain.* . . . 'TIS TIME TO PART. Even the distance at which the Almighty hath placed England and America, is a strong and natural proof, that the authority of the one, over the other, was never the design of Heaven. The time likewise at which the continent was discovered, adds weight to the argument, and the manner in which it was peopled increases [sic] the force of it. The reformation was preceded by the discovery of America, as if the Almighty graciously meant to open a sanctuary to the persecuted in future years, when home should afford neither friendship nor safety.

The authority of Great–Britain over this continent, is a form of government, which sooner or later must have an end: And a serious mind can draw no true pleasure by looking forward, under the painful and positive conviction, that what he calls "the present constitution" is merely temporary. . . .

It is the good fortune of many to live distant from the scene of sorrow; the evil is not sufficient brought to *their* doors to make *them* feel the precariousness with which all American property is possessed. But let our imaginations transport us for a few moments to Boston, ... The inhabitants of that unfortunate city, who but a few months ago were in ease and affluence, have now, no other alternative than to stay and starve, or turn out to beg. . . .

Thousands are already ruined by British barbarity; (thousands more will probably suffer the same fate) Those men have other feelings than us who have nothing suffered. All they *now* possess is liberty, what they before enjoyed is sacrificed to its service, and having nothing more to lose, they disdain submission. . . .

But where, says some, is the King of America? I'll tell you. Friend, he reigns above, and doth not make havoc of mankind like the Royal Brute of Britain. Yet that we may not appear to be defective even in earthly honors, let a day be solemnly set apart for proclaiming the charter; let it be brought forth placed on the divine law, the word of God; let a crown be placed thereon, by which the world may know, that so far we approve of monarchy, that in America THE LAW IS KING. For as in absolute governments the King is law, so in free countries the law *ought* to be King; and there ought to be no other. . . .

A government of our own is our natural right: And when a man seriously reflects on the precariousness of human affairs, he will become convinced, that it is infinitely wiser and safer, to form a constitution of our own in a cool deliberate manner, while we have it in our power, than to trust such an interesting event to time and chance. . . .

Ye that tell us of harmony and reconciliation, can ye restore us to the tie that is past? Can ye give to prostitution its former innocence? Neither can ye reconcile Britain and America. . . .

O ye that love mankind! Ye that dare oppose, not only the tyranny, but the tyrant, stand forth! Every spot of the old world is overrun with oppression. Freedom hath been hunted round the globe. Asia, and Africa, have long expelled her—Europe regards her like a stranger, and England hath given her warning to depart. O! receive the fugitive, and prepare in time an asylum for mankind.

From Moncure Daniel Conway, ed., *The Writings of Thomas Paine*, (New York: Putnam, 1894, Vol. I).

1. Comment upon Paine's comparison of the life of the colonies to that of an adolescent.

2. (a) What is the basis of Paine's argument against the continuation of the British connection?
(b) What ultimate argument does he make for independence?
3. To what extent is "Common Sense" a piece of war propaganda?

American Appeals to Canada, 1775-76

Many leaders in the Thirteen Colonies expected Quebec to join them in their struggle. The following excerpts consider both sides of this historic decision.

In 1775 George Washington issued the following proclamation to the inhabitants of Canada.

Friends and Brethren: The unnatural contest between the *English* Colonies and *Great Britain* has now risen to such a height that arms alone must decide it. The Colonies, confiding in the justice of their cause and the purity of their intentions, have reluctantly appealed to that Being in whose hands are all human events. He has hitherto smiled upon their virtuous efforts. The hand of tyranny has been arrested in its ravages, and the *British* arms, which have shone with so much splendour in every part of the globe, are now tarnished with disgrace and disappointment. Generals of approved experience, who boasted of subduing this great Continent, find themselves circumscribed within the limits of a single City and its suburbs, suffering all the shame and distress of a siege, while the freeborn sons of *America*, animated by the genuine principles of liberty and love of their Country, with increasing union, firmness, and discipline, repel every attack, and despise every danger. Above all, we rejoice that our enemies have been deceived with regard to you; they have persuaded themselves, they have even dared to say, that the *Canadians* were not capable of distinguishing between the blessings of liberty and the wretchedness of slavery; that gratifying the vanity of a little circle of nobility would blind the eyes of the views, but they have been deceived; instead of finding in you that poverty of soul and baseness of spirit, they see, with a chagrin equal to our joy, that you are enlightened, generous, and virtuous; that you will not renounce your own rights, or serve as instruments to deprive your fellow–subjects of theirs.

Come, then, my brethren, unite with us in an indissoluable union; let us run together to the same goal. We have taken up arms in defense of our liberty, our property, our wives, and our children; we are determined to preserve them or die. We look forward with pleasure to that day, not far remote, we hope, when the inhabitants of *America* shall have one sentiment, and the full enjoyment of the blessings of the free Government. Incited by these motives, and encouraged by the advice of many friends of liberty among you, the grand *American* Congress have sent an Army into your Province, under the command of General *Schuyler*, not to plunder, but to protect you; to animate and bring forth into action those sentiments of freedom you have disclosed, and which the tools of despotism would extinguish through the whole creation. . . . Let no one flee as before an enemy. The cause of *America* and of liberty is the cause of every virtuous *American* citizen, whatever may be his religion or his descent.

From G. Rawlyk, *Revolution Rejected, 1775-1776*, (Scarborough, Ont.: Prentice-Hall, 1968).

Military Realities and Canadian Reactions

Charles Carroll was sent to Quebec, along with Benjamin Franklin and Samuel Chase, to try and sway opinion in favour of the American cause. Here are his observations.

. . . The general apprehension that we shall be driven out of the province as soon as the King's troops can arrive, concurs with the frequent breaches of promise the inhabitants have experienced, in determining them to trust our people no further. . . .

Our enemies take the advantage of this distress to make us look contemptible in the eyes of the Canadians, who have been provoked by the violences of our military, in exacting provisions and services from them without pay, a conduct towards a people who suffered us to enter their country as friends, that the most urgent necessity can scarce excuse, since it has contributed much to the changing their good disposition towards us into enmity, and makes them wish our departure.

From K.M. Rowland, *The Life of Charles Carroll of Carrollton 1737-1832*, (New York: G.P. Putnam's Sons, 1898, I).

The Authority of the Church

One of the strongest opponents of the revolution was Bishop Briand. In May 1775 the Bishop issued the following instruction.

. . . Revolution was the anti–American policy adopted by Bishop Briand. . . .

A troop of subjects in revolt against their lawful Sovereign, who is at the same time ours, have just made an irruption into this province, less in the hope of maintaining themselves here than with a view of dragging you into their revolt or at least preventing you from opposing their pernicious design. The remarkable goodness and gentleness with which we have been governed by his very gracious Majesty, King George the Third, since the fortune of war subjected us to his rule; the recent favours with which he has loaded us, in restoring to us the use of our laws and the free exercise of our religion; and in letting us participate in all the privileges and advantages of British subjects, would no doubt be enough to excite your gratitude and zeal in support of the interests of the British Crown. But motives even more urgent must speak to your heart at the present moment. Your oaths, your religion, lay upon you the unavoidable duty of defending your country and your King with all the strength you possess.

From H. Tetu, Mandement of May 22, 1775, *Évêques de Québec* (Quebec: N.S. Hardy, 1889). Translation from R. Coupland, *The Quebec Act: A Study in Statesmanship* (Oxford University Press, 1925).

Quebec: Response to the Call to Revolution

With the Thirteen Colonies in open revolt, the security of the British Empire in North America suddenly depended upon two of its weakest links, the recently conquered Quebec and the isolated colony of Nova Scotia. In the following excerpts historians examine the reasons behind the Canadian response.

Francois-Xavier Garneau argued in 1846 that to have joined the Americans would have meant an end to French Canadian culture and identity.

. . . The fine names of "liberty" and "national independence" have always a charm for noble minds; a generous spirit is ever moved at their very sound. The polished Parisian, the Swiss herdsman, feel the sacred influence, in common, of proclaimed freedom. The address of the Congress, therefore, despite the recklessness of parts of its strain, caused a great sensation among the Canadian rural populations and the British townsmen. The latter, now no longer hopeful of dominating their fellow colonists of French race, mostly became American partisans. . . .

Through a fear of jeopardizing their religion and nationality by entering into a confederation both protestant and alien in blood,—an apprehension not groundless, for the man of that confederation had already incorporated the French settlements of Louisiana,—the clergy and seigniors [sic] resolved to resist every assault of the Anglo–Americans, and to retain our country for monarchic Britain, 3,000 miles distant; a patroness all the less likely, for that remoteness, to become perilously inimical to Canadian institutions.

Besides, even had the Canadians not been outraged by the declaration of Congress against catholicism and French jurisprudence, they ever preserved in their hearts that hatred for the British race, wherever born or located, which they had contracted during long wars; they thus made no distinction, in their minds, between those of it mingled with themselves, in Canada, and men of kindred blood dwelling beyond: viewing both alike as one body of turbulent and ambitious oppressors.

From M. Wade, *The French Canadians 1760–1945* (Toronto: The Macmillan Company of Canada, 1956).

American historian Victor Coffin wrote in 1896 that American mismanagement of the Canadian campaign had alienated their potential support in the colony.

Far from being effectual in keeping the mass of the Canadians loyal to the British connection, [*the Quebec Act*] had a strong influence in precisely the opposite direction. The Canadians were *not* kept loyal, and Canada was preserved at this crisis to the British Empire through the vigor and ability of its British defenders and through the mismanagement of their cause on the part of the revolutionists.

But my main purpose . . . is to enquire into the results of the Quebec Act on the French Canadians. The generally accepted view [is] that they were fully satisfied with the Act . . . . Overwhelming evidence shows that the French Canadians were not faithful to British rule at this crisis, . . . Further evidence, equally strong, if not so great in quantity, shows that the effect of the Act on the mass of the people was one of alienation rather than conciliation. . . .

. . . The ordinary judgement with regard to their conduct both from the British who saw in their neutrality even only the basest ingratitude, and from the Americans who experienced a very considerable change in the later months of disaster, is not sufficient or satisfactory. According to this, the people were moved mainly by fear and the desire of being on the stronger side; they embraced or acquiesced in that cause which was for the moment locally predominent. But to say that the Canadians were a timid race is to disregard wholly the facts of their military origin and training, and especially the strong testimony from both sides to their valor and conduct under the most disheartening circumstances in the last war. . . .

It must therefore be concluded that the Quebec Act had added no element of strength to the British cause in the Province; . . .

If the conclusion reached above be correct, we are confronted with a difficulty in the utter failure of the expedition. . . . it will be necessary to view the enterprise from the American side to see if any other factors enter into the situation. Such I think will be the case; it will be found that not only did the revolutionists fail to make any effective use of the Canadian alliance, but that the mismanagement and misconduct of both officers and men, the Canadians were from the first impressed with the incapacity of their would–be emancipators, and were gradually driven by actual ill–treatment to neutrality if not to hostility. The favourable moment was let slip and did not return. With the spring of 1776 not only was the British force strengthened to a degree which enforced caution upon the most hostile of the peasantry, but by that time that peasantry had had its revolutionary fervour cooled by treatment as arbitrary and injurious as anything that could be expected from the dreaded revival of the conditions of the old regime.

From W. Kingsford, *History of Canada*, (Toronto: Rowsell and Hutchinson, 1892).

In this essay, Canadian historian Hilda Neatby examines the reasons why Quebecois did not join with their American counterparts.

It has also been made clear by a number of scholars, French and English Canadian, that the old legend of Canadian nationalism provoked and inspired by love of France and by British tyranny, sanctioned as this legend was in some degree by the great Garneau, is without much foundation. . . .

From the very beginning the effect of British rule in Quebec was to stimulate, strengthen and at the same time irritate the newly acquired St. Lawrence community into an increasingly intransigent nationalism which, without any particular malice or ill–will, almost inevitably found its expression in a generalized animosity toward Great Britain and British traditions. This animosity has, however, proved quite consistent with an admiration of individuals, ideas, and institutions in spite of their British origin.

Nothing was further from the minds of the aristocratic oligarchy which became responsible for the security and well–being of the new possession than to provoke or encourage nationalism of any kind. . . . no one in those days thought much about "nationalism" as a moral force. . . . The basic problem of government in Quebec was seen in quite different terms. Canadians were looked at as individuals and not as an entity. As individuals no one wished to disturb them in their property or their customs; no one wished to harry them because of their religion. . . . Moreover it was hoped and expected that the country, three–quarters empty, would soon be filled by English or American immigrants. Purely from motives of simplicity and convenience it was taken for granted that a policy of gentle and steady transformation to a more or less British way of life, and especially to the Protestant Church of England, could be effected without harshness and with due regard for civil rights. . . .

As it happened the policy was never really tried at all, partly because of the normal indifference and lethargy of British statesmen of that period in relation to all but the most pressing colonial problems, but chiefly because their attention was diverted by a truly pressing colonial problem, the alarming activity and enthusiasm of colonists to the south. It is true of all periods of our history, but particularly of this one, that the historian who looks at Canada out of its historical context must be misled. During the first quarter of a century of British rule in Canada, the province of Quebec was only one, and one of the less important, of the American group. It had indeed been conquered and retained largely because of its nuisance value. . . . After the conquest it was natural that British policy in Quebec should be largely influenced by the total American situation.

Just as the French Revolution was to have a peculiarly unhappy effect on Britain by checking and diverting the necessary adjustments of an aristocratic and rural community to the rising urban and industrial society of the late 18th and early 19th century, so the immediate impact of the American Revolution, coming directly after the British conquest, was to embarrass and distort the necessary adjustments of the St. Lawrence community in coming to terms with a new age. . . . Had peace reigned in North America it is possible that Canadians might have made their own gradual and easy adjustments to the ways of their American neighbors, now in theory their friends, and even to the pressures of the British government. It is not certain that there was such religious fervour or such devoted loyalty to French culture and traditions as to have preserved a distinct community in the face of the steady attrition of an alien government and of alien influences from the south, so long as there was no active persecution.

II

It was the violent impact of the American Revolution involving as it did a new war between Britain and France which not only rendered impossible any steady and gentle policy of anglicization, but produced a type of British government which had a strong and perhaps a lasting effect on a people just awakening to political self–consciousness; a people exposed to a flood of radical ideas on church and state from the English–speaking merchants and traders who had entered the colony, and from the repeated communications that came up to them from the south.

The situation in the southern colonies, the threat and then the fact of the invasion of 1775, the impact of the ensuing war, and the operation of the peace resulted in a British policy which first divided from each other, and from the mass of the people, the literate classes in Canada who should have been the leaders of society, and then flung them once more into an uneasy unity based

less on mutual affection than on a common resentment against both arbitrary
government from above and against evils of arbitrary government. . . .
III
When, in 1775, Americans invaded the province, the bulk of the habitants
absolutely refused to take up arms against the invaders. They were, it was
reported, already disgusted and alarmed at the renewed and even novel preten-
tions of the seigneurs. They were attracted by American talk of liberty, and
still more by American offers of pay. . . .
    In fifty parishes in the lower part of the province affected by the invasion,
almost all the captains of militia compromised themselves by cooperating with
the enemy. These men had been trusted agents of the government under the
French regime. The British neglect of them in favour of the seigneur and the
church perhaps inclined them to listen to American persuasions more readily
than they might otherwise have done. Whether or not this is so, the anger of
the seigneurs against the recalcitrant habitants and the resentment of the habitants against the seigneurs who as the agents of the governments endeavoured
to force them into military service was yet another element of division in the
community.
    . . . It was the little group of seigneurs in council who throughout the war
steadily supported Carleton and his successor Haldimand in subjecting the habitant to the often arbitrary claims of the troops, including the German troops
used to garrison the province. Five years after the war was over a representative
of the radical Canadian merchant group in Montreal asked how the seigneurs
could dare to represent themselves as leaders of the country and protectors of
the people: "[These] famous protectors took very good care not to join their
voices to those of the oppressed when the Germans, sent to defend the colony,
came into it as if it were a conquered country. . . ."
IV
It seems certain then, that during the later part of the eighteenth century Canadian society had become sharply divided. If none of the divisions originated
with the Conquest all were accentuated by it. The seigneurs who, for all their
prominence as loyal councillors and subjects of the British King, had no real
power, were used as props by the government. . . .
    British policy, then apparently dictated by the kindest motives, had an
unhappy effect on the community. After having, during the early years of the
peace, governed the habitants with a mildness that they had grown to accept as
a natural right, the British in the crisis of war suddenly attempted to reimpose
the authority of the seigneurs in a new form, ...
    In every group in the Canadian community, therefore, there was frustration
and irritation. At the end of the war the socially divided Canadians may have
been more irritated with each other than with Great Britain. This situation,
however, was not to last. Although there were genuine movements of unity and
sympathy between Canadian radicals and English loyalists in the lower province, fundamental antipathies were not long in developing. It could hardly have
been otherwise. The loyalists, some of them at least, had lost much in position,
property, and friends. It was inevitable that they should place an exaggerated

importance on the convictions which had inspired their sacrifices. . . . Quebec was invaded by men who equated religion with protestantism, civilization with representative institutions, and culture with general literacy, newpapers, and public libraries. . . . Thus they contrived to alienate many Canadians whose views on politics were not far from their own, and whose religion was anything but fanatic.

Thus, the bad manners and bad humor of the loyalists and ultimately their insistence on more than their rights forced Canadians who were genuinely divided in their social, political and religious views into a defensive unity which ultimately became intransigent. . . . It is no wonder that the intoxicating sense of nationalism released by the French Revolution took on in Canada an especially tenacious form, expressing itself in a fashion peculiarly hostile to the British who had conquered and divided them, and the continuing Britishness even of the Americans who appeared to be engulfing them.

From Hilda Neatby, "French Canadian Nationalism and the American Revolution," in J.M. Bumstead, ed., *Canadian History Before Confederation*, (Georgetown, Ontario: Irwin Dorsey Ltd., 1972).

1. After reading these three accounts, write your own thesis, with defending arguments, as to why the inhabitants of Quebec refused to join with their American liberators.

The True Interest of America, 1776

In 1776 Anglican priest Charles Inglis of New York City published "The True Interest of America impartially Stated in Certain Strictures on a Pamphlet Intitled [sic] Common Sense." It was a direct response to the arguments put forward by Paine and remains an excellent statement of the Loyalist position at the outbreak of hostilities.

Inglis kept up his campaign throughout the war, to no avail. When he sailed for England in 1783 he stated: "I do not leave behind me an individual against whom I have the smallest degree of resentment or ill-will."

I think it no very difficult matter to point out many advantages which will certainly attend our reconciliation and connection with Great–Britain, on a firm constitutional plan. . . .

1. By a reconciliation with Britain, a period would be put to the present calamitous war, by which so many lives have been lost, and so many more will be lost, if it continues. . . .
2. By a Reconciliation with Great–Britain—Peace—that fairest offspring and gift of Heaven—will be restored. . . .
3. Agriculture, commerce, and industry would resume their wonted vigour. . . .
4. By a connection with Great–Britain, our trade would still have the protection of the greatest naval power in the world. . . .
5. The protection of our trade, while connected with Britain, will not cost us a *fiftieth* part of what it must cost, were we ourselves to raise a naval force sufficient for the purpose.

6. Whilst connected with Great–Britain, we have a bounty on almost every article of exportation; and we any be better supplied with goods by her, than we could elsewhere. . . .

Let us now, if you please, take a view of the other side of the question. Suppose we were to revolt from Great–Britain, declare ourselves Independent, and set up a Republic of our own—what would be the consequence. . . .

1. All our property throughout the continent would be unhinged; the greatest confusion, and most violent convulsion would take place. . . .

2. What a horrid situation would thousands be reduced to who have taken the oath of allegiance to the King; yet contrary to their oath, as well as to their inclination, must be compelled to renounce that allegiance, or abandon all their property in America! . . . A Declaration of Independency would infallibly disunite and divide the colonists.

3. By a Declaration for Independency, every avenue to an accomodation [sic] with Great–Britain would be closed; the sword only could then decide the quarrel, and the sword would not be sheathed till one had conquered the other. . . .

5. But supposing once more that we were able to cut off every regiment that Britain can spare or hire, and to destroy every ship she can send—that we could beat off any other European power that would presume to intrude upon this continent; Yet, a republican form of government would neither suit the genius of the people, nor the extent of America. . . . Limited monarchy is the form of government which is most favourable to liberty. . . .

Besides the unsuitableness of the republican form to the genius of the people, America is too extensive for it. The form may do well enough for a single city, or small territory; but would be utterly improper for such a continent as this. America is too unwieldy for the feeble, dilatory administration of democracy. . . .

But here it may be said—*that all the evils above specified, are more tolerable than slavery.* With this sentiment I sincerely agree—any hardships, however great are preferable to slavery. But then I ask, is there no other alternative in the present case? Is there no choice left us but slavery, or those evils? I am confident there is; and that both may be equally avoided. Let us only shew a disposition to treat or negociate in earnest—let us fall upon some method to set a treaty or negociation with Great Britain on foot; and if once properly begun, there is a moral certainty that this unhappy dispute will be settled to the mutual satisfaction and interest of both countries.

From G.N.D. Evans, *Loyalists*, (Toronto: Copp Clark Pitman 1968).

1. Contrast the arguments put forward by Inglis in favour of conciliation against those put forward for independence.
2. What argument does Inglis cite against republicanism?
3. Write a letter to Inglis from Thomas Paine in which he refutes his arguments.

The Loyalist Dilemma and the Loyalist Myth

The following excerpts are from contemporary accounts of the treatment afforded to Loyalist sympathizers. The first is from a letter from Ann Hulton written in Boston in

1774. The second is from a local Committee of Safety in New York City. The third is an early expression of the myth of loyalism, that would become so important in later Canadian history.

But the most shocking cruelty was exercised . . . upon a poor old man, a tidesman, one Malcolm. He is reckoned creasy, a quarrel was picked with him, he was afterward taken and tarred and feathered. Theres no law that knows a punishment for the greatest crimes beyond what this is of cruel torture. And this instance exceeds any other before it. He was stript stark naked, one of the severest cold nights this winter, his body covered all over with tar, then with feathers, his arm dislocated in tearing off his cloaths. He was dragged in a cart with thousands attending, some beating him with clubs and knocking him out of the cart, then in again. They gave him several severe whippings, at different parts of the town. This spectacle of horror and sportive cruelty was exhibited for about five hours.

. . . Before he was taken, [he] defended himself a long time against numbers, and afterwards when under torture they demanded of him to curse his masters, the King, Governor, etc., which they could not make him do, but he still cried, "Curse all traitors!" They brought him to the gallows and put a rope around his neck, saying they would hang him. . . .

These few instances amongst many serve to shew the abject state of government and the licentiousness and barbarism of the times. There's no majestrate that dare or will act to suppress the outrages. No person is secure. There are many objects pointed at, at the time, and when once marked out for vengeance, their ruin is certain. . . .

We are under no apprehension at present on our own account but we can't look upon our safety secure for long.

From Ann Hulton, *Letters of a Loyalist Lady . . . 1767–1776* (Cambridge, Mass., 1927).

Thomas Randolph, cooper, who had publickly proved himself an enemy to his country, be reviling and using his utmost endeavours to oppose the proceedings of the Continental and Provincial Conventions and Committees, in defence of their rights and liberties; and he, being judged a person of not consequence enough for a severer punishment, was ordered to be stripped naked, well coated with tar and feathers, and carried in a wagon publickly around the town; which punishment was accordingly inflicted. . . . The whole was conducted with that regularity and decorum that ought to be observed in all publick punishments.

From Peter Force, ed., *American Archives: Fourth Series*, 6 vols. (Washington, D.C.: M. St. Clair Clarke and Peter Force, 1837–1846), Vol. IV.

In no country upon the face of the Globe, and at no period in the history of any country, has appeared a higher or purer order of patriotism, than is written upon the pages of the history of British America. British connection is to mostly every son of the land dearer even than life itself. At least it has been so in respect to those of whom we write, the U.E.Loyalists. Co–equal with the love they have to the British Crown, is the hearty aversion they bear to Republicanism. Neither the overtures of annexation, nor the direct and indirect attempts to coerce, has produced a momentary wavering on the part of the descendants of the ancient stock. Americans in our midst have vainly tried to inoculate the minds of the people with the principles of Republican Government; but the Canadian mind was too free, the body politic too healthy, the system too strong to imbibe any lasting feeling of desire to change the tried for the untried. The few annexationists who have, from time to time, existed, were but the fungoid offshoot of a healthy plant. . . . The U.E.Loyalists have been as a barrier of rock against which the waves of Republicanism have dashed in vain. It has been the refugee–settlers and their descendants [sic], who prevented the Province from being engulfed in its dark waters. In 1812, in '37, and at all times, their loyalty has never wavered. . . .

From William Canniff, *A History of the Settlement of Upper Canada* (Toronto, 1869).

1. Based on the documents you have read here and additional research, write your own news account of the treatment of Loyalists, citing either their treatment at patriot hands or their reception by British officials in Canada.

The Neutral Yankees of Nova Scotia

Nova Scotians were torn between their sympathy for many of the aims of the revolution and a recognition of their isolation far from colonial support. These brief excerpts outline the two sides of the argument.

Anonymous Letter to General George Washington

The great contest between *Britain* and *America* has hitherto been only treated with speculation amongst us. A spirit of sympathy, I presume, for our brethren on the Continent, reigns in the breasts of the generality of the inhabitants. With gladness and cheerfulness would we be active in the glorious struggle, had our situation and circumstances been any way such that there was the least glimpse of success; but our remoteness from the other Colonies, and our form of Government, joined with the indigent circumstances of the inhabitants, render it in a manner impossible, without succour from some other quarter. . . .

. . . The straggling manner in which people have settled this new country makes it very difficult, and, in a manner, almost impossible for them to act either offensively or defensively. The people, in general, have great families, which will occasion a lamentable scene should *British* Troops arrived here before any succour comes from your Excellency. We would greatly rejoice could we be able to join with the other Colonies; but we must have other assistance before we can act publickly. I would observe to your Excellency, concerning the *Acadians*, I have dwelt among them . . . six–and–twenty years. I am well acquainted with their manners and ways. I have taken great pains in conversing with them concerning their commotions. They are, to a man, wholly inclined to the cause of *America*.

Peter Force, *American Archives*, Fourth Series Vol. 5, (Washington: 1844).

Resolutions of the Maugerville Inhabitants, May 1776

2ndly Resolved. That as tyrany [sic] ought to be Resisted in its first appearance we are Convinced that the united Provinces are just in their proceedings in this Regard.

3rdly Resolved. That it is our Minds and Desire to submit ourselves to the government of the Massachusetts Bay and that we are Ready with our Lives and fortunes to Share with them the Event of the present Struggle for Liberty, however God in his Providence may order it. . . .

6ly Resolved. That we will Immediately put ourselves in the best posture of Defence in our power, that to this End we will prevent all unnecessary use of gunPowder or other ammunition in our Custody. . . .

8ly Resolved. . . . we will share in and submit to the Event of this undertaking however it may terminate, to the true performance of all which we bind and obligate ourselves firmly each to other on penalty of being Esteemed Enemies and traitors to our Country and Submitting ourselves to popular Resentment.

From F. Kidder, *Military Operations in Eastern Maine and Nova Scotia During the Revolution*, (Albany: J. Munsell, 1867).

A Call To British Loyalty—The Voice of the Pro–British Element, 1776

. . . A sharply worded letter to the editor of a Halifax newspaper, dated September 10, 1776, clearly expressed [Nova Scotians'] views.

. . . The Demagogues, which raised this disturbance, are a motley crew of hungry lawyers, men of broken fortunes, young persons eager to push themselves in the world, others, gentlemen of opulence, vain & blustering— Amongst this medley there are several of good party, and great reading, but withal little versed in the complicated interests, and springs, which move the great political world, because untutored in the Courts of Europe, where alone that science is to be acquired—These could not miss perceiving the growing importance, as they call it, of America, and what she might one day arrive to: so far indeed they judged with propriety, if they would only give time, and leave her to herself; but the greatness of the object dazzled the eyes of their understanding; and they began to think Empire, without considering the infant state of their country, how much it is [in] want of every requisite for war, what a mighty nation they have to contend with, & that the united interest of every other nation in Europe likewise forbids their being anything more than dependent. . . .

From *Nova Scotia Gazette and the Weekly Chronicle*, Sept. 10, 1776 in Paul W. Bennett, *Emerging Identities*, (Toronto: Prentice Hall, 1986).

1. What problems are outlined in the anonymous letter to George Washington?
2. To what extent are the sentiments raised in the letter reflected in the resolutions of the Maugerville inhabitants?
3. Outline the arguments used against the colonial cause.

The Brebner Synthesis

In his classic 1937 work The Neutral Yankees of Nova Scotia *historian J.B. Brebner compiled the various theories as to why Nova Scotians remained neutral during the American Revolution. In this excerpt he outlines the reasons behind their actions.*

It would be a tedious and largely unprofitable task to set Nova Scotian behavior in detail over against the many elements of behavior which historians have arranged in various hypotheses to explain rebellion in other Colonies. Yet a few of these comparisons are valuable. Take, for instance, the thesis that the Colonial merchants, engaged after the Seven Years' War in keen competition with the British mercantile system, roused an American radicalism which grew too strong for them to restrain it. At once the flat difference emerges that by and large Nova Scotian merchants were in no position to fight British mercantilism. Nova Scotia was by nature nearly the perfect colony according to the mercantilist theory. . . .

There was not even a sense of solidarity in Nova Scotia. Settlements were scattered at intervals along the edges of a long, narrow peninsula whose rough surface defied the road makers. The unpredictable sea was the road between settlements. . . . There simply could not be integral Nova Scotia.

Perhaps, then, the principal clue to Nova Scotian behavior in this, as in many other problematical situations, lies in her insulation from the rest of North America. . . . Nova Scotia has always had to contemplate the possibility that she may be in North America but not of it, and this mold of circumstances has pressed with varying weight on some generations of Nova Scotians to modify their traditional loyalties and inclinations. France and England, New France and New England, tried to exploit her during the seventeenth century without accepting the responsibility for continuous reinforcement and aid to the inhabitants. . . . The Acadians, . . . were mere pawns in international politics. Small wonder, then, that their one persistent aim from 1710 to 1755, when it sealed their fates, was to be, and to be generally accepted as, neutrals—'the neutral French.' Small wonder, too, that after a brief flurry of conflicting aims in 1775, Nova Scotians a bare fifteen years out of New England naturally and almost inevitably, when confronted by the Revolution, made the same plea.

. . . It is now generally believed that in most of the thirteen rebellious American Colonies the majority of the population was passive, but that the radicals formed the larger of the two active minorities and thereby involved their communities. As events proved, the majority in Nova Scotia was also passive, and neither minority was able to rouse its members beyond individual acts or minor joint enterprises for or against Government. . . .

Clearly no summary phrase can be adequate to explain the behavior of so unintegrated a province. . . .

From J.B. Brebner, *The Neutral Yankees of Nova Scotia*, (New York: Columbia University Press, 1937).

1. Summarize Brebner's explanation of Nova Scotian behaviour.
2. Compare the response to the War of Independence of the Nova Scotians with that of the habitants of Quebec. What are the similarities and differences behind their common reactions to the Revolution?

The Loyalist Tradition in Canada

In this essay, historian David Bell outlines the impact of the American Revolution upon Canada. His basic contention that "the American Revolution produced not one country but two, a nation and a non-nation" is fundamental to an understanding of the concept of revolution and legitimacy.

To forget and—I will venture to say—to get one's history wrong, are essential factors in the making of a nation.
—*Ernst Renan*
In speaking of men who have left their impress upon their age, something I own, is due to the dignity of truth.
—*Lorenzo Sabine*

In its most important aspects, a nation is a psychological entity. To be sure, nations usually require certain minimal objective conditions of geography, economics, communications, etc. But nationalism is a state of mind. Non–nationalism, therefore, is also a state of mind. And a non–nation is a psychological non–entity.

The American Revolution produced not one country but two: a nation and a non–nation. By virtue of the Revolution, the nation (the United States) acquired a set of national symbols, a gallery of heroes, and a national identity that featured, among other things, an ideologically–based definition of citizenship.

Like all 'internal wars,' the Revolution had losers as well as victors. The Loyalists, as the losers were called, were not exterminated (as were many of the losers of the French Revolution); nor were they reintegrated into the community (as were the Southerners after the American Civil War); instead, they were expelled. Most of them migrated north and became the founders of the English–speaking component of the non–nation—modern Canada. With them they brought broken dreams, a distorted image of their experience, and a profound sense of indignation bordering on rage. . . .

There were some important differences in outlook between Loyalists and Revolutionaries, but they did not correspond to the categories denoted by "conservative" and "liberal." To the contrary, a careful analysis of the prerevolutionary debate between Whigs and Tories reveals that both groups *shared* liberal (Lockeian) assumptions about the nature of sovereignty, good government, the right of resistance, etc. The debate did not juxtapose one ideology with another; instead it featured the conflict of two views of the existing situation derived from identical premises. . . .

Thus, the Loyalists resembled fairly closely the persecutors from whom they fled. This fact deprived them of the luxury of unambiguous hatred of their own former adversaries. Rather, their attitude was one of ambivalence: the Loyalists found themselves hating America, but loving and envying it as well. As a result, the Loyalists were deprived of the opportunity of erecting their values—which were virtually identical to those of the Americans—into a national identity.

. . . The Loyalist was violently expelled, he was told, because he did not belong; he was 'un–American'. The Loyalist simply could not understand this. America was his home. The principles of John Locke were his principles. He knew no others. There is much room for sympathy with the Loyalist on this account. He had good reason to be baffled. He was expelled as a *political* exile, but on the basis of a false excuse: that he was also an *ideological* one.

This in turn involved him in an identity crisis that is at once poignant and profound. When the Loyalist asked 'Who am I?' his experience of expulsion precluded his giving the only conceivable answer—I am an American. An American in the sense of subscribing to the principles of John Locke. When the Loyalist refused to support the Revolution, he did not intend to sacrifice his home, his beliefs, and his hard–identity. . . .

The Many Facts of the Loyalist Myth

National sentiments rely heavily on mythical interpretations of the past. The nationalist believes that his is a "chosen" people, that his ancestors were divinely inspired, and hence that his nation is in a sense sacred. To this extent nationalism—and, therefore, non–nationalism as well—is a kind of civil religion. And the myths of the nation resemble the myths of the church: both celebrate the virtues of an earlier glorious age.

The loyalist experience provided the one element of glory in English Canada's history. All other achievements were subordinated and adapted to the idea of loyalism, which has functioned as the founding and integrating myth of the new society. . . .

. . . The loyalist myth of the American Revolution posed some temporary problems for democratization. But it had another consequence as well: it engendered among some 'liberal' Canadian historians in the present century a powerful countermyth. The Loyalists were identified as reactionary conservatives, universally opposed to change in politics (and by analogy changes in all spheres). According to this interpretation, the Loyalists represented the party of wealth and privilege, selfish tyrants and oppressors. (The similarity between the countermyth and *Whig* revolutionary propaganda is obvious.) The view of the Loyalists as a class–conscious group of would–be aristocrats is nevertheless no more accurate than the view the Loyalists held of the reformers as conspiratorial demagogues. Through a dialectic of mistruths, the true character of both groups has been distorted.

A further component of the loyalist myth is anti–Americanism. Loyalist attitudes to America were not entirely one–sided, however. Indeed, they featured agonizing ambivalence: hatred mixed with envious love; invidiousness tinged with pathetic admiration.

The ambivalent quality of the loyalist attitudes was evident even before the Loyalists arrived in Canada. Edward Winslow, later to become prominent of New Brunswick society and politics, epitomized the Loyalist outlook when he recorded this desperate aspiration: "By Heaven, we will be the envy of the American States." . . .

Winslow's hollow declaration of superiority has been echoed throughout Canadian history. It has led to an obsessive compulsion to make comparisons between Canada and the United States to demonstrate superior Canadian virtue or achievement. . . .

The American Revolution, like all revolutions, involved a crisis of legitimacy.

The policies pursued by Britain after 1763 were adamantly opposed, in part because important groups in the thirteen colonies no longer regarded them as acceptable or legitimate. By what standards were these policies judged? This question impels us to examine in general detail the bases of legitimacy. . . .

The leaders of the American Revolution opposed British policy on the grounds that the *substance* of the acts made them illegitimate on their face. The Acts, they argued, amounted to a "system to slavery." But the Revolutionaries also developed an embryonic theory of procedural legitimacy manifested in the cry "No taxation without representation." Thus, notions of *both* substantive and procedural legitimacy played a part in the philosophy of the American Revolution.

The break the British authority accomplished by the successful Declaration of Independence necessitated the development of a new theory of legitimacy to replace the old one that had been destroyed. . . . In at least this one sense, therefore, the Founding Fathers demonstrated a profound distrust of democracy. Furthermore, they transmitted to later generations a legacy of substantive limitations on power that in the twentieth century have seriously impaired the ability of the American political systems to adapt to rapid change.

Clearly, the Loyalists held to a substantive concept of legitimacy, almost to the exclusion of any procedural notions. Following the Revolution, the Assembly in the British North American colonies (like its predecessor in the thirteen colonies) was not an organ for the formulation of the 'general will' but a negative body, whose function was to oppose acts that were considered illegitimate. . . . Thus, Canadian developments tended to follow the British rather than the American pattern, with the result that the shift from substantive to procedural legitimacy, although (indeed, *because!*) slower and later, was in the end more complete and more successful. It took the form, not of the introduction of 'constitutional government', but of the achievement of 'responsible government' in which the exercise of authority is legitimated not in accordance with substantive principles outlined in a written constitution but through the subordination of the executive and administration to the elected body. This solution (i.e., responsible government), insofar as it permitted a larger ambit for the exercise of power, was more 'modern' than the American practice, which retained the Medieval notion of substantive limits embodied in 'higher law' and 'judicial review.' . . .

Nationalism and Non-Nationalism: The Melting Pot and the Mosaic
The American Revolution had differential effects on the two new communities in Anglo-America. For the new nation (the United States) the Revolution performed several vital nationalizing functions. In some ways it can be seen as a chemical reaction in which colonial society was broken down or 'analyzed' into its component groups, rearranged, and then separated into two parts. One part was then 'synthesized' into a new element; the other part was discarded through the Loyalist migration. ('Revolutionary waste material' would be an apt phrase to describe the 'leftover' [loyalist] groups.) The Revolution therefore laid the groundwork for American nationalism by (a) rapidly mobilizing previously iso-

lated groups, (b) providing a powerful precedent and experience for inter-regional cooperation, (c) providing a set of symbols, heroes, and 'values' for a national identity, and (d) eliminating a number of the most resistant minorities.
For the new non–nation (Canada) the Revolution performed obverse functions. The minority groups which, in an attempt to conserve their autonomy and culture refused to support the Revolution, became its victims. They migrated virtually *en masse* to Canada, and thus provided the basis for the cultural mosaic later discovered to be a Canadian phenomenon. Included in the migration were Highland Scots, Pennsylvania Germans (comprising several religious sects: Moravians, Mennonites, Dunkards, and "Reformed"), Hugenots, German Palatinates, Quakers, Indians, and a number of Blacks. Canada served as a sort of non–melting pot into which all these disparate ingredients were tossed. Thrown in gratuitously, so to speak, were a number of Hessian troops who had fought as mercenaries for the British.
Such diverse groups would pose problems for any nation to assimilate. But these were all bound together by the experience of the migration. Moreover, they achieved a loose, but lasting affiliation under "The Crown." In short, they took on a weak (non–) identity that did not prevent the preservation and persistence of their own peculiar cultures—they were all *Loyalists.*
Of course many minorities stayed behind in the new United States, but their fate further corroborates our thesis: they quickly became absorbed in almost every case. Those minority group members who supported the Revolution earned their credentials as "charter members" of the new nation. Those who did *not*, made a conscious effort to get 'lost' in the new society, probably to escape the stigma of suspected toryism.
Unlike the new nationalist identity in the United States, the loyalist identity in no way interfered with the continuation of ethnic culture. The ethnic group survived in Canada while it was being absorbed in the United States. A mosaic pattern appeared in Canada at precisely the point that it began to disappear in America: it was as central an aspect of the "counter–revolution" as the nationalization of leftover minorities was of the Revolution.

From David V.J. Bell, "The Loyalist Tradition in Canada," from *Journal of Canadian Studies*,V (May 1970) in J.M. Bumstead, ed., *Canadian History Before Confederation*, (Georgetown, Ontario: Irwin Dorsey Press, 1972).

1. Outline the problem faced by the Loyalists as explained by Bell.
2. What is the nature of the Loyalist "myth"?
3. Explain the concept of legitimacy.

Revolution and Legitimacy: Analysis and Application

1. Compare the writings of John Locke and Mercy Otis to the tenor of the American Declaration of Independence. To what extent were the ideals of the Thirteen Colonies in opposition to British political viewpoints?

2. Select and analyse the writings and career of one colonial theorist/publicist. In your analysis be certain to consider the viewpoint of the writer, her/his audience,

and the impact of her/his ideas upon the course of events. Based on your research create and defend your own thesis regarding the impact of ideas on the course of the revolution.

3. "While the 'natural leaders' of Quebec may have favoured the British position, the average *habitant* was a strong supporter of the colonial cause."
Defend or refute this statement with respect to the reaction of the inhabitants of Quebec to the outbreak of war in the Thirteen Colonies.

4. Assume that you are Guy Carleton. Write a counter-response to George Washington's proclamation. In an editor's note identify your target audience.

5. Stage a two-person debate between Bishop Briand and Charles Carroll centring on the fate of Quebec in 1776. One student should prepare a position paper reflecting Briand's viewpoint, while the other takes the position of Carroll.

Stage your debate allowing each participant an opportunity to state her/his position and to conduct a formal rebuttal. When you have finished step out of your role and consider the basic issue of Quebecois neutrality.

6. Re-examine the historians' debate over French-Canadian involvement in the revolutionary movement. Précis the arguments put forward by Garneau, Coffin, and Neatby. Based upon your analysis, formulate your own thesis about the events of this period.

7. "In the final analysis, the Loyalists were little more than gamblers who lost." Comment on this statement with regard to the Loyalist experience.

8. Précis Brebner's analysis of the Nova Scotian response to the Revolution. Based upon his analysis and your own research, create a political pamphlet reflecting one of the viewpoints current to the period.

9. Comment upon David Bell's view of the Loyalist myth. To what extent do you accept his contention that the "nation" and the "non-nation" took two different routes to legitimacy?

10. Defend the thesis that: "The American revolution should more rightly be called the 'North American' revolution for the outcome was the creation of two distinct nations on the continent." Write a brief paper, create an outline for a major research essay, or stage a debate to defend your view.

5
SETTLEMENT AND THE FRONTIER

In an address to a group of high-school students, Dr. Robert McClure, former moderator of the United Church of Canada, said that Canadians had little understanding of the needs of the developing world. He suggested that, because of the affluence of their society, Canadian students could not appreciate the difficulties inherent in trying to build a society in the face of enormous environmental obstacles. One student openly disagreed. Her position was that Canadian students could understand the problem based on the frontier experience of their ancestors who had struggled against nature and had endured. Dr. McClure sat back, smiled, and replied that it was too bad that the pioneer experience was not a hereditary one!

As North Americans, we have long prided ourselves in our collective pioneer past. Most of us believe that the influence of a wilderness frontier played a major role in the development of our national characters and values. Critics, on the other hand, have rejected this view, citing other societies with similar environments that developed in entirely different directions.

Most Canadian students are familiar with the characteristics of frontier life. However, the intellectual debate surrounding the significance of those characteristics and their influences are not as well known. Consequently, this chapter will take a slightly different approach, and will be devoted to the secondary interpretation of the impact of the frontier rather than an in-depth study of settlement patterns themselves.

These words opened an address to the Chicago Historical Society in 1893:

> In a recent bulletin of the Superintendant of the Census for 1890 appear these significant words: "Up to and including 1880 the country had a frontier of settlement, but at present the unsettled area has been so broken into by isolated bodies of settlement that there can hardly be said to be a frontier line . . ." This brief official statement marks the closing of a great historical movement.

The speaker was thirty-two-year-old Frederick Jackson Turner. His thesis on the impact of the frontier on American society was about to revolutionize historical thought in the United States.

Turner sparked a debate among historians that still rages today. The question posed by supporters and critics alike has been: "What was the role of the frontier in the development of the characteristics of North American society?" Many Canadians would immediately disavow even this question claiming that "frontierism" is strictly an American phenomenon. For us, however, the field is wide open.

To examine this question we must first define what Turner meant by the *frontier*. Traditionally, we think of a frontier as an edge or border. In the colonial sense it often refers to the line of settlement beyond which is wilderness. These definitions did not interest Turner. He saw the frontier not as a place, but as a process.

According to Turner, the frontier broke down the accepted conventions of society. It forced the settler to return to savagery and to build anew. This evolutionary process tended to result in an improved civilization. Frontier societies kept the best of the old society, and added the new experiences.

People on the frontier were isolated and had to cope with their own problems. As a result, individuals emerged from that experience more capable, more confident, and more self-reliant. Along with this newly found individualism was a rejection of any form of social control from above. The frontier, therefore, was the breeding ground of democracy.

As the United States grew, the exposure to the frontier continued to revitalize American society. People became more ambitious, more innovative, and more democratic. It was a natural process.

This being the case, the pronouncement of the closure of the frontier was terrible news for the Republic. Without the continual reversion to savagery, American society might stagnate. Nothing would ever be the same again. No wonder Turner concluded his paper with the words:

And now four centuries from the discovery of America, at the end of a hundred years of life under the Constitution, the frontier has gone, and with its going has closed the first period in American history.

Selections from two of Turner's papers appear in the readings along with excerpts from some of his critics.

Those who have supported Turner's ideas have done so with such conviction that they have often been described as disciples. Certainly in the decades following the publication of his ideas a whole generation of historians jumped on the frontier bandwagon. Canadian historians have also taken an interest in Turner's contentions. Although frontierism has never had the majority of support nor held the public imagination in this country the way it has in the United States, it has, nonetheless, had its share of distinguished Canadian adherents. In his book *The Canadian Frontier*, historian W.J. Eccles writes that: " . . . in the final analysis the habitant did not have to take to the woods, it was knowing that he could that was good enough." (See readings.)

A.R.M. Lower echoes Eccles' sentiments:

There can be little question but that American democracy had a forest birth and there also can be little doubt of the validity of the larger thesis that the frontier environment, or life lived on the margins of civilization, tends to bring about an equality of which the political expression is democracy. . . . It may be concluded that our own pioneering era plus the influence of American pioneer life brought about political democracy in Canada.

Critics of this viewpoint may be found on both sides of the border. American historian Louis Hacker states:

What is gained, except misunderstanding, by an ungracious exclusion of

Locke and Milton and Montesquieu, of Coke and Blackstone and Grotius, of Adams, Jefferson, Otis, Paine, and Madison from a share of the credit? . . . Democracy did not come out of the American forest unless it was first carried there.

Hacker's views are supported by Richard Hofstadter:

It became plain, as new thought and research was brought to bear upon the problem, that the frontier theory, as an analytical device, was a blunt instrument.

Canadian historian Donald Creighton has added:

I don't think that the frontier has been that important in Canadian history . . . the frontier . . . is not the main source of inspiration . . . for action or any kind of creative activity.

As you can see, the minds of historians are far from clear on the subject. How then should we consider the impact of the frontier? We must first consider the frontier thesis itself, then look at its applications on both sides of the border. Following this investigation we will examine the writings of the critics of frontierism and study some alternative schools of historical thought.

The Turner Thesis

Frederick Jackson Turner was thirty-two years old in 1893 when he read the paper that was to revolutionize North American historiographical thought, "The Significance of the Frontier in American History." Ten years later the historian reiterated his belief in the relationship between the frontier and the growth of democratic institutions in an essay entitled "Contributions of the West to American Democracy." Turner's thesis dominated American thinking for the first quarter of the twentieth century, partly because of the force of the idea and partly because of Turner's own power as a lecturer and teacher.

No discussion of the impact of Turner and his ideas may begin without an examination of the frontier thesis itself. The first two readings are taken from these pivotal essays.

The Significance of the Frontier in American History, 1893
Up to our own day American history has been in a large degree the history of the colonization of the Great West. The existence of an area of free land, its continuous recession, and the advance of American settlement westward, explain American development.

Behind institutions, behind constitutional forms and modifications, lie the vital forces that call these organs into life and shape them to meet changing conditions. The peculiarity of American institutions is the fact that they have been compelled to adapt themselves to the changes of an expanding people–to the changes involved in crossing a continent, in winning a wilderness, and in developing at each area of this progress out of the primitive economic and political conditions of the frontier into the complexity of city life. Said Calhoun in

Clearing the bush on the new frontier

Frederick Jackson Turner

1817, 'We are great, and rapidly—I was about to say fearfully—growing!' So saying, he touched the distinguishing feature of American life. All peoples show development; the germ theory of politics has been sufficiently emphasized. In the case of most nations, however, the development has occurred in a limited area; and if the nation has expanded, it has met other growing peoples whom it has conquered. But in the case of the United States we have a different phenomenon. Limiting our attention to the Atlantic coast, we have the familiar phenomenon of the evolution of institutions in a limited area, such as the rise of representative government; the differentiation of simple colonial governments into complex organs; the progress from primitive industrial society, without division of labor, up to manufacturing civilization. But we have in addition to this a recurrence of the process of evolution in each western area reached in the process of expansion. Thus American development has exhibited not merely an advance along a single line, but a return to primitive conditions on a continually advancing frontier line, and a new development for that area.

Each of these areas has had an influence in our economic and political history; the evolution of each into a higher stage has worked political transformations. But what constitutional historian has made any adequate attempt to interpret political facts by the light of these social areas and changes?

From the conditions of frontier life came intellectual traits of profound importance. The works of travelers along each frontier from colonial days onward describe certain common traits, and these traits have, while softening down, still persisted as survivals in the place of their origin, even when a higher social organization succeeded. The result is that to the frontier the American intellect owes its striking characteristics. That coarseness and strength combined with acuteness and inquisitiveness; that practical, inventive turn of mind, quick to find expedients; that masterful grasp of material things, lacking in the artistic but powerful to effect great ends; that restless, nervous energy; that dominant individualism, working for good and for evil, and withal that buoyancy and exuberance which comes with freedom—these are traits of the frontier.

From Frederick Jackson Turner, *The Frontier in American History*, (Gloucester, MA: Peter Smith, Publisher, 1920). Copyright 1948 by Caroline M.S. Turner.

Contributions of the West to American Democracy, 1903

From the beginning of the settlement of America, the frontier regions have exercised a steady influence toward democracy. In Virginia, to take an example, it can be traced as early as the period of Bacon's Rebellion, a hundred years before our Declaration of Independence. The small landholders, seeing that their powers were steadily passing into the hands of the wealthy planters who controlled Church and State and lands, rose in revolt. . . .

The "War of the Regulation" just on the eve of the American Revolution, shows the steady persistence of this struggle between the classes of the interior and those of the coast. The Declaration of Grievances which the back counties of the Carolinas then drew up against the aristocracy that dominated the politics of those colonies exhibits the contest between the democracy of the frontier and the established classes who apportioned the legislature in such a fashion as to secure effective control of government. Indeed, in the period before the outbreak of the American Revolution, one can trace a distinct belt of democratic territory extending from the back country of New England down through western New York, Pennsylvania and the South.

From Frederick Jackson Turner, "Contributions of the West to American Democracy," (1903) in *The Frontier in American History*, (Gloucester, MA: Peter Smith, Publisher, 1920). Copyright 1948 by Caroline M.S. Turner.

1. How does Turner describe the nature of the frontier?
2. What intellectual traits does the historian ascribe to the frontier?
3. What historical case does Turner make for the "revolutionary" character of frontier settlements?

Turner's American Critics

As American historians increasingly began to "bend" past events to fit Turner's thinking, a revolt began to grow in the intellectual establishment against some of the fundamentals of his thesis. In this excerpt, Benjamin Wright, a former professor of government at Harvard, challenges the contention that the frontier has been a democratizing influence in the past.

Political Institutions and the Frontier, 1934

The most brilliant and the most influential of American historians, Turner has colored all of our thinking about the growth of the American nation. His striking generalizations have been repeated countless times, but they have never been subjected either to the analysis or to the tests which the rudiments of scientific method would seem to suggest. A picture of the movement of political institutions is not one of sufficient scope to make possible a complete consideration of so inclusive a thesis. Indeed the whole canvas of American history is inadequate for the purpose; one must in addition take into account many aspects of Canadian, Latin American, and European history. But if a complete re-examination is neither possible nor intended here, a partial consideration may at least suggest the principal points of strength and of weakness in the frontier approach.

So far as I have been able to determine, there was no considerable desire among those who framed the early western constitutions to introduce governmental forms different from those long well established in the East. In all of the states of the Middle West the familiar pattern was adopted—a single executive, a bicameral legislature, and a hierarchy of courts.

As urban areas developed in these states, the forms of municipal government found in the older states were introduced even the cumbersome bicameral municipal council crossed the Alleghenies and found a home (fortunately temporary) in the new cities.

The new states occasionally made a few additions to the conventional list of reserved rights, but, without exception, they represented no genuine change in political ideals or constitutional practice.

Perhaps the most frequent claim made for the democratizing influence of the pioneer period is the lead taken by the states which passed through this phase during the late eighteenth and early nineteenth centuries in securing a broader suffrage. That these new states did help to accelerate a process under way before they were settled is clear. But it is equally clear that they did not attempt or even desire, to carry that process beyond the goal previously attained in several of the older states.

Benjamin F. Wright, Jr. "Political Institutions and the Frontier," in *Sources of Culture in the Middle West*, Fox ed., © 1934, reissued 1964, pp. 15-38. Reprinted by permission of Prentice Hall, Inc., Englewood Cliffs, New Jersey.

Louis Hacker of Columbia University questioned Turner's rejection of the intellectual basis for American democracy.

Sections—or Classes?, 1933

Frederick Jackson Turner was thirty-two years old in 1893 when he read his monograph, "The Significance of the Frontier in American History," before the American Historical Association. From that day, forty years ago, until now it may truly be said that he has so completely dominated American historical writing that hardly a single production in all that time has failed to show the marks of his influence.

If any one ever said that American democracy was the product of a single theorist's dreams, or, for that matter, the product of the entire residuum of political speculation, he probably was not taken very seriously. Obviously no theorist or group of theorists dreamed into existence the queer patchwork of institutions that we call American democracy. But what is gained, except misunderstanding, by an ungracious exclusion of Locke and Milton and Montesquieu, of Coke and Blackstone and Grotius, of Adams, Jefferson, Otis, Paine, and Madison from a share of the credit? One has but to compare the differences between the institutions of the English and those of the French, Dutch, and Spanish colonies in America to see that the foundations, and more, of our democracy were brought in the *Susan Constant* and *Mayflower*. That democracy did not come out of the American forest unless it was first carried there. On some frontiers democracy was not strengthened, rather the reverse. Free land gave the opportunity to establish slavery in Louisiana, oligarchy in the Mormon state, the hacienda system in Mexican California, while it was furnishing the opportunity for a "fit" people in the Middle West to establish the particular degree and kind of democracy that they favored.

If Turner's thesis had not been so widely relied upon, there would be no point at this late date in subjecting his generalizations to critical analysis. Certainly I have no desire to disparage his standing as an historian nor to minimize the stimulating effect that his writings had upon the American historiography of the last generation. He did have the genius to see in certain neglected factors extraordinarily useful instruments. If, in his zeal for his cause, he over-stated his case, that was more than pardonable, it was probably necessary. But the desirability of unquestioning acceptance of his sweeping doctrine vanished long ago. His thesis has, like previous interpretations, served its purpose. Continued reliance upon his unclarified and unmodified doctrine is more an indication of imaginative poverty than of loyalty to a dead leader.

From Louis M. Hacker, "Sections—or Classes?", in *The Nation* magazine, (New York: The Nation Company, Inc., 1933).

Yale professor George Wilson Pierson also highlights some of the shortcomings of Turner's thesis. In this excerpt he raises the spectre of the danger to intellectual and political thought when one concept rules unchallenged.

The Frontier and American Institutions, 1942

How much of Frederick Jackson Turner's frontier hypothesis is reliable and useful today? This problem has begun to trouble economists, sociologists, geographers, and most of all the teachers of graduate students in the field of American history.

For how shall we account for the industrial revolution by the frontier? Do American music and architecture come from the woods? Did American cattle? Were our religions born of the contemplation of untamed nature? Has science, poetry, or even democracy, its cradle in the wilderness? Did literature grow fertile with innovation in the open spaces? Above all, what happens to the intellectual history if the environment be all?

The predicament of the scholar, who has been living in a comfortable frontier philosophy, is beginning to attract some attention. Nor may we comfort ourselves with the assurance that ours is a purely academic debate. For frontier legends of one kind or another have now so permeated American thought as to threaten drastic consequences. Have not our most influential journalists and statesmen for some time been ringing *pessimistic* changes on the theme of "lost frontier," "lost safety-valve," "lost opportunity"? Such convictions can lead to legislation. In Congress the underlying issue could shortly be: was there but one economic frontier, was it really the "safety-valve," and are both now gone? The cultural historian meanwhile asks: is it true that the frontier was "the line of most rapid and effective Americanization"? More particularly, since we are now trying to define and safeguard the "American way of life," what share did the "frontier" have in its creation, and to what cultural influences must we henceforth look for its preservation?

From George Wilson Pierson, "The Frontier and American Institutions," in *The New England Quarterly* 15, (Boston, Massachusetts: Northeastern University, June 1942).

1. Write a synthesis of the objections to Turner raised by Wright, Hacker, and Pierson. To what extent do you feel these critics have successfully countered Turner's basic contention?

Canadian Historians Debate the Turner Thesis

Even before widespread opposition to Turner's ideas appeared in the United States, Canadian historians were considering how these theories applied to their own country. In excerpts from two essays written for the Canadian Historical Association in 1929, historians A.R.M. Lower and John L. McDougall consider the applicability of Turner to life in Upper Canada and New France.

A.R.M. Lower

Much has been written about the picturesque side of pioneer days. Everyone knows that the settler, leaving wife and children in a rude log cabin, was accustomed to trudge through the almost pathless woods for many miles with a heavy sack of wheat upon his back, and so on. But the general principles which underlay the whole process have not as yet been much canvassed. Has there been a frontier psychology in Canada as there was in the United States? Was the attack on the wilderness methodical despite its seeming confusion? Did certain classes of persons take upon themselves certain classes of work? Maria Chapdelaine's father with his self-appointed task of clearing a farm and then moving on again to the wilderness to do the same thing over again represented a type whose existence was well-defined on the American frontier. Did it exist in Canada? Hémon's novel is one bit of evidence showing that it did. There are doubtless others which would establish the point. Did the newly arrived person push on out to the frontier or did the biologic law of dispersion hold good, that law which teaches that it is the edge which moves and the old ground that is occupied by later comers?

In the United States, the innate genius of the Anglo-Saxon for self-government was illustrated over and over again as the frontier rolled westward by innumerable duplications of the Mayflower compact. Did anything of the sort occur in Canada or did government tread so closely on the heels of the settler that local arrangements were not necessary? If so, what has been the effect on our population of the orderliness of our development? Has it robbed us of some initiative? Or is our cautiousness a racial trait, to hazard a guess, Scottish in origin?

Both in Canada and the United States, democracy has been a condition, not a theory. It has been the spontaneous product of the frontier and the forest. In both countries it has had its battle to fight with the representatives of an older order of things. In the United States it had to contend with the propertied classes of the east and in Canada with propertied and privileged family compacts. Of the two survivals of aristocracy, the Canadian version was probably the more invidious and certainly the more petty. Not long after Andrew Jackson scored his ringing victory of 1828, Mackenzie led his guerilla raid against a foe akin to his. While other champions of the new order duly appeared, its victory in Canada was not as complete as in the United States and as a result there has always been an aristocratic tinge to our politics—or at least to our political system—not observable in those of the republic. . . .

Leadership and direction, the "tone" of life, have in Canada, tended to come from above, that is, directly or indirectly from English aristocratic tradition; the Americans, on the other hand, while not exactly getting these things from below, have at least made them up as they went along. The result is a fairly considerable difference in the political and social atmosphere of the two countries, a difference which has been reflected in laws and institutions. . . .

From A.R.M. Lower, "Some Neglected Aspects of Canadian History," *Canadian Historical Association Annual Report*, 1929.

John L. McDougall
No early settlement in North American was more thoroughly exposed to all the influences of the frontier than that of the French Canadians in the St. Lawrence Valley. All the frontier influences beat upon them with unparalleled force. . . .

. . . In view of these facts is it not proper to ask whether the external environment, the frontier, really was the dominant creative force which moulded American life? Would it not be more proper to describe it as a catalyst which set free elements in the American character not present in the same degree in other civilizations? . . .

That is the line of attack which gives the best returns. The distinguishing mark of French Canada is the degree of social cohesion which it possesses. The fur-trader with his word of good lands farther on was dynamite to the American society of his time; he was an alien curiosity in Quebec. To the French Canadian, living well meant living in community. The Coureurs des Bois were men who had surrendered that right and were more to be pitied for spiritual blindness than to be envied for their greater economic opportunities. The present colonizing activities in Northern Ontario and Quebec, so markedly at variance with the first seventy years of the last century, merely witness to that cohesion. The whole movement was begun by the Church and is carried on by it. It began as a relief movement to the older areas and as a counter-attraction to the mill-towns of New England. Nothing could be farther from the American experience—what is aimed at is not a haphazard response to the call of free land, but a carefully pre-arranged building of new communities. The raw frontier is not something whose passing is regretted as it has been in the United States. It is to be wiped out as soon as possible. Success is attained when the village spire is within the view of every settler and the angelus marks the beginning and the ending of his day. . . .

. . . And justification there may be for Professor Turner's thesis as an explanation of American history it could be little short of a calamity if Canadian historians were to attempt to deform the story of our own development to fit the Procustes bed of the frontier theory. One has heard England described as a land where bad German philosophies go when they die. One may at least hope that Canada will not stand in a similar relation to the United States.

From John L. McDougall, "The Frontier School and Canadian History," *Canadian Historical Association Annual Report*, (1929).

1. What are the differences identified by Lower between the American and Canadian experiences?
2. McDougall states that "no early settlement in North America was more thoroughly exposed to all frontier influences than that of French Canadians." In light of this contention, account for the differences between the experiences in New France and the American colonies.
3. Assuming the role of Turner, write a rebuttal of the arguments put forth by Lower and McDougall.

French Canada and the Frontier

In the following essay, A.I. Silver argues that the spirit of the frontier is more of a predisposition or attitude rather than a phenomenon created simply by moving there. He examines the attitudes of French Canadians living in the St. Lawrence Valley with regard to the rapidly expanding frontier opportunities in the West.

In the quarter-century after the Manitoba Act, . . . when English Canada was looking to the prairies as the land of promise, the key to Canada's future, and when thousands of Ontarians were pouring onto the plains, three main trends of opinion tended to keep French Canadians away from the region: a disbelief in the material value of prairie land; a fear that to go there was to expose oneself and one's national identity to danger; and a conviction that Quebec alone was the French-Canadian *patrie* so that to go west was to expatriate oneself. The letters of Taché's agents, reporting on their contacts in Quebec, seem to indicate that the first of these reasons was most important with farmers, the actual potential settlers, while the educated, the community leaders, were most concerned with the problem of expatriation and depopulation of Quebec.

Running through all these attitudes is a strain of pessimism, defeatism, or demoralization. . . . This frame of mind differs markedly from what has been typically represented as the frontier mentality. The frontiersman is supposed to be fearless, optimistic, independent, expansive. His boundless enthusiasm and self-confidence impel him to enterprise, often recklessly. Essential to the frontier hypothesis is the idea that these characteristics are "forest-born," are the result of the impact of the physical environment in changing the personality of the man who comes to the frontier. In this, the frontier hypothesis may well be psychologically questionable, for psychologists appear agreed that personality is established with virtual permanence by the time adulthood is reached. Far from being created by the frontier, the frontiersman was probably the kind of man whom his home society could create, and who was attracted by the frontier because he already was (at last latently) a frontiersman. Thus, J. B. Bickersteth, a young Protestant missionary on the north-west frontier, noted that 'an entirely English [European] settlement is seldom very progressive. The presence of a few bustling Americans or Canadians creates an atmosphere of push.' . . . One has to be born, or at least brought up, in the right kind of society to become a frontiersman—the kind of society that will mould a man's character so that he will be attracted by, and be able to survive at, the frontier.

Societies which have produced frontiersmen or colonizers seem always to have been characterized by a certain mobility or dislocation of their parts. The North American *Aufmarschgebiet* was a semi-settled area whose inhabitants moved around within it and moved out when more stable elements moved in. Nor was this frontier society created in a generation. Anglo-American colonists spent a century and a half in the Atlantic coastal area, gradually adapting to new conditions, still tied to Europe's lengthening apron string while facing the frontier, developing the society that would produce Turner's westerns. . . .

French Canada 1870 was far from the condition of any of the colonizing societies. . . . Not movement, but stasis, enforced by the very nature of the task of "survival," was the keynote of French-Canadian society. The conquest cut off prospects of French-Canadian growth by immigration, giving both conquerors and conquered the idea that the *Canadien* population was fully formed. So too, the Proclamation of 1763, by drawing the boundaries of the province close in around the limits of the seigneuries, created the impression that the province, if not already settled, was not so unsettled that the heirs of the present population would not fill it. Indeed, by 1824, the Montreal *Gazette* was reporting that land 'in situations fit for cultivation is now nearly all taken up.' This encouraged French Canadians to consider the country as already settled rather than being settled. Lord Durham noted the attitude: 'The English population . . . looked on the American Provinces as a vast field for settlement and speculation. . . .

'[The French Canadians] looked on the Province as the patrimony of their own race; they viewed it not as a country to be settled, but as one already settled; and instead of legislating in the American spirit, and first providing for the future population of the Province, their primary care was, in the spirit of the legislation which prevails in the old world, to guard the interests and feelings of the present race of inhabitants . . .' This attitude involved a rejection of mobility. Durham himself described French Canada as a 'stationary society,' and his chief investigator, Stewart Derbishire, was more emphatic, quoting Papineau as saying that French Canadians 'never want to go beyond the sound of their own Church Bells.' . . .

. . . Settlement was not a new start, but a way of preserving the old society of the St. Lawrence Valley. While the frontiersman went off to start a new, materially better life, French-Canadian colonizers saw in settlement very different goals: 'Prévenir l'émigration de nos compatriotes; ramener dans le sein de la patrie ceux dont la Foi est exposée à l'étranger; fixer notre peuple au sol; le détourner du luxe, de l'oisiveté, de l'ivrognerie, du blasphème; lui faire aimer la vie simple et paisable des champs. . . .'

French-Canadian attempts to colonization had, therefore, a very special form. The organization of the new parish had to be set up; in particular, a church had to be built and a priest brought in. Then, 'à son arrivée, le colon trouvera toutes choses bien chères à son coeur; le prêtre, l'église et l'école pour ses enfants.' This scheme for a frontier settlement aimed at making the move to the frontier as smooth as possible, at minimizing the differences between home and frontier, and therefore, tailored to the needs of a stable, home society, differed greatly from the typical frontiersman community. 'Everyone in the West,' wrote Bickersteth, 'is out to make every red cent they [sic] can, and the preacher is almost always considered to be on the same quest.' At the frontier, he continued, material ambition rules, and 'religion (if it stands in the way) must necessarily, like everything else, go to the wall.' English-language colonization propaganda played on material motives. A typical pamphlet on the North-West promised that 'a farmer in this vicinity SHOULD MAKE A FORTUNE in two or three years . . . .' How irrelevant, in contrast, seems the attitude of the great French-Canadian colonizer: 'Le Canadien . . . sait que l'homme ne vit pas seulement de pain, que s'il est pauvre sur la terre, il est riche dans le ciel et , si la mort se présente à lui, à sa femme, à ses enfants, avec son triste cortège, le médecin des âmes est là pour lui ouvrir les portes de la Jérusalem céleste. Peut-on reprocher à un chrétien de préférer le ciel à la terre?' Indeed, if the real frontier spirit was materialistic, the French Canadians must take special care not to appeal to material motives in their colonization propaganda. Thus a typical pamphlet begins with the warning: 'Le Manitoba et le Nord-Ouest Canadien ne sont ni bons ni avantageux pour le jeune monsieur qui voudrait vivre . . . sans ne jamais ôter son habit et sans ne jamais transpirer . . . .'

From A.I. Silver, "French Canada and the Prairie Frontier, 1870-1890," *Canadian Historical Review*, Vol. L, No. 1, (1969).

1. Contrast the expansive nature of English-Canadian society in the late nineteenth century with that of Quebec during the same period.
2. Describe the attitudes that contributed to the desire to maintain Quebec as a clearly defined homeland rather than as part of the larger homeland of Canada.
3. To what extent is the concept of Quebec as a "distinct society" in the Meech Lake Accord (see Appendix B) a product of the historical process described above?

The Metropolitan Thesis

Historian Maurice Careless argued that the development of Canadian society was less that of a gradually expanding frontier and more one of metropolitan centres reaching out into the hinterland. In this excerpt he calls into question the entire myth of the self-sufficient pioneer as part of the Canadian experience.

Well over a million people lived in the Province of Canada in 1841: 670,000 in the Lower Canadian half, now denominated Canada East; 480,000 in the Upper Canadian half, now Canada West. And the St. Lawrence-Great Lakes waterway linked them not only to each other but to the transatlantic British metropolis at one end and the core of the great republic at the other. The Canadian hinterland was supplied and shaped by both: British trade, immigration and political structure expressed the transatlantic connection; American-style enterprise, ways of life and social outlook, the influence of the continent. Remote as the world of Canada might seem, rimmed as it was by interminable forests and the timeless emptiness of the north, its people were still in decisive contact with the far wider worlds of Britain and the United States. . . .

Canada West generally was so full of recent immigrants, and so much in the stage of extensive rather than intensive growth, that its social structure was naturally ill-defined. Nevertheless, in the towns one could distinguish an upper class of officials, often sizable landholders (who were in close social contact with the officers of the British garrison, where that existed); a middle class of merchants, shopkeepers and skilled craftsmen, whose wealthy upper ranks might certainly be allied with the office-holders; and a lower class of wage labourers composed largely of immigrants, without the resources yet to farm. Many would never acquire them. Already Toronto and other towns were evincing the presence of the permanent poor, raising local problems of bad housing, sanitation, and winter relief, even in a society presumably characterized by the robust, self-reliant pioneer. There was also brawling and family suffering caused by the "liquor evil," which was endemic in this hard-drinking frontier society but was concentrated in the inns, farms, and squalid dram-shops of towns. In response, a temperance movement was developing. Toronto's temperance society, founded in 1839, had 1,300 members by 1841. Similar societies were being established in Lower Canada, where Roman Catholic 'cures' sponsored them for the parish poor.

The upper and lower strata of society were less in evidence in the Upper Canada countryside than in the towns. Small proprietors working their own farms constituted a broad agrarian middle class; though there were, of course, hired men on one hand, and on the other, an element of gentry in the government-appointed magistrates and British half-pay officers who managed to maintain themselves on the land. Moreover, there were differences within the middle class itself, between increasingly prosperous commercial farmers in more advanced districts and settlers in the still primitive backwoods, clearing land for their limited crops and lacking good roads out to market. Yet both groups produced for sale, and were dependent on purchased, imported goods, whether or not barter was the immediate means of exchange at the local mill or general store. The self-sufficient pioneer was largely a creature of myth. Almost from the start the Upper Canadian farmer had been part of a cash economy, specialising in wheat production for outside markets. To this the backwoodsman could add valuable potash from the trees he cleared and burned, while the more developed farmer had hides, meat and other produce to offer from his broader fields. However, those fields were not necessarily well-treated, too much being attempted with too little labour available. Canadian-born farmers and those from the States were frequently the worst land-butchers. Some, indeed, were professional pioneers who made their profit in clearing and selling farms rather than in working them. Lowland Scots or English made better "improving farmers" and the Irish often poor ones. . . .

Thanks to improving provisions for education, some of the crudities and cultural limitations of a half-fledged frontier society began to pass away. But the frontier age in any case was passing as a more thickly settled, better defined community took shape. In Canada East, good land in the Townships was rapidly disappearing, and other new areas looked too remote and rugged to invite ready expansion. Though much fertile wild land remained to be occupied in Canada West, that section, too, was rapidly approaching its limits of good arable soil, as settlement spread along the shores of Lake Huron towards the limestone Bruce Peninsula, or probed inland towards the inexorable rock barriers of the huge Precambrian Shield. The end of the open agricultural frontier would soon have to come. And while this still lay in the future, signs of a maturing consolidating community were already apparent in Canada by the early 1840's. . . .

Furthermore, despite the continuing problem of bad roads—mud pits in spring and fall, rutted tracks in summer—internal communications were steadily being developed to knit the community together. Yonge Street had been macadamized (graded with interlocking stone and gravel) nearly to Lake Simcoe by 1841. Governor Sydenham, by ordinance, had sought to improve the winter "snow roads" of Canada East. Wooden plank roads, which could be built for half the cost of macadamized ways, were increasingly being laid down. Traffic moved freely by steamboat or lake schooner along main water routes in open season, while canals would soon be building anew on the St. Lawrence. It only remained for the coming of the railway to provide sure, year-round heavy transport and lift the remaining burdens of inland isolation. Already lines were being talked of, charters sought; and a rail route from Toronto north to Georgian Bay had tentatively been surveyed.

Accordingly, the world of the united province was a world in process of vital change as it moved away from pioneering simplicity. The process, of course, would take years still to work itself out, but essentially the province of Canada was passing from the phase of extensive growth to one of intensive development. Ahead lay a different world, of the railway, steam-powered machinery, and the rising city; and a rural community with its own municipal life, well-developed commercial villages, and increasingly diversified agriculture. With the increase in wealth and population, class lines became more marked as advancing capitalism and the spread of wage-earning affected either end of the social scale. Old officialdom, backwood egalitarianism in the West, French-Canadian agrarianism in the East, all gave ground before the growing power of middle-class business interests.

From J.M.S. Careless, *The Union of the Canadas: The Growth of Canadian Institutions, 1841-1857*, (Toronto: McClelland and Stewart Limited, 1967).

1. How does Careless depict the urban environment of Upper Canada?
2. Account for Careless's statement that "the self-sufficient pioneer was largely a creature of myth."
3. What role did the transportation network play in minimizing the impact of the frontier in Upper Canada?

The North Americans: A Comparison

A.R.M. Lower in his "The Origins of Democracy in Canada" drew comparisons between the Canadian and American experiences. In his view, the frontier could only have the limited effect of building upon a predisposition that already existed.

The historical deductions from geography have been worked out in some detail for the United States by American historians of the school of F.J. Turner and they have shown very well how the frontier has conditioned the whole social setting, manners of thought and political reactions of the people of their nation. Turner's thesis has not yet been thoroughly applied to Canadian history and, indeed, there are factors present in the development of each country which are inconspicuous or absent in that of the other. It must therefore be a modified or adapted version of the thesis which can be fitted to Canada.

Probably the most striking and important aspect of the thesis is that one which dwells on the connection between the frontier and democracy. There can be little question but that American democracy had a forest birth and there also can be little doubt of the validity of the larger thesis that the frontier environment, or life lived on the margins of civilization, tends to bring about an equality of which the political expression is democracy. But it may be doubted whether social equality could work out into political democracy unless the society possessing it had not possessed certain theoretical positions as to its nature before it was projected into its frontier surroundings. The French Canadian and the American before 1763 both were faced with the same frontier conditions and within limits both made the same response to them. Both had much social equality, much rude good comradeship, the virtues of pioneer hospitality, adaptiveness and initiative in meeting the demands of forest life. Both were restive under control, making good scouts but poor regulars. There was infinitely more independence and assertiveness in French Canada, infinitely less readiness to do the will of a superior, than in old France; but it may be safely assumed that when the conditions which made for this independence had passed, the age-old controls of French life, the clergy and nobility, and the pressure of authority which was in the very air of the *ancien regime* would have made themselves felt and the independent Canadian would have had to bow the knee in the same manner as his ancestors.

Not so the American. He had all the independence of the *coureur de bois* and something more: he had behind him the consciousness that he was a free man, that his ancestors had been free men and that his whole society stood for the rights and privileges of the individuals. Thus when pioneer conditions had passed, the attitude toward life which they had induced remained as a conscious philosophy or creed, something to be fought for. It is only with the fading of the memory of the frontier and the elevation of the descendants of frontiersmen into a sort of aristocracy, at least a plutocracy, over an immigrant and alien bottom layer, that the old framework of American society tends to loosen. It has not loosened much yet but it is doubtful if the political ideals of the original population, reinforced as they were by a most intense frontier experience, can be indefinitely passed on to a citizenry much of which has little of them in its heredity and much of which is slowly becoming a lower class.

In Canada, democracy has been even more of a condition and less of a theory [than] it has been in the United States. Our political ideas have been British, not American, and in British political idealism, democracy, until recent days, had no place. In it freedom, it is true, had a large place, but a careful distinction must be made between the old English notion of freedom and the concept suggested by the word democracy. For three quarters of a century after the Loyalists came, lip-service was paid to freedom but "democracy" was discreditable, at least among the people who "mattered". It was something that caused French Revolutions or which was associated with the American tobacco chewers discovered by Martin Chuzzlewit. . . .

The Loyalists brought with them to Canada a bitter experience of popular action. Haldimand said, perhaps truly enough, that they had had all they wanted of Assemblies. Their chief men were aristocrats. Yet in half a century their settlements were being agitated by cries for responsible government. In so far as they supported this agitation and in so far as it did not obtain its chief support from the later comers, the frontier had done its work.

But it is probably necessary to distinguish between responsible government and democratic government. So far as the writer knows, Baldwin, Papineau and Lafontaine were not enthusiasts for democracy. Mackenzie probably was and he more than any other prominent figure represents the frontier at that period. Yet in Canada, the frontier, that is roughly, the countryside as opposed to the little governmental and mercantile centres of power and influence, never scored the ringing victory of Andrew Jackson and his frontiersmen in the United States.

It is curious to reflect how little support Mackenzie received. Logically most of the province should have supported him, for most of the province must have been affected by the grievances for which the ruling class was responsible, the conditions obtaining as to land and land-grants, the Clergy Reserves, the Anglican attempts at an established church, the tyranny of the semi-official Bank of Upper Canada. Similar conditions in the United States, both before and after the Revolution, had caused serious outbreaks. Bacon's Rebellion, the Alemance fight, Shay's Rebellion, the Pennsylvania Whiskey Rebellion, are familiar examples. A similar inspiration, if not actual grievances, had been at the bottom of the triumph of the frontier in 1828. Yet here was Upper Canada and, to a lesser degree, New Brunswick and Nova Scotia, suffering under more severe oppression [than] these others had been and to a remarkable extent taking it "lying down".

The explanation is two-fold. The character of the population differed from that of the western states. The democratic spirit in its political expression was a post-Revolutionary development in which Loyalist migrants had not shared. Later immigrants were not completely emancipated from old world modes of life and thought. The pioneer in his day-to-day life manifested all the characteristics of his American brother except the fierce desire of the latter to control the political situation. Mackenzie, a pioneer only by courtesy, a pioneer born in Scotland and seeing the frontier from the windows of a York printing house, was not an Andrew Jackson. . . .

The events of the rebellion period are not particularly creditable to a proud people. It should logically have been a great popular movement against undoubted grievances. Instead of that, its inherited social alignments, from which much of the meaning had evaporated, took all the fire out of it.

Though, partially as a result of the rebellion, self-government came, democracy did not prevail and as late as 1867, Sir John Macdonald could vigorously and without condemnation champion a property suffrage. Property and privilege is written into the British North America Act to a much greater extent than it is written into the American constitution, itself a document far from democratic. . . .

. . . With our traditions of political freedom working in the modern world, we must have come out somewhere near the point at which we have in fact arrived. Moreover we lay close to a country in which during the nineteenth century democracy was, so to speak, being continuously re-manufactured, recreated anew with every belt of new country opened up. In the tone of society as in every other particular, we were influenced by the United States and there is no doubt that the march of democracy in the United States influenced its march in Canada. The back-wash of western democracy forced political equality in all the eastern states and by the 'forties the last property qualifications and the last established church had disappeared from New England. Its effect on Canada must have been similar, for while the boundary tends to retard the spread of ideas northward it does not stop it. It may be concluded that our own pioneering era plus the influence of American pioneer life brought about political democracy in Canada.

. . . We like to think that our democracy does not shout as loud as that of America. These differences, for the most part small, probably proceed from three causes. The first is that our frontier experience, owing to differences in habitable area, has not been as intense and prolonged as has that of the United States. We have not been ground up quite as fine by it as the United States. Sir John Beverley Robinson was able to keep his coach and four and to pose as grand seigneur in "Muddy York" but it is unlikely that he could have done so in contemporary Cincinnati. The second cause is that the old world sentiment has been much sronger in Canada and the old world connection much more recent than in the United States. And the third lies in our monarchical form of government; in the old days we were governed and we have never quite got accustomed to governing ourselves. Government to many of us still seems a thing apart, not quite our own concern. The perpetuation of monarchical forms, even though the life has long since gone out of them, doubtless tends to act as a curb to the fullest expression of democracy. At any rate, the differences just mentioned between our democracy and that of the United States consist in a general way in this, that democracy in Canada has not had quite as thoroughgoing an expression as it has had amongst our neighbours.

From A.R.M. Lower, "The Origins of Democracy in Canada," *Canadian Historical Association Annual Report*, (1930).

1. How does Lower characterize life on the frontier?
2. Why does the historian contend that Canadians were willing to take political abuses "lying down"?
3. In the final analysis, how does Lower equate the experiences of the two neighbours?

The Frontier and Canadian Culture

Northrope Frye, in this essay, argues that the frontier was far more pervasive for Canadians than for the United States. In this brief excerpt he describes Canadians as being trapped in a frontier environment.

Canada began . . . as an obstacle, blocking the way to the treasures of the East, to be explored only in the hope of finding a passage through it. English Canada continued to be that long after what is now the United States had become a defined part of the Western world. One reason for this is obvious from the

142 The North Americans

map. American culture was, down to about 1900, mainly a culture of the Atlantic seaboard, with a western frontier that moved irregularly but steadily back until it reached the other coast. The revolution did not essentially change the cultural unity of the English-speaking community of the North Atlantic that had London and Edinburgh on one side of it and Boston and Philadelphia on the other. But Canada has, for all practical purposes, no Atlantic seaboard. The traveller from Europe edges into it like a tiny Jonah entering an inconceivably large whale, slipping past the Straits of Belle Isle into the Gulf of St. Lawrence, where five Canadian provinces surround him, for the most part invisible. Then he goes up the St. Lawrence and the inhabited country comes into view, mainly a French-speaking country, with its own cultural traditions. To enter the United States is a matter of crossing an ocean; to enter Canada is a matter of being silently swallowed by an alien continent. . . .

The mystique of Canadianism was . . . specifically the cultural accompaniment of Confederation and the imperialistic mood that followed it. But it came so suddenly after the pioneer period that it was still full of wilderness. To feel "Canadian" was to feel part of a no-man's-land with huge rivers, lakes, and islands that very few Canadians had ever seen. "From sea to sea, and from the river unto the ends of the earth"—if Canada is not an island, the phrasing is still in the etymological sense isolating. One wonders if any other national consciousness has had so large an amount of the unknown, the unrealized, the humanly undigested, so built into it. Rupert Brooke, quoted by Mrs. Waterston, speaks of the "unseizable virginity" of the Canadian landscape. What is important here, for our purposes, is the position of the frontier in the Canadian imagination. In the United States one could choose to move out to the frontier or to retreat from it back to the seaboard. The tensions built up by such migrations have fascinated many American novelists and historians. In the Canadas, even the Maritimes, the frontier was all around one, a part and a condition of one's whole imaginative being. The frontier was primarily what separated the Canadian, physically or mentally, from Great Britain, from the United States, and, even more important, from other Canadian communities. Such a frontier was the immediate datum of his imagination, the thing that had to be dealt with first. . . .

It is not much wonder if Canada developed with the bewilderment of a neglected child, preoccupied with trying to define its own identity, alternately bumptious and diffident about its own achievements.

From Northrope Frye, "Conclusion," in Carl F. Klinck, ed., *Literary History of Canada: Canadian Literature in English*, (Toronto: University of Toronto Press, 1965).

1. What geographic differences does Frye cite between Canada and the United States?
2. How does he contrast life on the Canadian frontier with American frontier life?
3. Cite specific examples of the use of isolation and survival as it pertains to the environment as an ongoing theme in Canadian literature.

How the Frontier Shaped the American Character

Contemporary American historians are not willing to completely dismiss the frontier thesis. To some extent its significance is increased by the impact which it had upon the generation raised believing it wholeheartedly. In this essay Ray Allen Billington discusses its implications for the United States.

. . . The belief in progress, both material and intellectual, that is part of modern America's creed was strengthened by the frontier experience.

Frederick Jackson Turner, then, was not far wrong when he maintained that frontiersmen did develop unique traits and that these, perpetuated, form the principal distinguishing characteristics of the American people today. To a degree unknown among Europeans, Americans do display a restless energy, a versatility, a practical ingenuity, an earthy practicality. They do squander their natural resources with an abandon unknown elsewhere; they have developed a mobility both social and physical that marks them as a people apart. In few other lands is the democratic ideal worshiped so intensely, or nationalism carried to such extremes of isolationism or international arrogance. Rarely do other peoples display such indifference toward intellectualism or aesthetic values; seldom in comparable cultural areas do they cling so tenaciously to the shibboleth of rugged individualism. Nor do residents of non-frontier lands experience to the same degree the heady optimism, the rosy faith in the future, the belief in the inevitability of progress that form part of the American creed. These are pioneer traits, and they have become a part of the national heritage.

Yet if the frontier wrought such a transformation within the United States, why did it not have a similar effect on other countries with frontiers? If the pioneering experience was responsible for our democracy and nationalism and individualism, why have the peoples of Africa, Latin America, Canada, and Russia failed to develop identical characteristics? The answer is obvious: in few nations of the world has the sort of frontier that Turner described existed. For he saw the frontier not as a borderland between unsettled and settled lands, but as an accessible area in which a low man-land ratio and abundant natural resources provided an unusual opportunity for the individual to better himself. . . .

. . . In Canada the path westward was blocked by the Laurentian Shield, a tangled mass of hills and sterile, brush-choked soil covering the country north and west of the St. Lawrence Valley. When railroads finally penetrated this barrier in the late nineteenth century, they carried pioneers directly from the East to the prairie provinces of the West; the newcomers, with no prior pioneering experience, simply adapted to their new situation the eastern institutions with which they were familiar. Among the frontier nations of the world only Russia provided a physical environment comparable to that of the United States, and there the pioneers were too accustomed to rigid feudal and monarchic controls to respond as Americans did.

. . . Franklin D. Roosevelt, declared: 'Our last frontier has long since been reached. . . . Equality of opportunity as we have known it no longer exists. . . . Our task now is not the discovery or exploitation of natural resources or necessarily producing more goods. It is the sober, less dramatic business of administering resources and plants already in hand, of seeking to reestablish foreign markets for our surplus production, of meeting the problem of under-consumption, of adjusting production to consumption, of distributing wealth and products more equitably, of adapting existing economic organizations to the service of the people. The day of enlightened administration has come.' To Roosevelt, and to thousands like him, the passing of the frontier created a new era in history which demanded a new philosophy of government.

Diplomats have also found in the frontier hypothesis justification for many of their moves, from imperialist expansion to the restriction of immigration. Harking back to Turner's statement that the perennial rebirth of society was necessary to keep alive the democratic spirit, expansionists have argued through the twentieth century for an extension of American power and territories. During the Spanish-American War imperialists preached such a doctrine, adding the argument that Spain's lands were needed to provide a population outlet for a people who could no longer escape to their own frontier. Idealists such as Woodrow Wilson could agree with materialists like J.P. Morgan that the extension of American authority abroad, either through territorial acquisitions or economic penetration, would be good for both business and democracy. In a later generation Franklin D. Roosevelt favored a similar expansion of the American democratic ideal as a necessary prelude to the better world that he hoped would emerge from World War II. His successor, Harry Truman, envisaged his "Truman Doctrine" as a device to extend and defend the frontiers of democracy throughout the globe. While popular belief in the superiority of America's political institutions was far older than Turner, that belief rested partly on the frontier experience of the United States.

These practical applications of the frontier hypothesis, as well as its demonstrated influence on the nation's development, suggest that its critics have been unable to destroy the theory's effectiveness as a key to understanding American history. The recurring rebirth of society in the United States over a period of three hundred years did endow the people with characteristics and institutions that distinguished them from the inhabitants of other nations. It is obviously untrue that the frontier experience alone accounts for the unique features of American civilization; that civilization can be understood only as the product of the interplay of the Old World heritage and New World conditions. But among those conditions none has bulked larger than the operation of the frontier process.

From Ray Allen Billington, "How the Frontier Shaped the American Character."

1. According to Billington, how did the American frontier experience differ significantly from that of other nations such as Canada?
2. What historical applications of the frontier theory does he cite?
3. To what extent do you think the frontier mentality is still a driving force in American society?

Turner Reconsidered

The pendulum that swung against Turner in the 1930s and 1940s has moved back again in modern historical writing. In this essay, Robert Riegel discusses the "middle ground" of the frontier thesis.

. . . The question of whether Turner was correct or incorrect in his analysis of the influence of the frontier is very possibly less important than the fact that he turned men's minds from traditional and increasingly sterile investigations to fields that were fresh and rewarding. His present biographer pays particular respect to Turner as an historical thinker—'the sole example of the species in the American scene at the time.' Another Turner admirer asserts about the Turner frontier theory that 'its soundness as well as its importance must in large measure be gauged in terms of its effects on the men of its own genera-tion.' Turner arranged American history in a new pattern that stimulated men to desert some of their preconceptions and see the nation's history in a com-pletely new light.

The United States, like other nations, is unique. Its distinctive characteristics must be the product of men of particular abilities and backgrounds operating in a certain geographic setting. An important part of the picture is certainly the long-term existence of a population frontier. Certain historians have been so anxious to correct and limit the Turner generalizations that at times they seem to deny that the frontier experience had any perceptible effect. Such an implica-tion must be wrong. No nation living on the edge of a wilderness for most of its national existence could fail to be affected by that experience.

Turner's concept of history as the handyman of current desires may itself have been a product of his own age and not necessarily true, but evidences of its validity are exceedingly numerous. Turner himself modified the historical thinking of his day by stressing such traits as individualism and democracy, but quite properly he did not eliminate the older values—he was modifying and not replacing. The present world tends to emphasize the actions of national govern-ments, both in the domestic and international spheres. Just as Turner pre-dicted, historians are now engaged in the task of rewriting history to make it pertinent to the new set of values.

Turner was definitely moving along with the trends of his day, for when there appeared in his mind a possible conflict between democracy and individu-alism he was willing to sacrifice some of the latter to obtain more of the former; like other liberals of his day he was willing to part with some of the older indi-vidualism to accomplish the improvement of the average man, which he identi-fied with democracy. He felt that the closing of the frontier, with the disappearance of free land and increasing urbanization, meant that the average man must more and more rely upon the government to protect him from forces which he as an individual could not control.

But did the end of the frontier really mean an important limitation of the opportunities of the average man? One of our more thoughtful present United States historians is of the opinion that individualism was limited not so much by the end of free space as by the development of machine culture and science which tended to outmode the trained amateur, and insists that the retention of the individualism is the pressing problem of our age—a problem that has only slight connection with the frontier.

Society can progress only to the extent that the powers and the abilities of the individual are challenged. From this point of view the study of the North American frontier is not only the study of a specific situation or even of a tradition, but a study of how human energies, both male and female, have been inspired to maximum effort, together with the results, both good and bad. The analysis of situations that have produced the greatest and most intense of human activities has particular value to the modern world, and the historian can perform no more useful function than to make as clear as possible the ramifications of human motivation.

From Robert E. Riegel, "Current Ideas of the Significance of the Frontier."

1. How does the author describe Turner's impact on his contemporaries?
2. What concepts does Riegel feel that Turner identified and brought into the mainstream of American political thought?
3. In the final analysis, what is the significance of the study of the frontier?

Toward a Theory of New Societies

In his book Canada in the North Atlantic Triangle: Two Centuries of Social Change, *John Finlay presents an excellent synthesis of the frontier theory and its relative applicability for North Americans on both sides of the border.*

The first full-scale theory to account for the specific qualities of American development appeared in 1893 when the young historian Frederick Jackson Turner presented a paper to the American Historical Association. What had sparked Turner's contribution, and what gave it its impact, was the finding of the 1890 census that there were no more unsettled areas available to homesteaders in the American west. Ever since the first colonists had precariously established themselves on the Atlantic coast in the early seventeenth century there had been land for settlement to the west of them. Turner undertook to explain to his fellow citizens 'The Significance of the Frontier in American History' (the title of his paper of 1893), the way in which this constant factor in the American experience had affected development.

At the outset it is necessary to understand what Turner meant by frontier. It was not a boundary between two areas in the way that the forty-ninth parallel is a boundary between the United States and Canada. Rather it was itself an area, a broad band of territory intermediate between the settled area in the east and the full wilderness in the west; thus the frontier would contain a fair number of people—explorers, traders, military men, missionaries, and settlers—but the density of population would be comparatively low. The frontier, then, was in advance of the more civilized east, and always in the process of being filled up and made over in the east's image. Thus it is perhaps helpful to stress that the frontier was not so much a place as an experience, a constantly shifting area in which the formative sensation was that of being free of fully developed civilization.

The most obviously distinctive characteristic of the frontier experience was its physical hardness. Western European man found himself in a strange environment devoid of any supportive institutions. . . . When it was a question literally of life or death it was not enough to take a line of action simply because that was the done thing back in Europe. Thus, for instance, it would not do to allow an individual to take charge simply because he was the son of the last leader, a member of the natural ruling class; that might be admirable in a settled community where continuity was prized, but on the frontier it would be necessary to ask if the would-be leader had the required qualities, was in fact the best man for the job.

But the rejection of the traditional went much further than this one instance, the rejection of oligarchy. . . . A more important casualty of the frontier . . . was culture . . . . Culture was a luxury that many communities simply could not afford, and it may be that that strain of anti-intellectualism that runs through American history had its strength in the continuing frontier experience. . . . American education, which has represented a tremendous commitment both of intellectual and material resources, has always stressed practical knowledge and directed expertise more than has European education, where the aim was the total moulding of the pupil.

The initial effect of the frontier, then, was to tear away much of the intellectual baggage that the settlers had brought with them from civilization, whether from Europe, or as time passed, from the eastern seaboard. But the frontier also had a positive role to play by fostering new values and then feeding them into the mainstream of American life. . . . In short, what the frontier valued were those things that worked, that enabled man to survive and prosper. Thus adaptability was praised, but even more so was inventiveness, technical inventiveness above all, and that tradition has been well-marked from the days of Whitney through Henry Ford down to the space triumphs. . . .

But if the frontier experience encouraged Americans to apply the test 'does it work?', 'is it useful?' it remains to ask for whom should it work? for whom should it be useful? The answer, of course, was: for the individual, and one of the major elements of frontier life was the emphasis given to the notion of the autonomous being. It may be seen in many different contexts. A good example would be the lawlessness of American life, a generalized attitude whose religious equivalent is antinomianism. It was the essence of the frontier that it was the area ahead of settled society, and this meant first and foremost ahead of law and order. On the frontier each man had to take the law into his own hands, a tradition that is kept alive in each cowboy epic. And when anarchy became too much to bear and some antidote became necessary, it was vigilante justice that was supplied, that is, a rough-and-ready popular justice devoid of abstractions and legalities; the punishments often fitted the rough extremism of the frontier, and lynch hangings were frequent.

This was the less pleasant side of frontier individualism. In a more elevated guise the same values could be seen in the kind of democratic theory worked out under American conditions. Those manifestations referred to throughout this account—Jeffersonism, Jacksonism, Populism—may be seen as the natural product of an agrarian frontier where the mass of people were alike in being upwardly mobile, property-owning individuals who instinctively reacted against the slightest sign of privilege and hierarchy. That these suspicious, resentment-filled movements should also have insisted upon elective institutions (school boards, judges, and so on) underlines the point already made that frontier conditions will breed a distrust of the specialist. At the same time it may be noted that it was the more westerly states, those that had had the largest exposure to the frontier mentality, that were first introducing 'progressive' legislation. Thus in the early nineteenth century, on the eve of Jacksonian democracy, it was the newer states that led the way in removing the last traces of property qualification for voting. It was western states in the latter portion of the nineteenth century that pioneered many of the social-security measures only later accepted by the east and federally, and it was in the western states that votes for women were earliest granted; after all, on the frontier a woman's worth was made abundantly evident as she took a full part in the work of winning a living from the land.

The frontier encouraged direct democracy, then, and an essential part of this was an emphasis upon localism. Unlike the British-Canadian practice, Americans have always insisted upon a representative's coming from the people he claims to represent; thus a senator from, say New York, must reside in that state. Then, too, there has long been a tradition of leaving the locality to settle its own affairs as far as possible without any interference from the outside. Schools, for instance, were always very local affairs, with control vested in a board locally elected. But the best example of frontier localism comes in religion. . . . Congregationalists, Methodists, and above all Baptists were ideally suited to frontier conditions and prospered accordingly. Even the Anglicans submitted to the frontier spirit. . . .

Above it was asked to whom the pragmatic test 'does it work?' was applied. The answer was for the individual, and these instances just given provide some idea of the dimensions of individualism in America. But the answer is not complete, for another question remains. Just what is the test of whether it works? What, in fact, is that 'it'? Here one needs to be reminded of a point in connection with the frontier thesis made most forcefully by a disciple of Turner, writing quite recently. In his valuable book *The Great Frontier*, W.P. Webb defines the frontier as the area of unappropriate surpluses; on the frontier are vast amounts of land, gold and silver, other mineral deposits, timber, grassland, and other resources that belong to no one (the Indians being in no position to withstand the Europeans), which can be seized without too great an outlay of effort, and which within a short while can be made to yield splendid profits. With these dazzling prospects in view the initial work of merely surviving is quickly transmuted into something very different, a determination to realize the tremendous possibilities that exist. In the absence of inherited restraints and alternative cultural ends, themselves stripped away by the frontier experience, work becomes not only a means but an end. Good is what conduces to wealth and the free mobilization of wealth. Hence the Yankee bustle, the concentration upon quick service, the time-is-money syndrome. Hence the impatience with primogeniture and entail, legal devices that stand in the way of an individual's developing his own full potential through the use of freely realized assets. As Webb has pointed out, the indigenous American folk heroes have been characters like Paul Bunyan and John Henry, giants able to work in herculean manner to tame the frontier and make it yield up its wealth. The American realizes his individualism less in being than in doing, and preferably in doing something tangible that will transform raw nature. It is in this sense that the American people are the people of the boom, not in the superficial sense of the Wall Street surge of the late twenties but in the deeper sense of four-hundred-year commitment to subduing challenge after challenge, each greater than the last.

One final point made by the frontier thesis may be noted here. The frontier acts as a safety valve. Whenever discontent builds up in the settled areas there will be a movement away from the sources of frustration to the new start possible in the west. In this way the pressure of reform within the main body of society is always kept within reasonable bounds and outright, fundamental rebellion is unlikely. At the same time it has been argued that the drain of manpower from the east meant a perpetual shortage of workers. Consequently those who remained were in a position to demand good wages, which further lessened the likelihood of revolution. . . . In particular the lack of long-contained discontent, together with the possibility of land on which a settler could become his own master and start moving upward in the socio-economic scale, was held to be a major factor in inhibiting the rise of an independent labour movement and above all of socialism. As indicated previously, the American worker thought less of overthrowing the bosses than of eventually joining them, and the continued existence of the frontier made this a valid belief over many years—and even after the 1890's, of course.

Naturally the Turner thesis came in for its share of criticism. It was pointed out that his terminology was vague and that certain of his observations were contradictory. Others went to the facts to claim that they disproved Turner; thus the safety-valve aspect was declared rejected when it was established that long before 1890 the urban areas were being peopled not solely from over-crowded Europe but also from the frontier. Then, too, it was urged that any aggressive, progressive attitudes discernible in the west might be due not so much to the frontier setting as to the fact that the population in these parts was a self-selected one, made up of younger, more ambitious types than those in the settled east; in other words migration rather than frontier might be the key. This is not the place to go into the revision in detail, and it may also be noted that the latest trend seems to be revising the revisers so as to re-establish the essence of what Turner was saying. The frontier thesis still provides valuable insight into American development, and may profitably be reflected upon.

And so presented, the frontier thesis is an environmentally determinist one; a transitional area between civilization and wilderness exists and has certain consequences for the total society. At the same time it is a thesis that stresses the independence of America from Europe. To take one major example; on the Turner theory, American democracy must be seen as something indigenous, not as the taking over of European ideas; as it is often put, American democracy was 'forest born'. Those who incline to the frontier hypothesis must play down the European heritage of American civilization, and at the same time must tend to see American civilization in its widest sense, i.e., not simply as the United States but possibly as the entire Northern and Southern American hemisphere, and certainly as the whole of North America: the United States and Canada. Thus the question inevitably arose, can Canadian history be explained in terms of the Turner hypothesis?

The attempt has been made on several occasions. Those eager to fit Canadian developments into the frontier thesis would point to the following facts. It was the intention of the authorities to impose absolutism in New France, an undertaking in which they were in the main successful. But there were certain departures from the blueprint. Thus the lightness of the feudal obligations is striking when set against those in the mother country. The tithe, in particular, is a case in point. It was not until 1663 that a tithe was made compulsory, and even then it was fixed at the low level of one twenty-sixth of the wheat crop as against (usually) one thirteenth of the total farm produce in France. This lightness was to be explained, it was held, by the fact that the frontier's existence made it possible for settlers, if pushed too far, to leave the main area of the colony and escape burdens altogether. Then it was noted that for a while at least the militia captains were elected officials, that is democratically selected, and that even the later appointments were a disguised form of popular choice. This fact pointed to the democratic spirit and the need to elect the best that marked frontier conditions.

Upper Canada was held to provide even better evidence of the frontier spirit. In its early formative years the province had been settled by the 'Late Loyalists', that is, by the natural westward push of settlement that even then was founding such states as Ohio. Thus in time Upper Canada produced its American-style democrats—Gourlay with his probing inquiries and 'conventions', and better still Mackenzie with his Jacksonian tinge. That it was the western, i.e. frontier, portion of Upper Canada that was prominent in the 1837 rising was taken as very powerful confirmation of the frontier thesis. And then when the democratic impulse revived in the 1850's and 1860's that same frontier spirit was committed to universal suffrage, elected governors, elected upper houses, elected public functionaries, and the secularization of the clergy reserves for public education along American lines.

And finally the Progressives of the inter-war years were pointed to as major examples of the frontier spirit. The roots of this movement had been laid down in Alberta on the eve of the war, at a time when that province represented the last significant frontier still open and when it was attracting a large proportion of settlers from America. The views of Wood and the repudiation of party government have been outlined above; they may be seen as manifestations of a frontier mentality.

But no sooner had the applications been made than the unsatisfactory nature of the case became evident. New France really yielded little confirmation of the theory. To set against the lightness of the tithe obligations and the existence of a quasi-elective official were the more important facts that individualism in the Turnerian sense did not develop in that society, that democracy was always a weak growth (witness the failure of the *Rouges* to develop into a viable political party), and that extensive genuine radicalness was, until the very recent period, missing from the province. Indeed the French-Canadian experience of colonization is a very significant one. By 1870 Quebec was over-populated and many French Canadians were moving to the north-eastern United States. This drift away from the traditional occupation on the land was viewed by many influential people with regret, and colonization societies were formed to keep the '*habitant*' on the land. Now just at that time Manitoba was opened to settlement. But very few French Canadians could be tempted there. What agricultural settlement there was went to the unpromising areas of northern Quebec; in other words the French-Canadian population lacked that pioneering spirit that, say, took the Mormons to Utah. Considerations like these have led A.I. Silver, writing the *Canadian Historical Review* of 1969 [see pp. 134-36] to question the frontier thesis by asking whether Turner did not have the cart before the horse; in other words, did a certain mentality form the frontier rather than the reverse?

Against this rejoinder it may be urged that French Canada never had a frontier in the sense that the United States did. Turner, who did not bother with comparative studies, instinctively took as the norm a frontier where the settler was cut off from more settled society and more civilized pressures and where the preferred unit of settlement was the individual family farm. It may be said that both these were lacking in New France—Quebec. There the power of absolutism was great from the start and there never was a significant time and area free from such control; the few exceptions were the *coureurs de bois* and they were by definition not settlers but traders incapable of communicating any positive values to a society (except, perhaps, that because the employer, the fur trade, needed Indian co-operation the French had a better record of Indian relations than the Anglo-Americans whose farming settlement was so dominant that possession of the land became all-important and Indians were driven off or exterminated; but such a point is peripheral to the main argument). And French-Canadian farms were never such individualistic enterprises, the basis of speculators' fortunes, as in the United States; the static farm, often subdivided among children, and the static parish, were the characteristics of Quebec. Thus, it is argued, the frontier as Turner assumed it had no chance to work its impact along the lower St. Lawrence.

Unfortunately for this counterargument, the example of Upper Canada is no better. Again the instances of frontier impact may be submerged in contrary examples. United States history has been full of frontier risings—the Regulators, Shays, and Kansas-Nebraska have been mentioned, and there have been many, many more both before and after these just mentioned. The same has not been true of Upper Canada. The one real rising, Mackenzie's, had to wait until 1837, and it took a world trading depression to trigger it off. Even then the impressive thing about 1837 is the lack of support that Mackenzie could drum up; the province was soon restored to peace and quiet with little bloodshed, and Mackenzie could eventually be allowed to return and to take part in political life. Basically the same may be said of the Grits; how quickly were their universal-suffrage ideas and elective proclivities forgotten in an acceptance of more British notions championed by George Brown and his *Globe* newspaper.

And briefly to round out his questioning of the applicability of frontier theory to Canada, the passing impact of Progressivism may be noted. The Progressive independence did not long maintain itself in its non-party guise but quickly transformed itself into the more British experiment of the socialist party.

And here the root failure of the frontier thesis for Canada is touched upon. Although Canada does share some North American traits with the United States, there is still an awkward amount of 'Britishness' (or possibly it would be better to say 'Old Worldness') about the country. In particular there is the fact that while the United States has failed to produce a socialist tradition, Canada, like Britain, has. Recognition of these facts has encouraged historians to develop alternative theories to account for Canada's distinctive evolution.

The origins of an alternative account, more sophisticated than the early theories that simply accepted that as a colony Canada would be essentially British, are to be found in the economic histories of H.A. Innis, many of which were studies of individual staple trades. Innis stressed the point that these trades required the financial help and marketing skills of the already developed mother country, and in particular that the dominance of the St. Lawrence as a continuation, so to speak, of the Atlantic helped to structure trade and society about that river. So prominent did this great highway loom in his writing, and in that of the similarly orientated D.G. Creighton, that a school of interpretation known as the Laurentian was recognized. And just a little later the impact of the Second World War encouraged other scholars to stress the trans-Atlantic links; J.B. Brebner's *North Atlantic Triangle*, first published in 1945, was originally intended to be a study in Canadian-American relations but was widened as the author felt more and more obliged to take note of British impact. More recently still, these strains have developed into the theory known as metropolitanism, a theory in Canada connected above all with J.M.S. Careless.

This theory seizes upon the fact that certain centres grow to unusual prominence. The economic historian who first used the term in this way, N.S.G. Gras, noted four stages in the growth of the super-centre; first the market in the surrounding area is organized to hinge on the centre; then the centre develops an industrial base; transportation is next improved so that industrial goods may be better distributed over the metropolitan hinterland and agricultural products and other goods may also flow easily in the reverse direction; and finally the metropolis develops major financial institutions and know-how, so that it may continue to finance and direct the economic activity of the area tributary to itself. But Careless's emphasis is upon the socio-cultural control that may parallel such economic dominance. Thus the entire St. Lawrence trading system down to 1849, when it was undermined by the establishment of free trade and the repeal of the Navigation Acts, was a means of ensuring the dominance of London and London values over the area, since the headquarters and finance of the trades were based there. At the same time, however, metropolitanism can operate at a subordinate level; thus within Canada itself Montreal acted as a metropolis, establishing its cultural imperialism over the hinterland. And at different periods and at different levels other Canadian centres have acted as metropolies; Toronto early became the focal point and 'organizer' of Ontario, especially the southern portion; Winnipeg performed the same function for the prairies, but as hinted earlier modern communication means that Winnipeg is losing that status as the emphasis moves as far afield as Toronto or Montreal. Meanwhile Vancouver, thanks to a growing Pacific orientation on Canada's part, has risen to metropolitan rank, and as the far north opens up Edmonton may do the same.

Careless would say that in terms of historical development the interaction between the metropolis and the hinterland is complementary. The hinterland is the area where grievances develop; thus in the 1830's the western Upper Canadian farmers felt discriminated against and exploited; in the fifties and sixties there was much the same feeling as the possibilities of further settlement became less and less; by the first decades of the twentieth century the prairies were convinced that eastern interests were ruining western potential. But it is in the metropolis that the solutions are worked out, that the grievances are formed into a political movement. Mackenzie was a newspaperman in Toronto and it was from there that his *Colonial Advocate* was put together and sent out to the smaller towns and rural areas, giving form to the inchoate protests of the backwoods. By the time of the Clear Grits it was George Brown and *The Globe*, again Toronto-based, that performed this service. And in the case of the western Progressives there was the Winnipeg-based *Grain Growers Guide* to offset the mainline liberalism disseminated through the *Winnipeg Free Press* of John Defoe.

It will be seen that metropolitanism does not wholly contradict the frontier thesis, for it too allows that frontier conditions may destroy the old loyalties and certainties. But whereas Turner held that the frontier could supply its own positive antidote to its negative work, Careless stresses the fact that more civilized forces were at work in the task of building up. And what makes metropolitanism more attractive to historians of Canada than to those of the United States is the realization that geography and history have helped in Canada's case to magnify the impact of the capital city. Canada has always been thinly populated, and with the exception of the *coureurs de bois* who were unable to make a lasting impact, the people always found it necessary to huddle together; the *'habitants'* of Lower Canada found this particularly natural since their religion and its parish structure held them to centripetal forces; in Upper Canada the Canadian Shield prevented the early spread of settlement and acted as a dam to keep the settlement relatively more compact and metropolis-bound than was the case in the American middle west. And when that dam broke in 1870 the settlement of the prairies coincided with the development of the railway and the tele-graph-telephone, methods of communication that enabled the 'frontiersman' of Canada to be kept in touch with the more settled values.

From John L. Finlay, *Canada in the North Atlantic Triangle: Two Centuries of Social Change*. (Toronto: Oxford University Press, 1975).

1. What case does Finlay make for the application of the frontier thesis to the United States?
2. What counter-case does the author make for rejecting the frontier thesis for Canada?
3. Create and defend your own thesis with regard to the influence of the frontier on the historical experiences of the North Americans.

Settlement and the Frontier: Analysis and Application

1. Account for the popularity of the concept of the frontier theory in the "age of imperialism" in the late nineteenth century.

2. Organize a panel discussion on the frontier theory. With two classmates create a panel of three: Turner (or one of his later supporters), an American critic, and a Canadian critic. Have each individual present her or his basic argument in support of or in opposition to the frontier thesis.

Stage the presentation in front of the class and then open the discussion for questions from the floor. You may wish to appoint a moderator to field questions and to summarize the discussion.

3. Select and expand upon one Canadian adaptation of the frontier thesis. You may wish to read the entire text of one of the original sources presented in the chapter, then analyse its arguments. In your analytical review, be certain to identify and comment upon the thesis developed by the author.

4. Conduct a book seminar on the impact of the frontier. Divide the class into seminar groups. Have each member of the group select a different work of fiction/ non-fiction based on the frontier experience. Examples might include *Roughing it in the Bush*, by Susanna Moodie, *Settlers of the Marsh*, by F.P. Grove, or *Klondike*, by Pierre Berton.

Have each member of the group give an oral summary of the book s/he has read, discussing such factors as:
(i) the nature of the frontier;
(ii) the social impact of the frontier experience; and
(iii) the applicability of Turner's thesis.
Group members should also prepare thought-provoking questions to stimulate discussion during the seminar.

5. Re-examine J.L. Finlay's interpretation of the relative differences in the frontier experiences of the two North American nations. Write a position paper in which you agree or disagree with his thesis. Give reasons for your point of view.

6
Identity and Nationhood

Today, Canadians and Americans tend to take their own sense of nationality for granted. Over the past two decades in Canada there has been a great deal of soul searching to attempt to define what is really meant by the Canadian "identity." In spite of this, a fundamental understanding that Canadians are not Americans in the national sense of the word has prevailed. It may seem odd to think of a country attempting to define its own nationality in terms of what it is not. However, if we examine the historical record, we can clearly see how this idea got its start.

The first three decades of the nineteenth century were years of consolidation and readjustment in eastern North America. At the beginning of the period, perhaps the only clearly defined national group existed in the colony of Lower Canada along the St. Lawrence River. Based upon two centuries of development and defended by the guarantees of the Quebec Act, the Canadiens had a clear vision of their nationality and homeland. Attitudes in the British colonies in North America were not so clear-cut.

The War of Independence had liberated the Thirteen Colonies from British rule. The Revolution had been against Britain but had not established a clear national purpose beyond that. In spite of efforts by people like linguist Noah Webster and artist John Trumbull to create a new national culture, events, such as the ratification controversy and the growth of political faction, showed that the new nation still thought in regional rather than national terms.

The new Loyalist colony of Upper Canada had an even vaguer notion of its own identity. Peopled by a combination of Loyalist migrants, veterans, and American settlers, by 1810 the colony was little more than a geographic location. No solid common ground had yet appeared.

For these three societies, the years 1812 to 1814 would provide a catalyst to speed up the process of national awareness. By 1820 the parameters of nationhood would be clearly established.

Nationalism and the War of 1812

Many American historians have referred to the War of 1812 as the Second War of Independence. In a real sense, the grievances that led to the conflict indicated that the British government, in the early nineteenth century, still failed to treat the young republic as a full member of the community of nations. One arena of conflict was at sea.

Britain and France were locked in conflict in the ongoing French Revolutionary/ Napoleonic wars. American ships were boarded and reboarded by French and British crews attempting to enforce the trade restrictions imposed by Napoleon's Continental System and the British Orders in Council, respectively. Although both European powers violated American sovereignty, it was the more powerful British navy that had the greatest impact upon American shipping. As if this indignity was not enough, a second maritime issue also poisoned relations between the two countries.

Many British seamen often jumped ship rather than endure the hardships of life in the British navy. Since they could not return to England, many travelled to the only English-speaking neutral country, the United States. There they took jobs on American merchant ships or in the United States navy where the life and pay were much better. If these men were found on American ships boarded under the Orders in Council, they were immediately arrested and returned to England.

The situation had reached crisis proportions for both sides. The British had a legitimate complaint. They had lost between four thousand and five thousand men since 1803. On the U.S.S. *Constitution* alone, about 150 of the crew of 419 men were British subjects. The Americans, however, rightly resented the obvious insult to their national pride that these incidents represented (see readings).

The issue came to a head in June 1807. The American warship *Chesapeake*, with a number of British deserters among its crew, was ordered to halt for boarding by the captain of the British frigate *Leopard*. Since they were only 16 km off of the American coast, the captain of the *Chesapeake* refused. The *Leopard* attacked and quickly disabled the *Chesapeake*. After boarding, the British seized four men; only one was a British deserter. The others included one man born in Maryland, one Black, and one Indian. The country was outraged, and war fever ran high in Congress.

The American president, Thomas Jefferson, responded with an economic measure of his own. Under his direction Congress passed an Embargo Act that forbade trade with all foreign nations. Jefferson planned to bring Europe to its knees. It didn't quite work out that way, however. For the next fourteen months, American shipping came to a standstill. Britain and France felt the pinch, but it was the United States that paid the highest price. There were some leaks, of course. Trade across the Great Lakes increased, as did smuggling. British North America benefitted from the arrival of a number of skilled shipbuilders and dock workers who could no longer find jobs in American ports. The South survived fairly well, but Jefferson's policies were particularly devastating in New England and along the Eastern Seaboard. Finally, Jefferson had to admit that he had been wrong.

In the face of a threatened secession movement in New England, Jefferson backed down. The Embargo Act was replaced by a much weaker "non-intercourse" bill. It left the door open to settlement and appeared to be a conciliatory move. In fact, it was an admission of failure. In one of his last official acts as president, Thomas Jefferson signed a bill on March 1, 1809, to end the embargo. Three days later his term was over and he headed into retirement.

The maritime conflict was only one concern. There was trouble on the frontier as well. In 1794, following the Battle of Fallen Timbers and the signing of Jay's Treaty, it appeared that the United States had a free hand in the Northwest. American settlement policy all but ignored the existence of the Native inhabitants of the region. The Indian nations, on the other hand, could not ignore the advance of settlers into their territory.

After 1805, two leaders emerged in the Northwest territory, Tecumseh, a chief of the Shawnee people, and his brother, the Prophet. Travelling from nation to nation, they began to overcome traditional hostilities and to forge a united Native confederacy against the growing invasion. Tecumseh's powerful skills of oratory, combined with his brother's vision of a new "golden age" of Native culture, had a significant impact upon their audience. By 1810 it appeared that a new independent Indian nation could be established in the West.

The United States moved to stop Tecumseh, but their means were questionable. In 1809, William Henry Harrison, the governor of Indiana Territory, rounded up a number of Indians, whom he described as "the most depraved wretches on earth." In a "formal" ceremony Harrison had these "representatives" sign over 1.2 million ha of land to the Americans. Tecumseh was incensed and denounced the deal:

> The white people have no right to take the land from the Indians, because they had it first. It is theirs. They may sell, but all must join. Any sale not made by all is not valid. The late sale is bad. It was made by part only. Part do not know how to sell. It requires all to make a bargain for all.

Following this Treaty of Fort Wayne, the confederacy stepped up its activities. American settlers in the region felt the impact of this move. Repeated Native attacks convinced local authorities that Tecumseh must be stopped. Under the leadership of Harrison a force of over eleven hundred American soldiers attacked Tecumseh's headquarters at Tippecanoe Creek in November 1811. The battle was indecisive, but Tecumseh was forced to abandon his camp, which was burned along with the local villages and crops.

The Indians were well-armed. Harrison, and most Americans, were convinced that the British were deliberately supplying the Natives with weapons to use against the settlers. The truth was quite the opposite. From 1807 on the Indian Department was increasingly active in its attempts to restrain the confederacy from attacking. They worried that any Indian attacks would result in American counterattacks against their own settlers in Upper Canada. The British were arming the Natives, but for defensive reasons. If they were to defend their sparsely populated colony they needed the Natives as allies (see readings).

Midwestern North America was in a state of cold war by the end of 1811. Only cool heads and reasonable negotiation could prevent hostilities from erupting. Would there be war, or would Washington and London provide a solution?

James Madison was elected president in 1809. Madison was a great statesman but a naive politician. Jefferson had left the country in economic turmoil. Now Madison had to find a way to restore order. He offered to resume trade with Great Britain if they would exempt the United States from the Orders in Council. They refused. He turned to Congress for help, but their ideas were no better than his.

First Congress reduced the size of the army and the navy; it was hardly a move that pressured either the English or the French, however. Secondly, in May of 1810, they passed Macon's Bill Number 2 which restored full trade with Europe. It included a clause that said that if either Britain or France repealed their laws against the United States, the Americans would renew their embargo against the other. Trade with England soon picked up, and New England began to recover from the suffering caused by the embargo.

A lithograph of the British attacking Washington in 1814
A medal struck to commemorate "Upper Canada" preserved in the War of 1812
Detail from a period painting of the battle of Queenston Heights

It was a short-lived solution, however. Napoleon saw the embargo clause as his opportunity to include the United States within his Continental System. He called off his action against the Americans. In March 1811, Madison acted against the advice of his advisors and renewed the embargo against Britain. It hurt the British who were struggling against Napoleon in Spain; it hurt New England who depended upon British business; and it pushed the countries closer to war. Had Britain responded quickly and exempted the United States from the Orders in Council there might have been peace. This eventually happened, but it was already too late.

"Free Trade and Sailors' Rights" was the rallying cry for war. This might have made sense in 1807, but not in 1812. In the final analysis, war probably came less because it had to, and more because people wanted it to.

There was a growing feeling of nationalism in the United States. Many people, particularly in the West, wanted a chance to prove themselves in the eyes of the world. One group in particular agitated for war. These Western congressmen, labelled "War Hawks," were led by Henry Clay of Kentucky. They agreed with Thomas Jefferson when he said that "the acquisition of Canada . . . would be a mere matter of marching." This sentiment was not held by all Americans, however. When Madison brought his "War Message" to Congress in June of 1812, eight New England senators voted against it, as did a majority of their representatives in the House; New York, New Jersey, and Maryland all joined in opposition. It was not enough. On June 18th the United States was officially at war.

Madison expressed his view of the reasons for the war in his "War Message" delivered to Congress on June 1, 1812.

> . . . The conduct of her [Great Britain's] government presents a series of acts hostile to the United States as an independent and neutral nation. British cruisers have been in the continued practice of violating the American flag on the great highway of nations, and of seizing and carrying off persons sailing under it . . .
>
> Not content with these occasional expedients for laying waste our neutral trade, the cabinet of Britain resorted at length to the sweeping system of blockades under the name of orders in council . . .
>
> We behold our seafaring citizens still the daily victims of lawless violence . . .
> We behold our vessels . . . wrested from their lawful destinations . . .
> We behold, in fine, on the side of Great Britain a state of war against the United States, and on the side of the United States a state of peace toward Great Britain.

The references to the "violations" of the American flag, to "seizures" of persons, to the "laying waste" of trade, and to "lawless violence" clearly indicate that Madison and his supporters believed that Great Britain was violating the rights of American citizens at sea. For Madison the slogan "Free Trade and Sailor's Rights" crystallized the basic nature of the dispute (see readings).

Although the war claimed to be about rights at sea, it was not a naval conflict. The main target was Upper Canada.

Those in Congress who opposed the war were not deceived. They refused to accept Madison's claim that naval concerns were the prime motive for war. John Randolph of Roanoake, Virginia, pointed out the inconsistencies:

Agrarian cupidity not maritime right urges this war. Ever since the report of the Committee on Foreign Relations came into the House, we have heard but one word like the whip-poor-will, but one eternal monotonous tone— Canada! Canada! Canada! Not a syllable about Halifax, which unquestionably should be our great object in a war for maritime security . . .

Go march to Canada! Leave the broad bosom of the Chesapeake and her hundred tributary rivers unprotected!

Randolph considered the issue of maritime rights to be simply the War Hawks' excuse to acquire Upper Canada. He saw the war as part of a larger movement to extend the boundaries of the republic to cover the entire continent. As Thomas Jefferson had said in 1786: "Our confederacy must be viewed as the nest, from which all America, North and South, is to be peopled."

The decision to attack Upper Canada was hardly surprising. The maritime colonies were strongly Loyalist and easily defended by the British navy. The inhabitants of Lower Canada (Quebec) were hardly pro-British, but they were certainly anti-American. Moreover, with its strong nationalism and well-organized militia system, Lower Canada represented a formidable opponent for the Americans.

The colony had been divided for almost a decade in a political dispute between the English minority and French majority. But when war was declared in 1812 the Assembly of Lower Canada voted more financial support for the conflict than any other colony in British North America.

In their one major attack against the French Canadians at Châteauguay in 1813, the invaders were soundly defeated. Remembering the experience of 1774-75, they quietly went home.

Upper Canada, however, was a different matter altogether. Although this British colony had received a number of Loyalists, by 1812 they were a minority of the population. Most of the settlers living in the frontier province were from the United States. These people had come, not to escape republicanism, but rather because of the attraction of available land safe from Indian attack. By 1812 eight out of ten Upper Canadians had been born in the United States. American politicans believed that these inhabitants would accept the incoming troops not as invaders but as liberators from British rule. The military leader of Upper Canada, Sir Isaac Brock, agreed with them:

My situation is most critical, not from anything the enemy can do, but from the disposition of the people–The population, believe me is essentially bad– A full belief possesses them all that this Province must inevitably succumb . . . Most of the people have lost all confidence. I however speak loud and look big.

For the most part Upper Canadians saw their best course of action as remaining neutral (see readings). This seemed sensible. On paper, the odds against the Canadians looked overwhelming. The United States had ten times the population; the American army numbered seven thousand, with an additional militia strength of almost seven hundred thousand; the British had fewer than five thousand regulars in North America; and while many Americans appeared to be consumed by "war fever" and eager to fight, the inhabitants of Upper Canada hoped to remain neutral.

In theory Henry Clay was probably right when he claimed in the Senate that "the militia of Kentucky are alone competent to place Montreal and Upper Canada at your feet." In reality, however, neither Kentucky nor any other state militia left its home state. The declaration of war was enough for most Americans. They had shown Great Britain that they would not simply lay down and submit each time that their former mother country rattled its sabre. When it came to actually disrupting their lives and going off to war, most wanted no part of it.

Although there was some militia support, particularly in Indiana and to some extent in New York, for the most part the fighting was left to the American army. These federal forces had been ignored and even reduced in number by Congress in 1810. Their leadership left a great deal to be desired as well; most of the generals in the American army were veterans of the Revolution.

Finally, the United States suffered from a lack of conviction. As we have seen, many parts of the country were opposed to the war. New England, in fact, continued to trade with Britain during the conflict, and even supplied the British troops with food! It is not surprising then that the war began on a note of indecisiveness and defeat.

The American "conquest" of Canada began from the western–most frontier of the colony. On July 12, 1812, Brigadier General William Hull landed at Sandwich (Windsor, Ontario) with a force of two thousand men. Hull had been a commander during the revolutionary war, and was fifty-nine at the time of the Sandwich invasion. On July 13, Hull issued a Proclamation that had been prepared by President Madison. It reflects the attitudes of the administration and is an excellent example of the typical war propoganda of the time.

> Inhabitants of Canada! After thirty years of peace and prosperity, the United States have been driven to arms. The injuries and aggressions, the insults and indignities of Great Britain, have once more left them no alternative but manly resistance or unconditional submission.
>
> The army under my command has invaded your country. . . . To the peaceable, unoffending inhabitant it brings neither danger nor difficulty. I come to find enemies not to make them. I come to protect, not to injure you.
>
> Separated by an immense ocean and an extensive wilderness from Great Britain, you have no participation in her councils, no interest in her conduct. You have felt her tyranny, you have seen her injustice. . . .
>
> I promise protection to your persons, property and rights. . . .
>
> Many of your fathers fought for the freedom and independence which we now enjoy.

Hull's message is clear. He leads an army of occupation. There is only passing reference to the causes of the war in the first line. After that the proclamation is one of liberation. Hull compares the situation in Upper Canada to that of the Thirteen Colonies in 1776. It is clearly his hope that there will be no war at all. Like many of the War Hawks, Hull felt that Upper Canada would fall into his lap.

Sir Isaac Brock responded to Hull's proclamation ten days later.

. . . Where is the Canadian subject who can truly affirm to himself that he has been injured by the Government in his person, his property, or his liberty? . . .

Settled not thirty years ago by a band of veterans exiled from their former possessions on account of their loyalty, not a descendant of these brave people is to be found who . . . has not acquired a property and means of enjoyment superior to what were possessed by their ancestors. . . .

Are you prepared, inhabitants of Canada, to become the willing subjects–or rather slaves–to the despot [Napoleon] who rules the nations of continental Europe with a rod of iron? If not, arise in a body, exert your energies, co-operate cordially with the King's regular forces to repel the invader, and do not give cause to your children, when groaning under the oppression of a foreign master, to reproach you with having so easily parted with the richest inheritance of this earth–a participation in the name, character, and freedom of Britons.

Brock made an effective counter to Hull's proclamation. Using the same vocabulary he addressed the same "inhabitants of Canada" in his appeal. In Brock's declaration we find the roots of one facet of Upper Canadian nationalism. But it would be the course of the war that would give rise to a new feeling of distinct identity for the young colony.

Hull's foothold at Sandwich was short-lived. News of an advancing force of regulars, militia, and Natives under Brock convinced Hull to retreat to Detroit. Brock, with about one-third of the men that the Americans had, threatened to take Detroit. A salvo of cannon was fired into the stronghold. One shell hit the officers' mess, killing four men. Hull panicked and surrendered, ending the first invasion of Canada. In this case the Americans had actually lost territory. Hull was later court-martialled. His excellent war record during the Revolution saved him from execution.

A second invasion attempt at Queenston Heights on the Niagara Peninsula was more successful. Brock was killed during the battle, but a British-Canadian counterattack managed to drive the American troops back across the Niagara River. A third attempt, this time against Montreal, came to an abrupt end when the New York militia refused to leave its state.

By the end of 1812, the war was going badly. All the attempted invasions had failed, and now the British held American territory in Michigan.

The next year was better. In April an American force invaded and burned York (Toronto), the capital of Upper Canada. On September 10th, in the Battle of Put

In Bay on Lake Erie, Captain Oliver Hazard Perry defeated a British naval squadron and took control of the lake. This isolated the British forces in Detroit. While retreating through Upper Canada, they were attacked by advancing American troops under Harrison. In the Battle of the Thames near Moraviantown on October 5th, the British suffered a decisive defeat. The greatest loss was the death of Tecumseh, who was killed in the battle. The year ended on a losing note, however. The French–Canadian victory at Chateauguay in October, followed by a defeat of the Americans at Chrysler's Farm on the St. Lawrence River in November, stopped any further advances.

These invasions had an unexpected effect in Upper Canada. At the outset of war, the population, for the most part, had been indifferent as to the outcome. Now they found their homes being attacked and their businesses, farms, and crops being burned by the invaders. A growing sense of nationalism began to emerge, based less on loyalty to Britain and more on the defence of their own land. Just as the British actions of 1774-76 had created rebels in the Thirteen Colonies where none had existed, the American invasions of 1812-13 created Canadians where they had not been before (see readings).

The final year of the war saw a British resurgence. With the collapse of Napoleon's empire in Europe, the British navy was finally freed up for a concerted attack on the Eastern Seaboard.

A British task force sailed up Chesapeake Bay and landed troops, who marched on Washington. Madison and the Americans deserted the capital. The president and his family left so quickly that when British troops arrived at the White House dinner was still warm on the table!

The capital was burned, and a subsequent unsuccessful attack on Baltimore gave rise to the American patriotic national anthem "The Star Spangled Banner." As American historian Glenn Tuckers points out, such retaliatory attacks did not have the demoralizing effect intended:

> Retaliation is an insatiable appetite, a pitcher that will not stay filled. When used against noncombatants it only adds to a war's inhumanity and tends to make victory more difficult–the United States lost Canadian sympathy when Americans burned the border towns . . . after the enemy devastated Washington, [President] Madison at last commanded a virtually united nation.

In spite of these attacks, the Americans were losing interest in the conflict. The British had the stronger hand in the negotiations, but they too had little desire to fight any longer. It was in everyone's best interest to reach an agreement. The Treaty of Ghent was signed on Christmas Eve, 1814. There was nothing in it about "Free Trade and Sailors' Rights!". The treaty dealt with the real issues of the war. Commissions were established to set an official boundary and to establish naval agreements with regards to the Great Lakes. In the final analysis, the war established the independence of British North America and had demonstrated to Britain that the United States was more valuable as a friend than an enemy.

The war had one more ironic twist. Before news of the peace could reach North America, one more battle was fought. On January 8, 1815, a British force of fifty

– three hundred attacked a well-covered and entrenched American force of thirty–
five hundred under General Andrew Jackson. The British marched into gun and
cannon fire from the defenders. When the smoke had cleared they had lost two
thousand men compared with American losses of thirteen dead and fifty–eight
wounded. This Battle of New Orleans gave the Americans the decisive victory
they craved, and helped elect Andrew Jackson president.

Although generations of American and Canadian students have been presented
with clear statements on the outcome of the war, they are differing versions of
history. Canadian historian C.P. Stacey states:

> It was the sober truth that the colony had been successfully defended against
> all odds. Upper Canada had come through a fiery trial. Great deeds had
> been done, and good blood spilled, upon its soil; and future generations . . .
> would look back to the years 1812-14 as a heroic age.

Compare this with the comments of American historian Edwin Fenton on the
impact of the War of 1812:

> Spectacular social and economic growth, coming after a second military
> victory over England, gave a tremendous impetus to national consciousness
> and pride. The United States had proved its right to be treated as an equal
> among the great nations of the world, and its people were proud to be called
> Americans.

The realities of the war soon vanished into the national myths of both countries.

The American System

The War of 1812 was a watershed on both sides of the border. The young American
republic entered an age of harmony and the pursuit of national goals. During the
decade from 1814 to 1824, economic, social, and political objectives were established for the country. This new national feeling was most clearly reflected in the
economy.

Beginning in 1816, Congress initiated a new thrust in economic development.
Senator Henry Clay, the former War Hawk from Kentucky, advocated a new
national policy. Clay's American System had three planks. First, it would encourage local manufacturing; second, it would create local markets in the West for
goods; and finally, it would develop an efficient internal transportation system.

The "new" West was rapidly becoming a major factor in the economic life of
the country. By the beginning of the War of 1812 the combined population of the
region was over 1 million, and there was regular trade in such commodities as
flour, pork, whiskey, tobacco, and hemp carried by flatboat up and down the Ohio
and Mississippi rivers. Things were changing rapidly. At the same time that
Tecumseh was trying to unite the nations along the Mississippi in his confederacy,
the first steamboats were making the trip south from Pittsburgh to New Orleans.

The rate of growth accelerated after 1814. Ohio had become a state in 1803; by 1820 it had a larger population than Massachusetts. In fact, the population of the entire region doubled during this period and four new states were created: Indiana (1816); Mississippi (1817); Illinois (1818); and Alabama (1819). These shifts began to change the face of the whole country. In 1800, 90 percent of the nation lived on farms or in small villages. Economic life was based upon a "family economy." The farm produced staples and bartered surplus crops for other goods. At the beginning of the century, almost five hundred thousand families lived this way, but it would not remain so for long.

The "new" West was not all rugged frontier. Cities sprang up as trade and commerce flourished in the interior. With wealth came the appearance of social classes. The prominent class was made up of merchants; they were followed in status by professionals, such as lawyers, doctors, and teachers; below these were skilled and unskilled labourers; finally, at the bottom of the social scale were the Blacks.

The upper classes frequented exclusive social clubs and private schools. In response, the working classes began to organize and to demand such improvements as better wages, shorter hours, adequate housing, and free public education.

The growing population of the West began to have an impact upon government policy. When Jefferson was elected president in 1801, the country consisted of little more than the original states. Two decades later what had been wilderness was now a powerful political force.

The West was to be linked to the South and East with a new transportation network. As John Calhoun proclaimed: "Let us bind the Republic together with a perfect system of roads and canals."

The only thing left was to find some way to safeguard the infant American manufacturing sector. As it stood, the small–scale local factories were no match for the growing industrial might of Great Britain and the continent.

Calhoun and Clay were convinced that the economy of the United States was too weak to survive in the face of European competition. In order to protect local interests from losing out to cheaper foreign products they proposed the creation of a tariff or import tax on certain foreign goods. Tariffs were hard on consumers because they forced them to pay higher prices, but they aided the growth of local industry. Calhoun believed that this move would protect the growing cotton trade and would result in the industrialization of the South. Clay and his constituents were convinced that the revenue from these tariffs would pay the cost of the roads and canals they wanted.

New England was opposed to the plan. Tariff walls would mean a decrease in transatlantic trade. Having just recovered from the embargo and the war, they did not need another recession. Daniel Webster of New Hampshire, considered by some to be the greatest orator in the history of the United States, voiced his opposition, but it was no use. On April 27th the Tariff Act was adopted. Duties of between 15 and 30 percent were applied to such imports as iron, textiles, leather, and paper.

Clay's plan worked but not in the way expected. Webster's New England developed a dynamic industrial base behind the tariff wall, while Calhoun's South became increasingly opposed to the measure as their growing cotton exports moved them toward the idea of freer trade.

Henry Clay's American System was built upon the belief that a strong industrial economy linked by an efficient transportation network to the markets of the West would make the United States a great nation. Such a vision might have seemed like an impossible dream to many in the early years of the nineteenth century. But it was a dream that quickly became a reality.

Initially one might think that the rapid growth of the Midwest would have drawn energy, people, and money away from the traditional financial centres in the East. This was far from the case. In fact, the opening of the West was a "shot in the arm" for the Eastern economy. The growing frontier society provided a much–needed new market for Eastern goods. At the same time, concentration upon the cultivation of cotton in the South meant that that society also began to depend heavily upon Northeastern manufacturing.

As we have already seen, the introduction of steamboats in the Ohio and Mississippi river systems was revolutionizing transportation in that region. By the 1830s over two hundred steamboats were active in the interior. The increased competition forced down rates. Cargoes transported from Louisville, Kentucky, to New Orleans cost $5 per 45 kg (100 lbs) in 1812. Steamboat travel reduced this to $2 by 1820; two decades later competition forced the price down to 25 cents!

This transportation system was of little use to the industrializing Northeast. Shipping goods by sea to New Orleans and then up the river to potential markets raised costs considerably. Business interests began looking for a short–cut, and with little government support they had to provide it themselves. In the first three decades of the nineteenth century, private interests built over 16 000 km of roads and turnpikes. Costing between three and seven thousand dollars per kilometre to build, the roads had to be supported by expensive tolls. This discouraged many farmers from using them to ship goods. Roads became settlers' routes but still did not seem to be the answer for interstate trade.

The problem was this: an excellent water transportation system existed in the interior. How could Eastern cities tap into it? The answer was to build canals. After a slow start (by 1816 there were only about 160 km of canals in the whole country), things began to pick up. Unlike roads, canals were too expensive for private development. It was now up to governments to step in. The first state to gamble on such a move was New York. In 1817 construction began on the Erie Canal to link Albany on the Hudson River with Buffalo on Lake Erie. It seemed like an impossible dream, but by 1825 the route was opened. It had cost $7 million, but was so successful that within ten years the entire cost had been recovered through tolls. By the time the canal stopped charging a fee, in 1882, over $120 million had been collected. Why were people so anxious to use the canal? Primarily because of time and cost. Before the canal was built it took twenty days to ship goods from Albany to Buffalo at a cost of about $100 per tonne. After completion the trip took six days at a cost of only $5.

The success of the Erie Canal sparked a rash of building throughout the Northeast and Midwest. By 1840, only twenty–five years after the canal boom had begun, over 5000 km had been built.

The great cities of the East were reaching into the West. These strong ties would be of critical importance in the sectional crisis to come. In the interim they represented the establishment of a national presence in the interior. Clay's "American System" had become the economic basis for a strong nation state.

Nationalism in the Canadas

It will be told by the future Historian, that the Province of Upper Canada, without the assistance of men or arms, except a handful of regular troops, repelled its invaders . . . and never, surely, was greater activity shewn in any country, than our militia have exhibited, never greater valour, cooler resolution, and more approved conduct; they have emulated the choicest veterans, and they have twice saved the country.

The speaker is likely John Strachan. His praise of the role of the militia (in stark contrast to the opinions of both Sir Isaac Brock and the future historians to whom he refers) was immortalized in the *Report of the Loyal and Patriotic Society of Upper Canada*, published in 1817. True or not, Strachan's view of a loyal and patriotic Upper Canada militia defending its homeland against hopeless odds formed the cornerstone of English–Canadian nationalism in the decades that followed. The War of 1812 guaranteed that such patriotism would be inexorably tied by loyalty to Great Britain. It is hardly surprising that among the names of the members of the "Loyal and Patriotic Society" we find not only such well–known members of the Family Compact as John Strachan and John Beverley Robinson, but influential reformers such as Dr. William Warren Baldwin as well. American republicanism found little support in either of the mainstream political groups in the colony.

This British connection and anti–Americanism inherent in the early development of English–Canadian nationalism, particularly in Upper Canada, bears little resemblance to the growth of national feeling downriver. Lower Canada, as Quebec was called from 1791 until 1841, was the homeland of the Canadiens. Even under French rule, the inhabitants of the St. Lawrence lowlands saw themselves as a national group based in a specific geographic "father land." The passage of New France into the hands of a British King did little to change this sentiment. British settlers, arriving either under the terms of the Royal Proclamation of 1763 or later as part of the Loyalist migrations, were expected by the habitants to integrate into this French–Canadian nation. The creation of Lower Canada by the Constitutional Act of 1791 seemed to guarantee its continued existence.

New democratically elected leaders such as Louis Joseph Papineau emerged during the first decades of the nineteenth century. They established a strong connection between the Canadiens and their government. More and more the assembly was seen as representing the legitimate voice of the people in economic, political, and cultural matters. Attempts by the British minority to restrict the power of the people through the operation of the appointed councils raised both democratic concern and national resentment.

The political issues in both Canadas in the 1830s were primarily economic in nature. In Upper Canada there were two main issues. The first was the system of land distribution and speculation. It interfered with systematic settlement and epitomized many of the worst aspects of the patronage system. The second dispute centred around control of the purse and the expenditure of monies. The councils in Upper Canada were attempting to initiate their own version of Clay's American System through the building of canals and the establishment of tariffs. The assembly, on the other hand, representing mainly agrarian interests, was far more concerned with road improvement and the extension of public services such as education. In Lower Canada too, the councils tended to represent commercial interests such as banking and trade. Their focus, like their Upper Canadian counterpart, tended to be upon industrial development and canal construction. For the assembly, representing a constituency reeling under an agricultural depression during the 1830s, such priorities were all wrong. In both colonies the elected representatives suffered from the same problem. They could air their grievances on the floor of the assembly, but they were powerless to implement even the most basic reforms. In frustration, individuals in both colonies eventually turned to violence. On the surface, then, the issues appeared to be the same; underneath, however, it was a different story.

As we have noted, the debate in Upper Canada was a domestic political one. Although some radicals, such as William Lyon Mackenzie, used republican models and even spoke of annexation, the vast majority of politicians took the British connection for granted. In Lower Canada, on the other hand, the English–dominated councils in opposition to the French–dominated assembly made the political debate appear to be one of a foreign minority wishing to usurp power from the democratically elected representatives of the majority.

By the time of the Rebellions, French Canadian political leaders had come to realize that the solutions to their grievances would not be forthcoming from the British Parliament. Individuals such as Papineau had exhausted the traditional routes of appeal and were left frustrated and disillusioned by the process. It was during this period that many French Canadians began to think of Lower Canada not in terms of one of five British North American colonies, but rather as the homeland of "la nation Canadienne". They looked to the example of the United States and saw in the American revolutionary experience a model of political independence and self-determination. This increasing radicalism would eventually undercut the support of the reform movement. The bulk of the population remained unmoved by republican ideas. They still looked for accommodation and compromise with their British neighbours. For them, Papineau and his supporters had moved too far, too fast.

As the Patriots deserted the corridors of the Assembly for the streets and fields, they increasingly lost support. Moderate French Canadians, the clergy and of course the English minority united in their opposition to the new tactics. Without popular support, and with no American aid forthcoming (President Van Buren enforced a strict neutrality in the conflict) the rebellion was doomed to defeat.

With the eventual defeat of the independence movement, la nation Canadienne did not disappear, rather it realigned itself to defend its rights and its culture within the larger context of British North America.

The resulting rebellions were as different as their causes. The British, however, in their desire to find a common solution, inadvertently created a forum for the development of a new Canadian nationalism. In an attempt to legislate French Canadians into a permanent minority, the Act of Union of 1841 created a combined legislature for the Canadas. The French–speaking representatives of Canada East, however, soon formed a political alliance with like–minded reformers from the English province, and over the next two decades they established a pattern of consultation of cooperation. As a result, the strong Canadien nationalism of Canada East combined with the pro–British and anti–American viewpoints of Canada West to form the compromise that would become Canada.

The French revolutionary wars gave rise to a wide variety of nationalist movements in Europe in the first three decades of the nineteenth century. This nationalist fervour was felt in North America also as the two future continental giants began to express their own ideas of national identity.

In the United States writers and artists gave expression to the vision of the new American nation early in the century. After the War of 1812 these sentiments found expression in such foreign policy initiatives as the Monroe Doctrine and in commercial ventures such as Clay's American System.

In the Canadas two different visions of North American nationhood emerged during the same period. The crisis of the rebellions of 1837–38 forced these visions of Canada to merge and gave impetus to the Confederation movement of the 1860s. The debates of the 1980s reflected the roots of this relationship. The Meech Lake Accord with its reference to a "distinct society" in Quebec touched a responsive chord in the descendants of the "patriotes" of 150 years earlier. Likewise the debate over free trade reflected the fundamental concerns about American domination that have haunted English–speaking Canadians since the War of 1812.

As with those of the 1830s, for the North Americans of the 1980s identity and nation still remain inexorably linked.

Washington's Farewell Address, 1796

Washington's farewell address has often been cited as the first articulation of isolationism as a thrust in American foreign policy. In another light, however, the outgoing president's warning to avoid "entangling alliances" represents a clear statement that neutrality was essential to establishing a clear national purpose and identity.

September 17, 1796

Friends and Fellow Citizens:

. . . It will be worthy of a free, enlightened, and at no distant period a great nation to give to mankind the magnanimous and too novel example of a people always guided by an exalted justice and benevolence. . . .

. . . Sympathy for the favorite nation, facilitating the illusion of an imaginary common interest in cases where no real common interest exists, and infusing into one the enmities of the other, betrays the former into a participation in the quarrels and wars of the latter without adequate inducement or justification. . . .

Against the insidious wiles of foreign influence (I conjure you to believe me, fellow–citizens) the jealousy of a free people ought to be *constantly* awake, since history and experience prove that foreign influence is one of the most baneful foes of republican government. But that jealousy, to be useful, must be impartial, else it becomes the instrument of the very influence to be avoided, instead of a defense against it. . . .

The great rule of conduct for us in regard to foreign nations is, in extending our commercial relations to have with them as little *political* connection as possible. So far as we have already formed engagements let them be fulfilled with perfect good faith. Here let us stop.

From Thomas P. Brockway, *Basic Documents in U.S. Foreign Policy* (Princeton, New Jersey: Van Nostrand, 1957).

The North American, 1783

In 1783 future president James Madison stated the case for a strong nation based upon a dominant central government.

The British Empire in America (prior to the late revolution) in the progress of population, and the rapid encrease [sic] of wealth and power, had no paralel [sic] in the annals of mankind.—These are proofs of the influence of mild and gentle forms of government and of an happy state of civil society, . . . which however of late discoloured by British insolence and barbarity, and veiled by necessary prejudices, may in the present stage of the contest, meet with the unreserved acknowledgements of the most strenuous assertors of American independence.—The principles too of political liberty, deeply rooted in the first establishments of the colonies, had flourished with such unrestrained luxuriance, that the anticipation of distant tyranny gave birth to opposition more firm and unanimous, than the iron rod of despotism wielded with unrelenting fury, had ever roused mankind to, in other climes.

The independence of the Thirteen States, has added dignity to our government, but it for *this* our peace and social happiness are to be exchanged; the splendour of sovereignty will only rescue from obscurity the wretchedness of our citizens, and transmit a melancholy lesson, to future ages, never to desert solid systems which have yielded freedom and tranquility, to pursue the dreams and phantoms of theory and speculation.

. . . What we dignify with the appelation of *patriotism*—that the exertion of this principle being as advantageous to a republic, as it is useful to a man,— whoever will make the interest of his country his own, and shew a blind devotion to its views and prejudices, will find the road open to its dignities and employments, and will be honoured with the flattering distinction of *patriot—*

and that the competition of interests and the desire of rulers to exalt their respective communities have laid the foundation of those wars which have desolated the world, and entailed misery on the human race.

Unhappily then for America, the separate sovereignties of our respective States, have left these principles to act with a force, but feebly restrained by the weak barrier of a nominal *union*.

From Irving Brant, *James Madison and American Nationalism* (Toronto: Van Nostrand, 1968).

1. Cite the arguments used by Washington in rejecting foreign influence in American affairs.
2. Refute Madison's case for a strong central government from the viewpoint of an advocate of states' rights.
3. To what extent did disparate loyalties, both internal and external, threaten the national identity of the young republic?

Natural Barriers to Nationalism, 1800

In 1889 American historian Henry Adams, grandson of President John Quincy Adams, wrote an assessment of the problems facing the first Jefferson administration. In this excerpt he describes the physical barriers to national unity.

America's physical problems had changed little in fifty years. The old landmarks remained nearly where they stood before. The same bad roads and difficult rivers, connecting the same small towns, stretched into the same forests in 1800, as when the armies of Braddock and Amherst pierced the western and northern wilderness. Only in 1800 these roads extended a few miles farther from the seacoast. Nature was rather man's master than his servant. The five million Americans struggling with the untamed continent seemed hardly more competent to their task then the beavers and buffalo which had for countless generations made bridges and roads of their own.

Even by water, along the seaboard, communication was as slow and almost as irregular as in colonial times. . . . The voyage to Europe was comparatively more comfortable and more regular than the voyage from New York to Albany or through Long Island Sound to Providence, Rhode Island. No regular packet [boat carrying mail and passengers] plied between New York and Albany. Passengers waited until a sloop was advertised to sail; then they provided their own bedding and supplies. A week on the Hudson River or on the Sound was an experience not at all unknown to travelers.

While little improvement had been made in water–travel, every increase of distance added to the difficulties of the westward journey. The settler, who after buying wagon and horses, hauled his family and goods across the mountains, might buy or build a broad flat–bottomed ark, to float him and his fortunes down the Ohio. The ark was in constant peril of being upset or being sunk. . . . Nearly all the rivers which penetrated the interior were unsafe. Freshets made them dangerous, and drought made them both dangerous and impassable.

Yet such as they were, these streams made the main paths of traffic. . . . The experience of mankind proved to be dependent on water communications, and, as yet, Americans did not dream that the experience of mankind was useless to them.

If America were to be developed along the lines of water communication alone, Nature had decided that the experiment of a single republican government must meet extreme difficulties. . . . The union of New England with New York and Pennsylvania was not an easy task, even as a problem of geography, and with an ocean highway. But the union of New England with the Carolinas, and of the seacoast with the interior, promised to be a hopeless undertaking. Physical contact alone could make one country of these isolated empires. To the patriotic American of 1800, struggling for the continued existence of an embryo nation, with machinery so inadequate, the idea of ever bringing the Mississippi River, either by land or water, into close contact with New England, must have seemed wild.

From Henry Adams, *History of the United States During the First Administration of Thomas Jefferson* (New York: Charles Scribner's Sons, 1889), in I. Bartlett, et al., *A New History of the United States*, (New York: Holt, Rinehart, and Winston, 1968).

1. How does Adams characterize communications by water?
2. To what extent would Adams's analysis be coloured by the transportation biases of his own period?
3. Contrast this view of the United States in the first decades of the nineteenth century with the evidence of road and canal building during the period.

The Road to War

The war hawks in the U.S. Congress outlined their clearly expansionist aims towards Canada in late 1811. In this excerpt from the annals of Congress for the period of the pro-war faction, representatives Felix Grundy of Tennessee and Richard M. Johnson of Kentucky are countered by John Randolph of Virginia.

Mr. Grundy, December 9

What, Mr. Speaker, are we now called on to decide? It is, whether we will resist by force the attempt, made by that Government, to subject our maritime rights to the arbitrary and capricious rule of her will; for my part I am not prepared to say that this country shall submit to have her commerce interdicted or regulated, by any foreign nation. Sir, I prefer war to submission. . . .

This war, if carried on successfully, will have its advantages. We shall drive the British from our Continent—they will no longer have an opportunity of intriguing with our Indian neighbors, and setting on the ruthless savage to tomahawk our women and children. That nation will lose her Canadian trade, and, by having no resting place in this country, her means of annoying us will be diminished. The idea I am now about to advance is at war, I know, with sentiments of the gentleman from Virginia: I am willing to receive the Canadians as adopted brethren; it will have beneficial political effects; it will preserve the equilibrium of the Government. When Louisiana shall be fully peopled, the

Northern States will lose their power; they will be at the discretion of others; they can be depressed at pleasure, and then this Union might be endangered—I therefore feel anxious not only to add the Floridas to the South, but the Canadas to the North of this empire.

From Richard Hofstadter, ed., *Great Issues in American History: From the Revolution to the Civil War 1765-1865*, (New York: Vintage Books, 1958).

Mr. Randolph, December 16

Sir, if you go to war it will not be for the protection of, or defence of your maritime rights. Gentlemen from the North have been taken up to some high mountain and shown all the kingdoms of the earth; and Canada seems tempting in their sight. That rich vein of Gennesee land, which is said to be even better on the other side of the lake than on this. Agrarian cupidity, not maritime right, urges the war. Ever since the report of the Committee of Foreign Relations came into the House, we have heard but one word—like the whip–poor-will, but one eternal monotonous tone—Canada! Canada! Canada! Not a syllable about Halifax, which unquestionably should be our great object in a war for maritime security. . . .

From Richard Hofstadter, ed., *Great Issues in American History: From the Revolution to the Civil War 1765-1865* (New York: Vintage Books, 1958).

Mr. Johnson, December 11

. . . Mr. J. said we must now oppose the farther encroachments of Great Britain by war, or formally annul the Declaration of our Independence, and acknowledge ourselves her devoted colonies. . . . The gentleman from Virginia (Mr. Randolph) has objected to the destination of this auxiliary force—the occupation of the Canadas, and the other British possessions upon our borders where our laws are violated, the Indians stimulated to murder our citizens, and where there is a British monopoly of the peltry and fur trade. I should not wish to extend the boundary of the United States by war if Great Britain would leave us to the quiet enjoyment of independence; but, considering her deadly and implacable enmity, and her continued hostility, I shall never die contented until I see her expulsion from North America, and her territories incorporated with the United States. . . .

. . . It has been said that Great Britain was fighting the battles of the world—that she stands against universal dominion, threatened by the arch–fiend of mankind. I should be sorry if our independence depended upon the power of Great Britain. If, however, she would act the part of a friendly Power towards the United States, I should never wish to deprive her of her power, of wealth, of honor, of prosperity. But if her energies are to be directed against the liberties of this free and happy people, against my native country, I should not drop a tear if the fast–anchored isle would sink into the waves, provided the innocent inhabitants could escape the deluge and find an asylum in a more favorable soil. And as to the power of France, I fear it as little as any other power; I would oppose her aggressions, under any circumstances, as soon as I would British outrages.

From Richard Hofstadter, ed., *Great Issues in American History: From the Revolution to the Civil War 1765-1865*, (New York: Vintage Books, 1958).

Madison's War Message, June 1, 1812

Aside from listing the maritime grievances that the United States held against Great Britain, Madison made a clear statement of the national goals of war.

Without going back beyond the renewal in 1803 of the war in which Great Britain is engaged, and omitting the unrepaired wrongs of inferior magnitude, the conduct of her Government presents a series of acts hostile to the United States as an independent and neutral nation.

. . . [This] is a solemn question which the Constitution wisely confides to the legislative department of the Government. In recommending it to their early deliberations I am happy in the assurance that the decision will be worthy the enlightened and patriotic councils of a virtuous, a free, and a powerful nation. . . .

From Thomas P. Brockway, *Basic Documents in U.S. Foreign Policy*, (Princeton, New Jersey: Van Nostrand, 1957).

1. What role does Canada play in the case put forward by Grundy and Johnson?
2. How does Randolph characterize the motives of the war hawks?
3. To what extent do the statements of the war hawks reflect the view of the War of 1812 as a second war of independence?

Nation-building under Fire: the War of 1812 and the Canadas

To a great extent, the defence of Upper Canada in 1812 depended upon the dynamic leadership and confidence of Sir Isaac Brock. Outwardly calm and positive, Brock harboured his own private doubts about the national sentiments of the local populace.

. . . My situation is most critical, not from any thing the enemy can do, but from the disposition of the people—The population, believe me, is essentially bad—A full belief possesses them all that this Province must inevitably succumb. This prepossession is fatal to every exertion—Legislators, Magistrates, Militia Officers, all, have imbibed the idea, and are so sluggish and indifferent in their respective offices that the artful and active scoundrel is allowed to parade the Country without interruption, and commit all imaginable mischief. . . .

What a change an additional regiment would make in this part of the Province!! Most of the people have lost all confidence. I however speak loud and look big.

General Brock to Colonel Baynes, 29 July 1812. From K.A. MacKirdy, et al., *Changing Perspectives in Canadian History*, (Toronto: J.M. Dent & Sons, 1971).

Early victories against the American invaders began to inspire local patriotism in the province. In two addresses in October and November of 1812, John Strachan, future bishop of Toronto and leader of the Family Compact, praised the role of the militia in the defence of the colony.

Permit me to express the great satisfaction I feel in meeting you on this occasion. . . . They rely on our conduct and courage not merely in defending the banner which they have presented, but in making it the admonisher of the most important services, in support of our king and country. . . .

The enemy against whom we contend are loud in their threats & enraged at the unexpected resistance which they have already experienced in this province, they will wreak the bitterest vengeance upon us should they prove victorious, but they can never be victorious while we are united, on the contrary they shall continue daily to receive bloody proofs that a country is never more secure, than when defended by its faithful, loyal, and industrious inhabitants. . . . Remember that we have made a noble use of the opportunity now presented of contributing to the defence, the safety, and the glory of this highly favoured portion of the British Empire.

From George W. Spragge, ed., *The John Strachan Letter Book: 1812-1834* (Toronto, 1946), in K.A. MacKirdy, et al., *Changing Perspectives in Canadian History*, (Toronto: J.M. Dent & Sons, 1971).

. . . It will be told by the future Historian, that the Province of Upper Canada, without the assistance of men or arms, except a handful of regular troops, repelled its invaders, slew or took them all prisoners, and captured from its enemies the greater part of the arms by which it was defended. . . . And never, surely, was greater activity shewn in any country, than our militia have exhibited, never greater valour, cooler resolution, and more approved conduct; they have emulated the choicest veterans, and they have twice saved the country.

From *The Report of the Loyal and Patriotic Society of Upper Canada* (Montreal, 1817), Appendix entitled "York, 22d November 1812. An Exhortation pronounced after the Sermon, or rather in continuation of it, to induce the Inhabitants to contribute to the comfort of the Militia fighting upon the Lines. . . ."

1. Account for Brock's appraisal of the temperament of the Upper Canadians in early 1812.
2. Contrast Brock's analysis with that of John Strachan. What factors led to the apparent change in attitude by late 1812?
3. To what extent may these early roots of English-Canadian nationalism be traced to anti-American sentiments?

War and the Growth of Nationalism

Writing in 1840, John Beverley Robinson assessed the impact of the American invasion upon Canadian nationalism.

. . . It is scarcely less certain that the war of 1812, which was engaged in by the United States, mainly for the purpose of subjugating the Canadas, has had the effect of binding them, as well as Nova Scotia and New Brunswick, much more strongly to the crown. Before that war the United States were scarcely looked upon by the subjects of the British empire as a foreign country; the probability of hostilities was not anticipated, and of course not guarded against; the citizens of the republic came in numbers to settle, especially in Upper Canada, and, but for the war, in a few years thousands of those fertile acres, which have since afforded a home to loyal and grateful emigrants from England, Ireland, and Scotland, would have been occupied in a manner much less conductive to the maintenance of British connexion.

The war was happily undertaken at a time when the adjoining states of America were but thinly inhabited, and when the invasion of Canada was, in consequence, attended with many difficulties which time has removed. It has had the effect of calling the attention of England to a danger which Lord Selkirk, in his very able book on emigration, pointed out to the government so early as the year 1805; it has produced in the British colonists a national character and feeling, and has taught both countries to appreciate their position more correctly.

From J.B. Robinson, *Canada and the Canada Bill* (London, 1840).

William Coffin was the first historian to clearly characterize the war as a pivotal event in the development of Canadian nationalism. The following excerpt is from his 1864 work 1812: The War and Its Moral: A Canadian Chronicle.

1812—like the characters on the labarum of Constantine—is a sign of solemn import to the people of Canada. It carries with it the virtue of an incantation. Like the magic numerals of the Arabian sage, these words, in their utterance, quicken the pulse, and vibrate through the frame, summoning, from the pregnant past, memories of suffering and endurance and of honourable exertion. They are inscribed on the banner and stamped on the hearts of the Canadian people—a watchword, rather than a war-cry. With these words upon his lips, the loyal Canadian, as a vigilant sentinel, looks forth into the gloom, ready with his challenge, hopeful for a friendly response, but prepared for any other.

The people of Canada are proud of the men, and of the deeds, and of the recollection of those days. They feel that the war of 1812 is an episode in the story of a young people, glorious in itself and full of promise. They believe that the infant which, in its very cradle, could strangle invasion, struggle, and endure, bravely and without repining—is capable of a nobler development, if God wills further trial.

The French population of Lower Canada are very proud of the victory of Chateauguay, and with just reason. The British population of the Upper Province had achieved a like success over the common enemy at Queenston Heights. It was gratifying to the natural pride of a great national origin, that the fortune of war should have thus equitably distributed her honourable distinctions. They had, moreover, a stronger motive, both for resentment and exultation. The American Government and democratic press, with unexampled effrontery, had cast upon a race *"sans peur et sans reproche,"* the dishonouring imputation of any easy political virtue. They had been charged with a readiness to violate plighted honour, and with disaffection to the British Crown. Truthful and generous in all relations, whether of peace or war, they resented this indignity, as a stain felt more keenly than a wound, and they gave the *"Bostonians"* their answer on the field of Chateauguay. . . .

Fifty years ago 300 brave men gave to the whole world the spectacle of one of the finest feats of arms of which our young country can be proud. Filled with the knightly courage which their ancestors bequeathed to them and marching in the steps of their valorous leader, De Salaberry, they repulsed and put to flight on the frontier of their homeland an army infinitely superior in numbers and full of the pride that past victories inspired. No doubt Mister Editor, you have already understood, and the victorious name "Chateauguay" has come involuntarily to your lips. . . . That memorable day, which gives the lie to the dishonest assertion that casts doubt on the bravery and courage of French Canadians, ought to be graven on the hearts of every good citizen, and its memory enshrined by some public mark that will transmit it to our most distant posterity. . . .

From William F. Coffin, *1812: The War and Its Moral: A Canadian Chronicle* (Montreal, 1864).

1. In what way does Robinson describe the change in British North American attitudes towards the United States and Britain as a result of the War of 1812?
2. Evaluate Coffin's account as a piece of patriotic literature. Assess its accuracy as a reflection of the impact of the War of 1812 upon his own generation.
3. Assess the impact of the War of 1812 upon the development of English-Canadian nationalism.

War and Literature

The following two poems capture the patriotic inspiration of the War of 1812. Each expresses the new feelings of national pride emerging from the conflict.

The Frontier Way
or
Canada Is Not Coming
As I stood on the frontier way,
I heard the indignant people say,
"Who fought and bled to save our rights
At Chateauguay and Queenston Heights?
Who is it fills each silent grave
That marks the hill or dots the plain?
The dust of patriots true and brave,
Who if they lived would cry again
"You're welcome as the flowers of May,
To Queenston Heights and Chateauguay!"
As I went up the frontier way,
I heard the patriot people say,
"No alien flat shall ever wave
Above the hero's honoured grave.
No alien heel shall e'er defile

Each green and grassy diadem;
No cunning tongue shall wean or wile
The shelter of our swords from them.
Their name shall never pass away,
From Queenston Heights and Chateauguay."

"The Khan" (National Archives of Canada: Denison Papers, Vol.35: scrapbook).

Grandfather's Gun of Eighteen-Twelve

Some blowin'-adder paper men
Out over there in Yankeedom,
Say we're to them as one to ten,
And woe betide us if they come,
"I've said before, 'twixt Christian lands.
It's time hard feelin's for to shelve:
But, Brock my boy, put in my hands
Grandfather's gun of eighteen-twelve.
She's not a beauty, but she did
Her duty in that ugly scrap;
The bay'net on her nozzle rid
Our Canada of many a chap
As thought we Canucks live in the snow
We're only fit to chop and delve.
But here's what taught 'em 'twasn't so:
Grandfather's gun of eighteen-twelve.

J. Cawdor Bell, (National Archives of Canada: Denison Papers, Vol.35: scrapbook).

The American System

In the decade following the War of 1812 a new feeling of Americanism began to emerge in the United States. Some historians have argued that westward expansion broke the hold of the states upon the affections of the people. Alone, or in small settlements, personal security and prosperity depended more upon a federal presence in the interior.

On the fiftieth anniversary of the signing of the Declaration of Independence Thomas Jefferson was asked to speak in Washington. In this excerpt, while turning down the invitation (he was ailing and would be dead in less than two weeks), Jefferson outlined the values represented by the United States.

. . . Respected Sir, The kind invitation I receive from you, on the part of the citizens of the city of Washington, to be present with them at their celebration on the fiftieth anniversary of American Independence, as one of the surviving signers of an instrument pregnant with our own, and the fate of the world, is most flattering to myself. . . . Our fellow citizens, after half a century of experience and prosperity, continue to approve the choice we made. May it be to the world, what I believe it will be, (to some parts sooner, to others later, but finally to all,) the signal of arousing men to burst the chains under which monkish ignorance and superstition had persuaded them to bind themselves, and to assume the blessings and security of self-government. That form which we have substituted, restores the free right to the unbounded exercise of reason and freedom of opinion. All eyes are opened, or opening, to the rights of man. . . .

From Paul L. Ford, ed., *The Writings of Thomas Jefferson*, (New York: 1899) X.

Henry Clay was a war hawk from Kentucky. In 1817 he described his vision of a new American system. A forerunner to John A. Macdonald's National Policy of the 1870s, Clay called for industrial growth, the development of western markets, and an expansion of the internal transportation system. One of Clay's staunchest allies was John C. Calhoun. In this excerpt, from a speech in the House of Representatives, Calhoun argues for the passage of legislation to implement Clay's vision.

. . . In many respects, no country, of equal population and wealth, possesses potential power equal to ours. In muscular power, in hardy and enterprising habits, and in lofty and gallant courage, our people are surpassed by none. In one respect, and, in my opinion, in one only, are we materially weak. We occupy an enormously large land area in proportion to our population. Only with great difficulty can the common strength of our nation be brought to bear on any point that may be menaced by an enemy.

It is our duty, then, in so far as possible, to counteract this weakness. Good roads and canals, carefully laid out, are the proper remedy. In the recent War of 1812, how much did we suffer for the lack of them? Our military movements were slow, while our transportation costs were high. In the event of another war, the savings in the cost of transporting materials and men would go far toward repaying us for the expense of constructing roads and canals.

What can be more important than a perfect unity of feelings and sentiments among the people in every part of the country? And what can help to produce unity more than a transportation system? No free state ever occupied a country as large as this one. Let it not, however, be forgotten—let it forever be kept in mind—that the size of our nation exposes us to the threat of disunity. We are great and growing rapidly. This is our pride and our danger, our weakness and our strength.

We must counteract every tendency to disunion. . . .

To aid us in this great work of maintaining the integrity of this republic, our country has most admirable advantages. It is belted around with lakes and oceans and intersected in every direction by bays and rivers. It is blessed with a form of government which combines liberty and strength. We may reasonably raise our eyes to a most splendid future, if we only act in a manner worthy of our advantages. If, however, we neglect them and permit a low, sordid, selfish, and sectional spirit to take possession of the House of Representatives, this happy scene will vanish. We will divide, and misery and despotism will follow.

From Richard K. Cralle, ed., *Works of John C. Calhoun*, (New York: D. Appleton and Company, 1856), vol. II.

The American spelling of words such as labour (labor), and centre (center) dates back to the work of Noah Webster. He advocated an Americanization of the English language, and although some words such as laf (laugh) and bred (bread) failed to catch on, his American Dictionary of the English Language *was a best seller upon publication in 1828. The following excerpt is from the preface to the dictionary.*

. . . It is not only important, but in a degree necessary, that the people of this country should have an *American Dictionary of the English Language.* Although the body of the language is the same as in England, and it is desirable to continue the sameness, yet some differences must exist.

Language is the expression of ideas; and if the people of one country cannot preserve an identity of ideas, they cannot retain an identity of language. Now, an identity of ideas depends materially upon a sameness of things or objects with which the people of the two countries are familiar. But in no two portions of the earth, far from each other, can such identity be found. Even physical objects must be different.

. . . Give rise to new terms or to new applications of old terms, unknown to the people of England. They cannot be explained by them, and will not be inserted in their dictionaries, unless copied from ours. Thus the terms *land-office, location of land, regent* of a university, *plantation, selectmen, senate, congress, courts,* and *assembly* are either words not belonging to the language of England, or they are applied to things in this country which do not exist in that. No person in this country will be satisfied with the English definitions of the words *congress, senate, assembly, court,* etc. Although these are words used in England, yet they are applied in this country to express ideas which they do not express in that country.

But this is not all. In many cases, the nature of our governments and of our civil institutions, requires an appropriate language in the definition of words, even when the words express the same thing as in England. . . .

Land-office was a government office which sold public lands to settlers and land speculators. Location of land is designated according to townships and sections set up by the Land Ordinance of 1785. A regent is a member of the governing board of a university. A selectman is a member of a board of town officers in New England chosen to manage certain public affairs.

A constitution is the group of basic principles by which a state or nation is governed. In the United States, it is a written document; in Britain, a group of documents and precedents. A law is any rule that a lawmaking body enacts.

In the United States, a plantation was a large farm on which cotton or tobacco was grown. In Britain, plantation meant a group of planted trees or plants.

From Noah Webster, *An American Dictionary of the English Language,* (New York: S. Converse, 1828), vol. 1, Preface.

1. How does Jefferson characterize the American experiment?
2. What economic arguments does Calhoun employ to ensure continued national union?

3. Respond to Webster's rationale for an American dictionary. Write your own argument for the existence of a Canadian version.

The Monroe Doctrine, 1823

In this famous declaration of American hegemony over the Western Hemisphere, President James Monroe was careful to combine American national goals with international reality. The doctrine conveniently leaves the door open for British involvement in the region. In 1823 Great Britain, which had first proposed a joint declaration, was the only nation powerful enough to enforce its provisions.

. . . As a principle in which the rights and interests of the United States are involved, the American continents, by the free and independent condition which they have assumed and maintain, are henceforth not to be considered as subjects for future colonization by any European powers. . . .

. . . The citizens of the United States cherish sentiments the most friendly in favor of the liberty and happiness of their fellow-men on that side of the Atlantic. In the wars of the European powers in matters relating to themselves we have never taken any part, nor does it comport with our policy so to do. It is only when our rights are invaded or seriously menaced that we resent injuries or make preparations for our defense. With the movements in this hemisphere we are of necessity more immediately connected, and by causes which must be obvious to all enlightened and impartial observers. The political system of the allied powers is essentially different in this respect from that of America . . . . We owe it, therefore, to candor and to the amicable relations existing between the United States and those powers to declare that we should consider an attempt on their part to extend their system to any portion of this hemisphere as dangerous to our peace and safety. With the existing colonies or dependencies of any European power we have not interfered and shall not interfere. But with the Governments who have declared their independence and maintained it, and whose independence we have, on great consideration and on just principles, acknowledged, we could not view any interposition for the purpose of oppressing them, or controlling in any other manner their destiny, by any European power in any other light than as the manifestation of an unfriendly disposition toward the United States. . . .

From Richardson, *Messages and Papers of the Presidents*, II, in Thomas P. Brockway, *Basic Documents in U.S. Foreign Policy* (Princeton, New Jersey: Van Nostrand, 1957).

1. What relationship does Monroe establish between European interests in the Americas and American interest in Europe?
2. Summarize the nature of the declaration.
3. Assess the Monroe Doctrine as an expression of nationalist sentiment.

Madison and National Unity

In the following series of excerpts James Madison warns against the divisive forces rising to prominence in the United States. His fears were justified; within thirty years the nation would be convulsed by civil war. This first excerpt is from a congratulatory telegram to Senator William Rives of Virginia in recognition of his opposition to the concept of secession.

The natural feelings which laudably attach the people composing a State, to its authority and importance, are at present too much excited by the unnatural feelings, with which they have been inspired against their brethren of other States, not to expose them, to the danger of being misled into erroneous views of the nature of the Union and the interest they have in it. One thing at least seems to be too clear to be questioned; that whilst a State remains within the Union it cannot withdraw its citizens from the operation of the Constitution and laws of the Union. In the event of an actual secession without the consent of the Co-States, the course to be pursued by these involves questions painful in the discussion of them. God grant that the menacing appearances, which obtruded it may not be followed by positive occurrences requiring the more painful task of deciding them!

From Madison to William C. Rives, March 12, 1833, Madison, *Writings*, IX, in Irving Brant, *James Madison and American Nationalism* (Toronto: Van Nostrand, 1968).

Around 1830, Madison wrote about the impossibility of re-establishing the Union should it ever dissolve.

. . . In all the views that may be taken of questions between the State Governments and the General Government the awful consequences of a final rupture and dissolution of the Union should never for a moment be lost sight of. Such a prospect must be deprecated, must be shuddered at by every friend to his country, to liberty, to the happiness of man. For, in the event of a dissolution of the Union, an impossibility of ever renewing it is brought home to every mind by the difficulties encountered in establishing it. The propensity of all communities to divide when not pressed into a unity by external danger, is a truth well understood. There is no instance of a people inhabiting even a small island, if remote from foreign danger, and sometimes in spite of that pressure, who are not divided into alien, rival, hostile tribes. The happy Union of these States is a wonder; their Constitution a miracle; their example the hope of Liberty throughout the world. Woe to the ambition that would meditate the destruction of either!

From "An Outline," February 1829, Madison, *Writings*, IX; Madison to Nicholas P. Trist, May 1832, Madison, *Writings*, IX, in Irving Brant, *James Madison and American Nationalism* (Toronto: Van Nostrand, 1968).

Even in death Madison was a nationalist. The following was written in 1834 for posthumous publication.

. . . The advice nearest to my heart and deepest in my convictions is that the Union of the United States be cherished and perpetuated. Let the open enemy to it be regarded as a Pandora with her box opened; and the disguised one, as the Serpent creeping with his deadly wiles into Paradise. . . .

From Madison, *Writings*, IX, in Irving Brant, *James Madison and American Nationalism* (Toronto: Van Nostrand, Toronto, 1968).

1. Trace Madison's arguments through the three excerpts.
2. Write a countering argument which might have been used by secessionist opponents to his viewpoint.
3. To what extent was the idea of secession simply a form of regional nationalism?

Nationalism and Manifest Destiny

By mid-century, nationalist sentiment was directed to continental expansion. The following four selections reflect the sentiments of the period. The first was delivered by Congressman John Wentworth of Illinois in 1845.

Many of this body would live to hear the sound from the Speaker's chair, "the gentleman from Texas." He wanted them also to hear "the gentleman from Oregon." He would go even further, and have "the gentleman from Nova Scotia, the gentleman from Canada, the gentleman from Cuba, the gentleman from Mexico, aye, even the gentleman from Patagonia." He did not believe the God of Heaven, when he crowned the American arms with success [in the Revolutionary War], designed that the original States should be the only abode of liberty on earth. On the contrary, he only designed them as the great center from which civilization, religion, and liberty should radiate and radiate until the whole continent shall bask in their blessing. . . .

From *Cong. Globe*, 28 Cong., 2 Sess., 200 (January 27, 1845), in Frederick Merk, *Manifest Destiny* (New York: Vintage Books, 1966).

Future presidential candidate Stephen Douglas was considered to be a moderate for his continentalist position.

[Douglas] would blot out the lines on the map which now marked our national boundaries on this continent, and make the area of liberty as broad as the continent itself. He would not suffer petty rival republics to grow up here, endangering jealousy at each other, and interfering with each other's domestic affairs, and continually endangering their peace. He did not wish to go beyond the great ocean—beyond those boundaries which the God of nature had marked out.

From *Cong. Globe*, 28 Cong., 2 Sess., 227 (January 31, 1845), in Frederick Merk, *Manifest Destiny* (New York: Vintage Books, 1966).

Andrew Kennedy of Indiana spoke in 1846:

Go to the West and see a young man with his mate of eighteen; and [after] a lapse of thirty years, visit him again, and instead of two, you will find twenty-two. That is what I call the American multiplication table. We are now twenty millions strong; and how long, under this process of multiplication, will it take

to cover the continent with our posterity, from the Isthmus of Darien to Behr-
ing's straits? . . .

From *Cong. Globe*, 29 Cong., 1 Sess., 180 (January 10, 1846), in Frederick Merk, *Manifest Destiny*
(New York: Vintage Books, 1966).

*In 1848 Daniel Dickinson of New York put forward the argument for a single North
American nation.*

But the tide of emigration and the course of empire have since been westward.
Cities and towns have sprung up upon the shores of the Pacific . . . . Nor have
we yet fulfilled the destiny allotted to us. New territory is spread out for us to
subdue and fertilize; new races are presented for us to civilize, educate and
absorb; new triumphs for us to achieve for the cause of freedom. North America presents to the eye one great geographical system . . .; it is soon to become
the commercial center of the world. And the period is by no means remote,
when man . . ., yielding to . . . laws more potent than those which prescribe
artificial boundaries, will ordain that it [North America] shall be united . . . in
one political system, and that, a free, confederated, self governed Republic. . . .

From *Cong. Globe*, 30 Cong., 1 Sess., App. 86-7 (January 12, 1848), in Frederick Merk, *Manifest
Destiny*, (New York: Vintage Books, 1966).

1. Outline the various justifications for expansion employed by the four authors.
2. What underlying nationalist theories supported every view?
3. To what extent was Manifest Destiny an attempt to divert political attention
from the national crisis in the East?

French Canada in the Age of Nationalism

*Sir James Craig, governor of Canada in the second decade of the nineteenth century,
assessed the nature of French-Canadian nationalism.*

. . . I speak of a Colony, the population of which . . . I myself believe to
exceed 250 000. Of these 250 000 souls about 20 000 or 25 000 may be English
or Americans, the remainder are French. I use the term designedly My Lord,
because I mean to say, that they are in Language, in religion, in manner and
in attachment completely French-bound to us by no one tie, but that of a Common Government, and on the contrary viewing us with sentiments of mistrust
& jealousy, with envy, and I believe I should not go too far, were I to say with
hatred.

In considering the probability of these people having in view their return to
their own Government, it may be urged that they have been hitherto quiet &
faithful subjects, during the long lapse of 50 years, in which it would rather be
to be supposed that their old attachment should have gradually decreased, so
that there should be the less likelihood of their assuming now a disposition, of
which they have hitherto shown no indication; to all this however it may be
replied, that no circumstance whatever has occurred to awaken their attachment
to their Mother Country, nor have any pains ever been taken to produce such a

change, their habits, language and religion, have remained as distinct from ours as they were before the Conquest. Indeed it seems to be a favourite object with them to be considered as [a] separate Nation; *La Nation Canadienne* is their constant expression, and with regard to their having been hitherto quiet & faithful subjects, it need only be observed that no opportunity has presented them an encouragement to shew themselves otherwise.

Sir James Craig to the Earl of Liverpool, 1 May 1810. From W.P.M. Kennedy, ed., *Statutes, Treaties and Documents of the Canadian Constitution, 1713-1929* (Toronto, 1930).

1. How does Craig characterize the colony?
2. To what does he attribute Lower Canada's lack of attachment to Great Britain?
3. Contrast the nationalist sentiment evident in Lower Canada with that described by Brock as existing in Upper Canada two years later.

De Tocqueville in Lower Canada

When French writer Alexis de Tocqueville toured the United States in 1831 he spent part of his time in Lower Canada. The following selection is taken from his comments on his visit.

Without comparison, Canada has the greatest similarity to France than any other portion of America we have visited up until now. . . .

. . . Although French is the language universally spoken, the majority of the newspapers, notices and even the signs of French merchants are in English. Commercial enterprises are nearly all in their hands. They are really the leading class in Canada. I doubt that this will be the case for long. The clergy and a great part of the classes which are not rich but are enlightened are French. They are beginning to strongly feel their secondary position. . . .

. . . If twenty years from now, French Canadians have not come out of their apathy, it will be too late for them. Everything indicates that their awakening is approaching. But if the middle and upper classes of the French-Canadian population abandon the lower classes in this effort, and let themselves be led into the English mainstream, the French race in America is lost. . . .

It was the habitants in which we were most interested. It surprises me that this country is so little known in France. . . . Today in the province of Lower Canada alone there are 600 000 French descendants. I guarantee that their origin cannot be disputed. They are as French as you and I. They resemble us even better than the Americans of the United States resemble the English. I cannot express what pleasure we felt to find ourselves again amid this population. We felt as if we were at home and everywhere we were received as fellow-countrymen, children of *Old France* as they call it. In my opinion, the epithet is poorly chosen. Old France is in Canada: the new France in France. We rediscovered there, especially in the outlying towns, the former French customs and morals. . . .

Would it not be a temptation to believe that the national character of a people is determined more by the blood from which it came than by political insti-

tutions or the nature of a country? Here are Frenchmen who have mingled for
years with an English population, who have been subject to the laws of England, who have been more separated from the mother country than if they lived
at the Poles. Now! they are still French, characteristic for characteristic. This is
true not only for the old but for all, down to the tiny tot spinning his top. . . .

From Alexis de Tocqueville, *Voyages 1. Tocqueville au Bas-Canada.* Introduced by Jacques Vallee
(Montreal: Editions du Jour, 1973).

1. To what extent does de Tocqueville identify a distinct society in Lower Canada?
2. Comment upon the author's assertion that "old France is in Canada: the new
France in France."

Immigration and the Canadiens, 1832-33

Le Canadien *was a French-language newspaper founded in Quebec City in 1806. In
1832-33 it launched an attack against the current immigration policy, which seemed to
be dumping "undesirables" on the colony.*

Le Canadien, October 12, 1832
. . . *Canadiens* will never look unfavourably on the honest and industrious
immigrant who arrives among them and who comes to help them work towards
the development of this new and vast country, without thought of infringing
upon and dominating the people. But, if *Canadiens* see that England's parishes
are banding together in order to rid themselves of their poor and burden a
young country like theirs with the dregs of England, Ireland and Scotland; if
they see rich and powerful companies assisted by the government and in connection with the party which in that colony has long dreamed of domination
and the destruction of every thing Canadian; . . . would they not have had to
renounce all feeling of honour and nationality if they did not look with some
suspicion on this multitude of foreigners who flock in every year under these
circumstances?

Le Canadien, August 2, 1833
. . . This statement would have gone unnoticed, if it were not linked to a
thousand other circumstances which serve to prove that there exists a long-
standing, systematic plan to erase, to wipe out, if possible, the *Canadien* people
and their institutions. Emigration has been seized upon as one of the many
ways of accomplishing this aim. . . . Our neighbours to the south invite European proletarians from every nation to come and reduce the huge western forests to cultivated land. Furthermore, the emigrant does not go there, nor is he
summoned there, to destroy the laws, customs and institutions of his adoptive
land; he arrives with the intention of conforming to the institutions, customs
and laws he will find established. Let it not be said that because the United
States has an independent, sovereign government, then what is good, just and
proper for these states is not so for Lower Canada because it is a dependent
province; since, as far as justice is concerned, we derive from treaties and actual
laws, the rights which our neighbours derive from their political position.

From Virginia R. Robeson, ed., *Lower Canada in the 1830s* (Toronto: O.I.S.E. Press, 1977).

1. How does the paper describe British emigration policy?
2. What impact does it predict such practices will have upon the "nation Canadienne"?
3. Write a letter to the editor opposing the viewpoint being expressed in these editorials.

The Crisis of the Rebellion, 1837-38

The movement for national independence reached a peak in the Rebellion of 1837. Unlike its Upper Canadian counterpart whose target was political reform, French Canada hoped for liberation from British rule. In his Histoire des Patriotes, *G. Filteau states the nationalist case.*

. . . Never did the Patriotes propose reforms just from a love of change, or in a spirit of opposition or simply to satisfy theories. They were neither democrats nor reformers nor liberals: they were first and foremost nationalists. What they wanted was not the overthrow of existing institutions but simply their employ-ment in the interests of the masses, according to the spirit that had erected them. . . .

The law of 1791 [the Constitutional Act] had the clearly proclaimed purpose of perpetuating French-Canadian national life. With rigorous logic the Patriotes wanted to put into pratice that principle and develop it to its fullest extent: the formation within the body of the Empire of a French state endowed with all the freedoms—political, intellectual, and material—necessary for its life and com-patible with the maintenance of allegiance to Britain. On the strength of the constitution of 1791 they postulated as an essential plank of their programme: Canadians ought to be masters of their own destiny, masters of their own Par-liament, masters of their own affairs, masters of their legislation, masters of the natural resources of the country won by their ancestors. . . .

From G. Filteau, *Histoire des Patriotes* (Montreal, 1938-9), Vol. 1 (translation).

The Constitutional Association of Montreal issued the following statement with regard to the outbreak of violence in the colony. Reflecting the view of the "British party," the association inadvertently makes a strong case for the French cause.

. . . The French Canadian population were . . . not only nationally inclined to mark their active opposition to their fellow-subjects of British and Irish origin, but they have been taught to consider them as strangers and trespassers upon their soil . . . they have in fine been taught to believe themselves oppressed by their fellow-subjects of British and Irish origin . . . desperate men made an open livelihood by influencing the population of French origin to acts of viol-ence . . . . In all cases, the object was attained, active discontent was intro-duced into the passive population, and noon day meetings gradually ripened into sedition and rebellion.

It is this exclusive French Canadian spirit alone which has given rise to all the discontent existing in this Province, it is this which has in fact made the question one of national origin and not of political party, in it is to be discovered the source of all the disturbances which have brought sedition and rebellion in their train, and in it alone is to be found a full and complete answer to the enquiry, to what causes the present unhappy condition of this Province is to be ascribed.

Address of the Constitutional Association of the City of Montreal to the Inhabitants of the Sister Colonies, December 13, 1837. From W.P.M. Kennedy, *Statutes, Treaties and Documents of the Canadian Constitution, 1713-1729* (Toronto: Oxford University Press, 1930).

Views of a "National-Democratic" Revolution

Marxist historian Stanley Ryerson places the revolt in the context of national self-determination.

. . . Inseparable from the parliamentary contest was the wide-ranging struggle over the innumerable economic and political grievances that landlordism and colonial-compact rule engendered. Gradually as the struggle sharpened, the fundamental political issue of *Canadian independence* was thrust to the fore. It was to be proclaimed in "declarations of independence" in both Canadas. . . .

In Lower Canada, the struggle involved not only colonial self-government, as in the other provinces, but the right of national self-determination for the French-Canadian nation. From the Conquest onward, this was to become the burning issue in the valley of the St. Lawrence. . . .

The struggle in Lower Canada started with the resistance of the French Canadians to national oppression. It soon embraced the issues of legislative control of the revenue, freedom of press and assembly, and colonial self-government. It thus paralleled the struggles in Upper Canada and those (in a less acute form) in the Atlantic provinces. Soon, as the contest sharpened, there came the first beginnings of joint effort and mutual support on the part of the national-democratic, patriotic forces in all three areas. . . .

But inseparable from the question of representative government was the issue of French-Canadian national rights. To the growth of the sentiment of nationality, of the existence of a "nation canadienne," Colonial Secretary Huskisson counterposed England's "duty and interest": having "carried our language, our free institutions, and our system of laws, to the most remote corners of the globe," it was now imperative to "imbue (the colony) with English feeling, and benefit it with English laws and institutions". . . .

[In an attempt to stifle French-Canadian rights] newspapers were prosecuted, judges removed from office, French-Canadian militia battalions dissolved. Petitions addressed to London protesting against the repression gathered the signatures of no less than eighty-seven thousand persons.

From Stanley Ryerson, *Unequal Union: Roots of Crisis in the Canadas, 1815-1873*, (Toronto: Progress Books, 1973, 2nd edition).

1. Contrast de Tocqueville's view of Lower Canada as "old France" with the evidence of emergent nationalism outlined in these excerpts.

2. Write a response to the arguments put forward by the Constitutional Association.
3. Compare the nature of nationalism in Lower Canada with that of other areas in British North America.

The Durham Report

Hailed as the Magna Carta of responsible government in Upper Canada, Lord Durham's report received far less praise in Lower Canada. In this excerpt Durham outlines the national issues involved in the conflict.

. . . I expected to find a contest between a government and a people: I found two nations warring in the bosom of a single state: I found a struggle, not of principles, but of races; and I perceived that it would be idle to attempt any amelioration of laws or institutions until we could first succeed in terminating the deadly animosity that now separates the inhabitants of Lower Canada into the hostile divisions of French and English . . . The national feud forces itself on the very senses, irresistibly and palpably, as the origin or the essence of every dispute which divides the community; we discover that dissensions, which appear to have another origin, are but forms of this constant and all-pervading quarrel; and that every contest is one of French and English in the outset, or becomes so ere it has run its course. . . .

Nor does there appear to be the slightest chance of putting an end to this animosity during the present generation. Passions inflamed during so long a period cannot speedily be calmed. . . . Their more discerning leaders feel that their chances of preserving their nationality would be greatly diminished by an incorporation with the United States . . . Yet none even of these considerations weigh against their present all-absorbing hatred of the English; and I am persuaded that they would purchase vengeance and a momentary triumph, by the aid of any enemies, or submission to any yoke.

There are two modes by which a Government may deal with a conquered territory. The first course open to it is that of respecting the rights and nationality of the actual occupants . . . and without attempting any change in the elements of the community, merely incorporating the Province under the general authority of the central Government. The second is that of treating the conquered territory as one open to the conquerors, of encouraging their influx, of regarding the conquered race as entirely subordinate, and of endeavouring as speedily and as rapidly as possible to assimilate the character and institutions of its new subjects to those of the great body of its empire. . . .

There can hardly be conceived a nationality more destitute of all that can invigorate and elevate a people, than that which is exhibited by the descendants of the French in Lower Canada, owing to their retaining their peculiar language and manners. They are a people with no history, and no literature. The literature of England is written in a language that is not theirs; and the only literature which their language renders familiar to them, is that of a nation from which they have been separated by eighty years of a foreign rule, and still more by those changes which the Revolution and its consequences have wrought in

the whole political, moral and social state of France. . . . In these circumstances, I should be indeed surprised if the more reflecting part of the French
Canadians entertained at present any hope of continuing to preserve their
nationality. . . .

I entertain no doubts as to the national character which must be given to
Lower Canada; it must be that of the British Empire; that of the majority of
the population of British America; that of the great race which must, in the
lapse of no long period of time, be predominant over the whole North American Continent. . . .

From Janet Morchain and Mason Wade, *Search for a Nation* (Toronto: Fitzhenry and Whiteside, 1984).

1. Précis Durham's analysis of the dispute between English and French in Lower
Canada.
2. What possible solutions of the racial problem does Durham identify?
3. Assess the French-Canadian response to Durham's report.

Search for a Nation

*In this essay French-Canadian historian Michel Brunet assesses the emergence of Quebec
as the fatherland of the French-Canadian nation.*

Did the *Canadiens* of 1763 conclude that they had failed and had to renounce
their collective goals? Not at all. A majority among them kept the conviction
that, even if they now owed allegiance to a new king, the St. Lawrence valley
was still their fatherland. . . .

. . . Lower Canada was the new name of their fatherland.

Thanks to the representative system, the *Canadiens* gave themselves new and
more responsible leaders. The former military and seignorial class had vanished.
The electoral process and the House of Assembly bred a new political class
closer to the mass of the people. Papineau became the first and only true
national leader of the *Canadiens*. He kept repeating that Lower Canada was the
fatherland of the *nation canadienne* and that the British immigrants who had
chosen to settle in the colony were bound to accept the leadership of the majority. He invoked democratic principles to bolster his viewpoint. These principles
served his national ends and those of his compatriots.

The English-speaking minority of Lower Canada had no intention of being
assimilated by the *nation canadienne*. On the contrary, its ambition had always
been to see the *Canadiens* melting away into a powerful British American
nation. One can easily understand their angry reaction and their stubborn opposition to the division of the colony in 1791. From 1818 to 1837 the leaders of
Lower Canada's English minority had the economic and political power—
thanks to the undemocratic composition of the Legislative and Executive Councils—to check Papineau's and the *parti canadien's* programme. They persisted in
demanding the union of the two colonies in order to put the *Canadiens'* representatives in a minority in the Lower House. Two collectivities were fighting

for opposed national ends in Lower Canada. They were both in search of a fatherland, a country where they could freely exert the powers of a majority.

The armed revolt of 1837-1838 gave to the Imperial government the opportunity of correcting the error committed in 1791. Lower and Upper Canada were united. The *Canadiens* protested against what they called an act of despotism. The fact is that Lower Canada was treated as a conquered land—which it was in spite of all the pious declarations to the contrary. The British American nation had triumphed over the *nation canadienne*. Canada would be a British and English-speaking country. Some leaders of the British American nation were even so naive as to believe that the *Canadiens'* complete assimilation was still possible eighty years after the Conquest. . . .

. . . It is not an ironic aspect of history that French-Canadian politicians of the 1840's were told that they had contributed to the building of the second British Empire. They might perhaps have satisfied themselves with the founding of a fatherland for the *Canadiens,* but now they could say to their constituency that in the cabinet there was an attorney-general for Lower Canada and that the French language had become official. The Church enjoyed more freedom than formerly and the influence of the priesthood had begun to become greater than that of the politicians. With the help of British capital, the British American entrepreneurs had given a new impetus to the economic development of the St. Lawrence Valley. The French Canadians' standard of living had somewhat improved; when their political leaders, who enjoyed for the first time the benefits of being associated as junior partners with the party in power, were repeating to them that they had nothing to complain about, they almost unanimously agreed. . . .

From Peter Russell, ed., *Nationalism in Canada* (Toronto: McGraw-Hill, 1966.)

1. What was the impact of the Constitutional Act upon the development of the French-Canadian nation?
2. How does the author describe the relationship between the French and English in the colony?
3. Create and defend your own thesis with regard to the emergence of a distinct French-Canadian nation during the first half of the nineteenth century.

Identity and Nationhood: Analysis and Application

1. Stage a two-person debate between a war hawk, such as Richard Johnson or Felix Grundy, and John Strachan of Upper Canada on the American plans for the "liberation" of Upper Canada.

a) Have each participant prepare a position paper outlining her/his point of view.
b) Using formal debating procedure, present the arguments face to face, allowing time for rebuttal.
c) Once the debate is completed switch position papers and, after studying the arguments of your opponent, switch sides and re-stage the debate.
d) In your analysis of the process consider the following questions:
Did you identify weaknesses in your own argument when you argued against it?

To what extent did the switching of sides result in a clearer understanding of the issues?

Having argued both sides, which party do you feel had the stronger case?

2. "The War of 1812 gave rise to two different brands of nationalism. For Americans it threw off the last bonds of British rule and set the stage for an expansive conquest of the continent. For English Canadians the war resulted in a defensive nationalism, unifying the nation in the face of a common enemy." Defend this statement with reference to the impact of the war on the two societies.

3. Compare the principles of Clay's American System with the National Policy of John A. Macdonald.

4. To what extent was nineteenth-century American expansionism a product of emerging nationalism?

5. Examine the conflict between the idea of state and nation in the United States during the first half of the nineteenth century.

6. Trace the development of French–Canadian nationalism from 1791 to 1840. Create and defend your own thesis with respect to the nature and origin of "la nation Canadienne."

7. Write a one-act play focusing on one aspect of the life of Louis Joseph Papineau. As much as possible, use primary source material from the period to provide the dialogue for your work. Together with a few friends, perform the play for a group or class. Have members of the audience critique the production from the standpoint of its historical accuracy.

8. Define nationalism in North American terms. Write a 250-word defence of your definition, citing specific examples from both Canada and the United States.

9. Canadians and Americans both established fundamental aspects of their national identity during the first half of the nineteenth century. Select an issue from the last quarter of the twentieth century. Compare the Canadian and American response to the issue from the perspective of each nation's national viewpoint.

10. Through outside research identify non-literary examples of North American nationalism evident during the period. Such examples might include: painting, sculpture, music, political cartoons, etc. Analyse the example chosen and create a thesis based on your research.

7
DEMOCRACY AND PARTY

Canada and the United States are both democracies. Each country is characterized by democratically elected institutions and political leaders who represent different social views. When voters go to the polls in a Canadian or American election, their vote is cast not simply for an individual, but for a political party as well.

Democracy and the party system grew up together in North America. What American President James Madison had denounced as "faction" in *The Federalist Papers* (1787–88) had become a fact of life on both sides of the border by the late 1820s. While in the United States party differences tended to represent opposing democratic options, in British North America party lines were more blurred. In fact, it would take another twenty–five years before the political lines would be clearly drawn north of the border. In both countries, the increasing democratization of society was reflected in the growth of the party system. As a result, we can see in the delayed appearance of clearly defined political groups in Canada an indication of the slower progress toward democratic reform.

Nonetheless, the period is marked by the emergence of champions of democracy on both sides of the border. Louis-Joseph Papineau, William Lyon Mackenzie, and Andrew Jackson all share a common political heritage.

The Growth of Democracy in the United States

Prior to 1810, the right to vote in the United States was the jealously guarded privilege of the well–to–do. Property qualifications were so restrictive in some states that in Rhode Island, for example, fewer than half of all adult white males were eligible to vote. The situation was gradually changing, however. Many of the new Western states required no property qualifications for voting, and even in those which did the availability of land extended the voting franchise considerably. Even so, prior to 1824 there was not an overwhelming interest on the part of eligible voters to cast their ballots. In the presidential election of 1824 only 355 000 men bothered to vote. By 1828, however, the number of votes cast tripled to over 1 155 000.

There were several reasons for this dramatic increase in voter interest, but perhaps the most significant was the re–emergence of distinct political parties in the mid–1820s. The election of 1824 was a hard–fought battle and the end results left the political process in a state of confusion. The Federalists had ceased to exist as a political force. As a result, all the major contenders for the presidency called themselves Republicans. There were four candidates for president, and as is often the case when several candidates run for the same office, no one received a majority of electoral college votes. Andrew Jackson was the most popular candidate. His 153 544 votes resulted in 99 electoral college ballots, winning Pennsylvania, New Jersey, and most of the South and West. Second, supported by 108 740 voters and 84 electors, mainly from New England and New York, was John Quincy Adams. William H. Crawford (46 618) had 41 votes, and Henry Clay (47 136) only 37. With no candidate holding a majority, the election was turned over to the House of Representatives to decide. Clay, in fourth place, was dropped from contention. Suspicious of Jackson, Clay threw his support behind Adams. That was enough to determine the outcome. Voting by states, Adams received thirteen votes, Jackson seven, and Crawford four. Jackson and his supporters were furious. They believed that a conspiracy had stolen the election from them.

The hard feelings that emerged as a result of the election soon split the Republican party. Supporters of Adams began calling themselves the "National Republicans" as distinct from Jackson's "Democratic Republicans." It was Jackson's "Democrats" that would form the basis of the modern Democratic party.

Political rivalry was encouraged by supporters of both groups. It has been said that the campaign for the election of 1828 began the day that Adams was declared president in 1824. Jackson condemned the "anti-democratic" deal that had "stolen" the presidency from him. His supporters wrote pamphlets, gave speeches, and formed local clubs and organizations, and although these "Democrats" were unclear what policies they were for, they knew what they were against.

The first "modern" presidential election took place in 1828, and the campaigning was rough and personal. Jackson's supporters accused Adams of squandering public funds on personal luxuries and of living a wild and dissolute life while serving as an ambassador in earlier years. When the president spent his own money on a billiard table and a set of chess pieces for the White House, Jacksonites labelled the purchases "gaming tables and gambling furniture."

Defenders of Adams dredged up tales of Jackson's military atrocities, including that he had shot six members of the militia for insubordination. The gloves were off, in spite of the fact that many of the accusations were unproven. In the end, however, it was no contest. Jackson had been preparing this campaign for years and the results were worth his efforts. Although relatively close in the popular vote (647 286 to 508 064) the results in the electoral college gave the challenger a clear victory. Sweeping the South and the West, Jackson won 178 electoral votes to Adams's 83. In reality, however, Jackson's victory was not a regional one but one of class. He had campaigned as the candidate of the common people, and the people had responded. (And what of John C. Calhoun, Adams's vice-president? Sensing which way the political winds were blowing, Calhoun abandoned Adams's campaign and ran as Jackson's running mate, winning re-election against his old partner!)

The election of 1828 clearly reflected a fundamental change in American politics. Power was beginning to shift away from the traditional ruling class to the hands of the common people.

Jacksonian Democracy

Although there was a dramatic increase in popular participation in the electoral process after 1824, it was still limited to white adult males. Democracy in the "Age of Jackson" was not as we consider it today. Blacks, Native people, and women were not part of the electorate. In fact, even Jackson's "conservative" opponents were more open–minded than the Democrats when it came to extending the voting franchise. Equality under the president they called "Old Hickory" really meant equality of opportunity for white men only. Jackson did appeal to the common people, however—the rural farmers of the West and the working classes of the East. His popularity was fostered by his image as a general and an Indian fighter. Many Jacksonians prided themselves on their ignorance and lack of education. When their political opponents compared them to a jackass, they were delighted; it has been the symbol of the Democratic party ever since.

Margaret Bayard Smith was a well-known Washington hostess during this period. The wife of the editor of the *National Intelligencer*, a Republican paper, she was also a contributer to various magazines. She described the party at the White House following Jackson's inauguration:

> The Majesty of the People [Jackson] had disappeared, and a rabble, a mob, of boys, negros, women, children, scrambling fighting, romping. What a pity what a pity! . . . The whole house had been inundated by the rabble mob . . .
>
> Old Hickory . . . had escaped to his lodgings at Gadsby's. Cut glass and china to the amount of several thousand dollars had been broken in the struggle to get the refreshments. Punch and other articles had been carried out in tubs and buckets, but had it been in hogsheads it would have been insufficient, ice-creams, and cake, and lemonade for 20 000 people . . .
>
> Ladies fainted, men were seen with bloody noses and such a scene of confusion took place as is impossible to describe.

This then was the "new democracy." The lower classes felt that they had finally elected "one of their own." But had they?

The Spoils System

"To the victors belong the spoils." This was the guiding principle of the early Jackson years. He was the first president to "clean house"—that is, to get rid of many of the appointees of his predecessors. He removed about 40 percent of these office holders (252 out of 612), creating considerable hardship for those who were displaced. In an age without pensions many elderly, hard–working public servants found themselves on the streets. Jackson justified his actions by claiming that in order to change policies, new people had to take control. In actual fact, the rapid growth of political parties had made these first "patronage" appointments essential. Loyal supporters expected more than just gratitude for their trouble. But such a system can and often does lead to corruption. A prime example during Jackson's presidency was the appointment of Samuel Swartwout as customs collector in New York. In less than ten years in the job, he managed to embezzle over $1 million.

Andrew Jackson was the champion of the common person. Although not a true "democrat" himself, his election was a symbol of a new democratic spirit in the country. The period surrounding his presidency has often been called a Second American Revolution. Certainly revolutionary changes were taking place in the

Patriotes at St. Denis defeat Col. Gore, 1837

Louis-Joseph Papineau   Andrew Jackson   William Lyon Mackenzie

social, intellectual, and economic life. But what about the political sphere? What made Jacksonian democracy so different from its predecessors?

Jackson's Views on Democracy

Jackson was frustrated with the events of 1824 which "robbed" him of the presidency. Once elected four years later he set out to change the system. In his first message to Congress as president he outlined his concern:

> To the people belongs the right of electing their Chief Magistrate; it was never designed that their choice should in any case be defeated, either by the intervention of electoral colleges or by the agency confided, under certain contingencies, to the House of Representatives. Experience proves that in proportion as agents to execute the will of the people are multiplied there is danger of their wishes being frustrated. Some may be unfaithful, all are liable to err. So far, therefore, as the people can with convenience speak, it is safer for them to express their own will.

The speech reflects Jackson's belief that the president, as the only nationally elected official, was the best representative of the will of the people. He demonstrated this idea clearly in 1834. Jackson had ordered the secretary of the treasury to remove $12 million in federal deposits from the Bank of the United States. The Senate, led by Henry Clay, censured Jackson for his action claiming that he had no constitutional right to give orders to the secretary. Jackson responded:

> The President is the direct representative of the American people, but the Secretaries are not. If the Secretary of the Treasury be independent of the President in the execution of the laws, then there is no direct responsibility to the people in that important branch of this Government to which is committed the care of the national finances. . . .
> If the censures of the Senate be submitted to by the President, the confidence of the people in his ability and virtue and character and usefulness of his Administration will soon be at an end, and the real power of the Government will fall into the hands of a body holding their offices for long terms, not elected by the people and not to them directly responsible. [Senators were not chosen by direct election until 1913.]

Jackson saw himself not just as the elected representative of the common people but also as a father figure. His vision of democracy was the election of a benevolent ruler who would look out for the interests of the average citizen. These sentiments were expressed in his remarks to the people of South Carolina in 1832:

> Fellow citizens of my native State, let me not only admonish you as the First Magistrate of our common country, not to incur the penalty of its law, but use the influence that a father would over his children whom he saw rushing to certain ruin. In that paternal language, with that paternal feeling,

let me tell you, my fellow countrymen that you are deluded by men who are either deceived themselves or wish to deceive you.

His opponents, however, did not always see him in such a benevolent light. A political cartoon from the period depicted Jackson not as the president of a democracy but as a king. He was shown with a veto in his left hand, one foot on the torn Constitution, and the other on the Bank of the United States.

Campaigns and Public Opinion

Universal white manhood suffrage radically changed the rules of the political game. Where in the past politics had been a type of exclusive social club, new factors were coming into play. Voters were not just looking for positions on certain issues but were seeking a candidate that would represent their interests in office. One such candidate was Davey Crockett. The following is a story from one of his campaigns for Congress.

I got up and told the people I reckoned they know'd what I had come for, but if not, I could tell them. I had come for their votes, and if they didn't watch mighty close I'd get them too. But the worst of all was, that I could not tell them anything about government. I tried to speak about something, and I cared very little what, until I choked up as bad as if my mouth had been jamm'd and cramm'd chock full of dry mush. There the people stood, listening all the while, with their eyes, mouths, and ears all open, to catch every word I would speak.

At last I told them I was like a fellow I had heard of not long before. He was beating on the head of an empty barrel near the roadside, when a traveler, who was passing along, asked him what he was doing that for? The fellow replied that there was some cider in that barrel a few days before, and he was trying to see if there was any then, but if there was he couldn't get at it. I told them that there had been a little bit of a speech in me a while ago, but I believed I couldn't get it out. They all roared out in a mighty laugh, and I told some other anecdotes, equally amusing to them, and believing I had them in a first-rate way, I quit and got down, thanking the people for their attention. But I took care to remark that I was as dry as a powderhorn, and that I thought it was time for us all to wet our whistles a little: and so I put off to the liquor stand, and was followed by the greater part of the crowd.

Jackson appreciated the value of having public opinion on his side. So critical was this to his way of thinking that, according to Daniel Webster, Jackson actually bribed and directed the press. This was a new approach to the political process, and Webster was clearly frustrated by it:

Mr. President, an open attempt to secure the aid and friendship of the public press, by bestowing the emoluments of office on its active conductors, seems to me, of every thing we have witnessed, to be the most reprehensible. It degrades both the government and the press. As far as its natural effect extends, it turns the palladium of liberty into an engine of party. It brings the agency, activity, energy, and patronage of government all to bear, with united force, on the means of general intelligence, and on the adoption or rejection of political opinions. It so completely perverts the true object of government, it so entirely revolutionizes our whole system, that the chief business of those in power is directed rather to the propagation of opinions favourable to themselves, than to the execution of laws.

The author James Fenimore Cooper also recognized the "power of the press" in politics. He wrote in 1838 that:

Publick opinion is the lever by which all things are moved, in a democracy. It has even become so powerful in monarchies, as virtually, to destroy all despotism in all really civilized countries, holding in check the will and passions of princes.
Publick opinion, however, like all things human, can work evil in proportion to its power to do good . . .
Publick opinion rightly directed is the highest source of national virtue, as publick opinion, which has taken the wrong direction, is the surest means of serving the devil.

Politicians and political observers in the Age of Jackson knew that they were experimenting with new forces in society. Mastery of the press, of public opinion, and of campaign style could decide victory regardless of the strength of the candidate. For many members of the traditional political elite it was a frightening time.

An outside observer of political events in America at this time was Alexis de Tocqueville. De Tocqueville arrived in New York on May 11, 1831, to investigate the state of prison reform in the United States on behalf of the government of France. But for him the real fascination lay in the nature of the American democratic experience. Together with his companion, Gustave de Beaumount, de Tocqueville quickly finished his prison investigation and then set out on a real voyage of discovery. Nine months later he returned to France with comprehensive notes that would later become a two–volume study entitled *Democracy in America*. His comments provide insight into an impartial outsider's view of Jacksonian democracy:

The very essence of democratic government consists in the absolute sovereignty of the majority . . .
The legislature is, of all political institutions, the one which is most easily swayed by the will of the majority . . .
When I see that the right and means of absolute command are conferred on any power whatever, be it called a people or a king, an aristocracy or a democracy . . . I say there is the germ of tyranny . . .

In my opinion, the main evil of the present democratic institutions of the United States does not arise, as is often asserted in Europe, from their weakness, but from their irresistible strength. I am not so much alarmed at the excessive liberty which reigns in that country, as at the inadequate securities which one finds there against tyranny.

In order that an association amongst a democratic people should have any power . . . means must be found to converse every day without seeing each other, and take steps in common without having met. Thus, hardly any democratic association can do without newspapers.

To call this period in American history the "Age of Jackson" may give too much importance to the role of one man. It is obvious that in many ways Jackson was an anti-democratic figure: he was a slave-holder; he dispossessed thousands of Native people; he was even ready to use troops to put down a political insurrection. In spite of all the negative aspects of his presidency, however, he remains a symbol of the growth of democratic ideas and practices during the era.

The Growth of Democracy in British North America

British North America was ripe for political change in the decades following the end of the War of 1812. The growing radicalism of the middle and lower classes in England and the democratic republicanism of the United States both found their way into the northern colonies through waves of immigration.

These new ideas found fertile ground in the disgruntled British colonies. Under the Constitutional Act of 1791, a deliberate attempt had been made to check the power of the democratically elected houses of assembly. The governor and lieutenant-governors and their appointed legislative and executive councils were designed to provide the aristocratic element which Britain felt had been missing in the governments of the pre-revolutionary Thirteen Colonies. First through the sale of crown and clergy reserves, and later through a system of legislative grants, the councils were able to maintain some degree of economic independence from the "power of the purse" held by the assemblies. By the 1830s the frustrations felt by those people on the outside of this system began to be expressed through the emergence of strong reform movements.

In the Maritimes (except Newfoundland), as in the Canadas, the move towards democracy followed a similar pattern. Unlike in the Canadas, however, the executive and legislative councils were combined in one body, which narrowed the target for reform. Local leadership in the assemblies called for such changes as a democratically elected council, and Joseph Howe of Nova Scotia even went so far as to lead the assembly to pass the Twelve Resolutions which called for widely increased powers for the assembly. The Colonial Office responded with a compromise solution which had been accepted already in New Brunswick. Under this arrangement, the governor of the colony was directed to bring members of the assembly into the council, thereby making the executive body more responsive to the electorate. It was not quite responsible government, but it was an improvement over the status quo.

Change did not come as smoothly in the two Canadas. In Lower Canada the conflict took on both economic and racial overtones. The democratically elected assembly reflected the needs and interests of the agrarian majority of French-speaking habitants. In contrast, the councils were dominated by the commercial interests of the British minority. A series of elections in the late 1820s and early 1830s heightened the polarization within the colony and propelled its citizens towards direct confrontation with the political establishment. In 1834 the assembly issued its own Ninety-Two Resolutions to the Colonial Office, in which they called for elective councils and an end to the patronage system which had grown up around what was known as the Château Clique.

The spoils system which was the cornerstone of Jacksonian America during this time had its parallel in the Canadas. However, in the British colonies it was not democratically elected politicians who were dispensing favours but rather the governor and the appointed councils. This system was described in Upper Canada as a "Family Compact" which controlled all government posts.

Opposition to the existing order in Upper Canada was less focussed than in Lower Canada. Popular support in the assembly wavered during the 1820s and 1830s between the Tories (supporters of the appointed councils) and the Reformers. While many Upper Canadians objected to the obvious abuses of power evident in the councils, most were unwilling to back more radical leaders such as William Lyon Mackenzie who called for a severing of British ties and the establishment of a republic. Even a majority of the rebels of 1837 in Upper Canada saw themselves as forces for reform, not independence. In comparison, sentiments in Lower Canada were much more radical, as expressed by the newspaper *The Vindicator*:

". . . the die is cast; the British ministry have resolved to set the seal of degradation and slavery on this Province, and to render it actually, what it was only in repute - the 'IRELAND' of NORTH AMERICA . . . One duty alone remains for the people of Lower Canada. Let them study the HISTORY OF THE AMERICAN REVOLUTION."

So clearly did the Patriotes of Lower Canada identify their cause with the Thirteen Colonies in 1776 that they even established their own "Fils de la Liberté" (Sons of Liberty) to terrorize government supporters.

Although local authorities saw their struggle against the radicals as the decisive battle against republicanism and the American style of government, the eventual defeat of the rebels in both Upper and Lower Canada in fact set the stage for the rebels attaining the goals they sought.

In the next decade, a reorganized government would see a rapid growth in democratic power and the emergence of new and vital political parties.

The Emergence of the Party System

"When a nobleman advocates democratic institutions, we give him full credit for the benevolence of his intentions, but we doubt his sanity."

This statement by Maritime satirist Judge Thomas Chandler Haliburton reflects the political response to the Durham report (see readings). There is no question that Durham's hope for a system of ministerial responsibility was still an idea of the future in 1841. Even so, British governors Sydenham and later Elgin, who were sent to the colonies to work with the councils in Upper and Lower Canada, recognized their grave shortcomings. Sydenham complained that the executive operated not as a government, but as a committee independent of legislative affairs. Elgin described the executive more bluntly, calling it "worse than useless."

There were two basic views of responsible government in the 1840s. Tories favoured the appointment of moderates who could win support in the assembly. Reformers, on the other hand, called for the appointment of assembly members who could already lay claim to a majority of support in the house. Eventually the reform view won out. In the process, the two old-line parties drew closer together philosophically. After all, in the 1830s their struggle had not been over policy, but over who would implement it. Once this issue was settled after 1849 they found little to distinguish their views. By 1854 they joined forces with the conservative "Bleu" party from Lower Canada to form the Liberal-Conservatives. Times had changed. This first coalition government was headed by Auguste-Nobert Morin, one of the authors of the "Ninety–Two Resolutions," and Sir Allan Napier McNab, one of the supporters of the Family Compact.

On the opposite side of the house was what some Conservatives referred to as an "unholy alliance." From Lower Canada came the Parti Rouge, representing a minority of citizens. They were fiercely democratic, but just as fiercely anti-British and anti-Protestant. From Upper Canada came the Clear Grits. The heartland of the Grit movement was western Upper Canada. The centre of the Duncombe uprising in 1837 (see readings), this area was greatly influenced by American ideas. The Grits called for more local autonomy with a smaller central government; for universal manhood suffrage; for assembly elections every two years; and for the replacement of patronage-appointed officials by elected ones. This rallying cry, however, and the issue which cost them most of their support in Canada East, was "representation by population." At the time of the Act of Union, Canada East had been the more populous of the two provinces. As a result, the equal representation provided by the act benefitted the western half of the new colony. By the late 1850s, however, the population balance had shifted. When George Brown, editor of the Toronto *Globe* and leader of the Grits, called for "rep by pop" it was seen as a direct threat to Canada East. Eventually the Grits would form the nucleus of the Liberal party, which would rule Ontario until 1905 and dominate federal politics for most of the twentieth century.

In spite of the emergence of political parties during this period, however, party leaders did not enjoy the same kind of control over their members as they do today. Administrations tended to be governments by coalition rather than by strict party loyalty; often a ministry would watch its support slowly dwindle away on successive votes in the House. On the other hand, British observers often commented on the pervasiveness of the Canadian party system. Lacking the rigid class structure of the mother country and a wider voting franchise, Canadian parties tended to reflect the electorate. In a relatively unstructured colonial society, political leaders built their bases of support on existing social structures. As a result, elections depended upon the loyalty of religious groups and social clubs such as the Masons and the Orange Order (see readings). The loyalty they displayed was rewarded through the careful dispensation of patronage following an election.

The birth of democracy in British North America was a slower and quieter process than in the United States but relentless just the same. While the frustrations with existing colonial oligarchies surfaced violently in the Canadas in 1837-38, the actual winning of responsible government came not through confrontation but through political cooperation. As Joseph Howe said, Nova Scotia achieved democratic self-government "without the shedding of a drop of blood [or] . . . the breaking of a pane of glass."

The evolution of political parties also followed a different path. By the 1850s, American parties had become sectional in nature, and the primary issue of the age, slavery, tended to dominate political life. In the final analysis, it was the breakdown of the party system in 1860 and the election of a minority president, Abraham Lincoln, which finally led to the dissolution of the Union. In the Canadas, on the other hand, for a political party to be successful it had to cut across regional and racial lines. The failure of the Grits and the Rouges to seriously challenge the strength of the Conservatives during this period lay in their inability to break out of a strictly regional power base. Although the emergence of the "double majority" (i.e., French–English) concept had virtually paralyzed government by the early 1860s, it had entrenched the concept of duality in Canadian politics. John A. Macdonald's observation in 1859 that the French–Canadian electorate was the "anchor" of any successful political party would come back to haunt his Conservative successor, Joe Clark, 120 years later.

The period from the end of the War of 1812 to the beginning of the 1860s saw the emergence of the forms and practices of modern political democracy in Canada and the United States. Although both nations still limited the right to vote to a minority of the population, the twin pillars of democracy and party would nevertheless form the basis for two strong democratic states in the twentieth century.

Aristocracy and Politics, 1813

The following two documents are excerpts from correspondence between Thomas Jefferson and John Adams. Part of the letters deal with the respective views of the two men with regard to the role of the aristocracy in a democratic society.

Jefferson to Adams, October 28, 1813

. . . I agree with you that there is a natural aristocracy among men. The grounds of this are virtue and talents. . . . There is also an artificial aristocracy, founded on wealth and birth, without either virtue or talents; for with these it would belong to the first class. The natural aristocracy I consider as the most precious gift of nature, for the instruction, the trusts, and government of society. And indeed, it would have been inconsistent in creation to have formed man for the social state, and not to have provided virtue and wisdom enough to manage the concerns of the society. May we not even say, that that form of government is the best, which provides the most effectually for a pure selection of these natural aristoi into the offices of government? . . . the best remedy is exactly that provided by all our constituents, to leave to the citizens the free election and separation of the aristoi from the pseudo-aristoi, of the wheat from the chaff. In general they will elect the really good and wise. In some instances, wealth may corrupt, and birth blind them; but not in sufficient degree to endanger the society.

. . . At the first session of our legislature after the Declaration of Independence, we passed a law abolishing the privilege of primogeniture, and dividing the lands of intestates equally among all their children, or other representatives. These laws, drawn by myself, laid the axe to the foot of pseudo-aristocracy. And had another which I prepared been adopted by the legislature, our work would have been complete. It was a bill for the more general diffusion of learning . . . to establish in each ward a free school for reading, writing and common arithmetic; to provide for the annual selection of the best subjects from these schools, who might receive, at the public expense, a higher degree of education at a district school; and from these district schools to select a certain number of the most promising subjects, to be completed at an university, where all the useful sciences should be taught. Worth and genius would thus have been sought out from every condition of life, and completely prepared by education for defeating the competition of wealth and birth for public trusts . . .

From Andrew A. Lipscomb and Albert E. Bergh, eds., *The Writings of Thomas Jefferson*, 20 vols. (Washington, D.C., 1905), Vols. XIII and XIV

Adams to Jefferson, November 15, 1813

. . . We are now explicitly agreed upon one important point, viz., that there is a natural aristocracy among men, the grounds of which are virtue and talents. . . . But though we have agreed in one point, in words, it is not yet certain that we are perfectly agreed in sense. Fashion has introduced an indeterminate use of the word talents. Education, wealth, strength, beauty, stature, birth, marriage, graceful attitudes and motions, gait, air, complexion, physiognomy, are talents, as well as genius, science, and learning. Any one of these talents that in fact commands or influences two votes in society, gives to the man who possesses it the character of an aristocrat, in my sense of the word. Pick up the first hundred men you meet, and make a republic. Every man will have an equal vote; but when deliberations and discussions are opened, it will be found that twenty-five, by their talents, virtues being equal, will be able to carry fifty votes. Every one of these twenty-five is an aristocrat in my sense of the word; whether he obtains his one vote in addition to his own, by his birth, fortune, figure, eloquence, science, learning, craft, cunning, or even his character for good fellowship, and a *bon vivant*.

. . . Your distinction between natural and artificial aristocracy, does not appear to me founded. Birth and wealth are conferred upon some men as imperiously by nature as genius, strength, or beauty. The heir to honors, and riches, and power, has often no more merit in procuring these advantages, than he has in obtaining a handsome face of an elegant figure. When aristocracies are established by human laws, and honor, wealth and power are made hereditary by municipal laws and political institutions, then I acknowledge artificial aristocracy to commence; but this never commences till corruption in elections becomes dominant and uncontrollable. But this artificial aristocracy can never last. The ever-lasting envies, jealousies, rivalries, and quarrels among them; their cruel rapacity upon the poor ignorant people, their followers, compel them to set up Caesar, a demagogue, to be a monarch, a master; *pour mettre chacun à sa place*. Here you have the origin of all artificial aristocracy, which is the origin of all monarchies. And both artificial aristocracy and monarchy, and civil, military, political, and hierarchical despotism, have all grown out of the natural aristocracy of virtues and talents. We, to be sure, are far remote from this. Many hundred years must roll away before we shall be corrupted. Our pure, virtuous, public-spirited, federative republic will last forever, govern the globe, and introduce the perfection of man; his perfectibility being already proved by Price, Priestley, Condorcet, Rousseau, Diderot, and Godwin. . . .

You suppose a difference of opinion between you and me on the subject of aristocracy. I can find none. I dislike and detest hereditary honors, offices, emoluments, established by law. So do you. I am for excluding legal, hereditary distinctions from the United States as long as possible. So are you. I only say that mankind have not yet discovered any remedy against irresistible corruption in elections to offices of great power and profit, but making them hereditary.

From Andrew A. Lipscomb and Albert E. Bergh, eds., *The Writings of Thomas Jefferson*, 20 vols. (Washington, D.C., 1905), Vols. XIII and XIV.

1. How does Jefferson distinguish natural aristocracy from the artificial variety?
2. What argument does Adams use to counter Jefferson's view?
3. What relationships do both men identify between society's aristocrats and the democratic process?

Democracy and Property, 1821

In 1821 the Constitutional Convention of New York decided to drop most of the property qualifications previously needed to vote. This was a radical departure from past practices, and although the measure was eventually adopted, it was not without considerable debate. In this excerpt, James Kent, a member of the New York Supreme Court, argues against the change.

Debate in the New York Constitutional Convention, 1821

Chancellor Kent . . . Let us recall our attention, for a moment, to our past history.

This state has existed for forty-four years under our present constitution, which was formed by those illustrious sages and patriots who adorned the revolution. It has wonderfully fulfilled all the great ends of civil government. During that long period, we have enjoyed in an eminent degree, the blessings of civil and religious liberty. We have had our lives, our privileges, and our property protected. . . .

These are some of the fruits of our present government; and yet we seem to be dissatisfied with our condition, and we are engaged in the bold and hazardous experiment of remodeling the constitution. . . . do we not expose ourselves to the danger of being deprived of the blessings we have enjoyed? . . .

The senate has hitherto been elected by the farmers of the state—by the free and independent lords of the soil, worth at last $250 in freehold estate, over and above all debts charged thereon. The governor has been chosen by the same electors, and we have hitherto elected citizens of elevated rank and character. Our assembly has been chosen by freeholders, possessing a freehold of the value of $50, or by persons renting a tenement of the yearly value of $5, and who have been rated and actually paid taxes to the state. By the report before us, we propose to annihilate, at one stroke, all those property distinctions and to bow before the idol of universal suffrage. That extreme democratic principle, when applied to the legislative and executive departments of government, has been regarded with terror by the wise men of every age because, in every European republic, ancient and modern, in which it has been tried, it has terminated disastrously and been productive of corruption, injustice, violence, and tyranny. And dare we flatter ourselves that we are a peculiar people who can run the career of history, exempted from the passions which have disturbed and corrupted the rest of mankind? If we are like other races of men, with similar follies and vices, then I greatly fear that our posterity will have reason to deplore, in sackcloth and ashes, the delusion of the day.

. . . The great body of the people are now the owners and actual cultivators of the soil. With that wholesome population we always expect to find moderation, frugality, order, honesty, and a due sense of independence, liberty, and justice. It is impossible that any people can lose their liberties by internal fraud or violence, so long as the country is parceled out among freeholders of moderate possessions, and those freeholders have a sure and efficient control in the affairs of government. Their habits, sympathies, and employments necessarily inspire them with a correct spirit of freedom and justice; they are the safest guardians of property and the laws. . . .

. . . The men of no property, together with the crowds of dependents connected with great manufacturing and commercial establishments, and the motley and undefinable population of crowded ports, may, perhaps, at some future day, under skilful management, predominate in the assembly, and yet we should be perfectly safe if no laws could pass without the free consent of the owners of the soil. That security we at present enjoy; and it is that security which I wish to retain.

The apprehended danger from the experiment of universal suffrage applied to the whole legislative department is no dream of the imagination. It is too mighty an excitement for the moral constitution of men to endure. The tendency of universal suffrage is to jeopardize the rights of property and the principles of liberty. There is a constant tendency in human society, and the history of every age proves it; there is a tendency in the poor to covet and to share the plunder of the rich; in the debtor to relax or avoid the obligation of contracts; in the majority to tyrannize over the minority and trample down their rights; in the indolent and the profligate to cast the whole burthens [burdens] of society upon the industrious and the virtuous; and *there is a tendency in ambitious and wicked men to inflame these combustible materials.* It requires a vigilant government, and a firm administration of justice, to counteract that tendency.

From *New York Constitutional Convention, 1821* in Richard Hofstadter, ed., *Great Issues in American History*, (New York: Vintage Books, 1968).

1. How does Kent characterize the situation in 1821?
2. Why does Kent say that this "extreme democratic principle . . . has been regarded with terror by wise men of every age."?
3. Defend or refute Kent's assertion that it requires "men of property" to ensure responsible governing. Pair up with a classmate. Represent the opposing viewpoints and stage a two-person debate on the isue.

Democracy in America, 1831

Alexis de Tocqueville travelled extensively through the United States and Canada in the early 1830s. Sent to investigate prison reform, he soon became interested in the whole process of government in the United States. The result was a two volume work entitled Democracy in America. *In this excerpt the young French liberal comments upon the power of the majority in American government.*

The very essence of democratic government consists in the absolute sovereignty of the majority; for there is nothing in democratic states which is capable of resisting it. Most of the American constitutions have sought to increase this natural strength of the majority by artificial means.

The legislature is, of all political institutions, the one which is most easily swayed by the will of the majority. The Americans determined that the members of the legislature should be elected by the people *directly*, and for a *very brief term*, in order to subject them, not only to the general convictions, but even to the daily passions, of their constituents. . . .

Custom has done even more than law. A proceeding is becoming more and more general in the United States, which will, in the end, do away with the guarantees of representative government: it frequently happens that the voters, in electing a delegate, point out a certain line of conduct to him, and impose upon him certain positive obligations which he is pledged to fulfil. With the exception of the tumult, this comes to the same thing as if the majority itself held its deliberations in the market-place.

Several other circumstances concur to render the power of the majority in America not only preponderant, but irresistible. The moral authority of the majority is partly based upon the notion, that there is more intelligence and wisdom in a number of men united than in a single individual, and that the number of the legislators is more important than their quality. The theory of equality is thus applied to the intellects of men; and human pride is thus assailed in its last retreat by a doctrine which the minority hesitate to admit, and to which they will but slowly assent. Like all other powers, and perhaps more than any other, the authority of the many requires the sanction of time in order to appear legitimate. At first, it enforces obedience by constraint; and its laws are not *respected* until they have been long maintained.

The right of governing society, which the majority supposes itself to derive from its superior intelligence, was introduced into the United States by the first settlers; and this idea, which itself would be sufficient to create a free nation, has now been amalgamated with the manners of the people and the minor incidents of social life.

... The majority, therefore, in that country, exercise a prodigious actual authority, and a power of opinion which is nearly as great; no obstacles exist which can impede or even retard its progress, so as to make it heed the complaints of those whom it crushes upon its path. This state of things is harmful in itself, and dangerous for the future.

From Alexis de Tocqueville, *Democracy in America*, (Boston, 1876).

1. According to de Tocqueville, how did the Americans guarantee that their legislators would be responsive to their wishes?
2. Why does the author state that the will of the majority is not only "preponderant", but "irresistible"?
3. Give your own opinion of de Tocqueville's general view of the danger inherent in the "tyranny of the majority."

The American Democrat, 1838

James Fenimore Cooper was one of the foremost literary figures of the Jacksonian era in the United States. In addition to a wide range of novels, Cooper also published a number of works of social criticism. Although a member of the Democratic party, in this excerpt from his book The American Democrat, *Cooper raises concerns about the unchecked power of public opinion.*

Publick opinion is the lever by which all things are moved, in a democracy. It has even become so powerful in monarchies, as virtually, to destroy despotism in all really civilized countries, holding in check the will and passions of princes.

Publick opinion, however, like all things human, can work evil in proportion to its power to do good. On the same principle that the rebound is proportioned to the blow in physics, there can be no moral agent capable of benefitting man that has not an equal power to do him harm. Publick opinion rightly directed is the highest source of national virtue, as publick opinion, which has taken a wrong direction, is the surest means of serving the devil.

In a democracy, as a matter of course, every effort is made to seize upon and create publick opinion, which is, substantially, securing power. One of the commonest arts practised, in connection with this means of effecting objects, is to simulate the existence of a general feeling in favor, or against, any particular man, or measure; so great being the deference paid to publick opinion, in a country like this, that men actually yield their own sentiments to that which they believe to be the sentiment of the majority. . . .

Whenever the government of the United States shall break up, it will probably be in consequence of a false direction having been given to publick opinion. This is the weak point of our defenses, and the part to which the enemies of the system will direct all their attacks. Opinion can be so perverted as to cause the false to seem the true; the enemy, a friend, and the friend, an enemy; the best interests of the nation to appear insignificant, and trifles of moment; in a word, the right the wrong, and the wrong the right.

In a country where opinion has sway, to seize upon it, is to seize upon power. As it is a rule of humanity that the upright and well intentioned are comparatively passive, while the designing, dishonest and selfish are the most untiring in their efforts, the danger of publick opinion's getting a false direction, is four-fold, since few men think for themselves. . . .

From James Fenimore Cooper, *The American Democrat*, (New York: Alfred H. Knopf, Vintage edition, 1956).

1. Explain Cooper's image of the two faces of public opinion.
2. How do people create public opinion?
3. What does Cooper see as the possible final consequence of adherence to public opinion?

The Tricks of the Democratic Trade, 1830s

Backwoods hero Davey Crockett was also a successful politician. Serving a number of terms as Congressman, Crockett was full of advice for aspiring "democratic" politicians. In the following excerpt, Crockett explains the tricks of democratic politics to an audience in Little Rock, Arkansas.

Having gone through with the regular toasts, the president of the day drank, "Our distinguished guest, Col. Crockett," and I soon saw that nothing would do, but I must get up and make them a speech.

I told them, that I was an old hand at the business, and as I was about to retire for a time I would give them a little instruction gratis, for I was up to all tricks of the trade.

"Attend all public meetings," says I "and get some friends to move that you take the chair; if you fail in this attempt, make a push to be appointed secretary, the proceedings of course will be published, and your name is introduced to the public. Intrigue until you are elected an officer of the militia; this is the second step towards promotion, and can be accomplished with ease, as I know an instance of an election being advertised, and no one attending, the innkeeper at whose house it was to be held, having a military turn, elected himself colonel of his regiment.

"If your ambition or circumstances compel you to serve your country, and earn three dollars a day, by becoming a member of the legislature, you must first publicly avow that the constitution of the state is a shackle upon free and liberal legislation; and is, therefore, of as little use in the present enlightened age. There is policy in this measure, for by making the constitution a mere dead letter, your headlong proceedings will be attributed to a bold and unshackled mind; whereas, it might otherwise be thought they arose from sheer mulish ignorance.

"When the day of election approaches, visit your constituents far and wide.

Treat liberally, and drink freely, in order to rise in their estimation, though you fall in your own. True, you may be called a drunken dog by some of the clean shirt and silk stocking gentry, but the real rough necks will style you a jovial fellow, their votes are certain, and frequently count double. Do all you can to appear to advantage in the eyes of the women. That's easily done you have but to kiss and slabber their children, wipe their noses, and pat them on the head; this cannot fail to please their mothers, and you may rely on your business being done in that quarter.

"Promise all that is asked. Promises cost nothing, therefore deny nobody who has a vote or sufficient influence to obtain one.

"Get up on all occasions, and sometimes on no occasion at all, and make long-winded speeches, though composed of nothing else than wind—talk of your devotion to your country, your modesty and disinterestedness, or any such fanciful subject.

"If any charity be going forward, be at the top of it, provided it is to be advertised publicly; if not, it isn't worth your while. None but a fool would place his candle under a bushel on such an occasion.

"These few directions," said I, "if properly attended to, will do your business; and when once elected, why a fig for the dirty children, the promises, the bridges, the churches, the taxes, the offices, and the subscriptions, for it is absolutely necessary to forget all these before you can become a thoroughgoing politician, and a patriot of the first water."

My speech was received with three times three, and all that; and we continued speechifying and drinking until nightfall. I went to bed, pleased and gratified with the hospitality and kindness of the citizens of Little Rock. There are some first-rate men there, of the real half horse, half alligator breed, with a sprinkling of the steamboat, and such as grow nowhere on the face of the universal earth, but just about the back bone of North America.

From Davy Crockett, "The Art of Democratic Politics," in *The Life of Colonel David Crockett*, (Philadelphia: Porter and Coates, 1865).

1. How do you think a modern audience would respond to Davy Crockett's view of politics?
2. Rewrite Crockett's speech using modern examples of the tactics he describes.
3. To what extent do you think Crockett's observations about politics are valid today?

Party Politics, 1840

In this excerpt, Whig leader Henry Clay comments upon the political events which had led to the election of William Henry Harrison in 1840. In it he raises serious concerns about the "cult of the presidency" which emerged during Jackson's term of office.

What are the positions of the two great parties of the present day? Modern democracy has reduced the federal theory of a strong and energetic executive to practical operation. It has turned from the people, the natural ally of genuine democracy to the executive, and, instead of vigilance, jealousy, and distrust, has given to that department all its confidences, and made to it a virtual surrender of all the powers of government. The recognized maxim of royal infallibility is transplanted from the British monarchy into modern American democracy, and the president can do no wrong! This new school adopts, modifies, changes, renounces, renews opinions at the pleasure of the executive. . . .

The whigs of 1840 stand where the republicans of 1798 stood, and where the whigs of the Revolution were, battling for liberty, for the people, for free institutions, against power, against corruption, against executive incroachments, against monarchy.

We are reproached with struggling for offices and their emoluments. If we acted on the avowed and acknowledged principle of our opponents, 'that the spoils belong to the victors,' we should indeed be unworthy of the support of the people. No! fellow-citizens; higher, nobler, more patriotic motives actuate the whig party. Their object is the restoration of the Constitution, the preservation of liberty, and rescue of the country. If they were governed by the sordid and selfish motives acted upon by their opponents, and unjustly imputed to them, to acquire office and emolument, they have only to change their names, and enter the presidential palace. The gate is always wide open, and the path is no narrow one which leads through it. The last comer, too, often fares best. . . .

If this state of things were to remain—if the progress of executive usurpation were to continue unchecked, hopeless despair would seize the public mind, or the people would be goaded to acts of open and violent resistance. But, thank God, the power of the president, fearful and rapid as its strides have been, is not yet too great for the power of the elective franchise; and a bright and glorious prospect, in the election of William Henry Harrison, has opened upon the country.

From Calvin Colton, *The Life, Correspondence, and Speeches of Henry Clay*, (New York, 1857), Vol. VI.

1. In what ways does Clay equate the Jacksonian presidency to a "modern" monarchy?
2. What political role does Clay attribute to his own party, the Whigs?
3. To what extent could Clay's concerns be applied to the American presidency in our own day?

Democracy in Lower Canada, 1833

Louis-Joseph Papineau called for the introduction of democratic institutions in the colony years before the rebellions. In this speech he calls for the replacement of the appointed Council with one more responsive to the will of the people.

In the colonies the people need democratic institutions because they are less costly and less burdensome than more expensive institutions. . . . It is in the customs, the nature and the common interests of colony and mother country that government institutions should be economical, for everything that is taken from the enjoyment of luxury is an endowment for new families that will marry earlier, will clear new land, will create a new productive capital to buy the useful manufactured products of cloth and iron rather than silks and liquors. . . .

Give institutions where there is no cause for flattery, and national distinctions will cease. In the present situation the Government is reaping the fruits that it has sown. There is need, they say, of a council to defend one part of the population that can't be a majority in the Assembly. . . . The complaints of this country against the evils of the Council's composition are too unanimous to make it necessary to say more on this subject. The Constitutional Act has given the Council a disastrous preponderance that allows it to paralyze all the work of the House of Assembly.

From *La Minerve*, February 27, 1834, in Fernand Ouellet, *Papineau: Textes choisis et presentes* (Quebec: Les Presses de l'Universite Laval, 1958).

1. Why does Papineau assert that democratic institutions are more economical than aristocratic ones?
2. What ills does Papineau cite to be plaguing Lower Canada?
3. Papineau's nationalism is reflected later in the same speech when he declares that the Constitutional Act has installed "Upper Canada in the Legislative Council of Lower Canada." What is your opinion of this observation?

The Ninety-Two Resolutions, 1834

In 1834 the assembly in Lower Canada passed the Ninety-Two Resolutions outlining its grievances against the appointed councils. Although even some members of the reform faction saw many of the complaints as being "false" or "ridiculous," still they remain the clearest statement of the popular sentiments of the period. Two of the main grievances are outlined in the following excerpt.

Resolved, That the most serious defect in the Constitutional Act . . . the most active principle of evil and discontent in the province . . . is that injudicious enactment . . . which invests the Crown with that exorbitant power (incompatible with any government duly balanced, and founded on law and justice, and not on force and coercion) of selecting and composing without any rule or limitation, or any predetermined qualification, an entire branch of the legislature, supposed from the nature of its attributions to be independent, but inevitably the servile tool of the authority which creates, composes and decomposes it, and can on any day modify it to suit the interests or the passions of the moment. . . .

Resolved, That since a circumstance, which did not depend upon the choice of the majority of the people, their French origin and their use of the French language, has been made by the colonial authorities a pretext for abuse, for exclusion, for political inferiority, for a separation of rights and interests; this House now appeals to the justice of His Majesty's Government and of Parliament, and to the honour of the people of England; that the majority of the inhabitants of this country are in nowise disposed to repudiate any one of the advantages they derive from their origin and from their descent from the

French nation, which . . . has never been behind the British nation, and is now the worthy rival of the latter in the advancement of the cause of liberty and of the science of Government; from which this country derives the greater portion of its civil and ecclesiastical law, and of its scholastic and charitable institutions, and of the religion, language, habits, manners and customs of the great majority of its inhabitants.

From Janet Morchain and Mason Wade, eds., *Search for a Nation*, (Toronto: Fitzhenry and Whiteside, 1984).

1. In your own words, summarize the complaint laid against the means of selecting the council.
2. To what extent are national concerns separated from political ones in this document?
3. Why might this document have driven some of the English-speaking reformers away from the *patriote* cause?

The Declaration of Saint-Ours, 1837

On May 7, 1837, the patriotes *issued the following Declaration from the town of Saint-Ours. It is a uniquely French-Canadian combination of the Declaration of the Rights of Man from France and the American Declaration of Independence. The declaration was published in the newspaper* La Minerve *along with the editorial comment that follows in the second excerpt.*

The people of this country have long awaited justice from the colonial administration at first, and later from the metropolitan government, and always in vain; . . . The high opinion that we had of the justice and honour of the English people made us hope that the parliament which represented it would provide a remedy for our grievances. . . . We have recognized at last how much this country has been mislead by the lying promises which made it fight against a people which offered it liberty and equal rights in behalf of a people who prepared to enslave it. Sad experience forces us to recognize that our true friends and natural allies were on the other side of the 45th parallel.

Regarding ourselves as no longer bound except by force to the English government, we shall submit to it as to a government of force, expecting from God, our valid rights and circumstances a better fate. . . . Meanwhile, . . . we regard it as our duty . . . to resist by all means now in our possession to a tyrannical power . . . and we resolve:

That . . . By preference we shall consume products manufactured in our own country. . . .

In order to effect more efficaciously the regeneration of this country, all should rally around a single man, . . . This man, already singled out by the country, is L. J. Papineau.

From Janet Morchain and Mason Wade, eds., *Search for a Nation*, (Toronto: Fitzhenry and Whiteside, 1984).

Friend Jonathan will supply us with the articles which we cannot make here.

Therefore let us aid the smuggler; from now on he is a brave fellow whom each of us will encourage. Vigorous youths, determined and well organized, must be trained for this career. Smuggling must be done on a grand scale. No more circumspection or temporizing. . . . The sources of the revenue must be dried up. The vaults will empty; the thieves will find nothing more there. Then England will listen to reason. Never has a struggle been more just. We have withheld the subsidies; this weapon is now taken from us and we must seek others more efficacious.

From Janet Morchain and Mason Wade, eds., *Search for a Nation*, (Toronto: Fitzhenry and Whiteside, 1984).

1. Why do the patriotes feel betrayed by the British?
2. What actions do they propose to take to offer resistance to British rule?
3. What does the editor of *La Minerve* feel that the result will be?

Do Not Be Seduced by Rebellion, 1837

On October 24, 1837, Bishop Lartique of Montreal urged his parishioners not to involve themselves in the revolt. His comments reflect conservative French thought during the period.

. . . Everywhere brothers are seen arrayed against brothers, friends against friends, and citizens against their fellow citizens; and from one end of the diocese to the other discord seems to have broken the bonds of charity which existed between the members of one body, the children of one Church . . . .

We shall not give you our opinion, as a citizen, on the purely political question as to which is right or wrong among the diverse branches of the sovereign power . . . but the moral question, i.e., what are the duties of a Catholic toward the civil power established and constituted in each state, this moral question, I say, is within our domain and competence. . . .

Do not let yourselves be seduced if some one wishes to engage you in rebellion against the established government, under the pretext that you form part of the "Sovereign People." . . .

Have you ever considered seriously the horrors of civil strife? Have you pictured brooks of blood flooding your streets and your countryside, and the innocent engulfed with the guilty in the same sequence of misfortune? Have you reflected on the fact that, nearly without exception, every popular revolution is a bloody business, as experience proves; and that the philosopher of Geneva, the author of the *Social Contract*, the demagogue of the sovereignty of the people, says somewhere that a revolution would be bought too dearly, if it cost a single drop of blood?

From *Mandements des eveques de Montreal* (Montreal, 1867), Vol. I, Lartigue, 24 October 1837. Translation in Robert Christie, *History of the Late Province of Lower Canada*, Vol. IV.

1. How does the bishop depict civil war?
2. What criticism does Lartique make of Jean-Jacques Rousseau?

3. How effective do you think the bishop's arguments were with his parishioners?

Democracy and the Frontier, 1820s and 1830s

The following three excerpts come from contemporary observations on the impact of the frontier on society.

Edward Talbot was a schoolmaster and journalist. In this excerpt from his book Five Years' Residence in the Canadas *(1824), he commented upon the levelling influence of the frontier.*

It is very remarkable, that although the present population of this fine Province is composed of emigrants from almost every European nation, and from every state of North America, there should be so little difference in their manners, customs, and habits of life. Germans, Hollanders, French, English, Scotch, and Irish, after a few years' residence in Canada, forget their national customs and peculiarities, and become, in almost every particular, entirely assimilated to the people of America.

These emigrants, having generally been of the lowest class of society in their respective countries, —and consequently mere cyphers except in their own immediate sphere, —as soon as they arrive in Canada, begin to assume an appearance of importance, and to be quite ashamed of their former unassuming manners and native customs. The most absurd notions of equality and independence take instant possession of their vertiginous and unreflecting minds. . . . They are indefatigable in acquiring a knowledge of the Rights of Man, the First Principles of Equality, and the True Nature of Independency and, in a word, of every thing which characterises an American; and thus they quickly become divested of common manners, and common civility, and not infrequently of common honesty too, indeed, this latter virtuous quality is rather uncommon on this side of the Western Ocean. . . .

From Edward Allen Talbot, *Five Years' Residence in the Canadas*, Vol. II, (London: Longmans, Hurst, Rees, Orme, Brown and Green, 1824).

Anna Jameson spent eight months in Toronto in 1837. Her husband, Robert Jameson, was a prominent member of the government in the colony, serving as attorney-general in 1833-34, and as an elected member of the assembly from 1835-37. The following excerpt is from her book Winter Studies and Summer Rambles in Canada.

February 17, (1837)

"There is no *society* in Toronto," is what I hear repeated all around me—even by those who compose the only society we have. "But," you will say, "what could be expected in a remote town, which forty years ago was an uninhabited swamp, and twenty years ago only began to exist?" I really do not know what I expected, but I will tell you what I did *not* expect. I did not expect to find here in this new capital of a new country, with the boundless forest within half a mile of us on almost every side, —concentrated as it were the worst evils of our old and most artificial social system at home, with none of its *agremens*, and none of its advantages. Toronto is like a fourth or fifth rate provincial town, with the pretensions of a capital city. We have here a petty colonial oligarchy, a self-constituted aristocracy, based upon nothing real nor even upon any thing imaginary; and we have all the mutual jealousy and fear, and petty gossip, and mutual meddling and mean rivalship, which are common in a small society of which the members are well known to each other, ...

There reigns here a hateful factious spirit in political matters, but for the present no public or patriotic feeling, no recognition of general or generous principles of policy and as yet I have met with none of these. Canada is a colony, not a *country:* it is not yet identified with the dearest affections and associations, remembrances, and hopes of the inhabitants: it is to them an adopted, not a real mother. . . .

Toronto is, as a residence, worse and better than other small communities—*worse* in so much as it is remote from all the best advantages of a high state of civilization while it is infected by all its evils, all its follies; and *better*, because, besides being a small place, it is a *young* place; and in spite of this affectation of looking back, instead of looking up, it must advance—it may become the thinking head and beating heart of a nation, great, wise and happy; —who knows? . . .

From Anna Jameson, *Winter Studies and Summer Rambles in Canada*, Vol. I, (London: Saunders and Otley, 1838).

Susanna Moodie emigrated to Upper Canada in 1832, settling near Cobourg. Her husband was actively involved in putting down the Rebellion of 1837, and years later she wrote about the experience and the attitude of her family and their neighbours towards the disturbances.

Buried in the obscurity of these woods [north of Peterborough], we knew nothing, heard nothing of the political state of the country, and were little aware of the revolution which was about to work a great change for us and for Canada. . . .

. . . My brother and my sister's husband had already gone off to join some of the numerous bands of gentlemen who were collecting from all quarters to march to the aid of Toronto, which it was said was besieged by the rebel force. . . .

The honest backwoodsman, perfectly ignorant of the abuses that had led to the present position of things, regarded the rebels as a set of monsters, for whom no punishment was too severe, and obeyed the call to arms with enthusiasm. . . .

From Susanna Moodie, *Roughing in in the Bush: or, Forest Life in Canada* Vol. II, (London: Richard Bentley, 1852).

1. Discuss Talbot's observations about the levelling influence of the frontier.
2. How does Anna Jameson view the political and social climate of Toronto in 1837?
3. What do Susanna Moodie's observations tell us about the general response to the rebellion in Upper Canada in 1837?

Election Corruption, 1836

The newly arrived lieutenant-governor of Upper Canada, Sir Francis Bond Head, actively intervened in the election of 1836 to ensure a Tory majority in the assembly. Following the election this editorial comment appeared in the Toronto Correspondent and Advocate.

. . . Previous to and even during the election a vast number of deeds under Sir F.B. Head's name and seal of office were issued by the Government, under unusual and extraordinary circumstances, and were distributed at the very hustings by Government Agents to poor men, whose integrity was not sufficient to bear up against such disgraceful corruption. This was notoriously the case in the County of Simcoe. Men only for a short time residing in the country were thus brought up to the hustings to exercise the elective franchise in favor of Sir Francis Bond Head, their mistaken benefactor, whilst the votes of many old inhabitants of thirty or forty years standing, who fought and bled in defence of the Province during the 1st war; men of considerable property and influence, whose right to the franchise was never before questioned, were ignominiously rejected, ostensibly because they could not immediately produce their certificate of sworn allegiance to His Majesty which, being never before required, they neglected to bring with them, but in reality because they were known to be favorable to Reform, and hostile to the policy of the Executive. . . .

From *Correspondent and Advocate*, (Toronto July 6, 1836).

Harmannus Smith was a reform candidate defeated in the election of 1836. In this excerpt he writes to his supporters.

Gentlemen—I thank you for the expression of approbation and confidence in my capacity of representative of this county, and agree with you that it was not public opinion that put me down, but was accomplished by many bad votes— votes on freeholds within the corporation of the town of Hamilton, that is represented by its own member—the foreign auxiliaries—the votes of married women, whose husbands voted at the some [*sic*] poll, which is a species of votes I never heard of being received by any returning officer in Canada before—and lastly, and most corruptly of all, by votes on patent deeds issued from the Government office for the express purpose, and some of them dated after the election commenced. A pretty effectual way this to get a verdict of the country. . . .

From the Public Archives of Ontario, Mackenzie–Lindsey Clippings, No. 2464 in Colin Read and R.J. Stagg, *The Rebellion of 1837 in Upper Canada*, (Toronto: Champlain Society and Carleton Library, 1985).

Born in Connecticut, Charles Duncombe moved to Upper Canada in 1819. He was a highly respected surgeon. Elected to the assembly for Oxford in 1830 and 1834, private and public grievances led him to become a member of the radical reform group. After his defeat in 1836, he submitted the following petition to the House of Commons.

Eventually, he led the rebellion in the Brantford area. Following this unsuccessful attempt, he fled the country and settled in California, where he was later elected to the California state legislature.

HUMBLY SHEWETH,

That your Petitioner has been deputed by the Reformers of that Province [Upper Canada] to lay before His Majesty's Government and your Honourable House the dangerous crisis at which the affairs of violence and outrage practised and sanctioned by Sir F. Head, the present Lieutenant Governor, and those under his immediate influence . . ., for the purpose of obtaining a majority in the House of Asembly.

. . . The . . . Returning Officer, in the early part of his election, while the contest was doubtful, refused to take the votes of many Reformers, long resident in the Province, though they had voted at former elections, and offered to take the oaths required by the Statute, . . . upon the ground that they had not the certificate with them of their having taken the Oath which had not formerly been required at any of your Petitioner's previous elections. . . .

That after the election closed in Oxford, your Petitioner, who is a freeholder of Middlesex, proceeded on the last day of the election to the polling for that Country; on arriving within a mile and a half of the village of London, where the election was held, he met Mr. Moore, one of the successful Reform Candidates, escaping from the Orangemen, whom he said had threatened his life, and that he should not be returned, and who were driving with clubs the Reformers from the hustings, and beating them wherever they found them. . . .

That Mr. Wilson, the Returning Officer, forbade the Magistrates from interfering with the rioters during the election, and when Mr. Talbot insisted on his right as a Magistrate to keep the peace, . . . the Returning Officer threatened to commit him to prison. . . .

That the Lieutenant Governor, the Attorney General, and Solicitor Generals, and in general every public functionary, made common cause with the Tories and Orangemen against the Reformers, using every means in their power to overcome the Reformers, and influence the Election in favour of the Tory Candidates. . . .

That the elections were fixed by the Lieutenant Governor at places to favor the Tory Candidates, and, as in Middlesex, where the place first appointed and where former elections had been held, were changed, because that place first fixed was considered favorable to the Reformers. . . .

That Sir Francis Head, in order to overwhelm these legally registered Electors, issued large numbers of patents or grants of lands, under the Great Seal, in many cases for only a quarter of an acre of wild uncultivated land, on which no buildings were erected. . . .

That such grants were distributed openly at the places of election, to persons who had not applied at that time for such patents, and who received them to enable them to vote, without paying the usual fees. . . .

That bands of Orangemen, supposed to have been organized by their lodges, committed acts of outrage and violence at many of the elections, and the

Returning Officers, as at London, refused to allow the Magistrates to interfere to prevent such breaches of the peace.

That at Leeds, these bands generally armed with clubs or knives, drove the Reformers and their candidates from the hustings—and at Leeds, procured the return of the Grand Master Ogle R. Gowan, as Member for that County.

From Charles Duncombe "Petition to the House of Commons," Public Record Office (PRO), CO 42, v. 437, p. 32, microfilm in Public Archives of Ontario in Colin Read and R.J. Stagg, *The Rebellion of 1837 in Upper Canada*, (Toronto: Champlain Society and Carleton Library, 1985).

1. What "strong-arm" tactics were used to control the people voting in the election?
2. What methods were used to enfranchise or disenfranchise voters?
3. Write a defence of the idea of rebellion based upon the experiences of the 1836 election.

Friends of Reform, 1837

A mass meeting was held in Toronto in late July 1837. At it members of the Toronto Union of Reformers passed a series of resolutions calling for the reform of government in the colony. The excerpts below outline the resolutions of the meeting and describe the meeting itself. Both documents appeared in William Lyon Mackenzie's newspaper The Constitution.

At a Meeting of Friends of Reform, . . . on the evening of Friday, the 28th of July, 1837, Mr. John Mills was called to the Chair, and Mr. John Elliot, appointed to act as Secretary.

[The Chairman and Secretary were of opinion that this was perhaps the largest assemblage of the Reformers of the City which ever met in Toronto.] . . .

Resolved, 2. That the Reformers of Upper Canada are called upon by every tie of feeling, interest, and duty, to make common cause with their fellow citizens of Lower Canada, whose successful coercion would doubtless be in time visited upon us. . . .

Resolved, 4. That it be an instruction to the said Convention to appoint seven persons of approved judgment, discretion and patriotism, to proceed to Lower Canada, there to meet the Delegates of any Congress of these provinces which maybe appointed to sit and deliberate on matters of mutual interest to the Colonies during the present year. . . .

Proposed by Mr. Mackenzie, . . .

Resolved, 6. That it is expedient to adopt the following project for uniting, organizing and registering the Reformers of Upper Canada as a political Union, for the establishment of the Constitution on the broad basis of freedom, peace, and justice. —Carried. . . .

From "Resolutions of the Toronto Union, July 28, 1837, *Constitution*, (Toronto: August 2, 1837).

The Reformers met, pursuant to adjournment, at seven in the evening, ...

Dr. Morrison, M.P.P., Chairman of the Special Committee appointed to report a Declaration of the Reformers of this City . . .: THE DECLARATION

OF THE REFORMERS OF THE CITY OF TORONTO TO THEIR FEL-LOW-REFORMERS IN UPPER CANADA.

The time has arrived, after nearly half a century's forbearance under increasing and aggravated misrule, when the duty we owe our country and posterity requires from us the assertion of our rights and the redress of our wrongs.

Government is founded on the authority and is instituted for the benefit of a people; when, therefore, any government long and systematically ceases to answer the great ends of its foundation, the people have a natural right given them by their Creator to seek after and establish such institutions as will yield the greatest number. . . .

The right was conceded to the present United States at the close of a successful revolution, to form a constitution for themselves; and the loyalists with their descendants and others, now peopling this portion of America, are entitled to the same liberty without the shedding of blood—more they do not ask; less they ought not to have. —But, while the revolution of the former has been rewarded with a consecutive prosperity, unexampled in the history of the world, the loyal valor of the latter alone remains amidst the blight of misgovernment to tell them what they might have been as the not less valiant sons of American Independence. . . . A painful experience has proved how impracticable it is for such a succession of strangers beneficially to direct and control the affairs of the people four thousand miles off; and being an impracticable system, felt to be intolerable by those for whose good it was professedly intended, it ought to be abolished, and the domestic institutions of the province so improved and administered by the local authorities as to render the people happy and contented. . . .

Under this mockery of human Government we have been insulted, injured and reduced to the brink of ruin. The due influence and purity of all our institutions have been utterly destroyed.

From "The Toronto Union to the Reformers of Upper Canada," July 31, 1837, *Constitution*, (Toronto: August 2, 1837).

1. How did the reformers view the *patriotes* in Lower Canada?
2. How do the reformers describe the purpose of government society?
3. What comparisons are made with the United States?

Mackenzie and Rebellion, 1837

William Lyon Mackenzie was a complex figure whose political views were never clearly defined. His writings ranged from reasoned pleas for a responsible application of British political principles in the colony to expressions of radical republicanism and espousals of Jacksonian democracy. In this excerpt it is the radical Mackenzie speaking as he attempts to rally the public to the rebel cause.

BRAVE CANADIANS! God has put into the bold and honest hearts of our brethren in Lower Canada to revolt—not against "lawful" but against "unlawful authority". The law says we shall not be taxed without our consent by the voices of the men of our choice, but a wicked and tyrannical government has trampled upon that law—robbed the exchequer—divided the plunder—and declared that, regardless of justice they will continue to roll their splendid carriages, and riot in their palaces, at our expense—that we are poor spiritless ignorant peasants, who were born to toil for our betters. . . .

CANADIANS! Do you love freedom? I know you do. Do you wish perpetual peace, and a government founded upon the eternal heaven–born principle of the Lord Jesus Christ—a government bound to enforce the connection with England would involve us in all her wars, undertaken for her own advantage, never for ours; with governors from England, we will have bribery at elections, corruption, villainy and perpetual discord in every township, but Independence would give us the means of enjoying many blessings. . . . Woe be to those who oppose us, for 'In God is our trust.'

. . . We, the people of the State of Upper Canada, acknowledging with gratitude the grace and beneficience of God, in permitting us to make choice of our form of government, and in order to establish justice, ensure domestic tranquility, provide for the common defense, promote the general welfare, and secure the blessings of civil and religious liberty to ourselves and our posterity, do establish this Constitution.

From Margaret Fairley, *The Selected Writings of William Lyon Mackenzie* (Toronto: Oxford University Press, 1960).

1. In what way does Mackenzie distinguish between lawful and unlawful behaviour?
2. What techniques does Mackenzie use in his "call to arms"?
3. How effective do you think a speech like this would be in inspiring rebellion? Defend your point of view.

American Influences in the Canadas, 1838

Robert Baldwin Sullivan, a member of the Family Compact, attributed the rebellions to the influence of the United States. He put forward this argument in a letter to the new lieutenant governor, Sir George Arthur.

In this country unfortunately the settlement of American citizens has been too much permitted and encouraged, and thus in the bosom of this community there exists a treacherous foe. The vicinity of the arena for the discussion of extreme political fantasies, infects this population, many of the natural born subjects of the Crown are carried away by the plausibility of republican doctrines. . . . Personal disappointments, disarrangement of private affairs, want of success in political intrigue, in short every circumstance which does not fall out precisely as every man . . . desires, is made a ground for organic change in government, a reason for revolution.

In such a state of things it is not wonderful that a considerable portion of this community may be said to be disaffected, and indeed it is much to the honour of the Upper Canadian people that the great majority are truly loyal.

It is for the British nation to judge whether it is for the interests of the empire to abandon this colony, or to give up its loyal inhabitants to the mercies of a demoralized American rabble, or its fair and fertile territory to the rapacity and avidity of American politicians.

. . . In many parts of the province the teachers are Americans. For the sake of obtaining employment they have swallowed the oath of allegiance which agrees so ill with them that the rest of their lives is spent in attempts to disgorge it. These men are utterly ignorant of every thing English and could not if they tried instruct their pupils in any of the duties which the connection of the province with England casts upon them. The looks they use are all American, filled with inflated accounts of American independence and the glorious wars with England. The exploits of General Jackson and the heroes of '76 fill the youthful mind to the exclusion of every thing glorious or interesting in English history. The young man grows up without a single prepossession in favor of his country; he looks upon a British soldier as a person whom it would be honorable and glorious to oppose with the rifle. . . .

From R.B. Sullivan to Sir George Arthur, 1838, in C.R. Sanderson, ed., *The Arthur Papers*, Vol. I, (Toronto, 1957).

1. What reasons does Sullivan cite for individuals joining the rebels?
2. What appeal does Sullivan make to Britain?
3. How does the author characterize American settlers and their influence on events?

The Durham Report, 1839

Lord Durham spent only five months in the Canadas (a mere two weeks in Upper Canada!) and yet his report on the causes of the rebellions had a profound effect on the future of the country. Its most lasting recommendation, the establishment of responsible government, set a pattern for the entire empire.

. . . The secure and honorable bond of connexion . . . exists in the beneficial operation of those British institutions which link the utmost development of freedom and civilization with the stable authority of an hereditary monarchy, and which, if rightly organized and fairly administered in the Colonies, as in Great Britain, would render a change of institutions only an additional evil to the loss of the protection and commerce of the British Empire.

. . . I rely on the efficacy of reform in the constitutional system by which these Colonies are governed, for the removal of every abuse in their administration which defective institutions have engendered. If a system can be devised which shall lay in these countries the foundation of an efficient and popular government, ensure harmony, in place of collision, between the various powers of the State, and bring the influence of a vigorous public opinion to bear on every detail of public affairs, we may rely on sufficient remedies being found for the present vices of the administrative system.

. . . It is not by weakening, but strengthening the influence of the people on its Government; by confining within much narrower bounds than those hitherto allotted to it, and not by extending the interference of the imperial authorities in the details of colonial affairs, that I believe that harmony is to be restored, where dissension has so long prevailed; . . . . It needs no change in the principles of government, no invention of a new constitutional theory, to supply the remedy which would, in my opinion, completely remove the existing political disorders. It needs but to follow out consistently the principles of the British Constitution, and introduce into the Government of these great Colonies those wise provisions, by which alone the working of the representative system can in any country be rendered harmonious and efficient. . . .

. . . Every purpose of popular control might be combined with every advantage of vesting the immediate choice of advisers in the Crown, were the Colonial Governor to be instructed to secure the co-operation of the Assembly in his policy, by entrusting its administration to such men as could command a majority; and if he were given to understand that he need count on no aid from home in any difference with the Assembly, that should not directly involve the relations between the mother country and the Colony. . . .

. . . I admit that the system which I propose would, in fact, place the internal government of the Colony in the hands of the colonists themselves; . . . The colonists may not always know what laws are best for them, or which of their countrymen are the fittest for conducting their affairs; but, at least, they have a greater interest in coming to a right judgment on these points, and will take greater pains to do so than those whose welfare is very remotely and slightly affected by the good or bad legislation of these portions of the Empire. If the colonists make bad laws, and select improper persons to conduct their affairs they will generally be the only, always the greatest, sufferers and, like the people of other countries, they must bear the ills which they bring on themselves, until they choose to supply the remedy. . . .

. . . I am inclined to go further, and inquire whether all these objects would not more surely be attained, by extending this legislative union over all the British Provinces in North America; . . . it would form a great and powerful people, possessing the means of securing good and responsible government for itself, and which, under the protection of the British Empire, might in some measure counterbalance the preponderant and increasing influence of the United States on the American Continent. I do not anticipate that a colonial legislature thus strong and thus self-governing, would desire to abandon the connexion with Great Britain. On the contrary, I believe that the practical relief from undue interference, which would be the result of such a change, would strengthen the present bond of feelings and interests; and that the connexion would only become more durable and advantageous, by having more of equality, of freedom, and of local independence. . . .

From J.J. Talman, "Durham's Report", *Basic Documents in Canadian History*, (Toronto: Van Nostrand Co., 1959).

1. What observation does Durham make about the state of affairs in the Canadas?
2. What argument does he present for placing greater power in the hands of the people of the colonies?

3. Outline Durham's recommendation regarding the political union of all of British North America. What were his motives in making the proposal?

Response to Durham, 1839-45

If the British government was initially lukewarm to Durham's recommendations, in British North America they became the focus of heated political debate. The following excerpts illustrate the range of response to the greater democratization of the colonies.

When a nobleman advocates democratic institutions, we give him full credit for the benevolence of his intentions, but we doubt his sanity.

From Thomas Chandler Haliburton, *Bubbles of Canada* (1839) in Janet Morchain and Mason Wade, eds., *Search for a Nation*, (Toronto: Fitzhenry and Whiteside, 1984).

The cause of popular agitation and of occasional collisions between the Assembly and other branches of government in the North American colonies is easily discerned. It lies on the surface. It is the tendency of democracy to swallow up everything, its impatience of any check . . . . If it be thought desirable to remove every obstacle to the absolute sway of the multitude whether their inclinations be just or unjust and whether their views be sound or unsound then undoubtedly the system recommended in these pages is admirably adapted to that object. But how it can be imagined that such a system will confer tranquility on a country is rather inexplicable.

From John Beverley Robinson, member of the Family Compact of Upper Canada (Draft in the Robinson Papers, Public Archives of Ontario, 23, 24, No. 18).

Seduced, distracted after a fashion by its details, we have for a long time lost sight of the object of that measure, which, however, is every day recalled to our recollection by that invasion of ideas and institutions, foreign to our ideas and institutions, which renders each day the most desirable, in the midst of the confusion of institutions, that perfect labyrinth of laws, of manners and of language, which imposes upon us a double nationality, so as to render the one necessary, the other useless, that is to say, to make us lose ours and adopt the other. . . .

From L'Avenir (*Rouge* journal) Janet Morchain and Mason Wade, eds., *Search for a Nation*, (Toronto: Fitzhenry and Whiteside, 1984).

Tell us, gentlement of *L'Avenir*, you who weep so much over the ruins of the past, and over imaginary evils—tell us at what period of our history has the French–Canadian nationality been more brilliant, more honoured, more respected, or has it occupied a higher position than it holds today? . . . The Union has saved us, and after powerful and well–directed efforts, after having won a position which permits us to avoid its inconveniences and evil consequences, after having obtained the political rights for which we have struggled for fifty years, now it is, that the devoted and generous gentlemen of *L'Avenir* raise their voices against it . . . .

But tell us, ye young and fiery apostles of French–Canadian nationality, what do you mean by the principle of nationality applied to the management of public affairs? . . . When our friends, the liberals of Upper Canada and those of Lower Canada of foreign origin, have made prodigious efforts to carry the elections and that together we have gained the most signal victory—it is not now that your appeal to prejudices and passions will have the least echo in the country.

From *La Revue Canadienne* (Journal of LaFontaine) in Janet Morchain and Mason Wade, eds., *Search for a Nation*, (Toronto: Fitzhenry and Whiteside, 1984).

The Union has completely failed in its purpose. It was enacted with the sole motive of reducing the French Canadians under English domination. And the contrary effect has resulted! Those that were to be crushed dominate! Those in favour of whom the Union was made are the serfs of the others! . . . I warn the ministry of peril . . . I warn it that the course it takes is likely to throw the people of Upper Canada into despair, and to make them feel that if they are to be governed by foreigners, it would be more advantageous to be governed by a neighboring people of the same race than by those with whom it has nothing in common, neither blood, nor language, nor interests.

From Sir Alan MacNab, leader of the Tory party in Upper Canada in Janet Morchain and Mason Wade, eds., *Search for a Nation*, (Toronto: Fitzhenry and Whiteside, 1984).

1. Prepare two responses to Durham's report, one in support of his recommendations and the other against. Write short presentations for each side in which you highlight the respective positions and debate the arguments put forth by the opposing side.

Democracy and Party: Analysis and Application

1. The concept of the "natural aristocracy" introduced by Thomas Jefferson had implications for both North American nations. Outline the interpretations of this idea that emerged on both sides of the border.

2. Sir Francis Bond Head once described democracy as having all the stability of turning a natural social pyramid "upside down." To what extent would Bond Head agree with the concerns raised by Alexis de Tocqueville?

3. Contrast de Tocqueville's impression of the state of "Democracy in America" with Papineau's assessment of democracy in Lower Canada.

4. Restage a debate in the Legislative Assembly in 1835. The issue in question is the need for a more responsible relationship between the assembly and the councils. Divide the class evenly between the Tory supporters of the existing system and the moderate and radical reform elements in the assembly.

5. Summarize the complaints raised by Charles Duncombe with regard to the election of 1836. Write a newspaper account or stage and videotape a "live-eye" television broadcast of a typical poll in the election of 1836.

6. The Durham mission to Canada in 1838 investigated the complaints that led to the rebellions of 1837-38. Recreate that investigation. Have a small group take

the roles of Durham and his aides. It will be their task to research the events of the period and then interview the participants. The remainder of the group should assume the roles of specific individuals involved in one of the rebellions, for example, in Upper Canada: William Lyon Mackenzie, John Strachan, Sir Francis Bond Head, Samuel Lount, Robert Baldwin, Egerton Ryerson, etc. Students should research the positions of characters they are playing, and should be prepared to answer questions posed by the Durham committee.

Once the committee has publicly interviewed each of the eyewitnesses they should write their own set of recommendations. All participants should then step out of role and compare their findings with those of the Durham Report.

7. Discuss the emergence of the party system in each country. To what extent did Canada avoid the regionalism which eventually paralysed the American system?

8
FEDERALISM AND CONFEDERATION

The 1980s in Canada have been marked by considerable debate over the structure and function of government. In the early years of the decade the focus of these discussions was on then Prime Minister Pierre Elliot Trudeau's efforts to patriate Canada's constitution, the British North America Act. Points of controversy included the entrenchment of a charter of rights and freedoms; the sharing of power with regard to nonrenewable resources; and the provision of an amending formula acceptable to both the federal government and the provinces. In the end, the Constitution Act of 1981/2 came close to meeting its objectives. The only shortfall was in the refusal of the government of Quebec to sign the final protocol. Although this did not present a legal problem, it remained a moral dilemma for Trudeau and his eventual Conservative successor, Brian Mulroney.

In 1987, however, Mulroney was able to unite all of the provinces with the signing of the Meech Lake Accord. Meech Lake not only lured Quebec "back into Confederation" through its declaration that the province represented a "distinct society" as the homeland of the French–Canadian people, but it also made sweeping changes in the balance of power between the federal government and the provinces. As a result, provincial governments gained the power to appoint Supreme Court justices and Senators as well as a veto power on any future changes to the constitution. As the political debate over the agreement raged on into 1988, many Canadians grew increasingly aware of the profound changes reflected in the agreement, and they began to turn to historical precedents to help sort out the issues.

For many Canadians Meech Lake represents a return to the beginning of the constitutional processes that began in North America in 1776. The gradual emergence of federal principles in the United States and Canada came, not as a clearly defined model, but through a complex and sometimes violent evolutionary experience. In this section we will investigate the nature of this process and consider the various viewpoints involved in this historical debate. In the process, we hope to gain some insights into our own current political state of affairs.

Tentative Beginnings

Unlike many revolutionary movements, the American revolution was not to establish new freedom from old oppressors. Rather, the War of Independence was fought to preserve old rights, not to establish new ones. There were no illusions among the revolutionary leaders as to what government should or could do. Although the rallying cry of the French Revolution a decade later would be to institute "the rule of reason," John Dickinson was able to state at the Constitutional convention that "Experience must be our only guide, reason may mislead us."

The leaders of the American Revolution were practical politicians whose main concern was to establish a workable form of government. It could be considered a "conservative" revolution: there were no purges, no counterrevolutions, and no military coups. The four who set out on the route to independence—John Adams, Thomas Jefferson, Benjamin Franklin, and George Washington—arrived together. The leaders of the revolution were members of a new generation of political thinkers. Well-educated, they were able to combine the ideas of classical political theory with the practical experience of the British Parliamentary system. For these men the concept of liberty was no vague political goal. It meant freedom to act, without infringing on the rights of others, under laws of their own making. Any constitution had to guarantee this liberty.

In this revolutionary atmosphere, new state constitutions began to be formulated. Based upon the old colonial system, these constitutions provided for a governor, and a bicameral, or two–house, legislature. Under British rule, many governors had asserted almost dictatorial powers. The new constitutions assured that this would not happen again. Elected by the legislature for one– or two–year terms, the powers of the governor were tightly checked by the representatives of the people. This is not to say, however, that the assemblies had unlimited power. The legislative, or law–making, branch was divided into two "houses." The lower house, modelled on the British House of Commons, was usually elected annually by the people. Its power was limited by the upper house, which was elected for terms of two to four years and was designed as a force for stability in the state.

The people were protected from abuse by this system through a bill of rights. In this way the courts could enforce a further check on the power of the legislature.

These local constitutions were usually the work of the political elite. Written and passed by conventions, they reflected the ideas of a relatively small group. The gap between these leaders and their constituents came to a head in Massachusetts in 1778. The people rejected the self-proclaimed power of the legislature to create a constitution. If such a body could write a constitution, they reasoned, they could also change it without consulting the people.

The resulting compromise set a precedent for the entire nation. In 1779 delegates were elected to a state constitutional convention. The draft constitution they wrote was then debated at town meetings throughout the state, and finally put to a popular vote for ratification. It was an important step towards real democracy. The new Massachusetts constitution embodied the ideas of a "mixed government." Written by John Adams, it established a system of checks and balances designed to prevent any one level of government from exercising too much power. It would form the basis for the national constitution to come.

The Articles of Confederation

The Declaration of Independence asserted that the united colonies "are and ought to be free and independent *states*." This was the prevailing mood at the Continental Congress in 1776. The new states, declaring their independence from one outside authority, were not about to subject themselves to another. As a result, the new government would have to be one in which the powers of the individual states would be greater than those of the central government. Such a system is called a *confederation*. On paper, the proposed new national Congress would have important powers. It would control the army and the navy, foreign policy, currency, Native affairs, and the postal and weights and measures systems. Although these powers seemed to be far–reaching, there were many areas that Congress did not control. It could not levy taxes, regulate trade, collect state debts, or in fact enforce *any* of its powers. If it wanted to raise an army, for example, it had to beg the states for money. If it wanted to sign a treaty with a foreign power it needed the states' approval for any clauses affecting trade. In effect, the Congress could pass laws, but it couldn't make anyone obey them.

In addition to the division of powers, the issue of representation was a critical one. The original Continental Congress was based on equality of representation by state; in other words, one state equals one vote. The more populous parts of the country, however, argued for representation by population. In the end, the larger states dropped their demands as they recognized the need for a unified effort against the British; internal political questions could be dealt with after victory.

The Articles of Confederation were passed in November 1777, with the expectation of quick ratification by the states. Although most states had ratified the articles by February 1779, Maryland refused to sign. It would eventually take the state almost three–and–a–half years to come to a decision. Against a common enemy the Thirteen States were united, but among themselves they were far from agreement.

The shortcomings of the Articles of Confederation were soon obvious to the new nation. After several local crises in the 1780s, twelve of the thirteen states sent representatives to a constitutional convention in Philadelphia in 1787. After five months of heated debate a compromise document was drawn up. It established a mixed government based upon a system of checks and balances. Under the Philadelphia plan, the executive, legislative and judicial branches of the central government would each exercise control over the functions of one another. In this way no one branch of government could gain too much power. (Note: the 1987 case of the appointment of Robert H. Bork to the Supreme Court is an excellent example of this system of checks and balances. In this instance, a Republican president, Ronald Reagan, attempted to shift the ideological balance of the Supreme Court through the appointment of a conservative justice, Robert Bork. His presence on the Court could have affected the way in which that body interpreted both existing and future pieces of legislation. The Democrat–controlled Senate debated the recommendation and eventually rejected the Bork appointment by a vote of fifty–eight to forty–two. Although Bork was only the fourth nominee to be voted down in this century, and the first in over fifty years to be rejected on the basis of ideological background, the action by Congress reaffirmed the strength of the checks and balances system in the American government.)

Far more controversial and critical to the survival of the young republic than the actual structure of the federal government was the definition of its relationship to the states.

In Canada in the late twentieth century, we take federalism for granted. A system in which there are two levels of government, each with specific powers and responsibilities, would seem to be logical in a nation as large as ours. For the United States in 1787, however, this federal system was a gamble. The writers of

The Declaration of Independence by John Trumbull

The Fathers of Confederation: The Quebec Conference, 1864

the Constitution had to balance the need for a strong central government with the jealously guarded local powers of the states. The fundamental question was where *sovereignty*—that is, the basic authority—rested. The preamble of the Constitution read: "We the People of the United States . . . ." But how should these words be interpreted?

Some people argued that the opening three words, "We the People," indicated that authority rested with "the people." Called popular sovereignty, this view held that the power of the individual states had been given over to a new government representing all of the people. Others argued that the phrase "We the People of the United States" must be read as a whole, and that the people referred to were the people of the individual states. As a result, it was as citizens *of those states* that they agreed to sign the Constitution.

The fundamental issue was clear: Was the Constitution a social contract entered into by the people and the new government, or was it a compact among thirteen sovereign states? It would take the Civil War several decades later to decide the issue.

A basic necessity in the structuring of any federal state is a clear division of powers. The American Constitution set out a series of *delegated powers* for the national government. A second set of powers, called *concurrent powers*, were to be held in common between the national and state governments. All remaining powers were reserved for the states. These residual powers should have, in theory, given the greatest power to the states. Such local potential prompted Alexander Hamilton to call the Constitution "weak and worthless fabric."

In spite of this, the national government was able to increase its original powers through the application of Section 8 (18) of Article I:

> The Congress shall have power: To make all laws which shall be necessary and proper for carrying into execution the foregoing powers, and all other powers vested by this Constitution in the government of the United States, or in any department or officer thereof.

Intended to allow the Congress to adapt to changing conditions in the country, this *elastic clause* has served to expand the power of the national government beyond the original intent of the convention.

Another interesting aspect of the American Constitution was the inclusion of clauses specifying actions which governments could *not* take. These clauses, under Sections 9 and 10, reflected the uneasy truce that was struck at Philadelphia. People whose rights had been violated once were not about to let it happen again.

The lack of unanimity in Philadelphia was typical of attitudes throughout the nation. When the convention approved the new Constitution, the delegates held no delusions that the process of acceptance by the states would be easy. As a result, Congress passed two "revolutionary" conditions for ratification. First, only nine of the states needed to ratify the new Constitution in order for it to be binding. Representing almost 75 percent of the states, this provision prevented any one state from exercising a veto over the wishes of the rest. Second, Congress declared that ratification be carried out by local conventions elected for that purpose. State governments could not make the decision. This, they hoped, would weaken the political interests who controlled the local legislatures.

Once the ground rules were set, the contest began.

Supporters of the new Constitution were called the Federalists. Led by influential writers such as Alexander Hamilton, John Jay, and James Madison, and supported by George Washington and Benjamin Franklin, the Federalist campaign faced an uphill battle. Federalists saw the new Constitution as striking a fine balance between a strong central government and the maintenance of states' rights. For them, any eroding of federal power would lead the new nation back into the turmoil it experienced under the Articles of Confederation (see readings).

Opponents of the new Constitution were called the *Anti-Federalists*. As their name suggests, the "Antis" were united more in opposition to the agreement than in pursuit of a common vision. Some of the Anti-Federalists wanted less federal and more state power; some decried the absence of a comprehensive bill of rights; still others accused the new Constitution, with its provision for an electoral college and six–year terms for senators, to be anti-democratic (see readings).

The contest was an unusual one. The dispute cut across social, economic, political and regional lines. Perhaps the greatest difference between the two sides was one of age. The Anti–Federalists were older. Politically active prior to the Revolution, they still harboured a mistrust of a strong central government, based on their experience under colonial rule. The Federalists, on the other hand, comprised a new generation of political leaders who were interested in the practical realities of running a country rather than revolutionary sentiments. In spite of the heated debate, however, the critical factors were not the details of the argument, but simply that people had seen that the old system did not work, and that both George Washington and Benjamin Franklin supported the new one.

Federalist support was strongest in the small states. They saw the power of the new central government as necessary to protect their rights. Delaware ratified unanimously in December 1787. Pennsylvania quickly followed. In Massachusetts it appeared as if the ratification proposal would be defeated. An informal vote before the convention opened showed 192 delegates against ratification and only 144 in favour. Careful political manoeuvring saved the day. John Hancock, who was wavering in his support, secured a promise (never to be fulfilled) from three prominent Federalists to back him for vice-president in return for his support. Sam Adams, an Anti–Federalist politician in Boston, was pressured to back the Federalists by his working class constituents from the Boston shipyards after they were guaranteed extra work by their Federalist employers if the Constitution was passed.

The final strategy to bring Massachusetts in line with the Federalist forces was a proposal to amend the new constitution. In a conciliatory move, the local Federalists proposed to add a bill of rights to the charter. This removed a major obstacle for many of their opponents. On February 6, 1788, Massachusetts voted 187 to 168 in favour.

The tide was turning. By June New Hampshire had become the ninth state to ratify. Legally, the Constitution had been accepted. However, there were still four states representing 40 percent of the nation's population that were holding out.

All attention turned to them in the summer of 1788. In Virginia, the contest was among giants. Lined up on the Federalist side were such figures as George Washington, James Madison, and John Marshall (future chief justice of the United States). On the Anti-Federalist side were George Mason and Patrick Henry. The debate raged with the fiery oratory of Henry on one side and the cool logic of Madison on the other. Finally the vote came. On June 23, Virginia ratified eighty–nine to seventy–nine. New York soon followed, and although North Carolina and Rhode Island did not come in until 1789 and 1790 respectively, the constitutional battle was no longer an issue.

Congress declared the new constitution to be in force, and elections were scheduled for January 1789. The Revolution was really finally over, and a new federal state had emerged. The nature of the relationship between the federal and state governments, however, remained a question of controversy through the first half of the nineteenth century. Many aspects of this issue were defined in favour of the Federalist viewpoint by judicial interpretation under Supreme Court Chief Justice John Marshall (see readings). Other issues were settled through political dealings, such as the Missouri Compromise and the Kansas–Nebraska Act. For many Americans, however, the issue was never settled. When South Carolina voted to secede from the Union in 1861 it did so based upon its own concept of its constitutional rights (see readings), and when Abraham Lincoln moved to bring the seceding states back into the fold, he did so with the same firm belief in the opposite viewpoint (see readings).

The Northern Experience

The lessons of the American experience were not lost on the British North American politicians of the mid-nineteenth century. The Act of Union which had combined the governments of the Canadas in 1840 had been originally intended as a means of legislating the francophone majority in Canada East (Quebec) into a permanent minority position. What actually developed was a form of "dualism." Politicians from the Canadas demanded equal participation from both halves of the combined colony. As a result, future executive councils would maintain a balance from Canada East and Canada West, and important measures in the legislature would demand a "double majority" to ensure passage.   In spite of this there were still serious problems. During the 1840s French-Canadian legislators complained that no fewer than seventeen issues of a purely local nature had been decided by the joint legislature on the basis of a majority consisting primarily of representatives from Canada West. Eventually the legislative process in the Canadas became deadlocked. As with sectional politics in the United States, one of the critical issues was that of western expansion. Legislators in Canada East saw the annexation of the Northwest as giving permanent political dominance to Canada West. English–Canadian politicians, on the other hand, worried about losing this vast territory to the Manifest Destiny aspirations of the United States.

Political leaders looked to constitutional change to resolve the stalemate. One plan called for a revised form of federal union between Canada East and Canada

West. Under such an arrangement, each province would be responsible for its own local affairs, while the combined government would handle mutual concerns. French-Canadians were wary of this arrangement, which many saw as placing Canada East in a perpetual minority position against a united opposition. For them the solution was not the dualism of the past, but a larger federation whose diverse interests would prevent permanent political alliances.

It was with these opposing views in mind that Canadian politicians travelled to Charlottetown, Prince Edward Island in 1864. The political problems of the two Canadas held little interest for the Maritimers. What did appeal to them, however, was the vision, articulated by Canadian leaders such as John A. Macdonald and George Étienne Cartier, of a British North American nation stretching from sea to sea. In the face of this grand dream, the Maritime colonies agreed to sit down and attempt to negotiate an agreement.

When the delegates met again in October of that year in Quebec City, it was an event unprecedented in Canadian history. Unlike the United States, which had controlled its own political destiny since the 1770s, the northern British colonies had always had their form of government dictated from abroad. The Seventy-two Resolutions that emerged from the Quebec Conference would eventually form the basis of the British North America Act and create the new nation of Canada.

The British North America Act was a hybrid. It was an attempt to graft British political forms to the federalist needs of the new continent. As in the American Congress, the Canadian Houses of Parliament were set up to balance representation by population with the protection of regional interests. Unlike the powerful United States Senate, however, with its two seats for each state, the new Canadian Senate had a more regional flavour. Canada East (Quebec), Canada West (Ontario), and the Maritime provinces (excluding Newfoundland) were each given twenty-four seats in the upper house. In theory this appeared to be a reasonable compromise. In reality, however, it gave a permanent majority to the commercial interests of the St. Lawrence Valley. Why, then, did the Maritime colonies agree to the arrangement? To begin with, many Maritimers rejected the agreement (see readings). Prince Edward Island and Newfoundland stayed out of Confederation, and an election in Nova Scotia in 1867 elected an overwhelming majority of anti-confederationists. For that province, however, it was too late. The British Colonial Office rejected the colony's petition to be exempted from the act; faced with the prospect of rebellion or acceptance, the province came to terms with its new political partners. PEI would come into the fold a few years later, but it would take a depression and two world wars to bring Newfoundland back to the bargaining table.

The second aspect of the Senate that raised controversy was the fact that as an appointed body it had little power against the will of the elected House of Commons. The whole debate over the role of the Senate continues to the present day, with current demands calling for an elected upper house to protect provincial interests (see readings).

In actual fact, however, the real defence of provincial rights existed not in the Senate, but in the division of powers between the two levels of government. The Fathers of Confederation drew up the Seventy-two Resolutions with one eye on the United States. The Civil War, which was raging during the Quebec Conference, prompted one early opponent of Confederation, Joseph Howe of Nova Scotia, to comment: "Have we not seen enough of federations. . .? Shall we not draw wisdom from the errors of others?"

It was with this in mind that the British North America Act was framed. Many observers felt that the Civil War was the result of conflicting interpretations of the American Constitution. The Confederate States of America, the South, held the view that individual states should have more power than the central government. The North, or Union as it was called, believed in the supremacy of the central government. The basic political debate, therefore, was between a federal and a confederal approach to government.

The British North America Act tried to avoid such conflict by investing all residual powers in the federal government. While Section 92 of the act gave certain specific powers to the provinces, Section 91, which dealt with the powers of the federal government, stated:

> It shall be lawful for the Queen, by and with the Advice and Consent of the Senate and House of Commons, to make Laws for the Peace, Order, and Good Government of Canada, in relation to all Matters not coming within the Classes of Subjects by this Act assigned exclusively to the Legislatures of the Provinces.

The strength of the federal government, however, was undercut by clause 16 of Section 92 which, after enumerating a series of specific powers belonging to the provinces, gave that level of government the power to "make laws in relation to": "Generally all Matters of a merely local or private Nature in the Province."

This *elastic clause*, supported by judicial interpretation (see readings), has stretched the powers of the provinces beyond the original intent of the act. (These powers were further extended first through the addition of Section 92A in 1982, and then through the additional rights granted in the Meech Lake Accord of 1987.)

In 1867, perhaps the only area of the country genuinely enthusiastic about the prospect of federal union was Ontario. John A. Macdonald had wanted to abolish the provinces and have simply one level of government, but knowing that this idea would never be accepted outside of his home province of Ontario he opted for the federal scheme. One of the most important proponents of the new government was George Étienne Cartier. Cartier had fought on the side of the patriotes in 1837 but he later became convinced that the only hope for the cultural and linguistic survival of Quebec lay within a strong Canadian federation. Without union, he felt that the scattered provinces would be doomed. In 1867 he stated: "The question reduces itself to this—we must either have a confederation of British North America or be absorbed by the American Union." Rather than accept the latter, Cartier proclaimed that:

> In our confederation there will be Catholics and Protestants, English, French, Irish and Scotch, and each by its efforts and success will add to the prosperity of the Dominion, to the glory of the new confederation. We are of different races, not to quarrel, but to work together for the common welfare."

For Cartier, and for the narrow majority of Lower Canadian legislators who voted for Confederation, a federal union represented the lesser of two evils in the mid-nineteenth century. The ambivalence of many French-Canadians toward the federal experiment would remain, however, and over a century later the same differences of opinion would surface in the Quebec referendum of 1980.

In both Canada and the United States, the desire for some measure of local autonomy, combined with the perceived need for a strong centralized state, led to the creation of a federal system of government. During the celebrations for the bicentennial of the American Constitution in 1987, many people praised the far-sightedness of the authors of that document and the lasting nature of the government it created. Such is the nature of myth, however. The original Constitution of the United States was an anti–democratic document withholding power from non-whites, women, and a large portion of the white male population. Further, the electoral college system is such that even today a president can win the popular vote but still lose an election. In addition, the deficiencies in the division of powers led to a schism so wide that it took a civil war to settle the issues, and the "perfect union" formed by the Constitution has required twenty-six amendments to keep it up to date.

By contrast, the Constitution Act of 1867 (the new name for the British North America Act) has proven to be an effective and flexible document for dealing with the changing conditions that have taken place since Confederation. Building upon the British parliamentary tradition and the American experience, Canada has been able to avoid some of the excesses that have stricken its neighbour.

Regardless of these differences, however, both countries have built strong and effective federal systems. In an age prior to the instantaneous communication of the late twentieth century, Canada and the United States developed strategies for providing a common focus for their widespread nations while still protecting local needs and aspirations.

Madison on the Duty of Government, 1783 and 1787

James Madison was a strong proponent of federal power. The following two excerpts outline his position which was formally articulated in "Federalist #10." In the first section Madison outlines the reponsibility of the thirteen state governments; for Madison, the protection of these rights required a stronger central authority. The second section, written four years later, presents an even stronger case for restraining the governments of the individual states.

. . . Let it be remembered finally that it has ever been the pride and boast of America, that the rights for which she contended were the rights of human nature. By the blessing of the Author of these rights, on the means exerted for their defence, they have prevailed against all opposition and form the basis of thirteen independent states. . . .

In this view the citizens of the United States are responsible for the greatest trust ever confided to a political society. If justice, good faith, honor, gratitude and all the other qualities which ennoble the character of a nation, and fulfill the ends of government, be the fruits of our establishments, the cause of liberty will acquire a dignity and lustre which it has never yet enjoyed; and an example will be set, which cannot but have the most favourable influence on the rights of mankind.

From James Madison, "Address to the States," *Journals of the Continental Congress*, April 26, 1783.

In republican Government the majority however composed, ultimately give the law. Whenever therefore an apparent interest or common passion unites a majority what is to restrain them from unjust violations of the rights and interests of the minority, or of individuals? Three motives only. 1. a prudent regard to their own good as involved in the general and permanent good of the community. This consideration although of decisive weight in itself, is found by experience to be too often unheeded. It is too often forgotten, by nations as well as by individuals, that honesty is the best policy. 2dly. respect for character. However strong this motive may be in individuals, it is considered as very insufficient to restrain them from injustice. In a multitude its efficacy is diminished in proportion to the number which is to share the praise or the blame. . . . 3rdly. will religion the only remaining motive be a sufficient restraint?

From James Madison, *Writings, II* in Irving Brant, *James Madison and American Nationalism*, (Toronto: Van Nostrand, 1968).

1. What rights and qualities does Madison attribute to the new nation?
2. Discuss Madison's concern with the problem of majority tyranny.
3. How might a federal state help to control the passions of a local majority group?

The Massachusetts Position, 1785

When discussions began regarding amendment to the Articles of Confederation, many state legislators were worried that the apparent weaknesses of the central government under the Articles might be replaced by a central government exhibiting too much power. Their refusal to introduce a resolution that would call for a constitution convention is explained in the following letter.

If an alteration, either temporary or perpetual, of the commercial powers of Congress, is to be considered by a Convention, shall the latter be authorized to revise the Confederation generally, or only for express purposes?—the great object of the Revolution was the establishment of good government, and each of the states, in forming their own, as well as the federal Constitution, have adopted republican principles. Notwithstanding this, plans have been artfully laid, and vigorously pursued, which, had they been successful, we think would inevitably have changed our republican governments, into baleful aristocracies. . . .

We are apprehensive and it is our duty to declare it, that such a measure would produce thro'out the Union, an exertion of the friends of aristocracy, to send members who would promote a change of government: . . . that we think there is great danger of a report which would invest Congress with powers that the honorable Legislature have not the most distant intention to delegate. . . .

Massachusetts has great weight, and is considered as one of the most republican states in the Union; and when it is known, that the legislature have proposed a general revision, there can be no doubt that they will be represented as being convinced of the necessity of increasing generally the powers of Congress, and the opinion of the state will be urged with such art as to convince numbers that the Articles of Confederation are altogether exceptionable. Thus, whilst measures are taken to guard against the evils arising from the want of one or two particulars of power in Congress, we are in great danger of incurring the other extreme—"More power in Congress" has been the cry from all quarters, but especially of those whose views, not being confined to a government that will best promote the happiness of the people, are extended to one that will afford lucrative employments, civil and military. . . .

We are for increasing the power of Congress as far as it will promote the happiness of the people, but at the same time are clearly of opinion that every measure should be avoided which would strengthen the hands of the enemies of a free government. And that an administration of the present Confederation with all its inconveniences, is preferable to the Risque of general dissensions and animosities which may approach to anarchy and prepare the way to a ruinous system of government.

From "Massachusetts Delegates in Congress, Letter on a Constitutional Convention, September 3, 1785" in Richard Hofstadter, ed., *Great Issues in American History*, (New York: Vintage Books, 1958).

1. What threats to liberty are identified by the delegates?
2. Comment upon the identification of the problems of over-reaction outlined in the letter.
3. What might account for the point of view being put forward in the letter?

The Need for Strong Government, 1786

In correspondence exchanged during the 1780s, John Jay and George Washington expressed concern about the lack of a strong central government in the new nation. In this letter to the future president, Jay raises doubts about the quality of leadership in the states.

June 27, 1786
To oppose popular prejudices, to censure the proceedings, and expose the improprieties of States, is an unpleasant task, but it must be done. . . . During the war . . . we had a fixed object, and though the means and time of obtaining it were often problematical, yet I did firmly believe we should ultimately succeed, because I was convinced that justice was with us. The case is now altered; we are going and doing wrong, and therefore I look forward to evils and calamities, but without being able to guess at the instrument, nature or measure of them. . . .

The mass of men are neither wise nor good, and the virtue like the other resources of a country, can only be drawn to a point and exerted by strong circumstances ably managed, or a strong government ably administered. New governments have not the aid of habit and hereditary respect, and being generally the result of preceding tumult and confusion, do not immediately acquire stability or strength. Besides, in times of commotion, some men will gain confidence and importance, who merit neither, and who like political mountebanks, are less solicitous about the health of the credulous crowd than about making the most of their nostrums and prescriptions.

From "John Jay to George Washington, June 27, 1786," in Richard Hofstadter, ed., *Great Issues in American History*, (New York: Vintage Books, 1958).

1. Discuss Jay's contention that the present system of government worked only when the states were faced with a common enemy.
2. Compare Jay's view of humanity with that expressed by John Locke or Thomas Jefferson.
3. To what extent did the centralization of power reflect a growing conservatism in the United States?

Federalist #10

The Federalist papers were a combination of essays written by Madison, Jay, and Alexander Hamilton. The most significant of these papers was #10 written by James Madison. In it he claims that conflict among different interest groups in society is inevitable. It was his assertion that in order to preserve freedom of expression in an atmosphere of domestic tranquility, a strong and balanced government was needed to prevent liberty from becoming anarchy.

To the people of the state of New York,

Among the numerous advantages promised by a well constructed Union, none deserves to be more accurately developed than its tendency to break and control the violence of faction. . . .

By a faction I understand a number of citizens, whether amounting to a majority or minority of the whole, who are united and actuated by some common impulse of passion, or of interest, adverse to the rights of other citizens, or to the permanent and aggregate interests of the community. There are two methods of curing the mischiefs of faction: the one by removing its causes; the other, by controling its effects.

There are again two methods of removing the causes of faction: the one by destroying the liberty which is essential to its existence; the other by giving to every citizen the same opinions, the same passions, and the same interests. . . . The most common and durable source of factions has been the various and unequal distribution of property. Those who hold, and those who are without property, have ever formed distinct interests in society. . . .

The inference to which we are brought is, that the causes of faction cannot be removed; and that relief is only to be sought in the means of controling its effect. . . .

If a faction consists of less than a majority, relief is supplied by the republican principle, which enables the majority to defeat its sinister views by a regu-

lar vote. . . . When a majority is included in a faction, the form of popular
government on the other hand enables it to sacrifice to its ruling passion or
interest, both the public good and the rights of other citizens.

Extensive Republics are most favorable to the election of proper guardians to
the public weal. . . . Extend the sphere [of government] and you take in a
greater variety of parties and interests; you make it less probable that a majority
will have a common motive to invade the rights of other citizens. . . .

The influence of factious leaders may kindle a flame within their particular
States, but will be unable to spread a general conflagration through the other
States.

From James Madison, *Federalist No. 10* November 22, 1787.

1. How does Madison define "faction"? How does he say it might be dealt with?
What problems would these "remedies" create?
2. What impact does property have upon faction?
3. If the causes of faction may not be cured, how then may governments control
the effects of the problem?

The Anti-Federalist Case

*Richard Henry Lee was one of the leaders of the anti-Federalist forces. A Virginian,
Lee was highly active in the Continental Congress, serving as its president in 1784-85.
Lee saw a danger to individual liberty in the drift toward a highly centralized government.
In the fall of 1787 he wrote five "Letters from the Federal Farmer to the Republican."
They remain an excellent statement of the anti-Federalist case.*

Dear Sir,

My letters to you last winter . . . anticipated the anxieties I feel, on carefully
examining the plan of government proposed by the convention. . . .

The first principle question that occurs, is, Whether, considering our situation we ought to precipitate the adoption of the proposed constitution? If we
remain cool and temperate, we are in no immediate danger of any commotions;
we are in a state of perfect peace, and are in no danger of invasions . . .
whether we adopt a change three or nine months hence, can make but little
odds with . . . circumstances. . . .

The plan of government now proposed is evidently calculated totally to
change, in time, our condition as a people. Instead of being thirteen republics
under a federal head, it is clearly designed to make us one consolidated
government.

Several orders of men [have taken part in an] abuse of power . . . which in
some cases has been charged upon the democratic part of the community, [and
this] has furnished aristocratical men with those very weapons, and those very
means [to defend creating] an oppressive government. . . .

The uneasy and fickle part of the community may be prepared to receive any
form of government; but I presume the enlightened and substantial part will
give any constitution present for their adoption a candid and thorough examina-

tion; and silence those designing or empty men, who weakly and rashly attempt to precipitate the adoption of a system of so much importance.

From "Letters from the Federal Farmer to the Republican," October 8, 1787 in Leonard Kriegel, ed., *Essential Works of the Founding Fathers*, (New York: Bantam Books, 1964).

1. What case does Lee make against immediate change?
2. What fears does he express with regard to the proposed changes in government?
3. To a great extent, Lee's concerns were answered by the Bill of Rights. Comment upon the balance provided between the Constitution and its first ten amendments.

The Debate over Federalism

Mercy Otis Warren, sister of James Otis, was an effective spokesperson for republicanism before, during, and after the Revolution. In this excerpt she expresses her concern about the corruptibility of men in government.

Some gentlemen with laboured zeal, have spent much time in urging the necessity of government. . . .

But the most sagacious advocates for the party have not by fair discussion, and rational argumentation, evinced the necessity of adopting this many headed monster; of such motley mixture, that its enemies cannot trace a feature of Democratick or Republican extract. . . .

It will be allowed by every one that the fundamental principle of a free government is the equal representation of a free people . . . And when society has thus deputed a certain number of their equals to take care of their personal rights, and the interest of the whole community, it must be considered that responsibility is the great security of integrity and honour; and that annual election is the basis of responsibility. Man is not immediately corrupted, but power without limitation, or amenability, may endanger the brightest virtue—whereas a frequent return to the bar of their Constituents is the strongest check against the corruptions to which men are liable, either from the intrigues of others of more subtle genius, or the propensities of their own hearts.

From Paul L. Ford, ed., Pamphlets on the Constitution of the United States, Published during its Discussion by the People, 1787-1788, (Brooklyn: privately printed, 1828).

Benjamin Franklin readily admitted that the constitution was not perfect. However, he argued that it was the best compromise that could be expected under the circumstances.

In these sentiments, Sir, I agree to this Constitution with all its faults, if they are such; because I think a general Government necessary for us, and there is no form of Government but what may be a blessing to the people if well administered, and believe farther that this is likely to be well administered for a number of years, and can only end in Despotism, as other forms have done before it, when the people shall became so corrupted as to need despotic Government, being incapable of any other. I doubt too whether any other Convention we can obtain, may be able to make a better Constitution. . . . It therefore astonishes me, Sir, to find this system approaching so near to perfection as it does; and I think it will astonish our enemies, who are waiting with confidence to hear that our councils are confounded like those of the Builders of Babel; and that our States are on the point of separation, only to meet hereafter for the purpose of cutting one another's throats. Thus I consent, Sir, to this Constitution because I expect no better, and because I am not sure, that it is not the best. . . .

Much of the strength and efficiency of any Government in procuring and securing happiness to the people, depends, on opinion, on the general opinion of the goodness of the Government, as well as of the wisdom and integrity of its Governors.

From Gaillard Hunt, *The Writings of James Madison*, (New York: Putnam and Sons, 1903).

1. In the first excerpt, what aspects of the Constitution would have caused Mercy Warren to raise these concerns?
2. In the second excerpt, what argument does Benjamin Franklin make for the need for a central government?
3. Create an exchange of correspondence between Mercy Warren and Ben Franklin in which they outline their views on the proposed constitution.

The Virginia Debates

In no state legislature was the debate more heated, the debators more powerful, or the outcome more critical than in Virginia. The most populous and powerful of all the states, Virginia's support was critical for the success of the scheme. In this excerpt, both viewpoints on the proposed change are clearly articulated.

Mr. George Mason

Mr. Chairman, whether the Constitution be good or bad, the present clause clearly discovers that it is a national government, and no longer a Confederation. The assumption of this power of laying direct taxes does, of itself, entirely change the confederation of the states into one consolidated government. This power, being at discretion, unconfined, and without any kind of control, must carry every thing before it. The very idea of converting what was formerly a confederation to a consolidated government, is totally subversive of every principle which has hitherto governed us. This power is calculated to annihilate totally the state governments. These two concurrent powers cannot exist long together; the one will destroy the other: the general government being paramount to, and in every respect more powerful than the state governments, the latter must give way to the former. . . .

But my principal objection is, that the Confederation is converted to one general consolidated government, which, from my best judgment of it, (and which perhaps will be shown, in the course of this discussion, to be really well founded,) is one of the worst curses that can possibly befall a nation. Does any man suppose that one general national government can exist in so extensive a country as this? . . .

Mr. Pendleton

Mr. Chairman, my worthy friend has expressed great uneasiness in his mind, and informed us that a great many of our citizens are also extremely uneasy, at the proposal of changing our government. What was the situation of this country before the meeting of the federal Convention? Our general government was totally inadequate to the purpose of its institution; our commerce decayed; our finances deranged; public and private credit destroyed: these and many other national evils rendered necessary the meeting of that Convention. If the public mind was then at ease, it did not result from a conviction of being a happy and easy situation: it must have been inactive, unaccountable stupor . . . .

We are perfectly free from sedition and war: we are not yet in confusion: we are left to consider our real happiness and security: we want to secure these objects: we know they cannot be attained without government. Is there a single man, in this committee, of a contrary opinion? What was it that brought us from a state of nature of society, but to secure happiness? And can society be formed without government? There is no quarrel between government and liberty; the former is the shield and protector of the latter. Where is the cause of alarm? We, the people, possessing all power, form a government, such as we think will secure happiness: and suppose, in adopting this plan, we should be mistaken in the end; where is the cause of alarm on that quarter? . . .

Who but the people have a right to form government? If the objection be, that the Union ought to be not of the people, but of the state governments, then I think the choice of the former very happy and proper. . . .

Then the question must be between this government and the Confederation. The latter is no government at all. It has been said that it has carried us, through a dangerous war, to a happy issue. Not that Confederation, but common danger, and the spirit of America, were bonds of our union. "United, we stand; divided, we fall!" echoed and reechoed through America—from Congress to the drunken carpenter. . . .

Mr. Madison

Before I proceed, I must take the liberty to make some observations on what was said by another gentleman, (Mr. Patrick Henry). He told us that this Constitution ought to be rejected because it endangered the public liberty, in his opinion, in many instances. If any dangerous and unnecessary powers be given to the general legislature, let them be plainly demonstrated; and let us not rest satisfied with general assertion of danger, without examination. If powers be necessary, apparent danger is not a sufficient reason against conceding them. If we consider the peculiar situation of the United States, and what are the sources of that diversity of sentiment which pervades its inhabitants, we shall find great danger to fear that the same causes may terminate here in the same fatal effects which they produced in those republics. . . . A federal government is formed for the protection of its individual members. Let me mention one fact, which I conceive must carry conviction to the mind of any one: the smallest state in the Union has obstructed every attempt to reform the government;

that little member has repeatedly disobeyed and counteracted the general authority.

From Jonathan Elliott, ed., *Debates in the Several State Conventions on the Adoption of the Federal Constitution* Vol. 3, (Washington, D.C.: Jonathan Elliott, 1836).

1. What basic argument is put forward by George Mason?
2. How does Pendleton counter Mason's view?
3. To what extent did the difference of opinion in Virginia reflect the fundamental issues which would lead to secession in 1861?

The Constitution: A Modern Assessment

American Historian Henry Steele Commager considered the nature of the constitutional debate and its long-term implications for the United States.

By June 26, 1787, tempers in the Federal Convention were already growing short, for gentlemen had come to the explosive question of representation in the upper chamber. . . .

What were the objects of the Federal Constitution? . . .

There were two grand objects—objects inextricably interrelated. The first was to solve the problem of federalism, that is, the problem of the distribution of powers among governments. Upon the wisdom with which members of the Convention distinguished between powers of a general and powers of a local nature, and assigned these to their appropriate governments, would depend the success or failure of the new experiment. . . .

How were they to enforce the terms of the distribution and impose limits upon all the governments involved? It was one thing to work out the most ideal distribution of general and local powers. It was another thing to see to it that the states abided by their obligations under the Articles of Union and that the national government respected the autonomy of the states and the liberty of individuals. . . .

The fact is that we look in vain in the Constitution itself for any really effective guarantee for property or any effective barriers against what Beard calls "the reach of popular majorities."

It will be argued, however, that what the farmers feared was the states, and that the specific prohibitions against state action, together with the broad transfer of economic powers from state to nation, were deemed sufficient guarantee against state attacks upon property. As for the national government, care was taken to make that sufficiently aristocratic, sufficiently the representative of the propertied classes, and sufficiently checked and limited so that it would not threaten basic property interests.

. . . Granted the wisest distribution of powers among governments, what guarantee was there that power would be properly exercised? What guarantees were there against the abuse of power? What assurance was there that the large states would not ride roughshod over the small, that majorities would not crush minorities or minorities abuse majorities? What protection was there against mobs, demagogues, dangerous combinations of interests or of states? What protection was there for the commercial interest, the planter interest, the slave interest, the securities interests, the land speculator interests?

It was Madison who most clearly saw the real character of this problem. . . . 'The truth was', he said on July 11, 'that all men having power ought to be distrusted to a certain degree.' . . . Listen to him on one of the early days of the Convention, June 6, when he is discussing the way to avoid abuses of republican liberty—abuses which 'prevailed in the largest as well as the smallest [states] . . .

> . . . the only defence against the inconveniences of democracy consistent with the democratic form of Government. All civilized Societies would be divided into different Sects, Factions and interests, as they happened to consist of rich and poor, debtors and creditors, the landed, the manufacturing, the commercial interests, the inhabitants of this district or that district, the followers of this political leader or that . . . In all cases where a majority are united by a common interest or passion, the rights of the minority are in danger. . . . The only remedy is to enlarge the sphere, and thereby divide the community into so great a number of interests and parties, that in the first place a majority will not be likely at the same moment to have a common interest separate from that of the whole or of the minority; and in the second place, that in case they should have such an interest, they may not be apt to unite in the pursuit of it.' . . .

What provisions did they write into the Constitution against what Randolph called 'democratic licentiousness'?

They granted equality of representation in the Senate. . . . But the decision for equality of representation was not dictated by considerations either economic or democratic, but rather by the recalcitrance of the small states. . . .

Senators and Presidents, then, would not be the creatures of democracy. But what guarantee was there that senators would be representatives of property interests. . . .

. . . What they did succeed in doing was to create a system of checks and balances and adjustments and accommodations that would effectively prevent the suppression of most minorities by majorities. They took advantage of the complexity, the diversity, the pluralism, of American society and economy to encourage a balance of interests. They worked out sound and lasting political solutions to the problems of class, interest, section, race, religion, party.

From Henry Steele Commager, "The Constitution: Was it an Economic Document?", *American Heritage X*, December 1958.

1. What considerations does Commager feel were paramount among the delegates?
2. To what extent was the United States safeguarded against democracy?
3. In 1987 the constitution celebrated its two hundredth anniversary. Discuss the assertion made by some historians that only a terribly flawed document could have caused a civil war and required twenty-six amendments to repair.

Lincoln Rejects Secession, 1861

Abraham Lincoln was a minority president who came into office without any support whatsoever in the South. By the time of his inauguration, the deep South had left the Union and within a few months, the nation had split in two. In an address to Congress in July 1861, Lincoln reaffirmed the nature of the American federal agreement. In his address he pointed out the ultimate result of the right of secession.

The purpose to sever the Federal Union . . . embraces more than the fate of these United States. It presents to the whole family of man the question whether a constitutional republic or democracy—a government of the people by the same people—can or cannot maintain its territorial integrity against its own domestic foes. It presents the question whether discontented individuals, too few in number to control administration according to organic law in any case, can always, upon the pretenses made in this case, or on any other pretenses, or arbitrarily without any pretense, break up their government, and thus practically put an end to free government upon the earth. It forces us to ask: Is there in all republics this inherent and fatal weakness? Must a government, of necessity, be too strong for the liberties of its own people, or too weak to maintain its own existence? . . .

The South . . . invented an ingenious sophism which, if conceded, was followed by perfectly logical steps, through all the incidents, to the complete destruction of the Union. The sophism itself is that any State of the Union may consistently with the national Constitution, and therefore lawfully and peacefully, withdraw from the Union without the consent of the Union or of any other State. . . .

This sophism derives much, perhaps the whole, of its currency from the assumption that there is some omnipotent and sacred supremacy pertaining to a State—each State of our Federal Union. Our States have neither more nor less power than that reserved to them in the Union by the Constitution—no one of them ever having been a State out of the Union. The original ones passed into the Union even before they cast off their British colonial dependence; and the new ones each came into the Union directly from a condition of dependence, excepting Texas. . . .

Having never been States either in substance or in name outside of the Union, whence this magical omnipotence of 'State rights', asserting a claim of power to lawfully destroy the Union itself? Much is said about the 'sovereignty' of the States; but the word even is not in the national Constitution, nor, as is believed, in any of the State constitutions. What is 'sovereignty' in the political sense of the term? Would it be far wrong to define it as 'a political community without a political superior'? . . .

The States have their status in the Union, and they have no other legal status. If they break from this, they can only do so against law and by revolution. The Union, and not themselves separately, procured their independence and their liberty. By conquest or purchase the Union gave each of them whatever of independence or liberty it has. The Union is older than any of the States, and, in fact, it created them as States. Originally some dependent colonies made the Union, and, in turn, the Union threw off their old dependence for them, and made them States, such as they are. Not one of them ever had a State constitution independent of the Union. Of course, it is not forgotten that all the new States framed their constitutions before they entered the Union—nevertheless, dependent upon and preparatory to coming into the Union. . . .

What is now combatted is the position that secession is consistent with the Constitution—is lawful and peaceful. It is not contended that there is any express law for it; and nothing should ever be implied as law which leads to unjust or absurd consequences. . . .

The seceders insist that our Constitution admits of secession. They have assumed to make a national constitution of their own, in which of necessity they have either discarded or retained the right of secession as they insist it exists in ours. If they have discarded it, they thereby admit that on principle it ought not to be in ours. If they have retained it, by their own construction or ours, they show that to be consistent they must secede from one another whenever they shall find it the easiest way of settling their debts, or effecting any other selfish or unjust object. The principle itself is one of disintegration and upon which no government can possibly endure.

From Abraham Lincoln, "Message to Congress, July 4, 1861 in Richard Hofstadter, ed., *Great Issues in American History*, (New York: Vintage Books, 1958).

1. What motives does Lincoln attribute to the leaders of the secession movement?
2. Do you agree or disagree with Lincoln's view of "states rights"?
3. What does Lincoln see as the ultimate result of secession?

Jefferson Davis Rejects Federalism, 1861

Jefferson Davis became the provisional president of the Confederate States of America in February 1861. In April of that year, he countered Lincoln's view of the nature of the union. For Davis, the United States was a compact among sovereign states, and as such the states could withdraw from the union at will.

Gentlemen of the Congress . . .

The declaration of war made against this Confederacy by Abraham Lincoln, the President of the United States . . . rendered it necessary, in my judgment, that you should convene at the earliest practicable moment to devise the measures necessary for the defense of the country. . . .

Strange indeed, must it appear to the impartial observer, but it is none the less true that all these carefully worded clauses proved unavailing to prevent the rise and growth in the Northern States of a political school which has persistently claimed that the government thus formed was not a compact between States, but was in effect a national government, set up above and over the States. An organization created by the States to secure the blessings of liberty and independence against foreign aggression, has been gradually perverted into a machine for their control above its creators; the principals have been made subordinate to the agent appointed by themselves. . . .

By degrees, as the Northern States gained preponderance in the National Congress, self-interest taught their people to yield ready assent to any plausible advocacy of their right as a majority to govern the minority without control. They learned to listen with impatience to the suggestion of any constitutional impediment to the exercise of their will, and so utterly have the principles of the Constitution been corrupted in the Northern mind that, in the inaugural address delivered by President Lincoln in March last, he asserts as an axiom, which he plainly deems to be undeniable, that the theory of the Constitution requires that in all cases the majority shall govern; . . . This is the lamentable and fundamental error on which rests the policy that has culminated in his declaration of war against these Confederate States. . . .

In the exercise of a right so ancient, so well-established, and so necessary for self-preservation, the people of the Confederate States, in their conventions determined that the wrongs which they had suffered and the evils with which they were menaced required that they should revoke the delegation of powers to the Federal Government which they had ratified in their several conventions. They consequently passed ordinances resuming all their rights as sovereign and independent States and dissolved their connection with the other States of the Union.

Having done this they proceeded to form a new compact amongst themselves by new articles of confederation, which have been also ratified by the conventions of the several States with an approach to unanimity far exceeding that of the conventions which adopted the Constitution of 1787. They have organized their new Government in all its departments; the functions of the executive, legislative, and judicial magistrates are performed in accordance with the will of the people, as displayed not merely in a cheerful acquiescence, but in the enthusiastic support of the Government thus established by themselves; and but for the interference of the Government of the United States in this legitimate exercise of the right of a people to self-government, peace, happiness, and prosperity would now smile on our land.

From Jefferson Davis, "Message to the Confederate Congress," April 29, 1861 in Richard Hofstadter, ed., *Great Issues in American History*, (New York: Vintage Books, 1958).

1. Outline Davis's view of the compact between states.
2. How does he describe the activities of Congress?
3. What rights does Davis say have been exercised by the Confederate states?

Federalism v. Confederation: the Canadian Experience

The collapse of the American federal state into civil war gave both impetus to the idea of political union in British North America and invoked cautious restraint among those who would draw up the terms of the agreement. The debate on the concept of Confederation (a misnomer seeing as the delegates were talking about a federal and not a confederal state) took place in two stages. The first was in the Parliament of the Canadas where the merits of the scheme were debated against the backdrop of English-French relations. The second debate took place in the Maritime colonies as anti-

Confederation forces rallied to prevent the loss of local autonomy in a union sure to be dominated by central Canada.

In the Legislative Council, the debates centred primarily on the question of whether a federal union would protect the rights of the individual provinces. Here former premier Etienne-Pascal Taché argues in its favour, as do two English Canadians, John Ross and Alexander Campbell.

Hon. Sir Etienne-Pascall Taché, Friday, February 3, 1865

If the opportunity which now presented itself were allowed to pass by unimproved, whether we would or would not, we would be forced into the American Union by violence, and if not by violence, would be placed upon an inclined plane which would carry us there insensibly. In either case the result would be the same. In our present condition we would not long continue to exist as a British colony. . . .

Lower Canada had constantly refused the demand of Upper Canada for representation according to population, and for the good reason that, as the union between them was legislative, a preponderance to one of the sections would have placed the other at its mercy. It would not be so in a Federal Union, for all questions of a general nature would be reserved for the General Government, and those of a local character to the local governments, who would have the power to manage their domestic affairs as they deemed best. . . .

Hon. John Ross, Wednesday, February 8, 1865

I will say that if the delegates who met at Quebec and prepared that instrument were incompetent for the task, I do not know where others can be found to do it better. . . .

Hon. Alexander Campbell, Friday, February 17, 1865

Do you desire to have a union of all the British American provinces, or do you desire to remain as you are? That is the issue . . . If the scheme is postponed now, it is postponed indefinitely. . . .

Honourable gentlemen, are you ready to take the responsibility of declaring that the people of Canada are opposed to Confederation? . . .

Those of you who know what difficulties and objections were met with—the selfish interests of the various sections of this and of the other provinces, which we had to overcome—must feel that a very great advance was made when the measure was brought to the present forward stage. . . .

If this harness of the Confederation of the country is to be put on, we cannot but expect that it will chafe here and chafe there; but time will give relief and provide the remedy, as it has done in other circumstances before.

From P.B. Waite, ed., *The Confederation Debates in the Province of Canada 1865*, Carleton Library Series, (Toronto: McClelland and Stewart, 1963).

In the Legislative Assembly the pro-Confederation forces were led by a triumvirate consisting of John A. Macdonald, George Etienne Cartier and George Brown. In these excerpts, the three leaders outline the advantages of the scheme.

Sir John A. Macdonald, Monday, February 6, 1865

By a happy coincidence of circumstances, just when an Administration had been formed in Canada for the purpose of attempting a solution of the difficulties under which we labored, at the same time the Lower Provinces, actuated by a similar feeling, appointed a Conference with a view to a union among themselves. . . .

We made this arrangement, agreed upon the scheme, and the deputations from the several governments represented at the Conference went back pledged to lay it before their governments, and to ask the legislatures and people of their respective provinces to assent to it. . . .

If we are not blind to our present position, we must see the hazardous situation in which all the great interests of Canada stand in respect to the United States. I am no alarmist. I do not believe in the prospect of immediate war. I believe that the common sense of the two nations will prevent a war; still we cannot trust to probabilities. . . .

The Conference having come to the conclusion that a Legislative union, pure and simple, was impracticable, our next attempt was to form a government upon federal principles, which would give to the General Government the strength of a legislative and administrative union, while at the same time it preserved the liberty of action for the different sections which is allowed by a Federal union. And I am strong in the belief that we have hit upon the happy medium in those resolutions, and that we have formed a scheme of government which unites the advantages of both, giving us the strength of a Legislative union and the sectional freedom of a Federal union, with protection to local interests. In doing so we had the advantage of the experience of the United States. It is the fashion now to enlarge on the defects of the Constitution of the United States, but I am not one of those who look upon it as a failure. (Hear, hear.) I think and believe that it is one of the most skilful works which human intelligence ever created; is one of the most perfect organizations that ever governed a free people. To say that it has some defects is but to say that it is not the work of Omniscience, but of human intellects. We are happily situated in having had the opportunity of watching its operation. . . .

They declared by their Constitution that each state was a sovereignty in itself, and that all the powers incident to a sovereignty belonged to each state, except those powers, which, by the Constitution, were conferred on the General Government. We have given the General Legislature all the great subjects of legislation. We have conferred on them, not only specifically and in detail, all the powers which are incident in sovereignty, but we have expressly declared that all subjects of general interest not distinctly and exclusively conferred upon the local governments, shall be conferred upon the General Government. We have thus avoided that great source of weakness which was the cause of the disruption of the United States. . . .

We thereby strengthen the Central Parliament, and make the Confederation one people and one government, instead of five peoples and five governments, with merely a point of authority connecting us to a limited and insufficient extent. . . .

If we do not take advantage of the time, if we show ourselves unequal to the occasion, it may never return, and we shall hereafter bitterly and unavailingly regret having failed to embrace the happy opportunity now offered of founding a great nation. . . .

Hon. George Etienne Cartier, Tuesday, February 7, 1865
Confederation was, as it were, at this moment almost forced upon us. We could not shut our eyes to what was going on beyond the lines, where a great struggle was going on between two Confederacies, at one time forming but a Confederacy. We saw that a government, established not more than 80 years ago, had not been able to keep together the family of states which had broken up four or five years since. We could not deny that the struggle now in progress must necessarily influence our political existence. We did not know what would be the result of that great war—whether it would end in the establishment of two Confederacies or in one as before. . . .

Hon. George Brown, Wednesday, February 8, 1865
I cannot help feeling that the struggle of half a life-time for constitutional reform—the agitations in the country, and the fierce contests in this chamber— the strife and the discord and the abuse of many years,—are all compensated by the great scheme of reform which is now in your hands. . . . We are endeavouring to adjust harmoniously greater difficulties than have plunged other countries into all the horrors of civil war. . . . We are striving to settle forever issues hardly less momentous than those that have rent the neighbouring republic and are now exposing it to all the horrors of civil war. . . .

. . . One hundred years have passed away since the conquest of Quebec, but here sit the children of the victor and the vanquished, all avowing hearty attachment to the British Crown–all earnestly deliberating how we shall best extend the blessings of British institutions–how a great people may be established on this continent in close and hearty connection with Great Britain. . . . And well, Mr. Speaker, may the work we have unitedly proposed rouse the ambition and energy of every true man in British America. . . . Our scheme is to establish a government that will seek to turn the tide of European emigration into this northern half of the American continent–that will strive to develop its great natural resources–and that will endeavor to maintain liberty, and justice, and Christianity throughout the land. . . .

. . .We imagine not that such a structure can be built in a month or in a year. What we propose now is but to lay the foundations of the structure–to set in motion the governmental machinery that will one day, we trust, extend from the Atlantic to the Pacific.

From P.B. Waite, *The Confederation Debates in the Province of Canada 1865*, Carleton Library Series, (Toronto: McClelland and Stewart, 1963).

1. What argument does Taché make for federal union?
2. What lessons does Macdonald say have been learned from the experiences of the United States?

3. What global destiny does Brown identify for the new nation?

Confederation: Guardian of French Canada

Some debators saw Confederation as the only practical alternative to the political dead-lock that had existed in the Canadas for almost a decade. In this excerpt J. Dufresne argues the case.

In examining this question, and in order to express more clearly and fully my opinion of these resolutions, I may say that I accept them for many reasons, but chiefly as a means of obtaining the repeal of the present legislative union of Canada, and securing a peaceable settlement of our sectional difficulties. I accept them, in the second place, as a means of obtaining for Lower Canada the absolute and exclusive control of her own affairs. I accept them, thirdly, as a means of perpetuating French-Canadian nationality in this country. I accept them, fourthly, as a more effectual means of cementing our connection with the Mother Country, and avoiding annexation to the United States. I accept them, fifthly and lastly, as a means of administering the affairs of the country with greater economy. Such are my reasons for accepting the Confederation scheme submitted to us by the Government.

Parliamentary Debates on the Subject of the Confederation of the British North American Provinces, (Quebec, 1865).

1. What are the specific reasons Dufresne gives for accepting the Confederation scheme?
2. Contrast Dufresne's practical reasoning with the lofty ideals of the sponsors of Confederation.
3. To what extent do you think Dufresne's logical arguments reflect the feelings of a large number of Canadians at the time? Why?

The Dorion View

Antoine A. Dorion was one of the most outspoken critics of Confederation in the Legislative Assembly of the Canadas. In this excerpt, he argues in favour of true Confederation.

I pronounced in favour of a Confederation of the two provinces of Upper and Lower Canada, as the best means of protecting the varied interests of the two sections. But the Confederation I advocated was a real confederation, giving the largest powers to the local governments, and merely a delegated authority to the General Government—in that respect differing *in toto* from the one now proposed which gives all the powers to the Central Government, and reserves for the local governments the smallest possible amount of freedom of action. . . .

Is the scheme represented to us the same one that was promised to us by the Administration when it was formed? . . . Since the scheme is so objectionable, especially as we are gravely told that it cannot be amended in the least, but that it is brought down as a compact made between the Government of this country and delegates from the governments of Nova Scotia, New Brunswick, Newfoundland, and Prince Edward Island–as a treaty which cannot be altered or amended in any particular. . . .

The whole scheme, sir, is absurd from beginning to end. It is but natural that gentlemen with the views of honorable gentlemen opposite want to keep as much power as possible in the hands of the Government–that is the doctrine of the Conservative party everywhere–that is the line which distinguishes the tories from the whigs–the tories always side with the Crown, and the Liberals always want to give more power and influence to the people. . . . We shall have the most illiberal Constitution ever heard of in any country where constitutional government prevails. . . .

Now, sir, when I look into the provisions of this scheme, I find another most objectionable one. It is that which gives the General Government control over all the acts of the local legislatures. . . . Now, knowing that the General Government will be party in its character, may it not for party purposes reject laws passed by the local legislatures and demanded by a majority of the people of that locality. . . . Do you not see that it is quite possible for a majority in a local government to be opposed to the General Government; and in such a case the minority would call upon the General Government to disallow the laws enacted by the majority? . . . There may, therefore, be matters not included in the enumeration, upon which the Parliament of Canada has the power to legislate, because they concern the peace, order and good government of the Dominion. But to those matters which are not specified among the enumerated subjects of legislation, the excerption from s.92, which is enacted by the concluding words of s.91, has no application; and, in legislating with regard to such matters, the Dominion Parliament has no authority to encroach upon any class of subjects which is exclusively assigned to provincial legislatures by s.92. These enactments appear to their Lordships to indicate that the exercise of legislative power by the Parliament of Canada, in regard to all matters not enumerated in s.91, ought to be strictly confined to matters as are unquestionably of Canadian interest and importance, and ought not to trench upon provincial legislation with respect to any of the classes of subjects enumerated in s.92. To attach any other construction to the general power which, in supplement of its enumerated powers, is conferred upon the Parliament of Canada by s.91, would, in their Lordship's opinion, not only be contrary to the intendment of the Act, but would practically destroy the autonomy of the provinces. If it were once conceded that the Parliament of Canada has the authority to make laws applicable to the whole Dominion, in relation to matters which in each province are substantially of local or private interest, upon the assumption that these matters also concern the peace, order and good government of the Dominion, there is hardly a subject enumerated in s.92 upon which it might not legislate, to the exclusion of the provincial legislatures.

From P.B. Waite, *The Confederation Debates in the Province of Canada 1865*, Carleton Library Series, (Toronto: McClelland and Stewart, 1963).

1. What abuses does Dorion foresee in the proposed federal arrangement?

2. What reasons does he give for placing residual powers in the hands of the provinces rather than the central government?

3. Compare Dorion's view of the potential danger of majority tyranny with those put forward during the Federalist debates in the United States. To what extent do you think Dorion might have been influenced by the observations of Confederate leaders such as Jefferson Davis?

The Political Case for Rejection, 1865-66

The following excerpts are taken from the speeches of various critics of Confederation. Christopher Dunkin was an English-speaking Member of Parliament from the Eastern Townships of Quebec. In February 1865, he foresaw an increase in English-French tensions resulting from the pact.

But the moment you tell Lower Canada that the large-sounding powers of your General Government are going to be handed over to a British-American majority, decidedly not of the race and faith of her majority, that moment you wake up the old jealousies and hostility in their strongest form. . . . you unfortunately countenance the idea that the French are going to be more unfair than I believe they wish to be. For that matter, what else can they well be? They will find themselves a minority in the General Legislature, and their power in the General Government will depend upon their power within their own province and over their provincial delegations in the Federal Parliament. They will thus be compelled to be practically aggressive, to secure and retain that power.

From P.B. Waite, *The Confederation Debates in the Province of Canada 1865*, Carleton Library Series, (Toronto: McClelland and Stewart, 1963).

Louis Auguste Olivier, in February 1865, echoed Dorion's belief that provincial rights would be crushed under the weight of a federal state.

My opinion is that as much power as possible should have been entrusted to the local governments, and as little as is consistent with the functions it will have to discharge to the Central Government, and my reason for entertaining this opinion is, that the Supreme Government, with its power of purse and its control of the armies, will always be more disposed to stretch its prerogatives and to trench upon the domain of the local governments than to narrow down and retain its authority. The scheme then, in my opinion, is defective in that it invests this order. . . . As it is now, if the scheme goes into operation, the local governments will be in danger of being crushed by the General Government.

From P.B. Waite, *The Confederation Debates in the Province of Canada 1865*, Carleton LibrarySeries, (Toronto: McClelland and Stewart, 1963).

Cornelius Howatt articulated the anti-Confederation view of a majority of Prince Edward Islanders when he spoke in the House of Assembly in May 1866. He foresaw the island being swallowed up by its larger partners.

I believe the day has come when we must make a stand for the preservation of our independence . . . If other Colonies go into Confederation, no doubt a pressure will be brought to bear upon us also, and then does it not remain for us to make a united effort to resist any attempt to take away our constitution, our revenue, and, I might almost say, everything else belonging to us? I was opposed to Confederation last year, for I saw there was danger even in admitting the principle of it, and I am just as much, or more opposed to it now. . . . I believe that, even if we should go into it with the most favourable terms, the Federal Government would have power to change the constitution, and therefore we would not be secure . . . and, considering that we would be such a small portion of the Confederacy, our voice would not be heard in it. We would be next to nothing.

From *The Charlottetown Examiner*, August 27, 1866, Vol. XVI, No. 42.

Nova Scotia elected an anti-Confederation government in September 1867. In fact, thirty-six of the thirty-eight members elected were declared repealers, as were eighteen of the nineteen members elected to go to Ottawa. The Nova Scotian government presented its case to Britain but was told that it was too late. Joseph Howe was one of the leading opponents of Confederation. After the British rejection and a meeting with John A. Macdonald in 1868, Howe emerged as a spokeman against repeal and instead for renegotiation.

Let us see what the Canadians desire to do. They are not, as we have shown, a very harmonious or homogeneous community. Two-fifths of the population are French and three-fifths English. They are therefore perplexed with an internal antagonism which . . . must ever be a source of weakness. They are shut in by frost from the outer world for five months of the year. They are at the mercy of a powerful neighbour whose population already outnumbers them by more than eight to one . . . on the opposite side of a naturally defenceless frontier. . . . it is evident that a more unpromising nucleus of a new nation can hardly ever be found on the face of the earth, and that any organized communities, having a reasonable chance to do anything better, would be politically insane to give up their distinct formations and subject themselves to the domination of Canada.

From J.A. Chisholm, *The Speeches and Public Letters of Joseph Howe*, (Halifax 1909) Vol. II.

William Miller, an independent member of the Nova Scotia Assembly, had argued for renegotiation as early as 1866.

If the Government will publicly abandon the Quebec scheme, and introduce a resolution in favour of a Federal Union of British America—leaving the details of the measure to the arbitrament of the Imperial Government, properly advised by delegates from all the provinces, I promise them my cordial support. This would be commencing rightly. By getting the endorsement of the Legislature at the outset—of the principles of Union, and its authority to enter on the settlement of the details of a scheme, the friends of the measure would occupy a very different position from that occupied by the delegates to the Quebec Conference, who went to Canada in 1864 without any authority from Parliament. . . .

The object of my present movement is—and I fearlessly avow it—to defeat
the Quebec scheme. Before it is too late—before we are borne down by the
powerful influences against which we are now contending—while yet we have
a formidable army in the field—while our opponents respect our strength and
hesitate at an engagement—is it not wise to seek the most advantageous terms
of compromise?

From Nova Scotia, House of Assembly, *Official Report of Debates*, 1866.

1. Identify the underlying themes of the anti-Confederation arguments.
2. To what extent does the failure of Nova Scotia to attain British support indicate
a change in colonial policy rather than specific imperial support for the scheme?
3. Discuss the parallels in the arguments used by the advocates of provincial rights
in Canada and the supporters of states' rights in the United States.

Confederation: Act or Pact?

*In the twentieth century considerable debate has centred around the fundamental nature
of the original Confederation agreement. Strong federalists such as former prime minister
Pierre Elliot Trudeau have argued that as an act of the British Parliament, no provincial
consent was required to make amendments. Other Canadians have seen Confederation
as a pact among sovereign colonies, and therefore one which cannot be changed without
mutual consent.*

*Professor Norman Rogers expressed the collective frustration of Canadians with this
issue in 1931.*

The compact theory of federalism in its Canadian form of expression is the
deferred result of a sin of omission on the part of the Fathers of Confederation,
a sin which in scriptural fashion has now been visited upon their children even
unto the third and fourth generation. Sometimes we are tempted to recall with
pride that the great task of the Quebec Conference was accomplished in the
brief period of sixteen days, and perhaps to congratulate ourselves that this
achievement compares favourably with the four months devoted to the framing
of the Constitution of the United States and the much longer period spent upon
the Constitution of the Commonwealth of Australia. No one can doubt that
those who drafted the Quebec Resolutions performed a difficult task with a
high degree of skill and a reasonable measure of foresight, but it is not easy to
forgive them for their failure to realize the necessity of providing the means
whereby the Constitution might be amended in future years without incurring
needless friction between the Dominion and the provinces. Certainly they
would be the more entitled to our gratitude today if they had continued their
sessions another week if need be in order to erect safeguards against the misunderstandings which must arise when changing conditions and new currents of
political and economic thought would lead to a demand for alterations of the
original terms of union.

From N. Rogers, "The Compact Theory of Confederation," in *The Canadian Political Science
Quarterly: Proceedings 1931* (Ottawa: The Canadian Political Science Association, 1931).

The Constitution Act of 1982 settled the issue temporarily by establishing an amending formula.

38.(1) An amendment to the Constitution of Canada may be made by proclamation issued by the Governor-General under the Great Seal of Canada where so authorized by
a. resolutions of the Senate and the House of Commons;
and
b. resolutions of the legislative assemblies of at least two-thirds of the provinces that have, in the aggregate, . . . at least 50 per cent of the population of all the provinces. . . .
  [Among the matters to be settled in this fashion are]
  . . . the principle of proportionate representation of the provinces in the House of Commons, . . . the powers of the Senate and the method of selecting Senators, . . . the Supreme Court of Canada, . . . [and] the establishment of new provinces.

The Constitution Act of 1982 also gave the provinces the power to opt out of such amendments when they involved the transfer of provincial power to the federal government. In such cases, Section 40 states that:

Where an amendment is made under Subsection 38(1) that transfers provincial legislative powers relating to education or other cultural matters from provincial legislatures to Parliament, Canada shall provide reasonable compensation to any province to which the amendment does not apply.

The Meech Lake Accord gave in to the pro-pact forces with its new agreement on amendments.

9. Sections 40 to 42 of the Constitution Act 1982 are repealed and the following substituted . . .
41. An amendment to the Constitution of Canada in relation to the following matters may be made by proclamation issued by the Governor-General under the Great Seal of Canada only where authorized by resolutions of the Senate and the House of Commons and of the legislative assembly of each province:
a. The office of the Queen, the Governor-General and the Lieutenant-Governor of a province;
b. the powers of the Senate and the method of selecting Senators;
c. the number of members by which a province is entitled to be represented in the Senate and the residence qualifications of senators;
d. the right of a province to a number of members in the House of Commons not less than the number of senators by which the province was to be represented on April 17, 1982;
e. the principle of proportionate representation of the provinces in the House of Commons . . .;
g. The Supreme Court of Canada;

h. The extension of existing provinces into the territories;
i. Notwithstanding any other law or practice, the establishment of new provinces; and;
j. an amendment to this part.
(A full text of the Meech Lake Accord appears in Appendix B.)
1. Trace the evolution of Canadian political thought concerning constitutional amendment.

The Role of Judicial Review

In the case of Marbury v. Madison, *Chief Justice John Marshall established the right of the United States Supreme Court to rule on the constitutionality of legislation. In Canada the same power was assumed first by the Judicial Committee of the Privy Council, and later by the Supreme Court of Canada.*

The landmark case for Canada was without question Russell v. the Queen. *It was the first time that the Judicial Committee had been asked to rule on the extent of the residual powers of the dominion government versus the elastic clause in section 92. In this case the justices decided for the federal government.*

In the Privy Council, 1882

. . . This is an appeal from an order of the Supreme Court of the Province of New Brunswick, discharging a rule nisi which had been granted on the application of the Appellant for a certiorari to remove a conviction made by the police magistrate of the city of Frederickton against him for unlawfully selling intoxicating liquors, contrary to the provisions of the Canada Temperance Act, 1878.

No question has been raised as to the sufficiency of the conviction, supposing the above-mentioned statute is a valid legislative Act of the Parliament of Canada. The only objection made to the conviction in the Supreme Court of New Brunswick, and in the appeal to Her Majesty in Council, is that, having regard to the provisions of the British North America Act, 1867, relating to the distribution of legislative powers, it was not competent for the Parliament of Canada to pass the Act in question. . . .

The general question of the competency of the Dominion Parliament to pass the Act depends on the construction of the 91st and 92nd sections of the British North America Act, 1867, . . .

The 91st section enacts, 'It shall be lawful for the Queen by and with the advice and consent of the Senate and the House of Commons to make laws for the peace, order and good government of Canada, in relation to all matters not coming within the classes of subjects by this Act, assigned exclusively to the legislatures of the provinces' . . .

What Parliament is dealing with in legislation of this kind is not a matter in relation to property and its rights, but one relating to public order and safety . . .

Few, if any laws could be made by Parliament for the peace, order, and good government of Canada which did not in some incidental way affect property and civil rights . . .

The Chief Justice of the Supreme court of Canada and the other judges . . . held that the Act, as a general regulation of the traffic of intoxicating liquors throughout the Dominion, fell within the class of subject 'the regulation of trade and commerce' enumerated in that section, and was, on that ground, a valid exercise of the legislative power of the Parliament of Canada.

From *In the Privy Council. (1882), 7 App. Cas. 829; 1 Olmsted 145* in Peter Russell, *Leading Constitutional Decisions*, Carleton Library Series, (Toronto: McClelland and Stewart, 1965).

1. What was the basic issue in the case?
2. How did the committee interpret the act?
3. Examine the significance of this decision for the future relationship between the two levels of government.

Meech Lake and the Lessons of 1787

Throughout much of 1988, the Senate, House of Commons, and the legislatures of various provinces debated over the issues involved in ratifying the constitutional amendments agreed upon in the Meech Lake Accord. Prime Minister Brian Mulroney argued that Meech Lake was a fragile package and that any tampering with its makeup could cause the whole deal to shatter. In this article that appeared in the Globe and Mail *on March 31, 1988, political columnist Gordon Crann argued that Canada should follow the American example when it came to ratifying the agreement.*

Uncle Sam's Example: Who says it has to be all or nothing when ratifying Meech Lake Accord?
Everyone debating the merits of the Meech Lake accord agrees that the reconciliation of Quebec is worth while. Beyond that, however, disagreement begins.

Those supporting the accord argue that it must be ratified unconditionally. To do otherwise, they maintain, would reopen the agreement and unravel the consensus reached by the First Ministers at Meech Lake last April 30.

Those who oppose the accord claim it is fundamentally flawed and constitutes a threat to Canada's national unity. They say the agreement must be amended significantly before ratification if the dire consequences they predict are to be avoided.

Unfortunately, the debate has seen both sides make increasingly extreme statements. Lost in the polarization has been any thought of developing a middle position. In particular, any suggestion that a province both ratify the accord as is and recommend amendments to be considered at later constitutional conferences has been called impractical.

Yet it is precisely this kind of give and take that has worked in the past. Specifically, the procedure of agreement followed by amendment was used effectively by several states when ratifying the U.S. Constitution 200 years ago. The result was the first 10 amendments, known as the U.S. Bill of Rights.

Considering the similarities between the Meech Lake debate today and the U.S. constitutional debate two centuries ago, Canadians could learn some lessons from the U.S. experience. Back in 1787, the constitutional convention held in Philadelphia was criticized for its secrecy. The document that was drafted took the citizenry somewhat by surprise. Due to the compromises required to get the representatives of the various states to agree, the end result differed from what people had expected.

Congress quickly voted on Sept. 23, 1787, to send the proposed constitution to the states for ratification. . . .

Those who favoured the constitution (known as the Federalists) argued that, without unconditional ratification, the consensus achieved at Philadelphia would unravel. The opposition (the Anti-Federalists) maintained that, by not entrenching civil liberties, the constitution would undermine the freedoms for which the American Revolution had been fought. . . .

John Hancock . . .proposed that the constitution be accepted—and that the various amendments be passed, not as conditions for ratification, but as recommendations for future constitutional action. . . .

The first 10 amendments, incorporating a number of states' recommendations into the Bill of Rights, were then adopted and came into effect three years later.

The similarities between the U.S. experience and Meech Lake are obvious. But what lessons should Canadians take from all this? Four points should be considered:

1. Any proposed amendment should have two attributes. First, it should have popular support. In 1788, it was important that the U.S. public believed in the protection of civil liberties. This meant there was continued public pressure to entrench civil liberties in the constitution. Today, only certain issues raised in terms of Meech Lake, such as multiculturalism, native rights, women's equality rights and minority language rights, could conceivably have the required popular support.

2. The amendment should not curtail provincial powers directly. Originally the U.S. Bill of Rights applied only to the federal government. . . . Therefore, the states ratified the first 10 amendments without perceiving a threat to their own powers. It follows that any amendments designed to restore unilateral federal power over appointments to the Senate and the Supreme Court of Canada or over national shared-cost program spending are doomed.

3. To be successful, amendments must have the support of more than one province. In 1788 it was essential that Massachusetts' suggestion to entrench a bill of rights was adopted by New Hampshire, Virginia and New York . . . Today, any recommendation for a future constitutional amendment probably needs the concerted efforts of at least three or four provinces. This would ensure the bargaining leverage required to give an amendment serious consideration at a constitutional conference.

4. Finally, adoption of the Meech Lake Accord with suggestions for future amendments might avoid certain long-term antagonisms that straightforward ratification could produce.

From Gordon Crann, "Uncle Sam's Example," *Globe and Mail*, March 31, 1988.

Federalism and Confederation: Analysis and Application

1. For many Americans, a federal state meant the submergence of local powers into a strong centralized government. For politicians in British North America, on the other hand, federalism meant a means to protect local rights. Account for this apparent difference in attitude toward the two federal schemes.

2. Canadian federalists considered the Charter of Rights an essential component of the patriated constitution in 1982. Compare this attitude with the American Anti-Federalists' demand for a bill of rights in 1789.

3. Canadian prime minister Brian Mulroney called the Meech Lake Accord "not perfect, but the best we could do." Discuss how this comment can be applied to the American constitution. Consider not only the problems expressed at the time of ratification, but also the constitutional questions that have been raised since.

4. In chart form, compare the division of powers under the Canadian federal system with that created by the American Constitution. Based upon your comparative study, formulate a thesis that expresses your opinion about the differences between the two systems of government.

5. Research *Marbury* v. *Madison* and *Russell* v. *the Queen*. What was the significance of these two cases with regard to the principle of judicial review?

6. Summarize the arguments put forward by Abraham Lincoln and Jefferson Davis with regard to the United States federal agreement. Compare their theses with those put forward during the Quebec referendum debate of 1980. Stage a "witness to yesterday" in which Davis applies his views to the Quebec situation.

7. Trace the evolution of Canadian political thought with regard to amending the constitution. To what extent has the nature of the British North America Act of 1867 precluded the need for extensive amendments as in the United States?

8. Create a clipping file on a current issue in Canadian federal/provincial relations. Prepare a report in which you identify and explain the issue; outline the federal and provincial positions; and summarize editorial opinions. Conclude your report with your own comments on the significance of the issue based upon your understanding of Canadian federalism.

9. As a follow-up to question 8, write a letter to the editor of your local paper outlining your analysis of the issue.

10. Assess the role of specific individuals in the development of federal systems of government in Canada and the United States. Select one political leader from each nation and compare their individual impact upon constitutional development. To what extent do the two individuals reflect a basic difference in the systems?

9
THE RESPONSE TO INDUSTRIALISM

The second half of the nineteenth century saw fundamental economic and social changes take place in North America. Primarily agrarian in 1850, by 1900 both Canada and the United States had taken great strides towards urbanization and industrial development. Many aspects of modern society, such as large corporations, labour unions, urban growth and development, and increasing government involvement in the economy, developed rapidly during this period. Although Canada tended to lag behind developments in the United States, the economies of the two countries took the same path. The pattern of bilateral interdependence taken for granted today had its origin in the final years of the last century.

This chapter will examine the pattern of industrial development in North America and its impact upon society, and the growth of labour unions in response to the new industrialism.

The Growth of Industry

The Civil War marked a turning point in the development of the American economy. Prior to 1860, six out of the ten states with the highest per capita income were the agricultural giants of the South. By 1880, however, the ten wealthiest states could be found in the rapidly industrializing states of the Northeast.

Several factors promoted this postwar industrial growth. Politically the war years were good for industry. The Morrill Tariff, passed in 1861, set up tariff barriers to protect American infant industries. This was followed two years later by a new National Banking Act, which established uniform federal bank notes and placed the country on the gold standard. This pre–industrial attitude extended to all aspects of business. Congress adopted a *laissez-faire* attitude towards industry; huge profits were made on war contracts, and railroad companies were given lucrative charters, land grants, and loans. Congress even gave corporations the same rights as citizens under the 14th Amendment.

Added to these political factors were the obvious economic advantages of a growing nation. A virgin continent, North America was blessed with abundant resources—fertile soil, untouched forests, and untapped mineral wealth. Northern victory had resulted in extensive profits, which were reinvested in the improvement of transportation and communications systems and the development of new products. The late nineteenth century was an age of innovation and invention. New technological changes, such as mass production and a system of interchangeable parts, revolutionized manufacturing.

With such advantages, the American economy took off following the end of the Civil War. The industrial states of the Northeast and the Ohio Valley began to extend their influence throughout the nation.

In spite of the war, there had been some expansion of the railway network during the early 1860s. As a result, by 1865 there were almost 60 000 km of track in the United States. Yet this was only the beginning. During the next eight years the number of kilometres of railway track doubled. Expansion was uneven, however. Of that 60 000 km of new track, only 8000 km were built in the South.

The growth of the railway system was not without its problems. There were scores of small railway companies, each with its own route and rate structure. In addition, the country had not yet established a standard gauge or track width, which meant that cargo travelling from one company's line to another often had to be reloaded to the other railway.

Consolidation of the railways began in the 1860s. One of the first major players was Commodore Cornelius Vanderbilt. Vanderbilt had made most of his money in shipping. However, with the decline in trade during the Civil War he decided to invest in railways. Through a series of shrewd stock moves, by the late 1860s he had bought up the New York Central line and extended its routes as far as Buffalo. Eventually the line ran to Chicago and to Omaha, Nebraska.

Vanderbilt was not just a speculator, however. To improve rail service, he introduced the practice of double tracking (running two parallel lines so that trains could pass each other) and improved existing tracks, routes, and bridges. He built Grand Central Station in New York City, and so much faster were his trains that they cut the travelling time from New York to Chicago in half, to only twenty-four hours. By the time he died in 1877, Vanderbilt had stretched his empire of over 7000 km of track west to Chicago and north as far as Toronto.

The New York Central was typical of the type of railway expansion taking place in the Northeast. Less concerned with actual construction, it was more a time for putting the pieces together to create a more efficient system. As well, construction was slow in the East as railways turned their dreams of expansion to the more appealing market in the West.

As early as 1862, two companies had received government charters to build lines linking the central plains and California. One, the Union Pacific, was given a charter authorizing it to lay track from Nebraska westward; another, the Central Pacific, could start in California and head east. Through grants, loans, double dealing, and profiteering the lines were finally built. Eventually the Union Pacific, hiring gangs of Civil War veterans and new Irish immigrants, started to make real progress. In one year alone they laid over 900 km of track. Eventually their 1700 km linked up with the 1100 km built by the Central Pacific. On May 10, 1869, the "last spike" was driven in Utah. The United States had its first trans-continental railway.

Investment and innovation continued unabated through the sixties, seventies, and eighties. In 1864 George M. Pullman developed the sleeping car; five years later George Westinghouse invented the air brake; the next decade saw the introduction of the refrigerator car. A railway business valued at $1 billion in 1865 had grown to $3.7 billion by 1873. New track brought the size of the empire to 150 000 km by 1880, and this almost doubled in the next decade. By 1890 the annual income of the railway industry was over $1 billion. By comparison, the federal government took in less than half of that amount.

Many Americans worried about the free rein given to the railway companies by the government. In the West in particular, railway monopolies meant that farmers often paid high rates for service. Shippers out of highly competitive Chicago, for example, paid less to send goods to England than did farmers transporting the same items only a few hundred kilometres in the West. Clearly something had to be done.

Attempts to control the railways at the state level were made during the 1870s and 1880s, but because as rail lines ran across state boundaries such laws were difficult to enforce. Consequently, in 1887 Congress stepped in and passed the Interstate Commerce Act. Although it initially had little effect, it established the right of the federal government to intervene in the affairs of private corporations.

The Industrialists

Although built upon a variety of economic and political factors, industrialization was largely the result of the efforts of a relatively small group. In the process of pursuing their own fortunes, these industrial entrepreneurs created the economic base for revolutionary change.

Today anyone driving across Canada or the United States comes into contact with the empire built by John D. Rockefeller. His Standard Oil Company is a worldwide, multinational corporation. Rockefeller started as a produce merchant in Cleveland. By the end of the Civil War, he had committed his resources to the newly expanding oil business. Oil was not used to drive engines in its early years; instead, it was refined into kerosene and used in lamps.

Like the early railways, oil refining was spread among a large number of small producers. Rockefeller wanted to consolidate the industry, and he wanted it under his control. His first attempts to buy out some of his competitors were rejected, and so he decided to force them out of business. By any standards, Rockefeller's tactics were ruthless. He would target a small business to destroy and then use any means to achieve his end. One approach was to set up a competitive business near by and sell the same product at a far lower price. Because his was a large operation he could afford a small financial loss. His competitors, however, could not. One small refining company after another was driven into bankruptcy. In other cases Rockefeller had company spies follow the competition's customers home, and then offer them a better deal. The competition's business would fall off drastically. The small refiner would have to sell out, never knowing what forces had been behind his demise. Through such practices Standard Oil grew bigger and bigger.

It was not only these backroom tactics that made Standard Oil successful, however. Rockefeller prided himself on efficiency and costcutting. He recognized the importance a small savings could make when multiplied by millions of barrels of oil. Every time he reduced the cost of refining one gallon (4.5 L) of oil by .082 cents he could increase his annual profit by over $600 000. No wonder, then, that by 1890 Standard Oil controlled over 90 percent of the nation's oil industry, and Rockefeller himself was worth over $800 million.

The secret of Standard's success was simple. The companies Rockefeller bought up were placed under the control of a committee of nine trustees. On the surface they all appeared to operate independently, but in reality they were controlled by

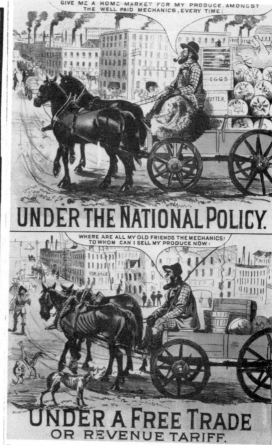

Political cartoon depicting life with and without the National Policy

Poster commemorating the completion of the Canadian Pacific Railway

a central administration. Thus Standard Oil maintained a monopoly without giving the appearance of doing so. Called a trust, Standard Oil became the corporate organizational model of the nineties.

Rockefeller's success in the oil industry was paralleled by Andrew Carnegie in iron and steel. Carnegie was the epitome of the self–made person. Immigrating to the United States from Scotland in 1848 at the age of thirteen, Carnegie took on jobs in a textile mill, as a messenger, and as a telegrapher. Eventually taking a position with the Pennsylvania Railroad, Carnegie came to see the potential market for the manufacture of steel for rails. He introduced a new system of steel manufacture called the Bessemer process. Prior to this, steel was very costly and time-consuming to produce; 10 to 20 kg of steel often took weeks to manufacture. With this new method, however, tonnes could be made in less than an hour.

In 1873, Carnegie invested all of his savings in a new steel plant which he built just outside of Pittsburgh. Using his connections with the railroads, Carnegie convinced the lines to invest in steel rails. By 1879 75 percent of all American steel production went into rails. While in 1870 the railway network comprised only 40 percent steel, by 1890 over 99 percent had been converted to steel.

Like Rockefeller, Carnegie attempted to buy up the small manufacturers in order to consolidate his holdings. Unlike the oil baron, however, Carnegie also invested in other industries that affected his business. He bought mines to produce the ore, railways to ship it, and factories to refine it. When he was finished he controlled the entire production process. Called *vertical integration*, Carnegie was the first to employ this system effectively, but it would soon catch on.

After decades of high pressure competition, however, Carnegie decided that he had had enough. In 1901 the Carnegie Steel Company was sold to financier J.P. Morgan for almost $500 million dollars, half of which went to Carnegie himself.

Vanderbilt, Rockefeller, and Carnegie—just three individuals, but individuals who had an impact on their era. There were others, but the stories of these three men provide an insight into the character of a rapidly changing period in North American history.

The Rise of Labour

As the nation industrialized the number of people working in factories also increased dramatically. A working class of 885 000 in 1860 had grown to over 3 million thirty years later.

Although the increased productivity in manufacturing resulted in a higher standard of living for most workers, there were still major problems. Unlike the old workshops, the new factories were impersonal places. The work was monotonous, and there was little communication between owner and labourer. Women and children, always available to supplement a family's income, were exploited ruthlessly. Actions to protect them were either rejected or suppressed. An Illinois court, for example, ruled as unconstitutional a law that restricted the number of hours a woman could be forced to work, declaring it a violation of her right to work for as long as she wanted.

In such an atmosphere it was not surprising that violence eventually erupted. The first outbreaks were in the late 1860s in the coal–mining regions of Pennsylvania. A secret miners' organization called the Molly Maguires decided to fight the mine owners with terrorism and violence. Property was burned, and bosses and supervisors were killed if they refused to accept workers' demands. After a decade of hostilities, the Molly Maguires were finally broken up in 1877, when ten of their leaders were brought to trial and eventually hanged.

Not all employers were ruthless towards their employees, however. Some, like Cornelius Vanderbilt, took a paternalistic approach. But even a benevolent attitude was no guarantee against employee dissatisfaction. In 1877, for example, after the announcement of a 10 percent cut in pay, the railway workers struck against the owners. However, the "Great Strike of '77" was cut short when federal troops were called in and the strikers were forced back to work.

The first postwar workers' organization was the National Labour Union. Formed in 1866, it encompassed a variety of skills and crafts within its membership. It was too idealistic, however, and when it went into politics, forming the National Labour Reform party in 1872, most members lost interest.

A more significant group was the Knights of Labour. The Knights were formed in 1869 by U.S. Stephens, who hoped to create "one big union" composed of individual members rather than representatives of numerous smaller trade unions. Idealists, they saw a day when workers would own the factories and would pay themselves through a portion of the profits. The Knights opened their doors to all workers, including Blacks and women, both of whom were often excluded from other organizations. In spite of this, the Knights remained relatively small until they were taken over by a Pennsylvania machinist named Terrence V. Powderly. Through a series of successful local strikes, Powderly's organization grew from a membership of forty–two thousand in 1882 to over seven hundred thousand just four years later.

Unfortunately, the leadership did not know how to cope with their success, and they found many activities getting out of their control. Matters came to a head in Chicago in May 1886. Workers in that city, supported by the Knights of Labour, conducted a general strike to demand an eight–hour work day. In that era, such an idea was revolutionary. In 1860 the average work day was about eleven hours; by the 1880s this figure had dropped to ten. Some manufacturers were beginning to realize that they maintained greater efficiency when their employees were rested and therefore more productive rather than over–tired from long hours of work. These manufacturers were in the minority, however. Because many factories were illuminated with natural light, owners wanted to take advantage of as many hours as they could. About eighty thousand workers joined the general strike. A group of one thousand were attending a rally in Haymarket Square on May 4th. When one speaker appeared to be inciting the crowd to violence the authorities moved in. From somewhere in the crowd a bomb was thrown at the advancing police. Seven people were killed and another sixty-seven wounded. The ringleaders of the strike were rounded up. Although there was no proof that any of them had been involved in the bombing, four were convicted and hanged.

The Haymarket riot discredited the Knights of Labour. Their membership began to decline almost as quickly as it had risen.

About five years before the Chicago riots a cigar industry worker named Samuel Gompers began to organize a new union. Eventually called the American Federation of Labour, it was quite different from its predecessors. Gompers insisted that the organization stay out of politics, which he believed had destroyed the National Labour Union. He was also against the idealist philosophy of "one big union," which he felt had been the undoing of the Knights of Labour.

The American Federation of Labour (AFL) was to be a federation of independent craft and trade unions. Its goal, Gompers said, would be "to increase the working man's welfare year by year." To do this, the AFL concentrated on every–day issues, such as higher wages, better working conditions, shorter hours, and closing shops to non–union labour. As president almost continuously from 1886 to 1924 Gompers used strikes or the threat of them to pursue his goals.

There were setbacks, however. A strike against Carnegie's Homestead Steel resulted in a riot and the death of seven private guards. The strike was crushed. In another case the American Railway Union, a member of the AFL, closed down the railway yards in Chicago. Government troops were called in to put down the workers. Eugene V. Debs, the leader of the railway workers, was so fed up with the political process that he decided to run for president himself, running five times on a socialist ticket.

Such activities hurt the AFL, but its membership still increased from 150 000 in 1886 to more than 1 million after the turn of the century.

The rapidly increasing industrial strength of the United States during this period was paralleled by rapid strides in agriculture. Farmers still felt that their influence in modern society was being eroded by the changes taking place in the cities. Frustrated with the old–line political parties, which seemed to be dominated by industrial and urban interests, farmers organized into a new people's party, the Populists, in 1892. Their concerns included high freight rates, industrial monopolies, the hardships of farming, and the impact of natural disasters.

Populist presidential candidate James Weaver did well in the election of 1892, attracting over 1 million voters and winning twenty electoral college votes. It was to be the peak of Populist strength, however. The old–line parties started to pay more attention to rural interests and when the Democrats nominated a populist–style candidate, William Jennings Bryan, to run in 1896, the Populists decided to back him rather than run their own candidate. It was the beginning of the end for the Populist party. When Bryan lost to William McKinley, they never recovered. Populism, however, had not been a failure. The Republicans and the Democrats had been forced to take note of the plight of the farmer, and the idea of third–party politics had gained a new respectability. In the early years of the twentieth century, the lessons learned by the Populists would be put to use by a new party, the Progressives.

The Progressive Era in the United States

The Nature of Progressivism

Many historians have argued that the Progressive era began with a single gunshot. On September 6, 1901, President William McKinley was shot in Buffalo, New York, as he attended the Pan–American Exposition. When he died eight days later, his vice–president, Theodore Roosevelt, was sworn in as his successor.

Roosevelt was considered the champion of Progressivism in the first decade of the twentieth century. But does he deserve the title?

Progressivism was a middle–class movement. Consisting of mainly urban, college–educated professionals and business people, Progressives were concerned about the plight of the working class, but were not a part of it. They saw the United States as a land of personal freedom, economic opportunity, and democracy, but they felt that many of these characteristics had been subverted by corruption. The basic aims of progressivism were simple: to preserve democracy against the dangers of plutocracy (government by the rich); to correct abuses of political power; to halt political corruption by the rich; to improve urban life; and to give the common person the chance to enjoy the economic rewards of industrialization.

Progressives shared some common traits with their Populist predecessors. Both spoke on behalf of honest, hard–working Americans, and both wanted to obtain a better deal for the people. Beyond these general similarities, however, there was a world of difference. Populists had tried to form their own political party, while Progressives tried to reform the existing ones. Populists had a rural base; the Progressives found their support in the cities. Populists included Blacks; Progressives tended to be members of the white middle class. Finally, Populists were idealists yearning to recreate the rural America of Thomas Jefferson. Progressives, on the other hand, were realists. Industrialization had taken place, and they were determined to take advantage of it.

Business, Labour, and Progressivism

Many business leaders saw themselves as progressives. Indeed, by 1909 it was unfashionable to be anything else. To some, progress meant increased efficiency. A more productive factory was a more profitable factory, and a more profitable factory meant better conditions for workers. Scientific managers such as Frederick Taylor introduced the concept of time and motion studies. Through careful observation of production techniques and worker behaviour, they demonstrated to employers how time—and therefore money—could be saved. Henry Ford was a firm believer in time management. "Save ten steps a day for each of 12 000 employees," he once claimed, "and you will have saved fifty miles of wasted motion and misspent energy." Ford's assembly–line process cut production time in half, and his company was able to turn out almost $300 million worth of cars per year by the early 1920s.

For many businesses, the ability to improve working conditions meant the ability to fend off unionization. In addition, the impersonal factories had a large turnover of workers. The employer who could bring a personal touch to the job kept employees longer and was saved the expense of constant retraining. This new program of paternal employer care was called *welfare capitalism*. Under this system companies paid for night school, liability insurance, unemployment compensation, and retirement plans. By 1905 over 1.5 million industrial workers were covered by such plans, and within ten years the number had doubled.

In most cases, employee benefit schemes were a means of keeping wages down and unions out. The system worked well from the employers' vantage point: workers in unionized shops worked ten hours less per week and received almost double the hourly wage of their non–union counterparts.

Roosevelt and Reform

Teddy Roosevelt did not begin the Progressive movement, nor did he alter its course. He did, however, bring about rapid change, and gave the idea of reform a new credibility among all facets of American society.

Roosevelt was a realistic reformer. He strongly believed in free enterprise and advocated the expansion of industry. On the other hand, he felt that only government had the power to control the giant corporations, and he believed that it was necessary to use that power to oppose corporations that used ruthless competitive tactics. These the president called the "bad trusts."

The first test of the new president's will to fight these bad trusts came in the Northern Securities case. Northern Securities was a holding company, the product of the merger of three railway companies in 1901; it monopolized a significant portion of the national railroad system, and was clearly in violation of the Sherman Anti–Trust Act of 1890. The act imposed severe restrictions on business combinations, and allowed for generous compensation to anyone who could prove damages against such a trust. Before Roosevelt's administration, however, little action had been taken.

In March of 1902, Roosevelt acted. It was a well–calculated move. Northern Securities was a well–known and almost universally despised monopoly. The public believed that its destruction would be a great victory for free enterprise and fair competition. What Roosevelt and his advisors knew was that National Securities was not as evil as people thought, and that its destruction would have little real impact upon the business community.

When the case was finally settled in the government's favour in 1904, Roosevelt became known as the "Trust Buster." In actual fact, the major investors were so happy at the way things had been handled that almost all of them contributed heavily to Roosevelt's re–election campaign that year.

Over the next few years the Roosevelt administration brought down indictments against twenty–five different trusts, ranging from the oil industry to tobacco to beef. Although the government lost most of the cases, it served notice that trusts would no longer be allowed to operate unregulated.

Other events of 1902 made it clear that business was not the president's only target. When, after a long and damaging strike in the anthracite coal industry the president of the United Mine Workers would not agree to submit to arbitration, Roosevelt stepped in. On October 16th he appointed an arbitration commission; five days later the strike was ended. When the board came down five months later with a reasonable settlement, including a nine–hour day and a ten percent wage increase, the president had won the support of both labour and business.

Throughout his two terms as president, Roosevelt continued to introduce reforms as part of his "Square Deal" program. Eventually, however, economic recession and the stock market panic of 1907 undercut public belief in the general benevolence of the financial and industrial giants. The age of cooperative change was over. Under Roosevelt's successors, the Progressive movement took a negative turn. (A more detailed discussion of this change can be found in chapter 12.)

By the beginning of the First World War, the United States had seen rapid industrial growth and the emergence of new political coalitions to deal with the changes in society. Canada too saw a similar pattern of development, but for the northern neighbors the political ramifications of change would be more far reaching.

The Industrialization of Canada

In the early 1870s many Canadians looked longingly across the border as they saw the United States racing towards an industrial society following the Civil War. For some, like Edward Farrer, an editorial writer for the *Globe*, the lure south was irresistible, and political union was the "manifest destiny of Canada."

Like today, some Canadians harboured an inferiority complex when it came to American economic growth. They believed that there was something in the Canadian character that prevented them from matching the vital growth of their powerful neighbour. In actual fact, however, Canada had no reason to feel ashamed. Between 1873 and 1896 Canada's gross national product rose from $710 million to $1.8 billion. Combined with a population increase from 3.7 million to 5.1 million during the same period, the per capita production of each Canadian had increased by over 83 percent during that twenty–year period.

Other economic indicators were equally as promising. Exports almost doubled; the number of kilometres of railway lines increased sixfold; annual manufacturing output grew from $217 million to over $500 million; and the iron and steel industry, which produced only half of local needs in the 1870s, produced triple the amount by the 1890s. Canada's economy was booming. If there were cyclical depressions, they were tied more to events in the United States and Britain than to local shortcomings.

The call for closer economic ties to the United States during this period were answered not in the field of business and industry, but in the political arena. In 1878 Sir John A. Macdonald declared:

> There has risen in this country a Canadian Party which declares we must have Canada for the Canadians . . . You cannot get anything by kissing the feet of the people of the United States.

This was the opening round in the proclamation of the new National Policy. In reality, there was little that was new in the National Policy. It rested on three pillars: protective tariffs, railway expansion, and increased immigration.

The tariffs reflected the country's economic goals. Agricultural products, such as raw wool and cotton, as well as the machinery to process them, were admitted duty free. Manufactured goods paid tariffs. Agricultural implements were taxed at 25 percent, railway cars at 30 percent, and steel rails at 35 percent. The agrarian and maritime interests in the West and East favoured the tariff structure. It was the industrialized provinces of central Canada who shouldered most of the tariff burden. The farmers, workers, professionals, and tradespeople of Ontario and Quebec represented the majority of the nation's consumers, and they were paying a heavy price for industrialization.

Tariff policy was critical to the young dominion. A Liberal opponent of increased tariffs, Sir Richard Cartwright, objected to this tax on "95 percent of the population" for the sake of "5 percent." But governments of the day had little choice. During the last three decades of the nineteenth century tariff income accounted for 70–75 percent of all government revenue.

In the United States, tariff walls had protected the growth and development of native infant industries who would have been easy prey for more efficient British and European businesses. Behind this protective barrier, higher consumer prices paid for the development of an industrial state. In Canada the situation was slightly different. The danger to Canadian business was the United States. On the other hand, the saviour of Canadian industry was also the American republic. Unable to export their products competitively through the tariff barriers, American industries built their own branch plants north of the border. Economically Canada benefitted. Jobs and tax revenues were generated at home, and the flow southward of the industrial work force was considerably slowed.

The price paid for industrialization is one over which Canadians have agonized ever since. Canadian economic vulnerability to decisions made in the United States provided impetus for the free trade negotiations of the late 1980s. The issues a century earlier were not much different. When the Liberal party proposed a commercial union with the United States in the late 1880s the Chicago *Times* responded with a call for the following constraint on any deal:

> Unless [Canada] . . . is prepared to make a complete and unconditional surrender of all control over its own tariff and accept whatever tariff our Congress may choose to enact from time to time, the scheme of commercial union . . . is entirely out of the question.

Although Canada experience rapid industrial growth during the period, it still remained vulnerable to every economic "twitch and grunt" from its southern neighbour.

The second pillar of the National Policy was the completion of a transcontinental railway. In the United States, the Union Pacific already reached the West coast, and branch lines were beginning to run north and south, linking the Canadian Northwest more closely to the United States than to the eastern provinces.

Earlier government and private efforts had built some sections of track, but by the late 1870s construction was at a standstill. Macdonald turned to George Steven of the Bank of Montreal and entrepreneurs Donald Smith and James J. Hill. Together they created the Canadian Pacific Railway Syndicate. Under the terms of the agreement, the CPR was to fill in the gaps in the present system. This meant laying track from Callandar, near Ottawa, to Port Arthur (modern–day Thunder Bay), and from Winnipeg to Kamloops, B.C. In return they received $25 million and over 25 million acres (10 million hectares) of land in the West. To further sweeten the pot they were given the right to operate the entire line, including the government–built section (valued at over $31.5 million); made exempt from taxation; and protected from all competition south to the U.S. border until at least 1900.

Many Canadians felt that their interests had been sold out by the government. The Edmonton *Bulletin* stated that the CPR bill had been pushed through Parliament by men "who think the sun rises in Halifax, shines all day straight over Montreal and Ottawa, and sets in Toronto."

For their part, Torontonians saw a railway line passing over their heads, linking the Northwest not with them but with their commercial rivals in Montreal. Nonetheless, the rail line was built, and when troops from Ontario arrived by train in Calgary during the 1885 Northwest Rebellion its value was finally accepted. As one contemporary observer commented:

> A great number of Albertans . . . until very recently . . . had a very faint conception of what the Canadian government and Canadian people could do. The military has swept away hostiles and rebels alike."

The third plank of the National Policy, immigration, is described in detail in chapter 10. These "new Canadians" eventually occupied many of the vast spaces on the Prairies, but in the late nineteenth century most of them arrived not with the dream of becoming farmers but with the hope of becoming members of the growing urban working class. Their experiences reflect the human side of the National Policy.

Working Class Canada

Investigating life for the working classes in Canada depends to a great extent upon the analysis of such secondary evidence as census data, industrial output, and domestic architecture. Unlike the wealthier segments of society, many working–class Canadians during this period were illiterate or lacked the leisure time needed to record their memories and experiences in diaries or letters for later generations to study.

Although labour organizations began to appear in the 1830s, it wasn't until the demand for a nine–hour day in the early 1870s that the working class rose to prominence in Canada. The majority of unions were limited to specific skilled trades—the "aristocracy" of labour. As a result, it is hardly surprising that the first major strike in post–Confederation Canada was conducted by the typographical union against the *Globe*. Although the strike failed to achieve its goals, it had a lasting political significance. George Brown, owner and editor of the *Globe* was a prominent Liberal; as a political move, John A. Macdonald and his Conservatives threw their support behind the union in the dispute. Macdonald's government repealed a section of the existing law, which called a strike "a conspiracy in restraint of trade." In so doing the Conservative party won the support of the working class in the election of 1872.

Early union activity had experienced few acts of violence. In the 1840s Montreal shoemakers had destroyed some "labour–saving" machinery, and railway workers belonging to the Brotherhood of Locomotive Engineers derailed trains in Belleville and Brockville in 1876. For the most part, however, Canadian unions were conservative, with limited aims.

In 1871 the coopers union spearheaded the formation of the Toronto Trades Assembly. This eventually led to the formation of the Canadian Labour Union (CLU) in 1873. The CLU started with lofty goals, directing its efforts at the securing of pro–labour legislation and the "repeal of all oppressive laws which now exist." Despite the energy with which the CLU was formed, within two years it had almost disappeared, the victim of forces beyond its control. First, the North American depression of the 1870s sapped union strength as unemployed workers provided a willing labour force for companies hit by strikes. Second, and perhaps more important, the Canadian labour movement began to be overshadowed by the increasing involvement of American unions in the country.

There had always been some American involvement in the Canadian labour movement. The American Federation of Labour had a foothold, as did other international unions, such as the Brotherhood of Locomotive Engineers. Under the National Policy, however, the pace accelerated rapidly. Branch plants of American companies brought American unions with them. The first chapter of the Knights of Labour was formed in Hamilton, Ontario, in 1881, and although the American branch of the organization collapsed in the 1880s, its Canadian counterpart lasted well into the twentieth century.

By the early years of this century, the Canadian labour movement could boast of some successes. The Ontario Factory Act of 1884 set standards for working conditions and regulated the use of child and female labour; the Dominion Conciliation Act of 1900 and the Industrial Disputes Act of 1907 both called for voluntary arbitration, and although arbitration usually meant a decision in favour of management, it at least resolved long and costly strikes. In addition, the government went so far as to create a new department of labour. Its first minister was the future prime minister, William Lyon Mackenzie King.

In spite of these gains, however, life was far from easy for the working classes. The average unskilled worker in Toronto received only about $10 per week; often over 70 percent of this went to housing and food. Montreal had one of the highest infant mortality rates in the world; in 1900, one in four children died. Thirty years after the Toronto typographical union went on strike for a nine–hour day, the majority of Canadian industrial workers still worked a ten–to–twelve–hour day; 20 percent of that labour force was made up of underpaid women, and a further 5 to 10 percent consisted of children.

It would take a world war to spark the real changes needed.

The Politics of Protest

The trade union movement experienced considerable growth during the First World War. From 166 000 in 1914, its membership grew to over 374 000 by 1918. In spite of this increase, the movement still represented only half of the nation's industrial work force. It was also primarily Eastern in focus. It should come as no surprise, therefore, that a combination of frustration with both the government and the conservative labour establishment resulted in an explosion of protest in Western Canada after the war.

In 1919 Western members of the Trades and Labour Congress formed the "One Big Union" (OBU). The OBU broke down the skilled/unskilled barrier and proposed a single union for everyone. The rhetoric of the OBU was Marxist in nature (see readings), and when the Winnipeg General Strike erupted in May of that year, many Canadians saw the beginnings of their own bolshevik revolution. In actual fact, the strike (see readings) had little to do with the OBU, whose founding convention would not be held until the strike was in its third week. Nonetheless, many Canadians saw a pattern in events, and approved government efforts to suppress the workers. Although subsequent investigations showed that the worker's demands had been legitimate and that there was no evidence of intended violence, many people continued to suspect that a revolution had been narrowly averted.

As with the Populist movement in the United States, it was the farmers who first began to organize politically. Provincially successful in Alberta and Ontario, they managed to elect sixty-five members to the House of Commons in 1921 under the banner of the National Progressive party. Although they held the balance of power in a Liberal minority government for the next four years, the Progressives had only a limited impact upon government policy. Unable to agree amongst themselves, and being too "democratic" to enforce party discipline, they eventually collapsed. After the election of 1925 there were only fourteen Progressives left sitting in the Commons; a year later that number had been reduced to nine. Eventually the platform of the Progressives was absorbed by the two mainline parties, and the existence of a third political party all but disappeared for a decade.

In the early 1920s labour leaders were still too conservative to go the route of their rural counterparts. Still hoping to influence the Liberals and Conservatives, they operated more as an external pressure group than as a political force. It would not be until the next decade that the impact of economic disaster would propel labour onto the political stage. What emerged was an urban/rural coalition strong enough to challenge the major parties. In the interim, the union movement continued to grow and remained content to bide its political time.

The last half of the nineteenth century was marked by rapid industrial growth on both sides of the border. Productive forces unleashed by the Civil War and protected by high tariffs resulted in an expansive and aggressive pattern of industrialization and urbanization in the United States. With the extension of rail lines across the continent, the western half of North America became a hinterland for

American industry providing both raw materials and a steadily growing market for production.

Canada tried to mimic this American phenomenon. The National Policy was a government attempt to do what private industry had done to the south. Industrial output underwent considerable growth: by 1914 two transcontinental rail lines spanned the Canadian West; and increasing numbers of immigrants gave some substance to Wilfrid Laurier's claim that "the twentieth century belong[ed] to Canada."

As with any process of rapid industrialization, there was a price to be paid. Working conditions and wages did not grow as fast as profits. Cyclical economic depressions created a new class of working poor. In both Canada and the United States, unions appeared to protect the interests of workers against the threat posed by both industry and the apparent indifference of government.

The Philosophy of Railroads, 1849

T.C. Keefer was a prominent nineteenth-century Canadian civil engineer. In his book The Philosophy of Railroads *published in 1849, he builds the classic case for the development of a rail network which would become the "arteries of the Canadian nation" in the 1800s. For North Americans in the nineteenth century, the train was the symbol of an expanding industrial economy. Later in his life Keefer would become disenchanted with the railroad, but in this early work, excerpted here, he was its biggest proponent.*

Old winter is once more upon us, and our inland seas are "dreary and inhospitable wastes" to the merchant and to the traveller;—our rivers are sealed fountains—and an embargo which no human power can remove is laid on all our ports. Around our deserted wharves and warehouses are huddled the naked spars—the blasted forest of trade—from which the sails have fallen like the leaves of the autumn. The splashing wheels are silenced—the roar of steam is hushed—the gay saloon, so lately thronged with busy life, is now but an abandoned hall—and the cold snow revels in solitary possession of the untrodden deck. The animation of business is suspended, the life blood of commerce is curdled and stagnant in the St. Lawrence—the great aorta of the North. On land, the heavy stage labours through mingled frost and mud in the West—or struggles through drifted snow, and slides with uncertain track over the icy hills of Eastern Canada. Far away to the South is heard the daily scream of the steam-whistle—but from Canada there is no escape: blockaded and imprisoned by Ice and Apathy, we have at least ample time for reflection—and if there be comfort in Philosophy may we not profitably consider the philosophy of railroads. . . .

Thus it is with the Railway System in Canada. We see, and to our cost, feel its effects around us;—we acknowledge its importance, the great results it has achieved, and the substantial expression of public opinion in its favour in the hundreds of millions which have been freely devoted to its extension in other civilized countries. . . .

The population, soil and wealth of Canada are not inferior to Vermont, New Hampshire, Michigan, Georgia, and other States which have Railways, and the local resources of some portions of our Province., where Railroads are wanting, are at least equal to those in Ohio and many other states where these advantages have been enjoyed for years. . . .

. . . We are placed beside a restless, early-rising, "go-a-head" people—a people who are following the sun Westward, as if to obtain a greater portion of daylight: *we* cannot hold back—we must tighten our own traces or be overrun—we must *use* what we have or *lose* what we already possess—capital, commerce, friends and children will abandon us for the better furnished lands unless we *at once* arouse from our lethargy; we can no longer afford to loiter away our winter months, or slumber through the morning hours. Every year of delay but increases our inequality, and will prolong the time and aggravate the labour of what, through our inertness, has already become a sufficiently arduous rivalry: but when once the barriers of indifference, prejudice and ignorance are broken down—no physical or financial obstacle can withstand the determined perseverance of intelligent, self-controlled industry.

We submit the foregoing view of the railway system and our position in relation to it, to the generous and patriotic consideration of every intelligent merchant, manufacturer, farmer, and mechanic—to every Canadian, native or adopted—and ask them:

Shall we have railroads in Canada?

From T.C. Keefer, *The Philosophy of Railroads, (1849)*, ed. by H.V. Nelles (Toronto: University of Toronto Press, 1972).

1. How does Keefer depict Canada without railroads?
2. What comparisons does the author draw with the United States?
3. In your own words, briefly summarize Keefer's "philosophy of railroads."

The Bunkhouse Man, 1903-1914

During the decade prior to the outbreak of World War I much of the expansion of the rail network in Canada was due to the establishment of an extensive construction "camp" system across the country. Over two hundred thousand men annually came and worked for low wages and substandard living conditions. It was a unique working and living experience. The workers were entirely male, without families, and tended to be new immigrants to the country trying to earn enough money to settle. With such a transient, immigrant population, it is not surprising that there was little union activity or pressure on management to raise the standard of living. Dr. Edmund Bradwin spent a decade studying life in the camps. His research first appeared in The Bunkhouse Man *in 1928. It remains the single-most important investigation of the topic.*

For twelve years following closely on the beginning of the century, the Dominion of Canada passed for the third time through a period of railway expansion. This activity in railway building culminated ultimately in the completion of a second and yet a third transcontinental extending across the Canadian provinces.

Material progress gives pride to any people. The country heard with much satisfaction of achievements, which, overcoming natural difficulties, bridged great rivers, gridironed the prairies, tunneled mountains and welded the far-sundered portions of the Dominion. But even prosperity may soothe—meanwhile other relationships, equally vital for the welfare of the country, had seemingly been overlooked: these pertained to the labour and housing of men employed on works throughout these various undertakings.

Occasional press reports, which multiplied toward the close of the period, told of discontent among the men at work in camps. Complaints were lodged by the workers themselves with the Federal authorities at Ottawa, resulting at times in official investigations being made locally into the nature and practical operation of wage agreements commonly existing between railway contractors and campmen during that particular period. All of which bespoke unsettled conditions of hire in frontier places across Canada, and a lack of accord in the commoner relationships of master and man. . . .

What were some of the causes that lay behind this unrest? . . .

An insight into the methods and conditions of employment on the National transcontinental will give, to those who desire it, an intelligent cross-section of frontier camps of whatever kind. It affords, also, the further opportunity to survey some of the problems that still confront the campman, and those who hire for work in the isolated places of the Dominion.

For, Canada is still a land of camps! Physical conditions compel it so. Great natural resources, combined with a climate that varies much, and often with suddenness, through its wide extent, give rise to seasonal works of diverse kinds.

There are years when three thousand large camps are in operation throughout the Dominion. Among other undertakings these activities are usually associated with lumbering, logging on the Pacific coast, and the cutting of pulp; railway work for both maintenance and along new construction; mining, in its earlier stages, and, in recent years, increasing numbers of hydro development camps. The number of men actually engaged on such enterprises is never constant, but in average years it may be safely inferred that fully two hundred thousand men in Canada, at different periods of the year, follow in some form or other the life of the camps.

Canada as a country owes much to its campmen. Down through whole generations the camps have played an important part in shaping the lives of all frontier workers; qualities incidental to such environments have characterized their ways. Yet, even in Canada, few of us seem to realize just all that this means. We overlook the debt which the country owes the workers in these important fields of labour. With the strides made by the Dominion since Confederation, in trade, in increasing wealth, and in education, there has been correspondingly a strange lack of recognition for the place and the needs of the bunkhouse man.

From Edwin Bradwin, *The Bunkhouse Man: A Study of Work and Pay in the Camps of Canada*, ed. by Jean Burnet (Toronto: University of Toronto Press, 1972).

1. Why does Bradwin call Canada "a land of camps"?

2. The camp system was a unique Canadian phenomenon. Account for its emergence in the early years of the twentieth century.

3. Investigate the differences between working conditions in the camps with those in a more traditional urban industrial setting.

Labour and the Police on the Railways, 1897

RCMP records from the turn of the century open a window on the sometimes violent state of life in the construction camps. Mountie reports are frequently critical of the attitude of company officials toward their employees. In these excerpts we see the type of work and contractual agreements being assigned to these men.

Extract from weekly report of Supt. Deane. . . .

. . . The works have not advanced to such a stage yet, as to require any particular Police protection.

All Patrols when passing near construction work have orders to go, out of their way if necessary, to look in upon working parties, enquiring of the foremen if there are many complaints.

As far as I have been able to learn, so far, the rate of wages does not exceed one dollar per day and rations. . . . I should judge from the appearance of the men, that I have seen, that they will not care to squander their money when they get it. . . .

In this connection I beg to report what, if true, is a disgraceful way of employing men in the East. Some 100 men, chiefly French-Canadian and axe men, have recently been employed and sent up by one Landry from Ottawa, acting as Agent of the CPR, and presumably on commission. All these, who had occasion to testify before me, swear to the fact that Landry engaged them as choppers for bush work: that they would have no blankets to pay for and, in some cases, no fares. Not one in ten can read English and do not know the text of the contract they signed. And it is safe to say that one in every five is physically unable to dump a scraper.

They have been placed to work with various contractors on the grade and very few have ever handled a pick, shovel and scraper. They naturally get into trouble and in a great many cases refuse to do work they did not engage to do and cannot do, and then we are called upon to compel them or send them to jail. They are completely discouraged and do not much care what happens to them.

Some have left families dependent upon what they can remit them, and they find themselves bound by a contract apparently signed under false pretences and a debt it will take them more than a month of uncongenial work to wipe out, whereas they would willingly work at their accustomed employment in the bush. . . .

Macleod, October 23rd, 1897.

From the Public Archives of Canada.

The Commissioner,
Regina.
Sir,
RE LABOUR ON CROW'S NEST CONSTRUCTION

I have the honour to bring to your notice the conditions of affairs in this district regarding labour on the construction of the Crow's Nest extension of the CPR.

Owing to the fact that all labourers are charged with their Railway fare from where they are hired to Macleod, and also in many instances, with their transport from Macleod to the particular camp at which they are to be employed, a great deal of dissatisfaction has arisen and much hardship experienced. This has been accentuated by the fact that the hiring Agents in the East, particularly about Hull and Ottawa, have misrepresented things and made promises to the men which the management of construction here refuse to ratify, they also send up men totally unfit for the work. . . .

There is no doubt whatever that a great number of these men would never have come out here had they known they had to pay their fare, which from Ottawa here at a cent a mile is $22.49. These men have families in the East and when they discover that after working six weeks or two months there is not a cent coming to them or more probably they are in debt to the Contractors, that they have no money to send to their families, and that they have nothing themselves, they as a rule leave that particular employer and wander around destitute, without blankets or even boots in some cases, looking for other work, and people have had to supply them with food and in some instances I have had to do so, and also give then a night's lodging.

There are numbers of men who are totally unfit for the work and what will become of them during the winter is hard to surmise. . . .

Where the men have clearly understood their agreement in the East that they had to pay their Railway fare, we have endeavoured to make them stick to their Contract. But where they were evidently brought up under false pretences, we have, as Magistrates, when the cases came before us, discharged them from their contracts.

No provision has been made by the Company for returning these men to their homes, winter is coming on and there is likelihood of much hardship and destitution. . . .

Some pressure ought to be brought to bear for fairer treatment of the men. I have the honour to be etc.

(sgd.) G. E. Saunders, Inspt.

From Public Archives of Canada, RCMP Records, Section A-1, Vol. 145, no. 56

1. What concerns are raised regarding the contracts and work assignments agreed to by the men?
2. What role does the RCMP appear to play in the protection of the rights of the workers?
3. Contrast these examples of life in the camps with the noble picture of camp life put forward by Bradwin.

The Nationalism of the National Policy

The building of the Canadian Pacific Railway was part of a three-pronged thrust of Sir John A. Macdonald's National Policy. Along with increased immigration and high protective tariffs, the National Policy was intended to build a strong industrial base in the young dominion. Historian Craig Brown argues that the National Policy was less about industrialization and more about nationalism. In this excerpt he argues that, faced with the expansion of the industrial and national might of the United States, the National Policy was "the price of being Canadian."

Debating nationalism is the great Canadian national pastime. Since Confederation it has been the pre-eminent preoccupation of politicians, journalists, scholars and plain ordinary citizens. All have wrestled diligently with the problem that Canadian nationalism—if such there be—does not fit any of the classic definitions of nationalism. Common language, religion, and ethnic origin must obviously be rejected. Except for the disciples of Harold Adams Innis, geography provided few satisfactory clues to the Canadian identity. And a common historical tradition, in the words of Mill, "the possession of a national history and consequent community of recollections, collective pride and humiliation, pleasure and regret, connected with the same incidents in the past," raises more questions about a Canadian "nationality" than it answers. . . .

I have tried to suggest that the National Policy was a manifestation of Canadian national sentiment. Its basic assumptions, protection against the United States, the need for a "Canadian economy" with a strong industrial base and secure markets, and the implicit assumption of achieving greater autonomy within the Empire all crystallized that ill-defined, but deeply felt, sense of difference that set Canadians apart from both their neighbours to the south and the mother country. But why did this desire to proclaim a national identity take its form in economic terms?

Perhaps a part of the answer rests in the dilemma posed at the beginning of this paper. Appeals to a common language, a common cultural tradition or a common religion were simply impossible for Canadians and when they were attempted they were rightly regarded by French Canadians as a violation of their understanding of Confederation. Most Canadians, especially those who built or paid for the building of the transcontinental railways, argued that the Canadian nation would have to be built in spite of its geography and regarded their efforts as "the price of being Canadian." Appeals to national history could also be a divisive rather than a unifying factor for, as often as not, the two ethnic groups disagreed as to what, in their historical tradition, was a matter of pride or of humiliation. What was necessary, then, as Cartier put it in the Confederation debates, was to "form a political nationality." And it is not at all surprising that the political nationalism of the early decades of Confederation was expressed in terms of railways and tariffs.

It is a commonplace to equate the politics of North America in the latter part of the nineteenth century with self-seeking capitalism. But we might remind ourselves that the age of Darwinism and of industrialism was also a great age of nationalism. The nationalism of the large assertive states of the age, the United States, Germany and Great Britain, was assuredly economic in its emphasis. In the United States, in particular, nationalism was equated with the problems of industrialism and industrial expansion. In keeping with Darwinian assumptions, bigness was a virtue for a nation state, and industrialism was the key to bigness. At the very time their own nation was being born, Canadians reasoned that industrialism was the determining factor in the victory of the North in the Civil War and in the apparent reunification of the United States. Industrialism meant power; power to withstand the pressures from the south and power to expand and consolidate the Canadian nation. And a political programme that emphasized expansion and industrialism has the added advantage of ignoring the potentially divisive issues that would disrupt a "political nationality."

In sum, then, the National Policy, a policy for a "Canadian economy" and a "Big Canada," a materialistic policy for a materialistic age, was the obvious policy to give expression to Canadian national sentiment. That policy was adopted in 1878 and accepted by the Liberal party in 1896. Three years later J.I. Tarte urged Laurier to do more than simply accept the National Policy, to expand upon it with more railways, canals and harbour improvements (and presumably with higher tariffs). "Voilà," he observed, "le programme le plus national et le plus populaire que nous puissons offrir au pays."

From Craig Brown, "The Nationalism of the National Policy," in *Nationalism in Canada*, ed. by Peter Russell (Toronto: McGraw-Hill Ryerson Limited, 1966).

1. What questions does Brown raise about the nature of the Canadian identity?
2. Why does he argue that there was a need for a Canadian economy?
3. Given Brown's basic arguments regarding the National Policy, what might his position be on the impact of freer trade with the United States in the 1990s?

Businessman as Hero

Canadian historian J. Michael Bliss contended in his 1974 study A Living Profit *that the industrial leaders were the heroes of their day. In this excerpt he presents his case.*

. . . To many, probably most, Canadians before the social disruption of 1914–1918, the country's business leaders were captains of industry; they were the men who were building a nation by driving steel through the wilderness, raising the tall chimneys of thriving manufactories, blasting metals out of the Canadian Shield, unlocking the power of Niagara. A popular poll in 1909 named four railway presidents among "Canada's Ten Biggest Men," and a journalist noted enthusiastically, "in the knapsack of every Canadian schoolboy there is—not a marshall's button—but a millionaire's bank book." Another writer could not believe Donald Mann and William Mackenzie were motivated by self-interest in the creation of their personal transcontinental railway, the Canadian Northern: their actions could only be explained as an act of patriotism. . . .

From Michael Bliss, *A Living Profit: Studies in the Social History of Canadian Business, 1883–1911* (Toronto: McClelland & Stewart, 1974).

1. Research a Canadian business leader of this period and test Bliss's thesis against your findings.

Wealth, 1889

Andrew Carnegie revolutionized the steel industry in the United States. A self-made man, Carnegie started out with nothing, and eventually sold his interests in 1901 for over $500 million. In this 1889 essay, he outlines the benefits capitalism brought to North America.

The problem of our age is the proper administration of wealth, so that the ties of brotherhood may still bind together the rich and poor in harmonious relationship. The conditions of human life have not only been changed, but revolutionized, within the past few hundred years. In former days there was little difference between the dwelling, dress, food, and environment of the chief and those of his retainers. The Indians are to-day where civilized man then was. When visiting the Sioux, I was led to the wigwam of the chief. It was just like the others in external appearance, and even within the difference was trifling between it and those of the poorest of its braves. The contrast between the palace of the millionaire and the cottage of the labourer with us to-day measures the change which has come with civilization.

This change, however, is not to be deplored, but welcomed as highly beneficial. It is well, nay, essential for the progress of the race, that the houses of some should be homes for all that is highest and best in literature and the arts, and for all the refinements of civilization, rather than that none should be so. Much better this great irregularity than universal squalor. . . .

It is easy to see how the change has come. One illustration will serve for almost every phrase of the cause. In the manufacture of products we have the whole story. It applies to all combinations of human industry, as stimulated and enlarged by the inventions of this scientific age. Formerly articles were manufactured at the domestic hearth or in small shops which formed part of the household. The master and his apprentices worked side by side, the latter living with the master, and therefore subject to the same conditions. When these apprentices rose to be masters, there was little or no change in their mode of life, and they, in turn, educated in the same routine succeeding apprentices. There was, substantially, social equality, and even political equality, for those engaged in industrial pursuits had then little or no political voice in State.

But the inevitable result of such a mode of manufacture was crude articles at high prices. To-day the world obtains commodities of excellent quality at prices which even the generation preceding this would have deemed incredible. In the commercial world similar causes have produced similar results, and the race is benefitted thereby. The poor enjoy what the rich could not before afford. What were the luxuries have become the necessaries of life. The laborer has now more comforts than the farmer had a few generations ago. The farmer has more luxuries than the landlord had, and is more richly clad and better housed. The landlord has books and pictures rarer, and appointments more artistic, than the King could then obtain.

The price we pay for this salutary change is, no doubt, great. We assemble thousands of operatives in the factory, in the mine, and in the counting-house, of whom the employer can know little or nothing, and to whom the employer is little better than a myth. All intercourse between them is at an end. . . . Under the law of competition, the employer of thousands is forced into the strictest economies, among which the rates paid to labor figure prominently, and often there is friction between the employer and the employed, between capital and labor, between rich and poor. Human society loses homogeneity.

The price which society pays for the law of competition, like the price it pays for cheap comforts and luxuries, is also great; but the advantages of this law are also greater still, for it is to this law that we owe our wonderful material development, which brings improved conditions in its train. But, whether the law is benign or not, we must say of it, as we say of the change in the conditions of men to which we have referred: It is here, we cannot evade it; no substitutes for it have been found; and while the law may be sometimes hard for the individual, it is best for the race, because it insures the survival of the fittest in every department. We accept and welcome, therefore, as conditions to which we must accommodate ourselves, great inequality of environment, the concentration of business, industrial and commercial, in the hands of a few, and the law of competition between these, as being not only beneficial, but essential for the future progress of the race. Having accepted these, it follows that there must be great scope for the exercise of special ability in the merchant and in the manufacturer who has to conduct affairs upon a great scale. That this talent for organization and management is rare among men is proved by the fact that it invariably secures for its possessor enormous rewards, no matter where or under what laws or conditions. . . . It is a law, as certain as any of the others named, that men possessed of this peculiar talent for affairs, under the free play of economic forces, must, of necessity, soon be in receipt of more revenue than can be judiciously expended upon themselves; and this law is as beneficial for the race as the others.

Objections to the foundations upon which society is based are not in order, because the condition of the race is better with these than it has been with others which have been tried. Of the effect of any new substitutions proposed we cannot be sure. The Socialist or Anarchist who seeks to overturn present conditions is to be regarded as attacking the foundation upon which civilization itself rests, for civilization took its start from the day that the capable, industrious workman said to his incompetent and lazy fellow, "If thou dost not sow, thou shalt not reap," and thus ended primitive Communism by separating the drones from the bees. . . .

From Andrew Carnegie, "Wealth," *North American Review*, v. 141 (June, 1889).

1. What beneficial changes to society does Carnegie identify?
2. How does he account for this radical change in the quality of life?
3. Why is he willing to pay the price for competition? Do you agree with his position?

Scientific Management

Proponents of industrialization always pointed to the existence of modern well-run factories as evidence of all that the machine age could be. In this 1885 report from the Toronto Globe, *the virtues of a Montreal boot and shoe factory are highlighted.*

. . . Your correspondent in making enquiries on the firm of J. & T. Bell, Notre Dame-street, finds that this firm is engaged in the finer class of boots and shoes, and is by the way the oldest manufacturing firm in Canada. . . . They were just now preparing samples for the coming season, and would start their travellers out with a wider range of goods than usual, having taken up men's boots in addition to ladies' boots, which had been their specialty, and that the prospects of a good trip were very bright. They had, of course, taken special precautions regarding the smallpox, such, for instance, as withdrawing all work previously given to outsiders and having it done in their own premises, having special visits of inspection from independent physicians, and having regular weekly visits from a medical man among their employees at the factory and at their homes, and these precautions, of which they had given proof to their customers, may have saved them from the results of panic among their own section of the trade. A visit through the factory seems to justify all that was claimed by the firm for their establishment. The factory is remarkably well equipped, and the light and sanitary advantages excellent. . . . As an instance of the progress made in boots and shoes manufacturing, it may be mentioned that the first introduction of machinery in the business in Canada was about 1845, when this firm imported from New York a Ginger machine for sewing the uppers: to-day they have machines capable of doing almost every branch of the work, from skiving and trimming of sole sewing and heeling—a revolution which has been wrought almost entirely within the last 30 years. Indeed, there were several employees of both sexes, some of whom came to the firm as children, whose experience compasses nearly all the improvements in boot and shoe machinery. . . . The operation of lasting is the only one which at present cannot be done to satisfaction on machines, but in most of the other processes it is said that the machines do the work not only more regularly and quicker, but with the result of a better finish than by hand.

From the Toronto *Globe*, November 18, 1885 in Paul W. Bennett et al., *Emerging Identities*, (Toronto: Prentice-Hall, 1986).

1. What steps had the company taken to ensure the health of its workers?
2. Comment upon the apparent working conditions in the factory.
3. Some critics of "scientific management" contend that the industrial paternalism described here resulted in almost tyrannical company rule. Investigate this claim further, then write a brief argument presenting your point of view.

Universal Male Suffrage: Should the Workers Vote?

In the nineteenth century, property qualifications prevented many workers from voting. An editorial in the Montreal Daily Witness *in December 1875 illustrated the general level of concern about the subject.*

The question has been before the Ontario Legislature, having been brought up by Mr. Currie, of Welland, a Liberal of good abilities and independent character. The subject, however, does not seem to be a very pressing one, for only one of the members, Mr. O'Donohue from Ottawa, thought it worth while to speak on the motion, and no one seemed to think it necessary to oppose it. It was negatived by a vote of two to one after Mr. Robinson, of Kingston, had caused some laughter by saying that he should like to see the females vote. The principal reason urged was, of course, that every one interested in the law should have some voice in making it, and this is a very strong one. Mr. Currie estimated that in his county one-fourth of the males above the age of twenty-one years were debarred from the franchise under the existing laws, which is perhaps a larger proportion than most people thought was the case. There never has been any very pressing demand for manhood suffrage in Canada, and the reason, no doubt, is that there are no class grievances, and that the extension of suffrage to all men of legal age, would not make any appreciable difference in the government of the country. . . .

From "Manhood Suffrage," in the Montreal *Daily Witness*, December 24, 1875.

1. Write a letter to the editor opposing the general view on universal male suffrage.

Women at Work, 1889

The following evidence was given to the Royal Commission on the Relations of Labour and Capital in Canada at its Nova Scotia hearings in 1889.

W.H. Gibson (of Doull & Miller, manufacturers of clothing), sworn.

By Mr. Walsh:

Q. You represent the firm of Doull & Miller here in connection with the clothing department? A. Yes.

Q. How many men do you employ, that is how many hands altogether do you employ in the manufacture of clothing? A. Well, it varies at different seasons of the year.

Q. Give us an average. A. There are just a hundred hands working now, but that is hardly a fair average; about a hundred and twenty-five would be a fair average.

Q. How many of those have you employed in the building? A. We have at present fifty-five.

Q. The balance would be outside? A. Yes.

Q. How many of these are men, I mean journeymen tailors? A. Eleven.

Q. What is the average wages of these journeymen tailors? A. About nine dollars.

Q. How many of your hands are women? A. There are forty-five employed inside.

Q. How many small children have you employed inside? A. None.

Q. Those inside—are they paid by the day or by the piece? A. By the piece, except for a few who are paid by the week. There are three or four paid by the week.

Q. Have you the kindness to tell us the wages per week earned by those women? A. They average three dollars a week all around.

Q. Then all the other hands are outside on piece work? A. Yes.

Q. Could you tell us about the average earnings of those people outside? A. I have taken them altogether. They average three dollars a week inside and out.

Q. Are you aware whether the people outside employ any help? A. I think nothing outside their own families. They may have a little assistance from some members of their own family.

Q. Have you ever had any labor troubles among your people? A. No. The only troubles we ever have are pic-nics.

Q. As a general rule are your hands pretty industrious? A. Yes; we have no labor troubles.

Q. Your men for the most part are sober and industrious? A. Yes.

By Mr. Heakes:

Q. Has there been any increase in the wages of your people in the last seven or eight years? A. No.

Q. Has there been any decrease? A. No; the wages are about the same.

Q. Do you furnish your hands with constant employment all the year around at the rates named? A. Yes.

Q. Have you separate conveniences for male and female help? A. Yes.

Q. How are they separated? A. They are practically one, with a division between the two.

Q. They are side by side? A. Yes.

Q. Is there any screen to prevent the men from seeing the females go in? A. No.

Q. They can see one another go in? A. Yes.

By Mr. Armstrong:

Q. Are your hands paid weekly or fortnightly? A. Fortnightly.

Q. Do you prefer that? A. We do it for our own convenience.

Q. Do they ask to be paid more frequently? A. No.

Q. Don't you think it would be a convenience to them? A. No; not to the class of people we employ.

Q. Are they wealthy people? A. No; but they are an industrious class; their money is perhaps more useful to them every two weeks.

Q. Can a person pay rent and support a family on five or six dollars a week? A. No; they don't have families.

Q. You say the average wage is three dollars a week? A. Yes.

Q. How much would the people who receive that amount pay for board? A. The girls mostly live at home and it does not cost them anything.

Q. Do you ascertain whether the girls you employ live with their parents? A. No.

Q. I suppose it is a matter of indifference to you? A. We don't care where they live.

Q. You don't know how much they pay for board? A. I suppose they would pay from two dollars to two and a half.

Q. Have you any in your employ that earn less than three dollars? A. Yes; that sum is the average. . . .

From Canada, Royal Commission of the Relations of Labor and Capital in Canada, 1889. Evidence—Nova Scotia in Michael S. Cross, ed., *The Working Man in the Nineteenth Century*, (Toronto: Oxford University Press, 1974).

1. How do wages compare between men and women in the clothing industry?

2. Based upon the evidence presented create your own thesis with regard to the general level of wages and working conditions.

3. Compare the image of life in this factory with that depicted in the Montreal boot and shoe operation.

Child Labour, 1906

In his book The Bitter Cry of the Children, *published in 1906, author John Spargo charged that "the great nation [the United States] in its commercial madness devours its babes." His revelations on the horrible conditions for children working in the United States were confirmed in a government-initiated study a few years later.*

The textile industries rank first in the enslavement of children. . . . According to Mr. McKelway, one of the most competent authorities in the country, there are at present time not less than 60 000 children under fourteen employed in the cotton mills of the Southern states. Miss Jane Addams tells of finding a child of five years working by night in a South Carolina mill; Mr. Edward Gardner Murphy has photographed little children of six and seven years who were at work for twelve and thirteen hours a day in Alabama mills. In Columbia, S.C., and Montgomery, Ala., I have seen hundreds of children, who did not appear to be more than nine or ten years of age, at work in the mills, by night as well as by day.

. . . It is true that the terrible pauper apprentice system which forms such a tragic chapter in the history of the English factory movement has not been introduced; yet the fate of the children of the poor families from the hill districts who have been drawn into the vortex of this industrial development is almost as bad as that of the English pauper children. These "poor whites," as they are expressively called, even by their negro neighbors, have for many years eked out a scanty living upon their farms, all the members of the family uniting in the struggle against niggardly nature. Drawn into the current of the new industrial order, they do not realize that, even though the children worked harder upon the farms than they do in the mills, there is an immense difference between the dust-laden air of the factory and the pure air of a farm; between the varied tasks of farm life with the endless opportunities for change and individual initiative, and the strained attention and monotonous tasks of mill life. The lot of the pauper children driven into the mills by the ignorance and avarice of British Bumbledom was little worse than that of these poor children, who work while their fathers loaf. During the long, weary nights many children have to be kept awake by having cold water dashed upon their faces, and when morning comes they throw themselves upon their beds—often still warm from the bodies of their brothers and sisters—without taking off their clothing. "When I works nights, I'se too tired to undress when I gits home, an' so I goes to bed wif me clo's on me," lisped one little girl in Augusta, Ga.

. . . During the Philadelphia textile workers' strike in 1903, I saw at least a score of children ranging from eight to ten years of age who been working in the mills prior to the strike. . . .

One evening, not long ago, I stood outside of a large flax mill in Paterson, N.J., while it disgorged its crowd of men, women, and children employees. All the afternoon, as I lingered in the tenement district near the mills, the comparative silence of the streets oppressed me. There were many babies and very small children, but the older children whose boisterous play one expects in such streets, were wanting. . . . At six o'clock the whistles shrieked, and the streets were suddenly filled with people, many of them mere children. Of all the crowd of tired, pallid, and languid-looking children I could only get speech with one, a little girl who claimed thirteen years, though she was smaller than many a child of ten. . . . If my little Paterson friend was thirteen, perhaps the nature of her employment will explain her puny, stunted body. . . .

From John Spargo, *The Bitter Cry of the Children*, (New York, 1906) in Richard Hofstadter, ed., *The Progressive Movement 1900–1915*, (Englewood Cliffs, N.J.: Prentice-Hall, 1963).

1. Outline the working conditions for children described by Spargo.
2. What do you think was the social cost of using child labour in the factories?
3. Investigate the conditions of child labour in both Canada and the United States. Write a report in which you compare and contrast your findings.

The Labour Movement

The preamble to the constitution of the Cigar Makers' International Union of America outlines why it is necessary for workers to band together. The second excerpt is taken from the testimony of Samuel Donnelly, president of the International Typographical Union, to Congress in 1899.

Labor has no protection—the weak are devoured by the strong. All wealth and power center in the hands of the few, and the many are their victims and bondsmen. In all countries and at all times capital has been used to monopolize particular branches of business, until the vast and various industrial pursuits of the world are rapidly coming under the immediate control of a comparatively small portion of mankind, tending, if not checked by the toiling millions, to enslave and impoverish them.

Labor is the creator of all wealth, and as such the laborer is at least entitled to a renumeration sufficient to enable himself and family to enjoy more of the leisure that rightfully belongs to him, more social advantages, more of the benefits, privileges and emoluments of the world; in a word, all those rights and privileges necessary to make him capable of enjoying, appreciating, defending and perpetuating the blessings of modern civilization. Past experience teaches us that labor has so far been unable to arrest the encroachments of capital, neither has it been able to obtain justice from lawmaking power. This is due to a lack of practical organization and unity of action. "In union there is strength." Organization and united action are the only means by which the laboring classes can gain any advantage for themselves. Good and strong labor organizations are enabled to defend and preserve the interests of the working people. By organization we are able to assist each other in cases of strikes and lock-outs, sickness and death. And through organization only the workers, as a class, are able to gain legislative advantages. . . .

From the preamble to the constitution of the Cigar Makers International Union of America, 1864. Reprinted in New York, *Third Annual Report of the Bureau of Statistics of Labor and the State of New York, for the Year 1885* (Albany, 1886).

Where trade unions are the strongest they are looked upon as reputable organizations, and their officers and people who are interested in their welfare as respectable and good citizens. The growth of the trade union is not entirely due to the efforts of the trade unionists themselves in the work of organization, or in proselytizing or preaching the gospel of trade unionism, but it is from the fact that capital in almost every case is tyrannical and unrelenting. . . . The capitalist who owns the factory in Massachusetts has been transferring his industry nearer to the cotton fields; and we find that, in the State of Georgia, where industrial conditions are not as good as in the State of Massachusetts, the man who has been under them, has been putting rails around his machinery, has been boxing in his belting, has been refusing to employ in his factory a child under the age of fourteen years, and has been putting on every floor of his factory separate closets for male and female labor, has been giving Saturday half holidays for his employees, and abolishing the company store and complying with the law of the State of Massachusetts—when he goes to the State of Georgia and transfers his business there he does not put any railing around his machinery; he does not box in his belting; he employs children nine, ten, or twelve years of age at wages as low as 15 or 20 cents per day, and works them from the time the light shines in the morning until it is dark at night; and in his factory he has no closets, no sanitary conditions, such as are required in the State of Massachusetts; he simply does as he pleases and acts in a most tyrannical and unChristian-like manner. There is nothing in the world that will protect the workers in those respects except organization. . . .

From the testimony of Samuel B. Donnelly, President of the International Typographical Union, May 9, 1899. U.S. Congress, House, *Report of the Industrial Commission on the Relations and Conditions of Capital and Labor Employed in Manufactures and General Business*, 56th Cong., 2d Sess., House Doc. 495 (Washington: U.S. Government Printing Office, 1901), VII.

1. What do the authors to this preamble see as the relationship between labour and capital?
2. Do you agree or disagree with the reasons given for the need for unions? Defend your answer.

3. How do you think labour might have responded to this appeal? Use evidence from the previous readings to support your position.

The Nine-Hour Movement, 1872

One of the first issues to unify Canadian labour was the Nine-Hour Movement. With its objective to reduce the work day from ten hours to nine, the issue gave great impetus to the trade union movement. The following editorial appeared in the Toronto Globe *following a public meeting on the issue in March 1872.*

We have no sympathy with those who object to organized movements for increasing the wages of the artisan or the elevation of his social position. On the contrary, our sympathy goes heartily in favour of whatever contributes to those ends. The best interests of the whole community are promoted by every fair and temperate step tending to increase the comfort and happiness of any large section of the people.

But to carry with it public sympathy, every such organized movement must have a clearly defined object in view; that object must be openly and honestly stated; and the demand made must be shown to be based on justice, common sense and the public well. No claim based on such grounds can be resisted for many days by any body of employers, however powerful, wealthy or united—in Canada at any rate, whatever may be done in other countries. And no claim that cannot stand examination by those tests can be permanently enforced.

We are glad at last to have an authoritative statement of what is the aim and scope of the Nine-hours movement. . . . One of the lecturers hired by the said League to peregrinate the United States and Canada and explain the objects of the Nine-hours movement. . . .

. . . Evidently he does not know that when you speak of the working man in Ontario, you include everybody. We all work. We all began with nothing. We have all got by hard work all we own—and the richest among us work on still, and like to do it. There is probably no country on earth where the whole people are more industrious or more reasonably frugal. Not many large fortunes are accumulated among us; but in very few countries, if in any, are there so large a proportion of the workers who achieve an ample independence. We have no such class as those styled capitalists in other countries. The whole people are the capitalists of Canada. . . .

In such a country it is utterly ridiculous to talk of the rapacity and despotism of the employer. The tyranny of the employed over his master would be an infinitely truer version of the case. In countries where the large mass of the people live from day to day on the wages of others, and in dread of the loss of work-excessive hours of labour and other injustice may be forced on the employed by the employer. But how can this ever be in a country where so vast a proportion of the people work for themselves—where so small a portion work for others, and can so readily find employment. . . .

. . . Not a fraction even of the forty thousand men who are within reach of his nostrums, we venture to affirm, have a particle of sympathy with him in the movement—and assuredly if the number was much more, they are mistaken if they flatter themselves for a moment that the other million and a half of their fellow-citizens, who do a full day's work for fair compensation will be coerced by any strikes or threats into paying them ten hours' wages for eight hours' work—or nine hours' either. . . .

. . . Not only are the people at large the real capitalists of Canada, but his [Mr President Trevellick, of the National Labour League of the United States] lights of oration about the political subjection of the working man are as ridiculous as his ideas on monetary despotism. The men who make our laws, who govern our Province, who administer our excellent institutions, who dispense justice admirably—almost to a man came from the people, are of the people still, and not a few of them are among the hardest-worked men in this or any other community. The people have entire political power in their own hands—what they wish done, must be done. All men stand here on an equal footing. . . .

From *Daily Globe* (Toronto), March 23, 1872 in Michael Cross, ed., *The Working Man in the Nineteenth Century*, (Toronto: Oxford University Press, 1974).

1. Summarize the main point of the editorial.
2. How is the leadership of the movement depicted?
3. What image is conveyed of the typical Ontario worker?

The Knights of Labor, 1885

T. Phillips Thompson, writing in the Palladium of Labor, *outlined the basic view held by the Knights of Labour toward the current social and economic order.*

. . . It is pretty generally understood by this time among those who are interested in Labor Reform that it is a much wider and more comprehensive question than the mere matter of wages or hours—that it includes everything relating to the mental, moral and physical advancements of the worker, and implies a war to the death against every influence which tends to depress the condition of Labor. Yet there are still many whose sympathies are with us to a certain extent who do not realize to the full the ideal which ought steadily to be kept in view. . . . Let us picture to ourselves

THE SOCIAL CONDITION

that would result were our ideals realized by the resolute determination of the masses in all civilized lands to use their power for the good of the whole people, instead of letting the selfish few play upon the prejudices and passions, and rule them for the benefit of the upper class. . . .

PAUPERISM WOULD BE UNKNOWN.

Those who were by disease, accident or old age unable to work would be pensioned not as a charity but as a right—as their share of the returns from the common inheritance—the earth. All industry would be co-operative. . . . The really necessary Labor of the world, all men being workers, could probably be done in three or four hours a day.

By this time, no doubt, the readers who have followed me so far are ready to exclaim "utopian!" "visionary!" "Altogether wild and impracticable!" I know it. Look back a little and you will see that I based the whole picture on the supposition that the great majority of

THE WORLD'S WORKERS

were educated as to their true interests and resolute in carrying out their purposes. Nobody can say that the state of things I have endeavoured to outline would not be to the best advantage of Labor—that we should not gladly welcome such a condition of society were it possible. Why then is it "utopian?"— why is it the dream of a visionary? If it would be for the benefit of the immense majority of mankind, why cannot it be realized? Why? Simply because the people who do the world's work, and physically at least have the immense advantage over all opposing forces

ARE NOT EDUCATED,

—are not self-reliant—are not ready to make sacrifices. There you have the whole thing in a nutshell. The picture is merely a faint presentation of what might be—what cannot be at present solely because of the blindness, ignorance and want of union among workingmen—but what I trust yet will be when the scales of error, of misleading education and of temporary self-interest have fallen from their eyes—so they can see the light. . . .

From *The Palladium of Labor*, December 26, 1885 in Paul W. Bennett et al., *Emerging Identities*, (Toronto: Prentice-Hall, 1986).

1. How does the author define the conflict between management and labour?
2. What image of future society is depicted in the account?
3. Comment upon Thompson's contention that the goals of the Knights are not utopian but a view of things as they must be.

The Patrons of Industry, 1895

In the 1890s a new party emerged in Western Canada in opposition to the National Policy espoused by the Liberals and the Conservatives. The following statement by a candidate representing the Patrons of Industry highlights Western grievances of the day.

. . . Some say that Patronism is no good; and at Ottawa they have said that the farmers are satisfied and all is well, for they are quiet, no sound is heard. Now, the fact is, it is pressure that makes the Patrons. There are some toys that when you press them on the stomach they cry out, and this is like the farmers, they have been pinched until they have become Patrons, for it seems impossible to get along, and each year things become worse . . . which no doubt has done great things for Ontario and Quebec, but only has produced evil for us. At the time it may have been wise, but now, at any rate, its work is done, it has grown old, corrupt, dead, and should be buried out of sight. Wheat has so far been the farmer's hope, and to Great Britain he has looked for his market. . . .

The cry, of course is "protect our infant industries," but these infants have been too long at the breast. Shame on them, children fifteen years old, and unable yet to stand alone. They have had their chance at our expense, and now it is our turn. . . . *As a friend remarked, when we first came to this country, we lived on faith, that failed, and we lived on hope, hope even is deserting us, and almost it seems as though at last, we should live on charity.* . . .

From speech by the Rev. J.M. Douglas at Saltcoats, Assiniboia, February, 1895 in *The Patrons Advocate*, February 13, 1895.

1. Compare the concerns raised by the Patrons of Industry in the 1890s with those of Western politicians a century later.

Labour and Unions

The increasing dehumanization of labour as a result of the factory system gave rise to frustration and discontent in the latter part of the nineteenth century. The first of the following two excerpts relates the testimony of machinist John Morrison to the United States Senate in August 1883.

By Mr. George:

Q. State your age, residence, and occupation.

A. I am twenty-three years old; I live in this city; I am a machinist, and have been in that business about nine years.

Q. Do you work in a shop?

A. Yes, sir; I work in different shops.

Q. Is there any difference between the conditions under which machinery is made now and those which existed ten years ago?

A. A great deal of difference.

Q. State the differences as well as you can.

A. Well, the trade has been subdivided and those subdivisions have been again subdivided, so that a man never learns the machinist's trade now. Ten years ago he learned, not the whole of the trade, but a fair portion of it. Also, there is more machinery used in the business, which again makes machinery. In the case of making the sewing machine, for instance, you find that the trade is so subdivided that a man is not considered a machinist at all. Hence, it is merely laborers' work and it is laborers that work at that branch of our trade. The different branches of the trade are divided and subdivided so that one man may make just a particular part of a machine and may not know anything whatever about another part of the same machine. In that way machinery is produced a great deal cheaper than it used to be formerly, and in fact, through this system of work, 100 men are able to do now what it took 300 or 400 men to do fifteen years ago. By the use of machinery and the subdivision of the trade they so simplify the work that it is made a great deal easier and put together a great deal faster. There is no system of apprenticeship, I must say, in the business. You simply go in and learn whatever branch you are put at, and you stay at that unless you are changed to another. . . .

Q. What is the prospect for a man now working in one of these machine shops, a man who is temperate and economical and thrifty to become a boss or a manufacturer of machinery himself from his own savings? Could a man do it without getting aid from some relative who might die and leave him a fortune, or without drawing a lottery prize, or something of that sort?

A. Well speaking generally, there is no chance. They have lost all desire to become bosses now.

Q. Why have they lost that desire?

A. Why, because the trade has become demoralized. First they earn so small wages; and, next, it takes so much capital to become a boss now that they cannot think of it, because it takes all they can earn to live.

Q. Then it is the hopelessness of the effort that produces the loss of the desire on their part; is that it?

A. That is the idea. . . .

From the testimony of John Morrison, August 28, 1883, U.S. Congress, Senate, *Report of the Committee of the Senate upon the Relations between Labor and Capital* (Washington: U.S. Government Printing Office, 1885), I in Leon Litwack, *The American Labor Movement*, (Englewood Cliffs, N.J.: Prentice-Hall, 1962).

In the second excerpt, G.W. Perkins of the Cigar Makers' Union outlined his duty as a union leader.

Real trade-unionists are not pessimists; they are not theorists; they are opportunists. We ameliorate as we journey along to a better industrial system. Emancipation, I do not know what it is—that is, I will not attempt to say what the system will be, when it arrives. I am an evolutionary trade-unionist. I hold that the human family is growing better morally, physically, and mentally. While perhaps some may dispute that we are growing better morally and physically—although they can not successfully do so—none can dispute but that we are growing better mentally. That being true, I hold that it is my duty to do all that I possibly can for myself and my fellowman under present conditions; and if we are growing better mentally, that future generations will know better what they want and how to get it; and it is none of my business to say what that system shall be. I concern myself chiefly with the present, and in my view our duty is to do all that we possibly can for the hired man, for the workingman as we find him today and under conditions we find him. What emancipation means I will leave to future generations to decide.

From the testimony of G.W. Perkins, president of the Cigar Maker's International Union of America—A.F. of L., May 5, 1899. U.S. Congress, House, *Report of the Industrial Commission on the Relations and Conditions of Capital and Labor Employed in Manufactures and General Business*, 56th Cong., 2d Sess., House Doc. 495 (Washington: U.S. Government Printing Office, 1901), V2.

1. Outline the changes that have taken place in the job of a machinist.
2. Would you agree or disagree with Morrison's contention that there is no opportunity for advancement among machinists? Give reasons for your answer.
3. Summarize Perkins's remarks about unionism.

The Company Town, 1890s

One of the greatest problems for industrial workers in the late nineteenth century was working and living in a "company town." Companies provided living quarters and stores, and gave employees credit in both. Often, however, company prices and rents were higher than elsewhere, and a worker once in debt to the company found her or himself a virtual slave with no possibility of escape. In the first of three excerpts, Samuel Gompers, president of the American Federation of Labor, gave the following testimony in Congress in 1899.

. . . There is not a case that I know of, or which has come under my observation in many years, where the people could not buy the things they needed from ten to twenty, and in some cases fifty per cent less in other stores than they were required to pay in the company's stores. The store-order system is in a measure a system of peonage, where a workman does not receive wages for his labor, but something in kind. A workman has a right to be paid his wages in the lawful money of the country, of which he can dispose to the best advantage, as he pleases. Under the store-order system the employers deduct from the wages the amount that the workers may be indebted to the store. This has led, first to overcharging; secondly, to compulsion of purchase at the place, whether they desire it or not, and has encouraged the custom of over-charging, not only in the price of the article but frequently items are added which the workmen or their families never had. . . . They are practically bound there; practically bound to the soil. They can not move; can not quit. Under the system they can not move; they are deprived of the right of American citizens, to move where they please. The strike there now is as much due to that as it is to an increase of wages—the strike of the textile workers there.

From the testimony of Samuel Gompers, president of the American Federation of Labor, April 18, 1899. U.S. Congress, House, *Report of the Industrial Commission on the Relations and Conditions of Capital and Labor Employed in Manufactures and General Business*, 56th Cong.,2d Sess., House Doc. 495 (Washington: U.S. Government Printing Office, 1901), V2.

The Pullman strikers in 1894 found themselves trapped by their obligations to the company. Their leaders made the following statement with regard to their situation.

Mr. President and Brothers of the American Railway Union: We struck at Pullman because we were without hope. We joined the American Railway Union because it gave us a glimmer of hope. Twenty thousand souls, men, women, and little ones, have their eyes turned toward this convention today, straining eagerly through dark despondency for a glimmer of the heaven-sent message you alone can give us on this earth.

In stating to this body our grievances it is hard to tell where to begin. You all must know that the proximate cause of our strike was the discharge of two members of our grievance committee the day after George M. Pullman, himself, and Thomas H. Wickes, his second vice-president had guaranteed them absolute immunity. The more remote causes are still imminent. Five reductions in wages, in work, and in conditions of employment swept through the shops at Pullman between May and December, 1893. The last was the most severe, amounting to nearly thirty per cent, and our rents had not fallen. We owed Pullman $70 000 when we struck May 11. We owe him twice as much today. He does not evict us for two reasons: One, the force of popular sentiment and public opinion; the other because he hopes to starve us out, to break through in the back of the American Railway Union, and to deduct from our miserable wages when we are forced to return to him the last dollar we owe him for the occupancy of his houses. . . .

Water which Pullman buys from the city at 8 cents a thousand gallons he retails to us at 500 per cent advance and claims he is losing $400 a month on it. Gas which sells for 75 cents per thousand feet in Hyde Park, just north of us, he sells for $2.25. When we went to him to tell him our grievances he said we were all his "children."

Pullman, both the man and the town, is an ulcer on the body politic. He owns the houses, the schoolhouses, and churches of God in the town he gave his once humble name. The revenue he derives from these, the wages he pays out with one hand—the Pullman Palace Car Company, he takes back with the other—the Pullman Land Association. He is able by this to bid under any contract car shop in this country. His competitors in business, to meet this, must reduce the wages of their men. This gives him the excuse to reduce ours to conform to the market. His business rivals must in turn scale down; so must he. And thus the merry war—the dance of skeletons bathed in human tears—goes on, and it will go on, brothers, forever, unless you, the American Railway Union, stop it; end it; crush it out.

From the Pullman Strikers' Statement at the Convention of the American Railway Union held in Uhlich Hall, Chicago, June 15, 1894. U.S. Congress, House, United States Strike Commission, *Report on the Chicago Strike of June-July, 1894,* (Washington: U.S. Government Printing Office, 1895).

The following year, the United States Strike Commission substantiated the union position in its report on the strike.

If we exclude the aesthetic and sanitary features at Pullman, the rents there are from twenty to twenty-five per cent higher than rents in Chicago or surrounding towns for similar accommodations. The aesthetic features are admired by visitors, but have little money value to employees, especially when they lack bread. The company aims to secure six per cent upon the cost of its tenements, which cost includes a proportionate share for paving, sewerage, water, parks, etc. It claims now to receive less than four per cent. . . . The company makes all repairs, and heretofore has not compelled tenants to pay for them. Under the printed leases, however, which tenants must sign, they agree to pay for *all repairs* which are either necessary (ordinary wear and damages by the elements *not* excepted) or which the company *chooses* to make.

The company's claim that the workmen need not hire its tenements and can live elsewhere if they choose is not entirely tenable. The fear of losing work keeps them in Pullman as long as there are tenements unoccupied, because the company is supposed, as a matter of business, to give a preference to its tenants when work is slack. . . . While reducing wages the company made no reduction in rents. Its position is that the two matters are quite distinct, and that none of the reasons urged as justifying wage reduction by it as an employer can be considered by the company as a landlord.

. . . No valid reason is assigned for this position except simply that the company has the power and the legal right to do it. . . .

From U.S. Strike Commission, *Report on the Chicago Strike of June-July, 1894*, (Washington: U.S. Government Printing Office, 1895) in Leon Litwack, *The American Labor Movement*, (Englewood Cliffs, N.J.: Prentice-Hall, 1962).

1. From what you have read, and using further research if necessary, create and defend your own thesis regarding the company town system.

On Strike

The Pullman strike of 1894 was finally broken by the issuance of an injunction against the strikers. The injunction was granted at the request of the company and the federal government. In this first excerpt Eugene V. Debs, five-time socialist candidate for president, describes the impact of the injunction on the morale of the workers.

. . . On the second day of July, I [Eugene Debs] was served with a very sweeping injunction that restrained me, as president of the union, from sending out any telegram or any letter or issuing any order that would have the effect of inducing or persuading men to withdraw from the service of the company, or that would in any manner whatsoever, according to the language of the injunction, interfere with the operation. . . . From Michigan to California there seemed to be concerted action on the part of the courts in restraining us from exercising any of the functions of our offices. That resulted practically in the demoralization of our ranks. Not only this, but we were organized in a way that this was the center, of course, of operations. It is understood that a strike is war; not necessarily a war of blood and bullets, but a war in the sense that it is a conflict between two contending interests or classes of interests. . . .

. . . As soon as the employees found that we were arrested and taken from the scene of action, they became demoralized, and that ended the strike. It was not the soldiers that ended the strike; it was not the old brotherhoods that ended the strike; it was simply the United States courts that ended the strike. . . . Our headquarters were temporarily demoralized and abandoned, and we could not answer any messages. The men went back to work, and the ranks were broken, and the strike was broken up by the Federal courts of the United States, and not by the Army, and not by any other power, but simply and solely by the action of the United States courts in restraining us from discharging our duties as officers and representatives of the employees. . . .

From the testimony of Eugene V. Debs, president of the American Railway Union, August 20, 1894. U.S. Congress, House, United States Strike Commission, *Report on the Chicago Strike of June-July, 1894*, (Washington: U.S. Government Printing Office, 1895) in Leon Litwack, *The American Labor Movement*, (Englewood Cliffs, N.J.: Prentice-Hall, 1962).

In this second excerpt Gompers defends the necessity of striking under certain circumstances.

The working people find that improvements in the methods of production and distribution are constantly being made, and unless they occasionally strike, or have the power to enter upon a strike, the improvements will all go to the employer and all the injuries to the employees. A strike is an effort on the part of the workers to obtain some of the improvements that have occurred resultant from bygone and present genius of our intelligence; of our mental progress. We are producing wealth today at a greater ratio than ever in the history of mankind, and a strike on the part of workers is, first, against deterioration in their condition, and, second, to be participants in some of the improvements. Strikes are caused from various reasons. The employer desires to reduce wages and lengthen hours of labor, while the desire on the part of the employees is to obtain shorter hours of labor and better wages, and better surroundings. Strikes establish or maintain the rights of unionism; that is, to establish and maintain the organization by which the rights of the workers can be the better protected and advanced against the little forms of oppression, sometimes economical, sometimes political—the effort on the part of employers to influence and intimidate workmen's political preferences; strikes against victimization; activity in the cause of the workers against the blacklist. . . .

. . . Workmen have had to stand the brunt of the suffering. The American Republic was not established without some suffering, without some sacrifice, and no tangible right has yet been achieved in the interest of the people unless it has been secured by sacrifices and persistency. . . . We recognize that peaceful industry is necessary to successful civilized life, but the right to strike and the preparation to strike is the greatest preventive to strikes. If the workmen were to make up their minds tomorrow that they would under no circumstances strike, the employers would do all the striking for them in the way of lesser wages and longer hours of labour.

From the testimony of Samuel Gompers, president of the American Federation of Labour, November 20, 1899. U.S.Congress, House, *Report of the Industrial Commission on the Relations and Conditions of Capital and Labor Employed in Manufactures and General Business*, 56th Cong., 2d Sess., House Doc. 495 (Washington: U.S. Government Printing Office, 1901), V II in Leon Litwack, *The American Labor Movement*, (Englewood Cliffs, N.J.: Prentice-Hall, 1962).

1. How does Debs describe the impact of the injunction?
2. What was the role of government in labour relations?
3. Comment on Gompers's defence of the right to strike.

Ida Tarbell and Standard Oil, 1902

When McClure's *magazine commissioned author Ida Tarbell to write the story of the creation of Standard Oil, the editor expected a positive article. What resulted was an exposé of the business methods used by John D. Rockefeller that was so damaging that he was forced to hire a public relations agent to improve his image.*

In the fall of 1871, while Mr. Rockefeller and his friends were occupied with all these questions certain Pennsylvania refiners, it is not certain who, brought to them a remarkable scheme, the gist of which was to bring together secretly a large enough body of refiners and shippers to compel all the railroads handling oil to give to the company formed special rebates on its oil, and drawbacks on that of others. . . .

The first thing was to get a charter—quietly. . . . The name of the charter bought was the "Southern [usually written South] Improvement Company." For a beginning it was as good a name as another, since it said nothing. . . .

. . . Three weeks after this increase of capital Mr. Rockefeller had the charter and contracts of the South Improvement Company in hand, and was ready to see what they would do in helping him carry out his idea of wholesale combination in Cleveland. There were at that time some twenty-six refineries in town—some of them very large plants. All of them were feeling more or less the discouraging effects of the last three or four years of railroad discriminations in favor of the Standard Oil Company. To the owners of these refineries Mr. Rockefeller now went one by one, and explained the South Improvement Company. "You see," he told them, "this scheme is bound to work. It means an absolute control by us of the oil business. There is no chance for anyone outside. But we are going to give everybody a chance to come in. You are to turn over your refinery to my appraisers, and I will give you Standard Oil Company stock or cash, as you prefer, for the value we put upon it. I advise you to take the stock. It will be for your good." Certain refiners objected. They did not want to sell. They did want to keep and manage their business. Mr. Rockefeller was regretful, but firm. It was useless to resist, he told the hesitating; they would certainly be crushed if they did not accept his offer, and he pointed out in detail, and with gentleness, how beneficient the scheme really was—preventing the Creek refiners from destroying Cleveland, keeping up the price of refined oil, destroying competition, and eliminating speculation.

The perfection of the scheme, the inevitableness of the result, the persuasiveness of its advocate, the promise of great profits were different reasons for leading many of the refiners to succumb at once. Some of them took stock—more took money. . . .

From Richard Hofstadter, *The Progressive Movement, 1900–1915* (Englewood Cliffs, N.J.: Prentice-Hall, 1963).

1. How did the Standard Oil Company take over its competitors?
2. What impact would stories such as Tarbell's have upon the image of businessmen as heroes, as described by Michael Bliss (see page 282)?
3. Would you agree with Teddy Roosevelt's depiction of writers such as Tarbell as "muckrakers"? Give reasons for your answer.

The Industrial Workers of the World, 1908

Founded in 1905, the Industrial Workers of the World (IWW) or Wobblies as they were called, attempted to organize all workers into one large union. Its most spectacular campaign was waged between 1909 and 1912 to defend the right of free speech. In the excerpt below, from the preamble of the constitution of the IWW, the basic philosophies of the organization are outlined.

The working class and the employing class have nothing in common. There can be no peace so long as hunger and want are found among millions of working people and the few, who make up the employing class, have all the good things of life.

Between these two classes a struggle must go on until the workers of the world organize as a class, take possession of the earth and the machinery of production, and abolish the wage system.

We find that the centering of the management of industries into fewer and fewer hands makes the trade unions unable to cope with the ever growing power of the employing class. The trade unions foster a state of affairs which allows one set of workers to be pitted against another set of workers in the same industry, thereby helping defeat one another in wage wars. Moreover, the trade unions aid the employing class to mislead the workers into the belief that the working class have interests in common with their employers.

These conditions can be changed and the interest of the working class upheld only by an organization formed in such a way that all of its members in any one industry, or in all industries if necessary, cease work whenever a strike or lockout is on in any department thereof, thus making an injury to one an injury to all.

Instead of the conservative motto, "A fair day's wage for a fair day's work," we must inscribe on our banner the revolutionary watchword, "Abolition of the wage system."

It is the historic mission of the working class to do away with capitalism. The army of production must be organized, not only for the everyday struggle with capitalists, but also to carry on production when capitalism shall have been overthrown. By organizing industrially we are forming the structure of the new society within the shell of the old.

From the convention of 1908. Reprinted in IWW, *Songs of the Workers*, 29th ed., (Chicago: Industrial Workers of the World, 1956) in Leon Litwack, *The American Labor Movement*, (Englewood Cliffs, N.J.: Prentice-Hall, 1962).

1. In what ways are the ideas and goals of the Wobblies influenced by the philosophy of Karl Marx?

The Resort to Violence

After a series of local successes in 1885, the labour movement attempted a nationwide strike on May 1, 1886. On that day over 300 000 workers walked off their jobs. The centre of the movement was in Chicago. Two days later violence erupted during a mass meeting at Haymarket Square. A bomb was thrown into a crowd of police sent to break up the demonstration. Over seventy officers were seriously wounded, seven fatally. The police retaliated by opening fire on the crowd, killing and wounding large numbers. This excerpt comes from the testimony of one of the eyewitnesses.

I reached the Haymarket about 7:30. I found no meeting there. I walked around among the crowd, which was scattered over the Haymarket, then I went to the DesPlaines Street station and shook hands with Captain Ward, whom I knew. He introduced me to Inspector Bonfield and I had a conversation with him. Later on I went back and remained throughout the whole meeting until the bomb had exploded. The speakers were northeast of me in front of Crane Brothers' building, a few feet north of the alley. I remember the alley particularly. As far as I remember Spies' speech, he said: "Please come to order. This meeting is not called to incite any riot." [Witness then gave a synopsis of the speech, which in no wise differs from that previously given as written out by Spies.]

He thought Mr. Parsons did say: "To arms, To arms," but in what connection could not remember. "Somebody in the crowd said 'shoot' or 'hang Gould, and he says, 'No, a great many will jump up and take his place. What socialism aims at is not the death of individuals but of the system.' . . ."

From Richard Hofstadter and Michael Wallace, eds., *American Violence: A Documentary History*, (New York: Vintage Books, 1971).

1. Discuss the reasons why violence erupted within the labour movement.
2. Write an editorial in which you either support or condemn the use of violence by labour unions. Give reasons to support your position.

Unionism and Personal Liberty, 1914-15

In the two excerpts below Dudley Taylor, lawyer for the Employer's Association of Chicago, and Clarence Darrow, the famous criminal and labour lawyer, present the two sides of the union issue.

Dudley Taylor (1914)

. . . What would you consider to be a proper method and proper organization of labor? . . .

Of course, that is hard to say, but I do feel this, that a labor organization ought to be in a position to merit the confidence of the public and of employers, for that matter, and ought not to rely upon coercion. But what do we see? We see members of labor unions who do not dare to go to the meetings of their union and raise their voice in protest. . . . They don't dare do it. They are coerced into the union; they are coerced to do as the union directs, and we see the evidence of it every day. Some trouble is experienced somewhere in this city; a man goes around and perhaps whistles, blows a tin whistle, or snaps his fingers and the men go on strike. Why? The chances are they don't know anything about it; the chances are they are opposed to it, because for the time being it takes their living from them or a considerable part of their living, but they have no choice but to obey. If those men were not coerced; if they were in fear of violence that would not be the case. . . .

From the testimony of Dudley Taylor, General Counsel for the Employers' Association of Chicago, July 22, 1914. U.S. Congress, Senate, *Final Report and Testimony Submitted to Congress by the Commission on Industrial Relations*, 64th Cong., 1st Sess., Senate Doc. 415 (Washington: U.S. Government Printing Office, 1916), IV in Leon Litwack, *The American Labor Movement*, (Englewood Cliffs, N.J.: Prentice-Hall, 1962).

Clarence S. Darrow (1915)

. . . Of course, there is a lot of nonsense talked about it. They talk about the inalienable right of a man to work; he has no such right; no one has a right to work, and the man who stands for the open shop does not care for anybody's rights to work, except the nonunion man, and they only care for him because they can use him. If a man has any constitutional right to work he ought to have some legal way of getting work. If the Constitution is going to guarantee the right to work, it ought to guarantee some place to work, and there is no such thing. A man can only work if there is a job; he can only work for a man who wants some man to work for him.

The workingman spends a good share of his waking moments in a shop. He does not need to invite a nonunion man into his house if he does not want to, and probably won't, and he is under no more obligation to work with him in a factory if he does not want to. If a Presbyterian does not want to work with a Catholic, he may be narrow and bigoted, but he does not have to. Of course, a union man has a direct reason for it; he believes and he understands and feels that the nonunion man is working against the interests of his class. . . .

The nonunion man comes along and says, "I will take your place." He is not loyal to the union, and the union man regards him as a traitor to his class, and he won't work with him, and he has a perfect right to refuse to work with him. . . .

From the testimony of Clarence S. Darrow, labor and criminal lawyer, May 18, 1915. U.S. Congress, Senate, *Final Report and Testimony Submitted to Congress by the Commission on Industrial Relations*, 64th Cong., 1st Sess., Senate Doc. 415 (Washington: U.S. Government Printing Office, 1916), XI in Leon Litwack, *The American Labor Movement*, (Englewood Cliffs, N.J.: Prentice-Hall, 1962).

1. Summarize Taylor's view of the union movement.
2. To what extent did Darrow support the attitudes of unionized workers towards their nonunion counterparts?
3. Assuming the roles of Taylor and Darrow, stage a debate over the issue of closed and open shops.

The Winnipeg General Strike, 1919

The spectre of bolshevism loomed large in Winnipeg in 1919. What was generally a peaceful and responsible strike was seen by many Canadians as having sinister implications. This series of excerpts includes various contemporary viewpoints of the crisis.

It is to the general public of Winnipeg that we speak in stating without equivocation that this is not a strike at all, in the ordinary sense of the term—it is revolution.

It is a serious attempt to overturn British institutions in this western country and to supplant them with the Russian Bolshevik system of Soviet rule. . . . Why is it that one finds many thousands of men and women among the strikers who state quite frankly that they had no wish to strike—that they did not want to strike, and yet, paradoxically, they are on strike?

It is because the "Red" element in Winnipeg has assumed the ascendency in the labor movement, dominating and influencing—or stampeding—the decent element of that movement, which desires the preservation of British institutions, yet is now striking unconsciously against them. . . . It is seriously to be feared that the strike cannot much longer be controlled and lawlessness averted. . . . The only way to defeat Bolshevism is for the people, the injured, the sufferers, those who are put to hardship through this strike, those who stand in the position of the proverbially "innocent bystander" who always gets shot in a riot, to organize. . . .

Law and order? Yes—in a way, law and order has prevailed, to the extent that rioting has not occurred. Law and order to this extent has been kept, solely because the industries and commercial houses have submitted to the strike dictum and suspended operations. Why should not business be carried on so far as possible by men whose legitimate right is to do business in this city?

From the Winnipeg *Citizen* (published by the Citizens' Committee of the employers), May 17, 1919 in J.H. Reid, et al., *A Source Book of Canadian History*, (Toronto: Longman Company Limited, 1964).

There is great cause for congratulation during this struggle, in that until the present moment the participants are more orderly than a crowd of spectators at a baseball game. . . . There has been evolved a weapon of great power—orderliness.

From *Western Labour News* (organ of the Central Strike Committee), May 17, 1919 in J.H. Reid, et al., *A Source Book of Canadian History*, (Toronto: Longman Company Limited, 1964).

The general public is up in arms. They have suffered inconvenience and loss. "Why should innocent non-combatants suffer?" The general public has not been innocent. It has been guilty of the greatest sin—the sin of indifference. Thousands have suffered through the years under the industrial system. The general public have not realized. It did not touch them. Now it is coming home to them. They blame the strikers. Why not blame the employers whose arrogant determination has provoked the strike. Why not, rather, quit the unprofitable business of trying to place blame and attempt to discover and remove causes that have produced this strike and will produce, if not removed, further and more disastrous strikes? . . . The crisis calls for extraordinary measures. Troops and more troops will not settle the question. Constructive radical action must come some time. Why not now?

From J. S. Woodsworth (formerly a Methodist minister, and then a labour leader), *Western Labour News*, June 12, 1919 in J.H. Reid, et al., *A Source Book of Canadian History*, (Toronto: Longman Company Limited, 1964).

It was essential that the greater issue raised by the assumption of Soviet authority—and it was nothing less on the part of those in control of the strike in Winnipeg—should be once and for all decided and be decisively beaten down before they should concern themselves with the smaller and much less important issue upon which certain men had originally gone on strike. That is the stand the citizens of Winnipeg took. That is the stand the Minister of Labour took. . . . Can anyone contemplate such an event? . . . Are we to have on the one hand a concentration of employers, and on the other a concentration of all the labour interests of the Dominion, fighting it out for supremacy?

The Rt. Hon. Arthur Meighen, Canada, House of Commons *Debates*, 1919 in J.H. Reid, et al., *A Source Book of Canadian History*, (Toronto: Longman Company Limited, 1964).

1. How did the Citizen's Committee depict the strike action?
2. Comment upon the remarks made by the Central Strike Committee and J.S. Woodsworth regarding the effect of the strike upon the general public.
3. Account for the inflammatory remarks made by future prime minister Arthur Meighen.

On the Brink: Business and Labour, 1928

In the following account from a meeting of the Taylor Society (Frederick Taylor founded a school of scientific management), the following observations were made about the changing role of labour in the 1920s.

. . . The present day job is characterized by two things, among others. It is being speeded up and it is being narrowed down. Through scientific management and careful time study, we have succeeded in packing every movement on the job with its sixty seconds worth of distance run. In the more scientific shops we have made Kipling's poem not merely an ideal, but a necessity for the man on the job. We have taken out of the job the chance to ruminate. If we look at a tradesman of the old school we shall recall how different the situation was before this speeding up occurred. At the same time, in giving out each job we have said, "This shall be done in this way and no other." A worker must work precisely, according to specifications. By these two means we have taken away from the working man the power of full expression of his personality—of his soul, or whatever you prefer to call it—in his work. At the same time, life is demanding more constructive thought from labor, for bit by bit the laboring class has become the governing class in America. They are becoming the governing class politically because they are becoming aware of their dominating numerical power in government. They are sharing in the government of industry either because they have won this share by their own organized efforts, or because more and more employers have realized that they need guidance of labor in order to manage well. Thus, on one hand, while the jobs we have prepared them for have made their working experience narrow and dry, society, on the other hand, is requiring of them an ever wider capacity for judgement.

From William Graebner and Leonard Richards, ed., *The American Record: Images of the Nation's Past*, (New York: Alfred Knopf, 1982).

1. How does the author feel that life has changed for the worker?
2. What new political role does he see for the labouring class?
3. Give your opinion of the author's contention that the scope of life was broadening for the worker in 1928.

Response to Industrialism: Analysis and Application

1. "From the very beginning, transportation in Canada was not a creature of private enterprise, but a product of public policy."

Based upon this contention, contrast Canadian railway policy with that of the United States.

2. Many Western Canadian historians have argued that the National Policy was not one of nation building, but of empire building, and that the industrialization of Eastern Canada was paid for by the West. Discuss this statement in groups of three or four. Bring out arguments on both sides of the issue. Following your discussion, see if your group has reached a consensus.

3. Compare Andrew Carnegie's view of the relationship between capital and labour with the testimony given by workers in the readings.

4. Research the origins and development of a local industry in your area that was established prior to World War II. In your investigation consider such issues as: the role of labour in its development; its impact upon the local community; the effect of modernization upon the industry; and the impact of government policy upon the industry. Prepare an oral report of your findings.

5. Research the origins and development of one Canadian labour union. In your investigation consider such issues as: the effect of the American labour movement upon the union; changes in its strength and influence over time; the evolution of working conditions as reflected by union contractual demands; and the impact of strikes or other labour disruptions. Develop a plan and thesis as if you were going to write a major research paper on the topic.

6. Working with a classmate, conduct a private debate on the resolution:
"Unions have been a positive contributor to the improvement of working conditions in Canada." Support your position paper along with a précis of the arguments put forward by your opponent.

7. Recreate a town meeting in Winnipeg in May 1919. Representatives on a panel could include: a member of the citizens' committee; a member of the central strike committee; J.S. Woodsworth; Arthur Meighen; and a representative of the North-west Mounted Police. Have the participants debate the issues involved in the General Strike, then open the discussion to questions from the floor.

8. Write a biographical profile of one industrialist or labour leader of the period.

9. Graph the growth of a particular industry in Canada during the period 1880-1930. If possible, compare the pattern and rate of growth with the same industrial sector in the United States.

10
IMMIGRATION AND NATIVISM

Canadians today take the multicultural nature of our society for granted. Many of our schools boast a wide cross-section of ethnic and racial groups learning and playing together. Around the turn of the century, however, attitudes were quite different. North America was largely a white, Northern European continent. There were other groups, of course. Both Canada and the United States were home to large numbers of non–white aboriginal people. In addition, the substantial Black population of the United States, a legacy from the era of slavery, had spread across the continent. To a great extent, however, these were "invisible" minorities, people who lacked many of the rights and privileges enjoyed by the majority of the white population.

In the closing decades of the nineteenth century and the early years of the twentieth, however, the cultural makeup of North America began to change. Lured by the prospects of available land, and freedom from persecution, immigrants from other parts of the world began arriving in North America.

This chapter looks at the process of immigration in both countries, and the reactions of the indigenous population to it. Facts and statistics alone cannot tell the real story of this chapter in North American history. Therefore, much of this section concentrates on the words of the people themselves. Only in this way can we hope to clearly understand the experiences of the newcomers and the reaction to their arrival of those who already called North America home.

Immigration and the Changing Face of American Society

Before the 1880s over 85 percent of new arrivals in the United States came from Great Britain, Canada, Germany or Scandinavia. The vast majority of these immigrants were English–speaking Protestants. Although some, such as the Irish, remained culturally and politically distinct, most blended into the existing white population.

After 1880, however, there was a dramatic change in this pattern. Hundreds of thousands of new immigrants arrived from Southern and Eastern Europe. These newcomers, from places such as Italy, Poland, Russia, Hungary and Bohemia, brought with them different languages and customs. It was in the Eastern cities that the greatest impact of this migration was felt. Arriving in the major ports, many of the new immigrants were taken in by families from their home lands.

This new wave of immigration brought a new richness to the American cultural fabric. American life became more diverse as the cultures and traditions of many nations blended together on the new continent.

Not all of the new arrivals were welcomed, however. Labour leaders opposed the new wave of immigration, believing foreign labour undercut their own workers and created further unemployment. In San Francisco, for example, the large Chinese population, which reached 17 percent of the city's total by 1880, was resented by other local residents. Brought to the country as cheap labour, the Chinese were blamed for keeping wages down. As hostilities mounted, riots broke out. Congress was finally forced to respond in 1882 with exclusion acts prohibiting all Chinese immigration, initially for a period of ten years, and later for an indefinite period. The Chinese soon discovered an aspect of American society that Blacks and Native people had known for centuries.

Of the large numbers of new immigrants who came to the United States in the late nineteenth century, more than two–thirds settled in the cities. The slum conditions in which many of these immigrants found themselves living were exposed by the newspaper muckrakers; but instead of receiving sympathy, the newcomers often found themselves objects of contempt. "Native" Americans blamed these newcomers for the squalid surroundings in which they found themselves.

Even some progressive social reformers had difficulty accepting the new immigrants. Jane Addams, whose work established a network of settlement houses for slum residents as well as nursery, recreation and cultural facilities for the children of working mothers, believed that many immigrants were culturally deprived. The background of Italian immigrants, for example, had resulted in "primitive habits" and "inherently unclean minds" which could only be cured by assimilation into American society. Some progressives went so far as to say that any immigrants who tried to preserve their European or Oriental ways of life in the United States were being "inconsistent with the American ideal of brotherhood, and [were] disloyal."

Such attitudes were not uncommon, nor were they confined to the American side of the border.

Sifton and the Open Door Policy

Sir Clifford Sifton was Canada's minister of the interior under the Liberal prime minister Sir Wilfrid Laurier. In this position he accomplished what the first phase of the National Policy had failed to do: he increased immigration to Canada from 49 000 in 1900 to 402 000 just thirteen years later. The secret of Sifton's success was in large part due to an extensive advertising campaign. Signs advocating the "last best west" appeared in dozens of languages in countries around the world.

Sifton's first principle of discrimination was based upon economic background. Canada wanted immigrants who would help develop the nation's vast farm lands. As his deputy minister, James Smart, commented in 1900: "If a settler is one who has been engaged in agricultural pursuits in the old land...we believe it most desirable to encourage him to occupy our land and to break up our soil and assist in developing the resources of the country." To further this goal, Sifton advised his foreign agents to discourage "labouring men and mechanics."

Preferred immigrants were either British or American—the British because they were thought to be culturally superior, and the Americans because they had money. (The average American immigrant arrived in Canada with over $850 in cash and belongings.)

Preferential treatment for Britons eventually backfired on the Canadian government. Successful at first, the number of immigrants from the British Isles increased from about twelve hundred in 1900 to over sixty–five thousand five years later. Eventually Canada became a dumping ground for the less desirable elements of the British population. By 1908 over 70 percent of all deportations from Canada were to Britain. As one Methodist minister said: "Now we know something of the dreadful conditions existing in the cities in England."

American immigrants tended to be the children of farmers who had moved to the northern states in search of available land. From an annual total of nineteen thousand in 1900, by 1912–13 almost one hundred and forty thousand American settlers were arriving each year. Not all were welcomed with open arms, however. W.E. Dubois, leader of the N.A.A.C.P. (National Association for the Advancement of Coloured People) commented that "all restrictions respecting health, money, etc. [were] strictly enforced" to limit the number of Blacks allowed into the country.

By contrast to the "wealthy" Americans, the average settler coming to Canada from Europe had only about $15 in her or his pocket. Even within this group the Canadian government had its preferences. Southern Europeans were subtly discouraged from immigrating to Canada. Sifton himself showed a great preference for Eastern Europeans from such points of origin as Poland, Russia, Austria–Hungary, and the Ukraine. Many of these people, such as the Doukhobors, the Ukrainians, and the Mennonites, established group settlements as a means of preserving their religious and cultural heritage. Unlike prevailing American attitudes, Canada was in no hurry to "Canadianize" its new settlers. Whether the product of more liberal thinking or simply a desire to attract and hold on to desperately needed settlers, the result was the same. The Canadian west became an exciting patchwork of cultures, languages, and religions existing under a common government.

The biggest attraction for non–farm labour during this period was construction work on the new transcontinental railway lines. Near the turn of the century one immigration official asked the railways to refrain from bringing Italian workers into the country, believing them to be undependable and incapable of making a positive contribution to the country. Instead they were encouraged to hire Central Europeans, who were "obedient and industrious" and who would "take the wages they [were] offered." In spite of this "advice," the CPR continued to bring in large numbers of Italian workers illegally through the United States. Once construction on the railways was finished, however, the Italian immigrants were unable to find work. By 1907 there were between six and eight thousand destitute Italian labourers living in Montreal. Finding themselves isolated and unable to speak the language, many were victimized by ruthless employers and ethnic crew bosses who took advantage of their dilemma to exploit their labour.

The second largest group of immigrants to enter Canada for railway work during this period were the Chinese and Japanese. John A. Macdonald, who advocated the importation of Oriental labour, advised British Columbians that they would not see "permanent degradation of the country by a mongrel race." Macdonald assured the public that once construction was finished the Oriental workers would be sent home. This did not turn out to be the case, however, and by 1891 10 percent of the population of British Columbia was Chinese.

This was only the beginning. The year 1904 saw four hundred Oriental immigrants arrive in Canada. This figure swelled to over twelve thousand four years later. Canadian "nativists" warned of a "yellow peril." Future Canadian prime minister R.B. Bennett warned British Columbians in 1907: "We must not allow our shores to be overrun by Asiatics, and become dominated by an alien race. British Columbia must remain a white man's country."

By 1907 anti–Oriental sentiment had reached crisis proportions. That year an Asian Exclusion League was formed to pressure the government to restrict immigration from the Far East. Anti-Japanese riots led to a deal between Canada and Japan to restrict immigration from that country; this, combined with federal legislation forcing immigrants to arrive directly from their country of origin, effectively stopped the flow of new citizens from Japan and India.

The *Komagata Maru* incident of 1914 reflects the height of the anti–Asian fervour. The *Komagata Maru* was a Japanese ship that arrived in Vancouver in the spring of that year. On board were 376 East Indians holding British passports who were eager to settle in Canada. Port authorities refused to let the ship dock. Eventually the Canadian navy, "with local citizens cheering it on," escorted the Japanese ship back out to the open seas. One local politician proclaimed: "I hold it to be the duty of the people of Canada to guard, and to cherish, . . . the real simon-pure Canadian life . . . and go as far as possible to keep pure and free from the taint of other peoples."

Massive immigration raised a host of social, cultural and political concerns. Immigrants who had failed in the agricultural fields drifted to the cities. They were forced to live in slums and further strain municipal social services. Immigrant voters were blamed for the defeat of prohibition and anti-prostitution legislation and many earlier immigrants decried the negative influence of these "foreigners" upon the development of a Canadian nationality. By 1900 the cooperative English–French development of the West envisioned by the Fathers of Confederation was clearly dead. French-Canadian leader Henri Bourassa most clearly expressed the nativist sentiment of this, the oldest group of European immigrants, when he stated that, "it never was in the minds of the founders of this nation . . . to make it a land of refuge for the scum of all nations."

World War I and the Re–emergence of Nativism

In the years prior to World War I, nativist sentiment continued to grow in Canada and the United States. Restrictive demands were placed upon many immigrants. In Canada the head tax, a per person duty on immigrating Chinese, was raised from $50 to $500 by 1903. In the United States, nativist "reformers" attempted to introduce a bill in Congress demanding a literacy test for all immigrants. President William Taft initially supported the measure as being good for American labour. It soon became clear, however, that the legislation would restrict the entrance of more than 25 percent of European Jewish refugees awaiting entry. Under pressure, Taft reversed his position and vetoed the bill. His flip–flop ended up offending both Jewish supporters and labour groups. This was a significant group, as over 1 million European Jews would eventually enter the United States between 1908 and 1925.

War and Repression

The First World War was the crisis that undercut progressive reform. Many economic changes were put on hold as the nation turned to the business community to produce the goods needed for the war effort. As controls were lessened, profiteering increased and corruption spread. In spite of these "evils," however, the real repression came not in the economic sphere but in the area of civil rights.

When Canada entered the First World War, there were over one hundred thousand native–born Germans and Austro–Hungarians living in the country. Added to this total were over four hundred thousand new citizens from "enemy" nations, creating the basis for nativist paranoia. In the first month of the war, the Toronto *Globe* called for the registration of "enemy aliens" and for their restriction under a strict curfew. Anyone violating these rules was to be "court–martialled and shot as a spy." Letters to the government warned of hundreds of thousands of German–Americans training in Milwaukee in preparation to invade Canada, and by 1916 an Anti–German League had been formed in Toronto. Meanwhile Canadian propagandists flooded the United States with anti–German articles and films. By 1917, they had taken their toll on American attitudes. When the United States finally entered the war in that year, it did so with a vengeance.

In the forefront of the anti–German movement in the United States was the Committee for Public Information. Run by muckraker George Creel, it wrote and distributed hate literature, falsified history, and corrupted the reporting of current events in order to foster anti–German sentiment across the country. Eventually, German–Americans became the targets of not only verbal abuse, but physical violence as well. Windows in German–American homes were frequently broken; some citizens of German descent were even stoned or tarred and feathered. At the height of the anti–German fervor in North America, Berlin, Ontario, became Kitchener, and in the United States sauerkraut was rechristened "liberty cabbage."

In Canada in 1917, Robert Borden's Conservative government, while preaching tolerance, took the persecution of immigrants one step further. The Wartime Elections Act disenfranchised all naturalized citizens who had been born in enemy countries and who had come to Canada after 1902. Allowed to enter Canada under the immigration policies of Sifton and his Liberal successors, the immigrants had tended to be Liberal supporters. Now their right to vote had been denied them. Nativism had become a useful political tool as well.

Similar anti–immigrant actions did not reach such a peak in the United States, which was at war for only eighteen months. At their worst, however, Americans still fostered racism and hatred, and created in the United States the mechanics of oppression that Americans were fighting against in Europe.

When the war ended, the campaigns against foreign agents and enemy spies did not disappear. Instead they simply found a new target. The hate campaign against the Germans, was quickly turned against a new enemy, communism.

The Bolshevik Revolution in Russia in 1917 had unnerved many North Americans. After the war, Canadians and Americans fought bolshevism on two fronts, abroad and at home. In Russia, American and Canadian soldiers supported anti-Bolshevik forces. Although they were eventually withdrawn, their presence in the first place helped fuel suspicion on both sides.

It was at home, however, that the real "Red Scare" took hold. A series of general strikes in Europe, followed by labour disruptions in the United States, gave some substance to the fear of a general revolution. The most significant outburst of labour unrest occurred in the steel industry. During the war, labour had put a hold on all negotiations, and had generally accepted employer demands for the sake of productivity. Once the war was over, production demands declined, yet the number of available workers climbed with the return of the war veterans. As a result, unemployment was high, and many companies used this situation to further erode workers' rights.

In September 1919 over 365 000 steel workers went on strike across the country. The strike soon became violent, and owners called upon the police and state militia to restrain the workers. Meanwhile, most companies continued to operate by hiring unemployed labourers as strikebreakers. After the dispute dragged on for almost five months, the union finally gave up. In January the workers returned to their jobs without obtaining one of their demands.

Other labour disputes, such as a general strike in Seattle and a police strike in Boston, worried average citizens. It seemed to them that the entire social order was breaking down, and they looked for someone to shoulder the blame.

Many Americans claimed that the new labour unrest was a product of immigration. Editorials and cartoons depicted hordes of undesirable immigrants flooding off the ships to swell an already underemployed work force. Among these were supposedly dangerous radicals who were bent on starting a communist revolution. There is no doubt that there were communists within the labour movement, and that in a number of instances they tried to turn legitimate strikes into revolutionary action. But there is also no doubt that they had little or no impact, and that they were never a serious threat to the political or social order. Nevertheless, the campaign to rid the country of these "dangerous" elements was given a boost by the explosion of a series of terrorist bombs in 1919.

In early 1919 President Woodrow Wilson said that to "save civilization from chaos—from a flood of ultra–radicalism that will swamp the world . . . Liberalism must be more liberal than ever." His sentiments were echoed by his secretary of state, Robert Lansing, who reminded the American people that "while we must set our faces sternly against the anarchy and the class tyranny and terror of Bolshevism, we must at the same time cut to the root of the sore and relieve the misery and exhaustion which form such a fertile soil for its rapid growth."

In the confrontational atmosphere that followed the war, such sentiments were soon set aside. Mitchell Palmer, the attorney general, attacked the problem head-on. On January 20, 1920, his agents made a series of sweeping arrests in thirty-three cities across the country. Thousands of people were held and then later released. About 5000 were formally charged, and 536 were deported as undesirables. There was never any proof of a conspiracy to overthrow the government, however, and after this action public attitudes changed. Most Americans rejected the use of force and the violation of constitutional rights that had taken place. The Red Scare was over, but suspicion of foreigners would continue to haunt the rest of the decade.

Canada too was gripped by the same fears that overtook the United States. While Borden was meeting at Versailles, acting prime minister Sir Thomas White cabled that: "Bolshevism has made great progress among workers and soldiers . . . we cannot get troops absolutely dependable in an emergency . . . [and] plans are being laid for revolutionary movement which . . . would bring about serious disturbances in Calgary and Winnipeg where socialism [is] rampant." The Winnipeg General Strike in 1919 served as "proof" to nativist forces suspicious of alien subversives. Within a few years "suspected" anarchists and spies appeared on the list of "undesirables" not allowed into Canada.

Restrictions on enemy aliens continued until 1923, the same year that the new Chinese immigration law practically eliminated immigrants from that country. Although Canadian authorities continued to encourage British and American immigrants throughout the decade, immigrants from other countries were first required to obtain visas in their country of origin. It was a process which would close the door to many potential Canadians.

In 1921 the United States Congress passed the Emergency Quota Act, which restricted the number of immigrants allowed into the country. The quota for each country was set at 3 percent of the number of Americans of that original nationality who were living in the United States in 1910. The policy did not prohibit immigration from within the Western Hemisphere, but was clearly aimed at reducing the number of so-called "dangerous" immigrants, such as Southern and Eastern Europeans and the Japanese. The restriction was tightened even further in 1924, when the quota was dropped to 2 percent and the base year changed to 1890. Under this restriction, Japanese immigration was banned altogether. Of the 152 000 people who arrived in the United States from outside the Western Hemisphere in 1929, only 20 000 were from areas other than Northern Europe. The Statue of Liberty had turned her back on the "huddled masses."

By the 1920s North America had begun to put up barriers to immigration and to reconsider its role in world affairs. The open borders and rapid expansion of the pre–war decades had been replaced by increasing caution and suspicion of all things foreign. An era was passing, but it had left an indelible impression upon the face of North America.

Statistics alone tell only a small part of the story of immigration to North America during the thirty years prior to World War I. In order to more fully appreciate the immigrant experience and the reaction to it, it is necessary to consider the thoughts of the people who lived it.

Peopling a Country: Immigration Policy, 1896-1911

In order to compete with the lure of the United States, Canada took a far more aggressive approach to attracting immigration in the late nineteenth century. The immigration leaflet shown here was published by the federal government to entice British immigrants to Canada.

CANADA
The New Home Land.

CANADA presents a strong appeal to all who wish to make a new home in a new land. This is especially true of its appeal to the people of Great Britain and Ireland. Canada is the nearest to the Motherland of all the great Dominions of the British Commonwealth—only a few days' journey lie between Britain and Canada. Modern ocean liners have brought the coast of Canada within five days of Liverpool.

Canada is situated mainly in the North Temperate Zone, in the latitudes in which the people of the United Kingdom have been born and brought up. The climate is particularly suited to the white race. It is a land of homes --the "New Home Land" of the British people --a land where all who are intelligent and industrious may reasonably expect success. British people soon find themselves at home in Canada. It is a British country, with British customs and ideals: Britons going to Canada do not change their allegiance: they are still under the British flag.

1. Comment upon the accuracy of the claims made in the advertisement.
2. Evaluate the document in terms of its ethnic or racial bias.
3. To what extent do you think that such an ad would be an effective lure to immigrants?

Not Wisely But Too Well: Immigration Policy, 1908

In this article from the Canadian Magazine, *author W.S. Wallace outlines the basic principles of Canada's immigration policy and evaluates the degree of its success.*

The present immigration policy of the Canadian Government dates, in its broad outlines, from the year 1897. In that year Mr. Clifford Sifton came into office at Ottawa as Minister of the Interior, and under his direction, the Department of the Interior entered on a policy, not merely of encouraging immigration into Canada, but of fostering it by all means in their power. The United States had been, previously to that, absorbing nearly all the immigration flowing from the old world to the new; it was the aim of the Department of the Interior, in striking out their new policy, to divert a fair share of that immigration towards Canada. . . . In Great Britain immigration affairs were taken out of the hands of the Canadian High Commissioner, who had carried the work on in a semi-diplomatic manner, and were placed on a business basis under the control of an official who had nothing else to do. This official, when appointed, applied himself to bringing before the notice of the people of Great Britain the advantages of Canada as a country for immigration. . . . Not only, however, did the Department attempt to capture the United States immigration at its sources, but it carried war into the enemy's country by establishing immigration agencies in the United States itself, in Omaha, Chicago, Kansas City, St. Paul, and most of the other large cities of the West. Between two and three hundred immigration agents were employed on commission. Advertisements of Canada were authorised in American papers, which reached 5 700 000 families. . . .

In the end perseverance has won the day, and immigration into Canada has now grown to proportions that have exceeded the most sanguine expectations. In 1897, the immigrants who came to Canada numbered 712; last year those who came over the border numbered 57 919. In 1897, the immigrants from the British Isles numbered less than 20 000; last year they numbered 86 796. In the last seven years, in the neighbourhood of 900 000 immigrants have settled in Canada.

Has this policy been on the whole in the best interests of the Canadian people?

It is not the aim of the present article to discuss this question fully or to answer it definitely. The subject of immigration is admittedly a difficult and complex one; and to attempt to deal with it exhaustively . . . would be to court the wrath of the gods. . . . It must be confessed that most of the discussion which has taken place with regard to immigration hitherto has been undisguisedly *ex parte* (one-sided) in character; and anything which serves, however inadequately, to suggest the different aspects of the question, must help to clear the air.

(1) What object or objects had the Department of the Interior in view in inaugurating the present policy in 1897? . . . The object of the immigration policy was to build up Canada to enable Canada to do business on a larger scale, to enable her to better herself in a financial and material sense; and so to keep at home those of her sons who were flocking over the border. Now, it is universally admitted that in these regards the Canadian immigration policy has been a success; it has attained the ends it contemplated. . . .

(2) Is this increased wealth and prosperity likely to have a good effect on the character of the Canadian people? This, of course, is one of those elemental problems which humanity, in its headlong pursuit of wealth, delights to ignore. Sweets are the uses of adversity, but most people prefer prosperity. . . .

(3) A very important feature of immigration is the question of its effect on the native stock. What effect is immigration likely to have on our native-born population? In this, as in so much else, Canada may learn from an article on American immigration in Vol. 179 of *The North American Review:*

> Back of all statistics of the criminality, pauperism, illiteracy, and economic value of immigration lies the great question of the effect of immigration on our native, or older, stock. . . . The immigration of the last fifty years has contributed millions to our population; has undoubtedly added enormously to the wealth of the country, but these things have been accomplished at the expense of the native stock. . . . As newer and lower classes of immigrants came to this country, Americans shrank more and more from the industrial competition which was thus forced upon them; they became unwilling to subject their sons and daughters to this competition; and hence these sons and daughters were never born. The stronger the competition, the greater the effort to maintain and raise the standards of living and social position above that of the majority of recent immigrants; and the greater this effort, the greater the voluntary check to population. . . . Many of our recent immigrants, not discouraged by the problem of maintaining high standards of living with their many children, are replacing native Americans. It is fundamentally a question as to what kind of babies are to be born; it is a question as to what race shall dominate this country. . . .

It is possible that this quotation rather overstates . . . the case; and it is possible that what applies to the United States may not apply wholly to Canada; but it appears to be shown here clearly that there are grounds for believing that the tendency of inferior immigration (and nearly all immigration is, in the nature of things, inferior), is to lower the birth-rate of the native-born population. . . .

(4) There are a number of the more detailed features of the immigration policy that call for consideration. Should the immigration of foreigners be encouraged? . . . What will be the effect on the country of a large foreign vote, unfamiliar with the spirit of our institutions and ignorant of our political history? Will they cast their votes intelligently? Or will they sell their franchise for

a mess of pottage? These are matters on which statistics will be forever unobtainable; but it is perhaps not false to say that there is a widespread impression that the foreign vote does not always stand for intelligence and integrity. It is a conceivable hypothesis which traces many of the ills from which the body politic of the United States is suffering to-day . . . to the great masses of unassimilated foreigners who are within her gates. It may be objected that the foreigner can be educated; but one can only reply by saying that the foreign immigrant puts a strain on the inadequate educational system of Western Canada that it cannot bear. Few foreigners could be transformed into good Canadians in five years' time by the best educational system.

(5) The evil of foreign immigration has been intensified tenfold by the "block system" of settling immigrants. Every Canadian knows what a solid French-Canada, impervious to outside influences, has meant to Canada. By establishing solid colonies of Doukhobors, Galicians, Mormons, Mennonites, etc., here and there in the West, the Department of the Interior has repeated the French-Canadian situation all over the country.

(6) Should there be a literacy test for immigrants as well as a medical test? . . . We require a modicum of education in the case of our youth; why not require it in the case of our immigrants? . . . (Are) immigrants of any sort an imperative and urgent necessity? Is not quality more than quantity? Is not safety better than speed? Here one touches, perhaps, on the very core of the immigration policy of the Government; it is essentially a policy of forcing immigration rather than merely a policy of welcoming it judiciously. It is a policy of making haste quickly, instead of slowly. Is it not possible that by forcing immigration into Canada, and thus filling Canada with aliens and illiterates as well as with immigrants of a higher type, the Immigration Department is fulfilling its duties not wisely, but too well?

From *The Canadian Magazine*, Vol. XXX (1907-8).

1. According to W.S. Wallace, what has been the relative success of Canadian immigration policy?
2. The author has frequently used rhetorical questions in his article. To what extent does he effectively build an argument using this method?
3. Explain Wallace's contention that Canadian immigration policy has worked "not wisely, but too well."

Warning, 1910

The poster on page 318 appeared as a warning to new immigrants leaving Britain for Canada.

1. Speculate as to the type of "service" being offered to unsuspecting immigrants to Canada.

Immigration to Canada, 1897–1905

The two charts on page 319 list the origins and destinations of immigrants to Canada from 1897 to 1905.

WARNING

TO

INTENDING EMIGRANTS.

The Public is again warned that the system of paying Premiums (or any sum above the ordinary steamship and railway fare) in this Country to gain instruction in Farming in Canada is liable to grave abuse, and is considered by the Canadian Government to be unnecessary. Young men who are going to Canada in order to obtain a knowledge of farming are strongly advised to pay no fee of the kind to any private agency, but to apply for information to the Canadian Assistant Superintendent of Emigration, 11 and 12, Charing Cross, London, S.W., or to the Chief Clerk at this Office.

Emigrants Information Office.
31. Broadway
Westminster. S.W.
April. 1910.

Table 10.1 Number of Immigrant Arrivals in Canada, 1897–1905

Year	Immigrant Arrivals From			Total
	United Kingdom	*United States*	*Other Countries*	
1897	11 383	2 412	7 921	21 716
1898	11 173	9 119	11 608	31 900
1899	10 660	11 945	21 938	44 543
1900*	5 141	8 543	10 211	23 895
1901	11 810	17 987	19 352	49 149
1902	17 259	26 388	23 732	67 379
1903	41 792	49 473	37 099	128 364
1904	50 374	45 171	34 786	130 331
1905	65 359	43 543	37 364	146 266

* 6 months, January to June inclusive

From *The Canada Year Book, 1919*, p. 123. Reprinted with permission of Information Canada.

Table 10.2 Destination of Immigrants into Canada, by Provinces, 1901–1905

Year	Mari-time Prov.	Quebec	Ontario	Mani-toba	Sas-katch-ewan*	B.C. & Yukon	Not Shown
1901	2 144	10 216	6 208	11 254	14 160	2 600	2 567
1902	2 312	8 817	9 798	17 422	22 199	3 483	3 348
1903	5 821	17 040	14 854	39 535	43 898	5 378	1 838
1904	5 448	20 222	21 266	34 911	40 397	6 994	1 093
1905	4 128	23 666	35 811	35 387	39 289	6 008	1 766

* Alberta figures included (neither Alberta nor Saskatchewan existed as provinces during these years).

From *The Canada Year Book, 1919*, p. 126. Reprinted with permission of Information Canada.

1. Create three pie graphs illustrating the origins of immigrants to Canada in 1897, 1901, and 1905.
2. Using bar graphs, show the destinations of immigrants to Canada between 1901 and 1905.
3. Create and defend your own thesis with regard to Canadian immigration patterns during the period.

Immigration to the United States, 1821-1980

The following graphs illustrate immigration patterns to the United States in the nineteenth and twentieth centuries.

Figure 10.1 Recorded United States Immigration, 1821–1980
Total: ca.50 Million

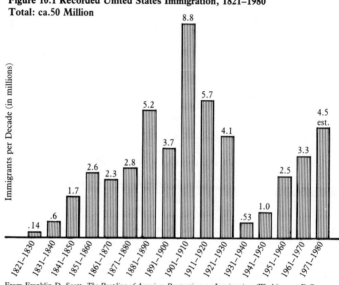

From Franklin D. Scott, *The Peopling of America; Perspectives on Immigration*, (Washington, D.C.: American Historical Association, 1984).

Figure 10.2 European Immigration to America 1900–1920

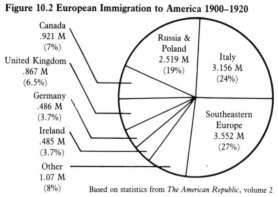

Based on statistics from *The American Republic*, volume 2

1. Compare the average annual per capita immigration to Canada and to the United States in the years around the turn of the century.
2. Compare the origins of immigrants to both countries.
3. Create and defend your own thesis based upon your comparison of immigration to the two countries.

No Streets of Gold, 1896-99

In her 1977 study of Ukrainian immigration to Canada in the late 1890s, Helen Potrebenko examined the reaction of Canadians to their arrival.

More and more Ukrainians came through Edmonton on their way to the settlement at Edna.

The country was going to be overwhelmed by them. All summer long the weird, menacing hundreds trekked east—"damned foreigners," "bloody bohunks."

The press couldn't immediately whip up a hate campaign because of the confusion about who exactly all these people were.

As a result of the recent visit of Professor Oleskow from Austria, there arrived on Monday's train 22 families, comprising about 70 souls in all, of Austrian Poles and naturalized Germans from Galicia. They are described as Ruthenian settlers. (Edmonton *Bulletin.* May 14, 1896) . . .

Almost as soon as the newspapers gave them a name, they began a hate campaign. The Ukrainians were reported to be "uncivilized" (Edmonton *Bulletin.* June 2, 1897) and not properly dressed. (June 10, 1897)

If our foreign immigration agents cannot send us a better class of immigrants than these it is almost time to consider whether we might not dispense with immigration altogether. The southern Slavs are probably the least promising of all material that could be selected for nation-building. (*Daily Nor'wester*, Winnipeg. December 23, 1896) . . .

Some Ukrainians went to work on the CPR's construction of the Crow's Nest Pass railway where the conditions were particularly bad. In some cases, they never got paid. They were told to go to Edmonton to collect their money, but after waiting around for months, could not persuade anyone to pay them.

The police insisted there was nothing wrong with the working conditions on the Crow's Nest Pass railway even though there were an extraordinary number of complaints. Workers always exaggerate, was the cop's attitude. Men who complained of not getting paid were accused of being drunk.

Numerous fatal accidents occurred. They were, as a rule, due to the carelessness of the victims . . . In no instance could they be ascribed to the negligence of the contractors. (L. W. Herchmer to Wilfred Laurier. *Sessional Papers.* Annual Report of the North-West Mounted Police for 1898. p. 40)

As in all such cases, it has most to do with who does the ascribing. Even the reactionary *Bulletin* was upset about the working conditions. Van Horne said the working conditions were no worse in the Crow's Nest Pass than they had been on the main line of the CPR, and that, said the *Bulletin*, was exactly the problem. . . .

In retrospect, it seems despicable that people who were poor and ill should be vilified for no other reason than that they were poor and ill, but it seems to be a capitalist tradition.

The first wave immigrants were usually easy to handle because they didn't speak English and many were illiterate even in their own language. Immigration agents simply told them where the "good" lands were, pointed them in the direction they were to go and never thought about them again. When a new area was opened to settlement, immigration agents took a group of people there, and then their friends and relatives had to follow.

Occasionally there were rebellions. In 1898 an agent named Speers planned to take a group of Ukrainians from Regina to Fish Creek. The people said they didn't want to be homesteaders at all, and at least they wanted to settle near friends and relatives near Edmonton. Speers put them on a train which he said was going to Edmonton. When they discovered it wasn't, they got off the train. Speers sent a pathetic telegram:

> Almost distracted with these people, rebellious, act fiendish, will not leave cars, about 75 struck out walking Regina, perfectly uncontrollable. Nothing but pandemonium since leaving Regina. Have exhausted all legitimate tactics to no avail. Policemen assisting-situation eclipses anything hitherto known. Edmonton, Edmonton, or die. Will not even go inspect country, have offered liberal inducements, threatened to kill interpreter. Under existing circumstances strongly recommend their return to Edmonton and few to Dauphin and get another consignment people special train leaving this afternoon. Could take them Regina. Answer immediately, am simply baffled and defeated. Quietest and only method will be their return. Waiting reply. Mostly have money and will pay fare. They are wicked. (Speers to W. F. McReary. *Sessional Papers*. Annual Report of the Department of the Interior for the year 1898.)

The *Alberta Tribune* of February 4, 1899, reported Father Morin as pushing French Canadians as the ideal settlers and quoted him as saying about Ukrainians:

> As for the Galicians I have not met a single person in the whole of the Northwest who is sympathetic towards them. They are from the point of view of civilization, ten times lower than Indians.

The papers and prominent men also complained frequently that Ukrainians didn't understand democracy and could not help maintain the high standard of "Anglo-Saxon civilization," and similar such absurdities.

What is this country coming to? Doukhobors pouring in by the thousands on the eastern slope, Galicians swarming over the central portions, and rats taking possession of Dawson City, one would imagine that Canada had become a veritable dumping ground for the refuse of civilization. (Calgary *Herald*. February 2, 1899)

No matter what was said about them, Ukrainians were more or less white people, and this was the major consideration in official minds.

A little dose of them may even in variation, do good, like a minute dose of poison in medicine. . . . I am not saying we should absolutely shut out and debar the European foreigner as we should and do shut out the Oriental. But we should in no way facilitate his coming. (Stephen Leacock, 1930)

From Helen Potrebenko, *No Streets of Gold*. (Vancouver: New Star Books, 1977).

1. Discuss the attitude of the local press toward Ukrainian immigrants.
2. Contrast local attitudes toward immigration with official government policy.
3. Account for Potrebenko's contention that "no matter what was said about them, Ukrainians were more or less white people, and this was a major consideration in official minds."

Life in the Camps, 1912

In his book The Bunkhouse Man, *E.W. Bradwin recounts the enticements used to attract immigrant labour to work building railway lines in the Canadian interior.*

It is intended to enter into the actual facts of daily life as they pertained to the hire, the housing, and the pay of men in camps during the last period of railway expansion in Canada.

The present selection will touch briefly on the system of hiring frontier workers through private employment agencies. . . . The following shows something of the system in operation, particularly in the five-year period following 1910.

Even until very recent years the private employment agency was always conspicuous in the various towns adjacent to camp-works. Indeed it was also much in evidence in the larger Canadian centres, such as Ottawa, Edmonton, Montreal, Winnipeg, as well as Fort William, Sudbury, North Bay and other large towns that commonly served as feeders for all kinds of camp labour, required on the various frontier works. . . .

The old "shipping-office" is still remembered: unpretentious and modestly located, perhaps at a corner adjacent to the station or in a nearby lane, these places were the rendezvous for unplaced men. Such an office had always an enticing display of ad-heads plastering the walls and windows. Notices were paraded to advantage on bulletins announcing: "Men Wanted"; "Good Wages Paid Teamsters"; "Labourers for Construction"; "Bushmen Wanted, $40. a month"; "Railway Contractor needs 100 men, $2. per day"; "Men for Station-work," etc., etc. A blackboard tilted at an angle for the advantage of the unemployed conveyed further detailed information of work to be had, while many items already erased showed the danger of delay. Even the sidewalk cement in the front of the stand, chalked in colours, would indicate particularly some tit-bit in the way of employment.

To the man who is down and out, and who has eagerly scanned the boards of different shipping offices, the natural thing to do is to inquire within. Occasionally, but not always, a fee is charged before imparting information as to the details of the work. That will depend on the arrangements already made by the employment agent with the employing company. It is always impressed as an inducement to the men seeking work that the wage offered is considerably higher—perhaps twenty-five cents or fifty cents per day—than that paid locally for a similar class of work.

A common objection raised by men looking for work under such circumstances is the distance to the camp and the railway fare incurred. This, also, is usually coupled with the fact that they have not a cent in their pockets. This predicament, however, while serious, may be easily overcome; the employment agent, because of his relations with the employing firms, can advance the fare. Meals and sleeping places for the whole time en route to the camp—often over a week is consumed in such trips—will be provided for the men, and the whole amount can then be deducted from wages accruing later, once they are located. Sometimes even tobacco is supplied and other inducements are made for the campman to sign up.

Who are the usual applicants at such places? The casuals, some tired of doing nothing, others sore after a big drunk, just the flotsam and jetsam who go to make up the migratory classes in frontier towns. There are others, too, men, foreign-born, newly arrived in the country, and glad of just such an offer to get immediate work with accompanying transportation to their tasks. . . .

With the continued influx of men from the continent to the camps of Canada, in those years immediately preceding the World War, many of the employment agencies paid particular attention to the foreign-born workers. Quite often such private offices were conducted by men who themselves were not naturalized citizens in the Dominion. Offices thus operated appeared to work in chains.

The methods of all private agencies, which catered particularly to the illiterate foreign-born, varied but little. The main thing was to get the newcomers from Central Europe, blessed as they are with strong arms and broad backs, hastily signed-up and forwarded. Duly informed of the prospective arrival of an immigrant ship, a representative of these agencies would meet the Atlantic boat, crowded with the new arrivals, at the docks. Some agents more enterprising than the others would, when permitted, come up the river from Quebec City with the men in the steerage.

Such labour recruits were, of course, pleased to learn so soon of profitable employment awaiting them. Upon landing at Montreal they were herded directly to the agency; there they were patted and stroked the right way until they signed up. Then they were soon hustled to a railway camp hundreds of miles distant somewhere in the hinterland. Not infrequently these newcomers from beyond the Atlantic were landed at a frontier work with little more real knowledge of the settled parts of Canada than was already surmised before leaving their native village somewhere in central Europe. Their first impressions of the new land, now that they had arrived, were gleaned intermittently from a car window, as the woods and rocks and lakes of the unsettled northland sped past in ever-widening circles.

Not uncommonly such workers were enticed by the smooth-tongued individuals, rich in dialects, who, while a countryman of theirs, was already experienced in methods of hire common through the Dominion. Such a man was indeed invaluable toward making for the success of any privately-conducted agency. To observe his tactics among his group of nationals, when, for days at a time, a construction train slowly makes its way out from the end of the steel, is to note his callous attitude toward the real interests of his fellow-countrymen. In doing work of this nature he is not unlike the trained steer of the stockyards which decoys into chosen channels its kindred brutes, yet always to its own advantage. . . .

From Edmund Bradwin, *The Bunkhouse Man* , (Toronto: University of Toronto Press, 1972).

1. Why would employment agents be so anxious to hire immigrant labour?
2. What impression of Canada did the employment agents give these new immigrants? Why was it not an accurate impression?
3. Read *The Bunkhouse Man*. To what extent did the treatment of immigrant labour differ from that afforded to Native Canadians?

Arrival

In the following excerpt, popular historian Pierre Berton describes the arrival of a Doukhobor immigrant to Winnipeg in 1902.

It is a crisp winter afternoon in Winnipeg, three days before Christmas, 1902. We are standing on the CPR platform, waiting impatiently for the eastern train, which is three hours late. A small knot of people has been here since noon and one, a woman, has waited since early morning. The anarchist Herbert Archer is here—that strange graduate from Purleigh who has dedicated his life to the Doukhobor cause and whom Wes Speers believes has had as much to do as anybody in stirring up the fanatics earlier this autumn. Crerar, the immigration agent from Yorkton, is here too. Three Doukhobor elders, an interpreter, and one reporter (from the *Free Press*, of course) make up the delegation.

At last the train hisses in. A crowd of holidayers surges forward to meet another crowd of holidayers pouring from the cars, their luggage stuffed with Christmas parcels. We crane our necks vainly for the object of our long wait. At last we spot him, towering over the throng. He alights from the coach and starts down the platform—a big man, half a head taller than his fellow passengers, with a luxuriant black beard and dark, thoughtful eyes. He is not dressed like the others: under his short gabardine coat we can see leggings, close fitting, dark grey, piped with black. He wears a black fedora, and around his neck, on a long cord, dangle a silver watch and a gold pencil.

The woman rushes toward him, followed by her Doukhobor companions. He drops his black nickel-studded valise, removes his hat, stretches out his arms to embrace her, and cries: "Anna!" She is his sister. He is Peter Verigin. They have not seen each other for fifteen years.

She clings to his arm as he walks quietly on toward the rest of the reception committee. We all repair to the immigration building where the acting commissioner, Moffat, who has replaced the ailing McCreary (now enjoying a well-earned rest as a Member of Parliament for Selkirk), greets him warmly.

"You'll be glad to be in a country where there is religious and individual freedom," says Moffat.

"I haven't looked around yet," replies Peter Verigin in his soft voice, "so I cannot yet tell whether this is a free country or not." . . .

From Pierre Berton, *The Promised Land: Settling the West 1896-1914*, (Toronto: McClelland & Stewart, 1984).

Here, Yuri Bruce describes his life in Moose Jaw in 1908 after immigrating to Canada two years earlier.

I was born in the village of Rashkiv, Horodenskoho county of Stanislavschina in 1886. When I was seven my father died, and we were left in the care of my eldest brother. My eldest brother went to Canada in 1903—to Winnipeg. In 1906 my mother died. We were left complete orphans. I was already 20 years old. My brother gave me money for the fare and I went to Canada.

. . . In Trieste the agent exacted from us some money, because he said he had heavy expenses because of us. Therefore we didn't have enough money to get to Winnipeg and had to get off the train in Sudbury.

We arrived in Sudbury on a Sunday. Here some people greeted us and asked us to stay at Copper Cliff. One man, named Kharuk, who had come to Canada in 1901, proposed that we look for work here. He said it was already May and warm, so we could go on foot to Sudbury and after that, wander down the main road and go find work somewhere. . . .

In Chapleau we got work cleaning a yard. After that we took *genok*. We dug six feet and cleaned the track for the laying of rails. Here I worked three months.

When my brother learned where I was, he wrote me to join him in Winnipeg without fail, because he had work for me. But the boss didn't want me to go, saying I was a good worker and could have a steady job. I waited for three days for him to release me so I could go to Winnipeg.

But I didn't go directly to Winnipeg, but stopped at Fort William and worked there between Ignace and Kenora. Again I worked three months. My brother wrote from Winnipeg that he had suffered enough in Canada and was returning to the Old Country.

It was already September when I got to Winnipeg. I earned a bit of money at various jobs and in 1908 sponsored my younger brother Wasyl. This was a difficult year. There were no jobs. Months went by, and people wandered around without a job. . . .

In Winnipeg, Main Street was being built, and they were paving it. I thought I might get work there, but they told me to leave town immediately, because there was no hope of getting a job.

I went from place to place, cut hay for a farmer, to survive somehow, to keep from starving. On Barber Street in Winnipeg people were dying of hunger. Many were returned home to Europe.

We used to go to the CPR office in Winnipeg. A clerk would come out and take one or two—and that's all. Then the police would appear from all directions and thrash the immigrants with clubs, scattering them from around the office.

They were signing up people for work in Moose Jaw. About 35 of us signed up. They brought us by train and uncoupled the car. In the morning we were given breakfast and told to go to work. It turned out that a strike had begun, and we had been brought as strike-breakers. We hesitated to go to work. The boss said that we had got breakfast, but if we didn't work, we wouldn't get dinner. We answered: We may die of hunger, but we won't be strike-breakers. And not one of us went to be a scab. From there we all went in different directions. . . .

In 1910 I returned to the Old Country. They punished me with a two-day jail sentence, because they said I hadn't registered for the draft soon enough. Immediately they put me in the 58th regiment, infantry, 4th battalion. It belonged to Bosnia-Herzegovina. All of 1910 I served in the army. We were drilled and told: Before you die, you must kill seven Russians!

I thought to myself, I was in Canada and saw different people, a different world, and I must die for the Emperor if the war begins? As soon as I was out of the army, I bought a ticket and in 1912 came to B.C., where I had previously worked. . . . When I first arrived in B.C., I was followed by a registered letter in which I was ordered to return without delay—not to the village, but straight to Bosnia-Herzegovina to the 58th regiment, 4th battalion. I sent the letter back and didn't obey the will of the Emperor.

Came the year 1914—no work. . . .

I went to the CPR office because I thought something might turn up for me, but the company police drove us away with clubs. Some people were badly beaten on their backs.

We then gathered to look for jobs in other places. When we left Moose Jaw, the police stopped us and asked for registration cards. We said we had none, because no one in Moose Jaw had told us anything about it. They arrested us and took us to Estevan, from there to Weyburn, then to Brandon. We were kept in Brandon for 12 months. We were kept in huge barracks under army guard—we were regarded as "enemies" because we came from Halychina which was under Austro-Hungary and fought against Canada. There were 1200 of us.

From Helen Potrebenko, *No Streets of Gold*. (Vancouver: New Star Books, 1977).

Sinefta Ribka came to Canada at the age of fourteen. Like many immigrants of the period, her father had come first in order to earn enough money to transport his family. In this excerpt she describes the war years in Calgary.

I came from the village of Shypintsi in Bukovina. My girlhood name was Senefta Ribka. I was born in 1898. My parents were poor peasants—they had a house, three-quarters of a *morg* of land, domestic fowl. We had no horses. Our family was made of up five persons. One child died in infancy. . . .

I went to school and finished five grades. Father twice went to Canada to earn money and then returned home. The third time he took the whole family with him. This was in 1912. We went from Antwerp and arrived in Montreal in April. We were brought on a cargo ship—one which normally transported cattle. The emigrants were poorly fed.

I shall never forget the moment we left our dear village, when Mother stood on the step crying bitterly that she was leaving her native land, parting from her people, going to an unknown foreign land. Father comforted her, saying there were many of our villagers in Canada.

Father had taken out a homestead there before his third trip home.

We arrived in Calgary and were to change trains there for Edmonton. At the station an acquaintance of my father's, who was a foreman on a railway construction project, began persuading him not to go to the homestead but to remain in the city. Father heeded his advice, and we stayed in Calgary. Here he worked at various city jobs.

I began to work as a domestic labourer for rich people for $10 a month.

In 1915 at the time of the First World War, I got a job washing dishes in a restaurant. One time some drunk soldiers broke into the restaurant and demanded that the owner fire "Austrians" because they were "enemies." The owner, afraid the drunk soldiers would break windows, had to fire us. Because of his "Austrianness," my father also lost his job. . . .

One time Father was almost taken to a concentration camp over nonsense. We had an empty tobacco can on which were some German *cherbi* or little flags, because the tobacco had been imported from Europe. One of us had covered a window with this box. A policeman passing by had seen this and thought it must be to demonstrate our "pro-German" sympathies. One day soldiers broke into the house to take my father to the camp. Mother cried and pleaded that the children would perish if they took him away. The soldiers took pity on us and left Father at home. . . .

We returned to Calgary to our house which had stood empty for a year. I got a job in a restaurant as a waitress. I was paid $7 a week. One time two people came into the restaurant and asked me how many hours I worked and how much I earned. They were organizing restaurant workers into a union. This was 1916 or 1917. Having organized the workers, they called a strike in restaurants and hotels in Calgary.

At the time of the strike I understood many things, experienced injustice, and saw great dishonesty among people. The results of this struggle were higher wages for restaurant workers.

Therefore, to the Ukrainian progressive movement I came, because of the union, because of the strike battle. . . .

In 1918 I met Hrehory Kizima, who came to Calgary from Canmore where he worked as a miner. He came from our village—Shypyntsi. The same year we were married. He was already a member of the Ukrainian Social Democratic Party. He took me with him to Canmore.

From Helen Potrebenko, *No Streets of Gold* , (Vancouver: New Star Books,1977).

1. Account for Peter Verigin's attitude toward freedom in Canada.
2. Discuss the experiences of Ukrainian immigrants during the first decades of the century.

3. Research your own immigrant roots. Write a brief analysis comparing your family's experience with those described here.

The Response to Immigration

Longtime residents such as Henry Starr from Qu'Appelle were typical of the nativist sentiment that greeted many immigrants to North America. In the first excerpted letter, Starr files a complaint with regard to German immigrants in the area. The second letter is from an officer of the Northwest Mounted Police who was sent to investigate the complaint.

PAC, RCMP Records, Section A-1, vol. 97, no. 587.
Starr's Point
Qu'Appelle Station,
Assa: N.W.T., July 17th, 1894
The Hon. T. M. Daly,
Minister of the Interior,
Ottawa.
My dear Sir,

The past year or two this part of the Territories, have had quite a number of German Emigrants settled here, who have turned out to be the very worst and lowest class of people under the sun, and who are considered quite a nuisance, and ought to be banished from the country otherwise they will be the means of driving every respectable settler out of the place. They steal and plunder whatever they can lay their hands on, and now, they go about, under cover of the night, and cut and steal and carry away Hay wherever they can get it and are not at all particular to whom it belongs, and every settler is complaining about them. I have had upwards of twenty tons of hay cut and taken away by them, even close to my crop, and not more than one mile from my residence, all done during the night. My object in writing is to draw your attention to the facts, and to ascertain whether anything can be done to put a stop to such doings, or must the settlers submit to it. Possibly if the Police had authority to be on the look out and watch their movements by night and by day, and when caught to have them imprisoned, and made to pay damages, it may have the effect of stopping their game both as with regard to stealing wood as well as Hay. Something must be done, and that very soon.

Kindly favour me with a reply immediately.
Believe me,
Yours faithfully,
"Sd." D. Henry Starr.
N.W.M. Police

Qu'Appelle, Aug. 14th, 1894.
The Officer Commanding
B. Division
Regina.

Sir,—

I have the honour to report as follows, re the enclosed communication. I proceeded to Mr. D. Henry Starr's residence to-day and, in reply to my questions he informed me, that he had no reasons to suspect the German settlers of being "the very worst and lowest class of people under the sun" only from what he has heard about them, having had no dealings with them himself. He suspects them of taking his hay from what he has heard about them and states, that he was informed, that a German was offering a load of hay for sale in Qu'Appelle Station which looked like what his hay would be when cut. In regards to his statement "they steal and plunder whatever they can lay their hands on," he is unable to prove it as he admits he never had anything stolen except hay which might just as likely be taken by any other class of settlers, as the hay crop being a failure this year, no one was particular where they obtained it. I visited a number of settlers in the vicinity, none of whom had any complaints regarding the conduct of those Germans beyond the fact that they suspected them of having taken hay where they had no right to it; but admitted that any other settler would do the same this year. The nearest German settler is about seven miles west of Mr. Starr's residence.

I might state, from my own experience with those Germans, I am not prepared to say they are any worse than other class of settlers. A few cases have been brought against some of them for wood stealing and they have been punished.

I have the honor to be,

Sir,

Your obedient servant

D. Holmes, Corpl.

From Public Archives of Canada, *RCMP Records*, (Ottawa, 1894)

1. What accusations does Starr lay against the German settlers?
2. To what extent are his charges substantiated by the Mounties?
3. Account for the nativist attitudes of Canadians such as Starr against immigrants arriving in the area.

Mountain of Gold: The Chinese Experience

Chinese-American author Betty Lee Sung examined the experience of Chinese immigrants to the United States in her book Mountain of Gold. *In an early chapter she describes the changes in attitude which led to the Chinese exclusion legislation of the 1890s.*

For their contribution to the early development of the West, the Chinese deserved recognition and gratitude. But as their ranks increased, alarm developed. Popular sentiment shifted from welcome to hatred and from praise to blame. Hounded and persecuted, the Chinese were driven from the West and excluded from the country.

How come? Why the abrupt about-face in attitude? Did the Chinese change for the worse? Were they at fault to cause the people to turn against them? No, the reasons were not logical; they grew out of the social, economic, and political climate of the West at that time. . . .

The East was experiencing a depression in the aftermath of the Civil War and Reconstruction. There had been hopes that the completion of the transcontinental railroad would open up boundless horizons and unlimited prosperity in the West. But the drain off of excess labor in the East only aggravated the conditions in the western labor market. . . .

Of those who swarmed into California, some were farmers who came with the intention of buying and tilling small tracts such as they had known at home. But small tracts were hardly ever sold; the few that were offered for sale were outrageously overpriced, their owners holding out for large profits. Meanwhile, they could hire farm hands to work the fields. The farm hands were recruited in the spring and laid off after the harvest.

The political climate of California led James Bryce to conclude in his *The American Commonwealth*:

> Both in the country and in the city there was disgust with politics and the politicians. The legislature was composed almost wholly either of office-seekers from the city or of petty country lawyers, needy and narrow-minded men. Those who had virtue, enough not to be "got at" by the great corporations, had not intelligence enough to know how to resist their devices. It was a common saying in the State that each successive legislature was worse than its predecessor. . . . County government was little better; city government was even worse. The judges were not corrupt, but most of them, as was natural, considering the scanty salaries assigned to them, were inferior men, not fit to cope with the counsel who practiced before them. Partly owing to the weakness of juries, partly to the intricacies of the law and the effects of the recently adopted code, criminal justice was halting and uncertain, and malefactors often went unpunished.

California was ripe for a demagogue, who emerged in the person of Dennis Kearney. Kearney, an Irish sailor, had ridden the tides of modest success, but on the advice of a friend, had committed himself heavily in mining stocks. Caught in the landslide, he was reduced to practically nothing. Embittered, he took to haranguing in the empty sand lots where construction was going up. At first, only a few hoodlums and vagabonds paid any heed to his thundering vituperations. These would have been passed off as the blubberings of another malcontent if the *Chronicle,* one of the two leading newspapers in San Francisco, had not championed him.

In keen rivalry with the *Morning Call,* the *Chronicle* was looking for a popular issue that would boost its circulation. A reporter was dispatched to the sand lots and instantaneously recognized the makings of a circulation booster. The reporter polished up Kearney's harangues, making them spit fire and venom. Each day, his "utterings" were reported faithfully by the *Chronicle* until he was built into a hero—champion of the "downtrodden workingman." His followers were organized into the California Workingmen's Party.

The *Morning Call,* having missed the boat in bidding for the support of the workingmen, made up for lost time. Each tried to outdo the other in reporting Kearney's demagoguery, most of which they helped write.

Kearney's targets were the land and rail monopolies and the Chinese. . . .

In this explosive social, economic, and political climate, the heavy concentration of Chinese in California made them a convenient scapegoat for the relief of pent-up frustrations and emotions. In 1870, there were 63 000 Chinese in the United States, 99 percent of whom were on the west coast. Every tenth person in California in 1860 was Chinese. Their large numbers, their physical differences, the retention of their national dress, the custom of wearing their hair in pigtails, their habits and traditions, so incomprehensible to the Occidental mind, made them a target easy to spot.

When employment with the railroad ceased, the Chinese sought work in the mines, on the farms, in land reclamation, in domestic service, and in the cigar and woolen factories. These were jobs which the white man scorned, for the white man was looking for a quick bonanza. Nevertheless, they were jobs that gave the Chinese employment while the white man was out of work.

So whereas the Chinese had been praised for their industry, their honesty, their thrift, and their peaceful ways, they were now charged with being debased and servile coolies, clannish, dangerous, deceitful, and vicious. They were accused of being contract laborers, although there was no shred of evidence to show that the Chinese were anything but Argonauts of a different skin coloring. Degenerate traits were ascribed to them, in direct contradiction to the praises heaped upon them a few years earlier. The workingmen accused them of undermining the white man's standard of living. It was alleged they could work for less because they subsisted on next to nothing. The word was spread that the land and rail monopolies hired Chinese instead of white men because the Chinese accepted employment at any price. Yet the books kept by Charles Crocker of the Central Pacific showed that white men were paid at the rate of $35 per month plus keep, and the Chinese were paid $35 per month without keep, mainly because the Chinese preferred cooking their own food.

The charge of accepting slave wages was shortly disproved after the exclusion laws took effect. The drastic curtailment in immigration brought about a shortage in Chinese laborers. Quick to take advantage of the situation, Chinese laborers demanded and got higher wages for their services—this in spite of a surplus in white labor.

However, reason and fact could not prevail. Elmer Clarence Sandmeyer wrote:

> . . . there would have been a depression in the 1870s if the entire population had been made up of lineal descendants of George Washington. . . . If the Chinese in California were white people, being in all other respects what they are, I do not believe that the complaints and warfare against them would have existed to any considerable extent.

But once the charges were made, they spread like a prairie fire, fanned red-hot by Dennis Kearney.

Kearney invariably began his speeches with an attack upon the monopolies—

the rich, huge corporate enterprises. He pointed out their owners' ornate mansions on Nob Hill and blamed these moguls for the plight of the workingmen. He accused the Chinese of working hand-in-hand with monopolies, of accepting slave wages, and of robbing the white man of his job. His wrath was directed against both the Chinese and the land and rail monopolies, but the latter were powerful, impregnable, organized, while the Chinese were docile, eager to avoid conflict, and ineffectual in court because their testimony could not be accepted as evidence. Kearney's speeches always ended with the slogan, "The Chinese must go!" So the blame fell upon the Chinese, and thus supplied with a hate object, the frenzied, incited mob would dash off to another orgy of attacks upon the defenseless Chinese.

During this period, the Chinese were stoned and robbed, assaulted and murdered. Hoodlums would organize attacks against the Chinese camps as sport, for they knew the Chinese could not obtain redress.

Professor Mary Coolidge wrote: "During the years of Kearneyism, it is a wonder that any Chinese remained alive in the U.S."

Murdering Chinese became such a commonplace occurrence that the newspapers seldom bothered to print the stories. Police officials winked at the attacks, and politicians all but incited more of the same. There were thousands of cases of murder, robbery, and assault, but in only two or three instances were the guilty brought to justice.

If murders were commonplace, the indignities, abuse, brutalities, and injustices practiced against the Chinese were outrageous. An oldtimer told of the indignities he suffered at the hands of drunken white men:

> Every Saturday night, we never knew whether we would live to see the light of day. We operated a laundry near a mining camp. Saturday was the night for the miners to get drunk. They would force their way into our shop, wrest the clean white bundles from the shelves and trample the shirts which we so laboriously finished. If the shirts were torn, we were forced to pay for the damages. One night, one of the miners hit his face against the flat side of an iron. He went away, but we knew that our lives were now in danger so we fled, leaving all of our possessions and money behind. The miner came back with a mob who ransacked our shop, robbed us of the $360 that was our combined savings and set fire to the laundry. We were lucky to escape with our lives, so we came east.

Whereas most Chinese had gone straight to San Francisco upon their arrival in the United States, they now began to disperse. Some had already gone north to work on the Northern Pacific and Canadian Pacific Railroads. Others sought work in the silver and coal mines of Nevada, Oregon, Wyoming, and Colorado. But prejudice and hatred confronted them everywhere. The anti-Chinese sentiments had spread like a cancerous growth to other parts of the West. . . .

The Chinese had no recourse. Neither the state, the federal, nor the Chinese government provided them any protection. . . .

The Scott Act redefined *Chinese* as any member of the Chinese race, whether subjects of China or any other nation. It callously prohibited the return of any

Chinese who had been employed as a laborer or miner, whether he held a validated return certificate or not. . . . This meant that 20 000 Chinese laborers who had gone back to China for a visit with re-entry permits and with every intention of returning to their jobs or their businesses here were locked out of the country. Many owned property and some had set up families, but they were denied re-entry. . . .

After the passage of the Scott Act, the Chinese Minister in Washington registered his government's protest with the State Department. He was not even given the courtesy of an answer or acknowledgement. . . .

The Republicans wanted to be on record as having outdone the Democrats on the Chinese question and they had demonstrated their ferocity. . . .

The election of 1888 passed, and the country settled down to another four years. With the coming of 1892, the whole story was repeated. Harsher measures were demanded and harsher measures were passed. This time, the bill was called the Geary Act of 1892. It practically stripped the Chinese of any protection in courts, singled out the Chinese to be denied the rights upon which western justice is based, and subjected to suspicion all Chinese in the United States. . . .

Chinese exclusion legislation rode the waves of political elections. And though Chinese immigration was a dying cinder, the heat of the elections generally managed to fan a little more life into it. The Chinese were yet to see many other acts of Congress directed specifically at them. . . .

Never in the history of the United States had the nationals of another friendly, sovereign state been so humiliated, so disgraced. Later, the Japanese were also excluded, but it was the Japanese government under a Gentlemen's Agreement with the United States that undertook to screen the emigrants. The Chinese were the only people specifically named in legislation to be excluded from the United States. It was an affront that still rankles in the hearts of many Chinese.

From B.L. Sung, *Mountain of Gold* , (New York: Macmillan, 1967).

1. How does Sung describe early life in California?
2. By 1860 one out of every ten Californians was Chinese. Why did society turn against them in the latter part of the century?
3. Account for the emergence of anti-Asian sentiment in American legislation in the late nineteenth century.

The Asian Experience in Canada

The following reports written by officers of the Northwest Mounted Police in 1892 provide graphic evidence of anti-Chinese sentiment in Calgary.

N.W.M. Police,
Calgary 3rd August 1892.
The Commissioner,
Regina.

Sir,

I have the honour to report the following circumstances:-

Yesterday evening the health Officer released the Chinamen who had been in quarantine. . . . The streets were in possession of a drunken mob and the Chinese habitations being sacked at about the same time (about midnight) a chinaman came to me asking for protection and another was brought by a citizen. They were being ill used, some had run out in the Country and 6 had been sheltered by Mr. Dean the Methodist clergyman in the parsonage. Realizing that mob law could not be allowed to prevail in the N.W.T. even in a Municipality and that serious trouble might ensue I turned out some men and went up town with the intention of acting under the statutes if necessary. The Town authorities seemed completely demoralized and in the absence of the Mayor none of them (including the Actg Mayor) knew what to do. There was a town constable visible but he was quite powerless to check the lawlessness. . . .

Three arrests were made and the streets cleared. The effect was so instantaneous that some of the crowd who were mounted left their horses behind. 10 chinamen sought shelter in Barracks going away again this morning.

We kept streets clear till 4 a.m., but everything was quiet after our first appearance. . . .

N.W.M.P.
Calgary, 6th August 1892.
The Commissioner,
Regina.
Sir,

Up to the present there has been no attempt at a disturbance re. the Chinamen, but I understand it is said by the hot headed ones that they will gain their ends in spite of the Mounted Police, this however may be only idle talk.

There are no new cases of small-pox & sixteen persons are to be allowed out of quarantine this evening.

The chinaman who was allowed out from quarantine on the 2nd inst and who ran away during the riot found by us at Langdon & brought in last night. At his own request he has been provided with a ticket & certificate of health by the Board of Health & leaves tonight for Vancouver.

The Mayor after his absence yesterday returned this a.m. and I presume will disappear again tonight.

The Council are ignoring him however & the respectable inhabitants speak of taking decided & vigorous measures in dealing with him.

All possible steps in so far as the strength of the Division will allow have been taken to deal with a disturbance.

I have etc. etc.,

(Sgd.) A. Ross Cuthbert, Insp.

N.W.M. Police,
Calgary, 19th August 1892.
The Commissioner,
Regina,

Sir, . . .

A man by the name of Locksley Lucas arrived here Wednesday to lecture against the Chinese. He did not succeed in arousing much sympathy in his subject and in his attempt to form an Anti-Chinese league he only received Mr. Orr as a member of a Provisional Committee and Mayor Lucas, who was also chairman of the entertainment. Being very down hearted at his treatment yesterday he attempted suicide at his hotel by taking opium. . . .

There is little talk now of Chinese disturbances and I have discontinued a day patrol, but still keep a N.C.O. and 2 men on Town duty from 8 P.M. till after train time. The scheme which the rabble contemplated of which I was privately informed and which was to start an uproar in some distant part of the town to draw the Mounted Police while a few of the leaders could wreak their will on the Chinese undisturbed, has evidently been abandoned. . . .

I have etc. etc.,

(Sgd.)A. Ross Cuthbert, Insp.

From Public Archives of Canada, *RCMP Records*, (Ottawa, 1892).

Anti-Oriental riots in Vancouver in 1907 resulted in a tightening of Canadian immigration regulations through the use of a head tax. To protect its own people, the Chinese Board of Trade issued the following warning to prospective immigrants.

At present business of all kinds is dull all over Canada, and employment in any kind of labor is hard to obtain. Only about one-third of the Canneries are in operation. The Shingle Mills, Factories of every industry, and Working Mines industry have shut down to more than one-half of their usual activity. Besides, Japanese and Hindu laborers have come in large numbers, hence wages have been reduced. White laborers look upon these with ill feeling, and are organizing to force out our people from all kinds of works.

On September last White laborers gathered in large numbers, marched through the streets, and smashed the doors and windows of our people. We were forced to stop business for several days. Besides all this, owing to the stringency of the money market in the States, business in Canada is greatly affected. At present many of our people are out of employment . . .

As all immigrants have to pay a head tax of $500 gold, which is more than $1000 in our money, and that money, many of them, may have to borrow or sell their property to obtain the same, thinking that they can easily earn it back and many times over on their arrival here, will be sorely disappointed. They will find that the conditions here are very hard, without work, and perhaps much harder than in China. It is doubly so, because the cost of living, here is about 5 times more than in our own country. If he should be without work for a single month he will find his savings will soon be gone.

Public Archives of Canada, W.L.M. King Papers, Vol. 13, MG26, J4. Translation of Circular Letter issued by the Chinese Board of Trade. From P.W. Bennett, et al., *Emerging Identities* , (Scarborough: Prentice-Hall, 1986).

1. Describe the situation for Chinese residents in Calgary.
2. Comment on the warning issued by the Chinese Board of Trade. What comment does it make about Canadian society?
3. Compare the anti-Oriental feelings evident in Canada and the United States during this period.

Making Room: "Civilizing" the Native People, 1881

The influx of European and Asian immigrants in the second half of the nineteenth century put a great deal of pressure on the availability of arable land in the West. To many Americans the solution was to "reclaim" much of the territory which had been deeded over to Native nations. In this message, President Chester Arthur offers his solution to "civilizing" Native peoples.

Prominent among the matters which challenge the attention of Congress at its present session is the management of our Indian affairs. . . .

It was natural, at a time when the national territory seemed almost illimitable and contained many millions of acres far outside the bounds of civilized settlements, that a policy should have been initiated which more than aught else has been the fruitful source of our Indian complications.

I refer, of course, to the policy of dealing with the various Indian tribes as separate nationalities, of relegating them by treaty stipulations to the occupancy of immense reservations in the West, and of encouraging them to live a savage life, undisturbed by any earnest and well-directed efforts to bring them under the influence of civilization.

The unsatisfactory results which have sprung from this policy are becoming apparent to all.

As the white settlements have crowded the borders of the reservations, the Indians, sometimes contentedly and sometimes against their will, have been transferred to other hunting grounds, from which they have again been dislodged whenever their new-found homes have been desired by the adventurous settlers.

These removals and the frontier collisions by which they have often been preceded have led to frequent and disastrous conflicts between the races. . . .

For the success of the efforts now making to introduce among the Indians the customs and pursuits of civilized life and gradually absorb them into the mass of our citizens, sharing their rights and holden to their responsibilities, there is an imperative need for legislative action. . . .

In return for such considerate action on the part of the Government, there is reason to believe that the Indians in large numbers would be persuaded to sever their tribal relations and to engage at once in agricultural pursuits. Many of them realize the fact that their hunting days are over and that it is now for their best interests to conform their manner of life to the new order of things. By no greater inducement than the assurance of permanent title to the soil can they be led to engage in the occupation of tilling it. . . .

Even among the most uncultivated Indian tribes there is reported to be a general and urgent desire on the part of the chiefs and older members for the education of their children. . . .

Boarding schools are doubtless much more potent for good than the day schools upon the reservation, as the pupils are altogether separated from the surroundings of savage life and brought into constant contact with civilization. . . .

From Chester A. Arthur, *First Annual Message*, (December 6, 1881), in William Graebner, Leonard Richards, ed., *The American Record*, (New York: Alfred Knopf, 1982).

1. How does Arthur describe the process by which valuable land was "lost" to Native peoples?
2. What role does education play in his plans?
3. Comment upon the underlying bias which characterizes the president's remarks.

Immigration—A World Problem, c.1905

In his book on the immigration problem in Canada, Strangers within our Gates, *J.S. Woodsworth opened his discussion by quoting the following passage from an American book of the period.*

Out of the remote and little known region of northern, eastern, and southern Europe forever marches a vast and endless army. Nondescript and ever changing in personnel, without leaders or organization, this great force, moving at the rate of nearly 1 500 000 each year, is invading the civilized world. . . .

It is a vast procession of varied humanity. In tongue it is polygot; in dress, all climes, from pole to equator, are indicated, and all religions and beliefs enlist their followers. There is no age limit, for young and old travel side by side. There is no sex limitation, for the women are as keen, if not more so, than the men; and babes in arms are here in no mean numbers. . . .

Gaining in volume and momentum with each passing year, without apparent regard for the law of supply and demand, the pressure of this army has already made itself felt upon the communities in which it finds its destination. The cry of protest has gone up from those who find themselves crowded from their occupations and their homes by the new arrivals, and peoples are demanding of their Governments that some steps be taken to check this alien invasion.

From J.S. Woodsworth, *Strangers within our Gates* , (Toronto: University of Toronto Press, 1972).

1. How does the author describe the immigration "stream"?

The Cartoonist Looks at Immigration

The editorial cartoon on page 339 appeared in 1879. In it we see a clear expression of American nativist sentiment.

1. Write an analysis of the cartoon. Include a clear statement of the thesis presented, a discussion of the issues, and your evaluation of the effectiveness of the message being conveyed.

"EVERY DOG" (NO DISTINCTION OF COLOR) "HAS HIS DAY."

February 8, 1879

RED GENTLEMAN TO YELLOW GENTLEMAN. "Pale face 'fraid you crowd him out, as he did me."

Winnipeg, Melting Pot of the Dominion, 1909

In this article which appeared in The Canadian Magazine *in September 1909, George Fisher Chipman commented upon the price paid by Winnipeg for the success of Canada's immigration policy.*

No other city of its age and size has been advertised throughout the world as much as Winnipeg, the gateway of the prairie region, which has added so greatly to the wealth and prestige of the Dominion. . . .

Up to the present time the immigrants have not all been of the hand-picked variety, but an improvement is now apparent. Men of the old lands in whose bosom there is the spark of hope or ambition are still stirred by the thought of homes in Canada free for the asking. . . .

Winnipeg holds a place by itself among Canadian cities. Less than half of its people are Canadians, while one-third are either foreign born or the children of foreign parents—which in many instances means the same thing. The rapid influx of immigration during the last fifteen years has been the cause. In the great Republic to the south immigration in proportion to the population has never been one-third as great as it has been in Canada. Yet the people of that glorious nation have failed miserably in the problem of the cities. Hardly a writer or public speaker of the present day touches on the subject of American humanity without deploring the fact of the poverty and suffering in the big cities.

. . . Proper precautions taken now will do much to avoid a repetition in Winnipeg where to-day is being worked out the greatest problem of assimilation ever cast upon a city of the same size on the continent. The fusion of races in the melting-pot is unceasing. . . .

The problem in Winnipeg is more serious than even the majority of people in that city appreciate . . . The mixed races were brough to the country by the Government, and once in the city the municipality has to deal with them. They are the unfortunate produce of a civilization that is a thousand years behind the Canadian; but nevertheless they are what they are, and that thousand years is a wide chasm to bridge. A generation seems a long time to transform people, but if Galicians can be made into representative Canadians in one generation it will be a good work. The hope lies with the younger members. The training of centuries cannot be cast off like a mantle and a new one taken on. . . . The older generation can only be pitied, regulated, aided, and endured, while the younger ones can be watched, fostered, and developed into Canadians through the regular channels.

From George Fisher Chipman, *The Canadian Magazine*. Vol. XXXIII (September, 1909).

1. Describe the pattern of immigration and settlement in Winnipeg.
2. Comment on the author's picture of Winnipeg as unique among Canadian cities of the period.

Strangers within our Gates, 1910

James Shaver Woodsworth, the future leader of the CCF, was alarmed by the rate of immigration to Canada around the turn of the century. He predicted that Canada would not be able absorb the numbers fast enough.

Immigration and transportation are the two questions of greatest importance to Canada. From the situation, extent and character of the country, transportation must always be one of the leading factors in industrial and commercial development. But as men are greater than things, so immigration is greater than transportation. Canada has many problems, but they all dwindle into insignificance before the one great, commanding, overwhelming problem of immigration. Of vital importance to us are the character, the welfare and the development of the peoples who are to be the peoples of Canada.

Perhaps we can best approach our subject by studying the immigration movement in the United States. Great social and economic developments over-ride political divisions. . . .

Now, who were these immigrants, and why did they come, and what did their coming mean to the American Republic?

Going back to the old colonial days, the "immigrants" to America were from England. . . .

How different they and their coming from the immigration of to-day! They made great sacrifices. They had to undertake a long, expensive and perilous journey. They came to an unexplored wilderness inhabited only by savages. They had to create a civilization. To-day our immigrants, or their friends, pay a few pounds' passage money, and in a week or so are safely transported to a land with institutions similar to their own, and in which they hope at once to "do better" than they did at home.

Besides the English of the early days there were the enterprising Dutch merchants who ventured forth across the seas and pushed their trade in regions unknown. Later two other elements were added, the German and the Scotch-Irish. . . .

A different and less desirable class of immigrants now began to arrive. Greatest in numbers and importance were the Irish. The potato rot in Ireland in 1846 drove thousands from their homes. Since then there has been a steady stream of those who sought to escape from poverty and from the hated rule of England. They have played no small part in the political life of the United States. Immigrants kept coming from England and Scotland and Germany. A large immigration of Scandinavians set in. Each decade drained a wider area of Europe; but the large majority were people fitted for the new civilization.

About 1882 a remarkable change took place in the character of immigration. Southeastern Europe had been tapped and the stream came with a rush.

. . . We are receiving immigrants from all parts of Europe—that is, we are taking our place side by side with the United States as the Old World's dumping ground. As the sluices are closed there, the flood will be diverted to Canada, whatever the policy of the Government may happen to be. As the free lands are taken in the United States, and the pressure of population begins to be felt, the flood will flow in upon us as surely as water finds its level.

Compare the population of Canada with that of the United States a century ago:

1790	United States	3 929 214
1891	Canadian	4 833 239
1800	United States	5 308 483
1901	Canadian	5 371 315

It will be seen that the United States stood a century ago, with regard to numbers, where we stand to-day. But what a difference in immigration!

From 1800 to 1810 there was an immigration to the United States of 70 000, or 7000 a year. During the corresponding decade it seems probable that the immigration to Canada will be between 2 000 000 and 3 000 000.

In Canada our immigration for 1901 was 49 149, a number not reached in the United States until 1831.

Last year our immigration was over a quarter million, a mark not reached in the United States until 1849.

When the United States contained our population they received one settler—and found it difficult enough to Americanize him. We receive thirty-six. What about our task? . . .

Fancy a family increased suddenly by the presence of several strange children! What a problem to feed and clothe them—to train them and educate them—to instill into them the family traditions and impart to them the family spirit!

English and Russians, French and Germans, Austrians and Italians, Japanese and Hindus—a mixed multitude, they are being dumped into Canada by a kind of endless chain. They sort themselves out after a fashion, and each seeks to find a corner somewhere. But how shall we weld this heterogeneous mass into one people? That is our problem.

From J.S. Woodsworth, *Strangers within our Gates* , (Toronto: University of Toronto Press, 1972).

1. How does Woodsworth distinguish the colonial from the immigrant experience?
2. Comment upon Woodsworth's statistical analysis of the current state of immigration to Canada.
3. What analogy does the author make?

Mass Migration, 1865-1914

Professor Franklin Scott of Northwestern University has studied the impact of immigration on the United States for almost forty years. In this 1984 pamphlet prepared for the American Historical Association he examines the period of the great migration.

The migratory stream from Europe to America both expanded and changed toward the end of the nineteenth century. Earlier immigration had come largely from northern and western Europe, and in the 1880s this movement reached its height. . . .

If the first American generation is included, the foreign stock of the United States (foreign or of mixed parentage) was almost twenty-four percent of the total white population in 1920.

Small wonder that people in both Europe and America became alarmed at this spectacular transfer of population. Investigating commissions were set up, and voluminous reports were issued in Italy, Sweden, and the United States. In Sweden a society against emigration attracted wide support from both employers and patriots who saw the young strength of the land disappearing. In the United States fear was expressed that industry could not continue to employ the burgeoning numbers of strangers, that they could not be assimilated into the society, and that if they were absorbed they would change the character of the nation.

The "new immigrants" who predominated in the statistics after the 1890s came for the same reasons as had their predecessors, but the people were indeed different. They differed in religious complexion, for they were mostly Greek Orthodox or Roman Catholic, entering a society that was basically Protestant; and a large segment were Jews. They came from southern and eastern Europe, and they spoke an unfamiliar variety of languages. Because they were generally poorer and less well educated than those who had come before, proponents of restriction advocated a literacy test. Many newcomers were frankly "birds of passage," seeking in the United States small but quick fortunes that would enable them to return home and live in ease. Fewer than before meant to settle on the land, and there was little cheap land available.

Powerful forces impelled this urgent exodus from Europe. The familiar imponderables—wanderlust, adventuresomeness, family problems—played their part. Basic religious, political, and economic discontent had major roles, and an exaggerated "myth of America" inspired hope in the hopeless. Underlying all was a very real population explosion. . . .

Emigration only partly relieved the pressure, but it did provide an alternative for those who were disgruntled but vigorous, who were poor but not destitute, who could not find work but who could dream of a better life overseas.

Reasons for the decision to emigrate had, by the late nineteenth century, changed in relative importance. . . .

Increasingly important was the effect of economic change. Both the threat and the promise of America were embodied in the tremendous production of wheat from the western prairies, which yielded bread but depressed prices for the small European farmer. . . .

But just as in earlier periods, before the discontented could leave they had to know of some place to go. Of course not all went to the United States, but the great majority did. A guiding influence again was the America letter. These America letters were like thousands of little magnets for Greeks, Portuguese, Italians, Poles, and Russians. The letters to Poland, for instance, show the gradual reorientation of the immigrant in a new environment, and the constant requests for money made by the people in the old country show that the milk-and-honey legend the immigrants themselves created was thoroughly accepted. One girl, working as a servant in Brooklyn, wrote her parents,

And now I am on duty and I do well, I have fine food, only I must work from 6 o'clock in the morning to 10 o'clock at night and I have $13 a month. And now, dear parents, I implore you don't grieve about me, thinking that I am without money. . . . As it is I have spent more than 50 roubles on myself for the coming winter. . . . I have brothers and sisters and I intend to help them all come to America.

From such letters simple peasants and urban laborers exaggerated the riches of the immigrants. Frequently letters back to America asked for money or steamship tickets, which, when received, evoked new requests. One letter began, "I thank you first for having sent the money," went on to explain how the writer had bought land, and ended, "send me about 100 roubles. . . . If 100 is too much for you, send at least 50." Not all letters from the West were favourable. One woman wrote back to her sister,

> My dear, in America it is no better than in our country: whoever does well, he does, and whoever does poorly, suffers misery everywhere. . . . Many people in our country think that in America everybody has much pleasure. No, it is just as in our country, and the churches are like ours, and in general everything is alike.

Immigration was also stimulated by growing organized promotion. . . .

Eager developers expanded state immigration programs after the Civil War and cooperated with the railroads—the Burlington and Missouri Railroad agent . . . was also the agent of the Iowa State Board of Immigration. . . .

Upon arrival in the United States the immigrant was met by conditions often strange and frightening. The officials in starched shirts at Castle Garden or Ellis Island in New York did not seem to understand the peasants from foreign lands. And the peasants, with the narrow outlook of their old life, suspected officials and distrusted interpreters. Probing questions about morals, politics, and previous conduct were looked upon as designed to trick those who knew no better. Even after the newcomers passed quarantine and official inspection many problems remained. Of the old immigrants many spoke English, and the British as well as the Germans and the Scandinavians often had family or friends well established in the new land. But how was an eastern European peasant expected to cope with problems of language, baggage, temporary lodging, and the purchasing of tickets?

Of course there were always some conationals who were eager to help, who greeted newcomers in their native language, snatched up their baggage, and, having won confidence, proceeded to fleece their victims unmercifully. Many who had hoped to go west no longer had the funds and were stranded in the port city. One story has it that a nice young man in New York helped an immigrant family bound for Kansas City by taking their money, buying their tickets, and putting them on the train—the only trouble being that the train was nothing but the Third Avenue elevated! Nor did these runners operate only in port cities. At big inland cities like Chicago they again hovered about, offering advice on baggage and railroad tickets. Other difficulties were due not so much to design as to indifference. Immigrant trains often ran as extras, going very slowly, and with inadequate accommodations, heat, and water. One observer asserted that better care was taken with cattle shipments.

From Franklin D. Scott, *The Peopling of America: Perspectives on Immigration* , (Washington: American Historical Association, 1984).

1. How does Scott characterize the "new immigrants" of the 1890s?
2. What conditions in Europe prompted the migration to North America?
3. How does the author describe the experience of arrival on this continent?

Reluctant Hosts

In a monograph included in Multiculturalism as State Policy: Report of the Second Canadian Conference on Multiculturalism, *author Howard Palmer comments on the nativist attitudes of Canadian "hosts" toward their new fellow citizens.*

. . . There is no need to catalogue here the extensive patterns of social, economic and political discrimination which developed against non-Anglo-Saxons. Patterns of discrimination parallelled preferences of immigrant sources with northern and western Europeans encountering relatively little discrimination, central and southern Europeans and Jews encountering more discrimination and non-whites encountering an all pervasive pattern of discrimination which extended to almost all aspects of their lives. Discrimination was one of the main factors which led to the transference (with only a few exceptions) of the same ethnic "pecking order" which existed in immigration policy to the place each group occupied on the "vertical mosaic," with the British (especially the Scots) on top, and so on down to the Chinese and blacks who occupied the most menial jobs. Non-British and non-French groups not only had very little economic power; they also would not even significantly occupy the middle echelons of politics, education or the civil service until after World War II.

The ethnic stereotypes which developed for eastern European and Oriental groups emphasized their peasant origins. These stereotypes played a role in determining the job opportunities for new immigrants and functioned to disparage those who would climb out of their place. Opprobrious names such as "Wops," "Bohunks" and especially "foreigner" indicated class as well as ethnic origin and these terms were used as weapons in the struggle for status. The very word "ethnic" carried, for many people, such an aura of opprobrium that even recently there have been attempts to expurgate the use of the word. Ethnic food and folklore were regarded by most Anglo-Canadians as not only "foreign," but "backward" and lower class. . . .

From Howard Palmer, "Reluctant Hosts: Anglo-Canadian Views of Multiculturalism in the Twentieth Century", in *Multiculturalism as State Policy: Report of the Second Canadian Conference on Multiculturalism* (Ottawa: Canadian Consultative Council on Multiculturalism and Supply and Services Canada, 1976).

1. Explain the concept of the "vertical mosaic."
2. Discuss the use of ethnic stereotypes in Canadian society during this period.
3. To what extent do you think that the criticisms levelled in this excerpt are still applicable today?

Canadianization, c.1914

The creation of a homogenous society in Canada was not an accidental process. In this excerpt from Immigrants: Portrait of the Urban Experience, *the authors point to a deliberate program of Canadianization in the decade prior to the First World War.*

. . . For some the task was a veritable Pygmalion effort. One speaker at the

1913 Pre-Assembly Congress of the Presbyterian Church in Toronto explained, "The problem is simply this: take all the different nationalities, German, French, Italian, Russian and all the others that are sending their surplus into Canada; mix them with the Anglo-Saxon stock and produce a uniform race wherein the Anglo-Saxon peculiarities shall prevail."

Rather than "Anglo-conformity," transforming the foreigner into a model Anglo-Canadian, some talked of an American style "melting pot" in which all peoples and cultures would blend to create a new and dynamic Canadian man. . . .

Yet this difference in imagery, melting pot versus Anglo-conformity, proved to be more a difference in rhetoric than in vision. To proponents of assimilation by whatever name, the foreign issue boiled down to one simple problem—Why can't they be like us?

The older generation, already set in its ways, was sometimes dismissed as beyond the possibility of Canadianization. In 1918 a University of Toronto researcher concluded, "Their hearts will remain, to a very great extent, bound up with the scenes of their childhood." However, if adults might remain beyond full assimilation, the teacher, social worker and settlement house volunteer regarded their children as more malleable material.

While compulsory school attendance laws prodded the few reluctant parents, the vast majority of foreigners dutifully, even enthusiastically, bundled their children off every weekday morning to study. Teachers, principals, inspectors and school board members, for their part, envisioned education not just as the process of learning but, perhaps more importantly, as the process of *becoming*. Under their watchful eye those children were marked for transformation from foreigners into useful young Canadians. From the morning's ritual opening exercises—the singing of "God Save the King," a salute to the flag, reciting the Lord's Prayer and usually a short Bible reading—until class was finally dismissed into the streets in the later afternoon, schools emphasized the Canadian way, a way which an educational spokesman defined in 1907 as "punctuality, regularity, obedience, industry, cleanliness, decency of appearance and behaviour, regard for the rights of others and respect for law and order." The formula was recited as if none of those values animated the immigrant home. One teacher stated more simply, Canadians are "tidy, neat and sincere"—foreigners are not.

Canadianization was not a hidden curriculum. Teaching of the Canadian way permeated every facet of the school's program. . . .

As late as 1928, Toronto's Chief Inspector of Schools boasted of one institution, "The teachers of this school are teaching English to their students, but they are also not losing sight of the broader aim, the Canadianizing of our foreign population." . . .

The neighbourhood schools returned children to the streets in the late afternoon. Here in the streets, however, the children of foreigners were again sought out by the guardians of the Canadian way. School Canadianization efforts were complemented, in some cases surpassed, by the work of settlement houses. Offering an atmosphere far more relaxed than that of the schools, settlement workers reached out into the streets, into the neighbourhood parks and play-grounds, to gather the children of foreigners for late afternoon and evening activities. . . .

Problems involving children proved especially trying. Settlement workers periodically confronted the outrages of child labour—not just in daytime factory or retail store jobs, but in the employment of children as late-night newspaper boys, pin-setters in night bowling alleys and, in rare instances, as prostitutes. On such occasions as seemed necessary, settlement workers functioned in loose alliance with police, truant officers and court officials to attack these pernicious social evils. . . .

Schools, settlement houses, the streets and the countless interactions children had with the outside world undoubtedly had their effect. In short order most children learned English and moved more confidently, more widely and, as often as not, more invisibly in that English-speaking world which lay beyond the home than did their parents. In this regard children took on new impor-tance. For the newcomers and "greenhorns," an English-speaking child became virtual ambassador to the outside world, privy to family secrets and exposed to issues normally deemed beyond the understanding of a child. It was left for the children to complete forms for this or that government agency, explain to the visiting nurse or the doctor at the free hospital clinic about a mother's abnormal discharge or unravel the mystery of printed immigration regulations. As a result, parents were often forced to reverse traditional roles with their children. Rather than the child being dependent on parents, non-English-speaking par-ents found themselves dependent on their children. . . .

The process of Canadianization did not go unchallenged. In an effort to chan-nel youthful energy toward a pride in traditional language, culture or religious heritage, many foreigners sought out their kinsmen and their co-religionists in order to organize their own classes. . . .

There children learned to read, write and appreciate the mother tongue, to perform the rituals of religious life, as naturally as they learned to walk. Here things were so different. Public schools promulgated Anglo-conformity beyond the classroom. If the mother tongue was to be preserved, religious traditions sustained and a sense of group consciousness developed, immigrants felt they had to support their own afternoon and Sunday schools—no matter the cost, no matter how meagre seemed the results.

In part because Canadianization did not go unchallenged, it is probably impossible to measure with any exactness the actual success achieved by the crusaders for assimilation. How can we ever know for sure whether teachers, social workers or visiting nurses played as great a role in Canadianizing the for-eigner as they claimed, as they might have hoped? We can be sure, however, that the teacher, missionary, visiting nurse and social worker regarded Cana-dianization, especially of the children, as a process with one clearly identifiable goal—the moulding of a new man out of an Old World clay. Within one gener-ation, two at most, the assimilationist believed the process would be complete; immigrants would be Canadianized and their strange ways be only an historical memory.

In part they were right; it was unavoidable that children of foreigners should look beyond the home, beyond their parents, for visions of tomorrow. With formal education the Italian, Jewish, Finnish, Hungarian, Ukrainian or Greek child was promised a chance to grow up as a Canadian. Social workers and educators sincerely believed, and children were repeatedly told, that Cinderella was not a fairy tale—it was the essence of a New World dream.

Yet, for many the sense of being a Canadian has not meant either melting pot or Anglo-conformity. It has meant the development of Canadian life in which traditional immigrant roots, family customs and religious beliefs have not been masked away but refined to complement a changing Canadian way.

1. What role did education play in the assimilation process?
2. What outside agencies played a role in Canadianization?
3. Account for the impact of this process on immigrant family life.

The Impact of Immigration on North America

In the conclusion to his analysis on the impact of immigration, Franklin Scott considered its effect on both North America and Europe.

Wave upon wave, the great outpouring of peoples from Europe through four hundred years had created new nations and cultures. The United States, Canada, Australia, New Zealand, South Africa, all were stamped with European birthmarks. Waves of immigrants have so infiltrated the countries of Latin America that these, too, are more European than Indian. Ripples of the flood have reached into almost every corner of the globe and, in cooperation with forces such as imperialism, commerce, war, and missions, have transformed the planet, have literally "Europeanized" it.

. . . People fled from overcrowding and injustice and hardship, but they had no desire to destroy the good in their past. They wished to preserve their culture, while at the same time they saw the need and the opportunity to refashion it.

A remolding of values and institutions was nevertheless inherent in migration. Sometimes it began early, if indeed the process of Americanization did not begin with the decision to migrate. A certain German immigrant barber, for instance, early in World War II, waved his razor over the head of a native-born, long-time customer and made a memorable speech:

> You think I'm a Nazi, don't you? Well, let me tell you. I fought in the German army in World War I, and I walked through France as a journeyman barber for three years in the 'twenties. I know what it's like over there. I read about America, I studied it. I made up my mind, that's what I want. I learned the Constitution, and I passed the citizenship exam. I chose America. I know what it means. You were just born here, you take it for granted. I bet you I'm a better American than you are!

Assimilation proceeded comparatively easily for such a man. . . .

The Europeanization of America and of the world thus preceded what some have called the Americanization of Europe. The latter term is, of course, a gross exaggeration, and what kernel of truth lies in it is due to many factors besides emigration. Yet, after the term and the idea have been hedged about with caution, it is obvious that both the emigration movement and the great emigrant-receiving country, the United States, have influenced Europe profoundly. This is a subject that has been curiously neglected by European historians and that Americans are only beginning to appreciate and study. At least some of the return effects of emigration are tangible and measureable, and an analysis of them might enhance understanding of some twentieth-century problems.

Not only did European descendants in Canada, Australia, South America, and United States provide food for Europe's increasing millions; they also served as markets for Europe's burgeoning industrial production. . . .

In addition the productive sons and daughters who had gone to America sent money home in amazing quantity. In Greece, for example, in the early years of the twentieth century such remittances totaled $5 000 000 per year, roughly one-fourth of the country's export income. . . .

In manifold ways the interchange of peoples and commerce between Europe and America was accompanied by an interchange of ideas, enriching and vitalizing both. Something of the provincialism of thought in the far corners of the European continent was shattered by knowledge of new societies across the sea. The opportunity of an alternative seemed open to everyone, even if he did not take it, and his life was expanded thereby. He became freer. . . .

In social ideas the construction of new communities in America, putting into practice some of the theories evolved by European philosophers, served as a challenge to the tradition-bound communities of the Old World and stimulated self-criticism, reform, and revolution.

The interaction of many forces unleashed the emigrant tide, and in its turn migration acted as a creative force in making new societies and transforming old ones. Contrary to the impression given in all too many treatments of immigration, it has not been simply an American manifestation but a phenomenon of worldwide proportions and impact. Although historically the "peopling of America" is primarily a European-American phenomenon it has been profoundly influenced by Africa, by America's neighbours in the Western Hemisphere, and increasingly by the recent surge from Asia.

From Franklin D. Scott, *The Peopling of America: Perspectives on Immigration* , (Washington: American Historical Association, 1984).

1. Comment on Scott's analysis of the "Europeanization of America."
2. What was the impact of emigration upon Europe?
3. Create your own thesis with regard to the immigrant experience.

Immigration and Nativism: Analysis and Application

1. Create your own advertisement to attract immigrants to Canada. Direct your appeal toward potential settlers from southeastern Europe. Write a brief compar-

ison of your advertisement with the one in the readings directed toward British immigrants.

2. Define nativism. In support of your definition cite specific examples of nativist response to new immigrants to Canada in the late nineteenth and early twentieth centuries.

3. Illustrate immigration patterns from 1897 to 1905 on a map of Canada. Assess the impact of the pattern of settlement upon the various regions of the country.

4. As a new immigrant, write a letter to your relatives in Eastern Europe. In your account be certain to discuss the problems of transit, adjustment, and finding work.

5. Many historians have compared the experience of the Chinese in California with the human rights abuses of Nazi Germany. Based upon evidence you uncover in library research, create and defend your own thesis with regard to this view of the treatment of Asian immigrants.

6. (a) "The Ballad of Crowfoot," a poem by singer/songwriter Willie Dunn, describes the process of assimilation of Native peoples in the Canadian West. For further research, find and read Dunn's poem. Write a personal response to his view of Native society.

(b) Dunn's poem has been illustrated in a National Film Board presentation. Watch the film. (It is available in most libraries and schools.) To what extent is your impression altered or intensified by the visual images?

(c) Which do you find more powerful—the words or the images? Why?

7. Stage a two-person debate on the resolution: "There should be strict limits on immigration to Canada."

8. Organize a book seminar on the immigrant experience. Each member of the group should read an account of the period. You may choose to all read the same book or to each read a different book. Possible selections include: *Mountain of Gold*, by Betty Lee Sung; *No Streets of Gold*, by Helen Potrebenko; *The Promised Land*, by Pierre Berton; or *The Immigrant Years*, by Barry Broadfoot.

Each person should read and make notes on her/his book. In addition, each seminar participant should prepare a series of five to ten thought-provoking questions to encourage seminar discussion.

Organize your seminar so that each person has a chance to lead the discussion and share some important insights from the book chosen.

9. In the late twentieth century the tactics used to "Canadianize" immigrants might appear to be heavy handed. Write a justification for this approach to dealing with new arrivals to the country.

11
IMPERIALISM AND ISOLATION

The thirty-year period from 1890 to 1920 saw the rise and fall of the philosophy of imperialism in Europe and North America. That is not to say that the global expansion of European powers in the seventeenth and eighteenth centuries, and the rapid continental expansion of the United States and Canada in the nineteenth century, were not fundamentally imperialistic in nature. But it is clear that imperialism, as a driving political and social force, in the late nineteenth century had reached a peak which would carry the European world on its crest until it came crashing down in the First World War.

The United States, like many European powers, perceived an imperialist mission for itself. This was based philosophically upon the extension of its enlightened culture and political institutions to the less fortunate peoples of the world, and economically upon its need to expand its markets and sources of raw materials. Canada, on the other hand, experienced a sort of "tag-along" approach to imperialism, hitching itself to the British world view rather than to a view of its own. Regardless of its form, however, imperialism had a great impact upon both nations, and eventually resulted in the full-scale commitment of both countries to total war on the European continent.

There was little in the decades following the end of the Civil War to indicate that the United States was about to embark upon a course of overseas expansion. In fact, prevailing attitudes during the period seemed to reinforce the opposite point of view. During the internal growth of the 1870s and 1880s most Americans wanted their country to remain in isolation from Europe, believing there was little to be gained from involvement in international affairs. The powerful Union army was demobilized as soon as the war was over, and the navy was allowed to decline into a state of uselessness. Even overseas trade was left to others, and by 1914 nearly 90 percent of all American exports sailed in foreign ships.

That is not to say that all interest in continental domination had disappeared. William Seward had negotiated the purchase of Alaska from Russia in 1867, and although many Americans ridiculed the purchase as "Seward's folly" or "Seward's Icebox," others saw the deal as the first step towards the inevitable absorption of Canada. The last cry for this form of Manifest Destiny was uttered in 1886 by Henry Cabot Lodge who proclaimed that "From the Rio Grande to the Arctic Ocean there should be but one flag and one country." But such ideas were already out of date. The next generation would be looking beyond the limits of the continent.

Canada too felt the lure of continental expansion. John A. Macdonald touched a responsive cord with his vision of a transcontinental nation in the 1860s, and the drive to complete the CPR was based upon the imperialist need to control the Northwest before the Americans did. Many Western Canadian historians point to the suppression of the 1885 rebellion as the epitome of Eastern Canadian imperialism. They contend that the actions of the Canadian army towards Native inhabitants of the Prairies were little different from British troops carrying out the "white man's burden" in India and Africa. Other historians point to the

National Policy of Macdonald and Laurier as the root of economic imperialism, by which the Eastern industrial establishment carved out a dependent empire west of the Canadian Shield. This vision is still strong enough to have been effectively used by Brian Mulroney in his 1988 campaign in favour of freer trade with the United States.

As in the United States, by the 1890s, most Canadians saw their continental mission as being complete. They too were ready to step on to a global stage under the banner of imperialism.

The Idea of Imperialism

Imperialism is a policy of extending the rule of one country over other countries or colonies. In the late nineteenth century many European nations pursued imperialist goals. While Russia, Austria-Hungary, and Turkey competed for continental territory, nations such as Britain, France, and Germany spread their influence overseas. The United States, preoccupied with settling and developing the North American interior, had little time for such pursuits. By 1890, however, this had changed.

Frederick Jackson Turner's "Frontier Thesis" worried many Americans, who felt that the nation had now reached its natural limits. Once the national goal of subduing the wilderness had been achieved, where should they go next? The closing of the frontier represented a crisis for Americans. For over a century they had followed a missionary impulse to bring civilization to the West. The mission had been accomplished; what Turner had called the first period of American history had come to an end, and it was time for a new direction.

In the early 1890s a new group of theorists appeared to fill the ideological gap left by the disappearance of the frontier. Some, like Josiah Strong, John Fiske, and John W. Burgess, saw a new mission for the United States as part of a world unified and dominated by an Anglo-Saxon alliance. This was not a new idea. The British had already absorbed large portions of the globe into their empire, and it was considered only natural that the United States should continue the process.

Although their ideas were grasped by the proponents of overseas expansion, these men were not actually imperialists. Instead they were idealists who believed in the gradual spread of the English language, the Christian church, and democratic institutions. Although often quoted by imperialist politicians, they had little impact on popular thought.

Canadian George Munro Grant, principal of Queen's University, saw Canada as the "living link" between the United States and Britain in this global mission. He expressed those same sentiments on behalf of the British Empire:

> We have a mission on earth. . . . Our mission was to make this world the home of freedom , of justice, of peace, and to secure these ends the British Empire was the highest secular institution the world has ever known.

His sentiments were echoed by Sir George Robert Parkin who stated, in defence of British imperial influence, "I am one of those who believe that power and influence are not given to some nation without divine purpose."

Parkin and Grant were proponents of the concept of Social Darwinism. To them, the "organism" of the state had to adapt to the changing "environment" of global power politics. For these men, the "mission" of the Empire was to provide benign protection for the "weaker races" of Asia and Africa. As interesting as these sentiments were, of more importance were the writings of naval historian Admiral Alfred Thayer Mahan. In his *Interest of America in Sea Power* (1897), Mahan wrote that the commercial and military interests of the United States necessitated the expansion of American sea power. For him, the goal of overseas expansion should not be the acquisition of colonies, but the development of markets. To this end he advocated that the navy be rebuilt with modern battleships, a canal be built across Central America, and naval bases be established worldwide.

Mahan's suggestions struck a responsive note. The decade following 1889 had seen a general economic decline in the United States. Farm prices were at an all-time low, and industrial production had run out of profitable markets. Over 75 percent of all American exports went to Europe but there were other possibilities. At the end of the century only 10 percent of U.S. foreign trade was with Latin American and less than 5 percent with Asia. If these markets could be tapped, then renewed growth might be possible.

This economic argument, coupled with Mahan's vision of a strong global naval presence, began to provide a focus for policy makers. As the nineteenth century drew to a close, the United States began to look beyond its borders once again. Canadians too read Mahan with interest. For some, his writings represented the telling argument for an integrated defence policy for the whole empire. For others, he was living proof of the direct link between imperialism and militarism in the modern world.

Reaching into the Pacific

Some limited American contacts had been made with Asia during the 1800s. To maintain these relationships in the age of steamships, the United States needed to establish coaling stations across the Pacific.

Strategists looked to the various island groups in the ocean to act as stepping stones to Asia. In 1889 conflict developed over one of these islands. American and British ships had been stopping to refuel in Samoa for many years. However, German economic interests gradually grew to dominate the island, and the other powers feared losing their rights. In a local struggle, German and American forces supported rival native factions, and it looked as if the two countries might actually go to war. At the height of the crisis, however, a freak storm sunk both the American and German ships, which were facing each other in the harbour at Pago Pago. In the wake of the disaster the two powers, along with Britain, agreed to share maritime access to the island.

The United States was willing to compromise on Samoa, but its sights were set on a more lucrative target: Hawaii.

SOLDIERS OF THE QUEEN.
"Where's the Coward that would not dare
To fight for such a Queen".

This commemorative envelope celebrates the Imperial Federalist ideal.

This recruiting poster invited men to join Canada's new navy.

The World's Constable

THE WORLD CONSTABLE.

The Hawaiian Islands had been a unified, independent kingdom since 1795. During the nineteenth century large numbers of American planters moved to the island to exploit the sugar cane industry. So extensive were these operations that by 1890, 99 percent of all Hawaiian exports consisted of sugar shipments to the United States. The plantations imported cheap labour from China and Japan and eventually became the targets of resentment by native Hawaiians. Finally in the early 1890s Queen Liliuokalani cracked down on the foreigners, restricting many of their privileges. The American residents responded in 1893 by rebelling against her rule and overthrowing her government. Their leader was Sanford Ballard Dole, the owner of major pineapple and sugar plantations in Hawaii. The rebellion would not have succeeded if it had not been for the presence of the American navy in the islands. Marines were sent ashore to protect American interests, and they remained to prop up the new American-dominated provisional government.

Benjamin Harrison advocated outright annexation of the islands, but the new president, Grover Cleveland, refused, stating that such a move would be "a perversion of our national mission . . . to build up and make a greater country out of what we have instead of annexing islands." In spite of these sentiments, Cleveland did not restore native government, and instead recognized the provisional government in 1894. When the Republicans returned to power under McKinley in 1898 the islands were annexed.

The United States had taken its first step towards Asia.

Reviving the Monroe Doctrine

Two factors encouraged the revival of the Monroe Doctrine during the Cleveland years. During his first administration the president was concerned by French attempts to build a canal across the Isthmus of Panama. Although the project eventually fell apart in 1889, many Americans felt that it was an affront to their rights in the region.

The second incident was more serious. In 1895 a border dispute arose between Venezuela and British Guiana. Cleveland offered to mediate the dispute, but the British told him to mind his own business. The president responded that under the Monroe Doctrine anything that any foreign power did in the Western Hemisphere was his business. The statement was especially insulting to self-governing nations such as Canada, but Britain backed off. With new alliances emerging in Europe they could not afford to alienate the United States.

Grover Cleveland shared the basic view of many Americans that overseas expansion was not morally correct. Anti-colonial sentiment had been a strong element in the American character since the time of the Revolution. But power was shifting in the United States. Many of the new generation of political leaders were being influenced by the theories of Turner and Mahan, and by the obvious successes of nations such as Britain and Germany. The election of 1896 would put these imperialist forces in power.

Stepping on to the World Stage: The Spanish-American War

The United States had no real dispute with Spain. In fact, the two countries had little to do with one another. Just off of the American coast, however, one Spanish possession had been the target of expansionists for decades. Cuba, with its rich sugar plantations, sat just 80 km off the tip of Florida. In 1895 Cuban nationalists revolted against Spanish control. It was not that the Spaniards were particularly cruel or oppressive. For the most part their regime was characterized by ineptitude and inefficiency. However, faced with rebellion, they quickly cracked down. The Spanish government sent over thousands of troops, led by their best general. Most of the fighting was quickly ended, but the armed forces continued to be harassed by guerrilla actions from bands hiding in the mountains. In response the government in Spain took an even harder line. A new governor, Valeriano Weyler, took charge in 1896. He brutally repressed the people, turning entire villages and towns into concentration camps. Within two years over two hundred thousand Cubans died of malnutrition and disease in these camps.

In the United States popular sentiment against Spanish rule was whipped up through a series of sensational stories in the "yellow press." Full of exaggerations and lies, these stories portrayed the Cuban rebels as akin to the patriots of 1776 fighting against foreign oppression. Anti-Spanish feelings were further aggravated when the New York papers published a secret letter written by the Spanish minister in Washington, Dupuy de Lome, to his government. In it, President McKinley was portrayed as weak and easily influenced. The Spanish quickly apologized, but another disaster was waiting to strike.

In January 1898 rioting broke out in Havana. To protect American interests, McKinley sent the battleship *Maine* to the city. Welcomed by the Spanish, there seemed to be no problem, until, on February 15th, the ship blew up in Havana Harbour, killing 260. The American press accused the Spanish of sinking the vessel and called for war. It is fairly certain, however, that the Spanish had nothing to do with the sinking; in all probability the ship was destroyed by Cuban rebels hoping to create trouble. Although this should have been a logical conclusion, few were thinking along rational lines. "Remember the Maine, to Hell with Spain!" cried the headlines.

In March the president delivered an ultimatum to the Spanish. He called for an immediate cease-fire between Spain and the rebels, peace negotiations with American mediation, and recognition of Cuban independence. If Spain did not meet these demands, war was inevitable. The Spanish hesitated. The American ambassador to Spain wired Washington that the Spanish were willing to grant Cuba some form of autonomy, and on April 9th they actually agreed to all of the American demands.

It was too late, however. McKinley ignored the Spanish response, and two days later went to Congress with his own interpretation of events. By this point war fever was running high in the United States. The president downplayed the Spanish message of goodwill and left the legislators with the impression that war was the only alternative.

From then on events took on a life of their own, and the nation began to mobilize for war. On April 19th Congress declared the independence of Cuba and authorized the president to use naval and military force to support the island. The Spanish responded five days later by declaring war on the United States. A formal declaration of war by the Americans came the following day, with an admission that a state of war had existed since April 21st.

The Spanish-American War demonstrated some basic principles of power. The Americans quickly discovered that an untrained, volunteer army was no real match for seasoned troops. American forces came close to suffering a crushing—and embarrassing—defeat in the Caribbean. They did learn, however, of the power and importance of a modern and disciplined navy. It was the American Pacific fleet under Commodore Dewey that spearheaded a convincing defeat of Spanish forces in the Philippines. By August 12th the war was over. The United States had inherited an empire and the global responsibilities that go with it.

It was a significant change in the American role on the world stage. Only seven years earlier George Grant (see readings) had denigrated American foreign policy, calling it "parochial" and had pointed to the role of Canadian troops in introducing "civilization into Africa and in preserving the Pax Britannica among the teeming millions of India and South-east Asia." Now it was the turn of the Americans, and the world watched to see how they would deal with these new responsibilities.

Consequences of War

American leaders quickly found themselves making excuses for the war. In the cold light of day there was little justification for it. The United States had wanted to "flex its muscles" for the world to see, but the war for Cuban independence had become something quite different. Attitudes had undergone a subtle change during the conflict. Hawaii had been quietly annexed in July, and McKinley had stated publicly that "when the war is over we must keep what we want."

Under the treaty signed on December 10th the United States acquired Puerto Rico, the Philippines, and the island of Guam in the Pacific. The Senate was uneasy with this new colonialism. In spite of the enthusiasm for the war, the treaty was only ratified by a two-vote margin.

Cuba was another matter. The war had been fought to free the Cubans from foreign rule, so it was impossible to annex the country to the United States. However, its independence was not immediately granted either.

After three-and-a-half years of rebellion and war, the island was in chaos. An American military government was appointed under the leadership of General Leopold Wood. Wood introduced several reforms in the areas of sanitation, education, agriculture, and urban renewal, but by 1900 the Cubans wanted him out. That year delegates to the Cuban Constitutional Convention started to draw up a new constitution for the island.

Under American pressure an additional clause was added to the document in 1901. Called the Platt Amendment it stated that Cuba could not make treaties or take loans which, in the opinion of the United States, could be detrimental to the island's independence. It also authorized the Americans to maintain two naval bases in the country and to send troops whenever necessary to preserve peace and stability on the island.

The Cubans ratified the amended version, and in May 1902 installed their first president. Two years later, the United States removed its troops, only to have them return in 1906 and again in 1917. Cuban independence was to be tolerated, but only under close supervision.

American intervention in the affairs of its Latin American neighbours worked well at first. A short war had resulted in the elimination of a foreign "threat" and the emergence of the United States on the global stage. The transition, however, was not easy. Its new international role meant a loss of innocence for the United States. It came first in the Philippines.

Crisis in the Philippines

Prior to the signing of the Treaty of Paris with Spain in 1898, McKinley declared that the people of the Philippines were "unfit for self-government." In spite of the fact that over 85 percent of the population was Roman Catholic and had been for three centuries, the president felt that it was necessary to wait until they had become properly "Christianized" before they were left to their own devices. As a result McKinley authorized a complete military occupation of the islands. The Philippine people were furious that the Americans had betrayed their hopes for independence. Within two months local rebels led by Emilio Aguinaldo launched their own guerrilla war against the occupying troops. In March of 1899 Congress authorized another force of thirty-five thousand volunteers to put down the revolt. This was followed six months later by a further contingent of military support.

American troops brutally suppressed the uprising. Eventually they introduced the same concentration-camp system that they had fought to destroy in Cuba. By the time the rebellion was finally put down in 1902, it had cost the United States more money than had the entire Spanish-American War.

This new role did not sit well with the American public. By 1907 an elected legislature had been introduced on the islands, and by 1916 a large degree of local autonomy was granted. Still, it would not be until after the Second World War that the Philippines would be granted full independence.

The new international prestige enjoyed by the United States was never more evident than in its dealings with China. John Hay was McKinley's secretary of state. A long-time political advisor to various Republican administrations, he began his career as a twenty-two-year-old secretary to Abraham Lincoln. Hay knew that mere possession of Pacific bases would not guarantee access to the lucrative markets of China; prior occupation by other powers still posed a major obstacle to American trade.

In 1889 China was divided into spheres of influence by the Europeans and the Japanese. Russia controlled the area around Port Arthur in the north; Japan dominated Korea and Formosa; Germany was in Kiachow; France was in Kwangchau Bay; and, of course, Britain was in Hong Kong.

Playing on the recent American naval successes in the region, Hay sent a series of Open Door notes to the governments of the various nations involved. He suggested three basic principles for the management of Chinese trade. First, no nation would prevent another country from trading within its sphere of influence. Second, any tariffs charged would be paid to the Chinese, not the occupying powers. Finally, no rail charges or port duties woud be paid to any foreign power.

This equal treatment or Open Door policy was ignored by the other countries. Hay took their lack of response as a sign of approval. On March 20, 1900, he publicly announced his policy, and stated that no one had expressed any objections. The United States was now firmly established in the Far East.

The "Big Stick" in the Caribbean

Theodore Roosevelt became president with the assassination of William McKinley in 1901. Roosevelt believed in an active foreign policy for the United States. He summarized his approach to diplomacy as the need to "speak softly and carry a big stick." For Roosevelt the "big stick" was the navy. A student of the ideas of both Turner and Mahan, Roosevelt was convinced that the next stage in American development depended upon the maintenance of a large and powerful fleet. He used the navy to protect American interests in the Caribbean basin. Warning European powers that they had no business interfering in the Western Hemisphere, he issued a redefined Monroe Doctrine. Addressing Congress he stated:

> Chronic wrongdoing or an impotence which results in a general loosening of the ties of civilized society, may in America, as elsewhere, ultimately require the intervention by some civilized nation, and in the Western Hemisphere the adherence of the United States to the Monroe Doctrine may force the United States, however reluctantly, in flagrant cases of such wrongdoing or incompetence, to the exercise of an international police power.

This Roosevelt Corollary to the Monroe Doctrine established the "right" of the United States to not only prevent European powers from intervening in hemispheric affairs, but to actively intervene in them itself. During the next decade the United States exercised this "right" in Venezuela, Santo Domingo, Panama, and Mexico.

Roosevelt's term as president ended with one last demonstration of American power. In late 1907 he sent the United States navy on a round-the-world cruise. By now the U.S. navy was the second largest fleet in the world, after Great Britain. This show of force by the "Great White Fleet" established the United States as a first-rank world power.

Canada and the Imperial Federalist Movement

For many Canadians in the late nineteenth century, imperialism meant closer ties within the British Empire. In 1884 the Imperial Federation League was founded in London, with branches in Canada. Imperial federalists called for colonial and dominion representation in the imperial parliament, an imperial preferential tariff, and a system of mutual defence. Canadian imperialists saw this proposal for participation in the larger affairs of the empire as being wholly consistent with national goals. Canada would retain autonomy in domestic matters, and would have a say in the running of the empire.

British and Canadian imperialists saw the relationship differently, however. Canadian supporters were attracted to the concept's trade provisions. Protected access to British markets, which were currently open to free trade, would be a great boost to Canadian farmers. The British, on the other hand, saw the dominions mainly as sources of income for imperial defence. Canada in the 1890s enjoyed the protection of the British navy. As in 1763, British taxpayers began to ask why the wealthy colonies should receive such a benefit free of charge. British colonial secretary Joseph Chamberlain agreed. He began consultations as the first step toward securing a financial contribution to defence.

In the 1890s most Canadians were not in favour of contributing to British war efforts. When war broke out in South Africa in 1899, Prime Minister Laurier resisted the imperial call for military support. Finally, under pressure, he agreed to authorize the recruitment of one thousand volunteers to serve in the campaign. In actual fact, over eight thousand Canadians fought in the war. Those against becoming involved in imperial conflicts believed this participation set a dangerous precedent.

Supporters of this South Africa "adventure" pointed to the fact that of the 224 Canadian dead, only 63 were actually killed in combat. The remainder had fallen victim to accident and disease. Such statistics caused the *Canadian Military Gazette* to proclaim that modern war was becoming a more humane affair in which "the proportion of killed, wounded and sick is steadily decreasing." It was a naiveté that would die in the trenches of Flanders.

Canadian imperialism during this time was simply another form of nationalism. Imperial federalists were not "anti-Canadian" but simply held a different vision of the character and mission of the nation.

Most Canadians saw the United States as the main threat to their sovereignty. When the British representative on the Alaska Boundary Commission sided with the American claim in the Alaska boundary dispute of 1903, it did not spark as much anti-British sentiment as it did the realization that Roosevelt's threat to "send a brigade of American regulars up to Skagway and take possession of this territory and hold it by all the force and power of the United States" was one against which Canada had no defence. Without the might of the empire behind them, what hope had 6 million Canadians against the 81 million citizens of the United States? As a result, while some Canadians viewed the continued dependence upon Britain as a holdover from colonial days, others felt that without the protection of the British Empire, Canada would have no chance for self-preservation.

John A. Macdonald had asked as early as 1890, "How long could we stand as an independent republic? . . . What could Canada do in the Bering Sea controversy without England at our back?" Many imperialists saw themselves as realists who recognized the precarious nature of a "little Canada" policy. George Foster warned in 1903 that an independent Canada "would live under the shadow of an overmastering power [who believed] that it is her destiny to possess the whole North American continent." For them the alternatives facing an independent Canada were either bankruptcy brought on by channelling national resources into defence, or compromising national integrity by living under the self-serving protection of the United States.

By contrast, the "new nationality" of imperial federalism offered Canadians a significant role as members of a vital global empire. Although the links provided by imperial conferences, transatlantic cables, and common postage fell short of tying the political bonds of the empire, in the closing years of the century the supporters of closer ties with Britain saw themselves as nationalists in the truest sense of the word. Their opponents asserted that the vision of imperial partnership predicted by British leaders was a thinly veiled ploy to extract military support from the reluctant dominions.

This debate was conducted against the background of a rapidly escalating naval arms race in Europe. As this crisis worsened, Canada was asked to make a significant financial contribution to the defence of the empire. Laurier proposed a compromise. There would be no financial contribution, but the government would create a Canadian navy. It would take responsibility for patrolling the seas around North America, leaving the Imperial fleet free for service elsewhere. The Naval Service Bill of 1910 called for the construction of a small naval force consisting of eleven ships. This compromise was rejected by the imperialists, who called it a "tin pot navy" which would be of no use in a time of crisis, and by French-Canadian nationalists, who saw it as a dangerous first step towards drawing Canada into international conflicts.

This issue, along with a proposal for reciprocity with the United States, brought about Laurier's defeat in the election of 1911. Early the next year, the new Conservative government, led by Sir Robert Borden, pledged $35 million for the building of battleships for coastal defence and also to be put at the disposal of the king in time of crisis.

Such a crisis was not long in coming. When Britain declared war on Germany two years later, Canada automatically became part of the conflict. However, the country was not dragged into the war against its will. In the summer of 1914 it was difficult to find any opposition to full Canadian participation in the Great War. Political leaders called for a great volunteer army to rush to the aid of Britain and France. In the early years of the conflict they were not be disappointed, but as the number of casualties escalated and the war bogged down into a mire of mud and death, interest and enthusiasm waned. The attitude of human expendability intrinsic to the strategies of both sides meant that by late 1916, the number of casualties far outstripped enlistments (see readings).

Borden had stated in the 1914 that "There has not been, there will not be, compulsion or conscription. Freely and voluntarily the manhood of Canada stands ready to fight beyond the seas." While that might have been true at the beginning of the conflict, by 1917 it was no longer the case. Borden returned from an Imperial War Conference at the beginning of the year convinced that conscription was necessary.

Many Canadians viewed the enlistment issue as a racial one. English-speaking

Canadians felt that French Canadians were not pulling their weight in the conflict. On the surface, that may have appeared to be true; English-speaking recruits outnumbered their francophone counterparts on a per capita basis. Careful analysis, however, shows that the English figures were radically inflated. By 1917 just under 50 percent of all anglophone enlistments had not been born in Canada at all. They were British immigrants who, having been in the country only a few years, were returning to fight to defend the land of their birth. As a result the gap between anglophone and francophone Canadians was much narrower than it seemed. There were other reasons as well.

There were few francophone officers. French-speaking recruits were split up among various English-speaking regiments, and in a peak of insensitivity, the chief recruiter for Quebec was an English protestant. In addition many French Canadians were nationalists who saw the conflict as a European affair in which Canada had no part. North Americans for centuries, these citizens retained few of the sentimental ties to the old continent that some of their English counterparts held. They saw the call for conscripts as simply the long arm of European imperialism reaching out to snatch Canada's sons and daughters. As one spokesperson said "Why have the Tories imposed conscription upon Canada? To create a precedent, in order that Canada may become for England a reservoir of men for the wars of the future. That is the basis of Imperialism."

This French-Canadian attitude was reflected in the response to the outbreak of war by the other North American nationalists, the Americans. When war broke out in Europe President Woodrow Wilson's first action was to appeal to the American people to remain "impartial in thought as well as in action." He believed that responsibility for the conflict lay in the hands of the European powers.

This attitude held for about the first fourteen months of the war. Staying out of the war, however, did not necessarily mean staying neutral. It was difficult to remain impartial in thought. The majority of Americans sided with the democracies. British propaganda, in the form of newspaper articles, films, and endorsements by prominent Americans, were particularly effective. Canada was an important base for these operations, and Canadian publications streamed into the United States during this period. By comparison, German newsreels of invincible marching armies seemed crude and only helped to reinforce many of the negative views that Americans had about militarism.

It was even more difficult to remain neutral in deed, however. Prior to the war, the United States had been in a recession. Business had been slow, and the country had been in debt to its European trading partners. All of that changed after August 1914. Large orders came pouring in from Europe, and soon the United States was back in full production. Before the war 77 percent of all American exports went to the Entente powers. This pattern continued during the conflict. These record sales, however, soon bankrupted the allies, and the United States was forced to either lend Britain and France the money to keep buying American goods or their sales.

In 1914 Wilson made it clear that "loans by American bankers to any foreign nation which is at war is inconsistent with the spirit of true neutrality." However, by 1915 the secretary of the treasury, William McAdoo, wrote the president that:

Great prosperity is coming . . . It will be tremendously increased if we can extend reasonable credits to our customers . . . The balance of trade is so largely in our favour . . . To preserve that we must do everything we can to assist our customers to buy.

Future secretary of state Robert Lansing wrote at the same time:

Can we afford to let a declaration as to our conception of the "true spirit of neutrality" made in the early days of the war, stand in the way of our national interests?

The president had little choice, the ban on loans was lifted and the United States became financially committed to the Allied cause. Wilson would have liked to do more business with the Germans as well. In fact between 1914 and 1917 over $56 million in loans and $70 million in goods were shipped to the Triple Alliance. This, however, was only a small fraction of the volume of trade with Britain. The fact was that the British navy controlled the sea lanes and little could get through its blockade. When criticized for this obvious favouritism in his policy, Wilson replied:

We can make and sell what any nation wishes to order . . . If it happens that only certain nations control the Atlantic, . . . that is not our fault or concern. Both the United States and the Atlantic Ocean have been here for a considerable time, and if any nation has not taken them sufficiently into account, it is obviously that nation's fault.

Wilson's policies of military neutrality, coupled with economic cooperation, struck a responsive note with the American people. They re-elected him president in 1916 on a campaign slogan "He kept us out of the war."

Circumstances were changing, however. The crisis in the lack of volunteers that prompted Borden to introduce conscription in 1917 put renewed pressure on the United States to step in to help its economic allies. British/Canadian propaganda and Germany's decision to renew unrestricted submarine warfare began to turn the tide of popular opinion.

In addition the February revolution in which the Russian people had overthrown the czar seemed to mark the beginnings of a new democratic regime. All of a sudden the division of power was clear: on one side were the aggressive monarchies and on the other three democratic regimes. The American mission was clear. On April 17th the president addressed the Congress:

The World must be made safe for democracy. Its peace must be planted upon the tested foundations of political liberty. We have no selfish ends to serve. We desire no conquest . . . It is a fearful thing to lead this great peaceful people into war, into the most terrible and disastrous of all wars, civilization itself seeming to be in the balance. But the right is more precious than peace and we shall fight for the things which we have always carried nearest to our hearts . . .

Two days later Congress responded to the president's message. By a vote of 82 to 6 in the Senate and later by 373 to 50 in the House, the United States went to war.

In the spring of 1917 the American mission, long applied to North America and the developing world, was finally turning its attention to Europe.

By May of 1918, over half a million Americans were in Europe. Each month after that, the navy delivered 250 000 more. American participation made the difference. By September Allied forces, bolstered by 1.2 million Americans, began to push the German army back. By November it was all over. The United States got off lightly. Of the over 2 million soldiers serving overseas, only 48 000 were killed in battle. By comparison, the Canadian military, numbering 650 000 over four years, saw over 60 000 killed and a further 173 000 seriously wounded. Other countries, of course, fared much worse: Germany lost 1.8 million soldiers; Russia, 1.7 million; France, 1.4 million; Austria, 1.2 million; and Britain 950 000.

There were reasons for the lower number of American casualties. The Americans had entered the war late, and although they had taken part in the great offensives of the last year of the war, for the most part they had escaped the devastating attrition of three years of trench warfare. Still, they suffered heavy losses over a relatively short period of time, and the American people would not soon forget the price of involvement in the wars of other nations.

North Americans made a critical contribution to the victory in Europe. Canadian troops earned their country a separate seat at the Peace Conference and in the new League of Nations. Among the casualties of the First World War was imperial federalism. Canada paid a bitter price for its ties to the empire. In the next two decades the country would turn toward continental concerns. The United States, unlike the other great powers, emerged stronger than ever from the war. The price of that power should have been greater global responsibility. The reality of the war, however, made many Americans reticent to take up that role. It would be a generation of isolationists who would succeed Woodrow Wilson.

Imperialism was seriously wounded by World War I, but not yet dead. It would take a second global disaster to finish the job.

World War I seemed to firmly establish Canada as an independent player in global affairs. When in 1921 Conservative leader Arthur Meighen called the British Empire "a league of autonomous nations" but one with "common burdens that all must share," his views seemed already out of date. Two years later Prime Minister Mackenzie King, speaking at an Imperial Conference, made it clear that "the decision of Canada on any important issue, domestic or foreign . . . should be made by the people of Canada."

King's statement reflected his outrage a year earlier when he learned in the press that Canadian troops were to be committed to support British forces during the Chanak Crisis. His government's refusal to cooperate, along with the independent signing of a Halibut Treaty with the United States the following year, made it clear that imperial federalism was a dead issue in Canadian minds.

Although not as insular as the United States during the 1920s and the early 1930s, Canadians still took little active interest in international affairs. A member of the League of Nations, Canada used its role to assert its autonomy rather than to intervene in times of crisis. The classic example of this "closet" isolationism came in 1935. When W.A. Riddell, Canadian representative in the League, recommended an oil embargo to stop Italian dictator Benito Mussolini's advance into Ethiopia, he was denounced and repudiated by his own government. In the final analysis, Canada did not want to get involved.

North Americans stepped on to the world stage in the late nineteenth and early twentieth centuries. Like most European nations, Canada and the United States saw a larger global mission for themselves. Taking different forms on each side of the border, imperialism was nonetheless a driving force for both countries. The harsh realities of the First World War brought the lofty ideals of most North Americans down to earth. The next twenty years would see them focus more directly on internal concerns.

The United States would continue to maintain its prewar "sphere of influence" but in the process would slowly divest itself of obligations in the Caribbean and the Far East. Canada too followed this isolationist path. Although its membership in the empire and involvement in the League of Nations would keep the country nominally active in international affairs, in the final analysis Mackenzie King's image of Canadians living in a "fire-proof house" was one to which most citizens could subscribe.

Not until German planes strafed Warsaw and Japanese bombers descended on Pearl Harbour would North Americans re-emerge from their shells to take an active international role.

Manifest Destiny, 1867

Proponents of Confederation in British North America did not have to look far to find annexationist sentiment in the United States. The following editorial appeared in the New York Herald *in April 1867.*

Preposterous . . ., in the United States at this day, "with all our modern improvements," is the fear entertained by our old time, slow-coach conservatives, that with the expansion of our boundaries the cohesion of States and sections must be more and more weakened until they fall to pieces. . . .

Manifest destiny, under all these advantages, marks out the North American continent as the future map of the United States. Men of the present generation may live to hear in Congress that the Speaker has appointed a member each from New York, Quebec, New Archangel, San Francisco, the city of Mexico, Panama, Havana, Haiti and Jamaica as the House Committee of Foreign Affairs. If within the last six years we have put down a rebellion of over half a million armed men, liberated four millions of slaves, reconquered eight hundred thousand square miles of territory, and purchased four hundred and fifty thousand square miles more, how long will it take us to absorb all North America?

From *The New York Herald*, April 17, 1867.

1. What point of view is being attacked by the editorial?
2. Outline the future vision of the Americas being described.

3. Account for the impact of this type of continental imperialism upon the British North American politicians of the period.

Canada: Key to the Union of English-Speaking Peoples, 1889

Benjamin Butler was a military leader during the Civil War and a former governor of Massachusetts. He ran unsuccessfully for the presidency in 1884 and wrote and lectured on American foreign policy until his death in 1893. In this excerpt, Butler argues for a global union of English-speaking peoples.

All know the fact that two English-speaking nations lie here side by side, divided by a conventional line only of more than six thousand miles in length. One the Dominion of Canada, a dependency of a European monarchy; the other the mightiest of republics, now beyond all peradventure a Nation, whose duty and mission it is to maintain the principles of self-government of the people of all nations. . . .

Why, then, is it necessary for statesman or priest to contemplate the declaration or enforcement of the independence of Canada, if there is a possibility of union of that country with the United States?

The problem seems to me to be this: Does Canada desire a union with the United States? If she so signifies her wish in a recognizable form, England has no power to prevent it. If Canada does not, then England has no power to enact it. She may throw Canada off as a dependency, but she cannot throw her upon the United States. Would not the more feasible, the more sensible, nay, the more statesmanlike and effective, manner of bringing together the United States and Canada, and ultimately both in a common bond of political union with Great Britain herself, especially as in a few years Great Britain may be a republic, the form of her government seeming to be not substantially in the way now, be to enter into negotiations for that purpose, carefully and in the most friendly spirit, the negotiators in charge having only one idea in common; that is, how can the three peoples best get together.

. . . Such a united power as I have sketched would save all the other nations of Europe from final and inevitable bankruptcy because of maintaining immense armies and navies, to the destruction of their people, to hold each other in check.

To that English-speaking league every nation would be obliged to submit for arbitrament every cause of differences, if not out of fear of its armed intervention, yet because of its holding the money of the world. No war could be carried on which that power should disapprove, and any nation might disarm who should be protected even by promise of financial aid from the pledge of the united English-speaking people of the earth.

With America and England uniting their means of production and transportation of that which sustains life and secures comfort, no want or famine could ever come; and within a century a universal language could pervade the world, thus relieving it from the punishment inflicted on mankind by the Lord Almighty at the tower of Babel.

From *Should There Be a Union of the English-Speaking Peoples of the Earth?* A dissertation, delivered before the alumni of Colby University . . ., July 2, 1889 Boston, 1889) in Milton Plesur, ed., *Creating an American Empire 1865—1914*, (New York: Pitman, 1971).

1. What relationship does Butler see between Canada and the United States?
2. What role should Canada play in the creation of a global English-speaking empire?
3. Why does Butler feel that the creation of this new power will lead to world peace?

The Influence of Sea Power upon History, 1890

Alfred Thayer Mahan was the foremost naval historian in the United States during the nineteenth century. In his book The Influence of Sea Power upon History *Mahan makes a compelling case for the creation and maintenance of a powerful fleet. In this excerpt he outlines the unique position of the United States to carry on world trade.*

Indications are not wanting of an approaching change in the thoughts and policy of Americans as to their relations with the world outside their own borders. For the past quarter of a century, the predominant idea, which has successfully asserted itself at the polls and shaped the course of the government, has been to preserve the home market for the home industries. . . .

For nearly the lifetime of a generation, therefore, American industries have been thus protected, until the practice has assumed the force of a tradition, and is clothed in the mail of conservatism. In their mutual relations, these industries resemble the activities of a modern ironclad that has heavy armor, but an inferior engine and no guns; mighty for defense, weak for offense. Within, the home market is secured; but outside, beyond the broad seas, there are the markets of the world, that can be entered and controlled only by a vigorous contest, to which the habit of trusting to protection by statute does not conduce.

At bottom, however, the temperament of the American people is essentially alien to such a sluggish attitude. Independently of all bias for or against protection, it is safe to predict that, when the opportunities for gain abroad are understood, the course of American enterprise will cleave a channel by which to reach them. Viewed broadly, it is a most welcome as well as significant fact that a prominent and influential advocate of protection, a leader of the party committed to its support, a keen reader of the signs of the times and of the drift of opinion, has identified himself with a line of policy which looks to nothing less than such modifications of the tariff as may expand the commmerce of the United States to all quarters of the globe. . . .

The interesting and significant feature of this changing attitude is the turning of the eyes outward, instead of inward only, to seek the welfare of the country. To affirm the importance of distant markets, and the relation to them of our own immense powers of production, implies logically the recognition of the link that joins the products and the markets,—that is, the carrying trade; the three together constituting that chain of maritime power to which Great Britain owes her wealth and greatness. Further, is it too much to say that, as two of these links, the shipping and the markets, are exterior to our own borders, the acknowledgement of them carries with it a view of the relations of the United States to the world radically distinct from the simple idea of self-sufferingness? We shall not follow far this line of thought before there will dawn the realization of America's unique position, facing the older worlds of the East and West, her shores lapped by the oceans which touch the one or the other, but which are common to her alone.

From *Atlantic Monthly*, LXVI (December, 1890).

1. How does Mahan characterize the previous twenty-five years of American economic development?
2. What relationship does he describe between the productive might of the United States and the desire for overseas markets?
3. What aspects of the British experience would have influenced Mahan's thinking?

The Imperialist Argument, 1898-99

With the outbreak of the Spanish-American War, many Americans attempted to justify the new imperialist face of the Republic. The following excerpts highlight various facets of the argument. In the first, Lymon Abbott, a Puritan clergyman from New England, outlined America's moral mission.

What are the distinguishing characteristics of American history; how do we differ, if at all, from other people? In the first place, we are on this continent forty-four independent sovereign states, and yet in a century there has been but one battle between these states. Why? Because we have contrived a method? No; not only that—because with that method we have possessed ourselves of a certain power of self-restraint and patience. . . . And it is not merely a tribunal which we have created; there is a principle which we have embodied in our national life—that controversies between communities as well as controversies between individuals shall be settled by right and by reason, not by force of arms.

Along with that has gone another—that we will depend chiefly on right and reason and conscience for the maintenance of law. We call this country a country of self-government. What do we mean by that? We mean, primarily, this: that we believe that men have wisdom enough to judge for themselves and conscience enough to respect the rights of their neighbor; and so, while we have our police and our armed force, and now and again we must call them into activity, in the main we depend, in this country, not on the police, not on the militia, to maintain the supremacy of the law; we believe there is a power in the human conscience and we trust to that power; in other words, we believe that if a law is a righteous law it will enforce itself. Or, to put it still more truly, we believe that God stands behind every righteous law, and that we can trust God Himself, by the force and operation of conscience speaking in man, to enforce righteous laws.

There is no other country that compares to America in its application of this principle of self-government; that is, trust to the conscience of men respecting the rights of their neighbors. . . .

Along with this is an attempt, at least, to give an equal and fair opportunity to all men. . . . In England, in France, in Germany, in Russia, in all European Powers, men are born more or less into classes and remain there; in this country a man is born an American; that is all. . . . I do not say we have equal justice to all men in America, but I say there are fewer obstacles and more opportunities for all men than in any other country on the globe. . . .

From *The Plymouth Morning Pulpit*, I (June 15, 1898).

Albert J. Beveridge was a Republican senator from Indiana. In the following excerpt, taken from a speech given in 1898, Beveridge, an imperialist, defends the right of the United States to expand overseas. Five years later, in the second excerpt, Beveridge looked forward to American global domination.

We are Anglo-Saxons, and must obey our blood and occupy new markets, and, if necessary, new lands. . . . [This is] the Anglo Saxon instinct of empire.

American factories are making more than the American people can use: American soil is producing more than they can consume. Fate has written our policy for us. The trade of the world must and shall be ours. And we will get it as our mother has taught us how. Like England, we will establish, trading posts throughout the world, we will cover the oceans with our merchant marine, we will build a navy to the measure of our greatness; great colonies will grow about our posts of trade, and American law, American order, American civilization, and the American flag will plant themselves on shores hitherto bloody and benighted.

. . . If it means Anglo-Saxon solidarity, if it means an English-American understanding upon the basis of a division of the world's markets, and English-speaking people's league of God for the permanent peace of this war-worn world, the stars will fight for us, and countless centuries will applaud.

All this is not the work of a day nor a year. Liberty and order and civilization are not planted by speeches, nor essays, nor editorials; their seed is borne on the talons of trade, and planted by the fingers of might. Fate puts the American people upon their decision between a Chinese policy of isolation and democracy, or a living policy of progress, prosperity and power. . . .

From R.W. Leopold, et al. *Problems in American History.* (New Jersey: Prentice-Hall, 1972).

Fellow Citizens:

It is a noble land that God has given us; a land that can feed and clothe the world; a land whose coast lines would enclose half the countries of Europe; a land set like a sentinel between the two imperial oceans of the globe, a greater England with a nobler destiny. It is a mighty people that He has planted on this soil; a people revitalized by the virile, man-producing working folk of all the earth; a people imperial by virtue of their power, by right of their institutions, by authority of their heaven-directed purposes—the propagandists and not the misers of liberty. It is a glorious history our God has bestowed upon His chosen people; . . .

Therefore, in this campaign, the question is larger than a party question. It is an American question. It is a world question. Shall the American people continue their resistless march toward the commercial supremacy of the world? Shall free institutions broaden their blessed reign as the children of liberty wax in strength, until the empire of our principles is established over the hearts of all mankind?

. . . And shall we reap the reward that waits on our discharge of our high duty as the sovereign power of earth; shall we occupy new markets for what our farmers raise, new markets for what our factories make, new markets for what our merchants sell—aye, and, please God, new markets for what our ships shall carry?

Shall we avail ourselves of new sources of supply of what we do not raise or make, so that what are luxuries to-day will be necessities to-morrow? Shall our commerce be encouraged until, with Oceanica, the Orient, and the world, American trade shall be the imperial trade of the entire globe? . . .

From Albert J. Beveridge, *Modern Eloquence*, XI (Philadelphia, 1903).

Future chairman of the Foreign Relations Committee, Senator Henry Cabot Lodge, in 1900, defended the American occupation of the Philippines.

I shall not argue our title to the [Philippine] islands by the law of nations, for it is perfect. No other nation has ever questioned it. . . .Equally plain is our right under the Constitution, by a treaty which is the supreme law of the land, to hold those islands, . . . The opposition . . . rests its weight on grounds widely different from these. They assert that on moral grounds we have no right to take or retain the Philippines, and that as a matter of expediency our whole Eastern policy is a costly mistake. . . . I deny both propositions. I believe we are in the Philippines as righteously as we are there rightly and legally. I believe that to abandon the islands, or to leave them now, would be a wrong to humanity, a dereliction of duty, a base betrayal of the Filipinos who have supported us . . . and in the highest degree contrary to sound morals. As to expediency, the arguments in favor of the retention of the Philippines seem to me so overwhelming that I should regard their loss as a calamity to our trade and commerce and to all our business interests so great that no man can measure it. . . .

Our opponents put forward as their chief objection that we have robbed these people of their liberty, and have taken them and hold them in defiance of the doctrine of the Declaration of Independence in regard to the consent of the governed. As to liberty, they have never had it, and have none now, except when we give it to them protected by the flag and the armies of the United States. . . .

From R.W. Leopold, et al. *Problems in American History.* (New Jersey: Prentice-Hall, 1972).

1. Compare the justificatons set out by the three defenders of imperialism. To what extent do they successfully counter possible opposing arguments?

2. Which of the three do you feel presents the most compelling argument? Defend your choice.

3. Write your own refutation of the position put forward by any of the three authors.

The Anti-Imperialist Case, 1899

The following excerpt is typical of the "cold water" thrown on the rhetoric of the imperialists during the period.

When the advocates of imperialism find it impossible to reconcile a colonial policy with the principles of our government or with the canons of morality; when they are unable to defend it upon the ground of religious duty or pecuniary profit, they fall back upon helpless despair upon the assertion that it is destiny. . . .

The people have not voted for imperialism; no national convention has declared for it; no Congress passed upon it. To whom, then, has the future been revealed? Whence this voice of authority? We can all prophesy, but our prophecies are merely guesses, colored by our hopes and our surroundings. Man's opinion of what is to be is half wish and half environment. Avarice paints destiny with a dollar mark about it, militarism equips it with a sword. . . .

If we embark upon a career of conquest, no one can tell how many islands we may be able to seize or how many races we may be able to subjugate; neither can any one estimate the cost, immediate and remote, to the nation's purse and to the nation's character, but whether we shall enter upon such a career is a question which the people have a right to decide for themselves. . . .

From R.W. Leopold, et al. *Problems in American History.* (New Jersey: Prentice-Hall, 1972).

1. How does the argument presented compare with the one which you built above?
2. What aspects of the argument would particularly appeal to an American audience?
3. Reread the last paragraph of the excerpt. To what extent has the author's prophecy come true?

Case for Continentalism, 1889

In the following excerpt, members of the House of Representatives debated a resolution calling for a commercial union with Canada.

The House having under consideration the joint resolution to promote commercial union with Canada, Mr. Butterworth said:

I cordially endorse what my friend had said touching the great advantage which would result to the people of the United States and to the people of Canada from removing the barriers which now intercept the sweep of our commerce towards the north. The resolution suggests commercial union. I believe that business relation would be of advantage to both countries. I have advocated full and unrestricted reciprocal trade. That relation being promptly rejected by

Sir John Macdonald's Government, political union is proposed as an alternative for imperial federation and as presenting advantages which are greater and more permanent than would result from any other possible arrangement.

I have never doubted, and do not doubt now, that unrestricted reciprocal trade is desirable; that commercial union is desirable; and that political union is still more desirable.

I have advocated removing every barrier and hindrance to full and free trade between Canada and the United States. I have believed, and do now, that such unhampered trade relations would lead to political union. I have deemed political union indispensable to the peace, prosperity, and happiness of our race in North America. I have believed, and do now, that we can no more avert it than we can change the course of the seasons.

The attitude of our Canadian friends toward political union is amusing and in some cases ridiculous. . . .

The proposition looks to the exaltation of Canada, not to her abasement. It looks to enlarging the opportunities of her people, not to restricting them.

★ ★ ★ ★ ★ ★

. . . I have often referred to the material advantage that would result to my countrymen if this union of the Dominion of Canada and the United States under one government could be consummated. It enlarges the opportunities of our people an hundred-fold. It secures to us with the blessings of lasting peace upon this continent the permanent supremacy of free institutions founded upon suffrage. It establishes upon an enduring basis an enlightened civilization based upon the precepts of Christianity. It would unite on this continent in indissoluble bonds the two great branches of the English-speaking family. . . .

Our Canadian kinsmen should discuss this proposition in the light of all the factors involved in its right solution. Loyalty to country is a noble sentiment, but a sentiment that should call practical common sense to sit in judgement with it.

1. What are the major arguments in support of the concept of political union?
2. How does the speaker characterize the nature of the Canadian position in the debate?
3. To what extent does the tenor of this excerpt reflect the concerns of modern anti-free trade forces in Canada?

Imperial Federation: the Canadian Alternative, 1888-1905

George Parkin was a staunch advocate of imperial federation. In 1888 he wrote that under such a scheme, the British Empire would be united under a common political and military banner. For many Canadians it was a preferable alternative to absorption by the United States.

Within a short time a remarkable change has come over public opinion in the British Isles themselves. Twenty years ago it almost seemed as if Great Britain was ready voluntarily to throw away her vast colonial empire. A whole school of politicians favored the idea, and seemed to have gained the public ear. 'The Times,' supposed to reflect public opinion, claimed that England was paying too high a price for enjoying the luxury of colonial loyalty, and warned the colonies to prepare for the separation that was inevitable. . . .

* * * * *

. . . Mr. Goldwin Smith still argues that trade interests will ultimately draw Canada into political connection with the United States, and apparently does not understand why this opinion is rejected with indignation by the vast majority of Canadians. Yet it seems impossible to conceive how, without a debasement of public sentiment quite unparalleled in history, a people whose history began in loyalty to British institutions, who through a hundred years have been sheltered by British power, who under that rule have attained and enjoyed the most complete political and religious liberty, who have constantly professed the most devoted regard for a mother land with which they are connected by a thousand ties of affectionate sympathy, should deliberately, in cold blood, and for commercial reasons only, break that connection and join themselves to a state in whose history and traditions they have no part. They would incur, and unquestionably would deserve, alike the contempt of the people they abandon and of the people they join. In a Great Britain reorganized as a federation, or union, or alliance, Canada would hold an honorable place, gained on lines of true national development; in annexation to the United States she could have nothing but a bastard nationality, the offspring of either meanness, selfishness, or fear.

From George R. Parkin. "The Reorganization of the British Empire". *The Century*, Vol. XXXV2 (December, 1888).

George Grant, principal of Queen's University, also supported Imperial Federation. For Grant, writing the next year, such a move would give Canada a greater voice in world affairs than it could ever enjoy as a small North American dominion.

Imperial Federation, from a Canadian point of view, means simply the next act in a process of political and historical development that began in 1763, when Canada—with the consent of all parties concerned—was declared to be British. From that day, the development of Canada from the position of a British colony into that of a British nationality has gone on steadily. The colonial condition is one of incomplete political development, and Canada has passed through various stages, each of which marks a greater measure of self-government than the previous stage. . . . The making of Canada into a nation has been a long process, and the process is not yet ended. . . .

This brief sketch prepares us for a definition. Imperial Federation, then, may be defined as a union between the Mother Country and Canada that would give to Canada not only the present full management of its own affairs, but a fair share in the management and responsibilities of common affairs. As British citizens, ought we to ask for more? As Canadians and full-grown men, ought we to be satisfied with less?

In the meanwhile the object of the Imperial Federation League is to form branches all over Canada to discuss the question from every point of view, with the confident expectation that in due time our Parliament will feel itself warranted by public opinion to instruct the Government of the day to enter into negotiations with the British Government on the subject. Then will be the time to draw up a scheme.

Before forming a branch of the league, all that is necessary is that a number of people in the locality should have two principles rooted and grounded in them: 1. that Britain and Canada must continue to have one flag, in other words that the present union must be maintained; 2. that Canadians are prepared for full citizenship, in other words that they are determined to be the peers and not the dependents of their fellow-citizens in the British Islands. . . .

From George M. Grant, "Imperial Federation": A Lecture Delivered in Victoria Hall, Winnipeg, on September 13, 1889 (Winnipeg: *Manitoba Free Press*, 1890).

Joseph Chamberlain was the British colonial secretary who first gave life to the concept of a federation of British nations. In a speech to the Colonial Conference of 1902, Chamberlain reiterated his support of the concept and pledged Britain's willingness to cooperate.

Gentlemen, we do want your aid. We do require your assistance in the administration of the vast Empire which is yours as well as ours. The weary Titan staggers under the too vast orb of its fate. We have borne the burden for many years. We think it is time that our children should assist us to support it, and whenever you make the request to us, be very sure that we shall hasten gladly to call you to our Councils. If you are prepared at any time to take any share, any proportionate share, in the burdens of the Empire, we are prepared to meet you with any proposal for giving to you a corresponding voice in the policy of the Empire. . . .

As regards Imperial defence, I propose to lay before you, for your information, a paper which will show the comparative amount of the ordinary naval and military expenditure of the United Kingdom and of the different self-governing Colonies. . . .

Now, no one, I think, will pretend that that is a fair distribution of the burdens of Empire. No one will believe that the United Kingdom can, for all time, make this inordinate sacrifice. While the Colonies were young and poor, in the first place they did not offer anything like the same temptation to the ambitions of others, and, in the second place, they were clearly incapable of providing large sums for their own defense, and therefore it was perfectly right and natural that the mother country should undertake the protection of her children. But now that the Colonies are rich and powerful, that every day they are growing by leaps and bounds, their material prosperity promises to rival that of the United Kingdom itself, and I think it is inconsistent with their position—inconsistent with their dignity as nations—that they should leave the mother country to bear the whole, or almost the whole, of the expense. . . .

From J.M. Bliss, *Canadian History in Documents*, (Toronto: Ryerson Press, 1966).

1. What argument does Parkin use to prove that Canada will never fall into the American orbit?
2. Account for Grant's thesis that imperial federation would mean an expanded role for Canada, and not a diminished one.
3. Outline the reasons behind Britain's support of the concept. How do they differ from Canada's position?

The Imperial Debate in Canada, 1902

Nationalists lined up on both sides of the imperialist debate. Unlike in the United States, the debate was not over the moral issues involved in imperial entanglements, but rather over the subservience of the nation to a larger whole.

Canadian humorist Stephen Leacock was serious about his imperialist sentiments. In Greater Canada: An Appeal *he set out the nationalist case for imperial federation.*

Now, in this month of April, when the ice is leaving our rivers, the ministers of Canada take ship for this the fourth Colonial Conference at London. . . . Shall we say to the people of England, "The time has come; we know and realize our country. We will be your colony no longer. Make us one with you in an Empire, Permanent and Indivisible."

This last alternative means what is commonly called Imperialism. It means a united system of defence, an imperial navy for whose support somehow or other the whole Empire shall properly contribute, and with it an imperial authority in whose power we all may share. To many people in Canada this imperialism is a tainted word. It is too much associated with a truckling subservience to English people and English ideas and the silly swagger of the hop-o'-my-thumb junior officer. But there is and must be for the true future of our country, a higher and more real imperialism than this—the imperialism of the plain man at the plough and the clerk in the counting house, the imperialism of any decent citizen that demands for this country its proper place in the councils of the Empire and in the destiny of the world. In this sense, imperialism means but the realization of a Greater Canada, the recognition of a wider citizenship.

I, that write these lines, am an Imperialist because I will not be a Colonial. This Colonial status is a worn-out, by-gone thing. The sense and feeling of it has become harmful to us. It limits the ideas, and circumscribes the patriotism of our people. It impairs the mental vigour and narrows the outlook of those that are reared and educated in our midst. . . .

Nor is it ever possible or desirable that we in Canada can form an independent country. The little cry that here and there goes up among us is but the symptom of an aspiring discontent, that will not let our people longer be colonials. 'Tis but a cry forced out by what a wise man has called the growing pains of a nation's progress. Independent, we could not survive a decade. . . .

Nor does our future lie in Union with those that dwell to the Southward. The day of annexation to the United States is passed. Our future lies elsewhere. Be it said without concealment and without bitterness. They have chosen their lot; we have chosen ours. Let us go our separate ways in peace. . . .

Not Independence then, not annexation, not stagnation: nor yet that doctrine of a little Canada that some conceive,—half in, half out of the Empire, with a mimic navy of its own; a pretty navy this,—poor two-penny collection, frollicking on its little way strictly within the Gulf of St. Lawrence, a sort of silly adjunct to the navy of the Empire, semi-detached, the better to be smashed at will. As well a Navy of the Province, or the Parish, home-made for use at home, docked every Saturday in Lake Nipigon! . . .

Thus stands the case. Thus stands the question of the future of Canada. Find for us something other than mere colonial stagnation, something sounder then independence, nobler than annexation, greater in purpose than a little Canada. Find us a way. Build us a plan, that shall make us, in hope at least, an Empire Permanent and Indivisible.

From J.M. Bliss, ed., *Canadian History in Documents*, (Toronto: Ryerson Press, 1966).

French-Canadian nationalist Henri Bourassa argued against imperialism in his work Great Britain and Canada. In it he attacked both the economic side of imperial attachment and the basic concept as being completely antithetical to Canadian nationalism.

The present feeling of the French-Canadian is one of contentment. He is satisfied with his lot. He is anxious to preserve his liberty and his peace. . . . Upon any proposed modification of the constitutional system of Canada he is disposed to look with distrust, or at least with anxiety. He cannot forget that all changes in the past were directed against him, except those that were enacted under such peculiar circumstances as made it imperative for the British Government to conciliate him. He asks for no change—for a long time to come, at least. And should any change be contemplated, he is prepared to view it, to appreciate its prospective advantages and inconveniences, neither from a British point of view nor from his own radical standpoint, but to approach the problem as it may affect the exclusive interests of Canada. He has loyally accepted the present constitution; he has done his ample share of duty by the country; and he feels that he is entitled to be consulted before any change is effected.

How thoroughly and exclusively Canadian the French-Canadian is should never be forgotten by those who contemplate any change in the constitutional or national status of Canada. This is so patent a fact, so logical a consequence of historical developments, that nothing short of absolute ignorance or wilful blindness can justify the language of those who talk of drawing him either by persuasion or by force to a closer allegiance to the Empire. As as matter of fact, he constitutes the only exclusively Canadian racial group in the Dominion. . . .

Now, apart from his instinctive reluctance to contemplate any political evolution, what are the feelings of the French-Canadian with regard to Imperial Federation or any form of British Imperialism?

First, as may be naturally expected, sentimental arguments in favour of British Imperialism cannot have any hold upon him. To his reason only must appeals on this ground be made. That the new Imperial policy will bring him, and Canada at large, advantages that will not be paid by any infringement on his long-struggled-for liberty, he must be clearly shown.

Towards Great Britain he knows that he has a duty of allegiance to perform. But he understands that duty to be what it has been so far, and nothing more. He has easily and generously forgotten the persecutions of the earlier and larger part of his national life under the British Crown. He is willing to acknowledge the good treatment which he has received later on, though he cannot forget that his own tenacity and the neighborhood of the United States have had much to do with the improvement of his situation.

In short, his affection for Great Britain is one of reason, mixed with a certain amount of esteem and suspicion, the proportions of which vary according to time and circumstances, and also with his education, his temperament, and his social surroundings.

Towards the Empire he has no feelings whatever; and naturally so. The blood connection and the pride in Imperial power and glory having no claims upon him, what sentiment can he be expected to entertain for New Zealand or Australia, South Africa or India, for countries and populations entirely foreign to him, with which he has no relations, intellectual or political, and much less commercial intercourse than he has with the United States, France, Germany, or Belgium?

By the motherland he feels that he has done his full duty; by the Empire he does not feel that he has any duty to perform. He makes full allowance for the blood feelings of his English-speaking partner; but having himself, in the past, sacrificed much of his racial tendencies for the sake of Canadian unity, he thinks that the Anglo-Canadian should be prepared to study the problems of Imperialism from a purely Canadian standpoint. Moreover, this absence of racial feelings from his heart allows him to judge more impartially the question of the relations between Canada and the Empire.

. . . The French-Canadians of the popular class look upon Canada as their own country. They are ready to do their duty by Canada as their own country; but considering they owe nothing to Great Britain or any other country, they ask nothing from them. Imbued with a strong sense of liberty, they have no objection to their English-speaking fellow country-men going to war anywhere they please; but they cannot conceive that Canada as a whole may be forced out of its present situation. They let people talk of any wise and wild proposal of Imperialism; but if any change were attempted to be imposed on them, they would resist the pressure, quietly but constantly.

To sum up, the French-Canadian is decidedly and exclusively Canadian by nationality and American by his ethnic temperament. People with world-wide aspirations may charge him with provincialism. But after all, this sentiment of exclusive attachment to one's land and one's nationality is to be found as one of the essential characteristics of all strong and growing peoples. On the other hand, the lust of abnormal expansion and Imperial pride have ever been the marked features of all nations of the verge of decadence.

From Henri Bourassa, "The French-Canadian in the British Empire," in *Monthly Review* of London, September/October 1902 (London: John Murray, 1902).

1. Outline Leacock's concept of a "greater Canada."

2. Account for Bourassa's assertion that imperial federation will have no benefit for Canada.
3. Write the script for a short debate between Bourassa and Leacock. Have each participant not only outline his own viewpoint, but also present consistent arguments to counter that of the other.

The World at War, 1914-18

The two North American nations were faced with a similar problem in the summer of 1914. Although Canada was technically at war when Britain was, the level of its involvement (as in the Boer War) remained Canada's decision. The United States, on the other hand, while having no political ties to the Entente powers, had strong personal and economic ties to the Western allies.

Sir Wilfrid Laurier rose in the House of Commons on August 19, 1914, during the emergency war session to speak as leader of the opposition. In his address, excerpted below, he called for Parliament to show that all Canadians were of "one mind" in their support of Britain and the Empire.

It is our duty, more pressing upon us than all other duties, at once, on this first day of this extraordinary session of the Canadian Parliament, to let Great Britain know, and to let the friends and foes of Great Britain know, that there is in Canada but one mind and one heart, and that all Canadians stand behind the mother country, conscious and proud that she has engaged in this war, not from any selfish motive, for any purpose of aggrandisement, but to maintain untarnished the honour of her name, to fulfil her obligations, and to save civilization from the unbridled lust of conquest and domination.

We are British subjects, and to-day we are face to face with the consequences which are involved in that proud fact. Long we have enjoyed the benefits of our British citizenship; today it is our duty to accept its responsibilities and its sacrifices. We have long said that when Great Britain is at war we are at war; to-day we realize that Great Britain is at war and that Canada is at war also. Our territory is liable to attack and to invasion. So far as invasion is concerned, I do not see that there is any cause for apprehension, for it seems to me obvious that neither Austria nor Germany, our foes in this war, can command any force able to make an attack so far from their base. But no one pretends that our maritime cities on the Pacific and the Atlantic, are free from the possibility of insult by an audacious corsair, who, descending suddenly upon our shores, might subject them to an insolent raid and decamp with his booty before punishment could reach him. . . .

. . . I have always said, and I repeat it on this occasion, that there is but one mind and one heart in Canada. At other times we may have had different views as to the methods by which we are to serve our country and our empire. More than once I have declared that if England were ever in danger—nay, not only in danger, but if she were ever engaged in such a contest as would put her strength to the test—then it would be the duty of Canada to assist the motherland to the utmost of Canada's ability. . . .

From J.J. Talman, ed., *Basic Documents in Canadian History*, (Toronto: Van Nostrand Publishing Company, 1959).

Neutral in Thought and Deed: the United States in 1914

The same day that Laurier was addressing the House of Commons, Woodrow Wilson issued the following statement to the people of the United States. In it he called for the American public to remain impartial and fair to both sides in the conflict.

The effect of the war upon the United States will depend upon what American citizens say and do. Every man who really loves America will act and speak in the true spirit of neutrality, which is the spirit of impartiality and fairness and friendliness to all concerned. The spirit of the Nation in this critical matter will be determined largely by what individuals and society and those gathered in public meetings do and say, upon what newspapers and magazines contain, upon what ministers utter in their pulpits, and men proclaim as their opinions on the street.

The people of the United States are drawn from many nations, and chiefly from the nations now at war. It is natural and inevitable that there should be the utmost variety of sympathy and desire among them with regard to the issues and circumstances of the conflict. Some will wish one nation, others another, to succeed in the momentous struggle. It will be easy to excite passion and difficult to allay it. Those responsible for exciting it will assume a heavy responsibility, responsibility for no less a thing than that the people of the United States, whose love of their country and whose loyalty to its Government should unite them as Americans all, bound in honor and affection to think first of her and her interests, may be divided in camps of hostile opinion, hot against each other, involved in the war itself in impulse and opinion if not in action. . . .

Such divisions amongst us would be fatal to our peace of mind and might seriously stand in the way of the proper performance of our duty as the one great nation at peace, the one people holding itself ready to play a part of impartial mediation and speak the counsels of peace and accommodation, not as a partisan, but as a friend. . . .

From R. Hofstadter, ed., *Great Issues in American History*, (New York: Vintage Books, 1958).

1. Why does Laurier say that Canada should enter the war?
2. What reasons does Wilson give for staying out of the conflict?
3. Why do you think that the North Americans reacted so differently in 1914?

The United States Goes to War, 1917

By 1917 the situation had changed in Europe. The resumption of unrestricted submarine warfare, coupled with the very real possibility of an allied collapse, prompted President Woodrow Wilson to step in. He defended his decision to Congress.

I have called the Congress into extraordinary session because there are serious, very serious, choices of policy to be made, and made immediately, which it was neither right nor constitutionally permissible that I should assume the responsibility of making.

On the third of February last I officially laid before you the extraordinary announcement of the Imperial German Government that on and after the first day of February it was its purpose to put aside all restraints of law or of humanity and use its submarines to sink every vessel that sought to approach either the ports of Great Britain and Ireland or the western coasts of Europe or any of the ports controlled by the enemies of Germany within the Mediterranean. . . . The new policy has swept every restriction aside. Vessels of every kind, whatever their flag, their character, their cargo, their destination, their errand, have been ruthlessly sent to the bottom without warning and without thought of help or mercy for those on board, the vessels of friendly neutrals along with those of belligerents. Even hospital ships and ships carrying relief to the sorely bereaved and stricken people of Belgium, though the latter were provided with safe conduct through the proscribed areas by the German Government itself and were distinguished by unmistakable marks of identity, have been sunk with the same reckless lack of compassion or of principle.

I was for a little while unable to believe that such things would in fact be done by any government that had hitherto subscribed to the humane practices of civilized nations. . . . I am not now thinking of the loss of property involved, immense and serious as that is, but only of the wanton and wholesale destruction of the lives of non-combatants, men, women, and children, engaged in pursuits which have always, even in the darkest periods of modern history, been deemed innocent and legitimate. Property can be paid for; the lives of *peaceful and innocent people cannot be.* The present German submarine warfare against commerce is a warfare against mankind. . . .

It is a war against all nations. American ships have been sunk, American lives taken, in ways which it has stirred us very deeply to learn of, but the ships and people of other neutral and friendly nations have been sunk and overwhelmed in the waters in the same way. There has been no discrimination. The challenge is to all mankind. Each nation must decide for itself how it will meet it. . . .

With a profound sense of the solemn and even tragical character of the step I am taking and of the grave responsibilities which it involves, but in unhesitating obedience to what I deem my constitutional duty, I advise that the Congress declare the recent course of the Imperial German Government to be in fact nothing less than war against the government and people of the United States; that it formally accept the status of belligerent which has thus been thrust upon it; and that it take immediate steps not only to put the country in a more thorough state of defense but also to exert all its power and employ all its resources to bring the Government of the German Empire to terms and end the war. . . .

From R. Hofstadter, ed., *Great Issues in American History*, (New York: Vintage Books, 1958).

1. Outline Wilson's description of the nature of submarine warfare.
2. The impartiality of which Wilson spoke in 1914 has been replaced by war rhetoric. Cite some examples of extreme language used in the speech to strengthen the pro-war argument.
3. To what extent do Wilson's arguments parallel those of Laurier three years earlier?

The Anti-War Argument, 1917

Not all Americans agreed with Wilson's decision. He had, after all, been reelected the previous fall on the slogan "He kept us out of the War."

Fred Britten, an Illinois congressman, argued that diplomatic alternatives should still be explored with Germany, and failing that that only volunteers should be liable for overseas service.

I am not a pacifist in any sense, but am firm in the belief that this resolution is being jammed through Congress against the wishes of a great majority of people all over the country. . . .

The wrongs of Germany, England, and all of the other belligerents which have been heaped upon us will not justify the loss of untold thousands of lives, the crippling and maiming of our American boys, nor the suffering and anguish which is bound to follow our flag to Europe.

It is not yet too late to diplomatically consider the differences between Germany and ourselves, and I am sure that a sincere effort in this direction would prove more valuable and creditable to the country than a declaration of war. . . .

Let us arm our whole Nation for its own defense and keep clear of any entangling alliances with European and Asiatic Governments.

By maintaining an attitude of armed neutrality we can rest secure until additional revolutions in Europe have done their work, and we can then assist in establishing a condition of universal peace. . . .

The truth of the matter is that 90 per cent of your people and mine do not want this declaration of war. . . .

Mr. Chairman, it is short and self-explanatory. You and I do not want our boys to go up against that liquid fire, noxious gases, and a trench warfare that has made wild animals out of human beings, just because our administration has convinced itself that the future safety of our country will be more secure in the defeat of Germany than in the defeat of England.

But let us not deceive ourselves that we are going into this war in the interest of humanity. . . .

From R.W. Leopold, et al., *Problems in American History*. (New Jersey: Prentice-Hall, 1972).

Claude Kitchin, floor leader for the majority Democrats in the House of Representatives, argued that it was a European concern in which the United States had no part.

Half of the civilized world is now a slaughterhouse for human beings. This Nation is the last hope of peace on earth, good will toward men. I am unwilling for my country by statutory command to pull up the last anchor of peace in the world and extinguish during the long night of a world-wide war the only remaining star of hope for Christendom. . . .

By passage of this resolution we enter the war. . . . Whatever be the future, whatever be the rewards or penalties of this Nation's step, I shall always believe that we could and ought to have kept out of this war. . . .

In my judgment, we could keep out of the war with Germany as we kept out of the war with Great Britain, by keeping our ships and our citizens out of the war zone of Germany as we did out of the war zone of Great Britain. And we would sacrifice no more honor, surrender no more rights in the one case than in the other. Or we could resort to armed neutrality, which the President recently urged and for which I voted of March 1. . . .

But we are told that Germany has destroyed American lives while Great Britain destroyed only property. Great Britain destroyed no American lives, because this Nation kept her ships and her citizens out of her war zone which she sowed with hidden mines.

But are we quite sure that the real reason for war with Germany is the destruction of lives as distinguished from property, that to avenge the killing of innocent Americans and to protect American lives war becomes a duty? . . .

Why can we not, why should we not, forego for the time being the violation of our rights by Germany, and do as we did with Mexico, and thus save the universe from being wrapped in the flames of war? . . .

War upon the part of a nation is sometimes necessary and imperative. But here no invasion is threatened. Not a foot of our territory is demanded or coveted. No essential honor is required to be sacrificed. No fundamental right is asked to be permanently yielded or suspended. No national policy is contested. No part of our sovereignty is questioned. Here the overt act, ruthless and brutal though it be, is not aimed directly at us. The purpose of the proposed enemy is not our injury, either in property or life. The whole aim and purpose and effort are directed at a powerful enemy with which she is in a life and death struggle. . . .

From R.W. Leopold, et al., *Problems in American History*, (New Jersey: Prentice-Hall, 1972).

1. How does Britten portray the two sides in the conflict?
2. What argument does Kitchin use against intervention?
3. Both authors claim that the United States can play a greater role in bringing about peace by staying out of the war. Outline and comment upon their argument.

The Conscription Crisis in Canada, 1917

When the Union government of Robert Borden introduced conscription in 1917 it tore the country apart. Many Canadians agreed with American isolationists such as Britten and Kitchin that the conflict was a European concern and that only volunteers should be expected to participate. The issue soon took on racial overtones as English and French Canadians split on the issue.

Borden defended his decision in the House of Commons by stating that the war was for the defence of Canada.

If it is conceded that there is an emergency, are we not fighting in France and Flanders for the defence of Canada? There are but few members of the House who, in speaking of the war, have not affirmed that truth. Let us look for a moment at Great Britain. . . . Her armies have sustained very nearly a million casualties on the soil of France and Belgium. Is Great Britain fighting in France and Belgium for the defence of her own territory? Yes, she is fighting to free the soil of France and Belgium from the unhallowed footsteps of the enemy, but she is no less truly fighting in defence of her own territory. . . . What about Canada? When the Canadians on the 22nd day of April 1915, barred the path of the German to Calais, I say that they barred his path also to Halifax, Quebec, St. John and Montreal. From the North Sea to the borders of Switzerland there is a line nearly 500 miles in length, which is being pressed back towards the German frontier. Along that 500 mile line there is a strip of territory of varying width over which this devastating struggle has swayed to and fro. It was once a glorious country with smiling fields, happy villages and prosperous towns. Today it is the abomination of desolation, a mass of shell-churned mud with no trace of road or street, house, habitation or village. . . . Its churches have been destroyed and even its graveyards desecrated. Imagine such scenes in this country of Canada, along a battle line extending from Quebec to Toronto. Where is Canada's first line of defence against such horrors and barbarities? It is in the North Sea, where the Empire's Navy holds back Germany's power, and in the trenches where the Canadians with the other Allied armies are slowly but surely freeing the soil of France and of Belgium from the insulting tread of the invader. If that is not our first line of defence, where is it? Who then will say that the Canadian Expeditionary Force is not fighting for the defence of Canada? . . . What security is there in mere distance, considering modern means of communication or attack not only on the sea, but through the air and under the sea? If this war continues for two more years, who shall say that we may not see German aircraft in Canada? Let us not forget that German submarines crossed the Atlantic nearly a year ago.

From the Parliament of Canada, *Debates of the House of Commons*, 1917, (Ottawa), 3.

Henri Bourassa had feared the spectre of conscription from the beginning of the conflict. In late 1914 he had made the case that the war was not in Canada's best interest.

To some, the Empire is all and every thing; others think of France only; another category, logical but narrow in their Canadian exclusiveness, see nothing beyond the borders of Canada: they seem to ignore our most conspicuous world's responsibilities.

These various feelings indicate a singular absence of a truly *national* patriotism. They show a marked contrast with that strong and practical sentiment which binds in one solid mass the people of other countries, the moment the vital interests of the nation are at stake. Since the outbreak of the war, the country has been flooded with "patriotic" speeches and writings; but those words have been followed with very few deeds for the good of Canada.

This marks all the difference between the thoughtful action of sovereign peoples, masters of their destinies, conscious of their responsibilities, and the thoughtlessness of a child-nation, deprived of international status, unable to measure the consequences of its actions and even to foresee the repercussion of the movements of other nations, including that from which it depends.

Everyone speaks of the duties of Canada to Great Britain or France. Who has thought of the duties of Canada to herself?

★ ★ ★ ★ ★ ★

Another point of great importance has been raised, in connection with Canada's participation in the war. It has been stated, in Parliament and out of it that Canada, as part of the British Empire, is in duty bound to participate actively in every conflict in which Great Britain may be drawn.

That doctrine is contrary to all traditions, to the basic principles upon which rests our constitution, to the long standing agreement between the motherland and her self-governing colonies.

Canada, as a mere irresponsible dependency of Great Britain, has no moral or constitutional *obligation*, nor any *immediate interest* in the present war.

Great Britain has entered the conflict of her own free will, in consequence of her entanglements in the international situation. She has framed her policy and decided her action with a sole view to her own interests, without consulting her colonies or considering in any respect their peculiar situation and local interests.

The territory of Canada is not exposed to the attacks of any of the belligerent nations. An independent Canada would be to-day in absolute safety. The dangers to which her trade may be exposed result from the fact that she is a British possession, subject to the consequences of British policy and the risks of a military intervention decided by the Imperial government upon their exclusive authority and responsibility. It is therefore the duty of Britain to defend Canada, and not the duty of Canada to defend Britain.

From Henri Bourassa, "The Duty of Canada at the Present Hour," (Montreal: *Le Devoir*, 1915).

1. Write a précis of the ideas and arguments put forward by the two leaders. To what extent are their arguments based upon the same feelings of nationalism?
2. Compare Bourassa's beliefs with those expressed by Wilson in 1914. Contrast that viewpoint with a comparison of Borden's ideas and those reflected in Wilson's declaration of war in 1917.
3. Discuss the commonalities of the response of the North Americans to the First World War.

The Debate over the League, 1919-20

North Americans were of two minds about the League of Nations. On both sides of the border there were concerns that membership might draw the continent into exclusively European conflicts.

Woodrow Wilson made the case for the League.

At the front of this great treaty is put the covenant of the League of Nations. . . . Unless you get the united, concerted purpose and power of the great Governments of the world behind this settlement, it will fall down like a house of cards. There is only one power to put behind the liberation of mankind, and that is the power of mankind. It is the power of the united moral forces of the world, and in the covenant of the League of Nations the moral forces of the world are mobilized. . . . They enter into a solemn promise to one another that they will never use their power against one another for aggression; that they never will impair the territorial integrity of a neighbor; that they never will interfere with the political independence of a neighbor; that they will abide by the principle that great populations are entitled to determine their own destiny and that they will not interfere with that destiny; and that no matter what differences arise amongst them they will never resort to war without first having . . . either submitted the matter of controversy to arbitration, in which case they agree to abide by the result without question, or submitted it to the consideration of the Council of the League of Nations . . . agreeing that there shall be six months allowed for the mature consideration of . . . the Council, and agreeing that at the expiration of the six months, even if they are not then ready to accept the advice of the Council with regard to the settlement of the dispute, they will still not go to war for another three months. In other words, they consent, no matter what happens, to submit every matter of difference between them to the judgment of mankind, and just so certainly as they do that, . . . war will be pushed out of the foreground of terror in which it has kept the world for generation after generation, and men will know that there will be a calm time of deliberate counsel. The most dangerous thing for a bad cause is to expose it to the opinion of the world. The most certain way that you can prove that a man is mistaken is by letting all his neighbors know what he thinks, by letting all his neighbors discuss what he thinks, and if he is in the wrong you will notice that he will stay at home, he will not walk on the street. He will be afraid of the eyes of his neighbors. He will be afraid of their judgment of his character. He will know that his cause is lost unless he can sustain it by the arguments of right and of justice. The same law that applies to individuals applies to nations.

From James R. Christopher, Bryan C. Vickers, *The American Challenge*, (Toronto: Oxford University Press, 1987).

William Edgar Borah was a senator from Iowa from 1907 until his death in 1940. In 1919 he led the isolationist fight against the League.

When the League shall have been formed, we shall be a member of what is known as the council of the league. Our accredited representative will sit in judgement with the accredited representatives of the other members of the league to pass upon the concerns not only of our country but of all Europe and all Asia and the entire world. Our accredited representatives will be members of the assembly. They will sit there to represent the judgement of these 110 000 000 people—more than—just as we are accredited here to represent our constituencies. We can not send our representatives to sit in council with the representatives of other great nations of the world with mental reservations as to what we shall do in case their judgement shall not be satisfactory to us. If we go to the council or to the assembly with any other purpose than that of complying in good faith and in absolute integrity with all upon which the council or the assembly may pass, we shall soon return to our country with our self-respect forfeited and the public opinion of the world condemnatory. . . .

. . . Can you hope for peace when love of country is disregarded in your scheme, when the spirit of nationality is rejected, even scoffed at? Yet what law of that moving and mysterious force does your treaty not deny? With a ruthlessness unparalleled your treaty in a dozen instances runs counter to the divine law of nationality. Peoples who speak the same language, kneel at the same ancestral tombs, moved by the same traditions, animated by a common hope, are torn asunder, broken in pieces, divided, and parceled out to antagonistic nations. And this you call justice. This, you cry, means peace. Peoples who have dreamed of independence, struggled and been patient, sacrificed and been hopeful, people who were told that through this peace conference they should realize the aspirations of centuries, have again had their hopes dashed to earth. . . . No; your treaty means injustice. It means slavery. It means war. And to all this you ask this Republic to become a party. You ask it to abandon the creed under which it has grown to power and accept the creed of autocracy, the creed of repression and force.

. . . Call us little Americans if you will, but leave us the consolation and the pride which the term American, however modified, still imparts. . . . We have sought nothing save the tranquility of our own people and the honor and independence of our own Republic. No foreign flattery, no possible world glory and power have disturbed our poise or come between us and our devotion to the traditions which have made us a people or the policies which have made us a Nation, unselfish and commanding. If we have erred we have erred out of too much love for those things which from childhood you and we together have been taught to revere—yes, to defend even at the cost of limb and life. If we have erred it is because we have placed too high an estimate upon the wisdom of Washington and Jefferson, too exalted an opinion upon the patriotism of the sainted Lincoln. . . .

From R.W. Hofstadter, ed., *Great Issues in American History*. (New York: Vintage Books, 1958).

Although a charter member of the League, as early as 1921, the Canadian delegation was filing protests against the binding provisions of Article X of the Covenant.

This article is open, in my judgment, to the very gravest objections, both generally, and from the point of view of countries in the condition and stage of development of Canada in particular.

Of the gravity of the obligations by it imposed upon the parties to the convention, there can be no question. It makes of the League, as the *The Times* expresses it, 'a mutual guarantee society of unlimited liability'. . . .

. . . Even if . . . it is right that a guarantee such as proposed should be given, it does not follow that it should be given by all the states. It may be right that one class of states should give it, and entirely wrong to exact it of another. Many reasons for such a distinction exist, and all of them justify Canada's being classed with those states upon which this onerous obligation should not be imposed. Canada has no say in, and no responsibility for, any settlement that may be made by the powers of general interests, after hearing those of particular interests directcy concerned therein, as to territory to be allotted to, or determined for, revived or newly created states, out of that formerly held by the vanquished powers. There is, therefore, in the fact of that settlement itself, to be found no reason why she should guarantee its being executed and continuously respected. . . .

From J.M. Bliss, ed., *Canadian History in Documents, 1762-1966*, (Toronto: Ryerson Press, 1966).

1. Do what extent do you agree with Wilson that the League was the only hope for the "liberation of mankind"?
2. Account for the major North American concern with regard to membership in the League.
3. Write a position paper to be submitted to Prime Minister Mackenzie King in 1921 either supporting or rejecting participation in the League of Nations.

The End of Imperialism: the Emergence of the Commonwealth, 1926

World War I put to rest the concept of Imperial Federation. In its place a new idea had emerged, a view of the empire as an organization of equals. Lord Balfour chaired a committee whose report was accepted by the Imperial Conference of 1926. The Balfour Report called for the formation of a British Commonwealth of Nations.

The Committee are of opinion that nothing would be gained by attempting to lay down a Constitution for the British Empire. Its widely scattered parts have very different characteristics, very different histories, and are at very different stages of evolution; while, considered as a whole, it defies classification and bears no real resemblance to any other political organization which now exists or has ever yet been tried.

There is, however, one most important element in it which, from a strictly constitutional point of view, has now, as regards all vital matters, reached its full development—we refer to the group of self-governing communities composed of Great Britain and the Dominions. Their position and mutual relation may be readily defined. They are autonomous Communities within the British Empire, equal in status, in no way subordinate one to another in any aspect of their domestic or external affairs, though united by a common allegiance to the Crown, and freely associated as members of the British Commonwealth of Nations.

A foreigner endeavouring to understand the true character of the British Empire by the aid of this formula alone would be tempted to think that it was devised rather to make mutual interference impossible than to make mutual co-operation easy. . . .

But no account, however accurate, of the negative relations in which Great Britain and the Dominions stand to each other can do more than express a portion of the truth. The British Empire is not founded upon negations. It depends essentially, if not formally, on positive ideals. Free institutions are its life-blood. Free co-operation is its instrument. Peace, security, and progress are among its objects. Aspects of all these great themes have been discussed at the present Conference; excellent results have been thereby obtained. And

388 The North Americans

though every Dominion is now, and must always remain, the sole judge of the nature and extent of its co-operation, no common cause will, in our opinion, be thereby imperilled.

Equality of status, so far as Britain and the Dominions are concerned, is thus the root principle governing our Inter-Imperial Relations. . . .

From J.M. Bliss, ed., *Canadian History in Documents, 1762-1966*, (Toronto: Ryerson Press, 1966).

1. Why does the report reject the idea of a common constitution for the empire?
2. How does Balfour redefine the nature of the members of the empire?
3. In what way does the report describe the new relationship which will exist within the Commonwealth?

Imperialism and Isolation: Analysis and Application

1. The fear of annexation has been a recurring theme in Canadian history since the time of Confederation. In graph form, chart the rise and fall of continentalist movements in Canada during the the nineteenth and twentieth centuries.

2. "The closing of the frontier, identified by Frederick Jackson Turner, gave great impetus to the drive for overseas expansion."

Account for this thesis with reference to the economic and philosophic justifications for American imperialism in the late nineteenth century.

3. Defend the following thesis: "The National Policy was not a product of Canadian nationalism, but rather Central Canadian imperialism."

4. (a) Select one spokesperson from the late nineteenth century in Canada, the United States, Great Britain, or some other expansionist European or Asian power. Research the individual selected and, based upon your research, write a first-person account entitled "The Duty of Imperialism." Or select one spokesperson from the late nineteenth century from Africa, the Americas, or Asia. Research the individual or the collective beliefs of people from her/his country and, based upon your research, write a first-person account entitled "The Crime of Imperialism."

(b) Together with your classmates, stage a panel discussion with representatives speaking for each point of view and from each nation or region. After the panelists have outlined their viewpoints, open up the discussion to questions from the floor.

(c) Following the panel, step out of role and in a general discussion compare the arguments for and against imperialism as perceived during the late nineteenth century.

5. "Imperial Federation was born in the glories of late Victorian England, and died in the mud and horrors of the Western Front."

Account for this statement with reference to the growth and decline of the Imperial Federalist movement.

6. "Rather than the responsibility of a single incident or nation, the outbreak of

war in 1914 was the result of the interplay of a series of complex forces and movements."

Defend this assertion with specific reference to the factors underlying World War I.

7. Trace the route by which the United States moved from a position of neutrality "in thought and deed" to one of armed intervention in Europe.

8. Compare the response of French Canadians to the call to fight in Europe with that of Americans between 1914-17. To what extent do these two groups reflect the "North American" attitude toward the war?

9. "At least Americans had the courage to say no to the League of Nations. Canadians joined and then pretended that it didn't exist."

Respond to this thesis with regard to Canadian involvement in the League of Nations.

10. Create a chronological graph tracing the development of Canadian autonomy in foreign affairs from 1890 until 1931.

12
THE URBAN EXPERIENCE

The fifty years from 1870 to 1920 saw a fundamental change in the lifestyles of North Americans. The face of the continent began to change from that of a rural-based society to one where more and more economic and political power rested in the urban areas.

In the United States this transformation represented a fundamental change in social thinking. The prevailing American myth of the first half of the nineteenth century, reflected in the writing of Frederick Jackson Turner, saw the frontier as a purifying factor against the corrupt and decaying city. Even if at one time this myth had been true, by 1870 it was no longer a reality. The city had become the symbol of the new America.

Development in Canada, on the other hand, had always followed a more urban pattern. Metropolitan centres were established, which in turn extended their influence into the wilderness. In the seventeenth and eighteenth centuries Paris and London, with their satellite cities of Quebec and Montreal, dictated settlement and commercial patterns in the colonies. In the 1800s new centres such as Toronto and Winnipeg emerged, and by the early decades of the twentieth century two transcontinental railway systems had made the entire nation the economic hinterland of the Eastern metropolitan giants.

The North American City

To understand the nature of the North American city, let's first look at examples from both sides of the border. In 1860 only about 16 percent of the population of the United States lived in towns or cities of eight thousand or more. By 1900 urban population had doubled and one in three Americans lived in cities.

Much of this growth took place in the industrial East and the Midwest. New York grew from a population of 2 million in 1880 to over 3.5 million by the end of the century. As phenomenal as this growth seems, it pales beside the development of the new financial capital of the West—Chicago.

In 1831 Chicago was a muddy village consisting of twelve families. However, its location at the foot of Lake Michigan and the connection with New York via Vanderbilt's railway line soon transformed it from a quiet hamlet into a thriving city. By 1880 Chicago boasted 440 000 inhabitants, and by the end of the century the population had swollen to 1.7 million. Much of this growth was the result of immigration. In fact, 75 percent of the city's population in 1900 was born on foreign soils.

Expansion made Chicago the transportation and distribution centre of the interior, but the city also paid a price for its success. Chicago was not a planned city in the modern sense. Radiating outward from the lake, as the city expanded into the country the wealthy middle class went with it. Left at the centre was a decaying core of factories, industrial dumping grounds and slums. Often ethnic groups were crowded into old tenement apartments, many of which had no running water; the unsanitary conditions made epidemics of typhoid alarmingly common. By 1890 only 30 percent of Chicago's streets were paved; spring run-off cleared the city of raw sewage, horse manure and dead animals, most of which ended up in the Chicago River. Water pollution was such a serious problem that most wealthy residents refused to drink from the city's water supply.

As imposing as these problems were—in Chicago and elsewhere—they were not unsolvable. What was needed were efficient, energetic, and honest civic governments. However, most American cities were run by corrupt and self-serving administrations. Many reformers claimed that the political "bosses" were kept in power by ignorant or indifferent electorates. They blamed recent immigrants, whom they felt were easily manipulated. British commentator James Bryce supported this opinion when he wrote in *The American Commonwealth* in 1888 that "in great cities we find an ignorant multitude, largely composed of recent immigrants, untrained in self government." There was some truth to this. Urban political clubs tended to take care of the needs of recent arrivals in ways that no other organizations did. They found them jobs, arranged for housing, and even provided legal advice and protection. In return all they asked for were their votes.

However, Bryce also noted that it was not the immigrant population alone who were enabling corrupt politicans to stay in power. Indeed, there was another more powerful group whose actions, or lack of them, helped to maintain the corrupt status quo: "We find able citizens absorbed in their private businesses . . . unwilling to sacrifice their time and tastes and comfort in the struggle with sordid wire-pullers and noisy demagogues."

Many of these business people supported the corrupt political systems because, although they cost money, they did accomplish some things (see readings). In addition, many legitimate politicians courted these groups for their political support, not because they needed their backing but because they could not afford their opposition.

Occasionally, however, even the comfortable middle classes could not tolerate the corruption. One notable example of an outraged public turning on its political machine was in New York in 1871. Led by cartoonist Thomas Nast and the editorial writers of the *New York Times*, corruption of the Tammany Hall political machine led by William "Boss" Tweed was exposed to public scrutiny. In just two years, the Tweed ring had defrauded the city of over $200 million. Tweed was tried and imprisoned. His real crime, however, lay not in his political actions but in his personal excesses. In the late nineteenth century, most American cities silently suffered from the same disease.

In Canada, another inland port city, Toronto on Lake Ontario was experiencing a similar growth. A city of 56 000 in 1871 with about 530 manufacturing firms, Toronto had more than tripled its population and quadrupled its industrial capacities only twenty years later. The ruling elements in late Victorian Toronto owed their status to wealth. The prominent families of the earlier colonial period were only a faded memory, replaced by new names such as Massey, Falconer, Atkinson, Gooderham, and Eaton. In the 1890s their homes lined the gentle curves of Queen's Park Crescent, and their proximity to the provincial legislature reflected the influence which they held over it. As one contemporary observer noted:

Society is pretty much what it is everywhere else, except that money is the chief requisite here. In smaller places a man who can boast of respectability and a character free from blemish are welcomed into good society with perfect good grace and as much warmth as if they were millionaires. In Toronto, an unprincipled knave . . . [with enough money] can secure entrance to the best social circles.

Toronto's middle class comprised commercial brokers, professionals, real estate dealers, and smaller merchants and factory owners. They mixed with their social "betters" in such organizations as the Albany Club, the Royal Canadian Yacht Club, the Toronto Cricket Club, and the Board of Trade.

As in all cities, however, the majority of the population was found in the working classes. Ranging from tradespeople and industrial workers to domestics and the unemployed, life was not quite so pleasant for many of these people. As one contemporary noted at the time:

In Toronto, poverty is not exactly a crime, but it is sufficient of an inconvenience to make everyone desirous of not possessing it.

The working classes had their own social organizations centring around the church, the union, or perhaps the Orange Order. Education, rather than cutting across class lines, only seemed to accentuate them. The wealthy sent their children to Upper Canada College or to one of the other private schools in the city; the middle classes dominated the public school system, while the poor, in spite of laws requiring children to attend school, usually remained uneducated. The *Globe* summarized the problem as early as 1867:

. . . among ourselves, the common schools, in cities, are indisputedly confined to the children of the industrious mechanic and tradesman; exclusive, on the one hand, of the wealthier merchant and professional man, and, unfortunately, on the other hand, to some degree, of the children of the poor and vagrant classes, who stand most in need of the free education they supply.

In spite of these problems, however, the educational system continued to develop. The city introduced kindergartens in 1883, and Jarvis Collegiate was joined in providing secondary education by Parkdale in 1889 and Harbord in 1892.

Toronto suffered from many of the same problems as Chicago. The expansion of public transit with a fare based upon distance meant that only the wealthier could afford to live in the more fashionable suburbs such as Yorkville, the Annex, or Rosedale. The lower classes remained near the waterfront within walking distance of the factories. As a result, slums gradually developed in the deteriorating inner core of the city. In Toronto, however, urban reform was blocked less by corrupt politicians than by the innate conservatism of civic officials.

Still, urban reforms in the United States had their parallels in Canada. Toronto's 1886 mayoral election saw the victory of a "citizen's" candidate, William Holmes

...ife in one room, New York City
...aying streetcar tracks in Montréal
...typical urban Canadian streetscape around the turn of the century

Howland. Over two terms in office, Howland eventually replaced the city council's old guard with reform-minded politicians. Roads were improved, liquor licensing was tightened up, and the beginnings of a professional civil service were established. A new public health department tackled such issues as the purity of the water supply, poor rental housing, foul privies, and garbage dumps. These reforms, combined with increased inspections of meat, milk, and ice deliveries cut the city's death rate from 21.3/1000 in 1883 to 15.18/1000 by 1896.

By the end of the century, Toronto and Chicago were both reflections of the new North American city. Now we can look at what life there was like.

Life in the New City

In spite of what might be called the "dark ages" in both municipal politics and living conditions, many positive changes did take place. Perhaps the greatest of these was the revolution in urban transit. The early cities of the East were "walking cities." With populations that travelled primarily on foot, nothing was too far away. By the late nineteenth century, however, this pattern was beginning to change. With the appearance first of horse-drawn trolleys and then of electric ones, urban settlement patterns were altered radically. In Chicago urban expansion meant that people moved farther and farther away from the city centre. Commuting became common by the late 1890s as train lines and trolley tracks whisked people into the city in the morning and then home again at night.

Electric streetcars appeared in Toronto in 1883. By 1890 the Toronto Railway Company boasted over 140 km of track and carried over 23 million fares a year. In a major political battle in 1897, working-class citizens won the right to have streetcar service on Sunday. With taxi cabs costing 25 cents a ride and bikes worth over $100, the TRC fare of six rides for a quarter made this an affordable means of travel.

Public transit had its impact. By 1912 the city proper had expanded to its modern limits. Advertisements of the period show the Belt line, which served the Annex, travelling through the wooded wilderness of the Don Valley.

While the electric trolley doubled the speed and tripled the passenger load of its horse-drawn predecessor, another innovation brough about even more rapid change. In 1897 Boston opened the continent's first subway; New York followed suit seven years later. And while the cities were changing, so too were their inhabitants.

Greater mobility changed the world of the working classes. Electric lighting in the factories made shift work more efficient and enabled employers to cut back the length of their employee's day. As the work week gradually became shorter many people found themselves with leisure hours for the first time in their lives. As a result there was a blossoming of cultural and recreational pursuits. The YMCA and YWCA, both founded in the 1850s, grew to a combined membership of over three hundred thousand in North America by 1897; thousands of North Americans enjoyed the facilities of the new public parks, community centres, and public bathing beaches.

Toronto's High Park, established in 1873, and Riverdale Park and Zoo, established in the mid-1890s, were favourite haunts of the middle and working classes during the summer months. The wealthy were indulging in more luxurious pursuits, spending their summers vacationing in Muskoka or on Georgian Bay.

Theatres were also popular. American cities drew European performers to them like magnets. Choices ranged from first-rate Shakespearean productions (for between 25 cents and $2.50 a seat) to one of the "10-20-30 cent" melodramas where patrons were encouraged to cheer for the hero and hiss and boo the villain!

In Canada, public libraries emerged as a common institution during the latter decades of the century; the first one opened in Toronto in 1884. In the United States, philanthropists such as Andrew Carnegie, who donated $60 million for library construction, set up libraries as institutions for the public betterment; by 1900, nine thousand had appeared across the nation.

Sporting events became common as well. Baseball was invented, so the legend goes, by Abner Doubleday of Cooperstown, New York, in 1839. Doubleday, a Union general, and his New York troops taught the game to their military cohorts during the Civil War. The Cincinnati Red Stockings (now known as the Reds) were the first professional team, but by 1876 there were enough teams (including the Chicago White Stockings—White Sox) to form an eight-team National League. After the American League was formed in 1900 the two began playoffs for the World Series starting in 1903.

American baseball was popular in Canada too, but it did not compare with the popularity of such sports as lacrosse, rugby, or curling. Hockey's first Stanley Cup was awarded in 1893, but the real sports craze during the last decade of the century was rowing. The Argonaut Rowing Club was founded in 1872, and Ned Hanlon brought world recognition to the city with his world rowing championship in 1877. In the United States basketball and football also appeared during this time; hockey and lacrosse were imported from Canada in the 1890s.

Two new "sissy" sports were gaining in popularity by the end of the century—tennis and golf. Future president Teddy Roosevelt once begged not to be photographed in his tennis clothes because it would damage his "macho" image and might hurt his political chances!

By the end of the nineteenth century the symbol of all that was the best and the worst about North American society could be found in the cities. On one side of the ledger were the squalid living conditions of the poor, political corruption, street gangs, illiteracy, unsanitary conditions, and disease. On the other side were increased leisure time, a general improvement in the lives of the working class and the new vitality of urban life. The symbols of the new age were the skyscrapers and department stores which spoke of a growing prosperity and importance. If America's cities were, as Bryce commented, its most "conspicuous failures," they were also the breeding grounds for success.

Many Europeans took to heart the poem written on the base of the new Statue of Liberty unveiled in New York's harbour in 1886. Written by Emma Lazarus, who worked long and hard helping immigrants to the city, it called out across the ocean:

"Keep, ancient lands, your storied pomp . . . Give me your tired, your poor,
Your huddled masses yearning to breathe free,
The wretched refuse of your teeming shore.
Send these, the homeless, the tempest-tost to me,
I lift my lamp beside the golden door."

As the cities swelled with the arrival of these hopeful immigrants, it became obvious that things could not remain the same. The reforming impulses of the latter half of the Progressive era would find their roots in the new city.

Curing Society's Ills: Urban Reform in the Early Twentieth Century

Many reformers at the turn of the century saw society as suffering from disease. These social ills took many forms, including the urban slums, the ghetto lifestyles of immigrants, labour radicalism, and alcoholism. The goal of reform activists during this period was to correct these ills through press exposure, legislation, and group actions such as protest marches and demonstrations. Before they were finished, every aspect of society would feel the impact of their actions.

The Muckrakers

"Muckrakers" was a name given to certain American magazines and their authors who made their names through sensational exposé articles. There were basically three different audiences during the period. The older, established magazines, such as *The North American Review*, *The Nation*, and *Scribners* were expensive (25-35 cents per copy) and tended to appeal to the upper classes. Their articles were reasoned and usually conservative.

At the other end of the scale was the so-called "yellow press." Led by the *New York Journal* of William Randolph Hearst and Joseph Pulitzer's *New York World*, these papers attacked public figures through distortion and scandal. Appealing to the urban working class, these papers sold for 3 cents an issue.

In the middle were the "muckrakers." Charging around 10 cents, these magazines were aimed at the middle class. Dedicated to public education and popular culture, they featured articles on science, technology, education, and family, as well as excellent short stories and serial pieces by popular American writers.

The most popular of these publications were *Cosmopolitan*, *Everybody's*, *Hampton's*, and, especially, *McClure's*. In October of 1902 *McClure's* began a series by Lincoln Steffens on the nature of the corrupt urban political machines. Later published as a book entitled *The Shame of the Cities*, the articles had a wide-ranging impact on urban reform.

One month after the first installment of Steffens's work began, *McClure's* followed with the first installment of "The History of the Standard Oil Company" by Ida Tarbell, which exposed the in-fighting and dirty tricks that had led to the creation of the Rockefeller empire.

While both of these articles were drawing considerable attention, a third series began. Ray Stannard Baker's work, "The Right to Work," criticized the "closed-shop" attitude of many unions. With the publication of the latter, McClure's had covered all of the bases. The threefold attack on big business, big labour, and big government was typical of this second phase of progressivism.

In spite of the violent attacks against business corruption and abuses, there was never a shortage of advertising for these magazines. By 1905, a typical issue of McClure's, for example, carried more than two hundred pages of ads.

Toronto boasted a similar range of publications during these years. Liberal politics were reflected in the Globe while the Mail and Empire (merged in 1895) represented the Conservative party. Other popular papers included the World, the News, and of course the Star. John Ross Robertson's Evening Telegram, founded in 1876, thrived on the sensationalism so prevalent in American publications. This focus, combined with its inclusion of Orange Order news, kept circulation high.

Magazine articles formed the mainstay of the muckraking movement, but they were by no means the only source of social criticism. Books, too, often denounced the social order. One such publication was John Moody's The Truth about Trusts, which examined the inner workings of the business giants of the day.

Many leading progressives grew tired of this constant diet of filth and corruption. Theodore Roosevelt gave the muckraker movement its name when he lambasted his critics for never having anything positive to say. He compared them to a character in the book Pilgrim's Progress who "could look no way but downward with the muckrake [manure rake] in his hand, who was offered a celestial [heavenly] crown for his muckrake, but would neither look up nor regard the crown he was offered, but continued to rake to himself the filth of the floor."

By 1906 muckraking was becoming a thing of the past. Even McClure's, which had reached a circulation of five hundred thousand a year before, dropped into obscurity. Ironically, just as the muckrakers disappeared, more people began to take their comments seriously.

The Temperance Crusade

The campaign against alcohol stands as an example of all that was wrong with this phase of the progressive movement, not because the motives of the reformers were necessarily bad, but rather because of the approach they adopted. Temperance advocates singled out alcohol as the single root cause of many of society's problems. Many approached the problem with the best of motives, but some rural reformers saw an attack on alcohol as an attack on the evils of city life in general. They believed that by forcing governments to prohibit the sale and consumption of alcohol they could end the problem.

As with many such campaigns, local politicans had no real argument against the idea, and eventually many states banned alcohol altogether. Under the Eighteenth Amendment to the U.S. Constitution passed in December 1917 the manufacture, sale, and transportation of liquor was prohibited, and so alcohol went underground during the 1920s.

Canadians had had their first taste of prohibition in 1878 when the government of Alexander Mackenzie passed a local option law which gave local authorities the power to forbid the sale and consumption of alcohol within their district. This was the extent of prohibition in Canada until the First World War. Under the theory that drunkenness reduced war production, and that the grains and hops used in distilling and brewing were needed by the troops in Europe, the Prairie provinces banned the production and consumption of alcohol in 1915. The other provinces (excluding Quebec) eventually followed suit for the duration of the conflict. Relaxation during the early twenties was followed by tighter restrictions again after 1924. This did not stop a healthy illegal export business from developing, however. While the United States remained officially dry, Canada was its unofficial source of liquor.

Urban reform in Canada during this period took a slightly different form from that advocated by Progressives in the United States. The publication *Industrial Canada* advocated that employers adopt a paternalistic attitude towards their workers, providing them with adequate food and housing. It warned that "Out of the slums stalk the Socialist with his red flag, the Union agitator with the auctioneer's voice, and the Anarchist with his torch."

Such an attitude saw reform in terms of its practical benefits, not its social worth. Over the previous two decades Canadian civic reformers had tried to cleanse their cities by improving sanitation and closing saloons and brothels. Improved public transit gave rise to the "Garden City" movement. It advocated the gradual depopulating of the corrupt city core, placing people in the suburban countryside. Eventually though real reform came in a typically Canadian fashion. Many civic reformers recognized the problems associated with private control of municipal services such as water, power, and transportation. Gradually this "gas and water socialism" won over converts, and by 1910 most cities had taken control over their essential utilities. One notable exception was Montreal (see readings); it became the centre of resistance to public control as reflected by the fact that while Ontario Hydro was created in 1906, Hydro-Quebec did not appear until 1963.

The Civic Improvement League, led by W.J. Hanna set out the minimum standards for urban life during this time. Their blueprint for reform was reflected in municipal legislation during the first decade of the century. So rapid was the rise in the cost of running a city that by 1907 the municipal governments of both Toronto and Winnipeg had budgets as large as their respective provincial governments.

Canadian urban reform found its greatest advocates not within the working class or the poor, but within the business community. Why did businesspeople and industrialists become involved in the potentially costly process of urban reform? The answer is simple: It was less expensive to clean up a corrupt civic administration than it was to work with one.

Canada's cities were not the centres of corruption that their American counterparts were. However, they were not models of honesty either. Many people vied for positions as aldermen or mayors in order to control the issuing of contracts for public services. There were occasional cases of bribery and patronage appointments were common, but these abuses were soon eliminated. Canadian businesspeople paid a heavy price for this corruption in the form of higher tax bills, expensive utilities, and pay offs to civic officials. To a great extent, it was these people who were behind the municipalization of utilities and the reorganization of the municipal civil service. When civic leaders refused to follow the lead of the business elite the local board of trade threatened—and often did—run its own candidates for office. Backed by society's wealthier citizens, they often displaced local administrations and effected the reforms themselves. This pattern of paternal control would continue until the Second World War and would guarantee the continued reform of the urban environment.

The differences in urban development between Canada and the United States during this period were more than just a matter of scale. The volunteerism and moral crusading of American Progressive reformers was replaced in Canada by the paternalism and social conscience of government. Witnesses to the widespread corruption of the urban political machine in the United States, Canadian civic leaders moved quickly to establish a responsible and non-political municipal civil service. Where American political leaders legislated to control private enterprise, Canadian urban politicians municipalized essential services, putting them directly under their control.

Still, the North American city was taking on a distinctive character. The growth of urban transit and the development of public parks and recreation facilities, coupled with the emergence of the city as a cultural centre, combined to shift the focus of society from rural to urban. A majority of North Americans continued to live in villages and towns well into the twentieth century, but the scale had tipped. The continent now belonged to the cities.

Life in the New City

In 1911 James Shaver Woodsworth wrote an impassioned plea for civic reform. In his book My Neighbour *the socialist leader discussed the collapse of traditional values as a result of urbanization. In this excerpt he contrasts the superficial appeal of the city with its grim reality.*

In the incident which was the occasion of the parable of the Good Samaritan, the lawyer desiring to justify himself said unto Jesus, 'And who is my neighbor?' . . .

Nowhere does the question come with greater force than in the latest and most complex product of civilization—the modern city. On the wild, lonely road between Jerusalem and Jericho the desperate plight of the stranger would arouse some sense of duty in the most promotive modern man. But when at breakfast this same modern man reads that, through the negligence of someone, ten workmen were maimed for life or hurled into eternity—well, what is that to him? He hardly pauses as he sips his coffee. His eye and his attention pass to the next news item—the rise in the price of wheat or the account of the great race. Even if he should own stock in the corporation in whose factories the unfortunate workman had been employed, it would hardly occur to him that he was even remotely responsible for their injury or death. The directors, the manager, the foreman, factory inspectors—a hundred officials come between him and the victims of the accident. . . .

Someone is responsible! Every unjustly-treated man, every defenceless woman, every neglected child has a neighbour somewhere. Am I that neighbour?

Not only do we need to learn who our neighbour is, but also how we can help him. . . .

They are part of a system as we are part of the same system. We as individuals cannot help them as individuals. The whole system must be reckoned with—possibly completely changed. . . .

We must learn to be neighborly not only in the wilderness, or in the comparatively simple life of a country community, but in the crowded city with its many and complicated interests. How? Well, to discover that is the purpose of our present study.

'The City'—what contrasted pictures are suggested! What varied emotions are aroused! To many who live in the country and only occasionally have the opportunity of an all too brief pleasure trip to the city, the word is full of charm. It means shopping and concerts and sight-seeing and all kinds of excitement. After the quiet, hum-drum existence of the farm, many a young man and woman sympathizes with the sentiment:

Had I but plenty of money, money enough and to spare,
The house for me, no doubt, were a house in the city square;
Ah, such a life, such a life, as one leads at the window there! . . . (Browning)

Such enthusiasm for city life is, however, that only of the visitor who views it from the window. The novel sights and sounds soon become familiar. The higher the buildings, the less sunshine; the bigger the crowds, the less fresh air. . . . We become weary in the unceasing rush, and feel utterly lonely in the crowded streets. There comes a wistful longing for the happy life of 'God's out-of-doors' with the perfume of the flowers and the singing of the birds. But our work now lies in the city and in the city we must stay. As we penetrate more deeply into its life, we discover evils of which we had hardly dreamed. Pitfalls abound on every side; dark crimes being committed; dreadful tragedies are being enacted in real life. We get behind the scenes; we see the seemy side. We look beneath the glittering surface and shrink back from the hidden depths which the yawning darkness suggests. . . .

H.G. Wells . . . writes:

But indeed, these great cities are no permanent maelstroms. These new forces at present still so potently centripetal in their influence, bring with them, nevertheless, the distinct promise of a centrifugal application that may be finally equal to the complete reduction of all our present congestions. The limit of the pre-railway city was the limit of man and horse. But already that limit has been exceeded, and each day brings us nearer to the time when it will be thrust outward in every direction with an effect of enormous relief.

The railway, the telephone, and similar inventions not only tend to bring the country into the city, but they carry the city into the country. So that we must, ultimately, look for the establishment of 'urban regions' in which the advantages of city and country will be combined.

Whatever the lines of future development, the importance of the city cannot well be overestimated. It is destined to exercise a dominating influence over the whole country. . . .

The cities are the . . . nerve centres of the whole of our social system. They are the very heart of the body politic. From the political, the social, the educational, the religious and the commercial standpoint, the city is the centre to which the whole nation is tributary, and which in turn moulds our national life. In *The American City*, Wilcox writes,

> There are many reasons why the city problem is assuming national proportions. First, democracy, the tool with which we are cultivating human nature in America, has been badly damaged by its contact with city conditions. . . . Secondly, the city, as the centre of civilization, and the distributing centre of the nation's intelligence, tends to impose its ethical and social ideals upon the whole people, irrespective of residence. Thirdly, as the accumulation of enormous wealth in the hands of one man without a corresponding responsibility for its use with reference to social welfare is a positive menace to the general well-being, so the concentration of wealth in a single city, without a clear recognition on its part of its duty to the state, becomes dangerous to the public weal.

Thus the city may become a menace to our whole civilization. Again let us listen to a warning voice from the Republic to the south,

> The city has replaced simplicity, industrial freedom, and equality of fortune with complexity, dependence, poverty and misery, close besides a barbaric luxury like unto that of ancient Rome. Vice, crime and disease have come in. The death rate has increased, while infectious diseases and infant mortality ravage the crowded quarters. The city has destroyed the home and substituted for it the hotel, flat, tenement, boarding-house, and cheap lodging-house. Our politics have suffered and corruption has so allied itself with our institutions that many despair of democracy. The city exacts an awful price for the gain it has given us, a price that is being paid in human life, suffering and the decay of virtue and the family.

And yet, making full allowance for this which he calls the loss account, Mr. Howe assures us that the city is the hope of Democracy.

> Despite current pessimism, the outlook for the American city is reassuring. The city contains the independent vote. . . . To the city we are to look for a re-birth of democracy, a democracy that will possess the instincts of the past, along with a belief in the powers of co-operative effort to relieve the costs which city life entails.

From James S. Woodsworth, *My Neighbour*, (Toronto: University of Toronto Press, 1972).

1. Discuss Woodsworth's contention that urban dwellers are indifferent toward their fellow citizens.
2. What factors have led to the extension of the influence of the city?
3. Contrast the concluding two paragraphs of this excerpt. Why do you think that Woodsworth has presented such contrasting points of view together?

The Working Poor in New York, 1885

As part of his testimony in front of a Senate investigating committee, machinist John Morrison commented on living conditions in New York City. In this excerpt, Morrison identifies the general decline in his own standard of living.

Q. What is the social condition of the Machinists in New York and the surrounding towns and cities?

A. It is rather low compared to what their social condition was ten or fifteen years ago. . . . When I first went to learn the trade a machinist considered himself more than the average workingman; in fact he did not like to be called a workingman. He liked to be called a mechanic. Today he recognizes the fact that he is simply a laborer the same as the others. . . .

Q. What sort of houses or lodgings do the machinists occupy as a general rule?

A. As a general rule they live in tenement houses, often on the top floor.

Q. How is it as to the size of the apartments that they occupy, the conveniences and comforts they afford, their healthfulness, the character of the neighborhood and the general surrounding?

A. That depends a great deal upon the size of the families. In most cases they are compelled to send their families to work, and of course they have rooms in proportion to the size of their families, and of course it often robs them of their earnings to pay rent; but as a rule the machinists live in the lowest quarters of the city. . . .

Q. I am requested to ask you this question: Dividing the public, as is commonly done, into the upper, middle and lower classes, to which class would you assign the average workingman of your trade at the time you entered it, and to which class would you assign him now?

A. I now assign them to the lower class. At the time I entered the trade I should assign them as merely hanging on to the middle class, ready to drop out at any time.

Q. What is the character of the social intercourse of those workingmen? Answer first with reference to their intercourse with other people outside of their own trade—merchants, employers, and others.

A. Are you asking what sort of social intercourse exists between the machinists and the merchants? If you are, there is none whatever, or very little if any.

Q. What sort of social intercourse exists among the machinists themselves and their families, as to visiting, entertaining one another, and having little parties and other forms of sociability, those little things that go to make up the social pleasures of life?

A. In fact with the married folks that has died out—such things as birthday parties, picnics, and so on. The machinists today are on such small pay, and the cost of living is so high, that they have very little, if anything, to spend for recreation, and the machinist has to content himself with enjoying himself at home, either fighting with his wife or licking his children.

Q. I hope that is not a common amusement in the trade. Was it so ten years ago?

A. It was not; from the fact that they then sought enjoyment in other places, and had a little more money to spend. But since they have had no organization worth speaking of, of course their pay has gone down. At that time they had a form of organization in some way or other which seemed to keep up the wages, and there was more life left in the machinist then; he had more ambition, he felt more like seeking employment outside, and in reading and such things, but now it is changed to the opposite; the machinist has no such desires.

Q. What is the social air about the ordinary machinist's house? Are there evidences of happiness, and joy, and hilarity, or is the general atmosphere solemn, and somber, and gloomy?

A. To explain that fully, I would state first of all, that machinists have got to work ten hours a day in New York, and that they are compelled to work very hard. In fact the machinists of America are compelled to do about one-third more work than the machinists do in England in a day. Therefore, when they come home they are naturally played out from shoving the file, or using the hammer or the chisel, or whatever it may be, such long hours. They are pretty well played out when they come home, and the first thing they think of is having something to eat and sitting down and resting, and then of striking a bed. Of course when a man is dragged out in that way he is naturally cranky, and he makes all around him cranky; so, instead of a pleasant house it is every day expecting to lose his job by competition from his fellow workman, there being so many out of employment, and no places for them, and his wages being pulled down through their competition, looking at all times to be thrown out of work in that way, and staring starvation in the face makes him feel sad, and the head of the house being sad, of course the whole family are the same, so the house looks like a dull prison instead of home.

From The testimony of John Morrison, August 28, 1883, U.S. Congress Senate, *Report of the Committee of the Senate upon the Relations between Labor and Capital*, (Washington, D.C.: U.S. Government Printing Office, 1885) in Leon Litwack, *The American Labour Movement*, (Englewood Cliffs: Prentice-Hall, 1902).

1. Account for the decline in status of machinist as described by Morrison.
2. Morrison identifies a number of social problems by inference. Outline some of the concerns of the urban poor.
3. Comment upon Morrison's contention that for the working poor in New York the "house looks like a dull prison instead of a home."

The Immigrant Poor in Toronto, 1889

The Royal Commission on the Relations of Labor and Capital in Canada called Mayor W.H. Howland of Toronto as one of its witnesses. In the evidence he presented to them, Mayor Howland described the plight of recent immigrants who had come to live in the city.

W.H. Howland, Toronto, called and sworn.

. . .

Q. You are Mayor of Toronto? A. Yes.

Q. This is your second term in the mayor's chair? A. Yes.

Q. You have been a resident of Toronto for a great many years? A. 32 or 33 years.

Q. As mayor, you come in contact with the poor of Toronto to a great extent? A. Not only as mayor, but for the last eleven years I have been working among them as a matter of love, and I have a very considerable knowledge of their ways, their difficulties and circumstances.

Q. Are there large numbers of people in Toronto requiring assistance? A. They require assistance from only two causes as a general rule, excepting extreme cases of misfortune, or cases where widows are left with large families. The first cause is, of course, drinking, and the second cause is sending out to this country people who are unsuited to make a living here—the sending out of great numbers of people who have got the poor-house taint, and who never will work or do any good anywhere.

Q. By whom are these people sent out? A. They are sent out in various ways. Up to the last two or three years our government machinery was very largely used for the purposes of relieving the poor-houses—not with their consent, but their machinery was perverted from its original intention and used in that way. Then, colonies have been sent out from time to time, with the kind intention of helping people in different districts. For instance there was a colony of a poor class sent out from some of the towns in Ireland some years ago; they are nearly all to be traced here at the present time, and to a large extent they have remained a charge on the people of this country. . . .

As a visitor of the House of Industry, I kept coming across a class of people from a certain place in Ireland; they were thoroughly unsuited for this country; they had been under the poor-house system very largely; they were demoralized, and all the spring was taken out of them for honest or faithful work. In the same way there has been progressing for sometime an immigration from England from the different poor-house Unions. You can trace them in particular streets; you come across a family at one time, sent out by certain poor-houses, or given means to come out. I have met several cases of that kind. For instance in East London they are now sending out families, and you cannot help being sorry for them, because they sent out people with large families— eight or nine children, and sometimes more. It makes you feel that the children might have a chance, but the parents are unsuitable; having no courage, or pluck, or hope, they drop at once into the old habit of getting help from others that they do not think of being able to help themselves; in fact they are a helpless immigration. In a great many cases they are chosen with some judgement as far as personal habits are concerned; many of those East London people that I have met with are not dissipated people, but they are corrupted with the poor-house character.

Q. They don't know how to help themselves? A. They have not got any spirit; they are absolutely helpless.

Q. Admitting this to be an evil can you suggest anything? A. I think we should adopt the American principle, which would prevent them from being sent. I think we should stop helpless people who are going to suffer—stop them at the border.

From Canada, Royal Commission on the Relations of Labor and Capital in Canada, 1889. Evidence—Ontario.

1. What two major reasons does Howland cite for people needing assistance in the city?
2. How does he describe the type of person currently arriving in Toronto?
3. Comment on his suggestion that unsuitable immigrants should simply be "stop[ped] . . . at the border."

Youth in the City, c.1900

Nobel Prize-winner Jane Addams saw the plight of working women as one of the greatest social concerns of city life. In this essay entitled "Youth in the City" she outlines some of the problems faced by young people living alone in an urban environment.

One generation after another has depended upon its young to equip it with gaiety and enthusiasm, to persuade it that living is a pleasure, until men everywhere have anxiously provided channels through which this wine of life might flow, and be preserved for their delight. The classical city promoted play with careful solicitude, building the theatre and stadium as it built the market place and the temple. The Greeks held their games so integral a part of religion and patriotism that they came to expect from their poets the highest utterances at the very moments when the sense of pleasure released the national life. In the medieval city the knights held their tourneys, the guilds their pageants, the people their dances, and the church made festival for its most cherished saints with gay street processions, and presented a drama in which no less a theme of history of creation became a matter of thrilling interest. Only in the modern city have men concluded that it is no longer necessary for the municipality to provide for the insatiable desire for play. In so far as they have acted upon this conclusion, they have entered upon a most difficult and dangerous experiment; and this at the very moment when the city has become distinctly industrial and daily labor is continually more monotonous and subdivided. We forget how new the modern city is, and how short the span of time in which we have assumed that we can eliminate public provision for recreation.

A further difficulty lies in the fact that this industrialism has gathered together multitudes of eager young creatures from all quarters of the earth as a labor supply for the countless factories and workshops, upon which the present industrial city is based. Never before in civilization have such numbers of young girls been suddenly released from the protection of the home and permitted to walk unattended upon city streets and work under alien roofs; for the first time they are being prized more for the products they manufacture than for their immemorial ability to reaffirm the charm of existence. Never before have such numbers of young boys earned money independently of the family life, and felt themselves free to spend it as they choose in the midst of vice deliberately disguised as pleasure.

This stupid experiment of organizing work and failing to organize play has, of course, brought about a fine revenge. The love of pleasure will not be denied, and when it has turned into all sorts of malignant and vicious appetites, then we, the middle aged, grow quite distracted and resort to all sorts of restrictive measures. We even try to dam up the sweet fountain itself because we are affrighted by these neglected streams; but almost worse than the restrictive measures is our apparent belief that the city itself has no obligation in the matter, an assumption upon which the modern city turns over to commercialism practically all the provisions for public recreation.

Quite as one set of men has organized the young people into industrial enterprises in order to profit from their toil, so another set of men and also of women, I am sorry to say, have entered the neglected field of recreation and have organized enterprises which make profit out of this invincible love of pleasure.

In every city arise so-called "places"—"gin-palaces", they are called in fiction; in Chicago we euphemistically say merely "places",—in which alcohol is dispensed, not to allay thirst, but, ostensibly to stimulate gaiety, it is sold really in order to empty pockets. Huge dance halls are opened to which hundreds of young people are attracted, many of whom stand wistfully outside a roped circle, for it requires five cents to procure within it for five minutes the sense of allurement and intoxication which is sold in lieu of innocent pleasure. . . .

One Sunday night at twelve o'clock I had occasion to go into a large public dance hall. As I was standing by the rail looking for the girl I had come to find, a young man approached me and quite simply asked me to introduce him to some "nice girl", saying that he did not know any one there. On my replying that a public dance hall was not the best place in which to look for a nice girl, he said: 'But I don't know any other place where there is a chance to meet any kind of girl. I'm awfully lonesome since I came to Chicago'. And then he added rather defiantly: 'Some nice girls do come here! It's one of the best halls in town.' He was voicing the 'bitter loneliness' that many city men remember to have experienced during the first years after they had 'come up to town'. Occasionally the right sort of man and girl meet each other in these dance halls and the romance with such a tawdry beginning ends happily and respectably. But, unfortunately, mingled with the respectable young men seeking to form the acquaintance of young women through the only channel which is available to them, are many young fellows of evil purpose, and among the girls who have left their lonely boarding houses or rigid homes for a 'little fling' are likewise women who openly desire to make money from the young men whom they meet, and back of it all is the desire to profit by the sale of intoxicating and 'doctored' drinks.

Perhaps never before have the pleasures of the young and mature become so definitely separated as in the modern city. . . .

Let us know the modern city in its weakness and wickedness, and then seek to rectify and purify it until it shall be free at least from the grosser temptations which now beset the young people who are living in its tenement houses and working in its factories.

From Jane Addams, "Youth in the City," (1900) in John Anthony Scott, ed., *Living Documents in American History*, (New York: Washington Square Press, 1963). Copyright 1963 by John Anthony Scott. Reprinted by permission of Washington Square Press, a division of Simon and Schuster, Inc.

1. What case does Addams build for the need for organized recreation in society?
2. Outline the social "pitfalls" which she identifies lying in wait for the naive new arrival.
3. What recommendations does she make with regard to changes in social policy?

The Classes and the Masses: Winnipeg, 1909

In this excerpt J.S. Woodsworth comments upon the social class distinctions which were a part of city life.

In country districts people are to a large extent on a level but in the cities we have the rich and the poor, the classes and the masses, with all that these distinctions involve. The tendency is that the well-to-do gather together in more or less exclusive suburbs, while the poor are segregated in slum districts, and between these there is comparatively little direct intercourse. The employer may meet his employee at business, but there is little bond of connection beside what Carlyle called the 'cash nexus'. A woman may superintend laundry operations in her own house, but she knows little or nothing of the home life of her washerwoman who has come several miles to give her days [sic] service. They live in two worlds . . .

The people who most need help are separated from those who best could help them.

From J.S.Woodsworth, "Some Aspects of the Immigrant Problem" in *The Young Women of Canada*, (December 1909).

1. Account for Woodsworth's contention that social equality in the country is replaced by stratification in the city.
2. What are the "two worlds" of the city?
3. Discuss Woodsworth's statement that "the people who most need help are separated from those who best could help them."

The White Slave Trade: Toronto, 1911

Lucy W. Brooking wrote a stinging condemnation of the extent of prostitution in Toronto as part of her 1911 book, Canada's War on the White Slave Trade. *In this excerpt she recounts some specific case studies of the "recruitment" of young girls.*

While this traffic in young girls is not perhaps so thoroughly organized in Toronto, as it is in some cities, quite enough proof of its existence comes to every rescue worker in this city. That there is a tremendous, and to those not thrown into immediate touch with the underworld, unsuspected, amount of immorality, both professional and unprofessional, is also most certain.

That there are in Toronto scores of attractive houses for professional immorality, is a well known fact to workers, and that there are also scores of dens and dives carried on by those who have sunk too low, or become too unattractive for the higher (save the mark) grade houses, is even more widely known for these last are continually brought to the notice of officials, and the occupants divided their time between the jail and Reformatories. My personal knowledge of these conditions has been gathered during nearly four years' experience as Superintendent of Toronto Haven. . . .

In one case known to me, a widowed mother struggled to bring up two little daughters in at least decency. One of them married a man apparently above her in station, who soon compelled her to support him by going to the streets and the old mother told me herself that the daughter was often driven out at night for the purpose of capturing men.

The other daughter was enticed away by a young man also much above her in station, and the last news was that she was out in Winnipeg living the unspeakable life and supporting the wretch who misled her.

A young West Indian girl with her little child was brought to us from the jail where she had served a term for attacking a man with a revolver. The truth lying behind the story was, that she had come to the country on the promise of well paid work, and under the protection of a male relative. This man took her to his 'home', soon found to be of very questionable character. There she lived and sank. When she found that not only was the promised marriage refused her, but even worse degradation was in store, her fiery tropical temper overcame everything and with a revolver she threatened the man who had led her into this pitfall. Then the law stepped in, and she was sent to jail for merely threatening the life of the man who had without interference wrought her ruin both soul and body. We kept her in charge for some time, but when finally she was placed in a situation this man tracked her up again and she was soon lost in the quagmire of the underworld. . . .

A young girl coming into the city to attend school took a room in an apparently respectable house on an apparently respectable street. The first evening she was invited to join the 'boarders' in the parlor. Having some unpacking to do, she excused herself. The prolongation of this 'social time' and amount of coming up and down stairs all through the evening rather surprised her, but she was too ignorantly innocent to be really suspicious. The next evening she was pressed to come down and even told by the house mistress that it was expected of all the boarders that they should make themselves agreeable during the evening. But this evening she had studies to prepare and again retired to her room. Becoming a little nervous she pulled some furniture against the door as well as locking it. Late that night her door was tried with a duplicate key, and she was plainly told where she was, and that resistance was useless. Having more of resource and courage than the average country girl she opened her window and screamed for the police and so was saved.

From Lucy W. Brooking, "Conditions in Toronto," in *Canada's War on the White Slave Trade*, (London, 1911).

1. How does Brooking describe the Toronto "underworld" of prostitution?
2. Outline the process of victimization by which these young women were trapped into prostitution.
3. What social services appear to have been available to help women caught in this cycle?

Playing in the Streets: Cleveland, 1913

The Chief Medical Inspector and Assistant Superintendent in charge of Physical Education in Cleveland conducted a play census of children under fifteen in June 1913. The results, shown in the chart on page 410, were very revealing. Among the conclusions drawn from the census were the fact that "just at an age where play and activity are the fundamental requirements for proper growth and development" 41 percent of the children were seen doing nothing, and over 50 percent were seen in the streets "in the midst of all the traffic, dirt, and heat, and in an environment conducive to just the wrong kind of play."

1. Comment upon the differences in activity between the boys and girls surveyed.
2. Assume that you were the officials conducting the survey. What possible plans of actions might you implement in order to alleviate the problem?
3. Conduct a similar survey in an old urban area in your own or a nearby city. To what extent have patterns changed in the last seventy-five years?

Urban Violence: Chicago, 1888

American sociologist Richard Sennett researched the ways in which local residents responded to the outbreak of violence surrounding and following the Haymarket Riot of 1886. His research focused in particular on the middle class attitudes of one mixed area, Union Park, towards the poor people of their neighbourhood.

In the years 1886 and 1888 an epidemic of violence broke out in the quiet neighbourhood of Chicago. The striking feature of this epidemic lay not in the violent acts themselves but in the reaction of shopkeepers, store clerks, accountants, and highly skilled laborers to the disorder suddenly rampant among their sedate homes. Their reaction to violence was impassioned to an extent that in retrospect seems unwarranted by events; indeed, it is the contrast between the limited character of the disorder and the sense residents had of being overwhelmingly threatened by anarchy that suggests that the response could have been the product of larger, seemingly unrelated social forces, such as the structure of family life.

The scene of the disturbance, which I shall name Union Park, was an area centered on the near West Side of Chicago around a rather large park formally

Table 12.1 What 14 683 Cleveland Children Were Doing on June 23, 1913				
		Boys	*Girls*	*Total*
Where they were seen	On streets	5241	2558	7799
	In yards	1583	1998	3581
	In vacant lots	686	197	883
	In playgrounds	997	872	1869
	In alleys	413	138	551
What they were doing	Doing nothing	3737	2234	5961
	Playing	4601	2757	7358
	Working	719	635	1354
What games they were playing	Baseball	1448	190	1638
	Kites	482	49	531
	Sand piles	241	230	471
	Tag	100	53	153
	Jackstones	68	257	325
	Dolls	89	193	282
	Sewing	14	130	144
	Housekeeping	53	191	244
	Horse and wagon	89	24	113
	Bicycle riding	79	13	92
	Minding baby	19	41	60
	Reading	17	35	52
	Roller-skating	18	29	47
	Gardening	13	14	27
	Caddy	6	0	6
	Marbles	2	0	2
	Playing in other ways, mostly just fooling	1863	1308	3171

From William Graebner and Leonard Richards, *The American Record*, (New York: Alfred Knopf, 1982).

landscaped in the early 1850's. Like most of the middle and lower middle-class neighborhoods of American industrial cities in the later nineteenth century, the area was considered so nondescript that it was never given a special name, as were the richer and poorer sections of Chicago. Its people were the forgotten men of the era, neither poor enough to be rebels nor affluent enough to count in the affairs of the city. . . .

During the middle 1880's, it was in modest, cheerless Union Park that a series of unexpected events broke out. A bloody encounter between laborers and police took place on its borders during the Haymarket Riot of 1886, to be followed eighteen months later by a series of highly expert robberies in the community, a crime wave that culminated in the murder of a leading Union resident. Union Park reacted by holding a whole class—the poor, and especially the immigrant poor—responsible for the course of . . . events. . . .

The fears of the foreign masses by a middle class group may have reflected something other than the actual state of interaction between bourgeoisie and proletariat. These fears may have reflected instead the impact of family life on the way people like those in Union Park understood their places in the city society.

Studies of overreaction . . . [were] given a clear definition in . . . *Frustration and Aggression* (1939). The authors wrote that 'aggression is always a consequence of frustration. More specifically . . . the occurrence of aggressive behaviour always presupposes the existence of frustration and, contrariwise, the existence of frustration always leads to some form of aggression.'

Applied in terms of social class, this frustration-aggression syndrome implies that when a group fails to achieve goals it desires, or when it is unable to maintain a position it covets, it becomes aggressive, and searches out objects on which it can blame its failure. This simple, clear idea Parsons has applied to the formation of the Nazi party in Germany: the fall in status in the 1920's of fixed-income, middle class groups breeding an aggressive desire to get back at their enemies, without knowing, or really caring, who they were. [Seymour Martin] Lipset has incorporated elements of the same idea in his essay on working-class authoritarianism in the United States after the Second World War. And of course the concept is now used to explain the hostility of lower-middle class whites toward blacks: the whites who have failed to rise high in the economic system they believe in are said to make blacks 'aggression objects' of the frustration they themselves have suffered.

If it is true, . . . then the nature of the fear of lower-class foreigners among Union Park families might tell something about the Union Park community itself. The Union Park men, during the time of the riot and robberies, accused their chosen enemies of being, first, lawless anarchists, which was transmuted, secondly, to be pushed by their base passions outside the bounds of acceptable behavior, which resolved itself, finally, to being emotionally out of control. If the poor were reasonable, if they were temperate, ran the argument, these violent things would not have come to pass.

From Richard Sennett, "Middle Class Families and Urban Violence: The Experience of a Chicago Community in the Nineteenth Century", in Thernstrom and Sennett, eds., *Nineteenth Century Cities: Essays in the New Urban History*, (New Haven: Yale University Press, 1969).

1. What situation had developed in Union Park by the late 1880s?
2. Comment upon the concept of "frustration-aggression" as applied to the Union Park experience.
3. Apply the Union Park experience to similar nativist or anti-labour incidents in Canada and the United States.

The Urban Environment

In his 1985 work The New City: Urban America in the Industrial Age, *urban historian Raymond Mohl outlined the rapidly changing face of transit within the urban area. In this short excerpt he traces the overnight transformation of the American city from horse-drawn to horsepowered.*

By the late 19th century, urban transit came to be defined as a necessary public service, but involvement in the political arena had its costs in the form of bribery, fraud and corruption.

Contempories hailed the horsecar system as a revolutionary improvement over the omnibus. The new innovation spread rapidly throughout urban America. By the mid-1880's, some 525 horsecar lines were operating in 300 American cities. Between the 1850's and about 1890, as urban geographer David Ward has noted, 'horsedrawn streetcars were the most important form of local transportation in American cities'.

The horsecar system had a more significant impact on urban spatial development than earlier transit innovations. Horsecar fares were lower—about five cents per ride. Urban politicians generally sought to keep fares low through their control over transit franchises. Thus, the luxury of riding to work rather than walking was no longer limited to the wealthy and business classes. Now middle-class urbanites, white-collar workers, perhaps even some skilled tradesmen could join the outward movement of population. As one Philadelphian observed in 1859, the streetcar was 'producing a complete revolution' in urban life by encouraging the 'spread of the city over a vast space with all the advantages of compactness and also the advantages of pure air, gardens, and rural pleasure.'

As horsecar lines radiated outward as much as five miles or more from the urban centre, new residential development sprang up along and near the transit arteries. Many transit companies were actively involved in real estate speculation and subdivision development in outlying areas. The availability of horsecar service to workplaces in the urban core hastened the suburban lot sales and house building. Suburban development, in turn, increased both the outward movement of population and the profits of the companies. Thus, at the very time when American industrial cities were experiencing explosive population growth, the horsecar lines permitted a dispersal of population to outlying city wards and new suburban towns. Indeed, it was the pressure of rising population that stimulated new technological innovation in transportation and many other fields. . . .

Through technological innovation, mechanically powered vehicles soon replaced the horsecar. In the 1870's, for instance, a number of cities experimented with the cable car. Introduced in San Francisco in 1873 by Andrew S. Hallidie, a wire manufacturer from Scotland, the cable car was put into motion by clamping onto a moving underground wire cable. A stationary steam engine provided the power to keep the cable moving, while the cable car operator could attach or detach the car from the cable by the use of a grip extending below the street's surface through a slot between the tracks. The cable car was superior to the horsecar as a means of urban transportation, especially in hilly cities such as San Francisco and Pittsburgh where horses often had difficulty traversing steep grades. The cable car was also faster, easily attaining speeds of 10 miles per hour. Larger cars meant more passengers, and the ride was smoother and more comfortable than that provided by the horsecar. . . .

Heavy construction and installation costs burdened most cable car systems. In 1893 in New York City, for example, the Metropolitan Traction Company completed a cable car line from lower Manhattan to 59th Street at a cost of $1 million per mile, or about 20 times that of a horsecar track. Other problems included broken cables, frequent breakdowns, high maintenance costs, hazardous conditions at curves and intersections, and the necessity to operate at a uniform speed regardless of traffic conditions. The limits of cable car technology stimulated the search for new alternatives in urban transit. The most important transit innovation of the late 19th century came with the electrification of the street railways. In 1888 Frank Sprague, a young engineer who had worked with Thomas Edison, successfully converted the horsecar system of Richmond, Virginia, to electricity. Drawing electrical current from overhead wires, the new streetcars—or trolleys, as they were called—proved vastly superior to horsecars and even the cable car system. Average speeds of 10 to 12 miles per hour made possible an even longer journey to work for residents of the urban periphery and the new suburbs. As electric trolley systems were built, densely settled areas in cities such as Boston and Chicago sprawled 10 and more miles from the urban core.

Electrified transit caught on quickly in the 1890's. City after city abandoned the horsecar and cable system in short order. By 1902 . . . 97 percent of urban transit mileage had been electrified. In that year, more than 2 billion urban passengers were carried on 22 000 miles of trolley car track . . .

Electrification stimulated two other mass transit innovations. . . . Frequent traffic jams in congested downtown areas slowed the streetcars considerably. In the most populous cities, engineers sought to avoid street-level congestion by building rapid transit systems both above and below ground. . . .

[In addition to elevated lines] electricity also permitted the establishment of subway systems, beginning with Boston in 1897, followed by New York in 1904, and Philadelphia in 1908. . . .

Subway building in the early twentieth century brought to an end more than a half century of technological innovation in urban mass transit. In 1908, the year the Philadelphia subway was completed, Henry Ford brought out his first Model T automobile. . . .

By 1920 more than 8 million automobiles were registered in the United States, along with over 1 million trucks and buses. As they were for the horse-car in the 1890's, the days of the electric streetcar were numbered. The future belonged to the automobile.

From Raymond Mohl, *The New City: Urban America in the Industrial Age*, (Arlington Hts, Ill.: Harlan Davidson, 1985)

1. Account for the contention that the street railway revolutionized urban life.
2. Outline the impact of electrification on urban transportation.
3. Defend or refute the thesis that "Nineteenth century cities were built for people; twentieth century cities were built for cars."

The Brooklyn Bridge, 1883

The Brooklyn Bridge was one of the wonders of the age when it was opened in 1883. It symbolized the promise that continual progress would ensure a shining future for the North American city. Democratic Congressman Abram Hewitt had the honour of delivering the keynote address at the opening. He would be elected mayor on the strength of the speech.

'What hath God wrought!' were the words of wonder, which ushered into being the magnetic telegraph, the greatest marvel of the many marvelous inventions of the present century. . . .

But when we turn from the unsightly telegraph to the graceful structure at whose portal we stand, and when the airy outline of its curves of beauty, pendant between massive towers suggestive of art alone, is contrasted with the over-reaching vault of heaven above and the ever moving flood of waters beneath, the work of omnipotent power, we are irresistibly moved to exclaim, What hath *man* wrought!

Man hath indeed wrought far more than strikes the eye in this daring undertaking, by the general judgment of engineers, without a rival among the wonders of human skill. It is not the work of any one man or any one age. It is the result of the study, of the experience, and of the knowledge of many men in many ages. It is not merely a creation; it is a growth. It stands before us to-day as the sum and epitome of human knowledge; as the very heir of the ages; as the latest glory of centuries of patient observation, profound study and accumulated skill, gained, step by step, in the never-ending struggle of man to subdue the forces of nature to his control and use. . . .

What message, then, of hope and cheer does this achievement convey to those who would fain believe that love travels hand in hand with light along the rugged pathway of time? Have the discoveries of science, the triumphs of art, and the progress of civilization, which have made its accomplishment a possibility and a reality, promoted the welfare of mankind, and raised the great mass of people to a higher plane of life?

This question can best be answered by comparing the compensation of the labor employed in the building of this bridge, with earnings of labour upon works of equal magnitude in ages gone by. The money expended for the work of construction proper on the bridge, exclusive of land damages and other outlays, such as interest, not entering into actual cost, is nine million dollars. This money has been distributed in numberless channels—for quarrying, for mining, for smelting, for fabricating the metals, for shaping the materials, and erecting the work, employing every kind and form of human labor. . . .

Taking all these kinds of labor into account, the wages paid for work on the bridge will thus average $2.50 per day.

Now if this work had been done at the time when the Pyramids were built, with the skill, appliances and tools then in use, and if the money available for its execution had been limited to nine million dollars, the laborers employed would have received an average of not more than two cents per day. . . . I shall not weaken the suggestive force of this statement by any comments upon its astounding evidence of progress. . . .

But this is not the only lesson to be drawn from such a comparison. The Pyramids were built by the sacrifices of the living for the dead. They served no useful purpose . . . Today the expenditures of communities are directed to useful purposes. Except upon works designed for defence in time of war, the wealth of society is now mainly expended in opening channels of communication for the free play of commerce, and the communion of the human race. . . .

. . . The tendency of modern civilization is towards the concentration of population in dense masses. . . .

With this rapid growth in urban population, have grown the contemporaneous complaints of corrupt administration and bad municipal government. The outcry may be said to be universal, for it comes from both sides of the Atlantic; and the complaints appear to be in direct proportion to the size of the cites. It is obvious, therefore, that the knowledge of the art of local government has not kept pace with the growth of population. . . .

Now we know that it is at least as difficult to govern a city as to build a bridge, and yet, as citizens, we have deliberately allowed the ignorance of the community to be organized for its government, and we then complain that it is a failure. Until we . . . organize the intelligence of the community for its government, our complaint is childish and unreasonable. But we shall be told that there is no analogy between building a bridge and governing a city. Let us examine this objection. A city is made up of infinite interests. They vary from hour to hour, and conflict is the law of their being. Many of the elements of social life are what mathematicians term 'variables of the independent order'. The problem is, to reconcile these conflicting interests, and variable elements into one organization which shall work without jar, and allow each citizen to pursue his calling, if it be an honest one, in peace and quiet.

Now turn to the bridge. It looks like a motionless mass of masonry and metal: but, as a matter of fact, it is instinct with motion. There is not a particle of matter in it which is at rest even for the minutest portion of time. It is an aggregation of unstable elements, changing with every change in the tempera-

ture, and every movement of the heavenly bodies. The problem was, out of
these unstable elements, to produce absolute stability; and it was this problem
which the engineers, the organized intelligence, had to solve, or confess to
inglorious failure. . . .

Now if our political system were guided by organized intelligence, it would
not seek to repress the free play of human interests and emotions, of human
hopes and fears, but would make provision for their development and exercise,
in accordance with the higher law of liberty and morality. . . .

No, let us rather learn the lesson of the bridge. Instead of attempting to
restrict suffrage, let us try to educate the voters; instead of disbanding parties,
let each citizen within the party always vote, but never for a man who is unfit
to hold office. Thus parties, as well as voters, will be organized on the basis [of]
intelligence.

From Abram Stevens Hewitt, "Address Delivered on the Occasion of the Opening of the New York
and Brooklyn Bridge," May 24, 1883 (New York: John Polhemus, 1883).

1. Précis Hewitt's contention that the building of the bridge was a symbol of the
accomplishments of industrialization.
2. What political parallels does Hewitt draw between the bridge and the city?
3. Write a news account of the opening of the Brooklyn Bridge.

Toronto the Ugly, 1906

*In an address to the Canadian Club of Toronto delivered on March 20, 1906, Byron
Walker outlined his plans to improve the cityscape of Toronto.*

Before we can hope to have any plan for the benefit of the city realized we must
secure the interest of the young men. They are looking back. We are told that
your young men shall see visions and your old men dream dreams. They must
not, like Shakespeare's Falstaff, dabble in green fields and think little about the
future. This trust in the future is the greatest impulse to any community. The
young men must bear the greater responsibility for they not only look forward
to the future but they inherit it.

This trust in the future is one of the essential elements in the successful life
of a new country. Yet temporary and ugly conditions are put up with which
would never be tolerated in anything but a new country. In the old world men
are mainly interested in the thing which they are to enjoy immediately and
hence they would not submit to the ugliness of the temporary expedients with
which we readily bear. The old world wouldn't put up with what we stand in
Toronto. In Mr Hyne's views we have seen tonight much of what can be—and
has been—accomplished. If he had gone over the whole of Europe, city after
city, he could have shown you further everywhere beautiful parks completed
and perfected. Compare them with the ugliness of Toronto. There are many of
these uglinesses. There are the trolley poles, hideous, antique, and years out of
date, disfiguring our streets. There are the telephone poles at least I thought so
until my friend Mr Dunstan, whom I see here tonight—convinced me that

there were no telephone poles, so they must be fire-alarm poles. But I know we could not take a picture of any of the Bank of Commerce buildings without including these unsightly relics of our ugliness. Then there are our wharves and waterfronts, ghastly and disgraceful; our wretched system of street signs and, worse still, our bill boards. It is a pleasure to visit Berlin where no billboards are allowed. They have what they call circular drums there.

Then there is also the ugliness of the undecorated interiors of our public buildings. Only Canada—and perhaps some new portions of the western United States—would put up with what we have put up with. Pray do not imagine that I do not regard as a virtue our readiness to accept the things which are possible, ugly though they be, until such time as we are able to accomplish better things. It is not always wiser to go without electric lights because we won't have an imperfect system. But the danger lies in becoming contented with temporary conditions. We may bear them for a time, but our faces should be set absolutely against them. We are wealthy and comfortable. Surely it is time for improvement. . . .

It is a curious anomaly that all our surroundings, not so immediately annexed to us as our back yards, shame us in every respect as citizens.

Some may say this is not fair. We have made great improvements in civic matters, in pavements, etc. Of course, and every part of Canada has improved. The question before us—and we should not seek to escape from it—is, do we in any sense measure with the other cities in the world with which Toronto naturally compares itself? I sometimes question whether we have any civic pride. As long as a question like this, of universal interest, fails to produce our enthusiastic interest and stir up our newspapers, we have it. We are comfortably interested in ourselves. And because of our indifference we do not improve our taste in public matters as we do in domestic matters.

We are ready to shift responsibility on the mayor and alderman. But we cannot expect the mayor and alderman to act without a mandate from the people. They will not act in advance of public opinion. This is not an excuse. We all know the condition for ourselves and we are all to blame. If we know that civic improvement ought to be made and don't give the mandate to the council then we must blame ourselves.

From Byron Walker, "A Comprehensive Plan for Toronto", Address to the Canadian Club of Toronto, March 20, 1906, *Saving the Canadian City: the first phase 1880-1920*, (Toronto: University of Toronto Press, 1974).

1. How does Walker depict the city?
2. What suggestions does he make for civic improvement?
3. What might Walker think of Toronto in the 1990s?

The City Beautiful

In his essay "The Fate of City Beautiful Thought in Canada, 1893-1930," Walter Van Nus examines the rise and fall of the city beautiful concept in Canada.

This paper seeks to summarize and account for the origins of major city beautiful concepts as advanced within the three professions that played the central role in the practice of town planning: architecture, engineering, and surveying. It also attempts to explain why, by the end of World War I, almost all advocates of town planning had ceased to urge implementation of those concepts. . . .

The notion of introducing beauty into the urban environment was, patently, not new to the 1890's and early 1900's, though many laymen and some professionals considered it the essence of city beautiful thought. What is more ambitious professional supporters thought innovative in the city beautiful idea lay in its scope. No longer should beauty be confined to scattered and isolated buildings, its effect more often than not spoiled by an ugly setting. Instead, professionals would plan and regulate the entire city so that people might be surrounded by beauty. Architects who shared in this vision grew impatient with their colleagues' preoccupation with individual commissions. . . .

What was the origin of this wider view? For those (relatively few) engineers and surveyors who actively supported city beautiful architects, no general answer seems possible. Many architects had in their training been exposed to pictures of marvellous vistas from Renaissance and modern European cities. Even when in their planning proposals to penurious municipal governments architects avoided any suggestion that the city be remade along such expensive lines, their wish to do so could not always be suppressed. . . .

In later years, when leaders in the Canadian planning movement talked of its beginnings, they often traced the North American planning movement back to the Chicago World's Fair of 1893. Though Canadian engineering and surveying journals show no significant response to the event, the Fair aroused considerable admiration among Canadian architects. . . .

A.T. Taylor told his Quebec colleagues in 1893 of 'the fair white city on the shores of Lake Michigan'. The discussion . . . drew the inference of architectural mastery over existing cities. But we must note the tone of resignation, the feeling that no architectural power could ever be wielded over a real city. . . .

Probably the most significant stimulus to city beautiful thinking among architects, though, was the contrast between the profession's commitment to the creation of beauty and the ugliness of Canadian cities around the turn of the century. A common self-image among architects was that of 'an artist, with the practical knowledge necessary to be able to carry out his dreams on a sound constructional basis.' . . .

Certainly downtown areas seemed to be getting uglier by the early 1900's, as overcrowding became ever more acute, as taller buildings began to disturb streetscapes, as the utility poles blemished most streets. The outrage which urban ugliness could arouse in the breasts of architects may be gauged by this outburst from Professor Nobbs:

'The Streets!—the numerous poles which make our main thoroughfares look like a Chinese harbour after a typhoon . . . the water tanks—the sky signs—the horrible advertisements painted in epic scale on the flanks of buildings—the lettering falling like a veil over many a fair piece of architecture—and the boardings bedight with playbills—all these things are without decency and contrary to the expression of any civic spirit or virtue.' . . .

On the face of it, planning cities to avoid visual monotony might seem at odds with regulation for similarity of neighbouring architecture. Architects recognized no contradiction here because the beneficiary of visual variety was always assumed to be a person travelling along city streets or through a city parks system. . . .

Professionals associated with prairie cities were particularly vexed on this point, especially in the early years of the century, when large trees had not had time to grow, thus leaving the expanse of dullness exposed throughout the year. In 1912 the Park Superintendent of Regina, Malcom N. Ross [argued that monotony] . . . was the most damaging feature of any visual environment, and nothing could be more monotonous than the long straight roads in Canada's new cities, due to the prevalent rectangular plan. . . .

Advocates of new civic centres and broad avenues had to concede that such projects would be costly, and this fact encouraged critics to question the proponents' sense of social priorities. The fact that the most grandiose of pre-war civic centre proposals—such as the truly monumental one for Calgary submitted by Thomas Mawson in 1914—seemed to come from foreign planning experts, did not lessen the vehemence of attacks on Canadian city beautiful advocates. . . .

By the end of 1915, attacks on city beautiful projects had become qualitatively different; instead of accepting their validity as part of improvement of the urban environment, though pointing out that decent housing had a higher priority, professional critics began to insist that society must choose either the city beautiful approach or the suburban regulation approach. . . .

Why did these critics insist, beginning about 1910, that provision of workers' housing must be the first priority in Canadian planning? . . .

The answer . . . is that after 1910, the shortage of decent housing became popularly regarded as Canada's greatest social problem, and suburban planning as the principal solution. The rate of population growth in the major centres of central and western Canada in the first decade of the century had been phenomenal. . . .

Private enterprise proved incapable of providing all of these people with decent housing at prices they could afford. . . .

By 1914 many thousands of families occupied only one or two rooms each. The severest cases of overcrowding were truly pitiable. In October 1909, a Winnipeg health inspector paid a midnight call on a boarding house, and came upon twelve occupants in one room measuring 13 x 12 x 7 feet. Inspector Allison of the Toronto Police discovered no fewer than 565 people in five houses on King Street East. . . .

The slum, with its damp and filthy houses, was pictured as the breeding ground 'wherein huge cultures of disease are growing, ready when ripe to rise and sweep the city streets.'

Many of the socially concerned citizens who were determined to overcome

the shortage of low-income housing had by 1914 come to the conclusion that
the realistic solution was to erect workers' suburbs. . . .

If enough slum dwellers moved to these suburbs, the surplus population
would be drained from overcrowded areas. As the exodus continued, slumlords
would be forced to improve their properties because of the competing attraction
of cheap and decent suburban housing.

From Walter Van Nus, "The Fate of City Beautiful Thought in Canada 1893-1930", *The Canadian
City: Essays in Urban and Social History* from CHA, *Historical Papers*, 1975.

1. According to Van Nus what was the impact of the concept of "city beautiful"
upon Canadian architects?
2. What political obstacles lay in the way of urban renewal?
3. Contrast the concept of urban orderliness with the monotony so dangerous to
the "city beautiful."

Urban Political Reform

The following anonymous analysis of urban politics in Montreal first appeared in
The Canadian Magazine *in March 1899.*

Writers on sociology agree that municipal reform is one of the most difficult
problems which confront the democracy of North America. The exposures of
boodling which occur from time to time in all large cities of the United States
and Canada, as well as the importance of the interests, both moral and material,
which are involved in municipal government, leave no doubt as to the urgency
of reform; while the frequent failure of sincere efforts to secure a better administration show that the obstacles in the way of improvement are both numerous
and difficult to overcome.

Some writers have contended that the salvation must be sought in a more
scientific system of municipal government. . . .

Others aver that good men alone can give an honest and efficient administration; and to get them in office a great deal of energy has been spent at times in
the organization of good government associations and people's parties. . . .
The moral, it seems is that both good men and good laws can only be had by
the observance of that old precept: 'Eternal vigilance is the price of liberty'.

Unfortunately, although the municipal taxes absorb a larger share of the people's income than those levied by either our provincial or federal governments,
the questions involved . . . are such that it is exceedingly difficult to excite
widespread and lasting interest among the people. . . .

To arouse their conscience the exposure must take the proportions of a
revolting scandal. And when you come down to questions regarding street-
making, parks, or public buildings, you find that the section of the city which
is directly benefited will generally favour the aldermen who supported the
scheme of improvement in spite of the fact that there is a suspicion of bribery
about the transaction and that the expenditure has been extravagant. . . .

The exposure of corruption in municipal affairs and the formation of public opinion against extravagance is rendered difficult by the absence of parties. Party government has its disadvantages, but it benefits the people by the rivalry and the animosity which it creates among two sets of public men. . . .

A party encourages its members to expose the misdeeds of the men of the opposite party; the work is considered meritorious and deserving of reward. In the ethics of municipal politics discreetness is considered essential to advancement. Although there may be two rival factions fighting for supremacy, the members must not expose the methods of the inner circle. . . .

I have touched . . . on obstacles to municipal reform which I believe exist in most cities.

From "A French Canadian," *The Canadian Magazine*, March 1899, 457-60, *Saving the Canadian City.*

1. Why did the "French Canadian" (the author) of the article contend that "municipal reform is one of the most difficult problems which confront the democracy of North America"?
2. What argument does he make in favor of party politics in urban government?
3. What role did English-French relations play in Montreal politics?

The Boss System, 1910

Mid-western Progressive leader William Allen White described the reform mood in American cities in the early years of the century. This excerpt is taken from his book The Old Order Changeth. *In it he outlines the nature of "bossism" and its replacement by a more democratic approach to urban politics.*

Now it is not pleasant to recall American political conditions as they were in the late nineties. Yet those conditions were founded so firmly on local public sentiment and represented so thoroughly the judgment of the average man, that— bad as they were—it becomes necessary to the uses of this discussion to record them here briefly. . . . Politics in America a dozen or fifteen years ago was founded upon the boss system. At the bottom, in the smallest political unit, was the precinct boss. Delegates to local party conventions were elected from precincts or wards or townships. . . .

Year after year the same men represented each precinct in the local convention. They were the men who obeyed the dominant precinct boss at the base of things. He was not an officer of the government, but he controlled delegates to local conventions which nominated candidates for all the offices of the local government, so he became an actual part of the local government of every community. . . .

[The] indomitable local boss had relations with the group of bosses that controlled the district or the great city. . . . If he was one of the larger groups, he was powerful enough to say who should be nominated for the legislature in his country, who should have the judicial and congressional nominations in his district, and who should attend the state convention as delegates to name the candidates for state office. His nose was above water. He had a status in the politics of his state. He was someone. . . .

The extra-constitutional place of the boss in government was as the extra-constitutional guardian of business. If a telephone company desired to put its poles in the street, and the city council objected, straightway went the owner of the telephone stock to the boss. He straightened matters out. If a street car company was having trouble with the city street department, the manager of the street railway went to the boss, and the street department became reasonable. . . . The boss, little or big, had the greatest respect for business, little or big. And this respect came to him not as a peculiar revelation . . . but because he realized that all of the people about him felt as he felt. He merely reflected his environment. . . .

[Eventually] the folly grew national . . . [and]the superficial government, in a most natural way, captured the Constitution.

But now conditions are changing. . . . The problem of democracy is at base the problem of individual self-sacrifice coming from individual good will. We cannot hope to socialize the forces of steam in our civilization until we control and socialize ourselves.

And now for ten years there has been a distinct movement among the American people . . . during the recent years last past that movement has been unmistakable. It is now one of the big self-evident things in our national life. It is called . . . Reform.

From William Allen White, *The Old Order Changeth*, (New York, 1910).

1. Outline the role of the political "boss" in the life of the American city.
2. Why does White feel that the public was willing to accept such abuses?
3. Account for White's feeling that real change was taking place in the United States.

The City Boss: a Modern Assessment

In his study of the nineteenth-century American city, Raymond Mohl considered the role of the political boss in the development of the new urban industrial centre.

Traditional interpretations [have] emphasized the evils of the boss system and the laudable ideals of the municipal reformers. The literature of the late 19th century is filled with complaints about the corruption of city government. As early as 1867, for instance, *New York Times* editor George Jones wrote that the government of New York City was 'worse than a failure . . . it is corrupt, inefficient, wasteful and scandalous. The people are overburdened with taxation and there is nothing to show for it. Millions are wasted and nothing is done. The streets are not cleaned; the public health is not cared for; waste and extravagance characterize every department; and although more money is spent than anywhere else in the world for the purpose of government, the government actually procured by it is the worst in the world.'

Twenty years later in his famous book *The American Commonwealth* (1888), a visiting Englishman named James Bryce criticized urban government as 'one of the conspicuous failures of the United States.'

This sort of criticism of machine-dominated city government continued through the 1890's and into the 20th century. One popular book, *The Twentieth Century City* (1898), written by Protestant leader and publicist Josiah Strong, described the American city as 'a menace to state and nation' because it was incapable of self-government. . . . Lincoln Steffens, the renowned muckraking journalist of the progressive era, blasted both corrupt municipal government and the apathetic citizens who made it possible in his book, *The Shame of the Cities* (1904). Viewing the city from the reform perspective, these writers and scores of others condemned the urban boss and the political machine.

In a sense, early historians of this era became moral critics. . . . Historians traditionally argued that immigrants and workers were easily led by corrupt machine politicians. The urban masses provided essential support for the city machines, selling their votes to the bosses or putting them in office in return for patronage jobs and other favours. By contrast, the reform interpretation held, middle-class urbanites and professionals supported efforts to root out corruption and restore morality to urban life. . . .

This reformist interpretation continued to dominate the writing of urban political history until fairly recently. . . .

The new interpretations of urban machine politics have followed several separate but nevertheless interrelated lines of analysis. . . .

According to [sociologist Robert K.]Merton, the bosses and the machines were able to 'satisfy the needs of diverse subgroups in the larger community', needs not adequately satisfied through legally approved or culturally acceptable channels. Earlier historians puzzled over the electoral success and longevity of the urban machines. Given the reform bias of these historians, it was easy to dismiss such political success as the result of bribery, corruption, and vote fraud. But as Merton and other scholars have made quite clear, the urban machines did not have to steal elections. Rather, they had consistently strong political support in immigrant and working-class neighborhoods during the industrial era. Why? In an age when official municipal welfare and social services were weakly developed or administered in a bureaucratic tight-fisted manner, the bosses and the machines provided very real and important services in the urban neighborhoods. . . .

The machine's local leaders provided jobs, entertainment, legal assistance, food and welfare, help of all kinds. . . .

Recent historical research has also demonstrated that strong links existed between machine politicians and certain segments of the business community. . . . The city bosses . . . provided services to businessmen as well as to the urban masses. . . . (By some interpretations, the bosses were great city builders.)

From Raymond Mohl, *The New City: Urban America in the Industrial Age*, (Arlington Heights, Ill: Harlan Davidson, 1985).

1. Account for James Bryce's contention that American government was "one of the conspicuous failures of the United States."
2. Comment on the belief that the boss system was necessary for the development of the modern city.
3. Based upon your reading create and defend your own thesis about the American urban boss.

The Canadian City: a Modern Assessment

In his essay "Tomorrow's Metropolis: the Urban Reform Movement in Canada, 1880-1920" Professor Paul Rutherford of the University of Toronto examines the process of urban reform in Canadian cities around the turn of the century. In this excerpt he considers both the goals of the movement and its actual accomplishments.

The Canadian response to the urban fact, especially to the appearance of the 'big city', was generally unfavorable. At one level, it is true, cities were regarded as the physical embodiment of progress, the home of literature and the arts. Yet many people, looking to the sad experience of Europe and America, feared the further spread of the city. Rural apologists emphasized the debilitating influences of city life upon the individual. Social conservatives inveighed against the rampant materialism of the new culture. Even urban writers admitted that there was a dark side to the city where crime, prostitution, and general misery flourished. In the city all the ills of modern society were concentrated and highly visible. By the beginning of the twentieth century, it was widely accepted that urban growth posed a serious menace to the future of the nation.

It is only in retrospect that reform seems the logical solution to the urban crisis. . . . During the 1880's, various daily newspapers, the exponents of what was called 'people's journalism', turned to the idea of urban reform, then attracting considerable attention in the United States. These papers appealed to the expanded reading public of their cities, which was as interested in urban affairs as in provincial and national problems. . . .

Though inspired as much by hopes of a higher circulation as civic spirit, these papers popularized the idea of reform long before intellectuals discovered urban problems.

By 1900 however, the journalist had been replaced by the expert. In 1897 Herbert Ames, a businessman, published 'The City Below the Hill', a statistical analysis of social conditions in Montreal. . . . In 1911 appeared J.S. Woodsworth's *My Neighbour*, an impassioned plea for the reform of living conditions in Canada's cities. . . .

Urban reform was less a single creed and more a common approach to a wide variety of urban problems. Early reformers concentrated upon the redemption of the urban environment, a theme which extended back to the mid-century. The old ideal of civic improvement had emphasized the construction of stately buildings, colleges and academies, eventually libraries and museums, to bolster the prestige of the city. But as the cities became more and more congested, this concern was replaced by the attempt to make the city more healthy, moral, and equitable. . . .

During the 1880's clergymen, temperance societies, and women's organizations set out on a long crusade to purify city life. . . . These crusaders were most famous for their attacks upon organized sin: the saloon, the gambling den, the house of prostitution, even the theatre. . . . They sponsored a variety of moral clean-up campaigns in each city to enforce these laws, a task which was not always easy or successful. . . .

It would be unwise to assume that the reform doctrine was wholly accepted by the urban middle class, much less by other groups in Canadian society. The rural myth, more especially the image of the 'evil city' retained a strong hold upon the Canadian mentality. . . . In fact the very success of urban reform government has inspired new anxieties, for the price of order was a reduction in the freedom of the individual and the neighbourhood.

From Paul Rutherford, "Tomorrow's Metropolis: The Urban Reform Movement in Canada, 1880-1920, *The Canadian City: Essays in Urban and Social History*, (Ottawa: Carleton University Press, 1984).

1. What social criticisms of the modern city does Rutherford identify?
2. Outline the impact of the city beautiful movement upon Canadian urban centres.
3. Comment upon Rutherford's statement that "then as now, reformers were continually foiled by civic apathy."

Toronto: Image of the North American City

In his 1985 paper "Toronto among North American Cities" author James Lemon opens his discussion with a quote from the American Journal of Science *praising Toronto: "I have seen civilization, and it works." In this excerpt Lemon provides an overview of the strength of Canada's largest city as a model for North America.*

'I have seen civilization, and it works.' So concluded the prestigious journal *Science*, when promoting the 1981 meeting of the American Association for the Advancement of Science in Toronto. . . .

Even in the 1930's, when Toronto still invited American experts to evaluate its problems, the city was said to possess 'a marvellous organization and the finest [public] health system in the world . . . a model among municipal health institutions' . . .

To Ernest Hemingway, a young *Star Weekly* reporter in the early 1920's, however, Toronto's stability could not compensate for its dullness: 'Christ I hate to leave Paris for Toronto the City of Churches.' . . .

In considering the place of Toronto among North American cities, then, two issues should be addressed. First, why is Toronto so different from US metropolises that it can conjure up the 'alternative' image? Second, what is Toronto's place among Canadian cities and regions? . . .

Toronto is distinguished most conspicuously from US cities by the spatial distribution of income groups in both the inner city and the suburbs. In the United States, inner-city residents have become poorer and the suburbs richer, while Toronto and other Canadian cities have halted and even reversed that pattern, though the pressures were never as strong as in the United States. In

American inner cities , new office construction, persisting enclaves of high and middle-income people . . . have all helped to support the property tax base. But the overwhelming reality has been a decline in the twentieth century. Canadian cities have been maintained far better than any large US city. In Toronto one is hard put to find an abandoned dwelling; in New York officials and the *Times* have argued for 'planned shrinkage' and 'dedevelopment'—the withdrawal of public services from the large areas of South Bronx and Brooklyn that now resemble bombed-out Dresden and Hiroshima. . . .

Canadian cities have been beneficiaries of a slower and more cautious pace of living. They are a considerable triumph for Canadian ingenuity. . . .

Living cheek by jowl with the American giant, Canadians, Ontarians, and especially Torontonians have been moved, it seems, to exercise restraint. In short, Toronto's success as an urban environment has been wrought by looking over its shoulders at American cities.

From James Lemon, "Toronto among North American Cities," in Victor L. Russell, *Forging a Consensus: Historical Essays on Toronto*, (Toronto: University of Toronto Press, 1984).

1. How does the author say Toronto distinguishes itself from other cities?
2. Comment upon Lemon's assertion that "Toronto's success as an urban environment has been wrought by looking over its shoulders at American cities."
3. Place modern Canadian cities within the urban reform traditions of the late nineteenth and early twentieth centuries.

The Urban Experience: Analysis and Application

1. Create a brief history of the development of your own city or town. Your account should consider such factors as patterns of development and growth and the introduction of services such as electricity, telephones, public transit, etc. You may wish to consider creating a photo essay highlighting these factors and including examples of buildings constructed during different periods of the area's development.

2. Compare the profiles of Toronto and Chicago presented in the chapter. Select a third city, either Canadian or American, and see how it fits into the patterns of these two cities.

3. Outline the emergence of uniquely urban problems during the late nineteenth and early twentieth centuries. Create and defend your own thesis with regard to the new institutions and services that emerged to deal with these issues.

4. Account for the impact of urban transit upon the development of a city. Using maps, illustrate the co-relation between the growth of public transit and changing neighbourhood patterns.

5. Write an editorial entitled "The car was the worst thing that ever happened to the city."

6. (a) Based upon editorials and editorial cartoons of the period, write an indictment of the "boss system" in urban politics.

(b) Based upon additional research, write a rebuttal to your own indictment.

7. To what extent has the concept of "the city beautiful" been revived in the late twentieth century?

8. If James Bryce could call cities "one of the conspicuous failures of the United States," to what extent could he have said that Canadian cities were by contrast a conspicuous success?

9. Defend or refute the statement: "In the United States the country attempts to control its cities, while in Canada the relationship is the opposite."

10. Create an editorial cartoon that reflects some aspects of the current situation in your own city or community.

13
THE NEW DEAL AND A NEW SOCIAL ORDER

For many, the stock market crisis of October 1987 raised the spectre of the great crash of 1929. News reports around the world pointed out the parallels between the two events, and warned that a total collapse of the economic system might be dangerously close.

For those who had lived through the crash of '29 and the subsequent depression, old images and fears surfaced. In reality, however, the world is very different than it was over half a century ago. The free market and laissez-faire attitudes of government that characterized the late twenties no longer exist. The decade of the 1930s was a turning point for North Americans. The crisis of the Great Depression resulted in a "New Deal" for some North Americans and a new social order for others.

The Collapse of the World Economy

The collapse of the world economic system had been coming for some time. The prosperity taken for granted in the 1920s was not as substantial as people thought. Some sectors, such as textiles, mining, and agriculture, reaped few benefits from the boom. Even the manufacturing sector had begun to slow down by the end of the decade.

Although real income had risen for workers, there was still a limit to what they could afford. Manufacturers, facing surpluses, tried extending credit to buyers to keep goods moving. Many of these items were consumer durables, however—items such as cars, stoves, refrigerators, and radios that had long life expectancies. Consequently, once people owned these items they were unlikely to replace them for several years. Thus while in the early twenties most North Americans were scrambling to buy these new innovations, by the end of the decade demand had levelled off. As demand dropped, so too did employment.

In spite of the rapid growth in manufacturing during the 1920s, considerable unemployment remained. Even during the height of the boom, over 1.5 million Americans were out of work, due in part to increased mechanization in the factories. (Technological displacement of workers is not just a modern labour problem; it was as much of a concern in the twenties as it is today.)

In Canada in 1927-28 only 2.7 percent of the country's 10 million people were unemployed. The following year, however, this figure had almost doubled to over 4.6 percent. It was only a taste of things to come.

Once factory owners had accumulated a huge backlog of goods they were unable to sell, they had no use for their workers. Plants ran at half-speed, then quarter-speed and finally shut down altogether. As more and more people were thrown out of work, their ability to buy declined. This increased surpluses, forced further plant closures, and caused higher unemployment. Clearly, the stock market crash was not so much the cause of the depression, but rather a symptom of a serious financial ailment.

There were a number of underlying weaknesses in the economy of the 1920s—over-expansion of agriculture; surplus production in industry (especially in consumer durables); technological displacement; over-extension of credit resulting in large personal debts; and over-speculation in the stock market.

We often think of the Great Depression as a time of extreme shortages. But in fact the cause of the depression was surplus rather than shortage. The country's ability to produce items simply outran its ability to consume them. Profits were concentrated in a few hands, and were reinvested in more labour-saving machines and factories when they should have been redirected to workers to enable them to buy more goods.

Humorist Will Rogers said that the United States had "more wheat, more corn, more food, than any nation ever had, yet we are starving to death." He predicted that America would be the only nation in history to go "to the poorhouse in an automobile." Socialist Norman Thomas raised the absurd image of Americans waiting "in bread lines" standing "knee deep in wheat."

There was only one hope in the early 1930s: North America must find a way to sell its surplus products abroad. As the new decade dawned, the hope for a return to prosperity depended upon overseas trade.

It was a faint hope, however. In the twenties, protective tariffs had increased as Europe tried to protect the rebuilding of its industries after the First World War, and the United States continued to shield agriculture. Agriculture was the most vulnerable part of the world economy and, in the fall of 1930, it was hit by the economic crisis. In November, the Soviet Union, in an attempt to gain some foreign currency, dumped a bumper crop of wheat on the European market. This devastated Austria, which had been struggling to rebuild its agricultural base. The principal banks of the country, which had extensive farm loans, collapsed, but not before withdrawing enough of their reserves from Germany to destroy that country's economy. American president Herbert Hoover tried to prevent German economic collapse by proposing a one-year moratorium on reparations and debt payments. It was too late. When the German banks folded, Hoover immediately froze the $1.6 billion in German assets held by American banks. Should their value decrease, much of the American banking system would fall apart.

Britain was caught next. Economic panic prompted overseas investors to withdraw their gold reserves from Great Britain. This finally forced Britain to go off the gold standard. Americans with hundreds of millions of dollars invested in the British economy panicked. Within two weeks, $500 million worth of American banking assets had collapsed. Ordinary citizens ran to the banks to withdraw their savings before it was too late. That only made matters worse. The withdrawal of over $1.5 billion in deposits led to the failure of two thousand banks by the end of the year. Those that remained were struggling for survival.

North American Reaction to the Crisis

President Herbert Hoover had the right ideas about how to help the economy. He felt that by building up the weaker sectors of society, the nation's natural prosperity would, in time, return. His programs were intended to help farmers, to cut taxes, to increase consumer spending, and to provide money for public works. He was, however, not ready to let the government intervene directly to help suffering individuals. He hoped that the "trickle-down" effect would improve the whole economy. As a result, Hoover was criticized for worrying about business while millions were lining up for bread.

A final obstacle to recovery was Hoover's belief that a balanced budget was essential to a strong economy. At a time when the government should have been pumping money into the country, it was cutting back. As a result, in spite of a $500–million public works program, government expenditure actually dropped by $1 billion in 1931.

Government spending in Canada followed the same pattern as that of the United States. During the twenties, Ottawa had little impact upon the economy, spending only 11 percent of the gross national product. In fact, during the last three years of the decade, governments in Canada collectively made a profit. As a result, when disaster struck there was little inclination to intervene within the House of Commons. In fact, between 1930 and 1933, spending at all levels of government withered away to almost nothing.

In fairness, it is unjust to criticize Americans and Canadians for their rejection of deficit financing. The majority of economists in the early 1930s believed that governments were doing the right thing by not intervening directly. In addition, in the United States Hoover faced an obstacle in the form of an uncooperative Congress.

Hoover approached Congress in December of 1931 with a sixteen-point program; Congress was not ready to go along. The Democrats controlled the House of Representatives, and many did not want to do anything that might make the Republican president look good in an election year. Others were interested in local relief for their constituents rather than a national package. Still other members of Congress simply did not understand what Hoover was trying to do, and voted against his proposals out of ignorance. This opposition resulted in only four of the president's sixteen major proposals being passed.

It was too little, too late. As the United States slipped into the depths of depression, it pulled the political fate of Herbert Hoover along with it.

Life in the Depression: The Urban Unemployed

In the summer of 1932, Herbert Hoover remarked that things might be bad, but "no one had starved." But with almost 12 million unemployed in the United States, and over eight hundred thousand out of work in Canada, it was only a matter of time.

Women were hard hit by the depression. Layoffs tended to affect them first, and their wages, already less than those paid to men, were depressed even further. By 1939 the average female clerical worker was being paid 71 percent of the wage her male counterpart in the same job received; as bad as this was, it was considerably better than the 44 percent of male salary being paid to women in the manufacturing sector.

Many people, evicted from their homes, became drifters, sleeping on the streets, in parks, or in alleys. They stood for hours to receive a meagre hand out in a bread line or at a soup kitchen. Photos taken during the period show the destitute, eyes downcast to avoid being recognized, patiently waiting for food and clothing. In spite of the thousands of citizens receiving relief, they represented only about 25 percent of the unemployed. What was happening to the rest of them?

Some people lived off their savings. That meant cutting corners and doing without certain things. They patched clothing, sharpened old razor blades, used low-watt bulbs, and heated only one room in the house. Others were simply too proud. They struggled along living in appalling conditions. In Los Angeles, men were living in old trolley cars; in New York, one person was living in a large baby carriage; and in Chicago it was estimated that over two hundred women a night were sleeping in one park alone.

Professionals in the United States were hard hit. An unemployed teacher and her children spent two winters in Iowa in a hole covered with a tent; an engineering graduate of the University of Colorado was arrested in Brooklyn, New York, for sleeping in a vacant lot for forty-six days. Many others were underemployed as clerks, doormen, or elevator operators.

In Canada, on the other hand, life was slightly better for white collar workers. Employment opportunities for them actually expanded. Professors and teachers received a steady income which, although less than they would have made in the 1920s, actually bought more at the now–depressed prices. One barometer of this hidden prosperity was the fact that the number of consumer luxury goods people owned increased substantially during the decade. By 1939 more Canadians owned refrigerators, radios, and cars than ever before.

In 1932, a group of American veterans from Oregon started a cross-country trek to Washington demanding payment of an advance on a bonus pension due to them in 1941. As they marched, the "Bonus Army" was joined by supporters, so that by the time they arrived in Washington they numbered almost twenty thousand. Their efforts had little effect, however. Congress rejected their appeal for money. Hoover offered to pay their way home, and most of them left. However, about two thousand remained and built a shanty town on the edge of the city. Hoover refused to meet the leaders of the group, claiming, incorrectly, that they were mostly radicals and troublemakers. Finally fed up with their presence, he called out the army. Led by General Douglas MacArthur, troops attacked the protesters with tear gas and tanks. The Bonus Army was driven from the capital, but the memory did not disappear from the public mind. The sight of government troops attacking war veterans and their families was more than many people could accept. Herbert Hoover was losing control (see readings).

Canada saw its own version of the Bonus Army three years later. Relief workers in Vancouver started an "On to Ottawa" trek to present their case to the federal government. Supported by radical workers' associations, the marchers had swollen to two thousand strong by the time they reached Regina. Here the government stepped in. When the RCMP attempted to arrest the leaders of the march, a riot broke out. While the journey was over, so too was the government's credibility. Prime Minister R.B. Bennett was soon on the road out of office (see readings).

The shanty town of the Bonus Army was not unique. Across the United States shanty towns known as "Hoovervilles" sprung up on the outskirts of major cities. A collection of "homes" made from old packing crates, sewer pipes, and scraps of sheet metal, the shanty towns illustrated the worst aspects of the depression. In Canada, rural workers and farmers, unable to buy gas for their cars, hitched them up to horses. These Canadian "Bennett Buggies" and "Bennett–boroughs" and the American Hoovervilles summed up the attitude of many North Americans towards their governments. But while the cities may have witnessed tragedy on a major scale, in the country it was worse.

Life on the Farm

The collapse of the domestic market for their produce devastated farmers in the early 1930s. Wheat remained unharvested and fruit rotted on the trees. The price of corn dropped so low that its selling price was lower than the cost of shipping it to market; some farmers gave up and just burned the corn for fuel. During the first three years of the depression, the average income of the American farmer dropped by 57 percent. In addition, between 1929 and 1932 the value of farm property fell by another third. Mortgages started to exceed the actual value of the land, and farmers got further and further in debt.

Canadian wheat in the 1920s had been marketed by the Wheat Pool. In 1928 the average field yielded 23.5 bushels (855 L) per acre (0.4 ha) worth $1.18 each. Over the next nine years that output dropped to just over 25 percent of that amount, and farm income in the Prairies, which had hit a record $450 million in 1928, dropped to under $100 million only three years later.

As if things weren't bad enough for the farmer, nature also decided to take its toll. Drought hit the Great Plains and the Prairies. For centuries the deep-rooted prairie grass had anchored the soil through dry spells and high winds. However, the rapid expansion of farm land during the wartime boom had caused farmers to plough more than a third of that grass under. During the wet years of the twenties, it hadn't mattered. But it was a different story when drought hit in the thirties.

Wind swept the dry soil into the air; the dust travelled for kilometres. Livestock, poultry, people, and even houses were buried by drifting dunes. Colorado, Kansas, New Mexico, Oklahoma, and Texas were all part of what became known as the Dust Bowl. In one day over 50 million tonnes of precious topsoil blew away. Hundreds of millions of tonnes drifted east in the winds. Clouds of dust from the Great Plains darkened the skies as far east as Albany, New York, and in the winter of 1935, New England had dirt-red snow. It was a national nightmare.

American novelist John Steinbeck described the inside of the dust storm in his novel *The Grapes of Wrath*. Canadian writer James Gray described driving across Saskatchewan past "empty farm after empty farm". Wind–whipped topsoil darkened the sky as far east as Winnipeg. Gray recalled one other plague as well. In Weyburn, Saskatchewan, "we made a deal with the son of a garageman to clean the grasshoppers off our car for a dollar. It took him almost two hours and a gallon of coal oil."

Clearly, the situation was out of the farmers' hands. All they could do was wait out the disaster or get out. Many chose to do the latter. Thousands of farm families strapped their belongings to cars or trucks and deserted their worthless properties.

By 1932 Americans had had enough. The government, in general, and Herbert Hoover, in particular, did not seem to have any answers for the problems that plagued them. If the country was ever going to recover, there would have to be a change in Washington.

The Election of 1932

Herbert Hoover and the Republicans appeared to be easy to beat in 1932. Consequently, several candidates scrambled for the Democratic nomination. The contest came down to two frontrunners: Franklin Delano Roosevelt of New York and John "Cactus Jack" Garner of Texas. With the help of powerful backroom organizers, such as Joseph Kennedy (father of a future president), Roosevelt came out on top. Garner agreed to run for vice-president, and the Democrats entered the campaign as a united force.

The contest was a vicious one. Roosevelt rejected Hoover's "trickle-down" philosophy, and called for a New Deal for what he called the "forgotten man"— the one at the bottom of the economic ladder. Hoover claimed that the contest was not between two men or two parties, but between two philosophies. He predicted that a Democratic victory would mean that "the grass would grow in the streets of a hundred cities." Both sides predicted disaster if the other won. Such fear tactics only aggravated an already bitter campaign. On election day 1932 the entire nation anxiously anticipated the results.

It was a landslide victory. Hoover, who had lost only eight states in 1928, won only six this time. Roosevelt received 22.8 million votes to Hoover's 15.8 million, and swept the electoral college by 472 votes to 59. FDR had the mandate for his New Deal.

Roosevelt called a special session of Congress to convene on March 9th. In his Inaugural Address, he made it clear that while he was "prepared under my constitutional duty to recommend the measures that a stricken nation in the midst of a stricken world may require," he expected Congress to do its part. If the House of Representatives and the Senate were not ready to "bring speedy adoption" of his plans, then he would be forced to ask for "broad executive power to wage a war against the emergency."

The president was convinced that, facing an army of 12 million unemployed, he needed to act, and act quickly. On the one hand, he believed that it didn't matter what the government did as long as the people could see that it was trying to do something. On the other hand, the policies that were soon enacted fell into an organized and recognizable pattern.

The New Deal

The New Deal was not a revolution. Government took a new, more active role in the economy, but still preserved private enterprise and democratic institutions.

Roosevelt was going to steer a middle course through the crisis. The three goals of the New Deal—relief, recovery, and reform—concentrated on a domestic program of economic rebuilding. Whatever his long-term goals, Roosevelt's first priority was to put people back to work.

The Hundred Days

Congress was greeted on March 9th with the Emergency Banking Act. It confirmed the steps that the president had already taken, and set the stage for the reforms to come. On March 31st, the Civilian Conservation Corps Reforestation Relief Act created a series of work camps for young men, eventually creating a job corps of over half of a million workers. In return for room and board and $30 per month, they worked on reforestation projects.

The Federal Emergency Relief Act (FERA) was passed on May 12th. It authorized the distribution of over $500 million in aid to the needy. This brought relief to millions of people. It was followed in June by the Home Owners Refinancing Act, which created an agency with $2.2 billion in assets to refinance home mortgages and prevent foreclosures. Over 1 million family homes were saved.

While these relief measures helped people in the short-term, the New Deal was also intended to help the long-term recovery of the economy as well. The same day that Congress passed FERA, Roosevelt signed the Agricultural Adjustment Act into law. It created an Agricultural Adjustment Administration (AAA) with the power to pay subsidies to any farmers who were willing to reduce their output. Although declared unconstitutional in 1936, the AAA proved to be a major gain for farmers. Farm income, which had been steadily declining for a decade, almost doubled by 1937.

Congress responded favourably to the president's lead. On May 18th, it created the Tennessee Valley Authority (TVA). Its mandate was to transform the depressed area of the Tennessee Valley through planned development. The TVA revolutionized life across seven states. Rivers were dammed; hydroelectric plants were built; new soil conservation policies were introduced; and factories and even new towns were constructed. Critics objected to this obvious social planning and government control, but there was no arguing with success. Even the most bitter opponents of the TVA had to admit that, if nothing else, the program put a lot of people back to work.

Perhaps the most controversial aspect of the "Hundred Days" was the passage of the National Industrial Recovery Act (NIRA). The act had three basic aims. To begin with, it created a Public Works Administration with the power to initiate major public works projects. It eventually spent over $7 billion and employed millions.

Secondly, NIRA created a National Recovery Administration (NRA) to set new codes for industry in such areas as the length of the work day, minimum wage, and child labour. The new codes, which covered over 23 million workers, eventually outlawed child labour, confirmed the eight-hour workday, and set the minimum weekly wage at $12.25. Businesses that cooperated with the new regulations were given a "Blue Eagle" sign that read "We Do Our Part." The public was encouraged to patronize businesses displaying this sign.

Finally, the NRA dictated that under the code all employees had "the right to organize and bargain collectively." In other words, they could form unions. Organizers used the boost given to them by the NRA to push the union movement. Claiming that "President Roosevelt wanted them to join," labour leaders increased union membership from 2.5 million in 1933 to over 10.5 million by 1941.

Many Americans blamed the financiers and the speculators for the depression. They felt that an unregulated stock market and semi-independent banking system had contributed heavily to the crisis. Consequently, Congress passed two measures in the spring of 1933 to bring these operations under control. The Federal Securities Act and, later, the creation of the Securities Exchange Commission brought the financial world under control. This was followed by the Glass-Steagall Act which created the Federal Deposit Insurance Corporation and tightened control on small banks. The results were impressive. Even during the boom years of the twenties, an average of seven hundred small banks failed each year. Under Glass-Steagall, this number dropped to about seventy, and then to almost nothing.

Congress adjourned on June 16th. In its "Hundred Days" since March 9th, it had enacted a long list of progressive legislation, but it didn't stop there. The rest of the year the president and Congress continued to institute reforms. In August, a National Labour Board was formed to oversee industrial disputes; October saw the creation of a Commodity Credit Corporation to provide loans to farmers.

In November the Civil Works Administration (CWA) was created. Run by Harry Hopkins, the CWA was established to create jobs for millions of unemployed Americans. Through local construction jobs, cultural performances, and public services over 4 million people were put back to work. Although the CWA was phased out the following year, it injected some much-needed life and money back into the economy during its brief lifespan.

By 1934 things were looking much better. Although there would be setbacks, conditions would never be so bad again. The United States had hit the depths of the Great Depression and had survived. The country was on its way up again.

Response to the New Deal

Not all Americans were pleased with the reforms of 1933–34. Many people feared that the government had gone too far. Power had been centralized in a federal bureaucracy at the expense of other levels of government. With the growing power of labour and minority groups within society, some class resentment appeared. Many wealthy people complained that the increase in their taxes was discouraging private initiative.

Fuelled by these complaints, the business community asked government to pass legislation to encourage private enterprise and cut back government regulations. In addition, a new organization, the American Liberty League, was highly critical of the radical actions of the administration. Led by conservative Democrats, including one of Roosevelt's old friends, Al Smith, they wanted the government to back off of its reform program completely.

On the other side of the political spectrum, radical leaders accused Roosevelt of not going far enough. One prominent leader of this group was Senator Huey Long of Louisiana. Called "the Kingfish," Long was genuinely concerned about the plight of the average American. Although he was a racist, he still believed in improving the lot of all poor people—Black or white. "I'm for the poor man—all poor men. Black and white they all gotta' have a chance."

Long proposed a Share-the-Wealth plan. Under this scheme, the government would confiscate all family fortunes with a value of over $5 million. The money collected would be used to provide every American family with a "homestead" (house, car, appliances, etc.) and an annual income of $2000 to $3000. He believed in social security, improved education, and veterans' benefits. His ideas became so popular that, by 1935, his movement had attracted 4.6 million members. Long did not live to benefit from this new-found political strength, however. He was assassinated on the steps of the Louisiana state legislature in 1935.

The New Deal might have survived these attacks had it been allowed to continue. The Supreme Court, however, had other ideas. It declared most of the reforms of the Hundred Days to be unconstitutional. The court's action may have been a good thing, however. The New Deal had been a temporary measure. It had not worked badly, but the economy was still sluggish. If Roosevelt was going to recapture the momentum of reform, he would have to act fast.

The "Second Hundred Days" began in the spring of 1935, and it was even more productive than the first. Roosevelt had been moving quickly. The Emergency Relief Appropriation Act was passed in April. It created a Works Progress Administration (later called the Works Projects Administration) to carry out a comprehensive public works program. The WPA built highways, bridges, and other public projects, but it also backed artists, writers, and actors, providing a cultural stimulus. By the time it was disbanded eight years later, it had created jobs for over 8.5 million people.

One aspect of the WPA was the National Youth Administration. Led for most of its history by Mary McLeod Bethune, it was designed to provide financial help to students to enable them to stay in school. Over 2 million young people were helped under the program.

A second major gain was the passage of the Wagner-Connery Act in July. It reestablished the rights of labour outlined in the earlier NRA codes. Congress went on to pass a Social Security Act, a Public Utility Act, and a Wealth Tax, and to establish a Rural Electrification Administration.

The government's motto for the 1936 election year was "Tax, tax, tax; spend, spend, spend; elect, elect, elect." How successful was the campaign?

The Election of 1936

The Republicans nominated Alfred Landon, the governor of Kansas, as their presidential candidate. Out to save America from "peril," the Republican campaign consisted of a series of stinging attacks on the New Deal reforms. It had little effect, however. Most people had benefitted under the New Deal; to them the Republicans represented the old business interests who had caused their problems in the first place. Radicals, on the other hand, threw their support behind William Lemke on the Left or Gerald Smith on the extreme Right, but neither had an impact on the final outcome. Roosevelt won over 61 percent of the popular vote, and captured 523 electoral college votes to Landon's eight. Landon won only the states of Maine and Vermont.

One major reason for the Democratic success in 1936 was the emergence of a new political alignment in the United States. This New Deal coalition comprised not only the traditional supporters of the Democratic party, but many new groups as well. Roosevelt's reforms had attracted labour, Blacks, and professionals into the party. This broad base of support would keep them in power until the 1950s (see readings).

The Canadian Response to the Great Depression

The Depression brought about a reassessment of the federal-provincial balance of power in Canada. Although some historians have argued that government did little or nothing during the decade, in actual fact fundamental constitutional changes were taking place to allow Ottawa to cope with national crises.

At the outset of the depression, the federal government wanted to stay as far away as possible from provincial relief payments. Prime Minister Mackenzie King went so far as to declare that he was not interested in giving federal money to the provinces for "alleged relief purposes" and that if they asked for any he was not inclined to even "give them a 5 cent piece." This display of insensitivity cost King the 1930 parliamentary election. Richard Bennett and the Conservatives were given a majority government to tackle the growing economic and social crisis.

In the election campaign Bennett had stated: "Mackenzie King promises you conferences; I promise you action. He promises you consideration of the problem of unemployment; I promise to end unemployment."

Expectations were raised that Bennett's Conservative government would be one of dramatic action. In reality just the opposite occurred. For the next four years, government policy drifted. Relief costs were bankrupting the provinces. More and more of the country elected local Liberal governments (Alberta elected a Social Credit one) in protest against the inaction of the Conservative government in Ottawa. Bennett during this period was intransigent. He refused to give any money to Ontario and Quebec, insisting that they "were rich and powerful enough to look after themselves," and he went so far as to state that if provincial governments were unable to cope with the crisis, then perhaps they should simply disappear.

Frustration with the lack of leadership offered by the old–line parties led to the emergence of new political alliances. The Social Credit party emerged as a powerful force in Alberta. Based upon radical economic theories and the force of personality of radio evangelist William "Bible Bill" Aberhart, the Social Credit swept 90 percent of the seats in the Alberta legislature in 1935. After an ill-fated attempt at implementing Social Credit theories, however, Aberhart retreated to a conservative approach to governing.

In actual fact, the left wing of Canadian politics was occupied by another new party. Delegates meeting in Regina in the summer of 1933 formed the Co-operative Commonwealth Federation (CCF). Based upon the principles of democratic socialism and led by long-time member of parliament J.S. Woodsworth, the CCF and its successor, the New Democratic Party (NDP), have remained a significant political force in Canada to the present day (see readings).

Finally in January of 1935, the prime minister decided to act. In a series of radio broadcasts intended to mimic the fireside chats of FDR, Bennett outlined the terms of his own "New Deal." "The old order...will not return," he said. "I am for reform" (see readings).

His reform package consisted of several measures dealing with unemployment insurance, minimum wages and hours, tax reform, and marketing boards. Many of these reforms were controversial. King denounced Bennett's policies as a sham intended to win over the Canadian people just prior to an election. King claimed that Bennett knew that his proposals would later be thrown out by the courts as unconstitutional; in this way Bennett could promote reforms without ever having to implement any.

The Election of 1935

Bennett called an election in October. In its campaign platform, the CCF called for an overhaul of the existing system. One pamphlet proclaimed that "Bank Robbers get millions, but the Big Shot Banker is a bigger criminal than the gunman." Most Conservatives backed the Bennett "New Deal," but for some the prime minister had not gone far enough. They broke away from the Conservative party and formed a splinter group, the Reconstruction party, which advocated more radical change.

Throughout the hotly debated campaign, Mackenzie King and the Liberal party advocated nothing. King promised not to take any rash actions, but rather to study the situation and govern carefully and prudently. "King or Chaos!" was his slogan.

In the end, inertia won out. The Liberals attracted almost 45 percent of the popular vote, capturing 173 seats out of a possible 245. Bennett finished a distant second with 30 percent of the vote and 40 seats. The Reconstruction party gained about 9 percent and elected one member; the CCF claimed slightly fewer voters but managed to win 7 seats; and the Social Credit, which attracted only 4 percent of the popular vote, concentrated its support in Alberta and took 17 seats. Mackenzie King had received his mandate to steer a cautious course through the remainder of the decade.

In spite of this mandate, however, King's government slowly increased the power and sway of the central government. The 1930s saw the creation of three future great instruments of public policy: the CBC (1932); the Bank of Canada (1935); and Trans-Canada Airlines (Air Canada, 1937). Another new agency to appear after King's return was the National Employment Commission, which was designed to find ways around the limitations the British North America Act placed upon the power of the federal government to directly support relief efforts. The commission recommended the adoption of the economic theories of John Maynard Keynes; Canada would have to spend itself out of the depression. The NEC called for an immediate reduction in taxes and for extensive government spending. King's cabinet wasn't willing to go quite as far as the recommendations, but in 1938 they took the first tentative steps towards deliberate deficit financing. The precedent had been set. When war broke out in 1939 the Canadian government would be ready to go deeply into debt to support the Allied cause.

Constitutional change was clearly needed to meet the challenges of the thirties and later the forties. In early 1937 King appointed a royal commission to investigate the existing division of powers and to make recommendations for constitutional amendment. The Rowell-Sirois Commission, as it came to be called, worked for over three years, finally reporting in May of 1940. Their recommendations were far-reaching, calling for a national standard in government social services that would not be dependent upon the willingness or ability of a particular province to pay.

The critical problems raised by the war, such as rationing, shifting tax burdens, and the financing of a large military force overseas, prompted the federal government to act upon the report. Unemployment insurance and old-age pensions were given to the federal government, and the provinces gave up their power of direct taxation in return for a guaranteed level of federal support. Social services in Canada became centralized. In this new order, the provinces became only administrative districts. The new social order would be drawn up and implemented by Ottawa.

The blueprint for this new Canada was laid out in 1943 in *The Report on Social Security for Canada*, or the Marsh Report. Pointing out that security against unemployment, illness, and old age was currently the privilege of the wealthy, it advocated a system within which it would become a national right. Unemployment insurance and old–age pensions were already law. To these benefits the King government added family allowances—the so-called "baby-bonuses" to supplement family incomes. As for health care, the end of the Second World War also saw a temporary end of the social reform movement. It would be twenty years before another Liberal prime minister, Lester Pearson, would adopt the CCF plan for universal medicare.

Franklin Roosevelt's New Deal set a pattern for government intervention in the economy. In the United States this amounted to a series of crisis–generated programs that faded away as the country returned to prosperity.

Canada's response, while not as spectacular, was long-lasting. Constitutional changes established the precedent that the federal government would accept responsibility for establishing and maintaining social programs across the country. In the late 1980s many Canadians view the decentralization of this responsibility as outlined in the Meech Lake Accord as an erosion of this traditional safeguard. Advocates point out that in the past forty years Canadians have come to expect such services as their right and would not allow any provincial government to decrease the level of service or the accessibility of programs. Still, in the 1990s the rising cost of supporting an aging population may prove to be the end of the principle of universality established during the Second World War.

Life in the Depression

These first excerpts are taken from letters written to Prime Minister R.B. Bennett during the first half of the 1930s. Part of a collection entitled The Wretched of Canada *they reflect what editors L.M. Grayson and Michael Bliss call the "bleak and still" lives of people struggling "for survival, monotonous and dreary.' Bennett, a wealthy individual, was often touched by such correspondence. All letters were read and virtually every letter with a return address received a reply. Such replies often included personal advice, or even a desperately needed gift ranging from $2 to $5.*

Sarnia Ont., Dec 1st/30
Hon. Mr. Bennet
Ottawa Ont.
Dear Sir:
I am taking this priviledge in my own hands of writing you which a person of my class should be ashamed to take such athoraty. But I am down and out and do not know what to do. We have six children and I don't beleive it right to see them suffer for the want of food. . . . I was in the second Canadian infantry Battalion as a private. I wrote to London see if I could get releif there. Enclosed you will find a coppy which they sent me. I will not take up too much of your time just now. But in my case I am a good worker but the work is not to be had. My name has been in the employment office since June but there is no jobs coming in so I have to do something might soon I hate to go out and steal but the family can't starve to death. . . . Kindly over look the privledge Im taking I think this is my last chance to get help. If this fails I do not know what we will do.
Thanking you very kindly in advance.
Yours very Truly,
Thomas M. Gibbs

From Michael Bliss and L.M. Grayson, ed., *The Wretched of Canada*, (Toronto: University of Toronto Press, 1971).

May 20/31
Mr Bennette
Since you have been elected, work has been imposible to get. We have decided that in a month from this date, if thing's are the same, We'll skin you alive, the first chance we get
Sudbury Starving Unemployed

From Michael Bliss and L.M. Grayson, eds., *The Wretched of Canada*, (Toronto: University of Toronto Press, 1971).

Ottawa Ont., Nov. 30th.32
Dear Sir
    I hope you will excuse me taken this liberty in writing to you. I know your

time is taken up with more important things than this but when I saw in the papers that you were going away I was desperate. Ive been going to write often, but I could not seem to get up enough courage. . . . Ime only asking for a loan as I shall pay every cent back. I have read lots about your kindness and oh sir its not much I ask for but it would mean a little bit of heaven for us both. We could be so happy away together from all this. I know I could work for us. I know you must be busy preparing for your trip and you must have lots of demands made on you But I hope you can spare a little of your time to read this. If I could only get enough to start us. I dont make many friends. I keep my troubles to myself. Your the first one I ever wrote to But Xmas is so near and I should like to spend a little happier one than last year. . . .
I am Yours respectfully
(Mrs) Henrietta Brown
P.S. I have to have my letters sent to here as ime afraid to have them sent home
(*Reply:* $5.00)

From Michael Bliss and L.M. Grayson, eds., *The Wretched of Canada*, (Toronto: Uniersity of Toronto Press, 1971).

Ferguson, N.B., March 21, 1933
Hon. R.B.Bennett
Ottawa, Can.
Dear Sir,
    The respectable people of this country are *fed up* on feeding the bums for that is all they can be called now. This "free" relief (free to the bums) has done more harm than we are altogether aware of. The cry of those who get it is "Bennett says he wont let anyone starve". They don't consider that the *people* (many poorer than themselves but with more spunk) have to foot the bill. . . .
    Getting relief has become such a habit that the majority think only of how to get it regularly instead of trying to do without once in a while. . . .
Yours respectfully,
Mrs. Ernest Ferguson

From Michael Bliss and L.M. Grayson, eds., *The Wretched of Canada*, (Toronto: University of Toronto Press, 1971).

1. Contrast the attitudes reflected in the letters.
2. Comment upon the statement that "these letters strip away the tawdry glamour and stupid nostalgia that somehow clouds the 1930s in retrospect."
3. Based upon your research, write your own letter to R.B. Bennett reflecting the situation in your family or community during the Depression.

Working for Eatons, 1934

This short excerpt is taken from the transcript of testimony given to the Royal Commission on Price Spreads and Mass Buying. It is an interesting illustration of the plight of the employed during the period.

Miss Nolan

Q. Miss Nolan, were you employed by the T. Eaton Company, Limited, of Toronto?

A. Yes, I was . . .

Q. And when you first went there what was your basis of pay?

A. $11 was guaranteed (per 44-hour week on piecework).

Q. And after that did it ever change?

A. Yes, I got $12.50. Toward the end of 1928, it was raised to $12.50.

Q. And what was the result, first of all, physically, from this drop in rates? (Piece-work rate of $3.60 for making a dozen voile dresses, which was dropped in 1933 to $1.75 a dozen for the same dresses and same work.)

A. Well, you had to work so hard, you were driven so fast that, it just became impossible to make $12.50, and you were a nervous wreck. The girls cried. I was hysterical myself. It almost drove me insane.

Q. Was that condition general or did it only happen to you?

A. It was general. All the girls were the same.

Q. And did you break down by reason of it all?

A. Yes, I went into hysterics several times and I had to go to the hospital and the nurse said, "What is the matter? You girls are always coming here."

Miss Amy Tucker

Q. It has been stated here that Eaton's do countenance and recognize Unions. Have you anything to say about that?

A. When we tried to organize, Mr. Clendining said, "You girls can form a Union if you please but that does not mean to say that this firm will recognize a Union. This firm will not recognize a Union."

Q. Who told you that?

A. Mr. Clendining.

Q. Anything else?

A. And then he went on to say "Of course we recognize Unions." And I said "You do in the printing, because it happens to be government work and it must have Union label on it. But otherwise you do not recognize Unions." And in all our talk he would try to bring in racial question, about the Jewish people, telling us we should not belong to the Union at all that was controlled by the Jews.

From Michael Horn, ed., *The Dirty Thirties*, (Canada: Copp Clark, 1972).

1. Account for the change in working conditions between 1928 and 1932.
2. Outline the situation with regard to unionization at Eaton's.
3. To what extent did working conditions differ for men and women during the 1930s?

Hard Times

American oral historian Studs Terkel interviewed a wide range of "survivors" of the Depression for his book Hard Times. *These two accounts illustrate the process of radicalization through which the political and social views of individuals were changed by the experiences of the period.*

Virginia Durr, whose husband went on to become a member of the Federal Communications Commission under Franklin Roosevelt, discusses her revelations at experiencing real poverty for the first time.

Oh, no, the Depression was not a romantic time. It was a time of terrible suffering. The contradictions were so obvious that it didn't take a very bright person to realize something was terribly wrong.

Have you ever seen a child with rickets? Shaking as with palsy. No proteins, no milk. And the companies pouring milk into gutters. People with nothing to eat, and they killed the pigs. If that wasn't the craziest system in the world, could you imagine anything more idiotic? This was just insane.

And people blamed themselves, not the system. They felt they had been at fault: . . . "if we hadn't bought that old radio" . . . "if we hadn't bought that old secondhand car." Among the things that horrified me were the preachers—the fundamentalists. They would tell the people they suffered because of their sins. And the people believed it. God was punishing them. Their children were starving because of their sins.

People who were independent, who thought they were masters and mistresses of their lives, were all of a sudden dependent on others. Relatives or relief. People of pride went into shock and sanitoriums. My mother was one. . . .

The young today are just play-acting in courting poverty. It's all right to wear jeans and eat hamburgers. But it's entirely different from not having any hamburgers to eat and no jeans to wear. A great many of these kids—white kids—seem to have somebody in the background they can always go to. I admire their spirit, because they have a strong sense of social justice. But they themselves have not been deprived. They haven't experienced the terror. They have never seen a baby in the cradle crying of hunger. . . .

I think the reason for the gap between the black militants and the young white radicals is that the black kids are much more conscious of the thin edge of poverty. And how soon you can be reduced to living on relief. What you *know* and what you *feel* are very different. Terror is something you *feel*. When there is no paycheck coming in—the absolute, stark terror. . . .

The Depression affected people in two different ways. The great majority reacted by thinking money is the most important thing in the world. Get yours. And get it for your children. Nothing else matters. Not having that stark terror come at you again. . . .

And there was a small number of people who felt the whole system was lousy. You have to change it. The kids come along and they want to change it, too. But they don't seem to know what to put in its place. I'm not so sure I know either. I do think it has to be done by democratic means, if possible. Whether it's possible or not—the power of money is such today, I just don't know. Some of the kids call me a relic of the Thirties. Well, I am.

Lewis Andreas was a doctor and a founding member of the first public medical centre in Chicago in 1932. He recounts treating the injured after the Memorial Day riots of 1937.

The Wagner Act had become the law—the right of labor to picket, to organize. Professionals, social workers, theological students—all kinds of people got into the thing. Some of the workers didn't like this. They must have wondered what we were doing there. But they didn't mind me, because I was a doctor and trouble was brewing.

A few days before Memorial Day, 1937, some steel workers picketed Republic Steel on the Far South Side. I received a call: "We've got a very nasty situation here. There're probably going to be some injuries. There's not a hospital for miles around, not even a drugstore. Would you come and get a few first aid stations started?"

There was a tavern called Sam's Place. I took a few supplies and got a first aid station started. The men who picketed that day got clobbered. There were a few split skulls and a few fractures. Everybody got mad and then decided to try it again on Memorial Day.

It was a holiday, so we had them from Indian Harbor and Gary and all kinds of places. Some were looking for trouble, but for many it was simply a family picnic sort of thing: little kids, people dressed up in their Sunday shirts. Many came just for the fun of it; they weren't expecting anything.

The police were standing in line in front of Republic Steel, quite a distance from the others. It was a hell of a hot day, about ninety. They had their winter uniforms on. The sun was strong, and all I could see were their stars glittering.

The people began wandering out. A long line. This was a mixed bunch. Some of them may have been planning to use the sticks they were holding the signs on for other purposes, for clobbering somebody. Nobody was armed. But the police got the idea these people were armed. At least, they were told so by Captain Mooney and Lieutenant Kilroy, who were managing this thing. Mayor Kelly was out of town.

I stayed behind. All of a sudden I heard some popping going on and a blue haze began rising. I said: My God, tear gas. What do you do for that? I couldn't remember what the medical books said. I ran back to Sam's Place. About three minutes later, they started bringing in the wounded, shot. There were about fifty shot. Ten of them died. One little boy was shot in the heel. I took care of him. One woman was shot in the arm. They were lying there, bleeding bullet wounds in the belly, in the leg and all over. All sorts of fractures, lacerations. . . . I had absolutely no preparation at all for this. I was there alone except for one guy sent by the Party. He tried to take over.

The communists didn't like the idea. I seemed to be doing what they wanted to be doing. I had no sympathy with them, I couldn't get along with them. I couldn't tolerate their dogmatism, their lack of tolerance and worst of all, their lack of humor. They were so grim. I couldn't understand this blind business of apologizing for everything—for all the Russian business. That I couldn't swallow.

We all wanted a better society, but I didn't want to deal with these boys, and they kind of resented my intrusion into their business. One of them helped me a little bit, but I was practically alone. . . .

What happened was this: There were a few rocks thrown at the police when the shooting started. Or even before. They all turned and ran. I said in my testimony before the La Follette Committee: like the shutters of a Venetian blind. As they were running, the police shot into them.

The police weren't all bad. Some of them quit the force because of the incident. They couldn't stand what happened. I know this as a fact because some of the boys came up here as patients and told me. . . .

From Studs Terkel, *Hard Times: An Oral History of the Great Depression*, (New York: Random House, 1986).

1. What conditions does Durr describe which made her change her views on society?
2. What criticisms does she direct at young protesters in the 1960s and 1970s?
3. Account for the escalation to violence of the Memorial Day riots in Chicago.

The Bonus Army

In 1932, World War I veterans staged a cross-country march on Washington to demand earlier payment of a "bonus" pension due in 1941. By the time they reached Washington the marchers numbered about twenty thousand. Their protest ended in failure and although most went home, about two thousand homeless veterans stayed behind and set up a shantytown just outside of the capitol. Hoover finally called out the army, and led by General Douglas MacArthur, General George Patton, and future president Major Dwight Eisenhower, the bonus "army" was driven from the city. In this exerpt Jim Sheridan, one of the veterans, relives the experience.

The soldiers were walking the streets, the fellas who had fought for democracy in Germany. They thought they should get the bonus right then and there because they needed the money. A fella by the name of Waters, I think, got up the idea of these ex–soldiers would go to Washington, make the kind of trip the hobos made with Coxey in 1898, they would be able to get the government to come through. . . .

We went down to the railyards and grabbed a freight train. Our first stop was in Peru, Indiana. We jungles up there for a little while, and then we bummed the town, so to speak. Go to different grocers and give them a tale of woe. They would give us sausage or bread or meat or canned goods. Then we'd go back to the railroad yards, the jungle, where we'd build a little fire and we'd cook it up in these cans. We'd sit around the fire and eat. . . .

Peru was the first division point outside of Chicago on the C & O (Chesapeake and Ohio Railway). We'd stop off and rest and scrounge up something to eat. We'd generally be told by the conductors the train was made up and ready to go out. Some of these fellas had come with their families. Can you imagine women and children riding the boxcars?

The conductor'd want to find out how many guys were in the yard, so he would know how many empty boxcars to put onto the train. Of course, the railroad companies didn't know this, but these conductors, out of their sympathy, would put two or three empty boxcars in the train, so these bonus marchers could crawl into them and ride comfortable into Washington. Even the railroad detectives were very generous.

Sometimes there'd be fifty, sixty people in a boxcar. We'd just be sprawled out on the floor. The toilet . . . you had to hold it till you got a division point. (Laughs.) That's generally a hundred miles. You didn't carry food with you. You had to bum the town. It was beggary on a grand scale.

In the town, D.C. Webb got up on the bandstand and made a speech. We passed the hat, even, among the local citizenry. The money was used to buy cigarettes for the boys. Townspeople, they were very sympathetic.

There was none of this hatred you see now when strange people come to town or strangers come into a neighborhood. They resent it, I don't know why. That's one of the things about the Depression. There was more camaraderie than there is now. Even more comradeship than the Commies could even dream about. That was one of the feelings that America lost. People had different ideas, they disagreed with one another. But there was a fine feeling among them. You were in trouble . . . damn it, they could help ya, they would help ya. . . .

When we got to Washington, there was quite a few ex–servicemen there before us. There was no arrangements for housing. Most of the men that had wives and children were living in Hooverville. This was across the Potomac River—what was know as Anacostia Flats. They had set up housing there, made of cardboard and of all kinds. I don't know how they managed to get their food. Most other contingents was along Pennsylvania Avenue.

They were tearing down a lot of buildings along that street, where they were going to do some renewal, build some federal buildings. A lot of ex–servicemen just sort of turned them into barracks. They just sorta bunked there. Garages that were vacant, they took over. Had no respect for private property. They didn't even ask permission of the owners. They didn't even know who the hell the owners was.

They had come to petition Hoover, to give them the bonus before it was due. And Hoover refused this. He told them they couldn't get it because it would make the country go broke. They would hold midnight vigils around the White House and march around the White House in shifts.

The question was now: How were they going to get them out of Washington? They were ordered out four or five times, and they refused. The police chief was called to send them out, but he refused. I also heard that the marine commander, who was called to bring out the marines, also refused. Finally, the one they did get to shove these bedraggled ex–servicemen out of Washington was none other than the great MacArthur.

The picture I'll always remember . . . here is MacArthur coming down Pennsylvania Avenue. And, believe me, ladies and gentlemen, he came on a white horse. Behind him were tanks, troops of the regular army.

This was a riot that really wasn't a riot, in a way. When these ex–soldiers wouldn't move, they'd poke them with their bayonets, and hit them on the head with the butt of a rifle. First, they had a hell of a time getting them out. A big colored soldier, about six feet tall, had a big American flag he was carrying. He was one of the bonus marchers. He turned to one of the soldiers who was pushing him along, saying: "Get along there you black bastard." That was it. He turned and said, "Don't try to push me. I fought for this flag in France and I'm gonna fight for it here on Pennsylvania Avenue." The soldier hit him on the side of the legs with the bayonet. I think he was injured. But I don't know if he was sent to the hospital.

This was the beginning of a riot, in a way. These soldiers were pushing these people. They didn't want to move, but they were pushing them anyway. . . .

The soldiers threw tear gas at them and vomiting gas. It was the one assignment they reluctantly took on. They were younger than the marchers. It was like sons attacking their fathers. The next day the newspapers deplored the fact and so forth, but they realized the necessity of getting these men off. Because they were causing a health hazard to the city. MacArthur was looked upon as a hero.

And so the bonus marchers straggled back to the various places they came from. And without their bonus.

From Studs Terkel, *Hard Times: An Oral History of the Great Depression*, (New York: Random House, 1986).

1. Describe the conditions suffered by the marchers and the attitudes of the residents of the towns through which they passed.
2. How did the government react to the marchers?
3. Assume that you are the Black veteran cited in the excerpt. Write a letter to Hoover expressing your concerns about the way you've been treated.

On to Ottawa, 1935

In 1932 over three thousand unemployed men descended upon Ottawa to demand government action. R.B. Bennett responded with local police, RCMP and military action. Even the conservative press was appalled by the over-reaction. Three years later, the workers tried again. Starting in Vancouver, the plan was to "ride the rails" east, picking up support along the way. As the "On to Ottawa Trek" picked up momentum, the Bennett government agreed to meet its leaders. These two excerpts describe the march, the meeting, and the subsequent end of the march in bloodshed on the streets of Regina.

Ronald Liversedge provided the following eyewitness account in his Reflections on the On-to-Ottawa Trek 1935. *It this exerpt he recounts the treatment of the trekkers and the reaction of the Bennett government.*

It was the afternoon of the second day when we pulled into Kamloops, and it was a stiff, sore, tired, and very hungry column of men which marched into the nearby city park to camp. Right away, it was obvious to all that our advance publicity group had done a poor job, or that the people of Kamloops lacked the imagination to conjure up the size and scope of the movement that we had started, and therefore had no idea of our needs.

There wasn't any welcoming committee, no girls with coffee,. . . no tables with food. Only a few curious people gathered to see what we were going to do. It was here that the breaking point was just about reached by some of the men, and the first time since our strike started that I had seen our self–discipline thrown to the winds. . . .

Here is a good place as any to mention our "pep" group, the Y.C.L.'ers, around a hundred strong, whose age averaged from seventeen to nineteen years, all members of the Young Communist League. Ever–ready to volunteer in any emergency, such as the one we faced in Kamloops. Whether tired, wet, or hungry, they were always cheerful, ready to step into the breach.

On the trek these young men sold the most papers, fanned out across the country to towns paralleling the railroad track, spoke to meetings, recruited unemployed for the trek, and with their unfailing cheerfulness, fortitude and discipline, were a stunning example to the rest of the men.

Nothing that I or anybody else could write about these young men would have been a sufficient tribute to their worth.

A couple of years after the events narrated above, most of these young men were in Spain, fighting against the fascist armies of Hitler and Mussolini, and many of them were killed there. . . .

The people of Golden knew about us, and our struggles, they knew about the relief camps. Their welcome of us was the welcome of pioneers, heartfelt, deep, and sincere, without fuss. Golden stood out in the memory of the trekkers as the most restful, tranquil episode of the whole trek. . . .

We left Golden with reluctance, but we had to push on. . . .

In Regina we tightened up our regulations, as we were receiving authentic news of police reinforcements arriving steadily, and being stationed around Regina. Militia being warned to be ready for call. Ominous signs. . . .

Then came the news of our negotiations. All of Canada was agog with the news that night. Our delegation, after a night's rest in an Ottawa hotel, had been summoned to the cabinet chamber for the meeting with the Prime Minister.

There sat Bennett behind his desk, surrounded by officials and guards. There were the press, and in front of Bennett the eight representatives of the trek. The Prime Minister wasted no time, but went into his diatribe of abuse, condemnation, and threats, his face crimson with hatred.

He then singled out Slim Evans, and roared, "We know you down there, Evans! You are a criminal and a thief!" At this Slim calmly rose to his feet, and looking the Prime Minister in the eye, he said, loudly and distinctly, "And you're a liar, Bennett, and what is more, you are not fit to run a Hottentot village, let alone a great country like Canada."

The delegation was hustled out, and that was our negotiations.

From Michael Horn, ed., *The Dirty Thirties*, (Canada: Copp Clark, 1972).

By late June the federal government had become convinced that the trek should be stopped. The RCMP was given the task of breaking up the march when it reached Regina. A few years later, the Canadian Annual Review *published the following account of the final confrontation.*

During the Spring and early Summer discontent had been growing in the relief camps for unemployed in British Columbia and on June 3 some 900 men broke camp and started eastward with the avowed intention of proceeding to Ottawa to place their grievances before the Dominion Government. Travelling by freight train, their ranks were swelled along the ways by recruits from other camps and other unemployed individuals. At Calgary on June 7 they were reported to be 1300 strong. This number increased at each city or camp on their forward march. On June 12, with the "army" at Swift Current, the Dominion authorities issued orders to the Royal Canadian Mounted Police that the march must be stopped at Regina. Two days later the men, now reported to number nearly 2000, were at Regina. . . . The next day on orders from Ottawa the R.C.M.P. mobilized to prevent the strikers moving eastward to Regina. An attempt by some of the men to move out by trucks was thwarted, and five men, including a Regina clergyman, were arrested and charged the next day under Section 98 of the Criminal Code dealing with unlawful associations. The R.C.M.P. warned citizens not to aid the strikers, announcing that no police action would be taken if the men would go to the Lumsden camp from where the Dominion authorities would provide them with transportation back to their relief camps or their homes.

Leaders of the relief strikers called a mass meeting of their followers and sympathizers in the market square of Regina for the evening of July 1 and in addition to the strikers thousands of Regina citizens attended. The R.C.M.P. and the Regina city police decided on this meeting as a suitable occasion for the arrest of leaders. Shortly after eight o'clock in the evening, forces of both bodies marched into the square as the meeting was in progress. Panic ensued. The police were attacked and fighting and rioting developed and continued for some three hours. Detective Charles Millar of the Regina city police lost his life being beaten to death by rioters using sticks and other weapons. Approximately 100 persons, including several members of the R.C.M.P. and city police, were injured, several seriously. Much property damage was caused. In the course of the attacks on the police shots were fired by the city police although the R.C.M.P. did not use guns. The police brought the situation under control, some 80 men being arrested. . . . The Provincial Government proceeded to take charge of the situation. In negotiations with representatives of the strikers they obtained their consent to return to their camps and homes. On July 5 about 1500 were moving westward on special trains engaged by the Provincial Government. . . .

The Commission was of the opinion that had the strikers reached Ottawa their numbers probably would have reached 5000 and a more serious riot might have occurred there.

From K.A. MacKirdy, J.S. Moir, Y.F. Zoltvany, eds., *Changing Perspectives in Canadian History*, (Toronto: Dent, 1971).

1. Compare the treatment of the Trekkers with that accorded to the Bonus Army.
2. What was the attitude of the government toward the marchers?
3. Prepare a position paper either for or against the resolution that: "The government was justified in using force to stop the On-to-Ottawa trek before it reached the capital."

Strikers' Nights, 1935

In May 1935 a relief-camp striker wrote the following letter to the Vancouver Sun.

We walk around the streets at night to kill time, so we can sleep in late the next day. By doing so we exist on two meals a day.

What do we see while putting in the hours? What do we think about?

We see a great many people going to shows, to this and that. Young couples who seem to be enjoying themselves, well–dressed and acting as if the world isn't so bad after all. People who have homes and kids and all the rest of it. People who seem to have faith in the future.

We think that something is wrong. We can't do as they do. We must go around lonely and dejected. No home life to enjoy, shut off from all social existence. No laughter in our hours, no hope in our young lives.

We see wonderful things in the stores. Food! Clothes! Books! And shiny cars line the streets. But none such for us. Outside looking in! Or in jail looking out. Are we criminals, unwanted in society? Are we lunatics who are to be shunned? What's wrong with us?

We think of marriage and homes, just like others have. Can't even have a friend or two! Shunned like lepers of early times, we are left to our fate. . . . Because we have the guts to fight for our inherited rights we are put in jail. . . .

. . . Would you like to have us lie down like a bunch of spineless whelps and be contented as slaves? Is that all our grandfathers toiled for? Canada . . . young nation . . . letting her youth go to hell! . . . we who should be the pride of the nation are the derelicts! The curse!

I leave it to you. Where do we go from here?

From Michael Horn, ed., *The Dirty Thirties*, (Canada: Copp Clark, 1972).

1. Write a newspaper editorial in which you respond to this letter sent to your paper by the striker.

The Political Response: Individualism, 1928

Herbert Hoover accepted the Republican nomination in 1928 from a nation brimming with hope and confidence. In his acceptance speech, he articulated the American belief in the individual and its benefits for society.

Commerce and industry have revived. Although the agricultural, coal, and textile industries still lag in their recovery and still require our solicitude and assistance, yet they have made substantial progress. While other countries engaged in the war are only now regaining their pre–war level in foreign trade, our exports, even if we allow for the depreciated dollar, are fifty–eight per cent greater than before the war. Constructive leadership and co–operation by the government have released and stimulated the energies of our people. Faith in the future has been restored. Confidence in our form of government has never been greater.

But it is not through the recitation of wise policies in government alone that we demonstrate our progress under the Republican guidance. . . . In this short time we have equipped nearly nine million more homes with electricity, and through it drudgery has been lifted from the lives of women. The barriers of time and distance have been swept away and life made freer and larger by the installation of six million more telephones, seven million radio sets, and the service of an additional fourteen million automobiles. Our cities are growing magnificent with beautiful buildings, parks, and playgrounds. Our countryside has been knot together with splendid roads.

We have doubled the use of electrical power, and with it we have taken sweat from the backs of men. . . .

Most of all, I like to remember what this progress has meant to America's children. The portal of their opportunity has been ever widening. While our population has grown but eight per cent, we have increased by eleven per cent the number of children in our grade schools, by sixty-six per cent the number in our high schools and by seventy-five per cent the number in our institutions of higher learning. . . .

One of the oldest and perhaps the noblest of human aspirations has been the abolition of poverty. By poverty I mean the grinding by under nourishment, cold, and ignorance, and fear of old age of those who have the will to work. We in America today are nearer to the final triumph over poverty than ever before in the history of any land. The poorhouse is vanishing from among us. We have not yet reached the goal, but, given a chance to go forward with the policies of the last eight years, we shall soon with the help of God be in sight of the day when poverty will be banished from this nation. There is no guarantee against poverty equal to a job for every man. That is the primary purpose of the economic policies we advocate.

From R.W. Leopold, et al., "The Fruits of Individualism," in *Problems in American History*, (Englewood Cliffs, New Jersey: Prentice-Hall, 1972).

1. How does Hoover depict the current "state of the union" in the United States?
2. To what extent does Hoover depict consumerism as a barometer of economic success?
3. What directions does the future president see for the country?

The New Deal, 1932

Franklin Delano Roosevelt was direct in his criticisms of the system which had led to the Depression. During the election campaign for his first term in office, FDR accused private economic interests of having betrayed the trust of the public. In his speech he called for sweeping changes and a reappraisal of basic values. Although the resulting

New Deal would be less dramatic than his rhetoric would indicate, this speech to the Commonwealth Club in San Francisco set the stage for the reforms to come.

A glance at the situation today only too clearly indicates that equality of opportunity as we have known it no longer exists. Our industrial plant is built; the problem just now is whether under existing conditions it is not overbuilt. Our last frontier has long since been reached, and there is practically no more free land. More than half of our people do not live on the farms or on lands and cannot derive a living by cultivating their own property. There is no safety valve in the form of a Western prairie to which those thrown out of work by the Eastern economic machines can go for a new start. We are not able to invite the immigration from Europe to share our endless plenty. We are now providing a drab living for our own people. . . .

Clearly, all this calls for a re–appraisal of values. A mere builder of more industrial plants, a creator of more railroad systems, an organizer of more corporations, is as likely to be a danger as a help. The day of the great promoter or the financial Titan, to whom we granted anything if only he would build, or develop, is over. Our task now is not discovery or exploitation of natural resources, or necessarily producing more goods. It is the soberer, less dramatic business of administering resources and plants already in hand, of seeking to re–establish foreign markets for our surplus production, of meeting the problem of underconsumption, of adjusting production to consumption, of distributing wealth and products more equitably, of adapting existing economic organizations to the service of the people. The day of enlightened administration has come. . . .

Every man has a right to his own property; which means a right to be assured, to the fullest extent attainable, in the safety of his savings. By no other means can men carry the burdens of those parts of life which, in the nature of things, afford no chance of labor: childhood, sickness, old age. In all thought of property, this right is paramount; all other property rights must yield to it. If, in accord with this principle, we must restrict the operations of the speculator, the manipulator, even the financier, I believe we must accept the restriction as needful not to hamper individualism but to protect it.

From R.W. Leopold, et al., "Roosevelt Pledges a New Deal," in *Problems in American History*, (Englewood Cliffs, New Jersey: Prentice-Hall, 1972).

1. Compare Roosevelt's description of America with that given by Hoover four years earlier.
2. Comment upon FDR's vision of "the day of enlightened administration."
3. Account for FDR's assertion that one must accept restriction "as needful not to hamper individualism but to protect it."

FDR and the "Trickle Down" Theory, 1932

When Ronald Reagan espoused supply-side economics he was not without precedent. Republican economic strategy in the election of 1932 called for the same kind of "trickle-

down" approach to prosperity. In this excerpt from a campaign speech on October 2, 1932, Roosevelt calls the basic premise into question and begins to build the basis of the New Deal coalition that would support the Democratic party for decades to come.

You know today is Sunday, and I am afraid that some of you people today in Detroit have been talking politics. Well, I am not going to. I want to talk to you about Government. That is a very different thing. And I am not going to refer to parties at all.

I am going to refer to some of the fundamentals that antedate parties, and antedate republics and empires, fundamentals that are as old as mankind itself. They are fundamentals that have been expressed in philosophies, for I don't know how many thousands of years, in every part of the world. Today, in our boasted modern civilization, we are facing just exactly the same problem, just exactly the same conflict between two schools of philosophy that they faced in the earliest days of America, and indeed of the world. One of them—one of these old philosophies—is the philosophy of those who would "let things alone." The other is the philosophy that strives for something new—something that the human race has never attained yet, but can and will attain—social justice, through social action.

From the days of the cave man to the days of the automobile, the philosophy of "letting things alone" has resulted in the jungle law of the survival of the so-called fittest. The philosophy of social action results in the protection of humanity and the fitting of as many human beings as possible into the scheme of surviving. I am sorry to say that among the followers of that first philosophy of "letting things alone" are a lot of people in my community back home, which is a little village, and in the farming districts of the Nation and in the great cities, such as yours. We can place in that philosophy a great many splendid people who keep saying, not only to themselves and to their friends, but to the community as a whole, "Why shouldn't we 'let things alone'? In the first place they are not as bad as they are painted, and in the second place they will cure themselves. Time is a great healer." An easy philosophy! The kind of philosophy, my friends, that was expressed the other day by a Cabinet officer of the United States of America, when he is reported to have said, "Our children are apt to profit rather than suffer from what is going on."

While he was saying that, another branch of our Government, the United States Public Health Service, which believes in my kind of philosophy, I think, said this: "Over six millions of our public school children do not have enough to eat. Many of them are fainting at their desks. They are a prey to disease. Their future health is menaced."

In which school do you believe?

In the same ways, there are two theories of prosperity and of well-being: The first theory is that if we make the rich richer, somehow they will let a part of their prosperity trickle down to the rest of us. The second theory—and I suppose this goes back to the days of Noah—I won't say Adam and Eve, because they had a less complicated situation—but at least, back in the days of the flood, there was the theory that if we make the average of mankind comfortable and secure, their prosperity will rise upward, just as yeast rises up, through the ranks. . . .

From Edwin C. Rozwenc, ed., *The New Deal: Revolution or Evolution?*, (Boston: D.C. Heath & Co., 1959).

1. What argument does FDR use to demonstrate that social justice is only attainable through social action?
2. How does he counter the trickle-down theory?
3. Outline the nature of the New Deal coalition that came together as a result of Roosevelt's policies.

The Liberal Way, 1933

In its summer conference in 1933, Canada's Liberal party embraced many of the concepts being implemented by the New Deal in the United States. In this excerpt, the New Deal is discussed as a natural progression for all North Americans.

The New Deal is of profound significance to Canada for two reasons. First, it is a polite name for the first real revolution that has struck Anglo–Saxon America and is taking place at our very doors, indeed, over our very threshold; second, its main principles are quite easily applicable to this country. For Canada is at about the same political, economic and intellectual stage in its development as the United States. As we investigate the New Deal, therefore, it is useful to remember that we are North Americans and observers of an experiment that was born in much the same political and commercial air as that which we normally breathe. . . .

As a social and political phenomenon the New Deal might be described as an historical climax: a man, a body of legislation, and a set of ideas. The swift chapter of events of last spring came at a time when many old ideas were being dropped in the United States, when the phrase "rugged individualism" and all that it stood for was passing into contempt and derision; when the Democratic Party was summarily and boldly changing its course, and when the financial and industrial world of the United States seemed ready to crash about their ears. . . .

Without a delay or compromise, the country saw decisive action taken by a properly constituted federal executive on all the major and most menacing questions of the day, and was duly encouraged. . . .

It is interesting to see how seldom the theory is given a name. It has been described as a communism based on the public will, as the next logical step to a social state; it has received the approval, though not the complete adherence, of the socialists, and it has been vilified by conservatives and communists for giving too much or not giving enough to labour. But even if we cannot give it a name we can, nevertheless, discern certain definite emphases, certain specific social objectives in the New Deal, which are of great importance in the interpretation of its legislative form. . . .

From Michael Horn, ed., *The Dirty Thirties*, (Canada: Copp Clark, 1972).

1. Why does the author state that the New Deal is as natural for Canada as it is for the United States?
2. What social philosophy is identified as underlying the program?
3. Account for the Liberal interest in adopting the ideas contained in the New Deal.

Radical Solutions: Canada, 1930s

The collapse of the economic system led to widespread criticisms of the existing social order. Solutions ranged across the political spectrum. These excerpts provide a sampling of the wide variety of opinion.

The prime minister, R.B. Bennett, was offered no end of "creative" solutions to the nation's problems. These two letters are typical.

. . . Why not put some of these foreigners and Indians in their own country and give a white man some show, as they are taking the work away from the Canadian men and I would think the Government could do something to prevent all of this. And the people wonder in Canada why so much robbing and bootlegging is carried on: Now why is it? If we have any government at all, why not look into it as our country is overrun by foreigners.

From Michael Horn, ed., *The Dirty Thirties*, (Canada: Copp Clark, 1972).

. . . I would like to suggest my . . . system, of how to help solve the *unemployment*. . . . First I would suggest a *method* or *law*, whereby Females would not be allowed employment as long as a Male can fill that or those posissions. . . . One cannot help but notice it these Days, practically in all Stores, Females are employed, of course the main cause of this, I think was the Grate War, no question about it, but why not change the system now? People will say for instance, Hello, Miss James, I hear you are going to get married. Oh no I am not, I would be foolish, I have a good place to work at, & I do not have to pay any of my Wages at Home, so she naturally is independent, on the other hand if the young men were in those posissions they would be able to support a wife, therefor would increase Population, & so we would not have so much unemployment. Also the young Females would stay at Home, & learn House keeping, Cooking, & etc. . . .

From Michael Horn, ed., *The Dirty Thirties*, (Canada: Copp Clark, 1972).

The Canadian Communist party gained new respectability when its ongoing warnings about the weakness of capitalism seemed to be borne out by the Depression. Communists looked to the relative economic calm of Stalin's isolationist Russia and believed that they saw the anwers to Canada's problems. The following two excerpts outline the pros and cons of the communist position.

Bennett's recent budget is a one hundred per cent 'HUNGER BUDGET'. . . .
We are convinced that these evils are inherent in any system in which private profit is the main stimulus to economic effort. We therefore look to the establishment in Canada of a new social order which will substitute a planned and

socialized economy for the existing chaotic individualism and which, by achieving an approximate economic equality among all men in place of the present glaring inequalities, will eliminate the domination of one class by another.

Such measures as the following are among the essential first steps for the achievement of the new social order:

(1) The creation of a National Economic Planning Commission. . . .

(2) Socialization of the machinery of banking and investment. . . .

(3) Public ownership (Dominion, provincial or municipal) of transport, communications, electric power and other such industries. . . .

(4) The development of co–operative institutions in every sphere of economic life where they are appropriate, notably in agricultural production and marketing. . . .

(5) The establishment of import and export boards for the regulation of foreign trade.

(6) Social legislation to secure to the worker adequate income, leisure, freedom of association, insurance against illness, old age, and unemployment, and an effective voice in the management of his industry.

(7) Publicly organized health, hospital and medical services.

(8) An aggressive taxation designed not only to raise public revenues but also to lessen the glaring inequalities of income. . . .

(9) The amendment of the Canadian constitution, without infringing upon legitimate provincial claims to autonomy, so as to give the Dominion Government adequate power to deal effectively with urgent economic problems which are essentially national.

(10) A foreign policy designed to obtain international economic co–operation and to promote disarmament and world peace.

The League will work for the realization of its ideal by organizing groups to study and report on particular problems and by issuing to the public in the form of pamphlets, articles, lectures, etc., the most accurate information obtainable about the nation's affairs in order to create that informed public opinion which is necessary for effective political action.

From Michael Horn, ed., *The Dirty Thirties*, (Canada: Copp Clark, 1972).

A few days ago two reputable English–speaking members of the Quebec Bar entertained to luncheon in Monteal a travelling agent of the Communist Party. These lawyers were prompted by curiosity to obtain a close–up of an avowed Communist and to hear him expound on his ideas. This man told his hosts that his job consisted of travelling between important cities coordinating the activities of the party. He said that the Communist program was now directed towards getting a footing in Municipal Councils and he confidently predicted that at the next Municipal elections in Winnipeg Communist candidates would sweep the boards.

"We know," he said, "that we can do nothing in Quebec until an anti–clerical movement can be got under way but from Port Arthur to the Rocky Mountains is *our* territory."

On its face there appears nothing very new about this declaration of Communist policy. However, if considered in the light of the prevailing trend of intellectual Bolshevism, it may be at once a sign and a portent. There is no gainsaying the fact . . . that public opinion just now is in a very disturbed and impressionable condition. Every second man one meets in the street is discontented and often enough distraught with the problem of gaining a living for himself and his family.

From Michael Horn, ed., *The Dirty Thirties*, (Canada: Copp Clark, 1972).

Maclean's magazine published the following exposé on the current state of fascism in the country in May 1938. Some Canadians saw the forced prosperity of Nazi Germany as a constructive model to follow.

There is a Fascist movement in Canada and it is growing. Whether it is a mighty force destined to turn this Dominion from a democratic into a totalitarian state, as its impassioned leaders assert; or whether it is nothing more than an ephemeral outbreak of anti–Semitic fanaticism, blown into unmerited prominence by the mouthings of a few crackpots, as some of its critics declare, it exists. It is here. It is a Fact. . . .

Canadian Fascism at the moment is divided into two groups. In Ontario and the West the official title of the organization is The Canadian Nationalist Party, and its membership for the most part is made up of English–speaking Protestants. . . . In Quebec the movement is headed by Adrien Arcand and is called the National Social Christian Party. . . .

The movement is frankly anti–Jew, anti–Communism, and is opposed to the Masonic Order, which its leaders claim is controlled by Jews. Almost all its literature—and it has an abundant supply, in French and English, some of it imported from Sir Oswald Mosley's headquarters in London—consists of violent attacks on Communism, Judaism, and Freemasonry. To its leaders, the hated Communism is a Jewish movement entirely. . . . The official "Program and Regulations" of the Party states: "Only members of the great races which have formed since its beginning as a country the population of Canada, and the other Aryan members of the population who will agree to identify themselves with the mother races, can be Canadian citizens." That is, Jews, negroes, and Asiatics would be denied the franchise. . . .

It is difficult to arrive at any authentic estimate of the number of the movement's supporters. Farr claims to have 10 000 dues–paying members in Ontario, as of April first, 8 000 of them in Toronto. Arcand says he has between 80 000 and 85 000 followers in Montreal alone, but admits that the actual membership is considerably less. . . .

It is difficult to imagine that the Canadian Nationalist Party will get very far on the strength of an appeal to the Canadian electorate based upon this "Program and Regulations" booklet. A foreward admits that the "Program" in its main lines and even in many details, is identical to the programs of the principal corporatist organizations of other countries. "We have chosen our fare where we found it." There follows a list of sixteen different countries in which corporatist states have been established. The second name on the list is that of Nazi Germany. . . .

Arcand's assertion that the Nationalist Party could win thirteen federal seats in Quebec and fifteen in the Prairie Provinces is a boast for the future, which now seems to have little value, however substantial it may have appeared so long as Adolph Hitler stayed out of Austria. . . .

From Michael Horn, ed., *The Dirty Thirties*, (Canada: Copp Clark, 1972).

1. Account for the growth of radicalism during the Depression.
2. Why do you think that North Americans rejected the radical solutions adopted in Europe?
3. What constructive role can radical groups play in society?

The Creation of the CCF, 1932

The League for Social Reconstruction was formed in 1931 as a "brains trust" to create the policy statements for a new political party. Led by Professors Frank Scott and Frank Underhill it hoped to become the intellectual wing of the Canadian socialist movement. Eventually its members became part of the Co-operative Commonwealth Federation—CCF. The following is an extract from the "LSR Manifesto."

The League for Social Reconstruction is an association of men and women who are working for the establishment in Canada of a social order in which the basic principles regulating production, distribution and service will be the common good rather than private profit.

The present capitalist system has shown itself unjust and inhuman, economically wasteful, and a standing threat to peace and democratic government. Over the whole world it has led to a struggle for raw materials and markets and to a consequent international competition in armaments which were among the main causes of the last great war and which constantly threaten to bring in new wars. In the advanced industrial countries it has led to the concentration of wealth in the hands of a small irresponsible minority of bankers and industrialists whose economic power constantly threatens to nullify our political democracy. The result in Canada is a society in which the interests of farmers and of wage and salaried workers—the great majority of the population—are habitually sacrificed to those of this small minority. . . .

From Michael Horn, ed., *The Dirty Thirties*, (Canada: Copp Clark, 1972).

Meeting in Regina in 1933, a year after its founding, the members of the Co-operative Commonwealth Federation issued a statement of their political aims and objectives. Part of this "Regina Manifesto" is excerpted below.

We aim to replace the present capitalist system, with its inherent injustice and inhumanity, by a social order from which the domination and exploitation of one class by another will be eliminated, in which economic planning will supercede unregulated private enterprise and competition, and in which genuine democratic self-government, based upon economic equality will be possible. The present order is marked by glaring inequalities of wealth and opportunity, by chaotic waste and instability; and in an age of plenty it condemns the great mass of people to poverty and insecurity. Power has become more and more concentrated into the hands of a small irresponsible minority of financiers and industrialists and to their predatory interests the majority are habitually sacrificed. When private profit is the main stimulus to economic effort, our society oscillates between periods of feverish prosperity in which the main benefits go to speculators and profiteers, and of catastrophic depression, in which the common man's normal state of insecurity and hardship is accentuated. We believe that these evils can be removed only in a planned and socialized economy in which our natural resources and the principal means of production and distribution are owned, controlled and operated by the people.

From K. McNaught, *A Prophet in Politics: A Biography of J.S. Woodsworth*, (Toronto, 1959) in K.A. MacKirdy et al., eds., *Changing Perspectives in Canadian History*, (Toronto: Dent, 1971).

1. What criticisms does the LSR level at the capitalist system?
2. To what extent are the aims of the LSR evident in the manifesto of the CCF?
3. Account for the fact that while the CCF emerged as a legitimate socialist force in Canada, there was no parallel party in the United States.

The Bennett "New Deal," 1935

Faced with an impending election in 1935, the Bennett government did a political about-face with regard to government intervention. In a series of radio broadcasts, intended to capitalize upon the successes of FDR, Bennett outlined a new program for Canada. In the first of two excerpts, Bennett accounts for his "conversion" in one of his radio addresses. In the second he outlines his new policy in a Speech from the Throne. It was too little, too late.

We will examine the system without prejudice of any sort. We neither hate nor love it. It is here to do you service. That is its only purpose. *If it has failed, then we must change it.* Quite properly, we have a regard for those things with which we have long been beneficially associated, but allegiance to a system does not involve our condonation of its defects. Possibly some of you will maintain that, because the system has served us well in the past, there is a presumption in favour of its continuing to do so in the future. But clearly, that is no proof that it will do so. Indeed, present conditions are surely proof enough that it will not. And, as I say, if it does not serve us, we must reform it. . . .

   I do not intend to trouble you just now with the history of the capitalist system. But in my opinion, it is important that you should carefully examine the origin of capitalism, its place in the early days, and the theory upon which it operated. It would be helpful to a clearer understanding of some of our present difficulties if you were to trace the development which carried the system from the simple practice of a simple theory to the complex practice of a theory strained and stretched out of its original form. You would then see that for the old checks and balances which ensured the proper working of the original system, the system today has provided no counterpart within itself. You would agree that free competition and the open market place, as they were known in the old days, have lost the place in the system, and the only substitute for them, in these modern times, is government regulation and control. You would understand that past depressions were caused by maladjustments in the operation of this system, and were corrected only after intense suffering and hardship, that these depressions were so many crises, dangerous and difficult to surmount, but that, in comparison with them, this depression is a catastrophe, and therefore demands the intervention of the Government. . . .

Selfish men, and this country is not without them,—men whose mounting bank rolls loom larger than your happiness, corporations without souls and without virtue—these, fearful that this Government might impinge on what they have grown to regard as their immemorial right of exploitation, will whisper against us. They will call us radicals. They will say that this is the first step on the road to socialism. We fear them not. We think that their ready compliance with our programme would serve their interests better than any ill–timed opposition to it. We invite their cooperation. We want the cooperation of all. . . .

J.M. Bliss, *Canadian History in Documents*, (Toronto: University of Toronto Press, 1966).

Better provision will be made for the security of the worker during unemployment, in sickness, and in old age.

The measures taken respecting public and private debts have done much to lighten the burden of the taxpayer and to improve the position of the farming community. . . .

Action will be taken to ameliorate the conditions of labour, to provide a better and more assured standard of living for the worker, to secure minimum wages and a maximum working week, ...

You will be invited also to enact measures to provide the investing public with means to protect itself against exploitation. . . .

You will be invited to authorize the constitution of an economic council, the functions of which will be to advise my ministers upon all economic questions which concern the national welfare. . . .

J.M. Bliss, *Canadian History in Documents*, (Toronto: University of Toronto Press, 1966).

1. What criticisms does the prime minister level at the captialist system?
2. How does Bennett portray his "new" political personna?
3. What reforms are promised in the Speech from the Throne?

This Challenge to Liberty, 1936

Herbert Hoover launched one last attack on Roosevelt and the New Deal in the election of 1936. In this speech, he claimed that the New Deal was destroying traditional American values.

Through four years of experience this New Deal attack upon free institutions has emerged as the transcendent issue in America.

All the men who are seeking for mastery in the world today are using the same weapons. They all promise the joys of Elysium without effort.

But their philosophy is founded on the coercion and compulsory organization of men. True liberal government is founded on the emancipation of men. This is the issue upon which men are imprisoned and dying in Europe right now. . . .

Freedom does not die from frontal attack. It dies because men in power no longer believe in a system based upon liberty. . . .

I gave the warning against this philosophy of government four years ago from a heart heavy with anxiety for the future of our country. It was born from many years' experience of the forces moving in the world which would weaken the vitality of American freedom. I grew in four years of battle as President to uphold the banner of free men.

And that warning was based on sure ground from my knowledge of the ideas that Mr. Roosevelt and his bosom colleagues had covertly embraced despite the Democratic platform.

Those ideas were not new. Most of them had been urged upon me. . . .

I rejected all these things because they would not only delay recovery but because I knew that in the end they would shackle free men.

Rejecting these ideas we Republicans had erected agencies of government which did start our country to prosperity without the loss of a single atom of American freedom. . . .

I am proud to have carried the banner of free men to the last hour of the term my countrymen entrusted it to me. It matters nothing in the history of a race what happens to those who in their time have carried the banner of free men. What matters is that the battle shall go on. . . .

Let me say to you that any measure which breaks our dikes of freedom will flood the land with misery.

From Richard Hofstadter, ed., *Great Issues in American History*, (New York: Vintage Books, 1969).

1. How does Hoover depict the philosophy of the Roosevelt administration?
2. Why does he reject that philosophy?
3. What do the Republicans offer in place of the New Deal?

The People's Front, 1938

The New Deal was not only under attack from the right in the 1930s. Socialists saw it as stealing much of their own political thunder. In this 1938 article, entitled "What Follows after the Roosevelt Victory," Earl Browder calls for the next step beyond the New Deal coalition. It is his contention that opposition on the right had disappeared and therefore there was a need to establish a political alternative on the left. This alternative was the People's Front.

. . . The employing class is naturally aware of the mounting spirit for struggle of the masses and they are trying to head it off. That is the significance of the large number of voluntary pay increases that have been announced since the elections.

Only the organization and struggle for the masses, independent of capitalist parties and politicians, will realize their demands and expectations, through Congress and outside of Congress, and prepare the way for greater concessions later on. . . .

Now more than ever there is a fear among many progressives of prematurely forming such a party and thereby narrowing it down, leaving behind and outside serious forces which can be brought in a little later or in a different form.

We want to hasten the formation of a national Farmer-Labor Party as much as possible. . . .

Roosevelt and his close supporters, of course, want to create the impression that the people already have achieved this goal through his re–election. This illusion if not fought against can become an obstacle to the further growth of the People's Front. It will be fully dispersed only in the course of struggle, in independent struggle on the economic and political field to realize the great expectation of the workers; first of all in the industries, in the fight for wages, hours and unionization, and, second, in the legislative assemblies of the states and the national congress in the fight for social and labor legislation.

We do not need to waste time, as some people do, in speculations as to whether Roosevelt will turn Right of Left, although our prediction of a Right turn by Roosevelt as expressed before election is being realized in the administration's relief policy today. From past experience we know that his course will be determined in its major aspects entirely by the course of the road. Roosevelt always tries to find the middle of the road. If the road turns right he turns right. If the road turns left, he will turn left. The road of national life will be determined not by Roosevelt's mind or tendency, but by the relationship of forces, by the independent struggle of the masses in the economic and political fields.

From Earl Broder, "What Follows After the Roosevelt Victory," in *The People's Front*, (New York: International Publishers Co., Inc., 1938, R. 1965).

1. What are identified as the expectations of the working class?
2. Why does the author feel that the Roosevelt victory has destroyed the two-party system?
3. What rationale is suggested for the creation of a new political force in the United States?

The Rowell-Sirois Commission, 1940

After many of the reforms initiated by Bennett in the closing days of his administration were declared to be unconstitutional, the new Liberal government of William Lyon Mackenzie King appointed the Royal Commission on Dominion-Provincial relations to "examine the economic and financial basis of Confederation and the distribution of legislative powers in light of the economic and social developments of the last seventy years." By the time its report was finished the country was in the middle of the Second

World War. Many of the recommended changes were implemented and as one historian has commented, by 1945 Canada was finally fully prepared to meet the challenges of the Depression.

The implications of the nature and extent of the world depression to Canada are obvious. The effects upon this nation, which obtains over one–third of its national income directly from abroad and two–thirds of whose exports consist of raw materials, were extremely drastic. For upwards of thirty years external influences and technical changes had played favourably upon Canada's resources and produced an era of almost unbroken expansion and prosperity. The Canadian economy had become delicately geared to the increasing foreign markets for foodstuffs, newsprint, lumber and minerals. For the production of these commodities a large and expensive transportation system was built and huge amounts were invested in power projects, processing plants, implements and machines. Much of the capital required for the provision of this immense equipment was borrowed from other countries. The application of this capital and of advanced techniques to virgin resources became the principal basis of our economic life. It involved a narrow specialization in the production of a few export staples, heavy fixed charges, and a precarious dependence upon the commercial policies of other countries.

As long as the conditions of international trade were favourable, specialization yielded a high standard of living. . . . Our social and economic institutions became closely related to the nature of the economy and rested on the condition of continuous expansion. When the bases for progress along the old lines disappeared and the full force of the world depression fell upon our specialized exports, the problems of adjustment were extremely difficult. Canada's political, public finance and economic organizations were not adapted to deal with sharp and prolonged economic reverses. . . .

The policies of Western settlement, all–Canadian transportation, and industrialization by protective tariffs had been designed to promote, and to function under the influences of, expansion. They had set the stage and in some measure had provided the incentives for the activities of private enterprise which were counted on to bring general prosperity and build an economically integrated and united nation. The success of the whole scheme depended upon the availability of extensive virgin resources and expanding foreign markets. . . .

The depression brought a set of problems almost entirely new in Canadian experience. Their solution or amelioration required new departures in federal policy. Broadly there were two alternatives. One was to try to *counteract the factors which were responsible for the slump* by attempting to maintain export values, to keep up activity in construction, and to prevent prices and costs from getting too far out of line. This would have involved what then appeared to be risky and unorthodox monetary measures. The other was carefully *to avoid risky and unorthodox monetary measures and to endeavour to maintain income in the sheltered and protected sectors of the economy* by drastic restrictions against imports, by following "sound" financial policies which would maintain confidence, preserve the public credit both internally and abroad, and thus facilitate the operation of the natural forces of recovery. While there could be no absolute certainty about which course would hold the total national income at the higher level, the latter would widen the disparities in the losses falling on the various groups . . . and hence would greatly increase the transfers of income which would have to be made through the public finance system to support the casualties of the unequal incidence of the depression. The second alternative describes briefly the policies which were actually adopted by the Dominion.

From K.A. MacKirdy, et al., eds., *Changing Perspectives in Canadian History*, (Toronto: Dent, 1971).

1. Why did the Depression have such an impact upon Canada?
2. What two alternatives were open to Ottawa during the Depression?
3. According to the commission, which choice was taken?

The New Deal and a New Social Order: Analysis and Application

1. What was it like to live in Canada during the Depression? Interview someone who was a teenager during the 1930s. You might approach the interview this way:
  Prepare a series of questions with regard to where the person lived, went to school or worked, what she/he did for recreation, etc. Give the interviewee a copy of your questions in advance. Ask her/him to cross out any questions which s/he might not wish to answer and to add others that she/he feels that you have left out.
  Conduct the interview. Be certain to take careful notes, or, with prior permission, to tape-record or videotape the session.
  Précis the information and write a personalized account of your "expert's" life during the period. This form of oral history is an important technique for capturing the recent past.

2. The wealth of documentary and first-person accounts from the 1930s provides us with the opportunity to more fully understand the feelings of people living during the period. One way to express this understanding is through the creation of a "docudrama." Create your own docudrama about the Depression.

(a) Divide the class into groups representing various factions, such as farmers, urban labourers, industrialists, politicians, etc. Have each group research the experiences, ideas, and remarks of their social class during the period.

(b) Based upon this research, and using only primary source material (including diaries, letters, film, music, photographs, interviews, etc.) have each group create approximately fifteen minutes of first-person drama. This should not be a block of material but rather a series of short vignettes.

(c) With the aid of an outside director (it could be the teacher but it's better if it is a member of the class), intersperse the vignettes created by the various groups to form an extended period of drama. Such drama should be supported, where possible, by music and contemporary pictures and props.

(d) After rehearsing your docudrama, perform the piece for another history or dramatic arts class.

(e) Following the performance, allow some time for debriefing. Students should feel free to discuss their feelings about the Depression as well as their thoughts about the docudrama as a means of investigating the past.

14
FOREIGN POLICY IN THE ERA OF THE COLD WAR

In the years since 1945 Canada and the United States have followed parallel but separate routes in foreign policy. Working in close cooperation in such areas as NATO, NORAD, and the United Nations, the two neighbours have followed quite divergent paths with regard to Latin America and the developing world.

Two weeks after his election as prime minister in September 1984, Brian Mulroney told a reporter from the *Wall Street Journal* that Canada had "good relations, super relations, with the United States [which] will be the cornerstone of our foreign policy." *Globe and Mail* correspondent Jeffrey Simpson saw this as a danger:

> The casualty is the independence of our foreign policy . . . [By] tying ourselves so tightly to American foreign policy . . . as an implicit trade-off for better [economic] treatment . . . whatever shreds of credibility we had as an "honest broker" or "mediator" have been reduced to nil.

Has Canada, as Simpson sees it, come to a crossroads in its foreign policy? Did the sentiments of the Shamrock Summit of 1985 mark the end of a distinctive Canadian approach to dealing with the world? This chapter will consider the two faces of the North American view of the world in the late twentieth century.

As the United States assumed leadership of the non-Communist world after the Second World War, it was left to Canada to eventually steer a careful middle course in the shadow of its powerful neighbour. During the first decade of the period, however, there was little to distinguish between the Canadian and American approaches to foreign policy. This was the era of the Cold War, and for most North Americans the lines were clearly drawn.

Origins of the Cold War

With the end of World War II in August 1945, most North Americans looked forward to a return to a more normal way of life. They could not have been more mistaken, however. Within two years a new and different kind of war had begun, the Cold War. What was the Cold War? How had it grown out of the ashes of Hitler's defeat? How had the high hopes of 1945 become the harsh realities of 1947? To understand the roots of this problem we must first look at an event that took place while the war in Europe was still raging—the Yalta Conference.

The Yalta Conference: February 1945
International conferences are like contract negotiations. Each participant comes into the meeting with two ideas. The first is what he or she would like to have; the second is what he or she is willing to give up. The most important of these demands are called the priority items.

Yalta involved a series of tradeoffs in which each party had to give in order to receive. The United States got the Soviets to approve the idea of the United Nations, but what did they have to give up? What Soviets demanded—and received—was the right to assist liberated countries in establishing acceptable governments and economic systems—in other words, to establish a Soviet sphere of influence. The British and Americans were promised Soviet aid against Japan, but in return they had to promise to award the Soviets all territory lost in Russia's war with Japan in 1904.

The biggest question at Yalta, of course, was how to deal with defeated Germany. All nations wanted to play a part in determining that country's fate. Stalin, Churchill, and Roosevelt finally agreed to divide Germany into separate zones of occupation. Each country, along with France, would control one section. Little did they know that forty years later, this "temporary" solution would have become quite permanent (see readings).

Who won at Yalta? The answer is really no one. No leader got everything he wanted, but neither did anyone go home empty–handed. Unfortunately, if the Western leaders believed that the conference resulted in a compromise that would bring about a better world, they were sadly mistaken. The period of agreement was short-lived. Within months the Soviet liberation force had become a brutal army of occupation. The hot war had ended. The Cold War had begun.

The Division of Europe
The first breach in the international contract involved Poland. Guaranteed free elections in the Yalta declaration, by the fall of 1945 it was clear that the occupying Soviets had no intention of carrying them out. What could the Allied leaders do?

Harry Truman was now president. He believed that the atomic bomb was the answer. In the late 1940s, only the United States, Britain, and Canada possessed the secret of the bomb. Truman thought that he could use Soviet fear of atomic destruction to make them do what he wanted.

Threats would not work, however. Instead, they only made Stalin more suspicious of the Americans. This growing distrust was not simply limited to Soviet-American relations. In February 1946, Soviet foreign minister Molotov called Churchill a hypocrit. The British leader was criticizing the Soviet occupation of Europe, while at the same time Britain controlled a global empire with troops in India, Africa, Greece, Palestine, Iraq, Indochina, and elsewhere. The Soviet Union had troops only in neighbouring countries which they believed to be a danger to them.

But if Molotov was right, Churchill certainly didn't agree. His response was given in a speech delivered in Fulton, Missouri, on March 5th. He stated that "God has willed that the United States, not some Communist or neo-Fascist state," possess the atomic bomb. He called for an Anglo-American alliance that would safeguard the world against the "iron curtain" that had been "extended across the continent" of Europe by the Soviets.

Stalin replied that Churchill and his American friends were like Hitler, advocating a theory that one race, in this case the English, "should rule over the remaining nations of the world." This, he claimed, was a "set-up for war, a call to war against the Soviet Union."

American policy soon changed to meet this new appraisal of the global situation.

American troops and financial support went to prop up pro-Western governments in both Greece and Turkey. Dubbed the "Truman Doctrine," the president stated that it was the duty of the United States to "support free peoples" who were resisting "armed minorities" and "outside pressures." It would eventually come to be applied not only to Europe but to the rest of the world as well. For Greece and neighbouring Turkey, it meant $400 million in economic aid and the military support necessary to crush internal communist opposition.

The Truman Doctrine was the centrepiece of American foreign policy in the Cold War years. The Greek experiment in some respects was a dry run. Over the next three years the full extent of North American financial and military commitment would become apparent.

The Marshall Plan

By 1947, the United States was beginning to realize that until Europe was back on its feet, Communist strength would continue to grow. They were also eager to reestablish their prewar buisness relationships with European nations; as long as their old customers were bankrupt they wouldn't be buying many American goods.

Like the Soviets, the United States offered to help their friends out. But the Americans had something the Soviets did not: an undamaged country with a strong economy. In 1947 they set out to capitalize on this advantage.

The method was the European Recovery Plan (E.R.P.). It had three goals:
1. The Americans refused to accept the Soviet division of Europe, so it was designed to offer aid to every country of Europe, Communist and non-Communist alike.
2. They assumed that communism's appeal was largely economic, so it would eliminate the poverty that fed its growth.
3. They felt that twentieth–century conflicts had been caused by economic competition, so by creating an international economy, the E.R.P. would break down the national rivalries which had led to two world wars.

The plan was unveiled by Secretary of State George Marshall in May of 1947. Even though he was not specific about the amount of money involved, Marshall's remarks gave the Europeans hope for massive aid. As a result the initial European requests totalled over $23 billion. However, it was a far cry from the $12 billion that Congress eventually authorized.

The Soviets tried to keep American aid out of Eastern Europe and denounced the Marshall Plan as the Truman Doctrine "of political pressure by means of dollars." They countered with the "Molotov Plan," which stressed bilateral trade agreements between themselves and their Eastern European friends. Any country within the Soviet sphere which showed interest in the Marshall Plan was quickly brought into line. When members of the Polish government suggested accepting the Marshall Plan and improving relations with the West, the Soviets had them removed from office. In Czechoslovakia, conservative and moderate leaders were manoeuvred out of power by the Communist party, backed by the Soviet army.

For Truman this was the last straw. He claimed that the Soviets' action had "sent a shock throughout the civilized world" and used the move to hurry the Marshall Plan legislation through Congress.

But it would not only be American dollars going to Europe. Truman wanted

Canadian peacekeeping troops in Cyprus
Reagan and Gorbachev take a "walk-about" in Red Square
U.S. marines cross a rice paddy in Vietnam

to be prepared on all fronts. He reintroduced the draft. The American armed forces were going to be ready to fight (see readings).

The Berlin Blockade

So far the Cold War was limited to words. But the real conflict was to come in defeated Germany.

At Yalta the Big Four had pictured postwar Germany as a neutral country with no armed forces. The Soviets also hoped that some of the damage done to their country by the Nazi invasion would be paid for by the Germans. By 1947 the Americans had changed their minds. They refused to allow any further payments from their zones to go into the Soviet Union. This was a violation of the Yalta agreements. Stalin responded by stripping the Eastern sector of resources and machinery. In contrast, under the Marshall Plan, aid flowed into the now–unified Western zones of the country. The differences between East and West became increasingly obvious, and nowhere was this more visible than in Berlin.

As part of the division of Germany, the capital city of Berlin was also divided between the Soviets and the West. Located in the Soviet–controlled Eastern sector of Germany, the city was chosen by the Soviets as the target for the Cold War. On June 24, 1948, their army blocked the land corridors that linked the democratic zones of the city with the West. The Soviet plan was simple: they would starve their former allies out of the city. The reunited Berlin would then become the capital of the new socialist East Germany.

Truman responded with what most thought to be a logistical impossibility, the Berlin airlift. For the next eleven months, food, coal, medical supplies, building materials—virtually everything the city required—was flown in from Allied bases in the West. At the peak of the airlift, transports were taking off and landing at West Berlin's airports every three minutes, twenty-four hours a day.

The Soviets hoped that the Berlin issue would divide the Western allies. Instead it made them realize that to stand up to the Soviet Union, they would have to work together. Faced with this policy failure, along with the incredible success of the airlift, the Soviets finally lifted the blockade the following May.

The move was too late to quell anti–Soviet hostilities in the West, however. The Soviet aggression in Berlin was all the evidence North American leaders needed to commit their nations to a mutual defence pact in Europe. In April 1949 the United States and Canada joined Britain, France, Belgium, the Netherlands, Luxembourg, Denmark, Norway, Portugal, Italy, and Iceland in signing the North Atlantic Treaty. It decreed that an attack on any one member nation would be considered an attack on them all. Eventually joined by Turkey and Greece in 1952, the Federal Republic of (West) Germany in 1955, and Spain in 1982 the North Atlantic Treaty Organization (NATO) has remained the prime focus of Canadian and American foreign policy in Europe (see readings).

This Western demonstration of solidarity was eventually countered by the formation of the Warsaw Pact alliance (consisting of Albania, Bulgaria, Czechoslovakia, East Germany, Hungary, Poland, Romania, and the Soviet Union) in 1955. The lines were clearly drawn in Europe. The iron curtain of Churchill's imagination had become a reality.

North America and NATO

The Second World War was a testing ground for American economic and military power. In the postwar world this new strength and global commitment was further put to the test.

The American and Canadian decisions to join NATO should have been a surprise to no one. In March 1948 Harry Truman addressed Congress, stating that: "I am sure that the determination of the free countries of Europe to protect themselves will be matched by an equal determination on our part to help them do so." Mackenzie King, upon hearing this pronouncement, commented that if there was "a league of free people . . . there could be no doubt on the part of anyone as to our being in."

The economic and military involvement of the United States in Europe had some Canadians worried. Economic historian Harold Innis called American policy a "gold curtain" to counter the Soviet "iron" one. Most Canadians, however, saw things differently. Minister of external affairs and future prime minister Lester Pearson remarked that the alliance "would provide the basis for the organization of an overwhelming preponderance of force . . . over the Soviet Union . . . [to be] used as to guarantee that the free nations will not be defeated one by one." Other Canadians pointed out that a strong and economically healthy free Europe would provide an alternative to increasing economic dependency upon the United States. Pierre Trudeau's "Third Option" of the 1970s had its roots in the formation of NATO.

Another new concept to emerge from the Canadian position was the idea of "Atlanticism." Pearson proposed that the new organization also contain a provision for cultural and economic cooperation. Although article 2, the so-called "Canadian clause," had little impact upon the actual running of the alliance, it gave a clear statement of the idealist Canadian dream of a democratic superstate spanning the Atlantic. Canada attempted to block the inclusion of dictatorships such as Portugal, but the military realists in Washington won out over the idealists from Ottawa.

Over the next thirty years, Canada would reassess its commitment to the alliance. After a foreign policy review, the Trudeau government drastically reduced Canada's European contingent (see readings). Although these numbers were marginally increased during the early years of the Mulroney government, by the 1980s Canadian defence priorities were concentrated elsewhere (see readings).

This ambivalence towards international military commitments was obvious from the start. Even with the formal signing of the North Atlantic Treaty, the Canadian government had still not been willing to reactivate its massive wartime military machine. Boasting the third largest navy and fourth largest army in the world in 1945, Canada by 1949 had fewer than fifty thousand women and men in uniform. In spite of the new commitments in Europe, things probably would have stayed that way if disaster had not struck elsewhere.

The United Nations

In April 1945 delegates from forty-five countries met in San Francisco to draw up the charter for the United Nations. The UN was to be an international organization dedicated to the preservation of world peace. In the preamble to the charter the member nations pledged to not only maintain peace, but also to abolish famine and disease and preserve human rights.

In theory the United Nations had three main powers, or sanctions, it could use against aggressor nations. The first was a moral sanction—that is, a condemnation of the actions of a country by the rest of the world. If moral sanctions had no effect then the UN could impose economic sanctions, such as a trade embargo or a blockade. As a last resort, the UN could impose a military sanction and intervene with an armed force. At various times, the United Nations has imposed all of these sanctions, with varying degrees of success.

In the 1940s the United States was embarking on a policy of "collective security." Although involved in local agreements with Canada, Latin America, and eventually NATO, Americans still saw the future in global, not regional, terms. This attitude was reflected in their dealings with the United Nations during the organization's early years.

The United Nations had a mixed record in the late 1940s. A successful attempt to get foreign governments out of Iran in 1946 was followed by an almost disastrous handling of the question of Palestinian independence. The real test, however, did not come in the Middle East, but on the opposite side of the globe. The world was on the brink of war over Korea.

The Korean Conflict

Korea had been under Japanese control since 1910. In the dying moments of World War II it had been liberated by the Soviet Union. After the final defeat of Japan in August 1945, American troops also landed in Korea and a joint occupation was arranged.

As a temporary measure, the nation had been divided on the 38th parallel of latitude. The heavily industrialized North was supervised by the Russians, while the agricultural South was under American control. In 1947 the UN tried to organize free elections in Korea in order to establish a national government that would reunify the country. Two-thirds of the population lived in the South, and so the Soviets, suspecting that their faction would lose in an open vote, refused to participate in the election. The result was the creation of two separate states. In the South, the Republic of Korea was created. Its leader was the democratically elected president Syngman Rhee. In the North, the Soviets helped establish the Korean Peoples' Republic based on the communist model.

By the middle of 1949 both the United States and the Soviet Union had withdrawn their troops from the country, and the two Koreas were left facing each other across the 38th parallel. Things were quiet, but it was only a matter of time before the underlying conflicts surfaced.

On June 25th the Korean "cold war" came to an end. Supported by Soviet-built tanks and aircraft, the North Koreans launched an invasion of the South. The UN Security Council condemned the North's actions. Two days later the members agreed to act to support South Korea. Both Security Council moves passed easily. The Soviets were boycotting the sessions over the Western powers' refusal to admit the Peoples' Republic of China to the Security Council as the legitimate government of that country, thus they were unable to exercise their veto.

The American army acted on behalf of the United Nations. Ground and air forces were sent in to shore up the South's defenses. The situation looked hopeless. Truman put General MacArthur in charge of the operation. The seventy–year-old general set up his command under the UN flag. Although troops from sixteen nations, including Canada, eventually fought against the North Koreans, almost 90 percent of the force remained American.

After initial North Korean successes, UN troops drove the Communist forces back close to the Chinese border. China, fearful that the war might be carried into its own territory, counterattacked in support of its North Korean neighbours. The Chinese drive took the impetus out of the UN offensive; eventually the war bogged down to a stalemate which lasted for eighteen months until the two sides agreed to an armistice. Negotiations were begun to settle the differences between North and South Korea, but twenty-five years later the problem still remains unresolved (see readings).

The Significance of Korea

Almost sixty thousand members of the UN forces, including 312 Canadians, lost their lives in Korea. What was gained?

On the positive side, both the United States and the United Nations demonstrated that they would not hesitate to fight to defend the rights of any nation in the face of aggression. On the negative side, the Korean War represented a fundamental shift in American policy making. Prior to their success in "containing" communism in Korea, most American officials believed that such a war was unwinnable and therefore it was not worth getting involved. Korea, however, demonstrated that a limited war could be fought and won in Asia. It was a lesson that would be applied in Vietnam with tragic results.

Canada maintained a brigade in Korea during the war as well as an air division. It was a token force at best. At the same time, however, Canada doubled its armed forces to one hundred thousand. Canadians were convinced that there was a danger to world peace, but they believed it was other than in Korea. Lester Pearson, in his role as president of the UN General Assembly, played a key part in the negotiations that led to a settlement. He saw the Korean conflict as drawing too much energy and attention away from Europe, and felt that the United States was becoming more and more inflexible in its Asian policy. Pearson's stand on Korea was a foretaste of things to come.

The McCarthy Challenge

In the tense atmosphere of the Cold War, many Americans became concerned about the infiltration of communists into their government. In response to this, Truman created a Loyalty Review Board in 1947. It was nothing new. Since 1938 the House of Representatives had conducted investigations of possible traitors through its Un-American Activities Committee (HUAC).

In a spectacular case in 1948, the committee went after a former member of the State department, Alger Hiss. Chief witness for the prosecution was a senior editor for *Time* magazine named Whittaker Chambers. Chambers confessed to being a former Communist spy. Now he was ready to point the finger at all of his former co-

conspirators. Hiss wasn't Chambers's only target, however; he and another repenting Communist, Elizabeth Bentley, named over fifty former agents. Hiss, however, was the only one to voluntarily come forward to face the committee. He denied everything that Chambers had said, but then made the fatal mistake of suing the journalist for libel. In his defence Chambers took members of the HUAC committee to his garden and retrieved, from a hollowed–out pumpkin, rolls of microfilm containing State department documents. These, according to Chambers, had come from Hiss. One of the men was lying. Hiss was charged with perjury. After one jury failed to reach a verdict, in February 1950 a second jury convicted him.

The Hiss case was only one of a number of spectacular revelations that winter. In another case, the British arrested atomic scientist Dr. Klaus Fuchs. Fuchs had worked on the Manhattan Project (the code name for the U.S. atomic project during WWII) from 1943 to 1946 and was discovered to have been passing information to the Soviets during that time. Fuchs implicated a courier, Harry Gold, who in turn pointed the finger at two Americans, Ethel and Julius Rosenberg. The Rosenbergs were found guilty of spying and were executed for treason in 1953.

The trials and apparent evidence of Soviet spy rings gave new life to right–wing forces in the United States. One immediate result was to block any possibility of recognizing the new government in Beijing (Peking). Republicans began accusing "Communist sympathizers" in the State department of having "lost" China. Into this emotionally charged environment of fear and suspicion stepped Joseph R. McCarthy. Soon he would become the spokesperson for the Right.

McCarthy was a junior senator from Wisconsin. After an undistinguished early career he jumped into prominence in February 1950. Speaking in Wheeling, West Virginia, he claimed to have in his hand a list of 205 known present or former Communists who were currently working in the State department. When pressed for more details, his story often changed. The numbers he quoted eventually came down to nine specific names. Of those, six had never worked in the State department and the rest held only minor posts.

In spite of these inconsistencies, McCarthy's popularity grew. When challenged on his facts, he simply made up new charges. Many of his claims were wild, but they fed the public fear and paranoia of the period. When a Senate investigating committee disputed McCarthy's charges, McCarthy used faked photographs to help defeat the committee chairman in his campaign for re-election.

Even more dangerous than McCarthy himself was the popularity of his methods. State legislatures and city councils copied his approach of vague charges and conviction by rumour. Employees were forced to sign "loyalty oaths," and some groups, like the entertainment industry, developed blacklists of former Communists.

Eventually McCarthyism burned itself out. His witch-hunting methods were held up to public scrutiny in the Army-McCarthy hearings of 1954. The army's lawyer, Joseph Welch of Boston, was soft-spoken and polite, but put devastating questions to the senator. McCarthy, by contrast, appeared ill-mannered and irresponsible. By the time the hearings were over, the issue had been settled in the public mind. McCarthy's short career was finished. Bolstered by public opinion, the Senate censured McCarthy for his actions. He fell into obscurity and died a bitter man four years later at the age of forty-eight.

Canada had its own sensational spy scandal soon after the Second World War.

In September 1945, Igor Gouzenko, a clerk from the Soviet Embassy, arrived at the Ministry of Justice with evidence of a Soviet spy ring in Ottawa. By the time the investigation had ended several people had been convicted of spying, including a Communist Member of Parliament. Unlike in the United States, however, Canada did not launch its own McCarthy–style witch hunt. Canadians were shocked, but they soon forgot the incident.

George Drew, the new leader of the Conservatives, tried to make the "red menace" an issue in Parliament. In January 1949 he accused the government of new prime minister Louis St. Laurent of covering up for a civil service full of Communists. Drew called for the outlawing of the Communist party and a purge of all of its supporters. St. Laurent, caught off guard, hesitated and then struck back. He accused Drew of using scare tactics and advocating dictatorship in the name of democracy. When the Conservative leader said that the members of the Liberal cabinet reminded him of Marx, one minister replied that Drew was like Marx too, but "Groucho, not Karl."

In April, St. Laurent went to the people. Drew's anti-Communist campaign proved to be a disaster. The Liberals won 193 seats to the Conservatives' 41. There would be no Joe McCarthy in Canada.

The Suez Crisis

Border incidents were common between Israel and Egypt in the early 1950s. Tensions came to the boiling point, however, in 1956. In that year the Egyptian president Gamel Abdul Nasser, was in the process of negotiating loans from Britain and the United States to build a giant dam across the Nile River near Aswan. At the same time, he was also buying arms from Czechoslovakia. American secretary of state John Foster Dulles warned Nasser that if he did not cancel his arms deal with the Czechs, the United States might be forced to cut off aid for the dam. Nasser responded that if the Americans would not help him then perhaps the Soviets would.

Furious with Nasser's threat, the Americans withdrew their loan. In response, Nasser nationalized the Suez Canal (which was owned by Britain and France) and declared that he would use the tolls collected from the canal to pay for the dam.

In a move prearranged with the governments in London and Paris, Israel attacked Egypt in the Sinai Peninsula. British and French paratroops landed to protect "their" canal. The Soviets backed Egypt. The prospect of a major war seemed inevitable.

Popular sentiment in the United States condemned the Western allies. Most people saw their actions as imperialistic and unfair to the Egyptians. Not all Canadians felt that way, however. St. Laurent's reference to France and Britain as the "supermen of Europe" who had yet to recognize that their day was over sparked a considerable national outcry. Meanwhile, the UN was paralysed, as Britain and France both threatened to use their vetoes if any action was proposed against them. The American government was caught in the middle. They could not support the actions of their allies, but it was their own policy that had caused the problem.

At this point the United Nations stepped in. Spearheaded by Canadian representative Lester Pearson, the UN proposed an immediate ceasefire. To keep the peace, an international army was sent to occupy the region. This United Nations Emergency Force (UNEF) was to become a principal arm of UN action in the future.

Pearson eventually received the Nobel Peace Prize for his efforts. At home, however, some Canadians condemned his stand (see readings). By refusing to back Britain, they claimed that Pearson was trying to turn Canada into an American satellite, a "banana republic." For the most part, though, Canadians emerged from the crisis thinking of themselves as a "middle power," an "honest broker" who could act as a buffer between the superpowers and other nations of the world. Canadian troops formed an important part of the first peacekeeping force. Since 1956 Canadians have served in that role in the Sinai Peninsula on the Golan Heights, and on Cyprus, and have offered their services in such diverse places as Vietnam, Namibia, Haiti, and Central America.

Canada and the United States had formed a joint board for continental defence in 1940. During the latter part of the decade many Canadians raised doubts about the stationing of American troops in the country, but for the most part people took the relationship for granted. In 1957 the new Conservative government of John Diefenbaker announced the creation of the North American Air Defence plan (NORAD) (see readings). It represented an integrated continental air defence network under American command. The nature of Canada's contribution to this arrangement remained a festering political issue for the next six years (see readings). In the final analysis, however, Canada took a middle road, accepting American aid at arm's length.

By 1960 Canada and the United States had established a joint approach to continental and European defence. Although each side might question the level of contribution or the motivations of one another over the next thirty years, for the most part the two neighbours stayed on track with each other. But if Canada and the United States were in step in these areas, their attitudes towards other foreign policy issues were far from compatible.

Vietnam and the End of Innocence

Canada and the United States both became actively involved in the internal affairs of Vietnam at about the same time. With the French withdrawal from Indochina following the Geneva Conference in 1954, the Americans stepped up logistical support to the non-Communist South. Canada, on the other hand, became the Western member of a three-nation International Control Commission designed to monitor the terms of the truce drawn up by the conference. Ostensibly neutral, Canada was seen as the American representative on the commission in balance to the Soviet client state, Poland.

U.S. president Dwight D. Eisenhower's commitment to help preserve South Vietnam cost the United States little more than money in the 1950s. While American advisors were training the soldiers and officers of the army of the Republic of Vietnam (ARVN), however, the North was making its own plans. By October 1957 Communist insurgents were actively at work in South Vietnam. Trained in the North, by 1959 they were also receiving arms and reinforcements from Hanoi. This support was reaching the South through Laos and Cambodia along what was known as the Ho Chi Minh Trail.

When President John F. Kennedy took office in 1960, he continued Eisenhower's policies in Vietnam, and responded to increased communist activity by increasing the American presence in the area. The number of American troops in Vietnam in 1961 totalled 3200; this figure had jumped to 16 000 by late 1963. These were not combat troops, however, and only 120 Americans had been killed so far.

In spite of American support, the 150 000-strong ARVN was still not able to overcome the 15 000 Vietcong (the Communist guerrillas). Part of the problem was the unpopularity of the Diem regime. Even though Vice-President Lyndon Johnson had called Diem "the George Washington of his country," most people were opposed to his rule. Finally an American-backed coup overthrew and killed the dictator in early November 1963. Kennedy was glad to be rid of Diem, and was looking forward to working with a new government in the South. He did not get the chance. Within three weeks he too was dead, and the war in Vietnam was handed over to his successor.

Lyndon Johnson had his hands full. Although the Eisenhower/Kennedy approach had accomplished little, it had not really cost the United States anything either. In early 1964 the new president sat on the fence, waiting for the Vietcong to make the next move. He did not have to wait long.

While acting in a supporting role to ARVN ships attacking North Vietnamese targets in the Gulf of Tonkin, two American destroyers, the *Maddox* and the *Turner Joy*, were attacked by Northern torpedo boats. On August 7th, five days after the *Maddox* was attacked, Congress passed the Gulf of Tonkin Resolution. It authorized the president to take "all necessary measures" to "repel any armed attack" and take any actions necessary to "prevent further aggression" in the future. This blank cheque passed the House by a vote of 416 to 0. The Senate tried to limit the president's freedom of action but eventually passed the resolution 88 to 2. Later that month the United States launched its first bombing raids against the North.

Johnson's restraint in dealing with North Vietnam helped him to win the presidential election in the fall of 1964. His opponent, Barry Goldwater, recommended extending the war to the north. Johnson hesitated, fearful that increased attacks might lead to Chinese involvement in the conflict. Soon, however, restraint was forgotten as Johnson and his advisors decided to plunge into the conflict head on.

In February 1965 the Americans launched Operation Rolling Thunder. It called for sustained American bombing of the North. In addition in March combat troops from the United States arrived in Vietnam for the first time. Starting with five thousand marines, American military involvement escalated rapidly. Johnson was convinced that without a substantial American military presence, a concerted offensive by the North would wipe out the ARVN. As a result, by the end of the year there were 185 000 American troops in the field. Within two more years Johnson had sent over half a million military personnel to the war-torn country.

In spite of this radical increase in American support, however, the war was far from over.

Canadians had become increasingly critical of American policy in Asia during the early sixties. Most Canadians advocated official recognition of Communist China, and when Johnson stepped up the war effort, Canada was quick to criticize. The Canadian government knew the bombing was coming. Canada's representative on the International Control Commission in Vietnam was the capable career diplomat Blair Seaborn. In April 1964 U.S. secretary of state Dean Rusk asked that Seaborn be given "the specific mission of conveying to Hanoi both warnings about its present course and hints of possible rewards in return for a change." Seaborn carried warnings of future American actions to the Hanoi government in hopes of sparking peace negotiations and of normalizing trade relations between the two countries. At the same time Johnson told Prime Minister Lester Pearson that should negotiations fail he would have no hesitation in beginning "punitive striking of discriminate targets" by non-nuclear bombs. The warnings were of no avail, and Operation Rolling Thunder went ahead as scheduled.

The Canadian government began to harbour serious doubts about the logic of American policy, but Pearson saw no hope of bringing the president to his senses. Finally his convictions forced him to break his silence. In April 1965, speaking at Temple University, he condemned the bombing, and called for its suspension, at least temporarily, as a sign of a willingness to negotiate. Johnson was furious. When Pearson visited the president at Camp David (see readings) he was physically and verbally assaulted. There would be no more bilateral discussions on Vietnam. As Pearson lamented in the House of Commons:

[All we can do] is to bring our worries and anxieties to the notice of those who are more immediately and directly involved in the hope that our advice and counsel will be of some help to them. I am thinking particularly of Washington.

For Canada it was the end of innocence. The friendly partnership had cooled. For the next twenty years Canada would have little influence in Washington.

Vietnam was very much a presidential enterprise by 1966. The powers granted by the Gulf of Tonkin Resolution meant that Johnson did not have to ask Congress for a declaration of war. The costs were staggering. By 1968 the war had a price tag of $25 billion a year with twenty-five thousand Americans dead and horrible Vietnamese military and civilian losses.

The bombing campaign took on a new and sinister phase in the late sixties. Because the Vietcong used the lush vegetation as cover for their activities, American military strategists decided to eliminate as much of this plant life as possible. Plant-killing herbicides (defoliants) were dropped on forest areas, napalm (jellied gasoline) was dumped on farms and villages, and industrial centres were saturated by conventional bombs. By the middle of 1967 the United States had dropped more explosives on North Vietnam than had been dropped on Germany during the entire Second World War. Yet still the war raged on.

Americans were confident that these tactics would eventually result in victory.

They were stunned when, in February 1968, the North Vietnamese launched the massive Tet offensive. American and ARVN forces were sent reeling back by surprise attacks throughout the South. Although they eventually recovered and gained back lost ground, the costs were enormous in human terms.

Calling a temporary halt to the bombing of population centres in the North, Johnson offered to open peace talks with Hanoi. The meetings, which opened in Paris on May 10th, dragged on for almost five years.

When Richard Nixon became president in 1968 the nation was in the midst of a domestic and foreign policy crisis. He rightly recognized that many of the problems at home could not be solved without bringing the war in Vietnam to an end. To do so, the new president announced two goals. The first was the beginning of the process of "Vietnamization." He wanted to turn back the clock to the early years of the conflict when the United States was fulfilling a supporting role, not a combat one. The second was the principle of "Peace with Honour." In other words, Nixon wanted to find some way to pull out of Vietnam without either side appearing to lose the war or without the Americans seeming to have deserted their allies in the region. For advice and support he relied on his national security advisor, Henry Kissinger. Kissinger, a German who had fled from Nazi persecution in 1938, was a former professor of defense studies at Harvard. He provided Nixon with the intellectual image that the president lacked.

To his critics Nixon's Vietnamization program seemed painstakingly slow. Still, by 1972 only 60 000 Americans were left in Vietnam of the 534 000 there when his presidency began. The process seemed uneven to some observers, however. As ground involvement declined, bombing escalated, including the 1970 invasion and bombing of neighbouring Cambodia.

Nixon's Cambodian adventure sparked an outburst of protest across the country. In two instances peaceful demonstrations took a tragic turn. At Kent State University in Ohio, the National Guard opened fire on a protest demonstration. When the smoke cleared four students were dead and nine more were wounded. A similar occurrence at Jackson State in Mississippi claimed two more lives.

Earlier that year it was revealed that American troops had massacred a village of over one hundred men, women, and children at My Lai in 1968. Fourteen officers were charged with concealing information from the military. William Calley, the army lieutenant who was in charge of the mission, was convicted in November and sentenced to life in prison.

The president was clearly shaken by events and announced that he would soon be withdrawing the troops from Cambodia. Protest mounted. On May 9th, five days after Kent State, one hundred thousand demonstrators met in Washington to protest the war. Later that year Congress revoked the Gulf of Tonkin Resolution. Nixon claimed that his position as commander–in–chief of the armed forces gave him the right to continue the struggle and ignored the new restriction.

In November, on the eve of the 1972 presidential election, Henry Kissinger announced that "peace is at hand." A ceasefire was enacted, but it was short-lived. To force the North Vietnamese back to the table, Nixon resumed intensive bombing in December. Finally in January talks resumed, and on the 27th an agreement was reached. It called for an immediate ceasefire and the complete withdrawal of American troops and advisors within sixty days. Within two months most American prisoners of war were freed. The pact won Kissinger and Le Duc Tho, the North Vietnamese negotiator, the Nobel Peace Prize. Le Duc Tho refused the honour. Possibly he knew what lay ahead. Two years after the American withdrawal a well-planned invasion from the North swept through the country. Saigon, which fell on April 30, 1975, was renamed Ho Chi Minh City and the country was finally unified under the name the Socialist Republic of Vietnam. Fifty-six thousand Americans and over 1 million Vietnamese died during the Vietnamese conflict, but in the final analysis, for the Americans the twenty-year war had been for nothing.

The Western Hemisphere

The United States initiated the creation of the Organization of American States (OAS) in 1947. Designed for mutual cooperation and security, it seemed to indicate a willingness on the part of the Americans to enter into an equal partnership with other American nations. Canada declined membership in this and all American defence groups except NATO. External Affairs in Ottawa regarded the organization merely as a tool for American policy in Latin America. They viewed the OAS as the Monroe Doctrine under a new guise.

The first evidence of this came in 1954. Guatemala, under the leadership of President Guzman Jacobo Arbenz, nationalized the holdings of the American-owned United Fruit Company, and redistributed its land to the peasants. Shunned by the United States and condemned as Communists by the OAS, the Arbenz government turned to the Eastern bloc for economic and military support. The Eisenhower administration, meanwhile, armed and supported anti-government exiles based in neighbouring Honduras. Supplied with planes and other military hardware by the CIA, and backed by the governments of Honduras and Nicaragua, these Guatemalan Contras successfully invaded their homeland and overthrew the government. (It was a tactic that would be applied less successfully in Cuba in the early sixties and in Nicaragua itself in the late 1980s.) The parallels with the Korean invasion were obvious, but the United States effectively blocked the United Nations from intervening, claiming this local "problem" would be dealt with at home by the OAS.

Throughout the decade American leadership increasingly supported dictatorial regimes in Latin America. Soon resentment against the United States spilled over into violence. On a goodwill tour to South America in 1958, Nixon was mobbed and his car pelted with eggs and rocks. It was clearly a time for a change in direction.

During the 1960 election campaign Kennedy called Eisenhower's policy towards Latin America unimaginative, and offered a new approach to relations with America's neighbours. He got a chance to try out his new approach sooner than he expected. The place was Cuba.

Cuba had suffered under the oppressive dictatorship of Fulgencio Batista throughout most of the 1950s. A growing guerrilla movement presented a serious challenge to the corrupt regime. In 1959 Batista was finally overthrown by rebels led by a young lawyer named Fidel Castro.

Castro had a genuine desire to reform Cuban society. Although his struggle against Batista was supported by the American government, Eisenhower was not ready for the reality of Castro in power. As one of his first actions, Castro announced a radical program of land reform. As in Guatemala, it involved the confiscation of a great deal of American–owned property. In order to calm fears in the United States, the Cuban leader visited Washington in April 1959. Convinced that the Americans understood his plan he went home to continue the revolution. Blood flowed as former Batista officials were executed. Many more fled into exile in the United States, where they agitated against the new government.

In February 1960 Cuba signed a trade deal with the Soviet Union. Castro hoped to diversify Cuba's export trade to reduce its dependence upon the United States. This was followed by the nationalization of British and American oil refineries in June. The United States retaliated by reducing Cuban sugar imports in July, followed by a complete trade embargo in October. Cuba was quickly being pushed into the Soviet camp.

Eisenhower was convinced that Castro and his economic advisor, Che Guevara, planned to export Communist revolution throughout Latin America. On January 3, 1961, the United States cut off diplomatic relations with its island neighbour.

Seventeen days later Kennedy was sworn in as president. But even as he called for a "new alliance for progress" in Latin America, plans were afoot to oust Castro from power.

Canada disagreed with the American approach to Cuba from the start. Although Eisenhower had informed John Diefenbaker that the situation in Cuba was "obviously inviting Soviet penetration of the Western Hemisphere," Canadians more accurately saw American policy as being the prime cause of Cuban disaffection, and made that opinion clear to the American government. Kennedy's secretary of state, Dean Rusk, angrily rejected this position, claiming that "this was primarily a matter of the Monroe Doctrine" and that "further U.S. policy was not going to be altered because Canada didn't like it."

The Bay of Pigs

Under Eisenhower, the Central Intelligence Agency (CIA) was planning the overthrow of the Cuban government. At a secret base in Guatemala anti-Castro Cuban exiles were training to invade and take over the country. Military analysts determined that with American air support the operation would go smoothly.

Upon becoming president, Kennedy was informed of the plan. He gave his approval, and on April 17th a force of fifteen hundred was put ashore in Cuba at the Bay of Pigs. It was a fiasco. Cuba was ready for them, and when significant American air support was withdrawn at the last minute, the invaders never had a chance. Within seventy–two hours it was all over. Twelve hundred men were taken captive, and the reputations of both Kennedy and the United States had taken a brutal beating.

The Missiles of October

Over the next eighteen months the Soviets continued to press the advantage that they had gained in Cuba as a result of the Bay of Pigs invasion. Soon another crisis was brewing.

On October 22, 1962, President Kennedy went on national television to drop a bombshell on the American people: U-2 spy planes over Cuba had spotted unusual construction. Close examination showed that the Soviets were building missile bases on the island. Faced with a possible nuclear threat in his own backyard, Kennedy acted quickly. A naval blockade or "quarantine" was set up around Cuba. Mobilizing the United States armed forces, the president notified Khruschev that either the Soviets cease shipping weapons to Cuba and dismantle the bases already there, or else there would be war. For two days the world held its breath. Finally the Soviets backed off. Soviet ships on their way to Cuba were redirected to Africa, and Khruschev cabled the American president, agreeing to "remove those weapons from Cuba which you regard as offensive." In return he demanded an American pledge that they would not invade the island. It was a face-saving move. Kennedy agreed and the crisis passed.

Diefenbaker was given a copy of Kennedy's television address about two hours before he went on the air. The expectation was that when American forces went on alert, those of its Norad ally would too. It was not the case. Diefenbaker hesitated, hoping that the crisis would not escalate. He lacked confidence in Kennedy, and indicated his doubts about the American intelligence findings by calling for an independent investigation of the charges by the United Nations.

Canada eventually issued a full military alert on October 24th, but by then the damage had been done. Most Canadians supported Kennedy and not their own prime minister. Public confidence was lost, and the administration in Washington began to look for a political alternative to their Conservative ally. American political strategists advised their Liberal counterparts in Canada in the election of 1963, and in spite of a Conservative resurgence built partly upon anti-Americanism and partly out of sympathy for the "Chief," Pearson and the Liberals regained power.

Over the next two decades attitudes and policies towards the Caribbean and Latin American nations widely diverged between the two North American neighbours. Two cases serve to illustrate their differences.

Ronald Reagan and the Monroe Doctrine

A new chapter in American relations with Latin America began in 1979. In that year two new Communist regimes appeared in the hemisphere. On the island of Grenada, popular Marxist leader Maurice Bishop took power. Bishop's attempts to establish normal relations with the United States were shunned by the new administration of Ronald Reagan; plans were laid for his overthrow. In October 1983 the opportunity came. Bishop was deposed by an even more radical Marxist faction in his government. Claiming that Grenada was about to become a new advance base for Communist aggression in the Caribbean, the United States launched a surprise invasion of the island. Unlike the Bay of Pigs over twenty years earlier, however, this was a smashing success. Over five thousand American troops moved against about fifteen hundred local defenders and seven hundred Cuban construction workers. The fighting lasted for three days. In the meantime, the press was kept out in order to avoid exposing any shortcomings in the operation. Once the smoke had cleared, the Americans claimed an unconditional victory (see readings).

The American action was supported by other political leaders in the region. Canada, however, was not even informed prior to the invasion. The Reagan administration knew that the government of Pierre Trudeau would oppose the move, and therefore decided to leave them in the dark.

Three years later, Reagan himself visited the island to the cheers of tens of thousands of residents. With such a success in his pocket, the president began to search for similar operations in Latin America. His prime target was Nicaragua.

A popular revolution in 1979 replaced the U.S.-backed dictator Anastasio Somoza with the left-wing Sandinista government led by President Daniel Ortega. Reagan saw the new regime as a danger to neighbouring El Salvador and Honduras and began a policy of full-scale military aid to those countries. At the same time he gradually increased military and financial support of the Contras, a force of about fifteen thousand anti-government rebels operating out of the countryside. In 1984 the CIA mined Nicaragua's harbours, a move which brought both Congressional and international opinion against the president's actions. In fact, by mid-1986 many Contras had been forced back over the Honduran border to hide from Sandinista forces.

At home, Reagan's Latin American policies raised the haunting spectre of Vietnam. Much of the same rhetoric, such as the domino theory, the defence of democracy, and national security, resurfaced in the vocabulary. At one point Reagan even warned that aggressive Sandinista forces were only two hours away from Texas!

Until the summer of 1986 Congress remained unconvinced. Restricted in their bid for financial support from Congress, members of the Reagan White House looked for other methods of providing aid to their anti-Communist allies. In an incredible turn of events, the administration authorized the sale of arms to the regime of the Ayatollah Khomeini in Iran. As this was illegal under American law, the entire operation was carried out in secret. Reagan later claimed that it was part of a strategy to normalize relations between the two countries and that in fact the arms were in exchange for American hostages being held prisoner in the Middle East.

There was, however, another agenda. Masterminded by CIA director William Casey, national security advisor William Poindexter, and Lieutenant-Colonel Oliver North, profits from the arms sales were siphoned off and earmarked for delivery to the Contras. In nationally televised Congressional hearings into the affair, North testified that in order to defend "democracy" in Nicaragua he had found it necessary to subvert the democratic process in his own country (see readings). His viewpoints raised serious doubts about the American commitment to peace in Central America.

Canada, on the other hand, continued to condemn Contra action and to call for support of the Arias peace plan in the region. Delegations of MPs and church and relief groups continued to visit the war-torn country, returning with positive observations about the accomplishments of the Sandinista regime. Official Canadian policy, however, remained confused. After a visit to the region by External Affairs minister Joe Clark in the fall of 1987, local officials commented on the Canadian government's lack of understanding of the issues. Clark drew heavy criticism both at home and abroad when he remarked that perhaps Canada could accept the Contras as refugees, thus eliminating the problem!

Today Central American leaders regard Canada as a potential mediator in the conflict, and still look for Canadian intervention with their powerful mutual neighbour (see readings).

The decades since the beginning of World War II have been marked by the active involvement of North Americans upon the world stage. Lacking the global empire and mission of the United States, Canada has often taken a more pragmatic view of events. A strong commitment to the defeat of fascism in the early forties was transferred to the Communist menace in the following decade. As Canadians began to take a less monolithic view of the world, their foreign policy goals began to diverge from those of their superpower neighbour. Maintaining a strong commitment to the containment of the Soviet Union in Europe, Canada did not accept the American contention that it was a global struggle in a number of different theatres. Canadian governments, influenced by the United States, were slow to normalize relations with the Soviet Union and the Peoples' Republic of China, although the leadership shown during the Trudeau era set the stage for an American thaw with each of those two nations.

In the field of nuclear arms, Canada, one of the original members of the nuclear club, debated the issue of staging nuclear weapons on its own soil in the early sixties. Eventually rejecting the option (see readings), Canadians went on to become strong advocates of disarmament. As a result, the members of the House of Commons were among the first to extend formal congratulations to Soviet premier Mikhail Gorbachev and American president Ronald Reagan when they signed the INF treaty removing intermediate–range missiles from Europe in December 1987. Such opposition to the use of nuclear weaponry, however, has not prevented the Canadian government from allowing nuclear–armed U.S. warships into Canadian ports, nor has it prevented the U.S. airforce from testing such nuclear delivery systems as the cruise missile over Canadian territory.

Although still perceived in many areas as a satellite of the United States, Canada has nonetheless established a reputation as a fair and moderate arbiter in international affairs. In Latin America Canada enjoys a level of credibility envied by many Americans. Within the Commonwealth Canada has emerged as a strong supporter of anti-apartheid forces in South Africa, to some extent supplanting Great Britain as the moral leader of the organization.

To the south, the United States has been reassessing its global position in the late 1980s. Improved relations with China and the Soviet Union have softened the hard anti-Communist line of many American political leaders. The revelations of the Iran-Contra affair demonstrated the degree to which the Reagan administration was out of step with its own people over its Latin American policy.

The rapport between Canadian prime minister Brian Mulroney and American president Ronald Reagan during the 1980s allowed for some progress in such areas as continental defence and trade. Closely interrelated with domestic trends, these issues will be discussed in later chapters. It is enough to say that by the late 1980s the United States was beginning to come to terms with "life in the middle lane." In this regard, many Americans have looked to the example of their northern neighbour for a fresh look at the outside world.

Canada Goes to War, 1939

The isolationism that had marked North American attitudes toward European affairs during the 1920s and 1930s disappeared in Canada first. There was no obligation for Canada to come to Britain's aid in World War II, but there was also no question but that it would. In this excerpt, Mackenzie King outlines his government's position in the House of Commons.

I noticed in the press last evening that one of the German papers which is supposed to be an organ of the administration had quoted Hitler as saying that if England wished to fight she must remember that if she entered this fight the prize of victory would be the British Empire. Well, that includes Canada. As my honourable friend has said, there is no portion of the globe which any nation would be likely to covet more than this Dominion of Canada. There is no other portion of the earth's surface that contains such wealth as lies buried here. Nowhere are there such stretches of territory capable of feeding for generations to come—not hundreds of thousands, but millions of people. No, Mr. Speaker, the ambition of this dictator is not Poland. . . . Where is he creeping to? Into those communities of the north, some of which today say they are going to remain neutral. I tell them if they remain neutral in this struggle, and Britain and France go down, there is not one of them that will bear for long the name that it bears at the present time; not one of them. And if this conqueror by his methods of force, violence, and terror, and other ruthless iniquities is able to crush the peoples of Europe, what is going to become of the doctrine of isolation of this North American continent? If Britain goes down, if France goes down, the whole business of isolation will prove to have been a mere myth. There will in time be no freedom on this continent; there will in time be no liberty. Life will not be worth living. It is for all of us on this continent to do our part to save its privileged position by helping others. . . .

From J.M. Bliss,"Canada Goes to War", in *Canadian History in Documents 1763-1966*, (Toronto: Ryerson Press, 1966).

1. What case does King make for Canadian involvement in the Second World War?
2. To what extent could the prime minister's arguments be applied to the whole continent?
3. To what extent does King's position establish foreign policy directions for the generation to come?

The Ogdensburg Agreement, 1940

August 18, 1940, has often been cited as the day that Canada officially moved from the British to the American sphere of influence. Mackenzie King and Franklin Roosevelt, meeting in Ogdensburg, New York, signed an agreement for joint continental defence. The creation of the Permanent Joint Board of Defence set a pattern of collaboration for the next half century.

The Prime Minister and the President have discussed the mutual problems of defense in relation to the safety of Canada and the United States.

It has been agreed that a Permanent Joint Board on Defense shall be set up at once by the two countries.

This permanent Joint Board on Defense shall commence immediate studies relating to sea, land and air problems including personnel and materiel.

It will consider in the broad sense the defense of the north half of the Western Hemisphere.

The permanent Joint Board on Defense will consist of four or five members from each country, most of them from the services. It will meet shortly.

From *Department of State Bulletin*, III, No. 61 (Aug. 24, 1940).

1. Discuss the long-term implications of the Ogdensburg Agreement.

Yalta, 1945

When Roosevelt, Churchill, and Stalin met at Yalta in February 1945, the war in Europe was almost over. Basic issues were discussed, including the creation of the United Nations, the liberation and reorganization of Europe, and the eventual entry of the Soviet Union into the Pacific war. The partition and occupation of Germany was left for future deliberations.

The Crimea Conference of the Heads of the Governments of the United States, the United Kingdom, and the Union of Soviet Socialist Republics which took place from February 4th to 11th came to the following conclusions.

I. World Organization. It was decided:

(1) that a United Nations Conference on the proposed world organization should be summoned for Wednesday, 25th April, 1945, and should be held in the United States of America. . . .

II. Declaration on Liberated Europe. The Premier of the Union of Soviet Socialist Republics, the Prime Minister of the United Kingdom and the President of the United States . . . jointly declare their mutual agreement to concert during the temporary period of instability in liberated Europe the policies of their three governments in assisting the peoples liberated from the domination of Nazi Germany and the peoples of the former Axis satellite states of Europe to solve by democratic means their pressing political and economic problems. . . .

III. Dismemberment of Germany . . .

VII. Poland. A new situation has been created in Poland as a result of her

complete liberation by the Red Army. This calls for the establishment of a Polish Provisional Government which can be more broadly based than was possible before the recent liberation of the Western part of Poland. The Provisional Government which is now functioning in Poland should therefore be reorganized on a broader democratic basis with the inclusion of democratic leaders from Poland itself and from Poles abroad. This new Government should then be called the Polish Provisional Government of National Unity. . . .
[sc]E. R. Stettinius, Jr.
V. Molotov
Anthony Eden[esc]

From *Foreign Relations in the United States, the Conferences at Malta and Yalta, 1945,* (Washington, 1955).

1. Compare the provisions of Yalta with the reality of events in Europe in 1945-46.

The Marshall Plan, 1947

When the United States unveiled the European Recovery Plan in November 1947 it was viewed with concern by the Soviet Union. North America alone had emerged economically stronger as a result of the war. The Soviet sphere of influence, maintained by military occupation and meagre financial support, was threatened with destruction by the infusion of vast sums of American capital. Eventually sixteen Western nations would accept money under the Marshall Plan. Although there were strings attached, there is no question but that American aid considerably hastened the recovery of Western Europe.

The excerpt below is taken from a speech given by secretary of state George Marshall at Harvard University the previous June.

This community before the war accounted for nearly one-half of the world's trade. They owned nearly two-thirds of the world's shipping. Their industrial production in terms of the basic commodities of coal, steel, and chemicals was before the war slightly greater than that of the United States. Their economy was highly integrated, each part depending upon the efficient working of the others.

The Committee of European Economic Cooperation, meeting in Paris, produced a recovery program extending over 4 years. . . .

. . . It is a program of construction, production, and recovery. It menaces no one. It is designed specifically to bring to an end in the shortest possible time the dependence of these countries upon aid from the United States. We wish to see them self-supporting. . . .

The automatic success of the program cannot be guaranteed. The imponderables are many. The risks are real. They are, however, risks which have been carefully calculated, and I believe the chances of success are good. There is convincing evidence that the peoples of western Europe want to preserve their free society and the heritage we share with them. To make that choice conclusive they need our assistance. . . .

We must not fail to meet this inspiring challenge. We must not permit the free community of Europe to be extinguished. . . .

Whether we like it or not, we find ourselves, our Nation, in a world position of vast responsibility. We can act for our own good by acting for the world's good.

From The Senate Committee on Foreign Relations, *A Decade of American Foreign Policy*, (Washington, 1950).

1. What rationale does Marshall use to justify rebuilding the economy of Europe?
2. What role does he outline for American involvement in world affairs?
3. Soviet foreign minister Molotov called the Marshall Plan, the "Truman Doctrine with dollars." To what extent would you agree with his analysis?

NATO: North America Commits to Europe

The Berlin Blockade convinced many North Americans of the need to maintain a Western military presence in Europe to counter the Soviet "threat." Even prior to the events of June 1948, however, many political leaders were calling for the creation of a "collective security league."

This first excerpt is taken from a speech in the House of Commons, in April 1948, in which Minister of External Affairs Louis St. Laurent outlines the rationale for the creation of such an organization. A year later, both Canada and the United States would become charter members of the North Atlantic Treaty Organization.

It is now, I believe, an accepted fact that practically everything of importance that happens in the international sphere is of interest to Canada—often of direct and immediate interest. For us there is no escape, even if we wish to seek one, in isolation or indifference. Recent events have brought home to all of us the increasing threat to our democratic national existence of the rising tide of totalitarian communism. . . .

Our foreign policy today must, therefore, I suggest, be based on a recognition of the fact that totalitarian communist aggression, endangers the freedom and peace of every democratic country, including Canada. . . .

It may be that the free states, or some of them, will soon find it necessary to consult together on how best to establish such a collective security league. It might grow out of the plans for "western union," now maturing in Europe. Its purpose, like that of a "western union," would not be merely negative; it would create a dynamic counter-attraction to communism—the dynamic counter-attraction of a free, prosperous and progressive society as opposed to the totalitarian and reactionary society of the communist world. The formation of such a defensive group of free states would not be a counsel of despair but a message of hope. . . .

From J.M. Bliss, "Louis St. Laurent Proposes an Atlantic Alliance, 1948," in *Canadian History in Documents 1763-1966*, (Toronto: Ryerson Press, 1966).

Louis St. Laurent, now prime minister, expanded upon these ideas during the House debate on the ratification of the NATO treaty.

Well, the fear of subversive communism allied to Soviet might is in fact the mainspring of the development leading up to this North Atlantic security pact. . . .

Under this treaty those signatory governments undertook that if any one of them should be the object of armed attack in Europe, the others would, in accordance with provisions in article 51 of the charter of the United Nations, afford the party so attacked all military and other aid and assistance in their power. . . .

. . . The treaty, if signed, will bring together in alliance against war the free nations of the North Atlantic community which share a common heritage, a common civilization, a common belief in the purposes and principles of the charter of the United Nations and a common desire to live in peace with all peoples and all governments. . . .

This treaty is to be far more than an old-fashioned military alliance. It is based on the common belief of the North Atlantic nations in the values and virtues of our Christian civilization. It is based on our common determination to strengthen our free institutions and to promote conditions of stability and well-being. It is based on the belief that we have in our collective manpower, in our collective natural resources, in our collective industrial potential and industrial know-how, that which would make us a very formidable enemy for any possible aggressor to attack.

★ ★ ★ ★ ★

This is, of course, a serious step for this young nation, but I think it is a step that will implement the desire of all the Canadian people that civilized Christian nations should at some time abandon trial by might for the rule of law.

From Canada, Parliament, *Debates of the House of Commons, 1949 (Ottawa)*, in Mackirdy et al., *Changing Perspectives in Canadian History*, (Toronto: Dent, 1971).

1. How does St. Laurent describe the two forces vying for control in Europe?
2. Discuss his argument for the creation of a collective security league.
3. To what extent do you think the basic premise for NATO's existence changed in the past forty years?

McCarthyism

No individual capitalized more effectively upon the anti-Soviet paranoia in the United States during the late 1940s and early 1950s than did Senator Joseph McCarthy. McCarthy energized an otherwise flagging political career by announcing in a speech in Wheeling, West Virginia, that he had in his hand the names of over two hundred known Communists in the State department. McCarthy's claims were eventually exposed to be inaccurate and widely over-stated and he was censured by the Senate for bringing that body into "dishonour and disrepute." In the meantime, however, his accusations destroyed careers and lives. The following excerpt provides a taste of the McCarthy approach.

I finally arrived at the conclusion that the only way to clean out the State Department, or any other Department which is infested with Communists, is not by the passage of any additional law. . . .

I have gone over it. Let me say, before starting, that I shall submit quite a large number of names. I think they are of importance. They all worked for the State Department at one time or another. Some are not there at the present time. Many of them have gone into work which is connected closely with the Department, for example, foreign trade, and some branches of the Maritime Commission. . . .

That is part of the usual modus operandi. If there is one Communist in the Department, he will get some other individual to recommend another Communist so that the breed can be increased. . . .

Next, Mr. President, I come to case No. 81. I think this individual has been doing this Nation untold damage because of the high position she holds in the Voice of America. This individual was in the Voice of America project, in the New York office, until some time ago. She was transferred to Europe, technically under control of the Commanding General, in the same type of work as the Voice of America, and subsequently the entire project was transferred back to the State Department, and she is today in the State Department. . . .

The file in this case contains a wealth of information indicating that this individual is an extremely dangerous and active Communist, completely disloyal to the United States, and loyal to Soviet Russia. Much of the information here, however, was given in strictest confidence but I shall try to give somewhat of a picture of this person.

It is perhaps sufficient to point out that the witnesses without exception have stated in essence that this individual has collected in her office a mixture of fellow travelers and pseudo liberals and outright Communists. These witnesses indicate that the group is close knit and attempts a vicious character assassination of anyone who attempts to disagree with them, and apparently rather successfully so. . . .

Mr. President, since this paper was dictated night before last I find that she is back in the State Department.

Immediate steps should be taken, in my opinion, to obtain not only the discharge but the prosecution of this individual.

From Allen J. Matusow, ed., *Joseph R. McCarthy*, (Englewood Cliffs, Prentice-Hall Inc., 1970).

1. In his outline of case 81, discuss McCarthy's use of rumour and innuendo rather than fact to prove his case.
2. Why was McCarthy able to wield so much influence over the political events of the period? Through further research, analyse the factors leading to the rise and subsequent fall of this demagogue.

Korea, 1950

The American strategy for the containment of communism faced its first crisis in June 1950. When North Korean troops launched a major offensive against their southern countrymen the United States was confronted with a problem. The choice was not over whether to intervene, but how. The decision to take the matter to the Security Council was based, in part, upon a recognition that the current Soviet boycott of that body would allow for speedy passage of a resolution of support.

This first excerpt is a statement issued by President Harry Truman to the American people, but it is also directed to the members of the UN Security Council.

In Korea, the Government forces, which were armed to prevent border raids and to preserve internal security, were attacked by invading forces from North Korea. The Security Council of the United Nations called upon the invading troops to cease hostilities and to withdraw to the 38th Parallel. This they have not done, but on the contrary, have pressed the attack. The Security Council called upon all members of the United Nations to render every assistance to the United Nations in the execution of this resolution. In these circumstances, I have ordered United States air and sea forces to give the Korean Government troops cover and support.

The attack upon Korea makes it plain beyond all doubt that communism has passed beyond the use of subversion to conquer independent nations and will now use armed invasion and war. It has defied the orders of the Security Council of the United Nations issued to preserve international peace and security. . . .

I know that all members of the United Nations will consider carefully the consequences of this latest aggression in Korea in defiance of the Charter of the United Nations. A return to the rule of force in international affairs would have far-reaching effects. The United States will continue to uphold the rule of law. . . .

From *Department of State Bulletin*, XXIII, No. 574 (July 3, 1950), in Thomas Brockway, ed., *Basic Documents in U.S. Foreign Policy*, (Princeton: Van Nostrand, 1957).

The United States was committed to aiding Korea regardless of the UN position on the war. For Canada, however, the issue was not so clear-cut. Without United Nations intervention, it is doubtful whether Canada would have sent troops at all. In his book The Diplomacy of Constraint: Canada, the Korean War, and the United States, *political scientist Denis Stairs comments upon the impact of Canadian involvement in the conflict.*

The North Korean attack was . . . perceived in the west, and especially in the United States, as an aggression authorized, if not actually engineered, by the Soviet Union. In accordance, therefore, with the view that "communism" had to be firmly opposed wherever and whenever it attempted to expand, the American government unilaterally decided to intervene in the hostilities and counter the North Korean assault. As an important but not crucial adjunct of its policy, it sought to take the United Nations with it, acquiring in the process a substantial measure of international legitimacy for its cause, together with a smaller portion of military support for its forces.

The American recourse to the Security Council in June 1950 nevertheless had profound implications for Canada, for without this formal involvement of the United Nations the government in Ottawa would no more have embroiled itself in the conflict in Korea than it did later in the war in Vietnam. To this extent American policy-makers were very successful in recruiting, through the UN, active support of a foreign government (Canada's was of course only one among several) that would otherwise have remained aloof. The price the Americans had to pay, and the advantage the Canadians (along with others who were similarly affected) were able to gain, was a measure of participation in the formulation of allied, or "United Nations" policy. . . .

From Denis Stairs, *The Diplomacy of Constraint: Canada, the Korean War, and the United States* (Toronto: University of Toronto Press, 1974), in P.W. Bennett, *Emerging Identities*, (Toronto: Prentice-Hall, 1986).

1. Discuss Truman's use of Cold War rhetoric in his account of events in Korea.
2. What price does Stairs indicate that the United States had to pay for international involvement in Korea?
3. What significant "lessons" did the United States and Canada learn from their involvement in Korea?

Suez, 1956

To some observers the Suez Crisis marked the peak of United Nations' influence in global affairs. For the first time Canada was caught in the middle of a conflict involving its two closest allies, the United States and Britain.

When on November 2nd the United States called for an immediate cease-fire, Canada abstained. Later, in an explanation of his reasons for taking this position, Lester B. Pearson outlined his counter-proposal for the creation of a United Nations Security Force to maintain the peace. The next day negotiations began in earnest to set up such a force. In this first excerpt, Pearson explains Canada's abstention.

This resolution does provide for a cease-fire, and I admit that that is of first importance and urgency. But, alongside a cease-fire and a withdrawal of troops, it does not provide for any steps to be taken by the United Nations for a peace settlement, without which a cease-fire will be only of temporary value at best. Surely, we should have used this opportunity to link a cease-fire to the absolute necessity of a political settlement in Palestine and for the Suez. . . .

★ ★ ★ ★ ★

I believe that there is another omission from this resolution to which attention has also already been directed. The armed forces of Israel and Egypt are to withdraw, or, if you like, to return to the armistice lines, where presumably, if this is done, they will once again face each other in fear and hatred. What then? What then, six months from now? Are we going to go through all this again? . . .

I therefore would have liked to see a provision in this resolution—and this had been mentioned by previous speakers—authorizing the Secretary-General to begin to make arrangements with member governments for a United Nations force large enough to keep these borders at peace while a political settlement is being worked out. I regret exceedingly that time has not been given to follow up this idea, which was mentioned also by the representative of the United Kingdom in his first speech . . . My own Government would be glad to recommend Canadian participation in such a United Nations force, a truly international peace and police force.

Abridged from text quoted in James G. Eayrs, *The Commonwealth and Suez: A Documentary Survey.* (Oxford: Oxford University Press, 1964).

Athough Lester Pearson would eventually receive a Nobel Peace Prize for his efforts, not all Canadians supported his stance. The following excerpts are editorials from the Toronto Globe and Mail, *written at the height of the crisis.*

The Canadian Government added nothing to its prestige—or to Canada's—by its conduct at the week's emergency meeting of the United Nations General Assembly. External Affairs Minister Pearson did not actually cast Canada's vote against the Anglo-French effort to restore peace in the Middle East, but his abstention from voting had the same effect—assisting, in a passive way, the adoption of a United States resolution urging the British and French to withdraw.

After the vote had been called, with Canada and five other nations abstaining, Mr. Pearson got up and explained. The Canadian delegation, he said, found the U.S. sponsored resolution "inadequate"; it called for all the nations involved in the Middle East fighting to lay down their arms—but offered nothing beyond that, no means of ensuring the arms would remain laid down.

★ ★ ★ ★ ★

Mr. Pearson wants no more of this nonsense; hence his proposal for a Middle East police force that would maintain order while a permanent settlement was being worked out between Israel and her neighbours. But why a UN police force? No such body exists, or has any prospect of coming into existence. It would have been more practical to suggest a force drawn from the North Atlantic Treaty Organization—which at least has men and arms.

From MacKirdy, et al., *Changing Perspectives in Canadian History,* (Toronto: Dent, 1971).

And why did the External Affairs Minister delay his criticism of the U.S. resolution until it had gone to a vote and been adopted; . . . Had he spoken before the resolution was voted upon, it could have been amended as he suggested . . .

It is not as if the idea of a Middle East police force hit Mr. Pearson suddenly, while the votes were being taken. He proposed it himself—had he forgotten?—in a House of Commons speech away back last February: saying then, as he said at the UN this week, that Canada would be willing to contribute to such a force. And this newspaper has been pressing the need of a Middle East force for the last five years. . . .

From the Toronto *Globe and Mail*, "Mr. Pearson Abstains," November 3, 1956.

Some of the extreme statements coming from some of the Opposition members in the Canadian Parliament—and the Government's angry reaction thereto—are giving the impression of a cleavage on foreign policy far greater than needs to exist. . . . Thus, the Government is stressing its deep attachment to the United Nations—all it has done was out of loyalty to the UN—and milking its proposal of a Middle East police force for all that proposal is worth.

For much more, in fact, than it is worth. The suggestion of a UN force was simply an expedient plucked out of thin air by a Government anxious to rescue itself from a position it should never have been in to start with. Ottawa has had no real confidence in the UN as an instrument of collective security; that is why, for almost ten years, the whole core of its stated foreign policy has been the North Atlantic Treaty Organization. By joining (indeed, it claims to have invented) NATO, the Canadian Government placed on record its lack of faith in the UN.

From "Our Only Real Hope", *Globe and Mail*, 29 November 1956, p.5, in MacKirdy, et al.,*Changing Perspectives in Canadian History*, (Toronto: Dent, 1971).

Reporting to the House of Commons, Pearson outlined the process that led to the eventual creation of the force.

On Saturday, November 3 . . . The Assembly was to meet at eight o'clock that evening. On that occasion I did produce a Canadian resolution for the setting up of a United Nations Emergency Force for this particular situation. . . .

It was a very short resolution, and it asked the Secretary-General merely to submit, within forty-eight hours, something we had been unable to do anything about for ten years, namely, a plan for setting up an emergency international United Nations police force with the consent of the governments concerned. . . .

We obtained 57 votes as sponsors for the resolution. There were 19 abstentions. Nobody voted against us. The United Kingdom and France did not find it possible to vote for that resolution at that time but they have indicated, both privately and publicly, their great appreciation of the initiative which resulted in its being adopted and they have also stated their support for it since then. . . .

Then on November 4 we started to work. Canada had something to do with this work because we were the sponsors of the resolution and had a certain obligation to help the Secretary-General to carry it out. We started to work on organizing a United Nations police force or at least to form the basis of the organization and report back in forty-eight hours. . . .

From J.M. Bliss, "Canada and the United States", *Canadian History in Documents, 1763-1966*, (Toronto: Ryerson Press, 1966).

1. Comment on Lester Pearson's explanation of the Canadian abstention on the American resolution.
2. Write a letter to the editor of the *Globe and Mail* in which you either support or oppose its editorial position on the Canadian action.
3. Discuss the following statement: "The United Nations Emergency Force is a prime example of the role that the United Nations should be playing in international affairs."

NORAD: The Case for Continental Defence

As a logical extension of the Permanent Joint Board of Defence established in 1940, the governments of Canada and the United States announced the signing of the NORAD agreement in August 1957. It created the North American Air Defence Command, a bilateral system for continental air defence. Under NORAD, Canada was relegated to the permanent role of junior partner in the air defence of its own territory. In the following excerpts, Prime Minister John Diefenbaker defends the agreement in the face of criticism from the leader of the opposition, Lester Pearson.

Mr. Diefenbaker: Collaboration in air defence was undertaken soon after the close of the last war, and a joint effort was made to develop a comprehensive air defence system for the common defence of North America. . . . In order to work out these intricate air defence problems of an operational and scientific nature, a joint Canadian-United States military study group consisting of service officers and scientists was set up.

One result of studies conducted by this group was a recommendation made to the chiefs of staff of both countries in December, 1956, for the establishment of a joint headquarters to provide for the operational control of the air defence of Canada and the United States. These recommendations of the joint study group were approved by the chiefs of staff of both countries and the United States Secretary of Defence approved these measures early in April.

This bilateral arrangement within the Canada-United States regional planning group of NATO is a further step in achieving the agreed NATO objectives for the Canada-United States regional planning group. . . .

★ ★ ★ ★ ★

Mr. Pearson: Interesting as his statement has been, Mr. Speaker, it certainly has not answered a great many of the questions in our minds concerning particularly the North American command, or NORAD, as it is called, and the implications of the action that has been taken by the government in regard to continental defence under that command. I refer to military implications and indeed political implications.

From MacKirdy, et al., *Changing Perspectives in Canadian History*, (Toronto: Dent, 1971).

1. How does Diefenbaker use the NATO agreement as justification for NORAD?
2. Pearson observed that NORAD has both military and political implications for Canada. In what ways is this so?
3. Defend or refute the following thesis:
"Dependence upon NORAD has cost Canada any hope of national sovereignty in the defence of its own territory."

The Vietnam Experience

Following the end of World War II, the United States maintained an active interest in the Far East. Aside from its military occupation of Japan, the United States focussed its attention on growing communist strength in China, Korea, and French Indochina.

As French power waned in the region, American policy makers weighed the merits of intervening themselves. The following excerpts are taken from the Pentagon Papers. *In 1967 Secretary of Defense Robert McNamara commissioned a top-secret history of the United States' role in Indochina. The final product consisted of forty-seven volumes containing over seven thousand pages of narrative and support documents and tracing American involvement from the closing days of World War II to May 1968. The* New York Times *obtained the bulk of the* Pentagon Papers, *and began publishing excerpts in June 1971. The government attempted to block publication of material but in an historic Supreme Court decision that same month, the Justices voted six to three that the public had a right to know and that the press had the right to inform them.*

In February 1945 an American diplomat stationed in Hanoi cabled the following message to the State Department in Washington.

Ho Chi Minh handed me 2 letters addressed to President of USA, China, Russia and Britain identical copies of which were stated to have been forwarded to other governments named. In 2 letters to Ho Chi Minh request USA as one of the United Nations to support idea of Annamese independence according to Philippines example, to examine the case of the Annamese, and to take steps necessary to maintenance of world peace which is being endangered by French efforts to reconquer Indochina. . . .

Outline of accomplishments of Annamese Government in Tonkin including popular elections, abolition of undesirable taxes, expansion of education and resumption as far as possible of normal economic activities:

Request to 4 powers: (1) to intervene and stop the war in Indochina in order to mediate fair settlement and (2) to bring the Indochinese issue before the United Nations organization. The petition ends with the statement that Annamese ask for full independence in fact and that in interim while awaiting UNO decision the Annamese will continue to fight the reestablishment of French imperialism. Letters and petition will be transmitted to Department soonest.

From Neil Sheehan, et al., *The Pentagon Papers*, (New York: Bantam Books, 1971).

U.S. Goals in Southeast Asia, 1952

In 1952 the National Security Council outlined the following objectives designed to prevent "the countries of Southeast Asia from passing into the communist orbit."

Objective

1. To prevent the countries of Southeast Asia from passing into the communist orbit, and to assist them to develop will and ability to resist communism from within and without and to contribute to the strengthening of the free world.

General Considerations

2. Communist domination, by whatever means, of all Southeast Asia would seriously endanger in the short term, and critically endanger in the longer term, United States security interests.

a. The loss of any of the countries of Southeast Asia to communist aggression would have critical psychological, political and economic consequences. In the absence of effective and timely counteraction, the loss of any single country would probably lead to relatively swift submission to or an alignment with communism by the remaining countries of this group. . . .

Courses of Action

Southeast Asia

7. With respect to Southeast Asia, the United States should:

a. Strengthen propaganda and cultural activities, as appropriate in relation to the area to foster increased alignment of the people with the free world. . . .

j. Make clear to the American people the importance of Southeast Asia to the security of the United States so that they may be prepared for any of the courses of action proposed herein.

Indochina

8. With respect to Indochina the United States should:

a. Continue to promote international support for the three Associated States.

b. Continue to assure the French that the U.S. regards the French effort in Indochina as one of great strategic importance in the general international interest rather than in the purely French interest, and as essential to the security of the free world, not only in the Far East but in the Middle East and Europe as well. . . .

(9) In the absence of large scale Chinese Communist intervention in Indochina, the United States should:

a. Provide increased aid on a high priority basis for the French Union forces without relieving French authorities of their basic military responsibility for the defense of the Associated States in order to:

(1) Assist in developing indigenous armed forces which will eventually be capable of maintaining internal security without assistance from French units.

(2) Assist the French Union forces to maintain progress in the restoration of internal security against the Viet Minh.

(3) Assist the forces of France and the Associated States to defend Indochina against Chinese Communist aggression. . . .

13. In the event the concurrence of the United Kingdom and France to expanded military action against Communist China is not obtained, the United States should consider taking unilateral action. . . .

From Neil Sheehan, et al., *The Pentagon Papers*, (New York: Bantam Books, 1971).

1. Summarize Ho Chi Minh's requests to the Americans.
2. Outline the "domino theory" as explained in the NSC briefing document.
3. Comment on the policy proposals contained in the NSC document.

The Canadian Connection, 1964-65

In August 1964 the United States government sent the following request to External Affairs. In it the U.S. sent instructions to Blair Seaborn, Canadian representative on the International Control Commission in Vietnam. Seaborn made two secret visits to Hanoi in an attempt to offer a "personal" explanation of American motives in the region. In this excerpt the detailed American instructions provide insight into their view of the conflict.

Canadians are urgently asked to have Seaborn during August visit make following points (as having been conveyed to him by U.S. Government since August 6):

A. Re Tonkin Gulf actions, which almost certainly will come to:

1. The DRV has stated that Hon Ngu and Hon Me islands were attacked on July 30. It should be noted that the USS MADDOX was all of that day and into the afternoon of the next day, over 100 miles south of those islands, in international waters near the 17th parallel, and that the DRV attack on MADDOX took place on August 2nd, more than two days later. Neither the MADDOX or any other destroyer was in any way associated with any attack on the DRV islands.

2. Regarding the August 4 attack by the DRV on the two U.S. destroyers, the Americans were and are at a complete loss to understand the DRV motive. . . .

3. The American response was directed solely to patrol craft and installations acting in direct support of them. As President Johnson stated: "Our response for the present will be limited and fitting." . . .

5. Mr. Seaborn should again stress that U.S. policy is simply that North Vietnam should contain itself and its ambitions within the territory allocated to its administration by the 1954 Geneva Agreements. He should stress that U.S. policy in South Vietnam is to preserve the integrity of that state's territory against guerrilla subversion.

6. He should reiterate that the U.S. does not seek military bases in the area and that the U.S. is not seeking to overthrow the Communist regime in Hanoi.

7. He should repeat that the U.S. is fully aware of the degree to which Hanoi controls and directs the guerrilla action in South Vietnam and that the U.S. holds Hanoi directly responsible for that action. He should similarly indicate U.S. awareness of North Vietnamese control over the Pathet Lao movement in Laos and the degree of North Vietnamese involvement in that country. He should specifically indicate U.S. awareness of North Vietnamese violations of Laotian territory along the infiltration route into South Vietnam.

8. Mr. Seaborn can again refer to the many examples of U.S. policy in tolerance of peaceful coexistence with Communist regimes, such as Yugoslavia, Poland, etc. He can hint at the economic and other benefits which have been accrued to those countries because their policy of Communism has confirmed itself to the development of their own national territories and has not sought to expand into other areas.

9. Mr. Seaborn should conclude with the following new points:

a. That the events of the past few days should add credibility to the statement made last time, that "U.S. public and official patience with North Vietnamese aggression is growing extremely thin."

b. That the U.S. Congressional Resolution was passed with near unanimity, strongly re-affirming the unity and determination of the U.S. Government and people not only with respect to any further attacks on U.S. military forces but more broadly to continue to oppose firmly, by all necessary means, DRV efforts to subvert and conquer South Vietnam and Laos.

c. That the U.S. has come to the view that the DRV role in South Vietnam and Laos is critical. If the DRV persists in its present course, it can expect to continue to suffer the consequences.

d. That the DRV knows what it must do if the peace is to be restored.

e. That the U.S. has ways and means of measuring the DRV's participation in, and direction and control of, the war on South Vietnam and in Laos and will be carefully watching the DRV's response to what Mr. Seaborn is telling them. . . .

From Neil Sheehan, et al., *The Pentagon Papers*, (New York: Bantam Books, 1971).

In April 1965, Prime Minister Lester Pearson spoke out against the U.S. bombing of North Vietnam in a speech at Temple University. After the speech the prime minister went on to a scheduled meeting with President Lyndon Johnson at Camp David. This excerpt is part of an account of that visit.

President Lyndon Johnson failed to appear at the helicopter landing area for Lester Pearson's arrival at Camp David. Like pallbearers, two advisers, who showed up in his place, escorted the uneasy Canadian prime minister to their master's cabin. Johnson greeted Pearson civilly there, but unmasked a truer disposition at the sound of newsmen's cameras clicking behind him. He turned to press secretary George Reedy. "Get those . . . out of here!"

Pearson knew the reason for his host's foul nature. In a speech in Philadelphia the previous evening, April 2, 1965, Pearson had denounced Johnson's decision to begin Operation Rolling Thunder—the bombing of North Vietnam. Coming from a friend and ally like Pearson, the dissent angered Johnson. Coming in the United States, "my own backyard," it enraged him.

As the luncheon dragged mercilessly on, Pearson finally chose to throw the raw meat on the table. "Well," he offered daintily, "what did you think of my speech?" LBJ's growl was audible. "Awwwful." He stretched his large hand across the table, clutched the prime minister by the upper arm, and led him on to the terrace where there was room for wrath. Striding the porch, his arms sawing the air, his sulphurous vocabulary contaminating it, Johnson ripped into Pearson full-voltage. The prime minister had betrayed the president. He had joined the ranks of ignorant liberals, "those know-nothing do-gooders," like "Walter Lippmann."

"Okay, you don't want us there [Vietnam], we can clear out, really clear out and then see what happens." Johnson was livid at the insinuation of Pearson and others that he was hawkish. The Pentagon, he stormed, had been advising him for weeks to fry the enemy area with nuclear weapons. But he had resisted. "Not bad for a warmonger!" . . .

For more than an hour he tore on until ultimately, in a piece of bilateral diplomacy knowing no equal, he moved beyond the realm of words. Having pinned the much smaller Pearson against the railing, the president of the United States grabbed him by the shirt collar, twisted it and lifted the shaken prime minister by the neck. The verbal abuse continued in a venomous torrent. "You pissed on my rug!" he thundered. . . .

Then it was time to meet the press, time to let the world in on the developments of the day. First up was President Johnson. "We had a general discussion," he said. "A friendly one." Pearson was next: "I haven't much to say except that it has been a very pleasant couple of hours and I am grateful to the President for giving me the chance to come to Camp David." . . .

Canadians went to bed that night satisfied, as usual, that all was well with the president and the prime minister, and that all was well with the Canada-U.S. relationship. In the prime minister's office there was relief and not a wholesale rush to amend the mistaken media reports. It was absolutely mandatory that the real story not get out. If it did, if Canadians discovered that the president had physically manhandled their prime minister, if they found out that their prime minister had been treated like the leader of one of the Soviet Union's eastern satellites, the damage to the bilateral bliss would be enormous. Irreparable. . . .

From Lawrence Martin, *The Presidents and the Prime Ministers*, (New York: Doubleday, 1987). Copyright 1987 by Literary Research, Inc. Reprinted by permission of Doubleday, a division of Bantam, Doubleday, Dell Publishing Group, Inc.

1. What concessions did the United States agree to make to North Vietnam?
2. To what extent did the Seaborn mission represent a threat to Hanoi?
3. Why might the incident between Pearson and Johnson have had irreparable damage on bilateral relations?

The Ronning Mission, 1966

Chester Ronning was the son of a Christian missionary to China and had a long and distinguished career as a Canadian diplomat. In 1966 the Canadian government sent Ronning to Hanoi to offer assistance in reaching a peace settlement with the United States.

In this excerpt, the purpose of the Ronning's mission is questioned in the House of Commons. It is interesting to note the parallel between the questions asked and the purposes of the still-secret Seaborn missions of 1964.

Statement to the House of Commons on July 8, 1966, by the Secretary of State for External Affairs, Mr. Paul Martin. (Extracts)
My right honourable friend [Mr. Diefenbaker] spoke of Mr. Ronning's two visits to Hanoi. . . .

First, I have said that this was a Canadian initiative and that it was carried out by Mr. Ronning on the instructions of the Canadian Government, and not on the instructions in any way of any other government. . . .

Second, I should like the House to understand that the assignment we have taken on is essentially in the nature of a good offices assignment. . . .

Third, I would like to restate the ultimate object of this initiative. It has seemed to us that, if a beginning is to be made in the long and patient process which we hope will lead to ultimate peace in Vietnam, we must find a basis on which both sides would be prepared to see such a beginning made. . . .

I do not wish to give the House a misleading impression of our results so far. We have not achieved any spectacular results and I think I can quite frankly say that we have had no illusions as to the pace at which progress was likely to be possible. . . .

I do not think, in a situation where a failure of communication may be crucial, we can discount the significance of such a channel for the time when the circumstances for the solution of Vietnam conflict are ripe.

From Arthur E. Blanchette, ed., *Canadian Foreign Policy 1966-1976*, (Toronto: Macmillan, 1980.)

Canada's Vietnam Policy, 1967

In early 1967 a group of professors from the University of Toronto personally delivered a letter to the prime minister and minister of external affairs expressing their concerns about Canada's policy with regard to the war in Vietnam. The first excerpt is taken from the letter and the second is from Pearson's reply.

The fact that the cruel devastation of Vietnam has been going on for such a long time does not render the continuing rain of explosives and chemicals more acceptable.

The fact that so many have already pleaded so often for an end to this terror does not make the suffering of the uncountable victims more bearable, nor does it make the situation less dangerous. Indeed, with each escalation, the possibility of Chinese intervention and a world war becomes more real.

We call upon the Canadian Government to demand, unequivocally, an immediate, unconditional and permanent end to the United States bombings of North and South Vietnam, and the earliest possible withdrawal of U.S. military forces from the area.

We further call upon the Canadian Government to reveal all military production contracts related in any way to the Vietnam war, and to consider following the example of Sweden in refusing to sell arms to the U.S. until this intervention ceases.

From *External Affairs*, Ottawa, DEA, April 1967.

I need hardly tell you that the situation in Vietnam is one to which the Government attaches great importance in the formulation of Canadian foreign policy. That importance reflects not only the implications of the problem for world peace and the international processes of change by peaceful means but also the concern which the Government shares with responsible citizens at the toll the hostilities are taking in terms of human suffering as well as of wasted resources and lost opportunities for human betterment. On these points, I think, there can be few differences of opinion.

The real problem, of course, for governments no less than for individuals, is in translating hopes and convictions into constructive action. Constructive action, in turn, depends on a realistic assessment of the nature of the situation which it is desired to change and of the likely consequences of any given action, whether public or private, in relation to the problem. Therefore, at every stage, we must ask whether any particular step is likely to advance the issue any distance towards a solution—or even towards a more satisfactory state of affairs. Any answer to this question becomes doubly difficult in the context of problems where the direct involvement and the direct responsibility for action rest essentially with others. . . .

1. Based upon these three documents, write an analytical summary of Canada's policy with regard to the Vietnam war.

Operation Rolling Thunder

In August 1966 the Pentagon Papers *presented an analysis of the current impact of American bombing upon North Vietnam. In spite of repeated raids against military and industrial targets, the report indicts the bombings for having had "no measurable direct effect on Hanoi's ability to mount and support military operations in the South."*

1. As of July 1966 the U.S. bombing of North Vietnam (NVN) had had no measurable direct effect on Hanoi's ability to mount and support military operations in the South at the current level.

Although the political constraints seem clearly to have reduced the effectiveness of the bombing program, its limited effect on Hanoi's ability to provide such support cannot be explained solely on that basis. The countermeasures introduced by Hanoi effectively reduced the impact of U.S. bombing. More fundamentally, however, North Vietnam has basically a subsistence agricultural economy that presents a difficult and unrewarding target system for air attack. . . .

2. Since the initiation of the ROLLING THUNDER program the damage to facilities and equipment in North Vietnam has been more than offset by the increased flow of military and economic aid, largely from the USSR and Communist China. . . .

3. The aspects of the basic situation that have enabled Hanoi to continue its support of military operations in the South and to neutralize the impact of U.S. bombing by passing the economic costs to other Communist countries are not likely to be altered by reducing the present geographic constraints, mining Haiphong and the principal harbors in North Vietnam, increasing the number of armed reconnaissance sorties and otherwise expanding the U.S. air offensive along the lines now contemplated in military recommendations and planning studies. . . .

4. While conceptually it is reasonable to assume that some limit may be imposed on the scale of military activity that Hanoi can maintain in the South by continuing the ROLLING THUNDER program at the present, or some higher level of effort, there appears to be no basis for defining that limit in concrete terms or, for concluding that the present scale of VC/NVN activities in the field have approached that limit.

The available evidence clearly indicates that Hanoi has been infiltrating military forces and supplies into South Vietnam at an accelerated rate during the current year. Intelligence estimates have concluded that North Vietnam is capable of substantially increasing its support.

5. The indirect effects of the bombing on the will of the North Vietnamese to continue fighting and on their leaders' appraisal of the prospective gains and costs of maintaining the present policy have not shown themselves in any tangible way. Furthermore, we have not discovered any basis for concluding that the indirect punitive effects of bombing will prove decisive in these respects. . . .

From Neil Sheehan, et al., *The Pentagon Papers*, (New York: Bantam Books, 1971).

1. What reasons does the report present for North Vietnam's ability to withstand the bombings?
2. To what extent does the report feel that further bombing will have a greater impact?
3. Based on this information, speculate as to why the United States continued to bomb North Vietnam after August 1966.

Vietnam and the End of the Johnson Presidency

The war in Vietnam consumed the presidency of Lyndon Johnson. Mired down in an unwinnable conflict abroad, and under seige by political rivals at home, on March 31, 1968, the president went on national television to announce that he would not seek reelection. His reason for not running, he stated, was so that he could devote his time to bringing the war to an end. In this emotional speech he outlined his view of the conflict.

Good evening, my fellow Americans:

Tonight I want to speak to you of peace in Vietnam and Southeast Asia.

No other question so preoccupies our people. No other dream so absorbs the 250 million human beings who live in that part of the world. No other goal motivates American policy in Southeast Asia.

For years, representatives of our Government and others have traveled the world—seeking to find a basis for peace talks. . . .

I believe that a peaceful Asia is far nearer to reality because of what America has done in Vietnam. I believe that the men who endure the dangers of battle—fighting there for us tonight—are helping the entire world avoid far greater conflicts, far wider wars, far more destruction, than this one.

The peace that will bring them home someday will come. Tonight I have offered the first in what I hope will be a series of mutual moves toward peace.

I pray that it will not be rejected by the leaders of North Vietnam. I pray that they will accept it as a means by which the sacrifices of their own people may be ended. And I ask your help and your support, my fellow citizens, for this effort to reach across the battlefield toward an early peace.

Finally, my fellow Americans, let me say this:

Of those to whom much is given, much is asked. I cannot say and no man could say that no more will be asked of us.

Yet, I believe that now, no less than when the decade began, this generation of Americans is willing to "pay any price, bear any burden, meet any hardship, support any friend, oppose any foe to assure the survival and the success of liberty."

Since those words were spoken by John F. Kennedy, the people of America have kept that compact with mankind's noblest cause.

And we shall continue to keep it.

Yet, I believe that we must always be mindful of this one thing, whatever the trials and the tests ahead. The ultimate strength of our country and our cause will lie not in powerful weapons or indefinite resources or boundless wealth, but will lie in the unity of our people.

This I believe very deeply.

From *Public Papers of the Presidents: Johnson, 1968,* (Washington, D.C, 1969).

1. Account for the emphasis in Johnson's speech not upon victory, but upon peace.

2. Comment upon the president's concentration on internal rather than external concerns.

3. Compare Johnson's position in 1968 with that of the U.S. policy objectives outlined in 1952.

Directions in Canadian Foreign Policy: the 1960s, 1970s, and 1980s

Canadian and American foreign policy followed roughly the same path during the late 1940s and 1950s. By 1960, however, many Canadians began to look in new directions.

In this excerpt from James Minifie's book Peacemaker or Powder-Monkey, *the author makes a case for a neutralist foreign policy for Canada.*

This book is written in the belief that Canada can contribute more to the defence of democracy, the West, the North American continent and to its own defence as a neutral than as a member of a lop-sided alliance in NORAD, or of the straggling military consortium into which NATO has been debased. I believe that Canada can speak to the world in the language of freedom and peace to inspire mankind, much as the United States did before the cares of paramountcy, the need to placate dictators, the burden of arming and subsidizing half the world, and the objective and subjective handicaps of wealth muffled the accents of Jefferson, Lincoln and Wilson.

★ ★ ★ ★ ★

In the world today Canada, although not a major power, may play a part if it chooses as inspiring and decisive as that of the United States in earlier times. But not as the client of a power committed to the struggle for paramountcy. An impregnable neutralism must be its warranty of independence.

From James M. Minifie, *Peacemaker or Powdermonkey,* (Toronto: McClelland and Stewart, 1960). Used by permission of the Canadian Publishers, McClelland and Stewart, Toronto.

In 1969 Prime Minister Pierre Trudeau unveiled a new "Canadianized" approach to the country's military commitments. Rejecting non-alignment, Trudeau nonetheless called for a substantial reduction in Canada's military presence in Europe. In addition, he moved to gain greater Canadian control over its NORAD commitments.

A Canadian defence policy, employing in an effective fashion the highly skilled and professional Canadian Armed Forces, will contribute to the maintenance of world peace. It will also add to our own sense of purpose as a nation and give renewed enthusiasm and a feeling of direction to the members of the armed forces. It will provide the key to the flexible employment of Canadian forces in a way which will permit them to make their best contribution in accordance with Canada's particular needs and requirements.

The Government has rejected any suggestion that Canada assume a non-aligned or neutral role in world affairs. Such an option would have meant the withdrawal by Canada from its present alliances and the termination of all co-operative military arrangements with other countries. We have decided in this fashion because we think it necessary and wise to continue to participate in an appropriate way in collective security arrangements with other states in the interests of Canada's national security and in defence of the values we share with our friends.

Canada requires armed forces within Canada in order to carry out a wide range of activities involving the defence of the country, and also supplementing the civil authorities and contributing to national development. Properly equipped and deployed, our forces will provide an effective multi-purpose maritime coastal shield and they will carry out operations necessary for the defence of North American airspace in co-operation with the United States. Abroad, our forces will be capable of playing important roles in collective security and in peace-keeping activities. . . .

Canada is a partner in two collective defence arrangements, which, though distinct, are complementary. These are the North Atlantic Treaty Organization and the North American Air Defence Command. For 20 years NATO has contributed to the maintenance of world peace through its stabilizing influence in Europe. NATO continues to contribute to peace by reducing the likelihood of a major conflict breaking out in Europe, where, because the vital interests of the two major powers are involved, any outbreak of hostilities could easily escalate into a war of world proportions. At the same time, it is the declared aim of NATO to foster improvements in East-West relations. . . .

The Canadian force commitment for deployment with NATO in Europe beyond this period will be discussed with our allies at the meeting of the Defence Planning Committee of NATO in May. The Canadian Government intends, in consultation with Canada's allies, to take early steps to bring about a planned and phased reduction of the size of the Canadian forces in Europe.

We intend, as well, to continue to co-operate effectively with the United States in the defence of North America. We shall, accordingly, seek early occasions for detailed discussions with the United States Government of the whole range of problems involved in our mutual co-operation in defence matters on this continent. To the extent that it is feasible, we shall endeavour to have those activities within Canada which are essential to North American defence performed by Canadian forces. . . .

From Arthur E. Blanchette, ed., *Canadian Foreign Policy 1966-1976*, The Carleton Library, No. 118 (Toronto: Macmillan, 1980).

Canada and the Reagan Challenge, 1982

Professor Stephen Clarkson raised concerns about Canadian-American relations in his 1982 work Canada and the Reagan Challenge. *In this excerpt he comments on the impact of the economic nationalism of the Trudeau government upon the administration of Ronald Reagan.*

Two factors account for the startling transformation of the Liberal government's orientation between May 1979, when it lost power, and February 1980, when it returned to office. First was the emergence of a new nationalism in certain sectors of the Canadian business community. In all parts of the economy, nationalist refrains, which a decade previously had only been sounded by dissident academic choruses, were now being heard from some of the most successful and aggressive business leaders in the country. . . .

This new thrust in the business community, which took a positive view towards government intervention, found a response in the second transmogrification—a drastic revision in the thinking of the Liberal party after it went into opposition in 1979. . . .

[In the ensuing 1980 election] the Liberals on the stump promised to launch a broad energy policy aimed at self-sufficiency, higher Canadian ownership levels, more industrial benefits for Canadian industry from mega-projects, and a price of energy maintained below world levels. Trudeau also committed his future government to expand the scope of FIRA's activities and to renegotiate the Auto Pact's disastrous imbalances. . . .

. . . The new centralism implied that the government was determined to play a larger role in directing the economy. Although greater government intervention in the economy would necessarily have a great impact on an industry overwhelmingly owned and controlled by American companies, there was no thought among the architects of the new Liberal strategy that their plans would lead them to a confrontation with Washington. Such features of the NEP as the target of 50 per cent Canadian ownership, which were later to be denounced by the *Wall Street Journal* and by enraged oil executives as nationalist and anti-American, were seen by their designers as necessary to achieve the centralizing goal of gaining greater revenues for Ottawa. . . .

The American and Canadian governments had been at loggerheads many times before over one issue or another without any crisis arising. The spat over the Cuban missiles in 1961, the arguments over the duty remission policies for the Canadian automotive industry in 1964, the criticism of the guidelines for American multinational corporations proposed in 1968 had, like many another issue, been resolved without the disputed issues escalating into a full crisis between the two governments. Now that a recentralizing, assertive, state-capitalist government on the banks of the Rideau Canal had set its sights on restructuring its energy industry, and that a remilitarizing, straight-capitalist administration had taken power on the banks of the Potomac River, future disputes might be less easy to reconcile. . . .

From Stephen Clarkson, *Canada and the Reagan Challenge: Crisis in the Canadian-American Relationship* (Toronto: James Lorimer & Company, 1982).

1. What aspects of Canadian government policy would aggravate the United States, according to Clarkson?
2. To what extent did the economic view of the world espoused by the Trudeau government contrast with that of Reaganomics?
3. Compare the economic relationship between Canada and the United States during the Trudeau years with that of the Mulroney administration. To what extent did Conservative government policy directly attempt to remove the economic irritants which divided the two countries?

Manifest Destiny and the Cold War

In the postwar era, American foreign policy in the Western Hemisphere has seen a re-emergence of a strong commitment to the principles of the Monroe Doctrine. During the period the United States has actively intervened in the political affairs of such nations as Cuba, Chile, Grenada, El Salvador, Honduras, Nicaragua, and Panama. In most of these cases American intervention has taken place in the name of keeping communism out of the hemisphere.

Following the Cuban Revolution and the Bay of Pigs fiasco, the United States saw Cuba as an advance base for a Soviet takeover of Latin America and the Caribbean Basin. In October 1962 the world was pushed to the brink of nuclear war over the Missile Crisis. After the fact a number of conflicting views of the crisis emerged.

The Soviet view of the crisis was outlined in December 1962 by Soviet premier Nikita Khruschev.

Flouting generally accepted standards of international relations, the United States reactionary forces have been doing everything from the first day of the victory of the Cuban revolution to overthrow Cuba's revolutionary Government and to restore their domination there. They broke off diplomatic relations with Cuba, were and are conducting subversive activity, established an economic blockade of Cuba. Threatening to apply sanctions, the United States began pressing its allies not only to stop trading with Cuba but even not to make available ships for carrying food to Cuba from the socialist countries which came to the assistance of their brothers. This is an inhuman policy—a desire to starve a whole nation. . . .

Revolutionary Cuba was compelled to take all measures to strengthen her defense. The Soviet Union helped her to build up a strong army standing guard over the achievements of the Cuban people. In view of the mounting threat from the United States, the Government of Cuba in the summer of this year requested the Soviet Government to render further assistance. ... .

What were the aims behind this decision? Naturally, neither we nor our Cuban friends had in mind that this small number of IRBM's, sent to Cuba, would be used for an attack on the United States or any other country.

Our aim was only to defend Cuba. We all saw how the American imperialists were sharpening their knives, threatening Cuba with a massed attack. We could not remain impartial observers in the face of this bandit-like policy, which is contrary to all standards of relations between states and the United Nations Charter. We decided to extend a helping hand to Cuba. We saw a possibility of protecting the freedom-loving people of Cuba by installing rockets there so that the American imperialists, if they really decided to invade, would realize that the war which they threatened to start stood at their own borders, so that they would realize more realistically the dangers of thermonuclear war. . . .

Indeed, had there been no threat of an invasion and had we had assurances that the United States would not invade Cuba, and would restrain its allies from this, had the United States guided itself by this course, there would have been no need for the stationing of our rockets in Cuba.

From *The Worker Supplement*, December 23, 1962, as quoted in Robert A. Divine, ed., *The Cuban Missle Crisis*, (Chicago: Quadrangle Books, 1971).

In response to Nikita Khruschev's statement, American president John F. Kennedy made the following remarks in a nationwide television interview.

I think in that speech this week he [Nikita Khrushchev] showed his awareness of the nuclear age. But of course, the Cuban effort has made it more difficult for us to carry out any successful negotiations, because this was an effort to materially change the balance of power, it was done in secret, steps were taken really to deceive us by every means they could, and they were planning in November to open to the world the fact that they had these missiles so close to the United States; not that they were intending to fire them, because if they were going to get into a nuclear struggle, they have their own missiles in the Soviet Union. But it would have politically changed the balance of power. It would have appeared to, and appearances contribute to reality. So it is going to be some time before it is possible for us to come to any real understanding with Mr. Khrushchev. But I do think his speech shows that he realizes how dangerous a world we live in.

The real problem is the Soviet desire to expand their power and influence. If Mr. Khrushchev would concern himself with the real interests of the people of the Soviet Union, that they have a higher standard of living, to protect his own security, there is no real reason why the United States and the Soviet Union, separated by so many thousands of miles of land and water, both rich countries, both with very energetic people, should not be able to live in peace. . . .

. . . Well, it is difficult. I think, looking back on Cuba, what is of concern is the fact that both governments were so far out of contact, really. I don't think that we expected that he would put the missiles in Cuba, because it would have seemed such an imprudent action for him to take, as it was later proved. Now, he obviously must have thought that he could do it in secret and that the

United States would accept it. So that he did not judge our intentions
accurately. . . .
. . . I think that anybody who looks at the fatality lists on atomic weapons,
and realizes that the Communists have a completely twisted view of the United
States, and that we don't comprehend them, that is what makes life in the sixties hazardous. . . .

From *Public Papers of the Presidents: Kennedy, 1962* (Washington, D.C., 1963).

*Kennedy's brinksmanship had its pacifist critics, who felt that his actions unnecessarily
pushed the country to the brink of war. At the same time, right-wing critics of the
administration, such as David Lowenthal, had their own view of events.*

The apparent vigor of President Kennedy's quarantine of Cuba, and the rapidity with which he effected the withdrawal of Russian missiles, left Americans
with a false impression. Only in contrast to the feebleness of our previous
Cuban policy was this a strong and vigorous act. Given the circumstances, it
was the weakest response open to us. It eliminated the most immediate and
obvious threat, but no more. And in the process it made concessions that will
assist the growth of Communist military power and subversion in this
hemisphere. . . .
  Because of our non-intervention, Khrushchev and Castro could proceed to
contrive a scheme that might have inflicted enormous damage on Western
power, influence and prestige. We cannot know for sure what motivated this
daring innovation in Russian missile policy. Was it to pressure our withdrawal
from bases in Turkey and elsewhere? Was it to prevent our invading Cuba?
Was it to give unmistakable proof of Soviet supremacy? Was the threat of these
nearby missiles meant to paralyze us during some momentous act of aggrandize-
ment in West Berlin, and protect Cuba from our retaliation at the same time?
Considering the nature of the missile move, it is probable that Khrushchev was
playing for the highest stakes. . . .
  Faced with solid evidence of the missile emplacements, what could the President do? . . .
  Here in our hands was the opportunity—only rarely afforded by a wily and
aggressive enemy—to inflict a drastic defeat upon him. The moment of crisis,
the magnitude of the threat to world peace, the incredible deceit practiced upon
the U.S., the heightened awareness and anger of allies and neutrals—all argued
for a comprehensive and decisive solution of the Cuban problem. . . . We
should therefore have demanded the departure of the Russians together with
their "offensive" weapons, and the holding of long-overdue free elections in
Cuba under UN supervision. . . . This policy had its risks, and there is no
assurance that blockade alone, without invasion, would ultimately have sufficed.
But there could be little doubt of the outcome, and we would have acted in full
justice, and consistently with our ideals. . . .
  Nothing closer to an explicit retraction of the Monroe Doctrine has ever been
made by any President.

From David Lowenthal, "U.S. Cuban Policy: Illusion and Reality," *National Review*, XIV (January 29, 1963).

1. Based upon your reading of these three views of the crisis, create your own thesis with regard to the appropriateness of the American response.

The Grenada Adventure, 1983

For the Reagan administration, the successful 1983 invasion of Grenada was no ad hoc adventure. The operation had been carefully planned long before the coup that had overthrown Marxist president Maurice Bishop.

In this 1982 interview, Bishop explained why he felt that the United States was "afraid" of the Grenada experience.

Interviewer: Why do you think that imperialism is so obsessively afraid of the Grenada Revolution, an obsession out of all proportion to the size of the country?

Bishop: There are several reasons for this. The first is the fact that Grenada was the first country in the English-speaking Caribbean to have had a successful revolution, and different US administrations have always shown a mortal fear of any revolutionary process, of any attempt by any people by revolutionary means to overthrow different dictatorships or oligarchies that are oppressing them. These administrations have, of course, conveniently forgotten the history of their own country and their own revolution in 1776. . . .

So for reasons such as these concrete benefits, imperialism is doubly worried and concerned about our revolutionary process, because they fear that the new socio-economic and political path of development which we have embarked upon may prove to be an example to the rest of the region, and therefore the people of the region may begin to press their own governments for a similar process to start in their own countries. Additionally, there is the fact that since the Revolution, Grenada has pursued an independent and nonaligned path, and different US administrations over the years—but in particular this present administration of President Ronald Reagan—is deathly afraid of any independence, of nonaligned commitment in the world, particularly by countries of the Third World, which they feel they have a divine right to dominate and exploit. . . .

Finally, we have gleaned from their own security reports which they have put out—not publicly, but which we have nevertheless seen—other insights. In one of these reports the particular point was made that Grenada's process has two big differences to the other two revolutionary processes in the region, in Cuba and Nicaragua. For on the one hand, we speak the same language—English— as the people of the USA, and on the other hand we have a largely black population. What they have pointed out from this is that the Grenada Revolution therefore has a facility of speaking directly to, and appealing directly in their own language to the people of the USA overall, but more so to the exploited majority. Then in the case of black Americans, meaning something like twenty seven million black people who are a part of the most rejected and oppressed section of the American population, US imperialism has a particular dread that they will develop an extra empathy and rapport with the Grenada Revolution, and from that point of view will pose a threat to their own continuing control and domination of the blacks inside the US. . . .

From Chris Searle, *Grenada: The Struggle Against Destabilization*, (New York: Writers & Readers Publishing, Inc., 1984).

Just prior to his overthrow and death, Maurice Bishop planned a visit to the United States to rally support for his country. In this excerpt Gail Reed, the American-born wife of the Cuban ambassador to Grenada, gave Bishop advice on how to handle his tour.

Dear Maurice—

I've given some thought to what you raised over the phone, and come up with a couple of ideas, although without [illeg.] the general picture of what the trip looks like and perspectives you have on it—a big limitation. But for what it's worth:

1) I think being pressured into coming up with a major announcement, declaration, etc. or even a gimmick along these lines is a bit of a trap. [illeg.] With all due respect to the power of the U.S. media, once you've got their attention, the agenda must be yours, not theirs. . . .

2) Why the visit? (Of course, you've given the answer to this one more thought than I.) But for the media, how does this sound: "Grenada and the United States have a long history of relations—many thousands of Grenadians live in the United States, their work contributing to the development of that country; many thousands of U.S. citizens travel to Grenada to enjoy its hospitality and natural beauty; cultural similarities united Grenada with cultural currents in the U.S.; other economic links, etc., etc. The purpose of the visit is to reaffirm and develop these ties at as many levels as possible, and by doing so to help lessen the tensions that have cropped up at one of these levels: the current White House administration [illeg.]." Thus, the importance of accepting the Black Caucus (*another governmental level*) and Transafrica invitations—*as important in themselves*—leaving open the possibility of meeting with the Reagan administration if it were to come off.

I think any suggestion that accepting these invitations is really a "cover" for another (larger) purpose (such as a meeting with Reagan) needs to be denied flatly, and strongly. After all, what is contained in the suggestion, besides the implication that the PRG is opportunist, is the *racist* and *anti-popular* implication—"why would he come here just because a bunch of Black folks invited him?" . . .

From Paul Salisbury, and W.A. McDougall, ed., *The Grenada Papers*, (San Francisco: Institute for Contemporary Studies, 1984).

1. Write a précis of Maurice Bishop's view of the concerns of the Reagan administration.
2. To what extent do you feel that the Grenadan leader misrepresented the American position?

3. Discuss the advice given to Maurice Bishop prior to his American visit.

The Nicaraguan Menace

The Sandinista revolution in Nicaragua became an obsession during the Reagan years. As congressional support for the contra rebels dried up in the winter of 1988 the president even went so far as to send troops into neighbouring Honduras under the pretence of an impending invasion from the south. However, by the spring of 1988 a truce and tentative settlement signed by both government and Contra leaders under the terms of the Arias peace plan, and the laying of formal charges against Oliver North and John Poindexter, had sent the Reagan initiative into disarray.

In this 1981 letter from Maurice Bishop to Daniel Ortega, the Grenadan leader proclaimed solidarity with the Nicaraguan government in the face of the American threat.

7/17/81

To: Commandante Daniel Ortega Saavedra
Commander of the Nicaraguan Revolution.
[My dear Daniel]
Warmest fraternal and Revolutionary greetings!
On the occasion of the second Anniversary of the glorious Nicaraguan Revolution Our Party, Government and People extend our total and complete solidarity with the FSLN, your Government of National Reconstruction and the fighting children of Sandino.

. . . I am certain, from the reports we have been receiving, that our two situations are under similar pressures. It is clear that U.S. Imperialism has decided to make an all-out onslaught on our two Revolutions. The propaganda war, the economic aggression, the Political and Industrial destabilisation and the threat of mercenary invasion all lead to the unmistakeable conclusion that imperialism has decided to attempt to overthrow our popular Revolutions this year. That is their decision; but we have made our own decision that our Revolutions will continue and undoubtedly we will win out. As our People say in Grenada—a united, conscious, organised and vigilant people can never be defeated.

In whatever way we can, and at whatever cost, the Grenada Revolution and the People of Grenada will always stand with the Nicaraguan Revolution and the People of Nicaragua.

Long live the Nicaraguan Revolution:
Long live the FSLN!
Long live the unbreakable bonds of friendship between the people of Grenada and Nicaragua!
Forward ever, backward never!
A Warm Embrace,
[Maurice]

From Paul Salisbury, and W.A. McDougall, eds., *The Grenada Papers*, (San Francisco: Institute for Contemporary Studies, 1984).

In 1986 Time *magazine interviewed both Reagan and Ortega about the future of Nicaragua. Their comments reflect contrasting views of the underlying issues.*

Reagan: "We Have a Right to Help"
On the U.S. goal. The cancer that has to be excised is Nicaragua. We can try and help those people who want freedom to bring it about themselves. We have a right to help the people of Nicaragua who are demanding what we think are any people's rights—the rights to determine their own government.
On the Sandinista regime. What happened there was a hijacking. The people of Nicaragua set out to get rid of a, certainly you could not call it a totalitarian government, but an authoritarian government: the Somoza dictatorship. The revolutionaries appealed to the Organization of American States and said, "Would you ask Somoza to step down so we can end the killing?" The OAS asked them, "What are your revolutionary goals?" They told them democracy, pluralistic society, free trade, freedom of religion. But among the revolutionaries there was an organization that had existed before the revolution—the Sandinistas, a Communist organization. The man who they honor, Sandino, he said he was a Communist. [Augusto Cesar Sandino, assassinated in 1934, was a guerilla leader and nationalist who in fact was not a Communist.] They ousted their other allies in the revolution , and then they established a totalitarian Communist regime, the same process that Castro employed in taking over Cuba.
On what the contras *could accomplish.* The Sandinistas have to look at one of two choices: the possibility of a military defeat and being totally overthrown, or a choice of having a political settlement in which, while they would have to give up this monopoly on power they have, at least they could be in a position to run for office if the could get the people's approval.
On possible U.S. intervention. All of this talk that I am nursing an ambition to send in the troops—no. To send in troops would lose us every friend in Latin America. They want us to help the *contras*, but not with troops. The only thing I've uttered is a warning that if this revolutionary, this Sandinista, group is allowed to solidify their base, they intend to spread that revolution to other countries. There might come a day when their acts—hostile acts—would be directly against us and a situation then when it wouldn't be going down to try and run someone else's government. It would be protecting ourselves.
On diplomacy. We've made ten attempts to negotiate with them. But when have we ever seen a Communist totalitarian government voluntarily give up their power and say, "Well, O.K., we want to have more democracy"? We haven't. diplomacy must have behind it strength. The Sandinistas are not going to agree to all the things that Contadora has been asking of them unless they feel the pressure of the *contras*.
On the strength of the contras. The Sandinistas felt pressured before 1984 and the *contras* were doing very well. But in 1984, the Congress shut off our ability to help. From then on, the *contras* have been shrinking in size.
On Daniel Ortega's comment that Reagan is not rational. I don't find *him* very rational. Well, he's rational in his belief, and that is he is a dyed-in-the-wool believer in the totalitarian Marxist government, which he has.

Ortega: "The Threat Is Still There"
On the House vote. It causes us no unhappiness. We have no reason to applaud.

The threat to Nicaragua is still there. U.S. troops are present in Honduras. The U.S. had a warship 60 miles off of Puerto Corinto. This is threatening.

On U.S. intentions. The U.S. is at war with Nicaragua. It is not formal, but it is open. First, Reagan got $27 million in humanitarian assistance; now he is asking for military advisors on the ground with mercenaries. [The *contras*] haven't been able to advance with the $27 million, they won't be able to advance with the advice, so the U.S. will have to put combat units with them. When they do so, U.S. troops will die too.

On diplomacy. We will never negotiate with the *contras*. We are prepared to negotiate and discuss with the chief of the *contras*, Ronald Reagan, and his functionaries. If the U.S. feels that Nicaragua is a threat to its interests in the region, we will look for mechanisms of security so the U.S. feels secure. Nicaragua's internal situation cannot be negotiated.

On Reagan's charges that Nicaragua supports terrorism and drug trafficking, commits atrocities and represses its people. He is lying to the American people. He loses credibility when he behaves this way.

On his private side. During my clandestine days, there was no room for a personal life. With the triumph, there are more possibilities for a personal life, but it is always shared with an obligation to the Nicaraguan people.

On what kind of preparation he had for becoming President. None [laughs]. I never thought I'd be President.

On decision making within the Sandinista directorate. We have lively discussions, and we decide by consensus. Our differences in the struggle to overthrow Somoza were tactical, but our objectives were the same. The fundamental contradictions outsiders try to find do not exist.

On his personal ideology. I admire Marx because I feel his thoughts are useful for humanity. But I identify first of all with Sandino. I rejected Somoza and U.S. intervention. I grew up with this reality. We were anti-Somoza and anti-Yankee. We didn't think there were any good Yankees.

On religion. I admire Christ as a fighter for the people, as an instrument of liberation. But I didn't respect the bishops who supported Somoza.

On what he would say to Reagan personally. I would invite him to normalize relations with Nicaragua, to have a friendly policy. I would invite him to convert himself into a factor for peace in Latin America and the world. If he says he is a Christian, that he believes in God, he would have a more Christian policy. He could be more humble. He could try a new type of relationship with a revolutionary government, a government that is not a threat to the United States.

From "Tough Tug of War," (New York: Time Inc. March 31, 1986).

This March 1988 editorial from the Toronto Globe and Mail *and coincidental editorial cartoon from the Victoria* Times Colonist *accurately reflected the attitudes of most Canadians toward American policy in the region.*

What a pleasure it is to read an article that begins, "Nicaraguans reacted with hope," even if that hope is tempered by the caution born of years of war. The Sandinista government and the U.S.-backed contras have reached a ceasefire agreement.

The prospect of peace in the beleaguered nation has predictably set a few nerves twitching in Washington, where anything that might leave Nicaragua and its government alone is regarded as a personal slight to President Ronald Reagan. Even by his lights, it will be harder to justify destabilizing Managua's government now that it has agreed to a gradual amnesty for political prisoners and the restoration of democratic freedoms, and the rebels have agreed to accept only non-lethal supplies, and those only from neutral groups.

Will the last contra soon be left sitting in the White House in mute frustration?

From "Nicaragua's Day," *Globe and Mail*, Toronto, March 26, 1988.

1. Write a letter to the editor of either the *Globe and Mail* or the *Times Colonist* opposing the viewpoint expressed in the editorial/cartoon.

American Foreign Policy in the Postwar World

In the late 1980s serious concerns were raised with regard to the directions being followed in American foreign policy. As early as 1961 outgoing president Dwight Eisenhower warned of the dangers inherent in a military-industrial complex. In his farewell address he gives a prophetic warning for the next thirty years.

. . . We now stand ten years past the midpoint of a century that has witnessed four major wars among great nations—three of these involved our own country.

Despite these holocausts America is today the strongest, the most influential and most productive nation in the world. Understandably proud of this preeminence, we yet realize that America's leadership and prestige depend, not merely upon our unmatched material progress, riches and military strength, but on how we use our power in the interests of world peace and human betterment. . . .

To strive for less would be unworthy of a free and religious people. . . .

Progress toward these noble goals is persistently threatened by the conflict now engulfing the world. It commands our whole attention, absorbs our very beings.

We face a hostile ideology—global in scope, atheistic in character, ruthless in purpose and insidious in method. Unhappily the danger it poses promises to be of indefinite duration. . . .

A vital element in keeping the peace is our military establishment. Our arms must be mighty, ready for instant action, so that no potential aggressor may be tempted to risk his own destruction. . . .

We can no longer risk emergency improvisation of national defense. We have been compelled to create a permanent armaments industry of vast proportions. Added to this, three and a half million men and women are directly engaged in the defense establishment. We annually spend on military security alone more than the net income of all United States corporations.

Now this conjunction of an immense military establishment and a large arms industry is new in the American experience. The total influence—economic, political, even spiritual—is felt in every city, every state house, every office of the Federal Government. We recognize the imperative need for this development. Yet we must not fail to comprehend its grave implications. Our toil, resources and livelihood are all involved; so is the very structure of our society.

In the councils of Government, we must guard against the acquisition of unwarranted influence, whether sought or unsought, by the military-industrial complex. The potential for the disastrous rise of misplaced power exists and will persist.

We must never let the weight of this combination endanger our liberties or democratic processes. We should take nothing for granted. Only an alert and knowledgeable citizenry can compel the proper meshing of the huge industrial and military machinery of defense with our peaceful methods and goals, so that security and liberty may prosper together. . . .

From Dwight D. Eisenhower, "Farewell Address," delivered to the nation, Washington, D.C., January 17, 1961.

In his 1984 book, Main Currents in American Foreign Policy, *York University professor Gabriel Kolko outlined the fundamental frustrations faced by the Americans.*

World War Two did not end with peace or a diplomatic settlement but only unleashed social, economic, and political forces which ultimately were not negotiable and transcended the capacity of the United States or any other nation to control. One may define the postwar decades as being a "Cold War" of Soviet-

American interaction, and it is from this perspective that postwar history is largely written. But that notion grossly misses the texture of a much larger, ultimately more decisive reality, bypasses the terror and virtually unlimited violence in which the United States was to engage and the revolutionary upheavals which repeatedly created disarray in Washington's priorities and strategy—the challenges to its ambitions and hegemony. And a myopic focus on Soviet-American affairs ignores, too, the fact that relations among capitalist states, the United States plans for their future, were ultimately to prove at least as decisive after the war as they had been before. The questions emerging from Washington's desire once and for all to create an integrated, cooperative world capitalism became inextricably linked to the manner in which the leaders of the United States confronted their problems with Russia and quite autonomous revolutionary struggles. If postwar American foreign policy therefore emerges as an indissoluble skein of events—in which the global framework is crucial, and priorities, crises, and needs are constantly mingling and clashing—the complexity of this picture to later viewers ultimately also gives them the sense of problems that confronted the American leaders who were ultimately to fail in imposing their essentially hegemonic goals on this bewildering diversity. It is true that to the men in Washington some questions were far more important than others, and they sought to stamp their priorities on what was to prove an uncontrollable world; but one cannot comprehend the final emergence of Vietnam as the most important war of epoch—if not the century for the United States—save as an aspect of these universal ambitions and the intersection of its numerous and unattainable objectives touching every corner of the globe after 1945.

. . . Ultimately, the history of postwar foreign policy was to reveal that along with its increasingly bloody and expensive successes, the constraints of its resources and the uncontrollable nature of the international situation were to leave the nation in what has become a permanent and ever more frustrating crisis involving both its power and its confidence. . . .

From Gabriel Kolko, *Main Currents in American Foreign Policy*, (New York: Pantheon, 1984).

A professor of international law at Yale Law School, Paul W. Kahn, raised the following concerns after the American bombing raids on Libya in 1986.

The U.S. air attack over Libya has underscored the fact that American foreign policy has turned dramatically toward the use of force.

Although it no longer formally declares war, it hesitates less and less to use its armed forces or to support groups committed to the use of armed force. Military power has regained a powerful place among the fools of U.S. diplomacy.

U.S. officials speak easily now of using force "to put pressure on" other states. They want to "pressure" Libyan leader Moammar Khadafy into ceasing support for terrorists, or to "pressure" the Sandinistas in Nicaragua into negotiations.

They say this use of "pressure" is not war—as if the use of force is not war unless its aim is the total destruction of the opposing state.

This distinction between war and "pressure" is a return to a legal framework that was specifically rejected by the nations of the world in the U.N. Charter. For 100 years, Western civilization has struggled with the problem of subjecting the international use of force to a legal order. The marriage of law and war has not always been happy, but the ideal was clear: Deliberate killing simply was not an acceptable means of achieving political objectives.

Before World War II, international law distinguished between war and other uses of armed force. The statesmen of the postwar era understood clearly that the distinction could no longer hold.

They recognized that every use of armed force represents deliberate state killing, and concluded that it was no longer acceptable to attempt to achieve political ends by asserting pressure through the deliberate killing of belligerents.

For that reason, the U.N. charter broadly prohibited "the threat or use of force" in international relations.

While the history of the struggle to control war by law has been uneven—in fact, in the first half of this century we seemed simultaneously to have more war and more law—the voice of law in the last century has responded vigorously to each outbreak of armed conflict.

Thus, the international community responded to World War I by declaring war illegal in a series of moves starting with the establishment of the League of Nations. Similarly, the international community responded to the horrors of World War II by creating the United Nations and by conducting the Nuremburg trials, in which individuals were brought before a court and condemned for violating the law of war.

Today, the Reagan administration seems to have lost the moral insight that wars kill individuals, not political abstractions.

From Paul W. Kahn, "U.S. resorts increasingly to use of force," in *The Sunday Star*, Toronto, April 20, 1986.

1. Based upon your readings and an analysis of current issues write your own personal analysis of American foreign policy.

Canada in the 1990s

In the late 1980s Canadian foreign policy became a top priority for the government of Brian Mulroney. The prime minister himself took a leadership role in such initiatives as anti-apartheid policy in the Commonwealth and free trade with the United States. In addition, cabinet ministers such as Perrin Beatty (National Defence), Barbara McDougall (Immigration), and Joe Clark (External Affairs) defined new goals for the nation in such areas as the modernization of the Canadian armed forces, a new refugee policy, and a reassessment of Canada's role in NATO in Latin America and the Middle East.

In this 1985 policy statement, Clark outlined some of Canada's new priorities.

The most direct threat to Canadian security derives from the Soviet Union's military capabilities and antipathy to our values, and from the consequent distrust and competition between East and West. Thoughtful people everywhere are concerned with the current state of East-West relations. Suspicions run high, contacts are sparse and the risk of misunderstandings persists. The recommencement of Soviet/American arms control negotiations is a welcome development, but the negotiations are likely to be lengthy.

There are also indirect threats to our security. There is always a risk of turmoil in Eastern Europe or in a Third World region producing a crisis which draws the superpowers into direct confrontation. At the same time, East/West rivalries are exacerbating Third World conflicts. And conflict in the Third World is being carried to North America and Europe by terrorist groups, some state-sponsored.

It is clear that it is in our security interests to play an active role between East and West and, in some cases, to work for stability in the Third World, as well. . . .

Nothing is more fundamental to statehood than the ability to exert control over sovereign territory. . . .

Control over our national territory, airspace and coastal waters is essential, both for the assertion of our sovereignty and for the preservation of our security. To be effective, control requires a surveillance and detection system able to provide a continuing picture of activities on land, in the air and at sea. . . .

Europe remains the most critical military region in the world. It is where the line is drawn most graphically between East and West, it is where the task of deterring aggression must start, and it is where we have stationed forces for 35 years as one component of our contribution to NATO and collective defence. Maintaining deterrence in Europe, without undue reliance on nuclear weapons, requires that the conventional military imbalance in favour of the Warsaw Pact be rectified. In the absence of a balanced force reduction, there is a case for increasing the effectiveness of the Canadian contribution to collective defence in Europe and the Government is taking steps in this direction. . . .

. . . It is in Canada's interest, and in the interest of the wider world community, that there be a general recommitment to the goals of the UN Charter, and an active effort by members to strengthen the UN system. A revitalized United Nations would facilitate managing some of the enormous problems in our century. The UN also helps to substantiate and validate Canada's position in international affairs and provides a vehicle for the exercise of our influence. . . .

Multilateralism is more than the UN. Other institutions, including the Commonwealth and La Francophonie, have key roles to play. In what ways can these organizations, and Canada in them, help to build international consensus on difficult issues?

From J. Clark, "International Peace and Security Issues," *Competitiveness and Security: Directions for Canada's International Relations*, (Ottawa: Ministry of Supply and Services Canada, 1985).

1. Select a current foreign policy issue. Outline Canada's position in terms of long-term foreign policy goals. Present your own opinion, either for or against Canada's position.

Foreign Policy in the Era of the Cold War: Analysis and Application

1. The Ogdensburg Agreement has often been described as the "watershed" in Canadian history, when the nation moved from the British to the American sphere of influence.

Cite three specific Canadian foreign policy initiatives from the period that would support this thesis.

2. (a) The year is 1945. The Big Three are meeting in Yalta. You are a policy advisor to Stalin, Roosevelt, or Churchill. Prepare a briefing paper to prepare your leader for the meeting. You should highlight the current state of the war; the costs to your country; your long-term and short-term aims; and a negotiation strategy.

(b) Team up with those classmates who researched the same leader. Select one from your group to play the role in a class re-enactment of the Yalta Conference. Meeting with the representatives from the other two nations, conduct your own negotiations.

(c) When you are finished, step out of role and discuss the issues with your classmates. Compare your settlement with the actual Yalta Protocol.

3. Write an editorial for the Soviet paper *Pravda* criticizing the Marshall Plan.

4. (a) Create a chart illustrating the response of Canada and the United States to various major issues dealt with by the United Nations.

(b) Create a thesis based upon the information illustrated in your chart.

5. Organize a book seminar based on an account of the war in Vietnam. Suggested sources might include *Rumour of War*, by Philip Caputo; *Garden of Stone*, by Nicholas Proffitt, or *Fire in the Lake: The Vietnamese and The Americans in Vietnam*, by Frances Fitzgerald. You may form your discussion groups by having each participant select the same book or by having each study a different work as in question 8 in chapter 10.

6. When Ronald Reagan decided to invade Grenada in 1983 he chose not to inform Canadian prime minister Pierre Trudeau. Sources in Washington admitted that the president knew that Canada would not approve of the action. To what extent does this incident reflect the contrast in Canadian and American attitudes toward Latin America?

7. Compare Canadian and American foreign policy objectives in the 1980s.

15
AFFLUENCE AND THE CONSUMER SOCIETY

Native peoples living on this continent thousands of years ago knew something that all immigrants have subsequently discovered: North America is a land of wealth. The shape of culture in Canada and the United States has been influenced profoundly by this undeniable fact. That is not to say that there is no poverty, no illiteracy, no unemployment, or no homeless in our nations. These problems all exist, but they exist outside of the continental dream. For North Americans, their lands have always held out the promise of material prosperity. While recognizing the existence of those who have not realized the dream, the focus of society is clearly upon those who have.

Perhaps no period in our history epitomizes this fixation on affluence and success as clearly as our own. If the heroes and heroines of previous generations were the explorers, generals, poets, painters, and leaders of business and politics, today they are the highly paid film stars, professional athletes, and rock musicians of our consumer society.

Escaping the physical horrors of war in the 1940s, North America emerged from World War II more powerful and dynamic than ever. If the world turned an envious eye towards this continent in the postwar years, it was not without cause. For our parents, and to some extent our grandparents, the past five decades have been a period of growth and affluence. American culture, long suffering from an inferiority complex, exploded onto the world scene. And in Canada, the recipient of the first shock waves, a new cultural nationalism arose to stake its claim in North American society.

Happy Days: the Fifties

Many students today picture life in the fifties as being something like a continuous diet of "Happy Days" reruns. Indeed, such pictures paint a fairly accurate image of the life and values of middle–class North America, but it is far from the whole story. Let's take a look at both sides of the coin.

White society developed a certain sameness during the 1950s. Differences tended to blend into a common culture. A number of factors helped to create the mould for this blend. The most obvious one was the advent of mass entertainment in the 1950s. Some institutions, like athletics, had always encouraged a group mentality. But, aside from the rapid growth in college and professional sports, a new and powerful medium had entered the field.

Television, for the most part, rejected any pretence of sophistication or depth. American programs such as "I Love Lucy," "The Honeymooners," and "Father Knows Best" catered to the lowest-common denominator on both sides of the border. Canadian viewers were able to add "The Plouffe Family," "Space Command," and of course "Hockey Night in Canada," but for the most part the regular television diet was American.

Television also reinforced the traditional stereotypes about the roles of women.

Often depicted as scatterbrained or helpless, they were invariably relegated to a role inside the home. "Rosie the Riveter" of World War II was replaced by "Hazel the Maid."

This conventional image of women portrayed on television was unrealistic. Women were changing. The fledgling feminist movement was beginning to make itself heard, and, propaganda to the contrary, a growing number of women were entering the work force. The statistics tell an interesting story. Between 1940 and 1960 the percentage of working wives doubled, and in the decade following 1949 more than 60 percent of all new workers were married women. Unlike the working woman of the eighties, however, the working wife of the fifties had other motives. Rarely did they talk in terms of job satisfaction or career goals. Instead they looked upon their jobs as a means of supplementing the family income in order to improve their lifestyle. Regardless of motivation, however, the emergence of large numbers of women in the work force would establish the pattern for the future (see chapter 16).

Other television innovations of the fifties included: children's programming, such as "Walt Disney" and "Howdy Doody"; variety shows like "The Ed Sullivan Hour"; and of course game shows!

The growth of television was phenomenal. In 1946 there were seventeen thousand television sets in the United States. By 1953 two–thirds of American families had sets, and within another four years there were 40 million televisions in homes across that country. Is it any wonder that one author, paraphrasing Karl Marx, claimed that television was the "opiate of the masses"?

Television was a family affair, but the music industry belonged to the youth of America. Blending rhythm and blues and country and western, rock and roll emerged as the favourite of the younger generation. Stars such as Elvis Presley were pretty conventional by modern standards. In the fifties Presley, who later developed a drug addiction, could honestly say that he neither smoked nor drank and he said his prayers before going to bed. Dick Clark, now a legend, used to defend his program "American Bandstand" by saying that he was only trying to "defend...my right to go to a church of [my] choice, or to buy the record of [my] choice." English Canada aired its own "TransCanada Hit Parade" but, with the exception of a few home–grown singers such as Paul Anka, it featured American Top 40 artists. When Elvis performed in Canada he drew the same screaming crowds that flocked to see him at home. Stars such as Bill Haley and the Comets and Buddy Holly were propelled to superstardom. But life was still fairly tame and bland, even in the music business.

The youth were still conformist in their outlook. University and college campuses were full of undergraduates whose sole ambition in life was to fit into the established corporate mould. Materialism and uniformity had replaced the individualism and self-sacrifice of the wartime generation. On the other hand, many people have characterized the fifties generation as being the most "free." They were free from the moral and radical baggage of other generations, and free to pursue their own interests without feeling guilt or anxiety. No matter what view you take, however, there was a quiet confidence in the 1950s (see readings).

Many North Americans felt that the complacency of youth was a product of the educational system. Canadian historian Hilda Neatby wrote as early as 1953 that North American education was failing its students. In her book *So Little for the Mind* she stated that: "Our schools seem to have missed the challenge of a brutal and dangerous but stimulating age"(see readings). Her prophecies seemed to be born out in October 1957. In that month the Soviet Union launched its first unmanned satellite, Sputnik I.

Sputnik was a shock to the American system. *Life* published a series entitled "The Crisis of Education," which condemned the lack of a rigorous program in math and science. Congress responded to the "crisis" by pumping money into the system in support of science education. A few months later, the United States was able to respond to the Soviet challenge with its own space launch, but the seed had been planted. America would not be caught offguard again (see readings).

Canada suffered a "brain drain" to the United States during the postwar years. Nowhere was this more evident than in the universities. As the first babyboomers reached the universities they found few teachers and faculty to teach them. This meant looking beyond our borders: by the end of the decade over 50 percent of Canada's university professors came from outside the country.

While most of North America conformed to one mould, there were some non-conformists in the 1950s. Some were merely beatniks who were supposed to live a romantic bohemian life in the core of the big cities. Others, such as artist Jackson Pollock; William Whyte, author of *The Organization Man*; and Canadian economist John Kenneth Galbraith, questioned the fundamental values of American society. Economic historian Harold Adams Innis of the University of Toronto broke inno-vative ground with such works as *Empire and Communications* and *The Bias of Communication*. His insights into the impact of the communication media would be extended by his student, Marshall McLuhan, in the decade to come (see read-ings). The ideas of this generation would help to mould the social criticisms of the next decade.

Suburban life became more of a norm in the fifties as bedroom communities became self-sufficient. The growth of local services, shopping plazas, movie the-atres, and of course television cut the suburb free from its dependency upon the city. Warren, Michigan, was a prime example. Located 22 km from downtown Detroit, this sleepy town of 757 people in 1950 swelled under the suburban boom. Within a decade it grew to over ninety thousand. As white blue-collar workers escaped the inner city for the "good-life" of the suburbs, more and more Blacks moved into take their place. This shifting balance of population would soon explode into a crisis. A new generation of urban Blacks in the United States was not going to put up with the old ways any more.

Canadian cities grew rapidly as well. While the population of the city of Toronto remained steady at 700 000 in the twenty-five years after 1939, its suburbs more than doubled in size to over 508 000. The creation of Metropolitan Toronto in 1953 resulted in the birth of a new urban metropolis of over 1.25 million. As farm land was transformed into housing subdivisions, four-lane highways replaced concession and side roads. The Gardiner Expressway was built in the 1950s and the Don Valley Parkway opened in 1961. Linked with the Queen Elizabeth Way and Highway 401, Toronto's expressway network made downtown increasingly

...iter/director Sandy Wilson talks to the cast of *My American Cousin*.

...rons of West Edmonton Mall are more likely tourists than shoppers.

..."ather Knows Best" characterized the values of white middle-class North America during the fifties.

accessible to commuters. And while life was improving for automobile drivers, Canadian public transit also began a new chapter. In 1954 Canada's first subway—Toronto's Yonge Street line—was opened.

As in American cities, the downtown cores of Canadian cities tended to depopulate during the 1950s. However, the Canadian cities never became the wastelands of their American counterparts. In the 1970s, when the new affluent middle class turned its attention back to the urban core, there was still much to preserve.

Credit became a fact of life during the fifties. Between 1946 and 1958 short-term consumer credit increased fivefold. Diner's Club had introduced the credit card in 1950. Within fifteen years it and American Express could each claim over 1 million cardholders.

In Canada there was a unique aspect to the nation's culture in the 1950s. In 1949 a commission was formed to investigate the state of Canadian culture. Nick-named the Massey Commission after its chairman, Vincent Massey (future governor-general and, ironically, the brother of an American television star!) it brought down its monumental report in 1951 (see readings). The Massey Commission looked at the National Film Board, the CBC, the National Gallery, and the arts in general. In its conclusions it recommended the formation of a Canada Council to oversee the arts and to help direct government and private funds to the support of a distinctive Canadian arts industry.

If nothing else the report reflected a growing interest in the arts in Canada. In 1950 the Royal Winnipeg Ballet was formed; the National Ballet of Canada and the Canadian Opera Company followed the next year. The Stratford Festival opened in 1953 and numerous other local theatres sprang up during the period. French-Canadian drama received a boost with the opening of the Theatre du Nouveau Monde in Montreal.

All in all, government and cultural industries responded well to the challenge posed by American mass culture during the decade. The institutions had been created. It would be up to the next generation to produce quality productions to preserve them.

Protest and Change: The Sixties in North America

Maclean's began the new decade with a special issue entitled "America 1960." There was a love affair in Canada, and indeed in much of the world, with everything American. The well-stocked shelves of the typical suburban supermarket were as great a marvel as the Soviet's Sputnik launch had been to much of the world. The Paris editor of *US News and World Report* returned home in 1960 after twelve years abroad. He was astonished at what he found. Where only one in ten families in France had hot running water and a bathtub, one in ten Californians had a pool in their backyard. He felt an alien in his own country, a land of "ready-mixed cocktails in envelopes . . . [and] striped toothpaste."

The winds of change were sweeping across North America. They struck first in Quebec City, where twenty-five years of Union Nationale rule was blown away by Jean Lesage and the Liberals and their simple slogan "It's time for a change."

Soon the continent would be basking in the reflected glory of the new "Camelot" of John F. Kennedy. His inaugural call set the tone for the first half of the decade:

We observe today not a victory of party but a celebration of freedom . . .
For man now holds in his mortal hands the power to abolish all forms of human poverty . . .
Let us explore the stars, conquer the deserts, eradicate disease, tap the ocean depths and encourage the arts and commerce . . .
[Let us create] a new world of law where the strong are just and the weak secure . . .
And so my fellow Americans: ask not what your country can do for you— ask what you can do for your country.

Many Canadians saw the new vitality as a means of democratizing the political process. To a great extent political leaders and policies had been made in the smoke-filled back rooms of the two main parties. The early sixties saw the emergence of new citizens' movements both in Canada and the United States. In the southern United States they protested against civil rights abuses (see chapter 17); on Parliament Hill in Ottawa they rallied against the nuclear bomb. Lester Pearson and the Liberals used the new mood of the people to open up the party and reach out to new members and new ideas. Even more ambitious was the creation, out of a coalition of labour and the old agrarian-based CCF, of the New Democratic Party in 1961.

Social institutions were also experiencing rapid change. The baby boomers were entering university, but the country wasn't quite ready. Enrolments increased from 70 000 in 1956 to over 110 000 in 1961, and the number would almost triple in the next five years. To deal with the influx of new undergraduates, existing universities expanded, and new universities sprang up to pick up the slack. When concerns were raised that a disproportionate number of university students were from the upper middle class, a new system of grants and loans was introduced. In addition, millions of dollars were invested in technical schools and community colleges to train graduates in the skills needed in the modern world. By the 1970s, most Canadians came to consider postsecondary education as a right, not a privilege.

On both sides of the border, the universities of the sixties became the home of the counterculture. Identified first with students at Berkeley in California, the culture of youth—the hippie movement—came to play a dominant role in the events of the latter part of the decade. The counterculture—primarily white middle-class youth—rejected the cold Aristotelian logic that had resulted in Vietnam, the nuclear arms race, and racism. Instead it called for a world based on love and peace, and advocated a liberal use of illegal drugs to "soften the edges" of reality.

The extremes of the counterculture posed a threat to the generation that preceded it; as a result, there were often over-reactions to it. For most young North Americans the real impact of the movement was reflected in some mild flirtations with soft drugs and "free love" and an increased interest in writers such as Ken Kesey, author of *One Flew over the Cuckoo's Nest*, Herman Hesse, Norman Mailer, and Edward Albee.

Music also reflected the times. The Beatles, whose early music owed a debt to artists such as Chuck Berry, began to acknowledge the influence of Eastern music, such as the sitar playing of Ravi Shankar. Performers such as Bob Dylan, Jimi Hendrix, Steppenwolf, Jefferson Airplane, Eric Clapton, Crosby, Stills, Nash, and Young, Cream, and The Who drew mammoth crowds wherever they performed. The epitome of this period was an event that gave its name to a generation: Woodstock. The Woodstock Music and Art Fair, held in upstate New York in August 1969, was a three-day "love-in." But as the memories of Woodstock faded, so did the era. The music continued but a tightening of drug laws, growing feminism, and tougher economic times made the counterculture a thing of the past.

The sentiments of the hippie era were summarized by sixties activist Jerry Rubin:

Screw work. We want to know ourselves. But of course the goal is to free oneself from American society's sick notion of work, success, reward, and status and to find and establish oneself through one's own discipline, hard work, and introspection.

Today Jerry Rubin is a stockbroker on Wall Street.

In Canada, the process stimulated by the Massey Commission continued to benefit the arts in the new decade. The sixties saw the creation of the Ontario Arts Council, the Place des Arts in Montreal, the Shaw Festival in Niagara-on-the-Lake, the St. Lawrence Centre for the Arts in Toronto, and the Neptune Theatre in Halifax. Appropriate to the age, the O'Keefe Centre in Toronto opened its doors in the fall of 1960 with a production of "Camelot."

Canadian literature, criticized in the previous decade for its parochialism, came into its own in the 1960s. The decade was ushered in with the publication of a flurry of outstanding works in 1959, including Mordecai Richler's *The Apprenticeship of Duddy Kravitz*; Hugh MacLennan's *The Watch that Ends the Night*; and Sheila Watson's *The Double Hook*. The decade saw the emergence of other talents, such as poet/songwriter Leonard Cohen, Malcolm Lowry, playwright James Reaney, Margaret Laurence, Earl Birney, Marie-Claire Blais, Al Purdy, Alice Munro, Dennis Lee, Graeme Gibson and Margaret Atwood.

Literary criticism also flourished during the period. The traditional university quarterlies had been joined in the fifties by *Fiddlehead* (1953) and *Canadian Literature* (1958); the popularity of these publications radically increased during the 1960s. Universities began to offer credits in Canadian literature, an idea that was unheard of a generation before. The graduates of these programs took the message one step further, introducing Canadian fiction into the high-school curriculum during the 1970s.

The mid-sixties saw the publication of analytical works on the role of print and non-print media, such as *Understanding Media* and *The Gutenberg Galaxy* by Marshall McLuhan. These were complemented by John Porter's seminal work *The Vertical Mosaic* in which he analysed all aspects of Canadian society, and in the political arena by Frank Underhill's *In Search of Canadian Liberalism*, *Lament for a Nation* by George Grant, and *Social Purpose for Canada* edited by Michael Oliver and containing an essay by future prime minister Pierre Elliot Trudeau (see readings).

It is not surprising that this increase in Canadian cultural activity also resulted in an increase in nationalism. The assassination of John Kennedy, the increasing violence of American urban life, and the escalation of the war in Vietnam all contributed to a growing Canadian disenchantment with the United States. As Canadian energy minister Joe Greene told a Denver audience in 1970:

> I say to you that a part of the cause for the rise of the new Canadian nationalism and determination to build something unique rests in the malaise that exists in your land—what appears to many as the sudden, tragic, disappearance of the American Dream, which, in some ways has turned into a nightmare.

As English Canadians increasingly began to look at themselves in a new light, so too did the Quebecois. Quebec was blossoming under the reforms of the Quiet Revolution during the early years of the decade, and a new vision of Quebec and of Canada was emerging (see chapter 17). A growing Canadian economic nationalism was epitomized by the budgets of Liberal minister of finance Walter Gordon. While approving the signing of the auto pact on one hand, Gordon remained concerned about the high degree of foreign (i.e., American) ownership, especially in Canadian resource industries. Although his attempts to protect certain economic sectors met with failure, they began a long process of economic reassessment that would later reappear as the Foreign Investment Review Agency (FIRA) and the National Energy Policy during the Trudeau years.

By 1967, according to a poll in the Toronto *Star*, 67 percent of Canadians thought that "the Canadian government [should] take steps to reduce foreign control of Canadian industry." The strength of this conviction would be illustrated twenty years later when the Conservative government of Brian Mulroney introduced a free trade agreement with the United States. Described by the *Globe and Mail* as "very limited" and a deal in which "little new ground was broken," almost 50 percent of the country opposed the agreement based on the suspicion that it might affect "Canada's sovereign power to shape its economic, cultural, and social future."

Brave New World: North America in the Seventies and Eighties

Canada entered the 1970s spending over ten times per capita the amount of money the American government did in support of the arts. Such funding reflected a social consensus favouring the extension and protection of the Canadian artistic community. In a sense this was a type of cultural "national policy." Some critics claimed that second-rate products were being supported because they could not make it on their own in the marketplace.

In the field of entertainment, Hollywood was rife with expatriate Canadians who had headed south in search of success. American television and film featured the work of such Canadian transplants as Norman Jewison, William Shatner, Lorne Greene, Monty Hall, Christopher Plummer, R.H. Thompson, Alex Trebec, Michael J. Fox, Hume Cronyn, John Candy, and Peter Jennings. So natural was this process that when CBC newscaster Peter Mansbridge decided *not* to accept a lucrative offer from the CBS network in the United States, it was front-page news across the country.

It was also during this period that Canada was "discovered" by Hollywood. Safe, clean, and, with a declining dollar, inexpensive, Canadian cities became the new back lots of the film industry. By the late 1980s movies and television series were being shot in locations across the country. Toronto, where filming always seemed to be underway, was dubbed "Hollywood North." That is not to say that Canada could not claim its share of home-grown success stories. Such films as *The Rowdyman, Mon Oncle Antoine, The Decline of the American Empire*, and *I've Heard the Mermaids Singing* won critical international acclaim, and Canadian television, once the brunt of a long string of bad jokes, actually began to export series ("King of Kensington," "The Beachcombers," "Night Heat," "Degrassi Junior High") and made-for-TV films *Anne of Green Gables, Empire Inc., The Newcomers*). The National Film Board continued to produce and support outstanding documentary productions, such as the Academy Award-winning *If You Love This Planet, Billy Bishop Goes to War*, and Gwynne Dyer's series *War* and *Defence of Canada*.

Regulations governing Canadian content on radio and television were introduced by the Canadian Radio and Television Commission (CRTC). The commission oversaw the percentages of Canadian content on the airwaves and approved or rejected the renewal of broadcast licenses based upon its findings.

In the field of Canadian literature, worldwide attention was paid to Margaret Atwood, Robertson Davies, and Antoinine Maillet. In addition, a new generation of writers such as Timothy Findley, Marion Engel, Rudy Wiebe, Erica Ritter, M.T. Kelly, and J.D. Carpenter began to attract attention on both sides of the border. The seventies and eighties also saw a rebirth of interest in Canadian history. Due largely to the work of popular historians such as Pierre Berton, Peter Newman, Michael Bliss, and Desmond Morton, more and more Canadians were put in touch with the rich texture of their collective past.

The affluent society in North America in the postwar decades meant for many people a radical growth in the popularity of armchair sports. Television had brought professional hockey, baseball, and football into the living rooms of almost every home on the continent. The NHL expanded from the original six teams of the late sixties, and eventually became so successful that Canadian superstar Wayne Gretzky was the American magazine *Sports Illustrated*'s athlete of the year. Canada also hosted the world's best twice during the last two decades. In Montreal in 1976 and again in Calgary in 1988, Canadians showed that they could not only stage the Olympic games but could compete successfully at them as well.

Prior to World War II, the United States had dominated the Olympics. After 1948, however, it was another story. The conflict between the superpowers erupted on the sports fields as well. As the Soviets and Americans struggled to emerge victorious, the games themselves began to take on political overtones. The Montreal Olympics suffered a boycott by African nations over the inclusion of New Zealand (which had played rugby against South Africa) and almost saw an American withdrawal over Canada's refusal to let Taiwan compete as the official representative of China. The United States and Canada refused to attend the Moscow games in 1980 in protest over the Soviet invasion of Afghanistan, a move which punished athletes and television networks and accomplished little else. Retaliation came four years later in Los Angeles when the Soviet Union and most of the Warsaw Pact nations refused to attend the 1984 summer games.

For most North Americans, however, the Olympics remained an interesting but temporary diversion. A Ben Johnson or a Mark Spitz might have a passing interest, but the real superstars were the ones seen in living rooms across the continent week after week. These heroes of consumption, with their six- and seven-figure salaries, most epitomized sports during the period. During a major league baseball strike in 1981, a comic strip appeared in the paper. It showed two firefighters rescuing a small girl from a burning building. One asked the other: "How much do you earn?" The reply: "$10 000 per year." "Do you think that we should go on strike?" the first one asked. The reply: "Who'd pay attention. It's not as if we did something important like play baseball!"

The early seventies were years of reappraisal for North Americans. In Canada the October Crisis (see chapter 17) ended the age of innocence and forced Canadians to take a more realistic approach to national concerns. The United States, having barely survived its Vietnam adventure, was rocked in the middle of the decade by the revelation that its president was suspected of obstructing justice and committing "high crimes and misdemeanours." The resignation of Richard Nixon in August 1974 finally brought the political horrors to an end, but many North Americans thought that the United States might never recover.

Historians may well look back upon the years 1976 to 1986 as a decade of renewal for the American Dream. It began with the Bicentennial. The United States began to re-establish contact with its roots. The values inherent in the Declaration of Independence had seemed almost out of date for Americans in the postwar world. Now they were beginning to reassess their meaning. It was a time of thought and reflection. As the eighties approached, Americans began to see new horizons opening up.

Ronald Reagan swept to power on a surge of American patriotism. For the first six years of his presidency it seemed that he might enable the country to recapture the optimism of the late fifties and early sixties. By 1987, however, the cracks were beginning to show. A Congressional investigation revealed that this president too had misled Congress, and perhaps even broken the law. Reagan's image as a doddering "absentee landlord" was accentuated first by the emergence of the dynamic Soviet leader Mikhail Gorbachev, and later by the collapse of the stock market and the dollar in the closing months of 1987.

One of the political casualties of the Reagan decline was Canada's prime minister and Reagan's good friend Brian Mulroney. The prime minister's emphasis on the "special relationship" between the two nations carried little weight by 1988. Another victim of the Reagan collapse was the resurgent American conservatism of the early part of the decade. Such myths as "supply-side economics" and the "trickle-down" theory of Reaganomics had been exploded, and Americans were once again looking to more concrete ways of helping the nation's poor and underprivileged.

Canada too went through its own form of renewal. The election of the Parti Québécois in 1976 jolted much of English-speaking Canada out of its complacency. The groundwork laid in the early Trudeau years to make Canadians think of themselves as citizens of a bilingual and bicultural country was put to the test, first by the election of René Lévesque and then by the referendum on sovereignty association held in May 1980. The victory for federalism was in reality little more than a breathing space for Canadians to try to define who and what they were. The patriation of the constitution, the Meech Lake Accord, and even the free trade agreement with the United States were all manifestations of this new Canadian determination. If Canadians were polarized by politics in the late 1980s, at least it was no longer a politics based upon language or region. It was based upon policy and performance, not upon prejudice and partisanship.

The Affluent Society in the Post-Industrial Age

Twenty-five years ago the concept of a personal computer would have been the stuff of science fiction. Even ten years ago it would have been an impossibility. In 1945 complicated circuitry that would have filled a large building can now be held in the palm of one's hand.

Today millions of North Americans have access to technology that was unheard of a generation ago. Pocket calculators, digital watches, portable Walkmans, and video games have all become a fact of life. Cable television, satellite dishes, and computer modems have brought the world into our homes. Alvin Toffler called this "the Third Wave." He said that we are living in a post-industrial society that depends more on the transfer of information than the shipment of goods. It is easy for us to see how in the past society progressed through the expansion of communications networks. In this book we have discussed the growth of the transportation systems that have integrated the continent. Electronic communications will probably be the transportation revolution of the future. Considering the impact previous changes have had upon North American society, can this be any different?

Industry too is changing. Robots are gradually taking the place of people on the assembly line. This has raised many fears among labour that such innovations will put people out of work. In countries such as Japan, robotics may only be used as a tool to free humans from dangerous or distasteful jobs; it may never take their place. That is not always the case. In Milwaukee, for example, modernization lowered blue-collar employment from a height of 223 600 in 1979 to just over 170 000 by the middle of 1986. In one factory this represented a drop from 4900 workers to just 750. The challenge of the computer age is to regear society in new directions without letting anyone "fall through the cracks."

Changing Values

North Americans take different social values for granted in the eighties. The changes in birth control that sparked the sexual revolution in the United States in the late sixties spread to Canada in the seventies. By the 1980s the pendulum had begun to swing again. Social pressures to defend gay rights and to secure equal access to abortions for all women began to result in a conservative backlash by the early 1980s. The emergence of the incurable and sexually transmitted AIDS (Acquired Immune Deficiency Syndrome) virus has resulted in a return to the more traditional values of sexual abstinence and marital fidelity.

Another factor that has begun to affect North American life is a gradually aging population. In the future, this will put a greater strain on social welfare programs and service industries.

The demographic shift has also been coupled with regional moves. The old Northeastern industrial states have been rejected in favour of the more attractive climates of the South and West. As a result, while the Northeast and Midwest remain fairly static in population (in New York and Rhode Island populations have actually declined), areas such as Florida have experienced substantial growth. A large percentage of this new Sunbelt population is Canadian. These "snowbirds" head south each winter to escape the cold, only to return the following spring. Such practices help to further integrate the people of the two nations.

As our individual differences have become more apparent in the 1980s, Canadians and Americans have generally become more tolerant of one another. Film, music, and television have helped to expose people to different ways of viewing the world. Much of this tolerance is now being translated into concern for others who are less fortunate. The consumer culture which was giving away $23 billion to charity in 1971 by 1986 was contributing almost four times as much. Some of this increase can be attributed to such charity extravaganzas as "Live Aid" which sent millions of dollars in relief aid to the starving people of Ethiopia; but the bulk of charitable donations are still channelled through the traditional outlets such as churches and the United Way.

The Institutionalization of Culture

Perhaps one of the things that makes North Americans more understanding of each other in the eighties is that today we have more in common. For most people popular culture has become the lowest common denominator. Whether they prefer football, baseball, hockey, tennis, or golf; whether they watch "Family Ties," "Cosby," or "The Beachcombers"; whether they prefer Richard Dreyfuss, Meryl Streep, or Charlie Sheen; or whether they listen to Wayne Newton, Bryan Adams, or Madonna, North Americans share a common popular culture. There may be differences in taste, but never in general outlook. As long ago as 1955 critics called pop culture a spreading ooze, but they recognized that "one of the functions of pop culture is to make it impossible to spot where a person belongs on the social hierarchy by what he's wearing, what he's drinking, what he's watching on TV."

More than any other factor, pop culture has become the great equalizer and unifier in North American society. Protesters who rioted against the inequities of the consumer culture in the sixties have, for the most part, embraced it twenty years later.

American pop culture also provides a common link around the world. Nowhere is this better illustrated than by that greatest of American institutions, McDonald's. Today the golden arches can be seen around the world. In July 1986, for example,

Japan opened its ten-thousandth branch of the restaurant chain. For Canada, such American institutions are taken for granted. The small maple leaf found at the bottom of the McDonald's big M to some extent symbolizes this country's position in the corporate scheme of things.

The economic power of the United States, coupled with its mastery of the new electronic media of the postwar age, has spread American culture around the globe in the last forty-five years. As the Japanese eat Big Macs, the Chinese drink Cokes, and the Germans watch "Dallas," what hope is there for Canada tucked up neatly underneath the American broadcast umbrella? The answer is, surprisingly, a great deal. Rather than be drowned in a sea of American cultural enterprises, Canadians have been nurtured by them. Canada has benefitted from the vitality, innovation, and money available from the United States. At the same time Canadian governments, from the late forties on, have provided the buffer necessary to protect a small nation from the cultural incursions of a neighbour ten times its size.

The result for the United States has been a cultural explosion. American film, television, and popular music is admired and emulated around the world. For Canada, the result, when we shake off our inferiority complex, has been the growth and flowering of a unique and interesting Canadian culture. A strong francophone base has been built upon by developing English culture, and the product has been enriching for both. Cultural nationalists in the late 1980s have raised the flag once again in opposition to the trade deal between Canada and the United States. Although few Canadians may agree with Pierre Berton when he says that "in a quarter of a century we may as well ask for a vote in Congress," the government was clearly reminded during the negotiations and subsequent public debate that Canadians are not willing to sell their cultural heritage.

The consumerism of North America has become a symbol of all that is good and bad about our societies. The material benefits envied by most of the world have been offset in some minds by a decline in traditional values. But this complaint has always been levelled at North Americans, whether it was Peter Kalm commenting upon the decolletage of the women of New France or Jerry Falwell evoking the idea of AIDS as the wrath of God. Affluence and its effects have always been an integral part of the culture of the continent.

Education and Society

In the postwar era no aspect of public policy has received more attention than education. For almost five decades, the pendulum of educational theory has swung back and forth across the curriculum. In these excerpts, we see some of the major proponents of change.

Canadian historian Hilda Neatby wrote a highly critical indictment of North American education in the early 1950s. In these excerpts she condemns the "new" humanistic curriculum.

A sad characteristic of this 'age without standards' is that words which once had dignity and strength, because they stood for things respected and clearly defined, have become like false money. Defaced by excessive use and frequent abuse they are now offered freely and hopefully as symbols for almost any kind of intellectual exchange. Democracy is one such word, now almost useless except for purposes of propaganda. Education is another. Both are used freely by those who exploit their traditional dignity and worth, to cover all sorts of mysterious and doubtful transactions. . . . Neglect of health and comfort, lack of sympathy, and harshness, drill and discipline for their own sakes are as unfashionable today as their opposites were a generation or two ago. The educational system which undertakes to care adequately for all, the dull, the lazy and the misfits, as well as for the bright and the industrious is indeed a new and notable achievement.

But in English-speaking Canada, as in the United States, there are signs of unrest and dissatisfaction which go beyond the normal grumbling bestowed on other universal institutions like the weather and the income tax. . . .

Few children are actively happy today; they all wend their way more or less willingly to school. But it cannot be said that they display any boundless enthusiasm for their work. Much noise, energy and cooperation go into 'extra-curricular activities' and sports, but even the traditional school children could shout at their play. About their work and even about much of their recreation, modern pupils are distinctly blase.

The bored 'graduates' of elementary and high schools often seem, in progressive language, to be 'incompletely socialized'. Ignorant even of things that they might be expected to know, they do not care to learn. They lack an object in life, they are unaware of the joy of achievement. They have been allowed to assume that happiness is a goal, rather than a by-product. . . .

As everyone who knows them will agree, those who pass as experts in Canadian education are, as a class, conscientious, hard-working and devoted, struggling patiently and hopefully to satisfy varied and exacting demands by means, both human and material, which may be entirely inadequate. Educators, like the rest of us, are the products and may be the victims of the society in which they live. They are all, in a sense, the slaves of our social defects. For all our talk of educators moulding the future, it is equally true, sometimes it is more true that they are completely in the grip of the follies and vices of the past and of the immediate present. It is strange, indeed, that educators united in glorifying democracy, for it is the democratic nature of society itself which holds them in bondage. . . .

There can be no serious discussion of education in any free society which does not provoke profound and even bitter disagreement. . . . But, however much disagreement there may be on this and on many other questions, on one matter there will be very general agreement among the thoughtful members of a free society. The present preoccupations with body building and character moulding are useless and may even be dangerous so long as we neglect and starve the mind.

From Hilda Neatby, *So Little for the Mind: An Indictment of Canadian Education*, (Toronto: Clark, Irwin and Co., 1953).

1. Why does Neatby refer to her society as "an age without standards"?

2. What is the relationship between education and society?
3. Précis Neatby's criticism of education in 1953.

Teaching as a Subversive Activity, 1969

The launching of Sputnik by the Soviet Union in the late fifties sparked a reassessment of the state of education in the United States. Most people came to the same conclusion as Hilda Neatby and saw a need for a return to stricter standards and more rigorous content. A decade later, the pendulum had swung back and critics of the structured school system, such as Neil Postman, professor of English Education at New York University, were calling for a radical rethinking of the system.

The basic function of all education, even in the most traditional sense, is to increase the survival prospects of the group. If this function is fulfilled, the group survives. If not, it doesn't. . . .

Survival in a stable environment depends almost entirely on remembering the strategies for survival that have been developed in the past, and so the conservation and transmission of these becomes the primary mission of education. But, a paradoxical situation develops when change becomes the primary characteristic of the environment. Then the task turns inside out—survival in a rapidly changing environment depends almost entirely upon being able to identify which of the old concepts are relevant to the demands imposed by the new threats to survival, and which are not. Then a new educational task becomes critical: getting the group to unlearn (to 'forget') the irrelevant concepts as a prior condition to learning. What we are saying is that 'selective forgetting' is necessary to survival.

We suggest that this is the stage we have now reached environmentally, and so we must now work to reach this stage educationally. The only thing that is at stake is our survival.

From Neil Postman and Charles Weingartner, *Teaching as a Subversive Activity*, (New York: Delta, 1969).

1. Contrast Postman's view of the needs of society with those of Hilda Neatby sixteen years earlier.

Back to Basics, 1979

In his book America Revised *author Frances Fitzgerald takes issue with the swing in the late 1970s back toward a strict compulsory curriculum.*

The Back to Basics people may be right about certain of the innovations, but since they condemn opposite theories and forms of education in the same breath—nineteen-fifties-style 'progressive education' and the New Math and Social Studies—they cannot show how or why, or even whether, they are right. The blanket indictment of all new methods makes for an implausible argument. In fact, the Back to Basics argument is not a theory at all but, rather, a mood that sweeps the country from time to time. It is not even a specific reaction to progressive education, since it is far, far older than that. Complaints about the decline in education due to modern permissiveness go back at least to the mid-nineteenth century. As a national mood, it often coincides with the ends of wars and with periods of economic downturn. Conservative, pessimistic, nostalgic, it seems to be some kind of quest for certainty in an uncertain world. The argument itself is not racist or anti-democratic, but it always seems to appear in the wake of efforts to democratize the school system, and its proponents always insist on the importance of maintaining middle-class standards and values. It also contains an undertone of curmudgeonliness with regard to the young: they've had it easy, and now they've got to be disciplined, toughened up, the way we were. In its distrust of experimentalism and its glorification of the past, it is the opposite of what might be called the progressive temperment. At bottom, it is not conservative but fundamentalist, for its proponents, too, have no interest in history and no sense that the whole culture is worth preserving. Then, too, the Back to Basics theorists are clearly warning teachers against any ambitions they might have to teach critical thinking or the uses of the imagination. The basics are to them grammatical rules, facts, dates—also, instruction in patriotism and filiopiety.

From Frances Fitzgerald, *America Revised*, (New York: Vintage, 1980).

1. What criticisms does Fitzgerald lay against the proponents of the "back to basics" movement?
2. What hidden agenda does he identify in the movement?
3. Contrast the "back to basics" movement with the criticisms raised by Hilda Neatby.

The Image of the Learner, 1980

The Ontario Guidelines for History and Contemporary Studies was published in 1986. It is the basis for courses such as "Canada in a North American Perspective." In the introduction to the guideline, the authors quote the "Image of the Learner" cited below.

The image of the learner implicit in Ministry of Education guidelines and policy statements is complex. Recognizing the diversity of individual abilities and interests, the Ministry views the learner as an active participant in education who gains satisfaction from the dynamics of learning. The concept of the learner as a mere processor of information has been replaced by the image of a self-motivated, self-directed problem-solver, aware of both the processes and uses of learning and deriving a sense of self-worth and confidence from a variety of accomplishments. This learner is guided by values consistent with personal religious-ethical beliefs, cultural traditions, and the common welfare of society. The image also reveals a methodical thinker who is capable of inquiry, analysis, synthesis, and evaluation, as well as a perceptive discoverer capable of resourcefulness, intuition, and creativity.

Lest it be thought that this image of the learner is too idealistic or valid only for students in advanced stages of cognitive development, it should be noted that in the educational system of this province even young children and older ones with learning disabilities are perceived as moving towards this image; in other words, it applies to all learners potentially. The point is that the kind of education provided for the learner envisaged here is quite different from what would be provided for a learner who was envisaged, for example, as requiring a strictly regimented program comprised largely of information to be assimilated or a reluctant learner who had to be coerced and directed at each step towards the acquisition of knowledge. Thus, the very goals of education flow from the image of the learner for whom the direction is being provided.

From *Curriculum Guideline: History and Contemporary Studies*, (Toronto: Ministry of Education, Ontario, 1987).

1. Summarize the "Image of the Learner" as defined in the excerpt.
2. To what school of educational thought, identified above, does this excerpt belong?
3. In February 1988 a ministry-sponsored report, written by George Radwanski, called for a "back to basics" approach to Ontario education. Place this document in its historical perspective.

Life in the Postwar Era

In his 1979 book Express Highway Politics, *Mark Rose outlines the highway "revolution" of the 1950s.*

'In highways, then, lies a new national frontier for the pessimist who thinks frontiers have disappeared. It challenges the imagination and spirit of enterprise which always have been the distinctive marks of American life. And even the gloomiest of men admit that America never ignores the challenges of a new frontier.'
Paul G. Hoffman, President,
The Studebaker Corporation, 1940
By 1960, a recorded voice promised visitors to General Motors' Futurama exhibit at the 1939 New York World's Fair, fourteen-lane express roads would accommodate 'traffic at designated speeds of 50, 75, and 100 miles and hour'. Spectators, six hundred at a time, rode around GM's 35 738 square foot mock up of a future America while the synchronized recording in each chair continued. Automobiles from farm and feeder roads would 'join the Motorway at the same speed as cars traveling in the lane they enter,' and motorists would be able to 'make right and left turns at speeds up to 50 miles per hour.' In urban areas, express highways would be 'so routed as to displace outmoded business sections and undesirable slum areas'. In cities themselves, man would construct buildings of 'breath-taking architecture', leaving space for 'sunshine, light and air'. Great sections of farm land, 'drenched in blinding sunlight' according to an observer, were under cultivation and nearly in fruit. Traffic, whether in rural or urban areas, flowed along without delays and without hazards at intersections and railroad crossings. 'Who can say what new horizons lie before us' asked the

voice on the record, 'new horizons in many fields, leading to new benefits for everyone, everywhere'. By mid-May 1939, only a few weeks after the fair opened, Futurama was the most popular attraction.

Actually, G.M.'s exhibit, if fanciful, contained concepts and plans well known to engineers, business leaders, urban and regional planners, and big highway-minded men. Yet between 1900 and 1939, these planners never managed to construct sufficient highway mileage, to speed-up traffic, to remodel city and farm areas, or to put everyone to work. . . .

Political problems—tollway development and competition with railroaders— added a special dimension to discussion of traffic tangles. . . .

Postwar urban politics revolved around many of the same issues, though the stakes were immeasurably greater. After World War II, urban businessmen and residents continued to flee to the suburbs, leaving behind declining property values, falling retail sales, and an unsightly collection of decayed buildings and unrented space in the cities. Traffic congestion, since the 1920's a headache for urban leaders, motorists, truckers, and residents alike, composed a particularly critical part of the dilemma.

From Mark H. Rose, *Interstate: Express Highway Politics*, (Lawrence, Kansas: University Press of Kansas, 1979).

1. Research the highway system serving the urban area nearest to where you live. To what extent did its development parallel the pattern described by Rose?

The Kitchen Debate, 1959

In 1959 American vice-president Richard Nixon visited the American National Exhibition in Moscow. While in the kitchen of the "home of the future," Nixon exchanged views with Soviet premier Nikita Khruschev. Nixon's remarks are an interesting window into the values of the period.

Nixon (pointing to America workmen): "With men like that we are strong. But these men, Soviet and American, work together well for peace, even as they have worked together in building this exhibition. This is the way it should be.

"Your remarks are in the tradition of what we have come to expect—sweeping and extemporaneous. Later on we will both have an opportunity to speak and consequently I will not comment on the various points that you raised, except to say this—this color television is one of the most advanced developments in communications that we have.

"I can only say that if this competition in which you plan to outstrip us is to do the best for both of our peoples and for peoples everywhere there must be exchange of ideas. After all, you don't know everything—"

Khrushchev: "If I don't know everything, you don't know anything about communism except fear of it."

Nixon: "There are some instances where you may be ahead of us, for example in the development of the thrust of your rockets for the investigation of outer space; there may be some instances in which we are ahead of you—in color television for instance."

Khrushchev: "No, we are up with you on this, too. We have bested you in one technique and also in the other."

Nixon: "You see, you never concede anything."

Khrushchev: "I do not give up." . . .

. . . The American system is designed to take advantage of new inventions and new techniques, [Nixon] said.

Khrushchev: "This theory does not hold water."

He said some things never got out of date—furniture and furnishings, perhaps, but not houses. He said he did not think that what Americans had written about their houses was all strictly accurate.

Gadgetry Derided by Khrushchev

Nixon (pointing to television screen): "We can see here what is happening in other parts of the home."

Khrushchev: "This is probably always out of order."

Nixon: "Da [yes]."

Khrushchev: "Don't you have a machine that puts food into the mouth and pushes it down? Many things you've shown us are interesting but they are not needed in life. They have no useful purpose. They are merely gadgets. We have a saying, if you have bedbugs you have to catch one and pour boiling water into the ear." . . .

Nixon (hearing jazz music): "I don't like jazz music."

Khrushchev: "I don't like it either."

Nixon: "But my girls like it." . . .

Russians Have It Too, Premier Asserts

Khrushchev: "The Americans have created their own image of the Soviet man and think he is as you want him to be. But he is not as you think. You think the Russian people will be dumbfounded to see these things, but the fact is that newly built Russian houses have all this equipment right now. Moreover, all you have to do to get a house is to be born in the Soviet Union. You are entitled to housing. I was born in the Soviet Union. So I have a right to choose between sleeping in a house or on the pavement. Yet you say that we are slaves of communism." . . .

Nixon: "To us, diversity, the right to choose, the fact that we have 1 000 builders building 1 000 different houses, is the most important thing. We don't have one decision made at the top by one government official. This is the difference." . . .

U.S. Models Stop the Debate, Briefly

Khrushchev (noting Nixon gazing admirably at young women modeling bathing suits and sports clothes): "You are for the girls too."

Nixon (indicating a floor sweeper that works by itself and other appliances): "You don't need a wife."

Khrushchev chuckled. . . .

From "The Two-Worlds: A Day-Long Debate," *New York Times*, July 25, 1959.

1. What American accomplishments does Nixon cite?
2. How does Khruschev counter his remarks?

3. Summarize American values as articulated by Nixon.

The Politics of Mandatory Retirement, 1977

In 1977 the United States Congress held hearings on the issue of mandatory retirement at age sixty-five.

Retirement of Bert Seidman, Director of Department of Social Security, AFL-CIO.

. . . It should be recognized that prohibition of mandatory retirement is no panacea and would do little to resolve the problems of most older workers. Legislation will benefit a small number of people who want to work beyond age 65 but do nothing to resolve the more serious problems faced by most older people. An effective full employment policy is the most important solution that could be made toward the resolution of these problems. . . .

. . . Therefore, we urge that if legislation is recommended barring mandatory retirement before a specified age, it should specifically exempt elected officers of trade unions. . . .

Senator Javits. Mr. Seidman, I must say that I find it extremely difficult to follow the argument you make that an antidiscrimination statute which is designed to protect the minority should have a collective bargaining exception. Now, if we are going to let collective bargaining wipe out the right of the minority, then we ourselves are supporting discrimination. In short, you say, the older worker should give way to the younger worker. That is true any time. You can do that when you are 45, 55, 65, or 75, and if that is the criterion, I must say I find it extremely difficult to follow how you justify an antidiscrimination statute against race or creed, but not against age. All we are dealing with is one of the shibboleths of our time. Somebody said 65. They probably should never have said it. How long do you keep your job? What kind of person are you? How can you perform? . . .

Statement of Gene F. Jankowski, Vice-President, Administration, CBS, Inc.

Mr. Jankowski. . . . Before [1960], as I mentioned in my testimony earlier on, there was no mandatory retirement policy [at CBS], but people went from year to year. The recent 1960 policy was put in when we discovered that people who were not competent enough to complete their job, and there were such people, wound up in constant squabbles which led us to put in a policy requiring everyone to plan on retiring at 65. We felt it was fair, despite the disadvantages. It was fair to all employees. They could plan better for their retirement, make better plans earlier on.

I would also like to point out that as far as CBS is concerned, of the 24 000 employees that we have in the United States, last year, we had age 65 reached by only 83 of those people. Only 83 retired last year.

Mr. [Congressman Claude] Pepper. Who retired at 65?

Mr. Jankowski. Yes, sir.

Mr. Pepper. That was a question that was directed to Mr. Morris. If there are relatively so few, why maintain that discriminatory policy? You could certainly

sift out the ones that should be permitted to remain in employment and those
who shouldn't out of 83 people. You have to let people go from time to time
for certain reasons, I suppose. I imagine you could find a way of determining
when people should be requested to retire or when they shouldn't be.

From U.S., Congress, House, Select Committee on Aging, *Retirement Age Policies: Hearings before the
Select Committee on Aging*, 95th Cong., 1st sess., March 16 and 17, 1977, 2 pts. (Washington, D.C.,
1977), 1:35-36.

1. What are the views of business and labour on retirement?
2. What counterarguments do Senator Jacob Javits and Congressman Claude Pepper put forward?
3. Account for the existence of a mandatory retirement age. To what extent is it
discriminatory legislation?

Empire and Communications, 1950

*Economic historian Harold Adams Innis lectured at the University of Toronto for thirty-
two years. His influence on one of his most noted students, Marshall McLuhan, is evident
in this excerpt from his 1950 work* Empire and Communications.

. . . The United States, with systems of mechanized communication and organized force, has sponsored a new type of imperialism imposed on common law
in which sovereignty is preserved *de jure* and used to expand imperialism *de
facto*. It has been able to exploit the tendencies toward imperialism which have
emerged in members of the British Commonwealth. Canada has been used as a
means of penetrating the British Commonwealth. Resistance to this influence
can be made effective by adherence to common-law traditions and notably to
the cultural heritage of Europe. The state and the Church have lost control in
large areas of Europe as a result of successive periods of occupation, and survival in the West depends on their continual subordination and on a recognition
of the cultural leadership and supremacy of Europe. States are destroyed by
lack of culture, and so too are empires and civilizations. Mass production and
standardization are the enemies of the West. The limitations of mechanization
of the printed and the spoken word must be emphasized and determined efforts
to recapture the vitality of the oral tradition must be made. . . .
   Concentration on a medium of communication implies a bias in the cultural
development of the civilization concerned either towards an emphasis on space
and political organization or towards an emphasis on time and religious organization. Introduction of a second medium tends to check the bias of the first and
to create conditions suited to the growth of empire. . . . In the United States
the dominance of the newspaper led to large-scale development of monopolies
of communication in terms of space and implied a neglect of problems of time.
Regional monopolies of metropolitan newspapers have been strengthened by
monopolies of press associations. The bias of paper towards an emphasis on
space and its monopolies of knowledge has been checked by the development of
a new medium, the radio. The results have been evident in an increasing concern with problems of time reflected in the growth of planning and the social-

ized state. The instability involved in dependence on the newspaper in the United States and the Western world has facilitated an appeal to force as a possible stabilizing factor. The ability to develop a system of government in which the bias of communication can be checked and an appraisal of the significance of space and time can be reached remains a problem of empire and of the Western world.

From Harold Adams Innis, *Empire and Communications*, 2nd edition (Toronto: University of Toronto Press, 1972).

1. Why does Innis state that "mass production and standardization" are enemies of the West?
2. Comment on his contention that concentration on one method of communicaton tends to bias a civilization.
3. Apply Innis's thesis of the "bias of communication" to modern North American society.

Understanding Media, 1964

Marshall McLuhan revolutionized thinking about the impact of media on society. In these excerpts from Understanding Media *he considers the impact of the media upon society and its application to advertising.*

In the mechanical age now receding, many actions could be taken without too much concern. Slow movement insured that the reactions were delayed for considerable periods of time. Today the action and the reaction occur almost at the same time. We actually live mythically and integrally, as it were, but we continue to think in the old, fragmented space and time patterns of the pre-electric age.

Western man acquired from the technology of literacy the power to act without reacting. The advantages of fragmenting himself in this way are seen in the case of the surgeon who would be quite helpless if he were to become humanly involved in his operation. We acquired the art of carrying out the most dangerous social operations with complete detachment. But our detachment was a posture of noninvolvement. In the electric age, when our central nervous system is technologically extended to involve us in the whole of mankind and to incorporate the whole of mankind in us, we necessarily participate, in depth, in the consequences of our every action. It is no longer possible to adopt the aloof and dissociated role of the literate Westerner. . . .

This is the Age of Anxiety for the reason of the electric implosion that compels commitment and participation, quite regardless of any "point of view." The partial and specialized character of the viewpoint, however noble, will not serve at all in the electric age. At the information level the same upset has occurred with the substitution of the inclusive image for the mere viewpoint. If the nineteenth century was the age of the editorial chair, ours is the century of the psychiatrist's couch. As extension of man the chair is a specialist ablative of the posterior, a sort of ablative absolute of backside whereas the couch extends the integral being. The psychiatrist employs the couch, since it removed the temptations to express private points of view and obviates the need to rationalize events.

The aspiration of our time for wholeness, empathy and depth of awareness is a natural adjunct of electrical technology. The age of mechanical industry that preceded us found vehement assertion of private outlook the natural mode of expression. Every culture and every age has its favorite model of perception and knowledge that it is inclined to prescribe to everybody and everything. The mark of our time is its revulsion against imposed patterns. We are suddenly eager to have things and people declare their beings totally. There is a deep faith to be found in this new attitude—a faith that concerns the ultimate harmony of all being. Such is the faith in which this book has been written. It explores the contours of our own extended beings in our technologies, seeking the principle of intelligibility in each of them. In the full confidence that it is possible to win an understanding of these forms that will bring them into orderly service, I have looked at them anew, accepting very little of the conventional wisdom concerning them. One can say of media as Robert Theobald has said of economic depressions: "There is one additional factor that has helped to control depressions, and that is a better understanding of their development." Examination of the origin and development of the individual extensions of man should be preceded by a look at some general aspects of the media, or extensions of man, beginning with the never-explained numbness that each extension brings about in the individual and society.

From Marshall McLuhan, *Understanding Media*, (New York: McGraw-Hill, 1964).

Keeping Upset with the Joneses

The continuous pressure is to create ads more and more in the image of audience motives and desires. The product matters less as the audience participation increases. An extreme example is the corset series that protests that "it is not the corset that you feel." The need is to make the ad include the audience experience. The product and the public response become a single complex pattern. . . .

It is the powerful mosaic and iconic thrust in our experience since TV that explains the paradox of the upsurge of *Time* and *Newsweek* and similar magazines. These magazines present the news in a compressed mosaic form that is a real parallel to the ad world. Mosaic news is neither narrative, nor point of view, nor explanation, nor comment. It is a corporate image in depth of the community in action and invites maximal participation in the social process.

Ads seem to work on the very advanced principle that a small pellet or pattern in a noisy, redundant barrage of repetition will gradually assert itself. Ads push the principle of noise all the way to the plateau of persuasion. They are quite in accord with the procedures of brain-washing. This depth principle of onslaught on the unconscious may be the reason why.

Many people have expressed uneasiness about the advertising enterprise in our time. To put the matter abruptly, the advertising industry is a crude attempt to extend the principles of automation to every aspect of society. Ideally, advertising aims at the goal of a programmed harmony among all human impulses and aspirations and endeavours. . . .

Since the advent of TV, the exploitation of the unconscious by the advertiser has hit a snag. . . . In the new cool TV world, the old hot world of hard-selling, earnest-talking salesmen has all the antique charm of the songs and togs of the 1920s. . . . That is one of the most edifying aspects of the huge educational enterprise that we call advertising, whose twelve-billion dollar annual budget approximates the national school budget. Any expensive ad represents the toil, attention, testing, wit, art, and skill of many people. Far more thought and care go into the composition of any prominent ad in a newspaper or magazine than go into the writing of their features and editorials. . . . The ad teams have billions to spend annually on research and testing of reactions, and their products are magnificent accumulations of material about the shared experience and feelings of the entire community. Of course, if ads were to depart from the center of this shared experience, they would collapse at once, by losing all hold on our feelings.

From Marshall McLuhan, *Understanding Media*, (New York: McGraw-Hill, 1964).

1. Account for Marshall McLuhan's analysis of the impact of media as the "extensions of man."
2. Why does McLuhan entitle this section "Keeping Upset with the Joneses"?
3. Summarize the author's arguments as stated here.

Response to McLuhan, 1967

The 1967 book McLuhan: Hot and Cold *was a collection of essays debating his ideas. The first of these excerpts is from "The New Life Out There" by Tom Wolfe. The second, by Susan Sontag, is taken from her essay "Our Culture and the New Sensibility."*

What if he's right What . . . if . . . he . . . is . . . right
W-h-a-t i-f h-e i-s r-i-g-h-t

W	IF	R	
H	HE	I	
A	IS	G	?
T		H	
		T	

There are currently hundreds of studs in the business world, breakfast food package designers, television network creative department vice-presidents, advertising "media reps," lighting fixture fortune heirs, smiley patent lawyers, industrial spies, we-need-vision board chairmen, all sorts of business studs who are wondering if this man, Marshall McLuhan . . . is right. . . . He sits in a little office off on the edge of the University of Toronto that looks like the receiving bin of a second-hand book store, grading papers, *grading papers,* for days on end, wearing—well he doesn't seem to care what he wears. If he feels like it, he just puts on the old striped tie with the plastic neck band. You just snap the plastic band around your neck and there the tie is, hanging down and ready to go, Pree-Tide.

But what if—all sorts of huge world-mover & shaker corporations are trying to put McLuhan in a box or something. Valuable! Ours! Suppose he *is* what he sounds like, the most important thinker since Newton, Darwin, Freud, Einstein, and Pavlov, studs of the intelligentsia game—suppose he *is* the oracle of the modern times—*what if he is right?* He'll be in there. It almost seems that way. . . .

Swell! But where did *this* guy come from? What is this—these cryptic, Delphian sayings: *The electric light is pure information.*

Delphian! *The medium is the message. We are moving out of the age of the visual into the age of the aural and tactile.* . . .

Oracle!—McLuhan sits in the conference room on the upper deck of an incredible ferry boat that Walter Landor, one of the country's top package designers, has redone at a cost of about $400 000 as an office and design center. This great package design flagship nestles there in the water at Pier 5 in San Francisco. The sun floods in from the bay onto the basket-woven wall-to-wall and shines off the dials of Landor's motion picture projection console. Down below on the main deck is a whole simulated supermarket for bringing people in and testing package impact and all sorts of optometric wonder wards for testing visual reception of metribergiarglebargle—and McLuhan says, almost by the way:

"Of course, packages will be obsolete in a few years. People will want tactile experiences, they'll want to feel the product they're getting."

But!—

McLuhan's chin goes down, his mouth turns down, his eyes roll up in his *of-course* expression: "Goods will be sold in *bins*. People will go right to bins and pick things up and *feel* them rather than just accepting a package."

Landor, the package designer, doesn't lose his cool; he just looks—*what if he is right?* . . .

From Tom Wolfe, "The New Life Out There" in G.E. Stearn, ed., *McLuhan: Hot and Cold*, (New York: Signet Books, 1967).

. . . The standard response to the problem of "the two cultures"—and the issue long antedates by many decades the crude and philistine statement of the problem by C. P. Snow in a famous lecture some years ago—has been a facile defense of the function of the arts (in terms of an even vaguer ideology of "humanism") or a premature surrender of the function of the arts to science. By the second response, I am not referring to the philistinism of scientists (and those of their party among artists and philosophers) who dismiss the arts as imprecise, untrue, at best mere toys. I am speaking of serious doubts which have arisen among those who are passionately engaged in the arts. The role of the individual artist, in the business of making unique objects for the purpose of giving pleasure and educating conscience and sensibility, has repeatedly been called into question. Some literary intellectuals and artists have gone so far as to prophesy the ultimate demise of the art-making activity of man. Art, in an automated scientific society, would be unfunctional, useless.

But this conclusion, I should argue, is plainly unwarranted. Indeed, the whole issue seems to me crudely put. For the question of "the two cultures" assumes that science and technology are changing, in motion, while the arts are static, fulfilling some perennial, generic human function (consolation? edification? diversion?). Only on the basis of this false assumption would anyone reason that the arts might be in danger of becoming obsolete.

Art does not progress, in the sense that science and technology do. But the arts do develop and change. . . .

The conflict between "the two cultures" is in fact an illusion, a temporary phenomenon born of a period of profound and bewildering historical change. What we are witnessing is not so much a conflict of cultures as the creation of a new (potentially unitary) kind of sensibility. This new sensibility is rooted, as it must be, in *our* experience, experiences which are new in the history of humanity—in extreme social and physical mobility; in the crowdedness of the human scene (both people and material commodities multiplying at a dizzying rate); in the availability of new sensations such as speed (physical speed, as in airplane travel; speed of images, as in the cinema); and in the pan-cultural perspective on the arts that is possible through the mass reproduction of art objects.

What we are getting is not the demise of art, but a transformation of the function of art. . . .

From Susan Sontag, "Our Culture and the New Sensibility", in G.E. Stearn, ed., *McLuhan: Hot and Cold*, (New York: Signet Books, 1967).

1. Comment on Tom Wolfe's argument and the style in which it's presented.
2. Why does Sontag say that the conflict between "the two cultures" is an illusion?
3. Compare the ideas expressed in these two essays with those of Marshall McLuhan.

The Media-Made Man: the Rise and Fall of Richard Nixon

After his "loss" in the televised debate with John Kennedy in 1960, Richard Nixon decided to use the media to his own advantage. The following excerpts trace the story of his presidency.

In this excerpt from his book The Selling of the President, 1968, *author Joe McGuinniss compares politics to advertising.*

. . . Politics, in a sense, has always been a con game.

The American voter, insisting upon his belief in a higher order, clings to his religion, which promises another, better life; and defends passionately the illusion that the men he chooses to lead him are of finer nature than he.

It has been traditional that the successful politician honor this illusion. To succeed today, he must embellish it. Particularly if he wants to be President.

"Potential presidents are measured against an ideal that's a combination of leading man, God, father, hero, pope, king, with maybe just a touch of the avenging Furies thrown in," an adviser to Richard Nixon wrote in a memorandum late in 1967. Then, perhaps aware that Nixon qualified only as a father, he discussed improvements that would have to be made—not upon Nixon himself, but upon the image of him which was received by the voter. . . .

Advertising, in many ways, is a con game, too. Human beings do not need new automobiles every third year; a color television set brings little enrichment of the human experience; a higher or lower hemline no expansion of consciousness, no increase in the capacity to love.

It is not surprising, then, that politicians and advertising men should have discovered one another. And, once they recognized that the citizen did not so much vote for a candidate as make a psychological purchase of him, not surprising that they began to work together. . . .

With the coming of television, and the knowledge of how it could be used to seduce voters, the old political values disappeared. Something new, murky, undefined, started to rise from the mists. "In all countries," Marshall McLuhan writes, "the party system has folded like the organization chart. Policies and issues are useless for election purposes, since they are too specialized and hot. The shaping of a candidate's integral image has taken the place of discussing conflicting points of view." . . .

Television seems particularly useful to the politician who can be charming but lacks ideas. Print is for ideas. Newspapermen write not about people but policies; the paragraphs can be slid around like blocks. Everyone is colored gray. Columnists—and commentators in the more polysyllabic magazines—concentrate on ideology. They do not care what a man sounds like; only how he thinks. For the candidate who does not, such exposure can be embarrassing. He needs another way to reach people.

On television it matters less that he does not have ideas. His personality is what the viewers want to share. He need be neither statesman nor crusader; he must only show up on time. Success and failure are easily measured: How often is he invited back? . . .

The TV candidate, then, is measured not against his predecessors—not against a standard of performance established by two centuries of democracy—but against Mike Douglas. . . .

From Joe McGuinniss, *The Selling of the President 1968*, (New York: Pocket Books, 1969). Copyright 1969 by Joemac, Inc. Reprinted by permission of Simon and Schuster, Inc.

1. What parallels does McGuinniss make between advertising and politics?
2. Account for the impact of television exposure on the Watergate hearings.
3. Assess the Nixon presidency in terms of the president's relationship with the media.

Actor as President, 1988

Ronald Reagan took the use of the media one step further. Through the use of teleprompters and photo opportunities the president directed news coverage like a Hollywood production.

Ronald Reagan's personal jet, which goes by the name of Free Enterprise II, flew in late for a Reagan Rally at the Transient Terminal of El Paso Airport, Texas. Practically everyone in the waiting crowd was either a journalist, a secret-serviceman, or a delegate, one of Reagan's local "people". We were all wearing prominent name-tags, something that Americans especially like doing. I strolled among the Skips and Dexters, the Lavernes and Francines, admiring all the bulging Wranglers and stretched stretch-slacks. This felt like Reagan country all right, where everything is big and fat and fine. This is where you feel slightly homosexual and left-wing if you don't weigh twenty-five stone.

The blue-jodhpurred Tijuana band fell silent as Reagan climbed up on the podium. "Doesn't move like an old man," I thought to myself; and his hair can't be a day over forty-five. Pretty Nancy Reagan sat down beside her husband. As I was soon to learn, her adoring, damp-eyed expression never changes when she is in public. Bathed in Ronnie's aura, she always looks like Bambi being reunited with her parents. Reagan sat in modest silence as a local Republican bigwig presented him with a pair of El Paso cowboy spurs to go with his 1976 El Paso cowboy boots. Then it happened: "Ladies and gentlemen! The next President of the United States!" And with a bashful shrug ex-Governor Ronald Reagan stepped up to the lectern.

"You know, some funny things happen to you on the campaign trail," Reagan mused into the mike. "Not so long back a little boy came up to me— he must have been, why, no more than eleven or twelve years of age. He looked up at me and he said, "Mister, you're pretty old." (*Forgiving laughter as Reagan cleverly defuses the age issue.*) "What was it like when you were a boy?" (*Long, wry pause.*) And I said . . . "Well, son. When I was a little boy, America was the strongest country in the world. (*Applause and cheers.*) When I was a little boy, every working American could expect to buy his own home. (*Applause.*) When I was a little boy, gasoline was twenty-five cents a gallon." (*Cheers.*) . . . The little boy looked up at me and he said, "Hey, mister. You ain't so old. Things were like that when I was a little boy too." (*Laughter, applause, cheers and whoops.*) . . .

From Norman Corwin, *Trivializing America: The Triumph of Mediocrity*, (Secaucus, N.J.: Lyle Stuart, Inc., 1986).

1. Account for the success of Ronald Reagan's style with the average voter.
2. To what extent does the Reagan approach reflect the political advice given by Davey Crockett over a century and a half earlier?
3. In 1987 the Conservative party in Canada began its own news service to supply local television and radio stations. To what extent has the difference between news and public relations become blurred in the 1980s?

The Free Speech Movement, 1964

In this first excerpt, from the National Task Force on Violence, the author outlines the origins of the Free Speech Movement at Berkeley.

Those who believe that disorder and conflict are unique to the campuses of the

1960's are unacquainted with the history of American colleges. Dormitory life in nineteenth-century America was marked by violence, rough and undisciplined actions, and outbreaks of protest against the rules and regulations through which faculties and administrations attempted to govern students. Although collegiate life became more peaceful after the turn of the century, protest, activism, and collective action continued to be part of college life. The depression of the 1930's and the pre-World War II period of the 1940's were marked by protest, often of a political character. An examination of college and university disruption even during the 1950's provides a notable record of activity.

Student activism during the 1960's appears, however, to have unprecedented qualities. Compared to earlier activism, that of the 1960's involves more students and engages them more continuously, is more widely distributed on campuses throughout the country, is more militant, is more hostile to established authority and institutions (including radical political organizations), and has been more sustained. . . .

Student activists, before the Free Speech Movement, had viewed campus issues as trivial compared to the civil rights struggle. The only way for white students to display their commitment to social change, to put themselves "on the line," was to move off the campus. The Free Speech Movement showed how the campus itself might become a front line. Students now saw that what happens on campus could really matter politically, and that a local campus uprising could have national and international importance.

From Jerome H. Skolnik, *The Politics of Protest*, (New York: Simon and Schuster, 1969).

The Strawberry Statement, 1968

James Kunen was a student radical at Columbia University in the 1960s. In this excerpt from his book The Strawberry Statement, *he describes the alienation of many students from society.*

Intro 1
About the Book
My question is a simple one; who am I to write a book? I don't know just writing it. You're just reading it. Let's not worry about it.
Intro 2
Who Wrote the Book
I wrote the book.
I should like to point out immediately that just because I happened to be born in 1948, it doesn't mean that what I have to say as a nineteen-year-old is worth anymore than what nineteen-year-olds had to say, in to pick a year at random, 1920. To say that youth is what's happening is absurd. It's always been happening. Everyone is nineteen, only at different times. This youth-fare scene is a disservice to everyone. I'm anticipating a severe psychological setback when I turn twenty, and I don't know what I'm going to do when the youth-fare card runs out. As for this "don't-trust-anyone-over-30" shit, I agree in principle, but I think they ought to drop the zero. . . .

Intro 3
Who We Are

People want to know who we are, and some think they know who we are. Some think we're a bunch of snot-nosed brats. It's difficult to say really what we are. We don't have snot on our noses. What we do have is hopes and fears or ups and downs, as they are called.

A lot of the time we are very unhappy, and we try to cheer ourselves up by thinking. We think how lucky we are to be able to go to school, to have nice clothes and fine things and to eat well and have money and be healthy. How lucky we are really. But we remain unhappy. Then we attack ourselves for self-pity, and become more unhappy, and still more unhappy over being sad.

We're unhappy because of the war, and because of poverty and the hopelessness of politics, but also because we sometimes get put down by girls or boys, as the case may be, or feel lonely and alone and lost. . . .

There is loneliness as you can exist only in the midst of numbers and numbers of people who don't know you, who don't care about you, who won't let you care about them.

Everywhere you walk you hear a click-clack. The click-clack of your walking never leaves you, reminding you all the time that you are at the bottom of a box. The earth is trapped beneath concrete and tar and you are locked away from it. Nothing grows. . . .

From James Simon Kunen, *The Strawberry Statement: Notes of a College Revolutionary*, (New York: Avon Books, 1968). Reprinted by permission of Sterling Lord Literistic, Inc. Copyright 1968 by Avon Books.

1. To what extent was student protest in the 1960s a natural phenomenon?
2. What were the origins of the Free Speech Movement?
3. How does Kunen depict the quality of life?

Anti-War Protest: Chicago, 1968

The prime target of student protest in the 1960s was American involvement in the war in Vietnam. On both sides of the border students marched, sat-in, and sometimes rioted against the existing order. This first excerpt places the anti-war protest in its historical context.

In the past three years, protest against American involvement and conduct in Vietnam has become so familiar to our national life that it has almost acquired the status of an institution. Few people today would think of asking why this social force came into existence or how it has sustained itself and grown; even the movement's opponents seem resigned to its inevitability. In many respects, however, the very existence of a broadly based, militant opposition to foreign policy marks a sharp departure from long-standing and deeply embedded traditions, and future historians will probably marvel at the outpouring of protest and seek to explain it by reference to unprecedented conditions. . . .

Few Americans are aware of the United States' invasion of Russian after World War I, coups in Iran and Guatemala, the intervention of U.S. troops in

Lebanon, the attempted overthrow of the neutralist government in Laos, and the quiet deployment of 55 000 troops in Thailand. Finally, in seeking to explain recent protest it is especially useful, for purposes of contrast, to recall the Korean War, which resembled the Vietnam War in several respects and occurred within the memory of many current protesters. Though the similarities between South Korea under Syngman Rhee and South Vietnam under Ngo Dinh Diem were extensive and profound, no mass protest against intervention occurred. Even today, fifteen years after the Panmunjom Truce, few Americans know about, and fewer question, the presence of more than 50 000 American troops in South Korea. It is thus evident that a tradition of anti-interventionism is not in itself a significant factor in the shaping of American public opinion. Obviously, something more is required to account for the growth of a broad protest movement in this country.

The case of Vietnam would thus appear to be a unique exception to the support which the American public habitually grants its leaders in matters of national security. . . .

From Jerome H. Skolnik, *The Politics of Protest*, (New York: Simon and Schuster, 1969).

Rights in Conflict

The Walker Report was the result of an investigation of the riots surrounding the Democratic National Convention in Chicago in the summer of 1968. The following is an excerpt from the report.

. . . at 7:57 P.M., with two groups of club-wielding police converging simultaneously and independently, the battle was joined. The portions of the throng out of the immediate area of conflict largely stayed put and took up the chant, "The whole world is watching," but the intersection fragmented into a collage of violence.

Re-creating the precise chronology of the next few moments is impossible. But there is no question that a violent street battle ensued.

People ran for cover and were struck by police as they passed. Clubs were swung indiscriminately.

Two Assistant U.S. Attorneys who were on the scene characterized the police as "hostile and aggressive." Some witnesses cited particularly dramatic personal stories.

"I saw squadrols [sic] of policemen coming from everywhere," a secretary quoted earlier said. "The crowd around me suddenly began to run. Some of us, including myself, were pushed back onto the sidewalk and then all the way up against . . . the Blackstone Hotel along Michigan Avenue. I thought the crowd had panicked."

"Fearing that I would be crushed against the wall of the building . . . I somehow managed to work my way . . . to the edge of the street . . . and saw policemen everywhere.

"As I looked up I was hit for the first time on the head from behind by what must have been a billy club. I was then knocked down and while on my hands and knees, I was hit around the shoulders. I got up again, stumbling and was hit again. As I was falling, I heard words to the effect of "move, move" and the horrible sound of cracking billy-clubs."

"After my second fall, I remember being kicked in the back, and I looked up and noticed that many policemen around me had no badges on. The police kept hitting me on the head."

Eventually she made her way up to an alley behind the Blackstone and finally, "bleeding badly from my head wound," was driven by a friend to a hospital emergency room. Her treatment included the placing of 12 stitches. . . .

Another witness said: "To my left, the police caught a man, beat him to the ground and smashed their clubs on the back of his unprotected head. I stopped to help him. He was elderly, somewhere in his mid-50's. He was kneeling and holding his bleeding head. As I stopped to help him, the police turned on me. "Get that ---- ------ out of here!" This command was accompanied by four blows from clubs—one on the middle of my back, one on the bottom of my back, one on my left buttock, and one on the back of my leg. No attempt was made to arrest me or anybody else in the vicinity. All the blows that I saw inflicted by the police were on the backs of heads, arms, legs, etc. It was the most slow and confused, and the least experienced people who got caught and beaten. . . .

"I was overcrowded in with the group of screaming, frightened people," an onlooker states. "We jammed against each other, trying to press into the brick wall of the hotel. As we stood there breathing hard . . . a policeman calmly walked the length of the barricade with a can of chemical spray [evidently mace] in his hand. Unbelievably, he was spraying at us." Photos reveal several policemen using mace against the crowd. . . .

There is little doubt that during this whole period, beginning at 7:57 P.M., and lasting nearly 20 minutes, the preponderance of violence came from the police. It was not entirely a one-way battle, however . . .

"Some hippies," said a patrolman in his statement, "were hit by other hippies who were throwing rocks at the police." Films reveal that when police were chasing demonstrators into Grant Park, one young man upended a sawhorse and heaved it at advancing officers. At one point the deputy superintendent of police was knocked down by a thrown sawhorse. At least one police three-wheeler was tipped over. One of the demonstrators says that "people in the park were prying up cobblestones and breaking them. One person piled up cobblestones in his arms and headed toward the police." Witnesses reported that people were throwing "anything they could lay their hands on. From the windows of the Hilton and Blackstone Hotels, toilet paper, wet towels, even ash trays came raining down." A police lieutenant stated that he saw policemen bombarded with "rocks, cherry bombs, jars of vaseline, jars of mayonnaise and pieces of wood torn from the yellow barricades falling in the street."

From Richard Hofstadter and Michael Wallace, *American Violence*, (New York, Vintage 1971).

In this second excerpt Yippie leader Abbie Hoffman read the following statement of the aims of the movement.

. . . Abbie read the Yippie platform. The little plaza became quiet. No smirking questions and wisecrack answers now. This was serious stuff. At last, the Yippie platform:

(1) An immediate end to the war in Vietnam, and a restructuring of our foreign policy which totally eliminates aspects of military, economic and cultural imperialism. The withdrawal of all foreign-based troops and the abolition of the military draft.

(2) Immediate freedom for Huey Newton of the Black Panthers and all other black people. Adoption of the Community Control concept of ghetto areas. An end of the cultural domination of minority groups.

(3) The legalization of marijuana and all other psychedelic drugs. The freeing of all prisoners currently in prison on narcotics charges.

(4) A prison system based on the concept of rehabilitation rather than punishment.

(5) A judicial system which works toward the abolition of all laws related to crimes without victims—that is, retention only of laws relating to crimes in which there is an unwilling or injured party, i.e., murder, rape, assault.

(6) The total disarmament of all the people beginning with the police. This includes not only guns, but such brutal devices as tear gas, Mace, electric prods, blackjacks, billy clubs and the like.

(7) The abolition of Money. The abolition of pay housing, pay media, pay transportation, pay food, pay education, pay clothing, pay medical help, and pay toilets.

(8) A society which works toward and actively promotes the concept of "full employment," a society in which people are free from the drudgery of work. Adoption of the concept "Let the machines do it."

(9) A conservation program geared toward preserving our natural resources and committed to the elimination of pollution from our air and water.

(10) A program of ecological development that will provide incentives for the decentralization of our crowded cities and encourage rural living.

(11) A program which provides not only free birth control information and devices, but also abortions when desired.

(12) A restructured education system which provides the student power to determine his course of study and allows for student participation in overall policy planning. Also an educational system which breaks down its barriers between school and community. A system which uses the surrounding community as a classroom so that students may learn directly the problems of the people. . . .

(13) The open and free use of the media.

From Thomas Axworthy, ed., *Our American Cousins*, (Toronto: James Lorimer, 1987).

After the Chicago riots the leaders of the movement, Abbie Hoffman, Tom Hayden, David Dellinger, Rennie Davis and Jerry Rubin, were tried by Judge Julius Hoffman.

As a result of their conduct at the trial the accused and their lawyers were also charged with contempt. The following excerpt is from the transcript for the contempt hearings.

The Court: This was a case marred by continual disruptive outbursts in direct defiance of judicial authority by the defendants and Defense Counsel. . . .
     Much of the contemptuous conduct in this case does not show, of record. The constant murmurs and snickering emanating from the defense table were not captured on the printed page. No record, no matter how skilfully transcribed, can adequately portray the venom, sarcasm, and tone of voice employed by a speaker. No record, no matter how skilfully transcribed, can adequately reflect the applause, the guffaws, and other subtle tactics employed by these contemnors in an attempt to break up this trial. I have not focused on these cheap theatrics, histrionics, and affectations. I note them for the record lest my silence be construed as approval. But for the sake of the citations of contempt in this case, I limit myself to that conduct which is clearly and adequately portrayed in the record. . . .
     The Court: Particularly reprehensible was the conduct of counsel, who not only disregarded a duty to advise and direct their clients to observe the rules of this Court but participated with their clients in making a mockery of orderly procedure. . . . I will first consider the conduct of the Defendant David Dellinger. . . .
     Defendant Dellinger: You want us to be like good Germans supporting the evils of our decade and then when we refused to be good Germans and came to Chicago and demonstrated, despite the threats and intimidations of the establishment, now you want us to be like good Jews, going quietly and politely to the concentration camps while you and this Court suppress freedom and the truth. And the fact is that I am not prepared to do that. . . .
     [Defendant Dellinger was sentenced to 29 months and 16 days on 32 counts of contempt.]
     Defendant Davis: You have just jailed one of the most beautiful and one of the most courageous men in the United States.
     The Court: All right. Now we will talk about you, Mr. Davis. . . .

From Mark Levine et al, ed., *The Tales of Hoffman*, (New York: Bantam Books, 1970).

1. Account for the violent outcome of the Chicago protests.
2. Comment on the aims of the Yippie movement as outlined by Abbie Hoffman.
3. Debate the contention that "Judge Hoffman gave the defendants the political victory they were looking for."

Searching for Values: North America in the 1970s and 1980s

In this excerpt, John Warnock, a professor of political science at the University of Saskatchewan, comments on the death of the myth of American liberalism in the war in Vietnam.

All nation-states live by myths. They are necessary for social cohesion. Yet there is no nation-state in the world today more committed to myths than the United States. The American myths of today are those of eighteenth century liberalism, a philosophy of myths that has died everywhere else but to which the Americans desperately cling.

The United States is the New World where traditional conservatism and power politics are dead. It is the great egalitarian society where everyone is created equal; advancement comes by recognition of ability, and those who do not succeed are judged to have been lazy or not ambitious. It is the nation-state that celebrates Locke and Montesquieu, where the acceptance of pluralism sees to it that no group or class can dominate society. Free enterprise and competition assure that the customer will get the best product at the lowest price. It is the nation of peace that rejects war and imperialism. It is the great melting pot, the haven for oppressed masses, the tired, and the weak. It is the society that has proven Marx wrong. It is the individual's paradise. It is the land of the free. It is the Great Society.

In the past, Americans have felt a profound need for these myths. This is still true today, but there is a rising group in the United States which is finally beginning to accept the truth. Two things in particular have contributed to this: the rebellion of the blacks and the vicious war that is being waged against the Vietnamese.

First, the crisis at home signals the end of one of the great American myths, that the United States is an egalitarian society. In the past, those who have described the existence of a governing class in the United States have been ignored or dismissed. . . .

However, the American establishment can no longer adequately deal with criticisms of the American system simply by issuing those familiar pious pronouncements. Even in the United States, it is becoming public knowledge that in the richest country the world has ever known there are vast inequalities of wealth, with millions living in the state of starvation, poverty, and deprivation. . . .

Until the war in Vietnam, the United States was able to maintain a generally favourable image abroad. Many people were willing to believe the myths of the great liberal society. American excesses overseas were seen as exceptions, not as the rule. This is now changing. Yet in the United States the majority of the people still want to believe that their country is a great, progressive, liberating force. How could the United States be an empire? After all, wasn't the United States the first to break away from the old colonial system? American expansion across the continent was not imperialism but Manifest Destiny. Expansion overseas was not for reasons of self-interest but for humanitarian ideals, to uplift, to Christianize, and to civilize backward peoples.

From Al Purdy, ed., *The New Romans*, (Edmonton: M.G. Hurtig, 1968).

1. How does the author describe the traditional view of the United States?
2. What has destroyed the American myths?
3. Do you agree with the author's analysis of American history? Explain your point of view.

The Politics of Experience

In his 1967 book, The Politics of Experience, *psychoanalyst R.D. Laing examines the human need to experience. In this excerpt Laing describes the barriers to true experience.*

. . . We are separated from and related to one another physically. Persons as embodied beings relate to each other through the medium of space. And we are separated and joined by our different perspectives, educations, backgrounds, organizations, group-loyalties, affiliations, ideologies, socio-economic class interests, temperaments. These social "things" that unite us are by the same token so many *things*, so many social figments that come between us. But if we could strip away all the exigencies and contingencies, and reveal to each other our naked presence? If you take away everything, all the clothes, the disguises, the crutches, the grease paint, also the common projects, the games that provide the pretexts for the occasions that masquerade as meetings—if we could meet, if there were such a happening, a happy coincidence of human beings, what would now separate us?

From R.D. Laing, *The Politics of Experience*, (Middlesex: Penguin Books, 1967).

1. Summarize R.D. Laing's argument. What is the logical extension of his reasoning?

The Coming American Revolution

In his book The Greening of America *author Charles Reich concludes by calling for a revolution led by the younger generation.*

There is a revolution coming. It will not be like revolutions of the past. It will originate with the individual and with culture, and it will change the political structure only as its final act. It will not require violence to succeed, and it cannot be successfully resisted by violence. It is now spreading with amazing rapidity, and already our laws, institutions and social structure are changing in consequence. It promises a higher reason, a more human community, and a new and liberated individual. Its ultimate creation will be a new and enduring wholeness and beauty—a renewed relationship of man to himself, to other men, to society, to nature, and to the land.

This is the revolution of the new generation. Their protest and rebellion, their culture, clothes, music, drugs, ways of thought and liberated life-style are not a passing fad or a form of dissent and refusal, nor are they in any sense irrational. The whole emerging pattern, from ideals to campus demonstrations to beads and bell bottoms to the Woodstock Festival, makes sense and is a part of a consistent philosophy. It is both necessary and inevitable, and in time it will include not only youth, but all people in America. . . .

From Charles Riech, *The Greening of America*, (New York: Bantam Books, 1970).

The Silent Spring, 1962

The 1962 publication of Silent Spring *about the effect of pesticides on the environment stunned North Americans and gave rise to a new concern with environmentalism. In this excerpt, author Rachel Carson describes life after the collapse of the environmental order.*

There was once a town in the heart of America where all life seemed to live in harmony with its surroundings. The town lay in the midst of a checkerboard of prosperous farms, with fields of grain and hillsides of orchards where, in spring, white clouds of bloom drifted above the green fields. In autumn, oak and maple and birch set up a blaze of color that flamed and flickered across a backdrop of pines. Then foxes barked in the hills and deer silently crossed the fields, half hidden in the mists of the fall mornings.

Along the roads, laurel, viburnum and alder, great ferns and wildflowers delighted the traveler's eye through much of the year. Even in winter the roadsides were places of beauty, where countless birds came to feed on the berries and on the seed heads of the dried weeds rising above the snow. The countryside was, in fact, famous for the abundance and variety of its bird life, and when the flood of migrants was pouring through in spring and fall people traveled from great distances to observe them. Others came to fish the streams, which flowed clear and cold out of the hills and contained shady pools where trout lay. So it had been from the days many years ago when the first settlers raised their houses, sank their wells, and built their barns.

Then a strange blight crept over the area and everything began to change. Some evil spell had settled on the community: mysterious maladies swept the flocks of chickens; the cattle and sheep sickened and died. Everywhere was a shadow of death. The farmers spoke of much illness among their families. In the town the doctors had become more and more puzzled by new kinds of sickness appearing among their patients. There had been several sudden and unexplained deaths, not only among adults but even among children, who would be stricken suddenly while at play and die within a few hours.

There was a strange stillness. The birds, for example—where had they gone? Many people spoke of them, puzzled and disturbed. The feeding stations in the backyards were deserted. The few birds seen anywhere were moribund; they trembled violently and could not fly. It was a spring without voices. On the mornings that had once throbbed with the dawn chorus of robins, catbirds, doves, jays, wrens, and scores of other bird voices there was now no sound; only silence lay over the fields and woods and marsh.

On the farms the hens brooded, but no chicks hatched. The farmers complained that they were unable to raise any pigs—the litters were small and the young survived only a few days. The apple trees were coming into bloom but no bees droned among the blossoms, so there was no pollination and there would be no fruit.

The roadsides, once so attractive, were now lined with browned and withered vegetation as though swept by fire. These, too, were silent, deserted by all living things. Even the streams were now lifeless. Anglers no longer visited them, for all the fish had died.

In the gutters under the eaves and between the shingles of the roofs, a white granular powder still showed a few patches; some weeks before it had fallen like snow upon the roofs and the lawns, the fields and streams.

No witchcraft, no enemy action had silenced the rebirth of new life in this stricken world. The people had done it themselves.

This town does not actually exist, but it might easily have a thousand counterparts in America or elsewhere in the world. I know of no community that has experienced all the misfortunes I describe. Yet every one of these disasters has actually happened somewhere, and many real communities have already suffered a substantial number of them. A grim specter has crept upon us almost unnoticed, and this imagined tragedy may easily become a stark reality we all shall know.

What has already silenced the voices of spring in countless towns in America? This book is an attempt to explain.

From Rachel Carson, *Silent Spring*, (Boston: Houghton Mifflin Company, 1962). Copyright 1962 by Rachel Carson. Reprinted by permission of Houghton Mifflin Company.

Vanishing Air

In this introduction to Vanishing Air, *consumer watch-dog Ralph Nader outlines the corporate dangers to the environment.*

. . . Air pollution (and its fallout on soil and water) is a form of domestic chemical and biological warfare. The efflux from motor vehicles, plants, and incinerators of sulfur oxides, hydrocarbons, carbon monoxide, oxides of nitrogen, particulates, and many more contaminants amounts to compulsory consumption of violence by most Americans. There is no full escape from such violent ingestions, for breathing is required. This damage, perpetuated increasingly in direct violation of local, state, and federal law, shatters people's health and safety but still escapes inclusion in the crime statistics. "Smogging" a city or town has taken on the proportions of a massive crime wave, yet federal and state statistical compilations of crime pay attention to muggers and ignore "smoggers." . . .

Rarely revealed publicly, but still operational, are corporate rationalizations that air pollution is the "price of progress" and the "smell of the payroll." This, of course, is justifying the means by the end—a policy strongly condemned by the business world when practiced by others such as activist students. Translated into tactics, these attitudes represent industrial extortion which threatens to move or close the local plant if the gasping and soiled citizenry objects too strenuously. Moreover, many corporate hardliners believe the "ecology thing" will blow over. . . .

What is needed is a sustained public demand for a liberation of law and technology to cleanse the air by disarming the corporate power that turns nature against man.

From Ralph Nader, in John C. Esposito, *Vanishing Air*, (New York: Grossman Publishers, 1970).

Not by Bread Alone

As part of the Massey Lectures in 1961, Barbara Ward of The Economist *broadcast these remarks over the CBC.*

All the great revolutions of our contemporary world had their origin round the North Atlantic. The revolution by which equality has become a driving force in political life, the new concern with material things, the absorption in scientific analysis, the spurt of growth in the world's population, the whole transformation of our economic system by the application of technology and capital: all these vast changes were launched in the North Atlantic arena. Yet if you look at these Atlantic nations today they make the strange impression of not being particularly concerned with the revolutions they have wrought. The changes have been unleashed on mankind. Blindly, blunderingly, with immense impact and immense confusion, they are remaking the face of the earth. But can one say that the Western powers follow their course with any intimate concern? Do they see them as direct projections of the Western way of life or accept responsibility for the fact that it was the Western colonial system that chiefly set in motion the present world-wide movement of revolutionary change?

I wonder why this is. After all, is it not strange to care so little for what we have launched; to lose interest in our inventions just when they are beginning to have their maximum impact? And if one asks why this is so, I suppose some of the answers are not entirely comfortable. It seems to be a law of life that when you become rich you tend to become complacent. What is the Biblical phrase? "They sat down to eat and they rose up to play." Since the post-war economic revival in the West, the feeling has become fairly general that things are not going too badly. Elections have been fought on the slogan: "You never had it so good"; great nations have been lulled with the promise of "peace and prosperity". The once militant working class substitutes "I'm all right, Jack" for "Workers of the world, unite". This mood of ease and complacency unsuitably limits our ability to understand the needs and hungers of the millions who have not yet found their way into the modern world. To be rich and to be complacent invites the nemesis of such a condition—which is by indifference and by a narrowing of the heart to lost contact with the urgent desires of the great mass of one's fellow men. This constriction of pity can happen to individual men and women. History has always shown it. Today perhaps we see a new phenomenon: rich communities succumbing to the same limitation of human understanding. . . .

I must confess that I can see no inherent reason why such a re-dedication of ourselves to great tasks should be impossible. We have the resources available; we have more resources at our disposal than any group of nations in the history of man. And it is hard to believe that we have run out of the moral energy needed to make the change. Looking at our society I certainly do not feel that it already presents such an image of the good life that we can afford to say that we have contributed all that we can to the vision of a transfigured humanity. Our uncontrollably sprawling cities, our shapeless suburbia, our trivial pursuits quiz shows, TV, the golf games hardly add up to the final end of man. We can do better than this. We also have the means to do better. If we do not feel the need there is only one explanation. We no longer have the vital imagination for the task.

From Barbara Ward, *The Rich Nations and the Poor Nations*, (Toronto: CBC Publications, 1961).

1. How does Reich describe the roots of the new revolution?
2. In what ways do Rachel Carson and Ralph Nader's observations summarize the problems of modern industrial society?
3. Comment on Barbara Ward's thesis with regard to world hunger.

America Revised

Frances Fitzgerald uses the medium of American textbooks to illustrate the changes in American thinking in the age of affluence and anxiety.

Ideologically speaking, the histories of the fifties were implacable, seamless. Inside their covers, America was perfect: the greatest nation in the world, and the embodiment of democracy, freedom, and technological progress. For them, the country never changed in any important way: its values and its political institutions remained constant from the time of the American Revolution. To my generation—the children of the fifties—these texts appeared permanent just because they were so self-contained. Their orthodoxy, it seemed, left no handholds for attack, no lodging for decay. Who, after all, would dispute the wonders of technology or the superiority of the English colonists over the Spanish? Who would find fault with the pastorale of the West or the Old South? Who would question the anti-Communist crusade? There was, it seemed, no point in comparing these visions with reality, since they were the public truth and were thus quite irrelevant to what existed and to what anyone privately believed. They were—or so it seemed—the permanent expression of mass culture in America.

But now the texts have changed, and with them the country that American children are growing up into. The society that was once uniform is now a patchwork of rich and poor, old and young, men and women, blacks, whites, Hispanics, and Indians. The system that ran so smoothly by means of the Constitution under the guidance of benevolent conductor Presidents is now a rattletrap affair. The past is no highway to the present; it is a collection of issues and events that do not fit together and that lead in no single direction. The word "progress" has been replaced by the word "change": children, the modern texts insist, should learn history so that they can adapt to the rapid changes taking place around them. History is proceeding in spite of us. The present, which was once portrayed . . . as a peaceful haven of scientific advances and Presidential inaugurations, is now a tangle of problems: race problems, urban problems, foreign-policy problems, problems of pollution, poverty, energy depletion, youthful rebellion, assassination, and drugs. Some books illustrate these problems dramatically. One, for instance, contains a picture of a doll half buried in a mass of untreated sewage; the caption reads, "Are we in danger of being overwhelmed by the products of our society and wastage created by their production? Would you agree with this photographer's interpretation?" Two books show the same picture of an old black woman sitting in a straight chair in a dingy room, her hands folded in graceful resignation; the surrounding text discusses the problems faced by the urban poor and by the aged who depend on

Social Security. Other books present current problems less starkly. One of the
texts concludes sagely:
  'Problems are part of life. Nations face them, just as people face them, and
try to solve them. And today's Americans have one great advantage over past
generations. Never before have Americans been so well equipped to solve their
problems. They have today the means to conquer poverty, disease, and ignorance. The technetronic age has put that power into their hands.'
  Such passages have a familiar ring. Amid all the problems, the deus ex mach-
ina of science still dodders around in the gloaming of pious hope.
  Even more surprising than the emergence of problems is the discovery that
the great unity of the texts has broken. Whereas in the fifties all texts represented the same political view, current texts follow no pattern of orthodoxy.
Some books, for instance, portray civil-rights legislation as a series of actions
taken by a wise, paternal government; others convey some suggestion of the
social upheaval involved and make mention of such people as Stokely Carmichael and Malcolm X. In some books, the Cold War has ended; in others, it
continues, with Communism threatening the free nations of the earth. . . .

From Frances Fitzgerald, *America Revised*, (New York: Vintage, 1980).

1. How does Fitzgerald describe the histories of the 1950s?
2. What changes does he identify as having taken place in the sixties and seventies?
3. Look at your own textbooks. Compare them to their 1950s counterparts. Create
and defend a thesis with regard to changing attitudes.

New Directions

In 1980 Marilyn Ferguson wrote the Aquarian Conspiracy. *It was her contention that
the world could undergo a paradigm shift if individuals made the decision to change it.
In this excerpt she introduces the idea of the conspiracy and discusses its implications
for society.*

A leaderless but powerful network is working to bring about radical change in
the United States. Its members have broken with certain key elements of Western thought, and they may even have broken continuity with history.
  This network is the Aquarian Conspiracy. It is a conspiracy without a political doctrine. Without a manifesto. With conspirators who seek power only to
disperse it, and whose strategies are pragmatic, even scientific, but whose perspective sounds so mystical that they hesitate to discuss it. Activists asking different kinds of questions, challenging the establishment from within.
  Broader than reform, deeper than revolution, this benign conspiracy for a
new human agenda has triggered the most rapid cultural realignment in history.
The great shuddering, irrevocable shift overtaking us is not a new political, religious, or philosophical system. It is a new mind—the ascendance of a startling
worldview that gathers into its framework break-through science and insights
from earliest recorded thought.
  The Aquarian Conspirators range across all levels of income and education,

from the humblest to the highest. There are schoolteachers and office workers, famous scientists, government officials and lawmakers, artists and millionaires, taxi drivers and celebrities, leaders in medicine, education, law, psychology. . . .

Whatever their station or sophistication, the conspirators are linked, made kindred by their inner discoveries and earthquakes. You can break through old limits, past inertia and fear, to levels of fulfillment that once seemed impossible . . . to richness of choice, freedom, human closeness. You can be more productive, confident, comfortable with insecurity. Problems can be experienced as challenges, a chance for renewal, rather than stress. Habitual defensiveness and worry can fall away. *It can all be otherwise.* . . .

Re-Choosing

In this century we have seen into the heart of the atom. We transformed it—and history—forever. But we have also seen into the heart of the heart. We know the necessary conditions for the changing of minds. Now that we see the deep pathology of our past, we can make new patterns, new paradigms. "The sum of all our days is just our beginning" . . .

The nations of the world, Tocqueville once said, are like travelers in a forest. Although each is unaware of the destination of the others, their paths lead inevitably toward meeting in the center of the forest. In this century of wars and planetary crisis, we have been lost in the forest of our darkest alienation. . . .

We are pressed ever more deeply into the forest, toward an escape more radical than any we had imagined: freedom with—not from—each other. After a history of separation and mistrust, we converge on the clearing.

. . . We can transform the present and future by reawakening the powerful past, with its recurrent message of defeat. We can face the crossroads again. We can re-choose.

In a similar spirit, we can respond differently to the tragedies of modern history. Our past is not our potential. In any hour, with all the stubborn teachers and healers of history who called us to our best selves, we can liberate the future. One by one, we can re-choose—to awaken. To leave the prison of our conditioning, to love, to turn homeward. To conspire with and for each other.

Awakening brings its own assignments, unique to each of us, chosen by each of us. Whatever you may think about yourself and however long you may have thought it, you are not just you. You are a seed, a silent promise. You are the conspiracy.

The Third Wave

In his 1970s bestseller Future Shock, *former journalist Alvin Toffler discussed the impact of radical change upon modern society. In 1980 he published* The Third Wave, *a discussion of the post-industrial world. After considering the impact of the First Wave of change, brought on by the agricultural revolution, and the Second Wave, which followed industrialization, Toffler looked at our own time. The Third Wave described by Toffler has been brought on by the decentralization of society which has been facilitated by electronic communications and the microcomputer. In this excerpt Toffler compares the society of the Second Wave with the one to follow.*

All complicated societies require a mixture of both centralized and decentralized operations. But the shift from a basically decentralized First Wave economy, with each locality largely responsible for producing its own necessities, to the integrated national economies of the Second Wave led to totally new methods for centralizing power. . . .

What we see . . . is a set of six guiding principles, a "program" that operated to one degree or another in all the Second Wave countries. These half-dozen principles—standardization, specialization, synchronization, concentration, maximization, and centralization—were applied in both the capitalist and socialist wings of industrialized society. . . .

The six principles that formed this code lent a distinctive stamp to Second Wave civilization. Today, . . . every one of these fundamental principles is under attack by the forces of the Third Wave. . . .

A new civilization is emerging in our lives, and blind men everywhere are trying to suppress it. This new civilization brings with it new family styles; changed ways of working, loving, and living; a new economy; new political conflicts; and beyond all this an altered consciousness as well. . . .

The dawn of this new civilization is the single most explosive fact of our lifetimes. . . .

We grope for words to describe the full power and reach of this extraordinary change. Some speak of a looming Space Age, Information Age, Electronic Era, or Global Village. Zbigniew Brzezinski has told us we face a "technetronic age." Sociologist Daniel Bell describes the coming of a "post-industrial society." Soviet futurists speak of the S.T.R.—the "scientific-technological revolution". . . . Yet none of these terms . . . is adequate. . . .

Humanity faces a quantum leap forward. It faces the deepest social upheaval and creative restructuring of all time. Without clearly recognizing it, we are engaged in building a remarkable new civilization from the ground up. This is the meaning of the Third Wave.

From Alvin Toffler, *The Third Wave*, (New York: William Morrow and Company, 1980).

1. Write clear, descriptive definitions of the characteristics of the First, Second, and Third Wave societies.
2. Speculate on the characteristics of Third Wave society that Toffler could use to support his arguments.
3. Read more of *The Third Wave*. Write a brief biography of someone you know from an earlier generation, and compare it with your projected view of your own life. To what extent do these two generations reflect the differences between Second and Third Wave societies?

Trivializing America

Norman Corwin opens his book with an account of the current state of the union of the affluent consumer society.

On July 10, 1985, among hundreds of newsworthy events around the world, were the following:

Bishop Desmond Tutu, Nobel laureate, charged into an angry mob to save a suspected police informer from being burned to death.

An Israeli court convicted 15 Jewish terrorists of murder and other acts of violence against Arabs.

A Turkish supertanker was struck by an Iraqi missile and heavily damaged.

Bolivia established full diplomatic relations with mainland China, and ordered Taiwan's ambassador to get out within 72 hours.

A Greenpeace vessel was blown up in Auckland harbor, killing the ship's photographer.

The government of Sri Lanka freed 643 political prisoners.

China and the Soviet Union signed a $14-billion trade agreement.

Egyptian police discovered six tons of hashish hidden under a shipment of tomato paste aboard a cargo vessel bound for South Yemen from Greece.

In Washington the House voted to repeal a nine-year-old ban on American aid to guerrillas fighting the Marxist regime in Angola.

Attorney General Meese refused to rule out kidnapping as a means of bringing terrorists to justice.

The Nuclear Regulatory Commission came under attack for not properly considering earthquake hazards at the Diablo Canyon plant.

Eight major fires in California destroyed 300 000 acres of forests and scores of homes.

A disaster emergency was declared for New York City and several counties to its north, because of an acute water shortage.

—All of this on the same day. But the lead story on two of the three major American news broadcasts that evening was the announcement that Coca-Cola had decided to go back to its old taste after experimenting with a new one. Had this been merely a flukey aberration in high echelons of broadcasting, it would be remarkable enough, but print journalism joined in the ecstasy. Most of the country's press featured Coke's turnaround on their front pages, at the expense of all but a few of the genuine news stories listed above. The main headline of *The Denver Post*, for example, in type as large as the name of the paper itself, read, "The Real Thing Is Back." The banner was fortified, on the same front page, by a six-square-inch depiction of a can of Coke. In two colors.

This, in the country of Joseph Pulitzer, Horace Greeley, William Allen White, Edward R. Murrow and Bill Moyers. This, two centuries after Thomas Jefferson declared that "to the press alone, the world is indebted for all the triumphs that have been gained by reason and humanity."

From Norman Corwin, *Trivializing America: The Triumph of Mediocrity*, (Secaucus, N.J.: Lyle Stuart, Inc., 1986).

1. Write your own personal analysis of the consumer society. To what extent is North America driven by the values of consumption?

Reagan's America

Garry Wills, professor of American culture and public policy at Northwestern University, has carried on an ongoing study of the American presidency. In his 1988 edition of Reagan's America *Wills discussed the "myth of individualism" in the United States.*

It is hard to understand why people should think capitalism is identical with, or even conduces to, individualism. . . . Modern techology has been created by the efforts of people using stores of abundance in increasingly complex patterns of interdependence. Each time we use such a typical product of the system as (say) a jetliner, we are trusting a vast army of unseen collaborators in our journey—all those who designed, built, sold, service, fly, guard, and guide the plane. One slip in the huge operation, and it ends in disaster. . . .

The American frontier was not settled by lone cowboys but by federal troops, civic organizations, community posses, and railroad combines, organizations whose first concern was to get guns out of the hands of lone operators. The West was not settled by the gun but by gun-control laws. In our day the same concerns are evident. If the test pilot in a jetliner's coach section can die because of some maintenance man's error, he can die just as well from a bomb concealed by a single traveler. . . . That is why the terrorist is the true individualist of our time, the lone defier (and defeater) of the common will. . . . The threat of bombs on planes is answered most effectively by exhaustive search procedures, to which people must submit with good grace in order to achieve mutual protection.

But though these are the workaday realities of life, they do not fit Americans' self-image, nurtured by myth, ideology, and special interests. We, not the terrorist, are supposed to typify modern individualism and its success. The truth about our actual behavior, whether on the old frontier or the new, is as threatening to our sense of identity as the terrorist himself. The truth is that the delicate capitalist machinery has lifted itself, like a lumbering jet that overcomes the tug of gravity, by a social discipline of standardization. Yet we fly on, connected to each other, dreaming of a disconnected past—as if each passenger on the jet had floated up independently into the air and settled into the seat he or she aimed for, using separate skill and willpower. In our social dream, the individual passengers are carrying the dead weight of the airplane, rather than vice versa.

From Garry Wills, *Reagan's America*, (New York: Penguin Books, 1988).

1. Account for Wills's thesis that capitalism is the antithesis of individualism.
2. In another excerpt Wills claims that the efficiency of communication and distribution of products makes modern society extremely vulnerable to the "lone gunman." Defend this thesis with reference to a current example of "social terrorism."
3. Write your own analogy illustrating the interdependence of society.

Affluence and the Consumer Society: Analysis and Application

1. You are an expert on the education system. After considering the various views on education in the readings section, write your own critique of the system.

2. (a) Review a rerun of a television program from the late 1950s or early 1960s. What view of society is reflected by the program? How do the values depicted differ from current social values?

(b) Compare and contrast the show with a contemporary production that deals with the same subject matter.

3. Canadian and American politicans in the late twentieth century tend to "play" to the media. Create and defend your own thesis with regard to the influence of the media on the political process in North America.

4. Working with a group of classmates, research contemporary film footage, periodical coverage, and personal commentary on the anti-war movement in the late 1960s. Make a presentation to the class in which you present the concerns of this era and the reactions to the movement.

5. Form a group with some of your classmates. Create a presentation on some aspect of popular culture during the decades following World War II. Your presentation should not only describe the topic chosen but should, through the use of primary material such as films, music, and photographs, recapture the mood of the period.

6. Select a current environmental issue. Monitor the press to identify the nature of the issue, the political positions of the major parties, and possible resolutions to the problem.

Write an editorial in which you express your opinion on the issue.

7. Investigate the life of the "have-nots" within the affluent society. Take an experiential approach to understanding the problems of such groups as the homeless, the working poor, and the unemployable by talking with staff at local social agencies. An ideal approach would be to volunteer some of your own time and energy to one of these agencies.

8. Survey your peers to determine how they believe they are influenced by such mass media phenomena as television, popular music, advertising, and fashion. Based upon your findings, create a thesis with regard to the nature and origins of the values of the consumer society.

9. Interview a series of individuals who were teenagers in the fifties, sixties, seventies, and eighties. Have each person describe her/his generation during the appropriate decade.

In chart form, summarize your findings for each decade.

10. Create a pictoral essay on "Affluence and the Consumer Society."

16
THE WOMEN'S MOVEMENT

The issues of employment equity, affirmative action, and equal pay for work of equal value appear frequently in the press in the late 1980s. In the past twenty years North America has become increasingly sensitized to the needs and desires of women within society. The male-oriented social structure that seemed to be securely entrenched in the postwar decade is rapidly becoming a memory. In spite of these gains, however, there is still much to be accomplished. The defeat of the Equal Rights Amendment in the United States and the potential threat to sexual equality perceived in Canada's Meech Lake Accord are clear indicators that the intellectual struggle is not yet over.

The women's struggle for equality is not a new battle. In the nineteenth and early twentieth centuries, however, the lines were more clearly drawn. During that period there was clear discrimination against women in the work force, in the courts, and at the ballot box. In order to better understand the issues of our own day, we must first examine these historical struggles.

Women's Rights in Nineteenth-Century North America

There is no question that women did not share equal status with men in nineteenth-century North America. They were not afforded equal protection by the law, and they were not allowed to vote. In the work force they were paid less then men, and in fact, many professions were closed to them altogether. Most early feminist leaders recognized that these injustices were not the result of deliberate suppression or bigotry on the part of men, but rather a product of the prevailing attitudes of the day. The reform movement therefore set out to change those attitudes.

One of the most important areas for change was education. Active feminists worked to establish educational facilities to meet women's needs. Emma Hart Williard founded the Troy Female Academy in 1821. Hartford, Connecticut, native Catherine Beecher, the author of "American Women Will You Save your City?", founded the Western Female Institute in 1832. Oberlin College for women was opened the next year and in 1838 the University of Iowa became the first American university to admit women as students.

Life for female teachers was similar to that of their male counterparts, but with a couple of important exceptions. To begin with, teaching was considered to be an acceptable profession for women. As a result, female teachers tended to be brighter and more highly skilled than men in the same job. In spite of this the pay for women in teaching was only five to six dollars per month compared to seven to twelve dollars for men; in addition, women were only allowed to teach young children and older girls.

One courageous female reformer of the period was Prudence Crandall. At the request of local citizens, Crandall founded the Canterbury Female Boarding School in Canterbury, Connecticut, in 1831. However, Crandall believed not only in equality of sex but also in equality of race. Two years after she opened the school she admitted her first Black student. The white community was outraged. When they threatened to pull their daughters out of the school, Crandall countered by dismissing the girls herself. The Canterbury Female Boarding School became an all-Black institution. For the next year Crandall fought the courts and the legislature to allow a racially integrated school. She was the victim of threats and midnight vandalism. Finally in the fall of 1834, Crandall had had enough. Along with her new husband, Prudence Crandall Philleo moved to New York. Fifty-two years later Connecticut finally made amends. After apologizing for their earlier actions they awarded the eighty-three-year-old Prudence a pension of four hundred dollars per year. She had been ahead of her time, but Crandall had helped to establish the role of women as a powerful force in society, and Connecticut became a centre of reform in the abolition struggle to come.

Another area where women were active reformers was in the treatment of the mentally ill. In the 1840s, Dorothea Lynde Dix was a teacher in the Boston area. In 1841 she taught a class in the Cambridge jail. While there she was appalled by the treatment of insane prisoners. In her report she said: "I have seen . . . insane persons in cages, closets, cellars, stalls, pens! Chained, naked, beaten with rods and lashed into obedience." Her revelations and subsequent campaigning inspired reforms in fifteen states.

Women in fact tended to be in the forefront of the reform movement. In many cases the fight for women's rights was secondary to other causes. Elizabeth Cady Stanton was one such reformer. Originally active in the movement for the abolition of slavery, she was outraged when, in 1848, women were not allowed to act as delegates to the World Anti-Slavery Convention in London, England. With Lucretia Mott, a social reformer and Quaker minister, Stanton organized her own convention with a different theme: Rights for Women. This convention, held in Stanton's home town of Seneca Falls, New York, proposed such reforms as equal political rights for women, fairer laws with regard to divorce and the ownership of property, and equality of opportunity in education. The policy proclamations of the Seneca Falls Convention echoed the political cries of other nations and ages. In a paraphrase of the Declaration of Independence one proclamation stated: "We hold these truths to be self evident, that all men and women are created equal." Echoing the ringing words of Marx's Communist Manifesto published the same year, another proclamation stated: "The history of mankind is the history of repeated injuries and usurpations on the part of man over women."

The leadership role played by Elizabeth Cady Stanton at the convention sparked a special visit from her father. Reading about her actions in the press, he was concerned that she had suffered a complete mental breakdown. Seeing that she was fine and determined to continue he is reported to have said: "My child, I wish you had waited until I was under the sod [i.e., in my grave] before you had done this foolish thing."

Stanton did not wait. She went on to become the editor of *The Revolution*, a militant feminist magazine, and was elected the first president of the National Women's Suffrage Association.

British North America experienced its own period of social reform during the 1840s and 1850s. The influx of immigrants to the colonies resulted in an increased interest in providing such social services as free public education and better hospitals, asylums, and prisons. Although some historians believe that the real force behind the reform movement was a general desire to instill the working-class immigrants with Victorian middle-class values, others see a more altruistic motivation. Certainly women played a major role, particularly in the areas of temperance and mental illness. In the less democratic British colonies, however, women did not speak out on the issue of suffrage. Still, novelists Susanna Moodie and Anna Jameson helped to maintain a female voice and to provide another perspective on life in Canada at the time.

Although the American Women's Suffrage Association was founded in 1869 by Lucy Stone and Julia Ward Howe of Boston, and feminist leaders such as Susan B. Anthony and Elizabeth Cady Stanton campaigned hard throughout the latter half of the 1800s, it was not until the next century that real gains were made.

The Right to Vote

During the Progressive era in the United States, women once again led the call for social reform. In 1889 Jane Addams (who would win the Nobel Prize for Peace in 1931) founded Hull House, a settlement house that acted as a community centre for the poor of Chicago. Addams saw working mothers and children as one of the greatest social ills of the day. By 1914 the National Child Labour Committee had pressured every state into passing legislation that fully or partially restricted child labour under the age of fourteen.

Two other reformers, Florence Kelly and Elizabeth Beardsley Butler, fought to improve the lives of working women. The importance of their cause was highlighted in 1911 when a fire in the Triangle Shirtwaist Factory in New York took the lives of 148 workers, the majority of whom were young girls. The fire took place on the seventh floor. Evidence later showed that there were not proper exits to evacuate the workers. Within three years, thirty-nine states passed legislation setting minimum safety and health standards for women workers. Together with new limits on the work day and new minimum-wage regulations, the working conditions for female employees slowly began to improve.

Such activism gave increased credibility to women's demands for the vote. The final catalyst in the battle was the First World War. Prior to the war, women played a major role in the American work force. By 1910 there were over 8 million working women. Although Teddy Roosevelt, the only candidate to advocate universal suffrage for women, was defeated in 1912, his campaign drew considerable attention to the issue.

The state-by-state campaign to gain the vote was painstakingly slow. As late as 1914 only eleven states allowed female suffrage. As a result, the leaders of the women's movement decided to launch a national campaign. Through picketing, mass demonstrations, petitions, and referenda they displayed widespread support for their cause.

Nonetheless, it was the war that decided the issue. No one could deny the essential contribution of women, both as part of the industrial and agricultural

Nellie McClung

Jeanne Kirkpatrick at her desk in the United Nations

Sandra Day O'Connor becomes the first woman to sit on the Supreme Court of the United States.

Mme. Jeanne Sauvé, the first woman to be appointed governor general of Canada, congratulates Rick Hansen.

work force, and in volunteer organizations like the Red Cross. Finally a grateful nation decided to act.

In June 1919 Congress passed the Nineteenth Amendment to the Constitution. It stated that the "right of citizens of the United States to vote shall not be denied or abridged by the United States or by any State on account of sex." It was ratified on August 26, 1920, in time for women to vote in the national elections of that year. American women had finally entered the mainstream of political life.

In Canada the suffrage movement got its start in 1876 with the formation of the Toronto Women's Literary Club. Although formed to fight for women's suffrage, the group disguised itself behind its literary title for seven years. It finally went public when its members declared themselves to be the Women's Suffrage Association.

Like their American counterparts, Canadian suffragettes were active in many areas of reform. One pioneer of the reform movement was Nellie McClung. McClung began as an activist with the Women's Christian Temperance Union. She travelled from school to school, lecturing children against the evils of alcohol.

The women's groups worked hard against the spread of alcoholism. When the National Council of Women discovered that Canadian soldiers in Britain were being given all the beer and alcohol they wanted before being sent to the front, they issued a statement. In it they said that not only were their loved ones in danger from bullets and shrapnel, but they were "subjected to influences, the result of which may be more deadly than shrapnel or shell."

Founded in 1893, the National Council of Women first concentrated its efforts on general social issues. It was not until 1910 that it finally endorsed women's right to vote. For many Canadian women, the right to vote was not a key issue. They saw education and employment opportunities as being more significant goals on the road to equality. Feminist leaders, such as journalist Cora Hind of the *Winnipeg Free Press* and Emily Murphy, creator of Janey Canuck and the first woman police magistrate in the British Empire, saw themselves as role models of what women could accomplish with or without the vote.

Nevertheless, the drive for the vote continued. As in the United States, it was the First World War that finally settled the issue. Single women who held property had been able to vote in municipal elections in parts of Canada as early as 1872. But it was not until 1916 that the Manitoba government became the first legislature to grant provincial voting rights to women. Saskatchewan, Alberta, British Columbia, and Ontario all soon followed. Then, first through the Wartime Elections Act and then through official enfranchisement in the spring of 1918, all Canadian women received the right to vote federally. Although the Maritimes gave provincial voting rights to women by 1922, it was not until 1940 that women in Quebec were granted the same right.

In contrast to the rhetoric and demonstrations of its British and American counterparts, the Canadian suffrage movement was a conservative one. In the final analysis, there was no real uprising of Canadian women. A small and determined leadership sold a generation of male politicians on the simple idea of equity and justice. The vote was won, but as one Manitoba suffragist warned in 1920:

Let no one be so simple or sentimental as to imagine that the vote has opened the door for women into the promised land. The key is in their hands. But they have not learned how to make use of it. Nor are they likely to do so for some time.

Women's Rights: A Current Assessment

As we have seen, the battle for women's rights made uneven progress throughout the nineteenth and twentieth centuries. By the 1950s women were an established part of the work force, but usually in a secondary role.

In spite of the conventional image portrayed on television during the period, women were changing. The fledgling feminist movement was beginning to take shape. A growing number of women were entering the work force. Between 1940 and 1960 the percentage of working wives in North America doubled, and in the decade following 1949 more than 60 percent of all new workers were married women. Unlike the working woman of the eighties, however, the working wife of the 1950s had motives other than job satisfaction or career ambitions. Instead they looked upon their jobs as a means to supplement the family income and thus improve their lifestyles. Regardless of the motivation, however, the growing numbers of women in the work force established a pattern for the future.

To some extent, the job opportunities available to women during the 1950s were a result of the small number of children born during the Depression. Twenty years later this resulted in a labour shortage. Not all women were able to take advantage of these opportunities, however. Daycare was still a thing of the future. Unless there was a willing grandparent or neighbour to take care of the children, the average middle-class wife and mother was destined to remain in the home.

Although the role of women was slowly changing, there was no real leadership or direction. By the mid-1960s, however, a new generation of feminist leaders was emerging. In her 1963 book *The Feminine Mystique*, which sold over 1 million copies, Betty Friedan argued that women were no more than prisoners in their own society. They had given up power to men, but it did not have to be that way. She wrote: "Women can affect society as well as be affected by it and in the end a woman has the power to choose."

Friedan's book sparked a host of other feminist works, among them Susan Brownmiller's *Against our Will: Men, Women and Rape*, Germaine Greer's *The Female Eunuch*, and Kate Millet's *Sexual Politics*. Friedan herself founded the National Organization for Women (NOW) in 1966, a lobby group aimed at redressing the sexual inequalities in the economy. Its aims were revolutionary for their day: equal pay for work of equal value; affirmative action in hiring; and universal daycare.

Women fought hard against sexual stereotypes. Advertising and television were the worst offenders. Gradually they began to respond to demands that they protray women accurately. But in spite of this heightened awareness, a national survey in 1970 showed that over two-thirds of American women believed they were fairly treated. Clearly, radical demands would not work on the majority of women. It would take time and reason to make gains.

The consciousness of both women and men was raised through the work of Gloria Steinem and the feminist magazine *Ms*. Slowly attitudes began to change and the radical bra-burners of the early seventies became recognized as the hard-nosed negotiators of the eighties. Still progress was slow. By 1980 the average woman still received only sixty cents to each dollar earned by a man.

The biggest American political battle of the era centred around the proposed passage of an Equal Rights Amendment to the Constitution. Introduced in 1972, the ERA struggled to obtain the requisite number of states. Finally time ran out, and in June 1982 the ERA died unpassed. On the practical level, however, things continued to change. In the eighties two out of every three workers entering the job market are female, and a growing number of professional and executive positions are being filled by women.

In 1967 the Canadian government of Lester Pearson created the Royal Commission on the Status of Women, but it drew little attention at the time. In a society concerned with foreign ownership, bilingualism, and growing student activism, the rights of women were not perceived as a pressing issue. However, when the commission's report was released two years later, the public finally took notice. The report listed 167 changes that were necessary to improve the status of women in Canadian society (see readings). Basically these were divided into two categories: equality in the work place and equality within marriage.

During the 1970s legislation was introduced to correct many of the existing inequities in the areas of family law and employment opportunities and wages. The role of men also changed. The idea of a househusband who raised the family while his wife worked emerged. As traditional sex roles dissolved or merged, new views of marriage began to evolve.

The increased number of women in the work force resulted in a rapid growth in the daycare industry. In Canada between 1971 and 1983 the number of available daycare spaces increased from 17 400 to over 140 000. This seems impressive until we consider that in Canada in 1983 there were over 963 000 preschool children in Canada with working mothers. The daycare crisis has continued into the late eighties. Some who favour government support call for larger tax breaks for parents or increased subsidies for daycare centres. Others argue that government funds should go into raising the qualifications and salaries of daycare staff. Working long hours and fifty-week years, daycare personnel are still paid only a fraction of the salary of their kindergarten counterparts. As a result, when the government of Brian Mulroney announced in the fall of 1987 that it would commit $5 billion to daycare over the next five years, it did little to settle many of the basic issues.

In contrast to the unsuccessful struggle for the Equal Rights Amendment in the United States, Canadian women won the exact guarantees as part of the Charter of Rights and Freedoms. Section 15 states: "1. Every individual is equal before and under the law and has the right to the equal protection and equal benefit of the law without discrimination and, in particular without discrimination based on race, national or ethnic origin, colour, religion, sex, age or mental or physical disability."

This guarantee is further reinforced in subsection 2 through a clause that allows for the initiation of affirmative action programs to "ameliorate" past injustices. Author Richard Gwyn cites this section of the charter as the most tangible evidence of the difference between Canada and the United States:

The 1982 Charter of Rights and Freedoms contains perhaps the most expressive of all the differences between the two cultures. Included in it, reinserted into it by overwhelming political pressure after the politicians had log-rolled it out for convenience, is an equal-rights clause, the same clause virtually, that the American women's movement has failed to achieve, for all its far greater intellectual vigour and public activism...it has happened as a response to an explicit declaration by the public of its definition of fairness and equity.

Another issue developing out of the women's movement was the debate over abortion. Many women asserted that they had the right over their own bodies, and that abortion was a matter of choice. Opponents argued that the fetus was a living being and that abortion constituted murder. In 1973 the United States Supreme Court ruled in favour of the pro-choice faction. In Canada, a 1988 Supreme Court decision declared the nation's abortion law to be unconstitutional. The resulting legislative vacuum left Brian Mulroney's Conservative government searching for a politically safe middle ground.

Another beneficiary of the open discussions of the women's movement was the gay rights crusade. Laws prohibiting discrimination on the basis of sex were gradually extended to sexual orientation as well. Although many existing statutes remain to be tested in the courts, this sector of society has made great strides in the last decade.

What makes the women's movement of particular interest in North American society is that it had to take place at all. From the matrilineal/matriarchal society of the Iroquoians to the present, women have played a significant role in the development of this continent. It is difficult to imagine in the late 1980s, that as recently as during the lifetimes of our grandparents half of the population was without the right to vote. Likewise it is difficult to understand that even the world in which our parents grew up had vastly different expectations for girls and women.

During the past twenty years, women have begun to take their rightful place as equal partners in society. There are still wrongs to be redressed and attitudes to be changed, but things are improving. It is the task of the next generation to not only preserve the legislative gains that have been made, but to complete the reformation of attitudes that made the old system possible.

Husbands and Wives, 1625

American John Demos outlined the role of women in early American society in his book, A Little Commonwealth: Family Life in Plymouth Colony. In this excerpt he examines the relationship of husband and wife.

No aspect of the Puritan household was more vital than the relationship of husband and wife. But the study of this relationship raises at once certain larger questions of sex differentiation: What were the relative positions of men and women in Plymouth Colony? . . .

We know in a general way that male dominance was an accepted principle all over the Western World in the seventeenth century. The fundamental Puritan sentiment on this matter was expressed by Milton in a famous line in *Paradise Lost*: "he for God only, she for God in him"; and there is no reason to suspect that the people of Plymouth would have put it any differently. . . . Within the family the husband was always regarded as the "head"—and the Old Colony provided no exceptions to this pattern. Moreover, the culture at large maintained a deep and primitive kind of suspicion of women, solely on account of their sex. Some basic taint of corruption was thought to be inherent in the feminine constitution—a belief rationalized, of course, by the story of Eve's initial treachery in the Garden of Eden. It was no coincidence that in both the Old and New World witches were mostly women. . . .

The views of the Pilgrim pastor John Robinson are also interesting in this connection. He opposed, in the first place, any tendency to regard women as "necessary evils" and greatly regretted the currency of such opinions among "not only heathen poets . . . but also wanton Christians." The Lord had created both man and woman of an equal perfection, and "neither is she, since the creation more degenerated than he from the primitive goodness." Still, in marriage some principles of authority were essential, since "differences will arise and be seen, and so the one must give way, and apply unto the other; this, God and nature layeth upon the woman, rather than upon the man." Hence the proper attitude of a wife towards her husband was "a reverend subjection". . . . Women, he wrote, were . . . weaker, most obviously, with respect to intelligence or "understanding." For this was a gift "which God hath . . . afforded (the man), and means of obtaining it, above the woman, that he might guide and go before her." . . .

From John Demos, *A Little Commonwealth: Family Life in Plymouth Colony*, (New York: Oxford University Press, 1970).

1. Outline Demos's view of women in the seventeenth-century Western world.
2. What specific beliefs did Puritans have with respect to the qualities of women?
3. Take careful note of the Demos view of the North American woman as a point of departure for the movement towards equality.

Woman's Sphere, 1856

In an address entitled "The Proper Sphere and Influence of Woman in Christian Society," Reverend Robert Sedgewick of Halifax "enlightened" the members of the local YMCA as to the role of women in society.

It seems somewhat strange that at this time of day there should be any necessity for discussing the subject which has just been announced, either from the pulpit or the press, or in the Lecture room, as on the present occasion. One would have thought that this at least was a settled question—that it had been decided by universal consent, and that the unanimous voice of civilized and Christian man had definitely and permanently fixed the sphere and influence of woman in Christian society; but it is not so, and at this present time, and especially on this continent, this very question is agitated with a freedom and a fierceness too which augur badly for its settlement on reasonable and scriptural grounds, by those who view it in its moral aspects.

The errors and blunders which are interwoven with the subject of woman's rights and woman's place in modern society are, as these points now engage public attention, to be traced either to the ignoring of the fact or omission of the fact that in the economy of nature or rather in the design of God, *woman is the complement of man.* . . .

. . . [W]oman is the equal of man, alike in the matter of intellect, emotion, and activity, and . . . she has shewn her capabilities in these respects, . . . It would never do, however, from these premises, to draw the conclusion that woman behoves and is bound to exert her powers in the same direction and for the same ends as man. This were to usurp the place of man—this were to forget her position as the complement of man, and assume a place she is incompetent to fill, or rather was not designed to fill. This were to leap out of her sphere and attempt to move in another, in which, to move rightly, the whole moral relations of society would behove to be changed, and suited anew to each other, but which, because they are unchangeable, every attempt is fraught with damage, it may be with ruin, and woman becomes a wandering star, which, having left its due place, and violated its prescribed relations, dashes itself into shivers against some other planet, whose path it crossed in the eccentricity of its movements, and goes out in the blackness of darkness for ever. . . .

. . . That the question of investing women with similar political rights with man, and demanding of her the discharge of similar political duties, should have arisen at this time of day, after such a world-wide and world-long experience, is indeed one of the wonders of the age. . . .

. . . As to the idea that woman has a self evident and inalienable right to assist in the government of the race, I reply she does assist in that government now, and would to heaven she would exercise a still larger share in its administration. But this great work, like all others, is naturally divided between the sexes, the nobler government of children belonging to women, the less noble government of adults to men. . . .

From Ramsay Cook, Wendy Mitchinson, eds., "The Proper Sphere," in *Woman's Place in Canadian Society* (Toronto: Oxford University Press, 1976).

1. Why does Sedgewick say that the role of women was a settled question "decided by universal consent"?
2. Account for the author's contention that women should not participate in the same areas of endeavour as men.
3. Comment on Sedgewick's view of the shortcomings of a female Parliament.

Against Woman's Rights, 1872

By the 1870s the debate on equality for women had begun in Canada in earnest. In this essay written for the Canadian Monthly and National Review, Goldwin Smith *argued against the extension of political rights for women.*

A movement has been set on foot, and in England and the United States has made considerable way, the object of which is to effect a sweeping change in all the relations of the sexes—conjugal, political, legal, educational and industrial. It may safely be said, that such a revolution, if it actually takes place, will be at once unparalleled in importance and unprecedented in kind. Unparalleled in importance, because female character and domestic morality lie so completely at the root of civilization, that they may almost be said to be civilization itself; unprecedented in kind, since history affords no example of so extraordinary a change in the fundamental relations of humanity, the progress of which has hitherto been in conformity with those relations as well as comparatively gradual, though not unmarked by exceptional and momentous efforts, such as seem to rebut the idea that humanity is under the dominion of mere physical law.

In the United States a peculiar impulse has been given to all levelling movements by negro enfranchisement; and demagogism pounces, by anticipation, on the female vote. In England, the movement, though Radical in its origin, is fostered by a portion of the Conservative party in the hope that the female vote will come to the rescue of existing institutions. In Canada, exempt from these disturbing causes, we have hitherto been touched by the educational part of the movement alone, and are therefore in a position to consider the question calmly in case it should ever present itself to us in the broader and graver form.

It is desirable, in the first place, to clear away certain fallacies by which a very invidious character has been needlessly given to the discussion. The advocates of Women's Rights, male and female, have represented woman as the victim hitherto of wilful and systematic injustice, against which she is at last about to rise in revolt; and their language is such as, if it could sink into the hearts of those to whom it is addressed, might turn all affection to bitterness and divide every household against itself. But these representations are without foundation in history, which shows that the lot, both of man and woman, has been determined from time to time by circumstances only to a very limited extent subject to the will of either sex, and which neither sex could be blamed for accepting or failing to reverse. Those who assume that the lot of woman has been through all the ages fixed by the will of man, and that man has willed that he should enjoy political rights and that woman should be a slave, have forgotten to consider the fact that in almost all countries down to a very recent period, man himself has been, and in most countries even at the present day remains, if not a slave, at least destitute of political rights. . . .

The question whether it is desirable that women should take part in politics is closely connected with those relating to their domestic and industrial position. It is a question not as to the relative intelligence or virtue of the two sexes, but whether politics are or can be woman's sphere. The argument that educated women are better qualified for the suffrage than uneducated men is, therefore, irrelevant and invalid. The disqualification, if there be a disqualification, is not one of intellect but of position, or at least of intellect only so far as intellect in regard to special functions, may be unfavourably influenced by position. White women, it is often said in the United States, are better qualified for the suffrage than black men. In the same sense, many white boys are better qualified for the suffrage than many white men or women, and they are excluded not on account of their want of intelligence, but because, as a general rule, being dependent on their parents, they are not in a responsible position. . . .

Supposing women to be emancipated legally, conjugally and industrially, in the Woman's Rights sense, and to have made their way completely into what has hitherto been the male sphere, the objections to their taking part in politics would obviously be diminished. . . . But with female suffrage, the position and the practical education of women being as they now are, we should have at every general election a woman's question, very likely one of a sentimental kind, which demagogues would take care to provide and which would make a clean sweep of all other questions and of all public men who hesitated to take the woman's side. . . .

From A Bystander [Goldwin Smith], "The Woman's Rights Movement," *The Canadian Monthly and National Review*, March 1872, vol. I.

1. Why does Smith warn that the right to vote will usher in a revolution in the relationship between the sexes?
2. How does he depict the arguments put forward by the advocates of equality?
3. Identify and support Smith's thesis with evidence from the article.

In Favour of Woman's Rights, 1879

An unnamed writer in The Canadian Monthly and National Review *in May 1879 wrote an article entitled "The Woman Question" in which the case in favour of rights for women was presented.*

One of the most interesting and important problems of modern civilization is indicated in the above title. Certainly no subject touches more numerous points of our life; or touches them more deeply and tenderly. It is a subject moreover, which has recently become quite prominent; engaging the attention of able minds of both sexes the world over, provoking the consideration of grave deliberative bodies, and awakening a very widespread and lively popular interest. In fact, whatever else it is doing, it is achieving a very general and thorough discussion. It has got itself before the world; and it will no more yield its present vantage-ground, until it has been satisfactorily investigated and rightly determined, than the unwelcome guest at the banquet would down at the bidding of the guilty king. . . .

Here then, is woman, a living, self-conscious, responsible, moral entity, endowed with all the instincts and faculties of her brother, man. Her's a bodily form, somewhat smaller upon the average, perhaps not less enduring, certainly more sensitive and more graceful than his. Her's every intellectual power, be it fancy or imagination, memory or hope, comparison or judgement. . . . Few are the men, on this continent at least, that in any mixed assembly would wish or dare insult, or show the least disrespect to, a woman who did not in some way invite it. Give woman the ballot, and the polling-place will soon be fit for her to enter. Even as it is, the man or the woman who does not shrink from many a public conveyance, with its filth, and vile air, and bad manners, need not be greatly shocked at the offensiveness of an ordinary election room.

But the concession of suffrage to woman, it is said, will beget different political convictions, and so endless bickering, in the family. Do differences in religion beget such discord? Between low and vulgar souls, Yes; and mainly because, amongst such, woman is not yet recognized as a self-determining being, having the right of independent convictions. Between noble and generous natures, No; and still less would different political opinions tend to domestic strife from the fact that the proposed change is based on woman's natural right to do her own thinking, and shape her own destiny. . . .

It may be said again, that the right to vote involves the right to hold office. Not necessarily. Many men now vote who have never been, who never expect to be, elected to any office; some of whom do not want to be, and others of whom are not fit to be so elected. But suppose no man voted, here for Mayor or Member of Parliament, or elsewhere for Governor or President, who is not qualified for, and might not properly aspire to, either of those positions, very few votes would be cast. Yet who, on that account, prizes any the less the sacred right of saying whom he prefers to have preside over the administration of city or country? Suppose, moreover, the right to vote does involve the right to hold office. What then? Have not many women already held office, one sort or another, and shown themselves fully equal to their duties? Were Maria Theresa, and Catharine, and Elizabeth, any the less rulers because they were women? Who for more than forty years has reigned over the vast British Empire, and reigned in the hearts of her subjects as well, but a woman? Have the women of England and the United States, appointed as school superintendents, members of charitable boards, post-mistresses, and clerks of various grades, proved themselves, as a class, either dishonest or incompetent? They have shown themselves just the opposite—able, efficient, upright administrators. . . .

It is objected, finally, that women do not want the right of suffrage; that they are entirely content to remain without other influence on public affairs than they now have. Of many women—perhaps the majority—this is unquestionably true. How greatly to their praise it need not be said. Certainly it is not to their praise if they could, by their votes, help the industrial, educational, and moral interests of their country. . . .

It is very far from true that *no* women wish to vote. Thousands, and tens of thousands, and they will soon be hundreds of thousands wait impatiently to be invested with this right. And if there were but one woman in all the land who claimed the right, with what justice could it be withheld? Is there any better reason for wronging one or a few than for wronging many? It seems quite evident moreover, that the time is not far distant when this right will be conceded in all free countries; for how rapid has been the progress of public opinion in this direction during the last twenty-five years. . . . It would seem that one risks little in predicting that another generation will see woman's claim to suffrage placed on the same basis with man's throughout the great Republic. . . .

From "The Woman Question", *The Canadian Monthly and National Review*, May 1879, vol. II.

1. How does this author describe the capabilities of women?
2. What benefits for the political process does the author see in female suffrage?
3. What right is the author not yet prepared to extend to women?

Later that same year, a female writer calling herself "Fidelis" extended the argument in the same magazine.

. . . In the long run, women will find themselves permitted to do whatever they shall prove themselves to do well—all *a priori* prejudices to the contrary notwithstanding. The world wants good work so much more than it wants old prejudices—that these must eventually yield to common sense, and the inevitable law of demand and supply. Even the much vexed question of the suffrage, so obstinate before mere agitation, will ultimately, doubtless, be settled by the women who quietly demonstrate their capability of discharging all other duties of life, and of organising and conducting even great undertakings with the calm and judicious judgement, the perseverance and the thorough conscientiousness of highly cultivated women, which, we believe, will not be found inferior to the same qualities in highly cultivated men. If the new ideal of womanhood shall advance as much during the next quarter of a century as it has done in the past, the principle of excluding the holder of otherwise unrepresented property from the franchise on the ground of sex will, we venture to believe, be regarded as an antiquated survival of a semi-cultivation. But this result will never come by empty agitation. . . . Charles Kingsley's counsel deserves to be ever borne in mind by all promoters of this movement. "By quiet, modest, silent, private, influence, we shall win."

From Fidelis, "The New Ideal of Womanhood", *The Canadian Monthly and National Review*, November, 1879, vol III.

Almost twenty years later the same arguments were still being put forward. In this speech to the National Council of Women of Canada, Lady Ishbel Aberdeen identified woman's mission in the world.

. . . How can we best describe this woman's mission in a word? Can we not best describe it as "mothering" in one sense or another? We are not all called upon to be mothers of little children, but every woman is called upon to "mother" in some way or another; and it is impossible to be in this country, even for a little while, and not be impressed with a sense of what a great work of "mothering" is in a special sense committed to the women of Canada.

It is one of the great glories of this country that almost all its people are workers, and that there are very few drones. Its sons are all engrossed in the battle of life, striving for a sufficiency for themselves and their dear ones; and therefore on the women, hard-worked though they often are with domestic duties, must devolve the duty of building up the homes of the nation in the truest sense. And what sort of homes? Homes where the love of all that is beautiful and artistic and cultured is natural; where the true dignity of labour of every kind is recognized and acted upon; where a spirit of patriotism inspires young men and maidens to count it a high privilege to serve their country with single-minded disinterestedness, in however humble a way; where mutual love, consideration, forbearance, are the common rule, and the spirit of self-sacrifice is accounted the first necessity in the glorious work of helping others. . . .

The woman who aspires to make home a place for rest after work and for strengthening before labor, a centre of holy associations and inspiring memories, has need herself to be in touch with every side of our manifold life. She must realize that no walls can shelter her dear ones from the temptations, the sorrows, the discouragements of life. She must [be armed then] with armour suited for the fray. She must learn that if the poor around her doors are not cared for, the orphans not housed, the erring not reclaimed, because she was too much engrossed in her own house to lend a helping hand, the results of her self-absorption may be in the future to provide pitfalls for her own children, whom she so desires to cherish. If she is to be truly her husband's companion, her children's friend and guide, the maker of a home that will shed light and blessing, not only on its own inmates, but on the strangers who pass from time to time within her gates, she must needs understand the changes that are taking place in social conditions, the progress of thought in all directions.

From *Women Workers of Canada* (Ottawa: National Council of Women of Canada, 1898).

1. What tactic is advocated by Fidelis in order to achieve ultimate success?
2. In what way does Lady Aberdeen extend the concept of mothering to embrace a larger mission for women?
3. What was the status of women at the turn of the century?

Unequal Pay for Equal Work, 1890

The struggle for equal pay for work of equal value finds its roots in the previous century. In this essay, Minnie Phelps outlined the inequities existing between male and female labourers.

It is a geometrical axiom, "That things which are halves of the same thing are equal to one another." It follows then, that woman being the one-half of the human whole, is equal to the other half, the male fraction, and they being "one," have a common interest in all that relates to either sex—their mutual aspirations—spiritual advances and the struggles for existence.

Two-thirds of the human family are laborers, either of brain or muscle. One-half of the whole is woman, and the question presents itself. What is the per cent of women as laborers, and as wage-earners, and what is the accredited value of that labor?

In 1840, that good and great woman, Harriet Martineau, visited America, and found seven employments open to women: teaching, sewing, keeping boarding-house, folding and stitching in binderies, work in factories, as compositors, or in domestic service. So great have been the changes since Miss Martineau's visit, that in the United States 300 doors are now open to women, and in our Canada, from the census of 1881, we find 227 occupations, where, in 1840, our mothers had but seven.

In the two main departments of manufacture in the United States, including boots and shoes, carpets, cotton goods, silks, woolen hats, there are employed 535 000, one-third of which are women, or about 180 000. In the Province of Ontario there are 18 650 women employed in the various trades and occupations, in the Dominion of Canada there are 45 889. In the factories of our Province there are 7 594 women, 247 girls between the ages of 12 and 14 years; 1 588 between the ages of 14 and 18 years. These women, working side by side of the male laborers, battling with the same physical struggles, full of the same higher aspirations, the value of the world's market of exchange being equal, find they receive from one-third to one-half less wages, doing the same work with as much skill as their brother workers.

Let me give a few instances of the wages paid to women in the great industry of underwear for women. We hear now-a-days of the cheapness of these garments. "So much cheaper," you say, "than you could make them yourself." You wonder at it. Here are the reasons, and the only reasons. For the underclothing that some of you are wearing at this very hour, some poor, needy sister has been paid the sum of 48 cents per dozen, or 4 cents a piece, for the manufacture of the same. She has been paid 40 cents per dozen for coarse drawers; night-dresses, tucked and trimmed, $1.30 per dozen; while for the white skirts, tucked ruffles, she gets $1.00 per dozen. This is not all. These women and girls must buy their own needles, thread, oil and soap; 20 cents for one spool of thread, 40 cents for another, which lasts two weeks. These women work nine and one-half hours per day, if late five minutes are fined five cents. These facts are from the City of Toronto—"the city of churches," and while you are reading these things, the rush of the shuttle and the hurrying needle is being plied while some of us wear these garments which mean life and virtue to some poor girl.

Do you not catch the echo of Tom Hood's "stitch, stitch," and do you not see finally the picture of "one more unfortunate?" This is but one example of a class of women who, compelled by necessity, are slaving for the merest pittance. There is a terrible affinity between vice and hunger, between low wages and the eating cancer of our cities—the social evil. . . .

Take again another class, school teachers, both male and female, giving the same amount of time, their standard of excellence being equal. What do we find? That women do the work and men get the wages. In my own city, St. Catharines, I have gleaned these facts. There are two teachers in our central school, both doing entrance examination work; last year the woman promoted 14, the man 2; the woman gets $600 the man $900. Giving as is granted $100 for the responsibility of head master, why is it that the woman, whose work is superior to the man's, gets $200 less wages? Answer, sex. . . .

In every line of occupation given, we have shown that woman is equal to man in the quality and quantity of work; the question naturally arises, if woman can do and does do the same kind of work as man, why should she not have the same wages, and along what lines can we remedy this inequality?

1st—By giving the same protection to woman as to man, by allowing woman a chance to enter any field of labor she may find open to her. The sphere of each man or of each woman is that which he or she can best fill with the highest exercise of their respective abilities; and all that I ask for woman is the same liberty of choice as that offered man, and the chance to prove by that liberty of choice her ability to do her chosen work. . . .

2nd—Give woman the same preparation for her chosen calling as that of her brother—all sons are expected to learn some trade or profession, why not all daughters. So that when reverses come, and some rich man is not on hand to marry the girl, she may find herself in a position to earn a respectable living. . . .

3rd—Back of the two plans for the bettering of woman as wage-earners, is the foundation upon which both must build, e.g.—the ballot—for as Canon Kingsley once said, "Women will never have social equity, until she has legal equity." . . .

I present these remedies to you from a trial and from experimental knowledge of the one-half of integral humanity—man. The steps by which man has developed and assumed his present position, are the steps that womanhood now and the womanhood of the future must tread. Some of you are fearful that if the ballot be given to woman, and with that, the ever opening doors of commerce and of trade, the widening doors of the legal profession, the doctor's healing art, the editorial chair, the preacher's desk, and the various occupations and trades, as various as the talents of woman, that somewhere possibly woman may lose her womanliness and aspire to the other sex.

From Miss Minnie Phelps, "Women as Wage-Earners," in Rev. B. F. Austin, *Woman: Her Character, Culture and Calling* (Brantford, 1890).

1. Analyse the argument being put forward by Phelps. Based upon her statistics, create your own thesis with regard to pay equity in 1890.
2. Compare your findings with equivalent data from a century later. Contact a local pay equity office and find out the extent to which women have "caught up" in the last one hundred years.
3. Create your own thesis on the current state of pay equity in Canada.

American Women at the Turn of the Century

Marie Van Vorst and her sister-in-law, Mrs. John Van Vorst, researched the life of the working woman by taking menial jobs in various factories and sweat shops. In 1904 they published their findings in a book entitled The Woman Who Toils: Being the

Experiences of Two Gentlewomen as Factory Girls. *The following account is an excerpt from their book.*

When my employer had left me I observed the woman at my side: an untidy, degraded-looking creature, long past youth. Her hands beggared description; their covering resembled skin not at all, but a dark-blue substance, leatherlike, bruised, ingrained, indigo-hued. Her nails looked as though they had been beaten severely. One of her thumbs was bandaged.

"I lost one nail; rotted off."

"Horrible! How, pray?"

"That there water: it's poison from the shoe-dye."

Swiftly my hands were changing to a faint likeness of my companion's.

"Don't tell him," she said, "that I told you that. He'll be mad; he'll think I am discouraging you. But you'll lose your forefinger nail, all right!" Then she gave a little laugh as she turned her boot around to polish it.

"Once I tried to clean my hands up. Lord! it's no good! I scrub 'em with a scrubbin'-brush on Sundays."

"How long have you been at this job?"

"Ten months."

They call her "Bobby"; the men from their machines nodded to her now and then, bantering her across the noise of their wheels. She was ignorant of it, too stupid to know whether life took her in sport or in earnest! The men themselves worked in their flannel shirts. Not far from us was a wretchedly ill-looking individual, the very shadow of manhood. I observed that once he cast toward us a look of interest. Under my feet was a raised platform on which I stood, bending to my work. During the morning the consumptive man strolled over and whispered something to "Bobby." He made her dullness understand. When he had gone back to his job she said to me:

"Say, w'y don't yer push that platform away and stand on the floor? You're too tall to need that. It makes yer bend."

"Did that man come over to tell you this?"

"Yes. He said it made you tired."

From my work, across the room, I silently blessed the pale old man, bowed, thin, pitiful, over the shoe he held, obscured from me by the cloud of sawdust-like flying leather that spun scattered from the sole he held to the flying wheel.

I don't believe the shoe-dye really to be poisonous. I suppose it is scarcely possible that it can be so; but the constant pressure against forefinger nail is enough to induce disease. My fingers were swollen sore. The effects of the work did not leave my hands for weeks. . . .

When the foreman had left me I turned to look at "Bobby." She was in the act of lifting to her lips a glass of what was supposed to be water.

"You're not going to drink that!" I gasped, horrified. "Where did you get it?"

"Oh, I drawed it awhile ago," she said.

It had stood gathering microbes in the room, visible ones evidently, for a

scum had formed on the glass that looked like stagnant oil. She blew the stuff
back and drank long. Her accent was so bad and her English so limited I took
her to be a foreigner beyond doubt. She proved to be an American. She had
worked in factories all her life, since she was eight years old, and her brain was
stunted.

At dinner time, when I left Marches', I had stood, without sitting down
once, for five hours, and according to Bobby's computation I had made the
large sum of twenty-five cents, having cleaned a little more than one hundred
shoes. To all intents, at least for the moment, my hands were ruined. At Wey-
man's restaurant I went in with my fellow workwomen and men.

. . . There are dozens, you remember, still in the unaired fourth and fifth
stories—at "lunching" over their sandwiches. Far more vivid, more poignant
even must be to me the vision of "Bobby." I shall see her eat her filthy sandwich with her blackened hands, see her stoop to blow the scum of deadly matter from her typhoid-breeding glass.

From Marie Van Vorst and Mrs. John Van Vorst, *The Woman Who Toils: Being the Experiences of Two
Gentlewomen as Factory Girls*, (New York, 1904).

Rheta Childe Dorr wrote a regular column for Hampton's *magazine. A feminist, she
followed the lead of the Van Vorsts in investigating the working conditions of women.
Her findings appeared first in* Hampton's *and later as a book,* What Eight Million
Women Want, *published in 1910.*

Men, ardently, eternally, interested in Woman—one woman at a time—are
almost never even faintly interested in women. Strangely, deliberately ignorant
of women, they argue that their ignorance is justified by an innate unknowable-
ness of the sex.

I am persuaded that the time is at hand when this sentimental, half contemptuous attitude of half the population towards the other half will have to be
abandoned. I believe that the time has arrived when self-interest, if other
motive be lacking, will compel society to examine the ideals of women. In support of this opinion I ask you to consider three facts, each one of which is so
patient that it requires no argument.

The Census of 1900 reported nearly six million women in the United States
engaged in wage earning outside their homes. Between 1890 and 1900 the number of women in industry increased faster than the number of men in industry.
It increased faster than the birth rate. The number of women wage earners at the
present date can only be estimated. Nine million would be a conservative guess.
Nine million women who have forsaken the traditions of the hearth and are
competing with men in the world of paid labor means that women are rapidly
passing from the domestic control of their fathers and their husbands. Surely
this is the most important economic fact in the world to-day. . . .

Not only in the United States, but in every constitutional country in the
world the movement towards admitting women to full political equality with
men is gathering strength. In half a dozen countries women are already completely enfranchised. In England the opposition is seeking terms of surrender.

In the United States the stoutest enemy of the movement acknowledges that woman suffrage is ultimately inevitable. The voting strength of the world is about to be doubled, and the new element is absolutely an unknown quantity. Does anyone question that this is the most important political fact the modern world has ever faced? . . .

I hope that I shall not be suspected of ascribing to women any ingrained or fundamental moral superiority to men. Women are not better than men. . . .

That the mass of women are invariably found on the side of the new ideals is no evidence of their moral superiority to men; it is merely evidence of their intellectual youth.

From Rheta Childe Dorr, *What Eight Million Woman Want*, (Boston, 1910).

1. Create a diary account written by a female factory worker of the period.
2. What employment pattern does Rheta Childe Dorr identify?
3. Discuss Dorr's contention that the political life of the world is about to change.

Canadian Women at the Turn of the Century

In this account Canadian historian Pierre Berton describes a "tour" of working conditions given to Manitoba premier Sir Rodmond Roblin just prior to World War I. Sir Rodmond's tour guides were feminist activists Mrs. Claude Nash and Nellie McClung.

Sir Rodmond Roblin, Premier of Manitoba, sits nervously in the rear seat of his limousine, his plump hands gripping the gold handle of his cane. He is a big, florid man in his sixties, more than a little pompous, and flanked now by two determined women: Mrs. Nash, in her grey lamb coat and crimson velvet hat, on one side and the splendidly attired Mrs. McClung on the other.

Sir Rodmond is engaged in a monologue about working women. It is good for them to work, he says; there is far too much idleness these days. He himself worked a full day as a boy, and loved every minute of it! Are the ladies not being too sentimental about factory conditions? These young girls in the factories: are they really underpaid? No doubt they live at home and work for pin money. At any rate, work won't hurt them; it will keep them off the streets. Anyway, most workers are foreigners from countries where life is strenuous. They are used to hard work. Let them understand how money is made. Extravagant women are the curse of the age. And so forth. The monologue drones on. Mrs. Nash and Mrs. McClung grit their teeth and say nothing.

They reach a grubby factory, lead their man down a set of dark, slippery stairs and into an airless basement where naked light bulbs hang from smoky ceilings. The floor is ankle-deep in apple peelings and discarded cloth. There is no ventilation, no heat. A long line of untidy women crouch over sewing machines. Roblin takes one look, tries to leave; but his companions urge him to speak to the workers. Finally a question occurs to him: doesn't anyone sweep the floors? He has to shout to make himself heard over the sound of the machines. No one answers. One woman shakes her head and keeps on working.

Mrs. McClung reminds the Premier that all are on piecework; they cannot afford the time for conversation.

Again he tries to leave, but they will not let him go. They push him through a side door into a foul passage to show him a queue forming before a door marked "Toilet." There are no separate facilities for women, and the plumbing isn't working.

"For God's sake, let me out of here," cries Rodmond Roblin. "I'm choking. I never knew such hell holes existed!"

But they are implacable. "These people work from 8:30 to 6:00, Sir Rodmond. Six days a week," Mrs. Nash tells him sweetly. "But no doubt they get used to it." Her sarcasm is lost on the Premier.

Back on the street, he suddenly remembers an important interview and tries to break away, but they coax him into a shirt factory to witness young girls who are being "kept off the streets." Here is a young woman whose hand, bound up with a dirty bandage, has been injured in a machine. Here is another who coughs continually with bronchitis but who cannot afford to stop work because she must support her family; if she takes time off somebody will be hired at once in her place. The manager arrives to tell the Premier that he doesn't need any factory inspectors because "all the girls are glad of the work. I have no trouble with them."

"How about the girl who coughs so much?" asks Nellie McClung. "Couldn't she be given a few days off with pay to get built up a bit?"

"The company is not a charitable institution," the manager tells her. " . . . If the girl is sick she can always quit!"

Roblin edges toward the door and escapes into the protection of his limousine.

"I still can't see why two women like you should ferret out such utterly disgusting things," he says.

Once again they urge upon him the need to appoint a trained social worker as a woman factory inspector.

The Premier grows impatient at the harangue. "I tell you it's no job for a woman," he says. "I have too much respect for women to give any of them a job like this." He admits he's greatly disturbed. He didn't know such places existed in the highly publicized Chicago of the North. He'll speak to his people about the problem. But he promises nothing.

From Pierre Berton, *The Promised Land*, (Toronto: McClelland and Stewart, 1984).

A number of Winnipeg female suffragists formed the Political Equality League in 1912. The following editorial by Nellie McClung appeared in the league's publication The New Citizenship.

Ideas are contagious and epidemic. They break out unexpectedly and without warning. Thought without expression is dynamic and gathers volume by repression. Evolution, when blocked and suppressed, becomes revolution.

At the present time there are many people seriously alarmed by the discontent among women. They say women are no longer contented with woman's

work and woman's sphere. Women no longer find their highest joy in plain
sewing and working in wool. The washboard has lost its charm and the days of
the hair wreath are ended. Many people view this condition with alarm and
believe that women are deserting the sacred sphere of home-making and the
rearing of children; in short, that women are losing their usefulness. We may as
well face the facts. We cannot drive women back to the spinning wheel and the
mat hook. We do hear more of discontent among women than we once did.
Labor saving devices have entered the home and women are saved the endless
labor of days gone by, when a woman's hours of labor were: 5 a.m. to 5 a.m.
The reason we hear of more discontent than formerly is that women have more
time to be discontented. . . .

But discontent is not necessarily wicked. There is such a thing as criminal
contentment and there is such a thing as divine discontent. Discontent means
the stirring of ambition, the desire to spread out, to improve, to grow. Discontent is a sign of life corresponding to growing pains in a healthy child. . . .

Women have never yet lived in their own world. Man has assigned woman
her sphere. Woman's sphere is anything a man does not wish to do himself.
This is a simple distribution of labor and easily understood and very satisfactory
to half the population. Men have given a great deal of attention to women.
They have told us exactly what we are like. They have declared us to be illogical, hysterical, impulsive, loving, patient, forgiving, malicious, vindictive, bitter, not any too honest, not very reliable. They have given us credit for all the
good in the world and yet blamed us for all the evil. They are very prone to
speak of women, as a class, of women—women in bulk, making each individual
woman responsible for the sins of all.

From Nellie McClung, *The New Citizenship* (Political Equality League of Manitoba, n.d.) in Ramsay
Cook and Wendy Mitchinson, eds., *The Proper Sphere: Woman's Place in Canadian Society*, (Toronto:
Oxford University Press, 1976).

1. The tour had little effect on Roblin. In a subsequent speech on woman's suffrage
he stated that: "Woman suffrage is illogical and absurd . . . placing women on a
political equality with men would cause domestic strife."
Write a personal letter from a female suffragist to Roblin countering his views.
2. Outline McClung's defence of discontent.
3. Respond to the arguments put forward in McClung's article.

The Debate over the Vote: Canada, 1913-14

*The reasoned arguments put forward by the suffragists were gradually wearing down
their opposition when the First World War broke out. Although the war hastened the
movement to enfranchisement, there is no doubt but that it would have soon come
regardless. During the prewar years there was an ongoing debate over the right to vote.*

In this excerpt from a 1913 article in the Grain Growers' Guide *Francis Marion
Beynon, a member of the Political Equality League, challenges the anti-suffragists.*

The theory that a woman should appeal to a man through her basest qualities—
her vanity, her weakness, for which a more honest word is incompetence; her

mental dependence, which is either ignorance or stupidity, revolts me, more especially as these attributes appeal to the basest side of man's nature—his vanity, his sensual passions and his arrogance. I refuse to believe that such a low appeal is necessary to the perpetuation of the human race. . . .

We have too long been contented with the kind of motherhood that can look out of the window and see little children toiling incredible hours in factories or canning sheds over the way, until their small heads grow dizzy and their little fingers are bruised and bleeding, and say calmly, "Thank God, it isn't my children," or who can see the poor wayward girl being driven into a life of disgrace and shame by economic conditions and turn coolly away, content that her own daughter is chaste; with the sort of motherhood that can know that in the poor districts of our cities tiny babies are dying like flies and yet feel no responsibility for the conditions that cause their death.

I tell you, sisters, this kind of motherhood isn't good enough for the present day.

From Francis Marion Beynon, "Answers to an Anti-Suffragist", *The Grain Growers' Guide*, 1 October 1913, vol. X.

In an address to the National Council of Women of Canada in Montreal later the same year, Sonia Leathes made a strong case for the vote.

A high authority on constitutional law says that it requires a great deal of time to have opinions. The object of every reformer is, therefore, not so much to convert people to any particular way of thinking, as to make them realize that in the vast mass of ready made statements—many of them handed down from generation to generation for centuries—there is a great deal which, in the light of an advanced or altered social and spiritual condition of society, no longer applies. In other words, the reformer's object is to make people realize that there is a problem, that there is something to think about with reference to matters which the average man and woman have taken for granted. . . .

The problem of women suffrage which, though only a part of a general movement, is its culminating point, has its roots in, and grows directly out of these problems. It is indeed but a further, perhaps the last, chapter in the great history of the emancipation of the individual, black or white, rich or poor, male or female, from social and political disability imposed upon him or her on account of birth alone. This is the true meaning of democracy. It is not that all persons shall, or indeed ever can, be absolutely equal in intellect, moral power, influence, and wealth, and in the position among their fellows which is determined by the possession of these qualities. Democracy does not imply identity or equality in social status. The essence of democracy is the removal of all artificial restrictions which bar the way to the progress, development, and advancement, be it economic, social, or political, of any individual or of any class on account of birth, colour, religious creed, or sex alone. . . .

Our divine sense of justice tells us that the being who is to be governed by laws should first assent to them, that the being who is taxed shall have a voice in fixing the character and amount of the financial burden which it is to bear.

Then, if woman is made responsible before the law, if she is admitted to the gallows, to the gaol, and to the tax lists, we have no right to debar her from the ballot box.

Practically all the arguments against women's suffrage fall under three categories: Some people say that they do not believe in women's suffrage, when really what they do not believe in is representative government. . . .

This brings us to the second category of the anti-suffrage arguments. Some people think that they do not believe in women's suffrage, when really what they do not believe is that women are persons. They have thought of women as "wives," "mothers," "daughters"; and though they have been obliged to admit the existence of the female stenographer, shop assistant, clerk, physician, even of the female mayor and city councillor, they cannot as yet fully grasp the fact that in addition to her private relationship to some man, a woman is still a social unit, a citizen, a subject, a person. The fact of her being somebody's wife, or daughter, or sister, has nothing to do with her being a tax-payer. She remains personally responsible for her observance or non-observance of the law of the land. She is equally affected by war, conditions of climate, finance, industry, national prosperity or adversity. All these matters affect women as well as men, and women should have the right to help decide all questions on policy for precisely the same reason that men possess this right.

From Sonia Leathes, "Votes for Women," a speech given to the National Council of Women of Canada, Montreal, 1913, in *University Magazine*, Feb. 1914, vol. XIII.

Some men were not willing to give up their privileged position that easily. In a 1914 article in University Magazine, *Andrew Macphail argued against female suffrage.*

Every generation has its own problems, and each generation creates problems which it leaves to a succeeding generation to solve. The fathers eat the bitter fruit: it is the children whose teeth are set on edge.

The nineteenth century was rich in experiment; and the people who lived in those ancient days have left to us the task of reaping as they sowed and gathering up what they strawed so recklessly. They tried everything. They invented machinery to free the world from labour, and we are bound in a hard mechanical routine. They gave liberty to the people, and a new slavery has arisen on the ruins of the old. They freed men from superstition, and we are left without religion, according to the degree of their success. They enfranchised adult males, and we vote wrongly or corruptly, or will not vote at all. They introduced free education, and now the educated ones bewilder their minds by reading not the best, but the worst. They emancipated women, and the women avenge themselves by brawling in public places. They opened every trade and every profession to women; yet women will persist in marrying and giving in marriage, and encumbering the earth with their progeny.

From the beginning of time men have done their best in their poor, blind way to make the world a better place for themselves and their womenkind to live in; yet they hear on every hand that the first misfortune for a woman is to be born, the second to be married, and the last to become a mother. Everything in these days seems to turn out wrong. If a law is made that women shall be paid the same wages as men for doing work which seems to be the same, it quickly follows that the women are driven out of that field of employment entirely. . . .

At this worst moment of scepticism, when men are assailed by the conviction of failure, they are met with the temptation of help of a new kind from a quarter to which they have always looked for consolation, and rarely failed to find it. Women are offering assistance of a less passive nature. Instead of contenting themselves with binding up the wounds of those who fight, they are demanding that they be given a place in the forefront of the fray.

The first equipment they demand is the right to vote. On the part of the gentler it is an appeal rather than a demand. They ask that they be allowed,—if one may be permitted for the time being, without offence even to the most petulant, to interpret their mind by the employment of a term which is hortative rather than mandatory,—to assume the privilege and undertake the duty of casting the ballot, so that they may work side by side with men, as comrades in social service for the uplift of humanity, if one may be permitted again to employ those flamboyant terms with which constant iteration has made us all so familiar. There is something pathetic in the appeal, and one but the most hardened can be insensible to it.

If men have shown little alacrity in welcoming these volunteers to their ranks, it is because they are not convinced of the value of the "work" which is proposed to be done. . . . If women choose to walk in the slums doing social work rather than in the parks to make themselves healthy and beautiful, if they elect to visit the vicious poor rather than the vicious rich, and offer unsolicited and ill-considered advice to those who are too humble to resent it openly as an impertinence, the result of their enquiry may be a revelation to themselves. It will present nothing new to the world at large. It will only be new to them by reason of their inexperience.

The whole controversy turns on the meaning of this word, "work." Voting only occupies a few moments each year. Law-making is an employment for the very few. The world of work is free to all who show desire and capacity to undertake it. No profession or trade is closed to women. They may be sea-captains, farmers, or plumbers. They have proved their capacity as physicians, lawyers, and ministers of at least one form of religion. One woman is now at the head of the prison system, and another at the head of a department of hygiene in New York. Still another has so completely mastered the practice of law that she has been indicted on the charge of taking a false affidavit and of altering a complaint in action. . . . Such women are everywhere received as comrades. It is the incapable, idle women who, neglecting the work which lies ready, come forth with wild cries, and seek sanctuary as soon as they are opposed—it is these who are received, first with anger and then with open contempt. The women who really work are solving the problem for themselves. They are freeing themselves from conventions which grew up in a different environment, and are creating an atmosphere in which they can move more freely. They only require to be left alone by the professional agitators, the show-women, the "m'as-tu vus," since there is a limit to the patience of men, when they have serious business in hand. . . .

There is something pathetic in this appeal by emancipated women to men for comradeship. They have so little in common with normal women that they are condemned to solitude or to the company of each other; and they are not sufficiently like men to make them preferable to a man itself.

From Andrew Macphail, "On Certain Aspects of Feminism", *University Magazine*, Feb. 1914, vol. XIII.

1. Together with some friends create a docudrama highlighting the debate over female suffrage. Participants could be encouraged to research and take the role of a specific participant in the debates of the period. One interesting twist might be to have the women take the male roles and vice versa.

Response to Freud, 1939

Sigmund Freud raised the ire of many feminists in his chapter "The Psychology of Women" which appeared in New Introductory Lectures on Psychoanalysis *(1933). In this brief excerpt Karey Horney challenged Freud's view.*

Freud believes that psychic peculiarities and difficulties in the two sexes are engendered by bisexual trends in both of them. His contention is, briefly, that many psychic difficulties in man are due to his rejection of "feminine" trends in himself, and that many peculiarities in woman are due to her essential wish to be a man. Freud has elaborated this thought in more detail for the psychology of woman than for that of man, and therefore I shall discuss only his views of feminine psychology. . . .

There remains, the emotional basis of self-confidence. If, however, one's self-confidence is dependent on giving or receiving love, then one builds on a foundation which is too small and too shaky—too small because it leaves out too many personality values, and too shaky because it is dependent on too many external factors, such as finding adequate partners. Besides, it very easily leads to an emotional dependence on other people's affection and appreciation, and results in a feeling of unworthiness if one is not loved or appreciated.

As far as the alleged given inferiority of woman is concerned, Freud has, to be sure, made a remark which it is quite a relief to hear from him: "You must not forget, however, that we have only described women in so far as their natures are determined by their sexual function. The influence of this factor is, of course, very far-reaching, but we must remember that *an individual woman may be a human being apart from this*" (italics mine). . . . "But we must take care not to underestimate the influence of social conventions, which also force women into passive situations. The whole thing is still very obscure. We must not overlook one particularly constant relation between femininity and instinctual life. The repression of their aggressiveness, which is imposed upon women by their constitutions and by society, favors the development of strong masochistic impulses, which have the effect of binding erotically the destructive tendencies which have been turned inwards."

But since he has a primarily biological orientation Freud does not, and on the basis of his premises cannot, see the whole significance of these factors. He cannot see to what extent they mold wishes and attitudes, nor can he evaluate the complexity of interrelations between cultural conditions and feminine psychology.

I suppose everyone agrees with Freud that differences in sexual constitution and functions influence mental life. But it seems unconstructive to speculate on the exact nature of this influence. The American woman is different from the German woman; both are different from certain Pueblo Indian women. The New York society woman is different from the farmer's wife in Idaho. The way specific cultural conditions engender specific qualities and faculties, in women as in men—this is what we hope to understand.

From Karey Horney, *New Ways in Psychoanalysis* (New York: W.W. Norton and Company, Inc., 1939).

1. What does Horney say with regard to personal self-confidence?
2. Outline the author's fundamental critique of Freud.
3. To what extent to you agree with her thesis?

Job Title: Housewife, 1953

In 1953 job analyst Harold Jacobson of Massachusetts created this not so tongue-in-cheek job decription for the career of housewife.

Grade: HIGH
Description:
 Functions in several capacities and offices performing a wide variety of duties semi-routine in nature but where the exercise of independent judgement is required in the application of practices and policies to situations not previously covered:
 Effects the purchase of a wide variety of organic materials for processing, giving special consideration to costs, market conditions, and state of material. Plan, layout, and schedule processing operations, maintaining strict control of flow and inventory to meet schedules. Conduct necessary chemical operations, using various heat treatments as required to transform basic organic materials into completed form for distribution to consumer;
 Maintains budgeting, cost control, and cost accounting systems, operating within a limited financial framework. Strike semi-monthly trial balances to determine relationship between accounts-payable and accounts-receivable and, as required, perform necessary magic to bring accounts into balance;
 Operates and maintains a variety of manually and electrically powered equipment for heating, cooling, stitching, suctioning, cleansing, etc.;
 Performs other miscellaneous duties of a routine nature not specifically mentioned, but where such duties are a normal outgrowth of the job.
Substantiating Data
 Education: This factor appraises the minimum amount of theoretical education required, however attained.

Broad general knowledge of several specialized fields such as chemistry, mechanical and electrical engineering, marketing, accounting, and fundamentals of human relations.

Complexity of Duties: This factor appraises the need for initiative, ingenuity, and independent judgement.

Perform a wide variety of semi-routine duties directed toward the attainment of a general objective: the physiological and psychic welfare of a small social group. Performance requires the use of judgement in devising new methods and modifying or adapting standard practice to meet new conditions.

Responsibility: This factor appraises the responsibility for equipment, material, process, and health, safety, and work of others.

Complete responsibility in terms of costs, methods, and personnel for equipment, material, process, etc. Supervise and direct one inept male in the performance of a limited number of routine duties such as: rub, scrub, sweep, brush, mop, polish, etc.

Effort: This factor appraises the mental and/or visual demand required.

High degree of concentration where the volume and nature of work require unusual coordination of hand and eye.

Working Conditions: This factor appraises the surroundings or physical conditions under which the job must be performed. It includes health and accident hazards.

Somewhat disagreeable working conditions due to exposure to dust, dirt, heat, etc. Exposure to accidents where results will probably be minor in nature: cuts, bruises, burns, etc., which, although painful, are not incapacitating in nature. Health hazards negligible. Fatigue factor high.

From Harold W. Jacobsen, "Job Title: Housewife," in *Personnel Journal*, 32, (Costa Mesa, California: *Personnel Journal*, September 1953). All rights reserved.

1. Update Jacobson's description to match the typical demands on a working mother in the late 1980s.

The Feminine Mystique, 1963

In her best-selling book author Betty Friedan argued that women were little more than prisoners in their own society. In this excerpt she called for women to liberate themselves and begin to grow as people.

Our society forces boys, insofar as it can, to grow up, to endure the pains of growth, to educate themselves to work, to move on. Why aren't girls forced to grow up—to achieve somehow the core of self that will end the unnecessary dilemma, the mistaken choice between femaleness and humanness that is implied in the feminine mystique?

. . . It is time to stop exhorting women to be more "feminine" when it breeds a passivity and dependence that depersonalizes sex and imposes an impossible burden on their husbands, a growing passivity in their sons.

It is not an exaggeration to call the stagnating state of millions of American housewives a sickness, a disease in the shape of a progressively weaker core of human self that is being handed down to their sons and daughters at a time when the dehumanizing aspects of modern mass culture make it necessary for men and women to have a strong core of self, strong enough to retain human individuality through the frightening, unpredictable pressures of our changing environment. The strength of women is not the cause, but the cure for this sickness. Only when women are permitted to use their full strength, to grow to their full capacities, can the feminine mystique be shattered and the progressive dehumanization of their children be stopped. . . .

. . . For women of ability, in America today, I am convinced there is something about the housewife state itself that is dangerous. In a sense that is not as far-fetched as it sounds, the women who "adjust" as housewives, who grow up wanting to be "just a housewife," are in as much danger as the millions who walked to their own death in the concentration camps—and the millions more who refused to believe that the concentration camps existed. . . .

The suburban house is not a German concentration camp, nor are American housewives on their way to the gas chamber. But they are in a trap, and to escape they must, like the dancer, finally exercise their human freedom, and recapture their sense of self. They must refuse to be nameless, depersonalized, manipulated and live their own lives again according to a self-chosen purpose. They must begin to grow.

From Betty Friedan, *The Feminine Mystique* (New York: W.W. Norton and Company, Inc., 1963).

1. How does Betty Friedan say that society conditions boys and girls?
2. Comment on Friedan's vision of the dehumanization of society.
3. To what extent has the status of women in North American society changed in the past quarter century?

The United Nations Declaration of Women's Rights, 1967

The following selection is excerpted from the UN Declaration on Women's Rights, which was adopted by the General Assembly in November 1967.

The General Assembly,

Considering that the peoples of the United Nations have, in the Charter, reaffirmed their faith in fundamental human rights, in the dignity and worth of the human person and in the equal rights of men and women,

Considering that the Universal Declaration of Human Rights asserts the principle of nondiscrimination and proclaims that all human beings are born free and equal in dignity and rights and that everyone is entitled to all the rights and freedoms set forth therein, without distinction of any kind, including any distinction as to sex,

Taking into account the resolutions, declarations, conventions and recommendations of the United Nations and the specialized agencies designed to eliminate all forms of discrimination and to promote equal rights for men and women,

Concerned that, despite the Charter, the Universal Declaration of Human Rights, International Covenants on Human Rights and other instruments of the

United Nations and the specialized agencies and despite the progress made in the matter of equality of rights, there continues to exist considerable discrimination against women,

Considering that discrimination against women is incompatible with human dignity, . . .

Convinced that the full and complete development of a country, the welfare of the world and the cause of peace require the maximum participation of women as well as men in all fields,

Considering that it is necessary to insure the universal recognition in law and in fact of the principle of equality of men and women, Solemnly proclaims this Declaration: . . .

From Declaration on the Elimination of Discrimination Against Women, adopted by the General Assembly of the United Nations, Resolution 2263 (XXII), Nov. 7, 1967.

1. To what extent does North American society live up to the spirit of the declaration?
2. Create and defend your own thesis with regard to the record of either Canada or the United States in promoting sexual equality.

Pie in the Sky, 1971

The following critique of the report of the Royal Commission on the Status of Women appeared in The Pedestal.

"Paid vacations for housewives!" So the *Vancouver Sun* announced the release of the report of the three million dollar, three year old Royal Commission on the Status of Women. Many of us read with some surprise the recommendations of the Commission: maternity leave with pay, free abortion on demand, a national day-care program, equal job and promotion opportunity, pensions and paid vacations for housewives, guaranteed annual income for all one parent families, an end to sex-typing in the classroom, liberalization of divorce laws, etc., etc.,

For two days the papers gloated over the promised liberation of women. Those of us who have been fighting so hard for many of these very demands could hardly help but be impressed.

And yet an actual reading of the report gives less reason for optimism. It is hardly surprising that the demands in many ways echo our own. Some of us made submissions to Commission hearings. The commissioners themselves have spent many months listening to accounts of the oppression of women in Canada, from sophisticated professional women in Montreal and Toronto to angry Indian women in the Yukon. The only surprising thing about the recommendations is that it should have taken three years to document our obvious needs.

In fact, given three years and three million dollars collected in taxes from 2.3 million underpaid working women, the recommendations of the Royal Commission are remarkably short-sighted. While the commissioners were shocked into recognizing that women are oppressed, they failed somehow to understand the root causes of our oppression. For example, they recommend equal job oppor-

tunities and lament the ineffectiveness of the existing legislation which is supposed to guarantee women's right to equal pay for equal work. They argue that
women should be admitted to the boards of directors of the major corporations,
federal boards, task forces and the Senate. It is hard to believe that they can be
so naive. . . .

The federal government itself has been notoriously lax in its hiring and wage
policies vis-a-vis women. The question to be asked is why a government closely
inter-linked with business and industry would effect laws which will cut off a
cheap pool of labour? Why equal pay? Why equal job opportunity? Big business is concerned about profit, not human equality. As women we are
oppressed by the kind of society we live in—an economic social system based
on the exploitation of many by a few powerful owners and a social system
dependent on racial, national and sexual chauvinism. A few token women or
even a significant minority of women sitting in corporation board rooms will not
and cannot liberate women whose exploitation is the key to profits in quite a
few industries. . . .

. . . Given the usual plight of the recommendations of Royal Commissions,
there is reason for a certain cynicism about the likely destiny of this report. . . .
The pitiful changes wrought by the much touted Bilingualism and Biculturalism
Commission should serve as a warning to us not to be fooled by mere words.

From "Pie in the Sky . . . royal commission recipe," *The Pedestal*, (January 1971).

1. What criticisms are levelled at the report?
2. To what extent has Canadian society met the challenge of these criticisms in
the last twenty years?

Women and Politics, 1978

*Laura Sabia is a former chairperson of the Ontario Council on the Status of Women.
She was instrumental in pressuring the government to create the Royal Commission on
the Status of Women. In this 1978 lecture from the Gerstein Series at York University
she called for greater female participation in Canadian political life.*

The relationship of the sexes is and always has been political, in the widest
sense of the term. Any examination of this relationship must consider politics:
the politics of the state—of the governed and the governing; the politics of religion—of the blessed and the damned; the politics of the marketplace—of the
haves and the have-nots.

Through the centuries this relationship has been a continuing power struggle
in which women have been idolized, patronized, and exploited. Society's most
arbitrary folly has been and continues to be its under-utilization of women's
brainpower. It is now time for women to be humanized, their brainpower
tapped, and their abilities recognized.

Women comprise the largest alienated element in our society. Yet it has
taken two thousand years for women to move from passivity, to alienation, to
their present anger. This anger, which is the basis of the entire sexual revolu-

tion, is directed against patriarchy—patriarchy, with God on its side, in the state, in religion, and in the marketplace. Such devastating concepts as "Anatomy is destiny" or "Her future is in her biology" must be buried forever in the graveyard of male supremacy. Until that is done, women will have achieved very little. . . .

From Laura Sabia "Women and Politics," in *Women on Women: Gerstein Lecture Series*, (Toronto: York University Press, 1978).

1. What basic argument does Laura Sabia put forward for increased female participation?
2. The election of 1984 saw more women elected to Parliament than ever before. To what extent does this reflect a shift in power in the Canadian political scene?
3. Defend the thesis "Political parties should be required to run an equal number of male and female candidates."

Women as Persons, 1980

In late 1979 the Canadian Research Institute for the Advancement of Women held a conference entitled "Women as Persons." The following excerpts are taken from papers presented at that conference, held in Edmonton.

In the first, Greta Hofmann Nemiroff of the New School of Dawson College argued that in order to address current inequities women must establish their own self-definitions and direction.

In my preparations for this conference, I had the opportunity to read through the abstracts of the papers which will be given over the course of the next two days. I was interested to see that almost all of the papers appear to focus on women as persons . . . that is, how we live out our personhood and what obstacles there are to its accomplishment. I also noticed that our struggle to participate as fully fledged members of our society is a theme running through virtually the entire conference. Underlying all the work on women (in the labour force, the criminal code, the professions, technology, as defined by the psychologists, the family and divorce, native women and women living in small communities, working in voluntary and educational institutions, or even the armed forces) was the fact that women in our country have struggled long and hard for self-definition and that the battle is not yet won. . . .

. . . We must recognize that although we have had the dubious honour of being recognized persons in Canada for half a century, we still are persons who live in a reality unequal to the one accorded men. While we form 39% of the labour force (1978), we earn less than half of the income of the average Canadian male. Women, because we form 71.5% of the part-time labour force in Canada, are sentenced to lives of insecurity both while we work and as we age. As part-time workers, we have the least job security, few benefits, and so will suffer the same poverty in old age as we do now. In Canada, 44.7% of female-headed families live below the poverty line while only 8.2% of the male-headed families do. Thus a working woman who cannot depend on a man for support not only faces, on the whole, a life of poverty but is very likely to perpetuate this poverty through her children as well. We know that as the myth goes, women were created as ancillary beings to man. As non-persons we still occupied that position. Right now, though, despite our brave words to the contrary, Canadian women still live lives which are often lesser than and ancillary to men's. . . .

. . . The fact is that we live in a patriarchal society and inevitably a moment comes when we realize with surprise that our aspirations, no matter how justifiable, basically run counter to the *status quo*.

From Greta Hofmann, "Achieving Personhood: Self-definition and Direction" in *Women as Persons: Special Publication #8*, (Toronto: Resources for Feminist Research, Fall 1980).

Glenda P. Simms of the University of Lethbridge took stock of the Women's Liberation Movement and its impact on minority women in Canada.

Toffler in *Future Shock* makes the point that society's major institutions, which gave people a sense of security, have changed radically and have not been replaced by any equally *definite* substitutes. Modern man, therefore, searches in vain for replacements for these traditional institutions. This is manifested in many instances, such as the equalling of divorce rates with remarriage rates and the desperate *cultural flirtations* through avenues such as Transcendental Meditation and Primal Screams. In short, the search for a new modus operandi for dealing with the human experience—for despite the magic pill, the dramatic moonwalk, the end of the Vietnam war, the gay liberation, the black liberation and the women's liberation, human existence has remained as mystifying and as painful—perhaps even *more so*. We are therefore living in an era where anxiety, depression and hypertension are the major complaints of the masses of the population in North America and in all other societies modelled on or aspiring to the North American way. As such, then, most people in these societies can be defined as being psychologically and psychically disadvantaged. My definition of the word disadvantaged and its implications for the definition of the minorities is based primarily on the foregoing realizations.

Seen from a wider humanistic perspective, which, as far as I am concerned, should be the perspective gained by *true* feminism, one must avoid being too shallow in one's definition of who are deprived, disadvantaged and, ultimately, the minority of the society. . . .

In Canada, Blacks, Third-World Immigrants and Native peoples face a large number of problems and must deal with a complexity of issues in their day to day lives. Observation of, and interaction and discussions with these groups have helped me to develop a feel for the issues that are of *immediate concern* to them. First and foremost, they are constantly confronted with the attitudes and pressures that are related to racism in the society. As Nagler points out, "Canadian society, although theoretically valuing equality, has seldom if ever granted her minorities the advantage of full Canadian citizenship status." . . .

Nagler asserts that both Blacks in the United States and Natives in Canada are over-represented in the areas of crime and alcohol related offences. Further investigation will show that relative to their numbers in the population, they are also over-represented amongst the poor, the *learning disabled*, and the school *dropouts* and are generally more victimized and oppressed than any other sectors of the society. . . .

In a new society, the Third-World woman, like all immigrants, is seeking acceptance but she is, like all others, torn between two value systems—that of the old and that of the new. In many cases these two sets of values are in direct conflict—especially as regards major issues such as male/female roles, expectations in male/female relationships, child rearing practices, responsibilities, and fertility myths. . . .

. . . The more a woman from these groups finds acceptance *in terms of the majority society*—its norms, values and aspirations—the more alienated she becomes from her own group which then rejects her for the very things that won her respect, namely, economic independence and the potential for mobility in the larger society. Numerous cases of these are evident amongst Blacks and amongst Native women who suffer not only because they are no longer "traditional" enough but must also remain manless or unmarried because of laws and attitudes which limit their possibilities of finding alternative mates. . . .

The *new woman* is the enemy of the minority women of any color or race because by and through her mythology she has neutralized our ability to focus on the real issues and problems of minority women. She has declared herself the "51% minority" and has co-opted for her own purposes the behaviour patterns which were responses to and symptoms of total oppression.

Society's focus of attention and assistance is distracted from the reality of the oppressed women whose manless and fatherless state was *not* a proof of independence but rather a manifestation of her economic and socio-psychological straits.

Society's focus of attention and assistance is distracted from the reality of the oppressed women whose manless and fatherless state was *not* a proof of independence but rather a manifestation of her economic and socio-psychological straits.

Michelle Russell (1977) appealed to the middle class Rapunzels who are directing the Movement and who are indirectly and perhaps unconsciously perpetuating the suffering of the oppressed by the creation of new myths of womanhood to let down their hair and "make of it a rope for their descent from the tower to the earth; from the house to the world; from isolation to community; from bondage to freedom." . . .

From Glenda P. Simms, "Rapunzel, Can You Hear Me?: The Women's Liberation Movement and Its Relationship to Minority Women," in *Women as Persons: Special Publication #8*, (Toronto: Resources for Feminist Research, Fall 1980).

1. What evidence does Nemiroff cite of the lack of employment equity in Canada?
2. How does Simms characterize the current state of North American society?
3. What is the relationship between the status of minority women and that of the mainstream in Canadian society?

Women and Children First

In this excerpt from her 1982 book, author and columnist Michelle Landsberg
examines the various factions that exist within the women's movement.

. . . I have never read a radical attack on the family that takes the task of parenthood as seriously as it takes the self-fulfillment of the adults. Vague mutter-
ings about communes won't do; for the foreseeable future, family communes
will not be appealing or accessible to ordinary Canadian parents. Such hasty
and ill-thought-out solutions are almost flippant, considering how important a
question this must be for most women.

Neither is single parenthood a real answer. There may be, somewhere, a
woman who is strong, skilled, brave, and resourceful enough to raise children
from infancy, work for a living, put up the storm windows, file her own income
tax, change diapers, pay the day care, and still have enough money, leisure, and
buoyancy to enjoy her own life and enrich those of her children. If so, I've
never met her. People are often forced into such lonely situations, but few of
them would claim that it is an ideal set-up for child-rearing. From the viewpoint of the average mother, nothing could be more desirable than a loving and
steady marriage, in which the new mother is freed to give intense and undis-
tracted attention to her infant, with enough comfort, emotional support, and
companionship from her husband to allow her to go on giving, albeit with
diminishing intensity, over the next several years. (There's nothing in this
approach to say that it can't work the other way around too, of course, with
wife supporting the husband.)

Having cut loose from the left bank this way, I find myself looking the other
way and wondering why all those women over there on the right are keeping their
feet dry. Well back from the water's edge are women who may now and then
concede the rightness of a feminist insight, but who nevertheless refuse the bap-
tism. They do not call themselves feminists; they do not view events through the
critical eyes of the women's movement. Is it cultural conditioning, I wonder? Is it
the way we've all been taught to think of any group of strongly identified
women—Amazons, bluestockings, teetotallers—as faintly ridiculous? After all, it
still comes as a shock to youngsters today when they are prodded into realizing
that the suffragettes were honourable democrats, not a bunch of demented extremists running around in funny bloomers to get—ha ha—the vote.

Feminism, I think, has been tinged with the same militant-governess over-
tone. Because feminism questions male and female sex-roles, the subliminal
image of the feminist has come to be a mixture of the Dutch Cleanser woman
and a prohibitionist—an angry battleaxe, bursting into an uproarious gin-mill
with her scolding tongue and upraised rolling-pin, a spoilsport determined to
put the damper on sex, booze, and fun.

But what of these women who see through these mocking stereotypes, who
share feminism's commitment to justice and equality, but still decline to join
forces with their sisters? I see them over there on the right bank, grazing peacefully in those green pastures, quite removed—they think—from the currents

that buffet other women. Until the boss harasses them, or the husband leaves them on the begging end of child-support payments, they simply cannot make the larger feminist analysis fit their own personal situation. Women have not been trained to think politically, to see themselves as pieces in a pattern. Besides, such an insight is poison to people who have been brought up in the North American daydream of limitlessly free individualism. Those women who have not joined forces with feminism are not necessarily antagonistic; they simply have not experienced that famous "click" of connection that entered our vocabulary from the pages of *Ms.* magazine, that moment of astonished clarity when a woman sees that her life is shaped, not by random free choices, but by imposed and limiting gender roles. . . .

Still, I would rather be here in the middle than in either of the two rigidly opposing camps: Housewives who stubbornly refuse to consider any of the radical questions about marriage strike me as dully defensive; radicals who are unrelenting about the human seductiveness of marriage and babies have often seemed to me to have a bitter fixity of viewpoint. . . .

Most Canadian women will, like me, go through marriage, motherhood, and paid employment. I hope that some of them, through seeing their own joys and trials mirrored here, will come to share my conviction that until we all enjoy a perfect social, cultural, legal, and financial equality with men, none of us— however privileged we may be individually or temporarily—is really anything more than a second-class citizen.

From Michelle Landsberg, *Women and Children First*, (Toronto: Macmillan of Canada, 1982). Reprinted by permission of Macmillan of Canada, A Division of Canada Publishing Corporation.

1. How does Michelle Landsberg define the positions of the various factions?
2. Respond to her statement that "until we all enjoy . . . equality with men, none of us . . . is really anything more than a second-class citizen."

The Feminist Movement in the 1980s

These three excerpts examine various facets of the feminist movement as it has evolved in the United States over the past twenty-five years.

In the excerpt "Feminism and Teen Romance: 1966-1983," Sharon Thompson argues that second-wave feminists have become isolated from the next generation of support. She claims that their gains have taken much of the lure out of the movement.

For those early second-wave feminists who formed their sexual politics outside liberal feminism where the romantic ideal was the two-V.I.P. family, the sexual quest was for freedom. Tempered and sharpened by a critique of the double-standard and a sexual revolution designed for male pleasure only, the claim to female sexual territory informed most of the classics of the late 1960s and early 1970s women's liberation literature—for example, Shulamith Firestone's *The Dialectic of Sex* and Kate Miller's *Sexual Politics* (both 1970); a number of works of fiction [the most notorious are probably Erica Jong's *Fear of Flying* (1975) and Rita Mae Brown's *Rubyfruit Jungle* (1973)]; as well as many essays and articles collected in such volumes as *Sisterhood is Powerful* (1970): *Out of the Closets* (1972); and *Beginning to See the Light* (1981).

Women's liberation activists generally assumed that teenage girls and feminists shared the same interests and history. The assumption led to a defense of teenage sexual freedom and reproductive rights on the conviction that teenage girls, like all women, had the right to control their own bodies. . . . At adolescence, girls became candidates for feminism.

By the late 1970s, history was separating the teenaged from those who made the nervy opening bids of second-wave feminism. Partly because of the gains of the women's movement—the right to abortion and contraception, in particular—feminism no longer seemed a natural conclusion of adolescent experience. . . .

From Sharon Thompson, "Feminism and Teen Romance: 1966-1983," in Sohnya Sayers, et al., *The Sixties Without Apology*, (Minneapolis: University of Minnesota Press, 1984).

In her article "Putting Feminism Back on its Feet," Silvia Federici states that the movement has to redefine its goals in terms of the 1980s.

Almost fourteen years have passed since I became involved with the women's movement. At first it was with a certain distance. I would go to some meetings but with reservations, since to a "politico" like I was it seemed difficult to reconcile feminism with a "class perspective." . . . [I] read . . . Mariarosa Dalla Costa's *The Power of Women and the Subversion of the Community* (1970), a pamphlet that was to become one of the most controversial feminist documents. At the last page I knew that I had found my home, my tribe and my own self, as a woman and a feminist. From that also stemmed my involvement in the Wages for Housework campaign that women like Dalla Costa and Selma James were organizing in Italy and Britain, and my decision to start, in 1972, Wages for Housework groups also in this country.

Of all the positions that developed in the women's movement, Wages for Housework was likely the most controversial and often the most antagonized. I think that marginalizing the struggle for wages for housework was a serious mistake that weakened the movement. It seems to me now, more than ever, that if the women's movement is to regain its momentum and not be reduced to yet another pillar of the meritocracy system, it must confront the material condition of women's lives.

Today our choices are more defined because we can measure what we have achieved and see more clearly the limits and possibilities of the strategies adopted in the past. For example, can we still campaign for "equal pay for equal work" when wage differentials are being introduced in what have been traditionally the strongholds of male working class power? . . .

When the women's movement started in the late 60s we believed it was up to us women to turn the world upside down. Sisterhood was a call to build a society free from power relations where we would learn to cooperate and share on an equal basis the wealth of our work and the work of other generations before us have produced. Sisterhood also expressed a massive refusal to be housewives, a position that, we all realized, is the first cause of the discrimination against us. Like other feminists before us we discovered that the kitchen is our slaveship, our plantation, and if we want to liberate ourselves we first have to break with our identification with housework and, in Marge Piercy's words, refuse to be a "grand coolie dame." We wanted to gain control over our bodies and our sexuality, to put an end to the slavery of the nuclear family and of our dependence on men, and explore what kind of human beings we would want to be once we free ourselves from the scars centuries of exploitations have left on us. These, despite emerging political differences, were the goals of the women's movement and to achieve them we gave battle on every front. No movement, however, can sustain itself and grow unless it develops a strategic perspective unifying its struggles and mediating its long term objectives with the possibilities open in the present. This sense of strategy is what has been missing in the women's movement, which has continually shifted between a utopian dimension posing the need for a total change and a day to day practice that assumed the unchangeability of the institutional system.

One of the main shortcomings of the women's movement has been its tendency to overemphasize the role of consciousness in the context of social change, as if enslavement were a mental condition and liberation could be achieved by an act of will. . . .

From Silvia Federici, "Putting Feminism Back on its Feet," in Sohnya Sayers, et al., *The Sixties Without Apology*, (Minneapolis: University of Minnesota Press, 1984).

"Radical Feminism and Feminist Radicalism" by Ellen Willis is a retrospective on the radical feminist movement. Willis argues that the radicals were the shock troops who were swept aside as the movement became culturally acceptable.

I was a radical feminist activist in the late 60s. Today I often have the odd feeling that this period, so vivid to me, occurred fifty years ago, not a mere fifteen. Much of the early history of the women's liberation movement, and especially of radical feminism (which was not synonymous with the w.l.m. but a specific political current within it) has been lost, misunderstood or distorted beyond recognition. The left, the right, and liberal feminists have all for their own reasons contributed to misrepresenting and trivializing radical feminist ideas. To add to the confusion, radical feminism in its original sense barely exists today. The great majority of women who presently call themselves "radical feminists" in fact subscribe to a politics more accurately labeled "cultural feminist." That is, they see the primary goal of feminism as freeing women from the imposition of so-called "male values," and creating an alternative culture based on "female values." Cultural feminism is essentially a moral, countercultural movement aimed at redeeming its participants, while radical feminism began as a political movement to end male supremacy in all areas of social and economic life, and rejected the whole idea of opposing male and female natures and values as a sexist idea, a basic part of what we were fighting. Though cultural feminism came out of the radical feminist movement, the premises of the two tendencies are antithetical. Yet on the left and elsewhere the distinction is rarely made. . . .

It was radical feminism that put women's liberation on the map, that got sexual politics recognized as a public issue, that created the vocabulary ("consciousness-raising," "the personal is political," "sisterhood is powerful," etc.) with which the second wave of feminism entered popular culture. Radical feminists sparked the drive to legalize abortion and created the atmosphere of urgency in which liberal feminists were finally able to get the Equal Rights Amendment through Congress and most of the states. Radical feminists were also the first to demand total equality in the so-called private sphere—equal sharing of housework and child care, equal attention to our emotional and sexual needs. It's no exaggeration to say that the immense transformation in women's consciousness over the past fifteen years has been inspired by the issues radical feminists raised. One exasperating example of how easy it is to obliterate history is that Betty Friedan can now get away with the outrageous claim that radical feminist "extremism" turned women off and derailed the movement she built. Radical feminism turned women on, by the thousands.

Yet this movement collapsed as quickly as it had grown. By 1975 radical feminism had given way to cultural feminism. The women's liberation movement had become the women's movement, in which liberals were the dominant, not to say the hegemonic force. Socialist and Marxist feminism, which had come out of other tendencies of the w.l.m. and segments of the left influenced by it, were theoretically confused and practically marginal. Feminism had become a reformist politics, a countercultural community, and a network of self-help projects (rape crisis centers, battered women's shelters, women's health clinics, etc.).

How and why did this happen? Like other left social movements, feminism had to contend with the institutional and ideological power of American liberalism, which succeeded in marginalizing radical feminists while channeling the aspirations they aroused into demands for reform on the one hand, a cult of the individual "liberated woman" on the other. In addition, radical feminism had surfaced only a short time before the expansive prosperity and utopian optimism of the 60s and succumbed to an era of economic limits and political backlash. The conservative retrenchment of the 70s had a critical negative impact, not only in strengthening political resistance to feminist demands but in constricting women's personal choices, making rebellion of any sort more difficult and risky, and undermining faith in the movement's more radical possibilities. Yet these external pressures, heavy as they were, do not wholly explain why radical feminism fell apart so easily and thoroughly. Contradictions within the movement, problems with its basic assumptions, played a crucial role.

From Ellen Willis, "Radical Feminism and Feminist Radicalism," in Sohnya Sayers, et al., *The Sixties Without Apology*, (Minneapolis: University of Minnesota Press, 1984).

1. Create a synthesis of the process being discussed in the three articles.
2. Write a personal analysis of the gains made by the feminist movement in the past twenty-five years.
3. Predict feminist goals for the next twenty-five years.

The Women's Movement: Analysis and Application

1.(a) Organize a series of class tutorials. Select readings from the chapter and group them in some fashion, such as by historical period, issue, or viewpoint.

Assign one group of readings to a group of classmates. Read the selections in your group and prepare notes and five to ten discussion-provoking questions. Organize a round-table, tutorial discussion with your group members.

(b) Write a summary of your tutorial discussion.

2. Write a position paper either for or against women's suffrage. Team up with a friend and stage a two-person debate on the issue. After your debate, step out of role and assess the merits of both positions in terms of the society that produced them.

3.(a) Assess the ideas of radical feminism. Create your own thesis with regard to the objectives of the women's movement in the 1960s and 1970s.

(b) Prepare the outline for an essay intended to defend your thesis.

4. "Rather than being a period of growth and extension for women's rights, the 1980s saw a re-emergence of the forces of male chauvinism and female indifference." Account for this statement with reference to the characteristics of the women's movement in the 1980s.

5. Contrast the struggle for the Equal Rights Amendment in the United States with the entrenchment of sexual equality in the Canadian Charter of Rights and Freedoms.

6. Design and conduct a survey of friends, teachers, and other adults with regard to their attitudes towards such issues as equal pay for work of equal value; affirmative action hiring; government support for daycare; the abortion controversy; and the constitutional entrenchment of equal rights. Summarize your findings in a brief press release.

7. Conduct a study of sexual stereotyping in current advertising. Analyse the images of men and women as illustrated in such ads, and relate your findings to the objectives of the women's movement.

17
CULTURE, INTEGRATION, AND IDENTITY

Canadian professor John Porter, author of *The Vertical Mosaic*, made this comment about our society in 1967:

> Canada has always been characterized by dualisms: the historic dualism between French and English Canada, and the dualism which all are expected to feel between their Canadian identity and their identity with the ethnic and cultural origins, mostly European, of their forefathers.

This view of Canada coincides with the image presented in many classrooms across the country of our nation as a mosaic of ethnic and cultural groups. By contrast, Canadian students are told, the United States is a melting pot in which all new immigrants are expected to conform.

Traditionally there has been both truth and fiction in this simplistic analysis. The examination of the treatment of immigrants in chapter 10 provides evidence of this. It would be difficult to sell Canada's mosaic culture to immigrants arriving in Canada at the turn of the century. Frequently, these people were given English names by immigration authorities and were told to forget the culture of their homeland.

By the same token, when Pope John Paul II visited the southern United States in the summer of 1987 he might as well have been in Latin America. The language of the crowds he spoke to was Spanish, not English. In the late twentieth century the American melting pot seems to be cooling.

The pluralism that has increasingly come to characterize the continent is a relatively new phenomenon. Prior to World War II, minorities in North America were usually isolated from the mainstream. In the United States, Blacks and Hispanics lived in certain areas, attended particular schools, and aspired to limited goals. In Canada, Quebec emerged as a bastion of French Canadianism, while francophones in other parts of the country usually found themselves isolated and often unable to communicate with the government in their own language. At the height of the Quiet Revolution in Quebec, Canada was governed by two unilingual anglophones, John Diefenbaker and Lester Pearson. Today it is difficult to be a credible candidate in a federal leadership campaign without the ability to speak French. In the United States Jesse Jackson's bid for the Democratic presidential nomination in 1988 shows how far North American society has come in the past twenty years.

These accomplishments have not come easily. The fifties, sixties, and seventies were decades of turmoil and confrontation. Racial strife almost tore the United States apart as Blacks took to the streets to agitate for their rights. Canada too was almost irrevocably divided as the people of Quebec followed their charismatic nationalist leader, René Lévesque, to the brink of separation. The parallels between Blacks in America and the French in Canada were not lost on radical separatists. Pierre Vallières referred to French Canadians as the "White Niggers of America" (see readings), and it was not uncommon during the sixties to hear someone respond to a francophone speaking his own language by saying "Come on, speak white"!

Although Canada and the United States have actually matured since these troubled times, the process has been a difficult one.

The Struggle for Equality in the United States

Separate but Equal

It was the policy throughout much of the twentieth century to provide racially segregated facilities for Black and white citizens. This concept of "separate but equal" access to goods and services was at the heart of the problem of discrimination in the United States.

As the affluent consumer culture spread across the United States, a growing number of Blacks began to express their resentment at being kept outside of the mainstream of prosperity. The televised image of happy white suburban life only fuelled the resentment of people living in the deserted inner cities. (Series depicting Black families were unheard of in the fifties and during most of the sixties.)

The American government was often embarrassed by its segregation policy. In one incident, a visiting diplomat from Ghana was refused a glass of orange juice at a Howard Johnson's in Delaware. He was informed by the waitress that Blacks were not permitted to eat or drink in the restaurant. The image of the great democracy was on shaky ground.

The greatest challenge to the "separate but equal" concept came in the schools. Universities had slowly recognized that it was economically impossible to provide separate but equal facilities. Black lawyers systematically challenged the equality aspect of the provision of scientific equipment, library resources, and even entire faculties. Gradually the academic community relented. By the early fifties, universities and colleges were well on the way to full integration.

The next target was the public school system. On May 17, 1954, Chief Justice Earl Warren of the Supreme Court gave the unanimous opinion of his colleagues on the *Brown v. the Board of Education of Topeka*. The Court ruled that the concept of "separate but equal has no place" in the field of public education (see readings). Segregation of school children on the basis of race "generates a feeling of inferiority as to their status in the community that may affect their hearts and minds in a way unlikely ever to be undone (see readings)." The Warren Court eventually required that segregation be ended, not immediately but at least with "all deliberate speed." In the border states, such an order was all that local legislators had been waiting for. Things moved quickly, and in cities such as Washington and Baltimore the whole system was overhauled.

Response was quick in the Deep South. There was not one Black child attending school with a white in any of the eight most southern states in 1955, and most people were determined to keep it that way. Moderate southerners found the way to reform blocked by their more hard-line compatriots. In 1957 the school board in Little Rock, Arkansas, decided to institute a six-year plan for integration. As a beginning they agreed to admit nine Black children to Central High School.

Upon arriving the students found themselves face to face with the rifles of the Arkansas National Guard. The governor of the state, Orval Faubus, had ordered the children to be stopped on the front steps. After another attempt to admit the students was foiled by a hostile mob ringing the school, President Dwight Eisenhower stepped in. Putting the Arkansas troops under federal authority and adding one thousand paratroopers, the president forced the admission of the nine students.

In response the governor shut down the schools. The battle raged on for years, and although some progress was made, by the mid-sixties only 1 percent of all Black students attended integrated schools in the South. Equality still had a long way to go.

The Montgomery Bus Boycott
Local by-laws in Montgomery, Alabama, were typical of the discrimination facing Black Americans in the 1950s. For example, Blacks riding on a crowded bus were forced to give up their seats to white passengers. Many people felt that this was a ridiculous, unfair rule, and one day it was put to the test. In December 1955 Rosa Parks was on her way home from a long day's work as a seamstress. Tired, the Black woman refused to give up her seat. She was arrested. Local Black leaders moved fast. Spearheaded by a well-educated minister from the Dexter Avenue Baptist Church, the Black community decided to take direct action. The leader's name was Martin Luther King, Jr. Reverend King had been born in Atlanta, but had chosen to go to Boston University. Now returning to the South, he was determined to make changes.

King's newly formed Montgomery Improvement Association organized a boycott of the transit system. As the majority of riders were Black, the buses ran almost empty. For a year the contest of wills dragged on. As it did, the Black position hardened. Originally willing to take only the seats at the back of the bus on a first-come, first-served basis, by the time the struggle was over, King and his supporters were willing to settle for nothing less than totally equal access.

While the protest continued in Montgomery, lawyers such as Thurgood Marshall of the NAACP fought the antiquated "Jim Crow" laws in the courts. Finally in November 1956 the ruling came down. Alabama's segregation laws were unconstitutional. The bus company agreed to comply with the ruling, and even to begin to hire Black drivers. On December 21, 1956, Martin Luther King boarded a Montgomery bus. The boycott was over.

The Campaign Spreads
The administration eventually began to respond to the demands for change. In 1960 an expanded civil rights bill was passed. In particular, it was aimed at protecting the right of Blacks to vote. Change was coming, but for many young Blacks and whites it was not coming fast enough.

Groups of students had started to act on their own. Copying King's non-violent approach they organized "sit-in" campaigns to try to force integration. Their targets were all-white restaurants, stores, laundromats, and movie theatres. Protesters held "kneel-ins" at churches and "wade-ins" at pools. All in all, between sixty and seventy thousand young Blacks and whites participated in the campaign.

By the end of 1960 integration had come to lunch counters in more than 120 cities in the Deep South. Soon it would reach over 200.

The driving force behind such actions was a group of new organizations: the Southern Christian Leadership Conference (SCLC) led by King; the Congress of Racial Equality (CORE); and the Student Non-Violent Coordinating Committee (SNCC). Representing among them a mixture of North and South, white and Black, they presented a formidable force for change. The next decade would see them emerge victorious.

Civil Rights and Black Power

The Non-violent Movement

The Freedom Rides of 1961 built on the successful "sit-in" movement of 1960. This new movement consisted of groups of whites and Blacks travelling by bus from Washington to the Deep South. The strategy was simple. These antisegregation "shock troops" would oppose the practice wherever they found it. The response in the South was electric. Instead of welcoming throngs the Freedom Riders were greeted by angry mobs resenting this outside agitation. Attorney General Robert Kennedy was forced to send in over six hundred armed marshalls to keep the peace, yet still the problem mounted. Undaunted by these setbacks the Freedom Rides continued on into the next year, with little result. In fact in some areas they served only to create animosity between Blacks and whites where it had never existed before.

There was little action in Washington either. A bill outlawing literacy tests for voting was introduced but defeated in the Senate, and a constitutional amendment banning poll taxes was not passed until the practice had all but disappeared anyway.

The NAACP made some gains during the period. Their lawyers won the right for Black student James Meredith to attend the University of Mississippi. His admission resulted in a pitched battle between protestors and police. The resulting casualties numbered 2 dead and 375 wounded. But Meredith survived. He attended and graduated from the university.

The true leader during the early sixties, however, was the Reverend Martin Luther King. King orchestrated massive marches and demonstrations in the heart of segregation, Birmingham, Alabama. Police reacted by arresting King and almost twenty-five hundred other women, men, and children. The city finally gave in and negotiated. King had used the techniques of non-violence which had proven so successful for Mahatma Gandhi in India a generation earlier. Violent response by the local authorities only strengthened the popularity of the Black cause and gave further impetus to the movement.

King's "Letter from the Birmingham Jail" outlined the basic justice of his cause (see readings). It put in rational terms the argument against the status quo. The system could not remain much longer.

In the face of this new round of protest, the White House acted. President John Kennedy introduced a comprehensive civil rights bill that would remove segregation in virtually all public places. This was coupled with the encouragement to bring the issue to the front door of Congress. On August 28, 1963, they did.

Over two hundred thousand Blacks and whites converged on the Washington Mall to listen to their leaders. Almost twenty-five years later Martin Luther King's words still echo from that day:

> I say to you today, my friends, that in spite of the difficulties and frustrations of the moment I still have a dream. It is a dream deeply rooted in the American dream.
>
> I have a dream that one day this nation will rise up and live out the true meaning of its creed: "We hold these truths to be self-evident; that all men are created equal."
>
> I have a dream that one day on the red hills of Georgia the sons of the former slaves and the sons of former slaveholders will be able to sit down together at the table of brotherhood. . . .
>
> I have a dream that my four little children will one day live in a nation where they will not be judged by the colour of their skin but by the content of their character.

Martin Luther King's dream was cut short five years later. On April 4, 1968, he was shot and killed in Memphis, Tennessee. On his gravestone were engraved the words with which he finished his Washington speech: "Free at last, free at last, thank God almighty I'm free at last."

The Long Hot Summers
Lyndon Johnson managed to pass the long overdue civil rights legislation in his first year in office following the assassination of John F. Kennedy in 1963. As a result, by 1965 most white Americans thought that the civil rights issue was well on its way to being solved. They could not have been more wrong.

On August 11th the Black neighbourhood of Watts in Los Angeles exploded into violence. Burnings and lootings exacted a toll of thirty-four lives and $35 million in damages. Before the riots ended, more than four thousand people had been arrested. White America was stunned. Watts had been considered a success story. The riot laid bare the underlying bitterness still felt by many Blacks against the smug values of the majority culture. Watts had been bad, but it was only the beginning.

The next summmer saw outbreaks in Chicago, and in early July 1967 Newark erupted. Twenty-six people were killed and over twelve hundred wounded. No sooner had some calm and order returned to the New Jersey city then the greatest explosion of them all took place. On "Black Day in July" as Gordon Lightfoot called it, Detroit was devastated by more than four thousand fires. Forty-three people died and over two thousand were injured.

Detroit had been a model city. Blacks were influential in government and were paid equitably and well in the automotive industry. What had happened? A new concept was emerging. Not really a philosophy, it was more of a "cry of rage." It was called Black Power, and it was moving to centre stage.

Black Power
Since the early sixties a vocal group of Black leaders had rejected King's philosophy of non-violence. Elijah Muhammad, for example, led a faction known as the Black

Muslims. Although advocating violent separatism from white society, the Black Muslims actually became an effective agent for social improvement in the Black urban ghettos. One of Elijah Muhammad's chief lieutenants was a minister named Malcolm Little. Little rejected his "slave" name and simple called himself Malcolm X. He was an electrifying speaker. He finally split from Elijah Muhammad after visiting Mecca and learning about Islam firsthand. He felt that the Black leader had corrupted the teachings of the Koran. Soon after, Malcolm X was assassinated. However, he was even more influential after his death. His autobiography, ghost written by Alex Haley who would later write *Roots*, spread his ideas to every corner of Black America.

Extremist leaders such as Stokely Carmichael, Rap Brown, and Floyd McKissick rejected cooperative effort and preached violent revolution. Their advance guard became the Black Panthers, which operated as an underground army for a short period in the late sixties.

The upsurge in violence brought into sharp focus the "state of the union" in race relations. Monumental legislative gains had been made during the past decade, but attitudes still lagged far behind. It would take the relative calm of the seventies to allow Blacks and whites to adjust to their new relationship.

Towards a Pluralist Society

The struggle for equality that characterized much of the relationship between Black and white during the 1950s and 1960s was bound to spill over into other sectors of American life. From the mid-sixties on, two other racial groups emerged to pressure society for meaningful change. Although their struggles were not as dramatic as those of Black Americans, nonetheless they were able to force some real change in social attitudes and practices.

Bury My Heart at Wounded Knee

After the 1930s, Native Americans were encouraged to take on the task of self-government. Judge N.B. Johnson took a lead in this area when he became the first president of the National Congress of American Indians in 1944. Johnson, like a modern-day Tecumseh, knew that to counter the bureaucracy of white society, Native peoples needed an organizational voice of their own. The NCAI eventually became an effective lobby on Native issues in Washington, and through a succession of effective executive directors, such as Ruth Muskrat Bronson, Helen Peterson, and Vine Delora, by the 1960s it exercised considerable influence. Younger Natives joined the National Indian Youth Council, which adopted the tactics of Martin Luther King in its struggle. In one instance in 1964 its members staged a "fish-in" to protest the loss of traditional fishing rights in a number of rivers. For the most part, however, these organizations only represented those Native Americans who still lived in and around their ancestral homes. By 1970 that was less than 25 percent of the total. The rest were urbanized, disappearing into the big cities of the East.

To attempt to tap the growing national pride of this group, Dennis Banks and Clyde Bellecourt organized the American Indian Movement (AIM) in 1968. Committed to confrontationist tactics, AIM made the headlines when, in March 1973, its members seized a trading post and church at Wounded Knee, South Dakota. Receiving little popular support for their demands to have Senate hearings convened on their treaty grievances, they finally gave in peacefully.

Native peoples have struggled throughout the twentieth century to pressure the government to make amends for the wrongs of the past. By the 1980s most Americans had come to realize the legitimacy of their demands and were willing to move towards a just and equitable settlement.

Unfortunately the same could not be said for another group in American society. Lacking ancient claims and historical sympathy, Hispanic Americans have had to struggle against overwhelming odds.

Hispanic Americans: the Forgotten Minority

Since colonial times, what is now the United States has included a substantial Spanish-speaking population. Territorial changes as a result of the Mexican War, and the acquisition of Spanish-speaking islands such as Cuba and Puerto Rico in the Spanish-American conflict, resulted in the establishment of a substantial minority of Spanish-speaking citizens. In the fifties and sixties migrant workers flooded across the Mexican border in search of jobs in California. As their numbers grew, so did discrimination against them. Similar attitudes were expressed against Puerto Rican immigrants on the Eastern seaboard, and, after the Castro revolution, Cuban exiles in Florida.

In California, Chicano (Mexican American) grape pickers organized against discriminatory working conditions and wages. Led by Cesar Chavez they launched a successful nationwide boycott of California grapes. Chavez's goal was to organize all migrant workers into his United Farm Workers' Union. By the seventies, he had attained considerable success, but by then Spanish-Americans were facing even greater problems.

In the Southwest, large numbers of illegal immigrants were filtering across the border. Afraid of being turned in to the authorities, they settled for substandard jobs and low pay. This "wetback" labour continues to be a hidden racial problem, particularly in California.

In addition, over 125 000 Cuban refugees sailed to Florida in 1980. By the mid-eighties many of those immigrants still lived in guarded refugee compounds in the South.

The Cuban problem reached crisis proportions in the late fall of 1987. Many refugees found themselves imprisoned in Southern jails. While some were serving time for serious crimes, many minor offenders, who had served their sentences, languished in jail while the government decided what to do with them. It was an explosive situation, and it finally erupted. Riots broke out in a number of prisons and hostages were taken. For days the authorities were helpless. As the story of the Cubans became known, public sympathy turned in their favour. Finally the government agreed that there would be no wholesale deportations and that an equitable settlement would be arrived at for each inmate.

Some gains have been made by Hispanic Americans, but there is still considerable resentment against this Spanish tint to American society. As late as the early eighties, two congressmen attempted to introduce a constitutional amendment that would make the United States officially unilingual. They wanted to take no chances that someday Spanish might be an acceptable means of communicating in their country.

This, however, is a minority view. Slowly, but with certainty, the United States is moving towards a more pluralist twenty-first century.

Canada at the Crossroads: The French Fact

In 1944 the Union Nationale, under the leadership of Maurice Duplessis, returned to power in Quebec. For the next fifteen years the Duplessis "machine" dominated politics in that province. In a postwar version of "la survivance" and French-Canadian nationalism based upon provincial autonomy, the Union Nationale set out to strengthen the economic base of the francophone homeland. Foreign (meaning American and English-Canadian) firms were encouraged to invest in Quebec through lucrative tax breaks and the promise of a docile labour force. The result was a rapid growth in the industrial, hydroelectric, and mining sectors of the provincial economy.

Quebeckers paid a high price for this growth, however. Duplessis' promise of no labour unrest could not be fulfilled. Violent strikes erupted at Asbestos, Shefferville, and Thetford Mines. The Quebec Provincial Police had to be called in to control the situation. The union power that resulted was what the Duplessis regime referred to as the "democratic influences of trade unionism" as opposed to the traditional rule of the business elite. In reality the Quebec labour movement experienced a rapid politicization that was unprecedented in the rest of the country. For the trade union movement, the enemy was not the industrialists but the government. Effectively harnessed, this antagonism would become an effective impetus for change in the next decade.

For his part, Duplessis saw Quebec as his own personal fiefdom. When asked in the National Assembly about the fact that much more money went to government-held ridings than to those held by the opposition the premier replied: "The budget of the province is not big enough to meet all needs. . . . If I had a loaf of bread that was too small to allow me to share it with both my friends and my enemies, I would share it exclusively with my friends." (See readings.)

During the fifties, Union Nationale support was based in rural, francophone Quebec. In that sense, their investment policies eventually became their undoing. Industrialization meant urbanization, the growth of trade unionism, and the development and expansion of a non-parochial, public education system. Such modernization would eventually undercut the very basis of Union Nationale support. But while Duplessis led the party, the opposition was unable to make significant gains. In his last election as leader in 1956, the UN won seventy-two seats to a mere twenty for the opposition Liberals. Three years later, however, Duplessis was dead, and Quebec was on the verge of a new era.

The election of 1960 brought Jean Lesage and the Liberal party to power on the simple slogan "Time for a change." This was the beginning of the "Quiet Revolution" in Quebec. The immediate result was a flurry of social legislation designed to help Quebeckers catch up to the rest of the country. After two years Lesage went back to the people for a new mandate. This time the call was for Québécois to become "Maîtres Chez Nous" (Masters in our own House), and the new thrust was economic. The Duplessis era had entrenched an English economic elite in the province. Now the government wanted to slowly buy them out. One major tact was to nationalize the privately owned power industry. Under the leadership of Minister of Natural Resources René Lévesque, Hydro-Quebec expanded as proof of the government's recognition that control of power meant control of industrial development.

Under the Liberals and their eventual successors, a revitalized Union Nationale, Quebec demanded a new status in Canada. No longer was the province satisfied to raise barricades and isolate itself from the rest of the country. By the mid-sixties, Quebec City wanted to renegotiate its relationship with Ottawa. For most Québécois this renegotiation took one of three forms: a radical rejection of Confederation (separatism); a renegotiation of the British North America Act, with a wide increase in provincial powers (special status); or a new effort to entrench francophone goals within the existing system (federalism).

Radical separatists such as Marcel Chaput (see readings) saw Confederation as a dead end that did nothing but limit the freedom of the French-Canadian nation. He called for the "independence of Quebec, [our] true native land, which will make [us] masters of [our] own destiny." In 1960 a new political party, the *Rassemblement pour l'independence nationale* (RIN), was formed with the political goal of an independent Quebec.

At the same time the mainstream of Quebec politics was making increasingly radical demands of the federal government. Led not only by Lesage but by the leaders of the Union Nationale as well, this group called for a recognition of the "special status" of Quebec. For them it was time to recognize the bicultural nature of Canada and to accept Quebec as the homeland of all Canadian francophones. There needed to be more French in the federal government and its services and a renegotiation of the British North America Act to give the province the power to carry out its linguistic and cultural duties (see readings).

Finally there were the federalists. Typified by future prime minister Pierre Elliot Trudeau, this group claimed that for too long Québécois had blamed the English for their problems. Trudeau called for the people of Quebec to get their own house in order and then to work responsibly to secure recognition from the rest of the country.

In the sixties and early seventies Lesage's viewpoint dominated Quebec politics. At the same time Trudeau and the federalists were drawn into the heart of the federal Liberal party, who hoped to utilize their ideas to revive their political fortunes in Quebec. As early as 1963 Prime Minister Lester Pearson had created a Royal Commission on Bilingualism and Biculturalism to investigate the emerging reality of the country. At the same time the Liberals made a commitment to create a truly bilingual public service. When the Bi and Bi Commission presented its interim report in 1965 it sounded a warning to the country: "Canada, without being fully conscious of the fact, is passing through the greatest crisis in its history."

After two unsuccessful attempts to secure a majority government, Pearson finally stepped down as prime minister. He was succeeded in April 1968 by Pierre Trudeau. Five months earlier René Lévesque, who had quit the provincial Liberals when they had rejected his *Option Quebec* (see readings), had become the leader of a new party, the Mouvement Souveraineté-Association (MSA). By the end of 1968 he assumed the leadership of a new separatist coalition, the Parti Québécois. Thus, the battle lines were drawn. The next decade would see a bitter contest between the two powerful and influential francophones to determine the future of Quebec and Canada.

The Road to the Referendum: Radical Separatism

When Trudeau became prime minister most English Canadians associated the separatist movement not with the political actions of the RIN or the MSA but with the terrorist attacks of the Front de Liberation du Quebec (FLQ). During the sixties the FLQ attacked such symbols of English imperialism as the post office and the banks. Through a series of robberies and bombings, the FLQ maintained a high public profile. The peak of its power and its public sympathy, however, came in October 1970. In April of that year the Liberals had been returned to power in Quebec under the leadership of Robert Bourassa. Bourassa's Liberals had captured 42 percent of the popular vote, which translated into seventy-two seats. Their chief opposition in the cities was the urban-based Parti Québécois. While the PQ finished second with 23 percent of the popular vote, it elected only seven members to the assembly. By contrast, the rural-based Union Nationale won seventeen seats but placed third with only 20 percent. The right-wing Creditistes elected eleven candidates with only 11 percent support. For some Québécois the election outcome was the last straw. They denounced what they called the "election riggers," claiming that the election had been stolen from the people.

One group of these disaffected idealists decided to take matters into their own hands. On October 5, 1970, James Cross, the British trade commissioner in Montreal, was kidnapped. Cross's abductors demanded a half-a-million dollars in gold and the release of all "political prisoners" held by the government. Trudeau called the so-called political prisoners "bandits" and bank robbers. The government did agree, however, to read the FLQ's manifesto, which laid out its grievances and demands (see readings) on television. Dismissed as nonsense by much of English Canada, it nonetheless struck a responsive chord with many francophones; if opposed to the methods of the terrorists, they nevertheless could sympathize with their motives. When the government refused to react further, a second kidnapping took place. On October 10th, a group calling themselves the Chenier cell of the FLQ kidnapped Quebec's minister of labour, Pierre Laporte.

Many political and business leaders in Quebec panicked. In Ottawa, military personnel were assigned to protect cabinet members. As the Bourassa government continued to negotiate with the FLQ, the federal government prepared to act. At three a.m. on Friday, October 16th, the federal cabinet invoked the War Measures Act. It suspended all civil liberties in the country and placed Montreal and vicinity under martial law. Over 430 people were arrested in a general dragnet across the province. Of those, only sixty-two were actually charged, and only twenty were convicted of a crime.

The War Measures Act was an extreme measure (see readings) but one of which most Canadians approved. Over 89 percent of English Canadians and 86 percent of French Canadians supported the government's actions. Unfortunately, however, the act came too late for Pierre Laporte. The night after it was invoked his body was found stuffed into the trunk of a car.

James Cross was eventually found and released after his kidnappers were guaranteed safe passage to Cuba. (It would be nine years before they would return to their homeland to face trial.) Laporte's killers too were tracked down and sentenced for their crimes.

The October Crisis was a watershed for the separatist movement in Quebec. The FLQ had been the shock troops of the drive for independence. With the October Crisis they lost their popular support, and many Québécois turned their attention to the political arena. In the election of 1973 Bourassa called for a decisive victory over separatism. At first glance it would seem to have worked. Anti-separatist forces concentrated their vote (54 percent) behind the Liberals, winning 102 seats. The PQ, by comparison, won only six. In doing so, however, they attracted over 30 percent of the popular vote and became the official opposition. English Canadians breathed a sigh of relief, and even Trudeau felt moved to declare that "Separatism is dead." Such pronouncements, however, were premature.

The Quebec Liberals now represented the complacent business class. The PQ increasingly appealed to the "new" Quebec. Their supporters were the young, the university educated, the trade unions, and the civil service. In the election of 1976 the Parti Québécois emphasized its social democratic platform. Promising an energetic, honest government, Lévesque used the old Liberal "time for a change" theme, and it worked. Liberal support dropped to 34 percent and only 21 seats. The PQ jumped to 41 percent and seventy-one seats.

Lévesque had won a considerable amount of moderate support by downplaying the separatist option. He promised that he would wait for two years, after which time he would hold a provincial referendum on the question of independence. It was a shrewd move. Polls showed that even with the massive PQ victory only 20 percent of the population favoured separatism. Lévesque now had time to build his power base.

The Contest for Quebec

Lévesque quickly made his mark on the province. Legislation was passed for labour and electoral reform and to legalize a referendum. Perhaps the most controversial piece of legislation was Bill 101. It declared that French was the only official language of Quebec. Although later softened through court challenges, in its original form Bill 101 restricted access to English schools and eliminated the use of English in advertising, menus, and signs.

By 1979 the government was ready to launch its referendum campaign. A white paper was issued outlining Lévesque's proposals for "political sovereignty" and "economic association." Sovereignty-association was the best of both worlds, and to the PQ it seemed to be a sure-fire winner.

Ottawa had not been idle either during the latter half of the seventies. Slowly but surely Canada had moved towards bilingualism. French had become the co-language of government business across the country. Middle-class Canadians, recognizing the trend, began to demand that local boards of education institute French immersion classes for their children. So extensive were the changes that many English Canadians felt their own rights were being threatened. A 1977 book entitled *Bilingual Today: French Tomorrow* accused Trudeau of conspiring to conquer English Canada through government legislation. But by the end of 1979 Trudeau was gone. The Liberals had been defeated by the Conservatives under the leadership of Joe Clark. Clark had achieved victory with fewer votes than the Liberals (35 percent to 39 percent) and with only two seats in Quebec; it was an election that polarized the country more than any other since 1917. For Lévesque it was the perfect opportunity to launch his separatist drive, and he committed his government to hold the referendum the following May.

By May, however, things had changed. In a vote of non-confidence, Clark's government was defeated in November, and in a February election Trudeau and the Liberals were swept back into power. This time the country was polarized the other way, with the Liberals holding only two seats west of Ontario. What they did control, however, was seventy-three out of seventy-four seats in Quebec (voting in one riding was postponed due to the death of one of the candidates). As the referendum campaign began, the people of Quebec were faced with choosing between two of their own leaders.

Lévesque and the PQ were careful to phrase the referendum question in a way that could be supported by as many people as possible. It read:

The government of Quebec has made public its proposal to negotiate a new agreement with the rest of Canada, based upon the equality of nations: this agreement would enable Quebec to acquire the exclusive power to make its own laws, administer its taxes and establish relations abroad—in other words, sovereignty—and at the same time, to maintain with Canada an economic association including a common currency;
no change in political status resulting from these negotiations will be effected without approval from the people through another referendum;
On these terms do you give the Government of Quebec the mandate to negotiate the proposed agreement between Quebec and Canada?
Yes   No

The question itself soon became a non-issue. The real question was the future of Quebec and Canada. The "Oui" forces were led into battle by Lévesque and his cabinet. The "Non" troops were marshalled by Jean Chretien and provincial Liberal leader Claude Ryan. The real symbol of federalism, however, was Trudeau. His popularity was never higher in Quebec. Even among francophones he personally outpolled Lévesque by more than two to one. In the end the "Non" forces won out. Just under 60 percent of Quebeckers voted against the referendum. More importantly, a majority—52 percent—of francophones also voted against Lévesque's vision of a new Quebec. Although the PQ leader remained as premier until his retirement in 1984, for the time being, separatism was a spent force in the province.

During the referendum campaign Trudeau committed his government to patriate the constitution from Britain to Canada. In the process he promised a new Charter of Rights (see Appendix A) which would guarantee many of the rights for which the PQ had fought.

The 1987 Meech Lake Accord signed by Prime Minister Brian Mulroney and the ten provincial premiers took the 1982 constitution one step further. In return for Quebec's signature, it recognized the "unique character" of the province and took the relationship back to the "special status" days of the mid-sixties. In addition, both the Charter of Rights and the Meech Lake Accord provided another offshoot for Canadians. Minority groups, who had claimed some limited protection under the Canadian Bill of Rights, were finally given constitutional guarantees to protect their "rights and freedoms . . . subject only to the reasonable limits prescribed by law as can be democratically justified in a free and democratic society."

The Charter of Rights proclaims all Canadians to be "equal before and under the law . . . without discrimination based on race, national or ethnic origin, colour, religion, sex, age, or mental or physical disability." Such a statement is a reflection of the changing face of North America. Although Canada and the United States have taken different approaches to immigration policy over the last twenty years (see readings) both nations have undergone fundamental transformations. The white, British elite of the prewar period has been supplanted by a new reality. Political parties in both countries boast candidates, congressmen, and parliamentarians who reflect a wide range of ethnic, racial, and religious origins. Traditional Christian laws such as Sunday closings for businesses have been increasingly questioned as the social values and religious beliefs of the population continue to change.

The race riots and FLQ bombings of the sixties seem far removed from the cooperative mood of the late eighties. For students growing up in the eighties and nineties it is difficult to imagine the emotions and logic that fuelled the debates of the day. That is not to say that racism, sexism, and prejudice are dead in North America. Legal guarantees are only valuable as long as there is the political and social will to back them up.

Brown vs the Board of Education of Topeka, Kansas

In a landmark decision the United States Supreme Court ruled that the doctrine of "separate but equal" did not apply to education. In this excerpt, Chief Justice Earl Warren gave the majority report of a unanimous court.

. . . We come then to the question presented: Does segregation of children in public schools solely on the basis of race, even though the physical facilities and other "tangible" factors may be equal, deprive the children of the minority group of equal educational opportunities? We believe that it does.

. . . In *McLaurin v. Oklahoma State Regents, supra,* the Court, in requiring that a Negro admitted to a white graduate school be treated like all other students, again resorted to intangible considerations: " . . . his ability to study, to engage in discussions and exchange views with other students, and, in general, to learn his profession." Such considerations apply with added force to children in grade and high schools. To separate them from others of similar age and qualifications solely because of their race generates a feeling of inferiority as to their status in the community that may affect their hearts and minds in a way unlikely ever to be undone. . . .

Segregation of white and colored children in public schools has a detrimental effect upon the colored children. The impact is greater when it has the sanction of the law; for the policy of separating the races is usually interpreted as denoting the inferiority of the Negro group. A sense of inferiority affects the motivation of a child to learn. Segregation with the sanction of law, therefore, has a tendency to retard the educational and mental development of Negro children and to deprive them of some of the benefits they would receive in a racially integrated school system. . . .

We conclude that in the field of public education the doctrine of "separate but equal" has no place. Separate educational facilities are inherently unequal. Therefore, we hold that the plaintiffs and others similarly situated for whom the actions have been brought are, by reason of the segregation complained of, deprived of the equal protection of the laws guaranteed by the Fourteenth Amendment.

From R. Leopold, et al., eds., *Problems in American History*, (Englewood Cliffs, New Jersey: Prentice-Hall, 1972).

1. What questions did the Court ask itself?
2. What arguments are presented against segregation?
3. Comment on the long-term significance of the decision.

Segregation and Desegregation

In 1954 future Supreme Court Justice Thurgood Marshall argued the case on behalf of Oliver Brown, who sought admission to a "white" school for his eight-year-old Black daughter Linda Carol Brown. In this speech, given just prior to the announcement of the ruling, Marshall summed up the achievements of the desegregation movement.

There has been much discussion during recent years concerning the question of the removal in this country of dual citizenship based solely on race and color. The primary emphasis has been on the elimination of racial segregation. No one denies that progress is being made. There are, however, some who say that the progress is too slow and others who say that the progress is too rapid. The important thing to remember is that progress is being made. We are moving ahead. We have passed the crossroads. We are moving toward a completely integrated society. North and South.

Those who doubt this and those who are afraid of complete integration are victims of a background based upon long indoctrination of only one side of the controversy in this country. They know only of one side of the controversy in this country. They know only of one side of slavery. They know only the biased reports about Reconstruction and the long-standing theory which seems to support the "legality" of the separate-but-equal doctrine. . . .

Our government is based on the principle of the equality of man, the individual, not the group. All of us can quote the principle that "All men are created equal." Our basic legal document, the Constitution of the United States, guarantees equal protection of laws to all of us. Many state constitutions have similar provisions. We even have a "Bill of Rights" in the Constitution of Louisiana. These high-sounding principles we preach and teach. However, in the eyes of the world we stand convicted of violating these principles day in and day out.

. . . Constitutionally protected individual rights have been effectively destroyed by outmoded theories of racial or group inferiority. Why is this true? How long can we afford the luxury of segregation and discrimination?

One reason this condition of dual citizenship exists is because we have been conditioned to an acceptance of this theory as a fact. We are the products of a misunderstanding of history.

From P.S. Foner, *The Voice of Black America*, (New York: Simon and Schuster, 1972).

1. What constitutional arguments does Marshall use?
2. Why does he claim that American Blacks are "the products of a misunderstanding of history"?
3. Compare Marshall's point of view with that of the Warren Court.

Wallace and Segregation, 1963

On the centennial of the Emancipation Proclamation, Alabama governor George Wallace served notice that segregation was still alive and well in his state.

It is very appropriate then that from this Cradle of the Confederacy, this very Heart of the Great Anglo-Saxon Southland, that today we sound the drum for freedom as have our generations of forebears before us done, time and again down through history. Let us rise to the call of freedom-loving blood that is in us and send our answer to the tyranny that clanks its chains upon the South. In the name of the greatest people that have ever trod this earth, I draw the line in the dust and toss the gauntlet before the feet of tyranny . . . and I say . . . segregation now . . . segregation tomorrow . . . segregation forever.

From R. Leopold et al., eds., *Problems in American History*, (New Jersey: Prentice-Hall, 1972).

1. How does Wallace describe Alabama?

2. What does Wallace mean by "the tyranny that clanks its chains upon the South"?
3. Account for the continued existence of support for segregation as late as 1963.

Letter from Birmingham Jail, 1963

While Martin Luther King sat in jail in Birmingham, Alabama, his postion came under attack from a number of his more conservative colleagues. Begun in the margins of a newspaper, King later finished and polished this articulate statement of his aims and defence of his tactics.

April 16, 1963
My dear fellow Clergymen:
   While confined here in the Birmingham city jail, I came across your recent statement calling my present activities "unwise and untimely." Seldom do I pause to answer criticism of my work and ideas. . . . But since I feel that you are men of genuine good will and that your criticisms are sincerely set forth, I want to try to answer your statement in what I hope will be patient and reasonable terms. . . .
   You deplore the demonstrations taking place in Birmingham. But your statement, I am sorry to say, fails to express a similar concern for the conditions that brought about the demonstrations. I am sure that none of you would want to rest content with the superficial kind of social analysis that deals merely with effects and does not grapple with underlying causes. It is unfortunate that demonstrations are taking place in Birmingham, but it is even more unfortunaate that the city's white power structure left the Negro community with no alternative.
   In any nonviolent campaign there are four basic steps: collection of the facts to determine whether injustices exist; negotiation; self-purification; and direct action. We have gone through these steps in Birmingham. There can be no gainsaying the fact that racial injustice engulfs this community. Birmingham is probably the most thoroughly segregated city in the United States. Its ugly record of brutality is widely known. Negroes have experienced grossly unjust treatment in the courts. There have been more unsolved bombings of Negro homes and churches in Birmingham than in any other city in the nation. These are the hard, brutal facts of the case. On the basis of these conditions, Negro leaders sought to negotiate with the city fathers. But the latter consistently refused to engage in good-faith negotiation. . . .
   You may well ask: "Why direct action? Why sit-ins, marches and so forth? Isn't negotiation a better path?" You are quite right in calling for negotiation. Indeed, this is the very purpose of direct action. Nonviolent direct action seeks to create such a crisis and foster such a tension that a community which has constantly refused to negotiate is forced to confront the issue. It seeks so to dramatize the issue that it can no longer be ignored. My citing the creation of tension as part of the work of the nonviolent-resister may sound rather shocking. But I must confess that I am not afraid of the word "tension." I have ear-

nestly opposed violent tension, but there is a type of constructive, nonviolent tension which is necessary for growth. Just as Socrates felt that it was necessary to create a tension in the mind so that individuals could rise from the bondage of myths and half-truths to the unfettered realm of creative analysis and objective appraisal, so must we see the need for nonviolent gadflies to create the kind of tension in society that will help men rise from the dark depths of prejudice and racism to the majestic heights of understanding and brotherhood.

The purpose of our direct-action program is to create a situation so crisis-packed that it will inevitably open the door to negotiation. I therefore concur with you in your call for negotiation. Too long has our beloved Southland been bogged down in a tragic effort to live in monologue rather than dialogue. . . .

I have tried to stand between these two forces, saying that we need emulate neither the "do-nothingism" of the complacent nor the hatred and despair of the black nationalist. For there is the more excellent way of love and nonviolent protest. I am grateful to God that, through the influence of the Negro church, the way of nonviolence became an integral part of our struggle.

If this philosophy had not emerged, by now many streets of the South would, I am convinced, be flowing with blood. And I am further convinced that if our white brothers dismiss as "rabble-rousers" and "outside agitators" those of us who employ nonviolent direct action, and if they refuse to support our nonviolent efforts, millions of Negroes will, out of frustration and despair, seek solace and security in black-nationalist ideologies—a development that would inevitably lead to a frightening racial nightmare.

Oppressed people cannot remain oppressed forever.

From Martin Luther King, Jr., *"Letter from a Birmingham Jail."* Reprinted by permission of Joan Daves. Copyright © 1963, 64 by Martin Luther King, Jr.

1. Précis King's description of a non-violent campaign and the reasons for it.
2. Comment upon King's assertion that the failure of non-violence would result in a "frightening racial nightmare."
3. With the benefit of a quarter century of hindsight, write a letter back to Martin Luther King commenting upon the accuracy of his predictions.

The Black Muslims, 1963

Elijah Muhammad was the leader of a militant Black nationalist organization that gained prominence in the early sixties. The Black Muslims rejected integration and called for the creation of an independent Black state within the continental United States. This is an excerpt from one of Elijah Muhammad's speeches.

This is the question of today among the black people of America: Shall we have or get justice? The answer is yes. . . .

We want justice for the so-called Negroes regardless of the price. We are fast learning that nonviolence is not respected. Church services, praying and singing glory hallelujah are not regarded any more than singing the blues.

It was pitiful to look at college students headed by a college leader, Mr. Martin Luther King, on TV singing and praying to the devils to allow him and his followers to share in with them (whites), respect the Negroes, and be able to dine and have everything in common together, while the devils were shaking their heads saying no, no.

One poor brother leading the others said to the devil, "Why not? Why not? Am I not a human being?"

The police and his dogs were sicked upon the whole group of beggars, and the poor people were driven off without the respect of dogs. Shall we have justice? . . .

We are falling on our knees praying to a merciless enemy (the white American), begging and pleading with blood and tears streaming down our bodies, without the slightest sympathy from the universally known murderers (the white race of devils). The so-called Negroes have been fooled in the knowledge of the American white race. The average so-called Negro thinks he is dealing with a people that are of the God of righteousness, but they (white race) have just become rich and wicked.

The so-called Negroes must remember the poorer the whites are, the more wicked they are when it comes to the so-called Negroes. The entire black nation must know that God has revealed this race of people to be the true race of devils, and there is no righteousness in them. . . .

Now let us go from them and build a nation ourselves that God and the nations of the earth will respect. Your loving to live and become one of the race of devils, who have proven to you for four hundred years that they do not want you for anything but to enslave you in their behalf, is outright foolish and ignorant. Do not you want your own black nation to see you in a better light of understanding?

The government wants to enforce integration, and will be successful after some bloodshed, wherein, the so-called Negro will lose the most blood. . . .

What future will we, the twenty million blacks in America, have in a forced integration? Seeking equal employment and equal recognition would only be temporary, but some of this earth that you can call your own where you can build your own employment would be permanent! . . .

From Elijah Muhammad, "We Must Have Justice," in Roy L. Hill, *Rhetoric of Racial Revolt*, (Denver: Golden Bell Press, 1964).

1. How does Elijah Muhammad depict the non-violent Black movement?
2. What goals does he set out for his movement?
3. What impact do you think Muhammad's ideas would have upon the majority of American Blacks?

I Have a Dream, 1963

In August 1963 Martin Luther King led over 250 000 Americans in a march on Washington. In a mass rally in front of the Lincoln Memorial, King delivered the following speech.

Five score years ago, a great American, in whose symbolic shadow we stand, signed the Emancipation Proclamation. This momentous decree came as a great beacon light of hope to millions of Negro slaves who had been seared in the flames of withering injustice. It came as a joyous daybreak to end the long night of captivity.

But one hundred years later, we must face the tragic fact that the Negro is still not free. One hundred years later, the life of the Negro is still sadly crippled by the manacles of segregation and the chains of discrimination. One hundred years later, the Negro lives on a lonely island of poverty in the midst of a vast ocean of material prosperity. One hundred years later the Negro still languishes in the corners of American society and finds himself in exile in his own land. So we have come here today to dramatize an appalling condition.

In a sense we have come to our nation's capital to cash a check. When the architects of our republic wrote the magnificent words of the Constitution and the Declaration of Independence, they were signing a promissory note to which every American was to fall heir. This note was a promise that all men would be guaranteed the unalienable rights of life, liberty, and the pursuit of happiness.

It is obvious today that America has defaulted on this promissory note insofar as her citizens of color are concerned. Instead of honoring this sacred obligation, America has given the Negro people a bad check; a check which has come back marked "insufficient funds." But we refuse to believe that the bank of justice is bankrupt. We refuse to believe that there are insufficient funds in the great vaults of opportunity of this nation. So we have come to cash this check—a check that will give us upon demand the riches of freedom and the security of justice. . . .

I am not unmindful that some of you have come here out of great trials and tribulations. Some of you have come fresh from narrow jail cells. Some of you have come from areas where your quest for freedom left you battered by the storms of persecution and staggered by the winds of police brutality. You have been the veterans of creative suffering. Continue to work with the faith that unearned suffering is redemptive. . . .

I say to you today, my friends, that in spite of the difficulties and frustrations of the moment I still have a dream. It is a dream deeply rooted in the American dream.

I have a dream that one day this nation will rise up and live out the true meaning of its creed: "We hold these truths to be self-evident; that all men are created equal."

I have a dream that one day on the red hills of Georgia the sons of former slaves and the sons of former slaveowners will be able to sit down together at the table of brotherhood.

I have a dream that one day even the state of Mississippi, a desert state sweltering with the heat of injustice and oppression, will be transformed into an oasis of freedom and justice.

I have a dream that my four little children will one day live in a nation where they will not be judged by the color of their skin but by the content of their character.

I have a dream today.

I have a dream that one day the state of Alabama, whose governor's lips are presently dripping with the words of interposition and nullification, will be transformed into a situation where little black boys and black girls will be able to join hands with little white boys and white girls and walk together as sisters and brothers.

I have a dream today.

I have a dream that one day every valley shall be exalted, every hill and mountain shall be made low, the rough places will be made plains, and the crooked places will be made straight, and the glory of the Lord shall be revealed, and all flesh shall see it together. . . .

This will be the day when all of God's children will be able to sing with new meaning, "My country 'tis of thee, sweet land of liberty, of thee I sing. Land where my fathers died, land of the pilgrim's pride, from every mountainside, let freedom ring."

And if America is to be a great nation this must become true. So let freedom ring from the prodigious hilltops of New Hampshire. Let freedom ring from the mighty mountains of New York. Let freedom ring from the heightening Alleghenies of Pennsylvania.

Let freedom ring from the snowcapped Rockies of Colorado!

Let freedom ring from the curvaceous peaks of California!

But not only that; let freedom ring from Stone Mountain of Georgia!

Let freedom ring from Lookout Mountain of Tennessee!

Let freedom ring from every hill and molehill of Mississippi. From every mountainside, let freedom ring.

When we let freedom ring, when we let it ring from every village and every hamlet, from every state and every city, we will be able to speed up that day when all of God's children, black men and white men, Jews and Gentiles, Protestants and Catholics, will be able to join hands and sing in the words of the old Negro spiritual, "Free at last! Free at last! Thank God Almighty, we are free at last!"

From Martin Luther King, Jr., "I Have A Dream," in P.S. Foner, *The Voice of Black America*, (New York: Simon and Schuster, 1972).

1. How does King depict the previous one hundred years?
2. Summarize the nature of King's "dream."
3. Discuss the effectiveness of King's message to American Blacks.

The Autobiography of Malcolm X

After Malcolm X broke with Elijah Muhammad he became a powerful leader in his own right. His autobiography, published after his assassination, gives us some insight into his ideas and goals.

My thinking had been opened up wide in Mecca. In the long letters I wrote to friends, I tried to convey to them my new insights into the American black man's struggle and his problems, as well as the depths of my search for truth and justice.

"I've had enough of someone else's propaganda," I had written to these friends. "I'm for truth, no matter who tells it. I'm for justice, no matter who it is for or against. I'm a human being first and foremost, and as such I'm for whoever and whatever benefits humanity *as a whole.*"

Largely, the American white man's press refused to convey that I was now attempting to teach Negroes a new direction. With the 1964 "long, hot summer" steadily producing new incidents, I was constantly accused of "stirring up Negroes." Every time I had another radio or television microphone at my mouth, when I was asked about "stirring up Negroes" or "inciting violence," I'd get hot.

"It takes no one to stir up the sociological dynamite that stems from the unemployment, bad housing, and inferior education already in the ghettoes. This explosively criminal condition has existed for so long, it needs no fuse; it fuses itself; it spontaneously combusts from within itself. . . ."

They called me "the angriest Negro in America." I wouldn't deny that charge. I spoke exactly as I felt. "I *believe* in anger. The Bible says there is a *time* for anger." They called me "a teacher, a fomentor of violence." I would say point blank, "That is a lie. I'm not for wanton violence, I'm for justice. I feel that if white people were attacked by Negroes—if the forces of law prove unable, or inadequate, or reluctant to protect those whites from those Negroes—then those white people should protect and defend themselves from those Negroes, using arms if necessary. And I feel that when the law fails to protect Negroes from whites' attack, then those Negroes should use arms, if necessary, to defend themselves."

"Malcolm X Advocates Armed Negroes!"

What was wrong with that? I'll tell you what was wrong. I was a black man talking about physical defense against the white man. The white man can lynch and burn and bomb and beat Negroes—that's all right: "Have patience" . . . "The customs are entrenched" . . . "Things are getting better."

Well, I believe it's a crime for anyone who is being brutalized to continue to accept that brutality without doing something to defend himself. If that's how "Christian" philosophy is interpreted, if that's what Gandhian philosophy teaches, well, then, I will call them criminal philosophies.

I tried in every speech I made to clarify my new position regarding white people—"I don't speak against the sincere, well-meaning, good white people. I have learned that there *are* some. I have learned that not all white people are racists. I am speaking against and my fight is against the white *racists*. I firmly believe that Negroes have the right to fight against these racists, by any means that are necessary."

But the white reporters kept wanting me linked with that word "violence." I doubt if I had one interview without having to deal with that accusation.

"I *am* for violence if non-violence means we continue postponing a solution to the American black man's problem—just to *avoid* violence. I don't go for non-violence if it also means a delayed solution. . . .

When the white man came into this country, he certainly wasn't demonstrating any "non-violence." In fact, the very man whose name symbolizes non-violence here today has stated:

"Our nation was born in genocide when it embraced the doctrine that the original American, the Indian, was an inferior race. Even before there were large numbers of Negroes on our shores, the scar of racial hatred had already disfigured colonial society. From the sixteenth century forward, blood flowed in battles over racial supremacy. We are perhaps the only nation which tried as a matter of national policy to wipe out its indigenous population. Moreover, we elevated that tragic experience into a noble crusade. Indeed, even today we have not permitted ourselves to reject or to feel remorse for this shameful episode. Our literature, our films, our drama, our folklore all exalt it. Our children are still taught to respect the violence which reduced a red-skinned people of an earlier culture into a few fragmented groups herded into impoverished reservations." . . .

I am in agreement one hundred per cent with those racists who say that no government laws ever can *force* brotherhood. The only true world solution today is governments guided by true religion—of the spirit. Here in race-torn America, I am convinced that the Islam religion is desperately needed, particularly by the American black man. The black man needs to reflect that he has been America's most fervent Christian—and where has it gotten him? In fact, in the white man's hands, in the white man's interpretation . . . where has Christianity brought this *world?* . . .

Well, if *this* is so—if the so-called "Christianity" now being practiced in America displays the best world that Christianity has left to offer—no one in his right mind should need any much greater proof that very close at hand is the *end* of Christianity.

1. What role did violence play in Malcolm X's thinking?
2. Contrast his point of view with that of Martin Luther King.
3. How does Malcolm X depict racism in the United States?

Racial Attitudes of White Americans

In 1969 a special task force report was submitted to the National Commission on the Causes and Prevention of Violence. Part of the report considered the racial attitudes of whites in the United States.

The most significant conclusion of the National Advisory Commission on Civil Disorders (The Kerner Commission) was that "White racism is essentially responsible for the explosive mixture which has been accumulating in our cities since the end of World War II." Yet most Americans reply "not guilty" to the charge of racism. In an opinion survey conducted in April of 1968, white Americans disagreed by a 53 to 35 percent margin with the contention that the 1967 riots were brought on by white racism.

Figure 17.1 Percent of White Americans Who Say White Students and Negro Students Should Go to the Same Schools.

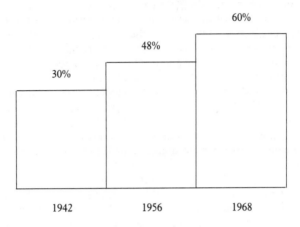

Data furnished courtesy of the National Opinion Research Center.

Figure 17.2 Percent of White American Who Do Not Object to Residential Integration.

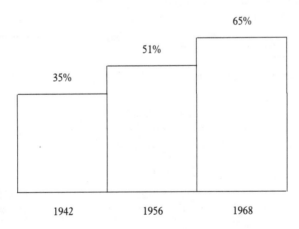

Data furnished courtesy of the National Opinion Research Center.

Perhaps part of the disagreement between public opinion and the Kerner Commission stems from different definitions of "white racism." The average person is likely to reserve the emotionally loaded term "racism" for only the most extreme assertions of white supremacy and innate Negro inferiority. Finding that few of his associates express such views, he rejects the central conclu-

Figure 17.3 Responses of White Americans to the Question: "If colored people came to live next door, would you move?"

	1963	1965	1966	1967
Yes, definitely	20%	13%	13%	12%
Yes, might	25	22	21	23
No	55	65	66	65

From *Gallup Report* press releases. Furnished courtesy of the American Institute of Public Opinion.

Figure 17.4 Responses of White Americans to the Question: "Would you move if colored people came to live in great numbers in your neighborhood?"

	1963	1965	1966	1967
Yes, definitely	49%	40%	39%	40%
Yes, might	29	29	31	31
No	22	31	30	29

From *Gallup Report* press releases. Furnished courtesy of the American Institute of Public Opinion.

sion of the riot commission. Perhaps he would be somewhat more likely to agree that *historically* white racism is responsible for the position of the black man in American society. . . . A society in which most of the good jobs are held by one race, and the dirty jobs by people of another color, is a society in which racism is institutionalized, no matter what the beliefs of its members are. For example, the universities of America are probably the least bigoted of American institutions. One would rarely, if ever, hear an openly bigoted expression at schools like Harvard, Yale, the University of Chicago, the University of California. At the same time, university faculties and students have usually been white, the custodians black. The universities have concerned themselves primarily with the needs and interests of the white upper middle and upper classes, and have viewed the lower classes, and especially blacks, as objects of study rather than of service. In this sense, they have, willy-nilly, been institutionally "white racist."

. . . We will examine the available data on white attitudes toward black Americans. . . . we will see that although there have been some favorable changes in the past twenty years, a considerable amount of racial hostility and opposition to integration remains. . . .

From Jerome H. Skolnick, *The Politics of Protest*, (New York: Simon and Schuster, 1969). Copyright 1969 by Jerome H. Skolnick. Reprinted by permission of Simon and Schuster, Inc.

1. How does the report define racism?
2. Create a thesis based on the information in the charts that accompany the report.

French and English in Canada

In 1960 Jean-Paul Desbiens published a satirical attack of Quebec society under the pen name of Frère Untel (Brother Anonymous). His critique of the old order was a clear indication that the winds of change were blowing through the province and that the Quiet Revolution was about to begin.

I work with the axe, though I don't like to. By temperament I am rather delicate, and nostalgic about the past. I enjoy Oka cheese and coffee laced with brandy. But in the land of Quebec this is no time for delicacy. . . . If a man is asleep in a house on fire, the neighbours don't wake him up with Mozart's *Eine Kleine Nachtmusik.* They yell at him, and if he still sleeps soundly, they kick him out of bed. . . .

Joual, this absence of language, is a symptom of our non-existence as French Canadians. No one can ever study language enough, for it is the home of all meanings. Our inability to assert ourselves, our refusal to accept the future, our obsession with the past, are all reflected in joual, our real language. Witness the abundance of negative turns of speech in our talk. Instead of saying that a woman is beautiful, we say she's not bad looking; instead of saying that a pupil is intelligent, we say he's not stupid; instead of saying that we feel well, we say we're not too bad. . . .

Now we approach the heart of the problem, which is a problem of civilization. Our pupils speak joual because they think joual, and they think joual because they live joual, like everybody around here. Living joual means rock'n roll, hot dogs, parties, running around in cars. . . .

. . . We live joual because our souls are impoverished, and so we speak it. I am convinced there is no substantial difference between the degradation of our language and the slackness of our attitude to the fundamental liberties. . . . When our youth has surrendered those liberties, as they seem to have done in practice if not in theory—the word liberty is still respectable—they easily give up on grammar. The apostles of democracy, like the apostles of good speech, appear like gentle madmen. Our people keep their admiration for machines and technique. They are impressed by nothing but money and luxury; the graces of syntax do not interest them. I flatter myself that I speak correct French—not elegant, but correct. My pupils nonetheless speak joual; I make no impression on them. Indeed I fancy that they sometimes do not understand me. To be understood, I often must have recourse to one or another joual expression. We speak two different languages, my class and I, and I am the only one who speaks both. What can we do? The whole French Canadian society is floundering.

From J.M. Bliss, *Canadian History in Documents, 1763-1966,* (Toronto: The Ryerson Press, 1966).

1. Discuss Frère Untel's contention that joual is more than a language, it is a way of life.

White Niggers of America, 1968-69

Pierre Vallières was a spokesperson for the Front de Libération du Québec (FLQ). He wrote White Niggers of America *while in prison in New York. It remains the clearest statement of the revolutionary goals of the organization.*

In writing this book I claim to do no more than bear witness to the determination of the workers of Quebec to put an end to three centuries of exploitation, of injustices borne in silence, of sacrifices accepted in vain, of insecurity endured with resignation; to bear witness to their new and increasingly energetic determination to take control of their economic, political, and social affairs and to transform into a more just and fraternal society this country, Quebec, which is theirs, this country where they have always been the overwhelming majority of citizens and producers of the "national" wealth, yet where they have never enjoyed the economic power and the political and social freedom to which their numbers and labor entitle them. . . .

Let us kill Saint John the Baptist! Let us burn the papier-mâché traditions with which they have tried to build a myth around our slavery. Let us learn the pride of being men. Let us vigorously declare our independence. And with our hardy freedom, let us crush the sympathetic or contemptuous paternalism of the politicians, the daddy-bosses and the preachers of defeat and submission.

It is no longer time for sterile recriminations but for action. There will be no miracles, but there will be war. . . .

To be a "nigger" in America is to be not a man but someone's slave. For the rich white man of Yankee America, the nigger is a sub-man. Even the poor whites consider the nigger their inferior. They say: "to work as hard as a nigger," "to smell like a nigger," "as dangerous as a nigger," "as ignorant as a nigger." Very often they do not even suspect that they too are niggers, slaves, "white niggers." White racism hides the reality from them by giving them the opportunity to despise an inferior, to crush him mentally or to pity him. But the poor whites who despise the black man are doubly niggers, for they are victims of one more form of alienation—racism—which far from liberating them, imprisons them in a net of hate or paralyzes them in fear of one day having to confront the black man in a civil war.

In Quebec the French Canadians are not subject to this irrational racism that has done so much wrong to the workers, white and black, of the United States. They can take no credit for that, since in Quebec there is no "black problem." The liberation struggle launched by the American blacks nevertheless arouses growing interest among the French-Canadian population, for the workers of Quebec are aware of their condition as niggers, exploited men, second-class citizens. . . .

Often, in writing this book, I have asked myself: Am I right? Am I wrong? But really, what do I care about being right?

It is not a question of being right, my friends, but of overcoming the exploitation of man by man, of overcoming without betraying oneself or one's people.

And if we are to overcome tomorrow, we must begin to fight today. To be sure, we must make every effort to see clearly. That is essential. But we must avoid the trap of imaginary certainties, of postwar dreams. We are at war, and have been for centuries, against those who exploit us. Let us not think that we shall win someday by a divine miracle. Neither let us wait until we know precisely what our world will be like after our revolution. But starting now, let us organize ourselves in such a way as to make this world as human as possible. Because we are forced to *make* history every day; we are not going to wake up one morning and find ourselves in a radically transformed society without having brought the transformation about ourselves. . . .

Let us not wait for a Messiah to bring us a magical solution to our problems. Let us reflect, let us sharpen our tools, roll up our sleeves and *all together* set to work! The revolution is *our* affair, the affair of the niggers. Let us not wait to get started on it until the Pope or the President of the United States gives us the word. The word can come only from us, the niggers: white, black, yellow . . . the men with dirty hands!

We are the strongest, my friends, but we do not know it because we are still dominated by fear.

I can understand that we are afraid of freedom when we see the price the Vietnamese are having to pay for theirs!

But we have no choice. Slavery is not a life. Others are doing all they can to free themselves from capitalism and imperialism. Why not us? Can it be that we are cowards, my friends, men of delicate constitution who shiver when winter comes? No. We are not cowards, but we are still a little too much like sheep. . . .

It is because I cannot bear to be a nigger that I joined the FLQ; that I will stay in the FLQ until the victory of the white niggers of Quebec over capitalism and imperialism; that I will stay there on *my feet*, in or out of prisons of the established Order; that in every possible way I will bear witness to our will, the will of all of us, to free ourselves from our condition as niggers.

I have enough confidence in you—in us—not to be afraid of the future.

The Quebec revolution will not stop.

From Pierre Vallières, *The White Niggers of America*, (Toronto: McClelland and Stewart, 1971).

1. Why does Pierre Vallières refer to Québécois as the "white niggers" of America?
2. What goals does he set for Quebec?
3. Comment on Vallières' statement in 1972 that the FLQ had outlived its purpose.

The October Crisis, 1970

The FLQ had conducted a series of attacks against the English establishment throughout the latter half of the 1960s. For the most part these attacks consisted of bank robberies and letter bombs in federal mailboxes. In 1970, however, things changed. Following two political kidnappings and a murder, the public took the FLQ threats seriously. This FLQ declaration in 1969 set the tone for the events to come.

. . . In a little while the English, the Federalists, the exploiters, the toadies of the occupiers, the lackeys of imperialism—all those who betray the workers and the Quebec nation—will fear for their lives and they will be right.

For the FLQ will kill.

. . . Our present cells look like amateurs when our elite groups go into action.

Have you ever seen a bus full of the English blow up?

Have you ever seen an English library burning?

Have you ever seen the president of a Yankee corporation under fire?

Have you ever seen a pellet micro-bomb?

Have you ever seen a miniature incendiary bomb?

Have you ever seen a can explode on the shelf of a supermarket in the British quarter?

Have you ever seen a Protestant church burning?

Have you ever seen Westmount without telephones or electricity and with its water supply poisoned?

Have you ever seen sharp-shooters ambushed on roofs, shooting down traitors?

Be sure you soon will!!!

From *Victoire*, internal liaison organ of the FLQ, No. 3, March, 1969, in G. Pelletier, *The October Crisis*, (Toronto: McClelland and Stewart, 1971).

As part of negotiations with the kidnappers during the October Crisis, the government agreed to broadcast the FLQ Manifesto on radio and television. Although extreme and often confused, many parts of the manifesto struck a responsive chord with the people of Quebec.

1. The Front de Libération du Québec is not the Messiah, nor a modern-day Robin Hood. It is a group of working people of Quebec who are committed to do everything they can for the people of Quebec to take their destiny in their hands.

2. The Front de Libération du Québec wants the total independence of the Québécois, brought together in a free society, purged forever of its band of voracious sharks, the patronage-dispensing "big bosses" and their servants who have made Quebec into their private preserve of "cheap labor" and of exploitation without scruple. . . .

25. Working people of Quebec, begin today to take back what belongs to you; take yourselves what is yours. You alone know your factories, your machines, your hotels, your universities, your unions, do not wait for a miracle organization.

26. Make your revolution yourselves, in your neighborhoods, in your workplaces. And if you do not make it yourselves, more usurpers, technocrats or others, will replace the handful of cigar puffers we now know, and everything will have to be done over again. You alone can build a free society.

27. We must fight, no longer one by one, but together, until victory, with all the means at our disposal, as did the Patriots of 1837-1838 (those whom our

holy mother the Church hastened to excommunicate, the better to sell itself to British interests).

28. Let all those, in every corner of Quebec, scornfully dismissed as "lousy French" and drunkards, take up with vigor the battle against the club-smashers of freedom and justice, and strip their power to harm from the professionals of hold-ups and fraud: bankers, "businessmen", judges, sold-out politicians. . . .

30. Our struggle can only be victorious. Not for long can we hold in misery and scorn a people once awakened.

Vive le Quebec libre!

Vive les camarades prisonniers politiques!

Vive la revolution Québécoise!

Vive le Front de Libération du Québec!

From G. Pelletier, *The October Crisis*, (Toronto: McClelland and Stewart, 1971).

1. Although intended to terrorize English Quebec, the "FLQ Will Kill" statement had little impact in 1969. Why might this have been so?

2. Why would defining the FLQ as "a group of working people of Quebec who are committed to do everything they can for the people of Quebec to take their destiny in their hands" be a popular sentiment with the general public?

3. What were the long-term implications of the October Crisis for the separatist movement in Quebec?

Freedom and Order

Gérard Pelletier was a cabinet minister in the Trudeau government when the War Measures Act was invoked. In this excerpt he outlines the justification for taking extreme action.

In an open and democratic society a politician is continually obliged to reconcile freedom and the requirements of public order. This is not a comfortable position. Especially in a period of crisis it is not likely to satisfy a mind of logical or Cartesian bent. One of my friends summed up this ambivalence very well when he said: "Today I recognize that the reasons for the emergency measures are well founded. But at the same time I agree in advance that I am likely to change my mind tomorrow and go to the defence of one of my friends who has been unjustly arrested." Such an attitude may appear very dull or tepid compared to the blazing, absolute intransigence of extremists on both sides: one demanding that an absolutely free hand be given to the police, and the other proclaiming on radio and television and in full-page statements in the newspapers that "Freedom of expression no longer exists in Quebec." Personally I found it difficult during the crisis not to be caught up in this simplistic dichotomy, not to allow myself to impose a dialectic of opposites. When intellectuals accuse one of supporting a police state, one is tempted to adopt a defensive attitude and systematically take the opposite position—that is to say, to caricature one's own thought. It is not easy to account for the fact that the Government to which one belongs has considerably augmented the powers of the police. One knows that such an operation is not without risks. One fears abuses and one's only desire is to be in a position to rescind all exceptional measures. . . .

. . . Strictly speaking, what is involved here is not a policy but rather an attitude of the moment, dictated by circumstances. When the lives of two men are at stake, discrimination and balance are imperative. . . .

. . . In a democracy the possession of power has a moderating effect. And since the parliamentary opposition is required to participate to some extent in decisions that affect the destiny of the community, it too is compelled by the internal logic of its position to take greater account of reality.

But there are opposition forces that do not participate in parliamentary exchange and have no way of being heard except by influence exerted directly upon public opinion. Since they are farther from the centres of decision, these groups or factions are not explicitly bound to *negotiate with reality*, and often yield to verbal extremism and scaremongering.

Authoritarianism is the temptation of power; alarmism that of opposition.

From Gérard Pelletier, *The October Crisis*, (Toronto: McClelland and Stewart, 1971).

1. What balance does Gérard Pelletier identify in a democratic society?
2. How does he respond to the accusations that the government is trying to create a police state?
3. What is the role of opposition in a democratic society?

Culture in Quebec

Quebec has always had a distinct culture based upon its own sense of identity and nationality. In this essay Professor Ben-Z. Shek of the University of Toronto outlines the strength of French-Canadian culture.

De mon grand pays solitaire
Je crie avant que de me taire
A tous les hommes de la terre
Ma maison c'est votre maison
Entre mes quatre murs de glace
Je mets mon temps et mon espace
A préparer le feu la place
Pour les humains de l'horizon
Et les humains sont de ma race . . .

The above words are from *Mon pays*, written and composed by Quebec's most famous *chansonnier*, Gilles Vigneault. This song is practically a hymn today in Quebec, because its sensitive creator has been able in it to touch certain chords common to thousands of his compatriots. In spite of what we have been told by those in high places that French-Canadian nationalism is to all intents and purposes a reactionary, xenophobic phenomenon, Vigneault's song is proof of the contrary. The word "race," is so much a part of the inward-looking, mythical vocabulary of traditional right-wing Quebec nationalism, has here been turned into its opposite, and is now applied to all of humanity, equally welcome to sit before the singer-poet's cosy fireplace. The neo-nationalism so evident today in Quebec's burgeoning culture is largely a positive, confident and realistic acceptance of the Québécois by themselves. Its approach is open to the world, and not chauvinistic, and stresses, as poet Fernand Ouellette said recently during a visit to Israel with other Quebec cultural leaders, that one contributes to universal cultural values by developing one's own people's artistic and psychological talents. . . .

From B.W. Hodgins et al., *Canadiens, Canadians and Québécois*, (Toronto: Prentice-Hall, 1974).

1. Account for the popularity of *Mon pays* in Quebec.
2. Comment on the fact that cultural industries display more vitality in Quebec than in the rest of Canada.
3. To what extent is culture linked to nationalism?

My Quebec: René Lévesque, 1977

Between 1976 and 1979 René Lévesque was at the peak of his power and popularity in Quebec. The Conservative electoral victory of the latter year would eventually provide the impetus to finally call for the referendum on sovereignty-association. In a speech to the French National Assembly in 1977, Lévesque outlined a confident vision of the new order.

We are speaking of a people that for a long time has been content, to let itself be forgotten in order to survive. But then it said that in order to survive validly, one must assert one's identity, and subsequently that, in order to properly assert one's identity, it must become desirable and even necessary to be emancipated. . . .

It is therefore more and more assured that a new country will soon appear, by democratic means, on the map, where until now a federal state would have preferred to see only one of its many provinces, and where those whom you often call *"les Français du Canada,"* an apparently simple expression, which rejoins the essential facts, but whose meaning has nonetheless become ambiguous over the course of time, have their home.

. . . Outside Europe we are therefore the only large community which is of French stock. We can, like you, seriously evoke our ancestors, the Gauls! And as we are only six million in the corner of a continent which numbers forty times as many anglophones, we sometimes even feel encircled, like Asterix in his village. . . . And imagine that the entire continent of North America ought to have been French instead of . . . neo-Roman. . . .

This is not a nostalgic idealization of a tiny society of some tens of thousands of poor people who, in 1760 in the Saint Lawrence Valley, had to submit to a foreign domination which was destined to remain for a long time. . . .

. . . This was a nation, and a French nation certainly, but a nation which was just as able to live its own life and to be a presence in the world as any other.

This is what defeat broke up, but it did not manage to dispel the dream. It was a dream which, though normally unacknowledged, was strong enough to nourish, even today, a national identity and a national idea that only numerical weakness and total isolation prevented us from realizing. . . .

Inevitably this metamorphosis owed it to itself to create an instrument for its political expression and to try to conduct it to its logical conclusion. This instrument is the Parti Québécois. We were just a few hundred, then a few thousand, to bring it into being in 1967-68, with two objectives which have remained coupled since then: sovereignty and association. This means a sovereign State of Quebec which will accept, or rather offer in advance, new links of interdependence with Canada, but links which will this time be negotiated between equal peoples, as a function of their geographic and other unquestionable common interests. . . .

But there is, in addition, the constant, pressing, daily worry of maintaining a linguistic and cultural identity which has lost the old security of an isolated, rural and prolific Quebec, an identity which is today exposed as never before to the major transcontinental influences of the American culture, and which risks, in addition, being swamped by the immigration policy of a federal state which we will never control, and by the excessive weight in Quebec of an anglophone minority, the managing circles, which have exercised a truly colonialist influence for too long. This identity, after almost four hundred years, is so much a part of the intrinsic soul of Quebec that, without it, it would no longer have any reason to be. . . .

Whatever happens, Canada as a whole now knows, almost as well as Quebec, that at the very least some profound changes are required. . . .

For us Quebecers, this is literally a question of our right to live.

From René Lévesque, Speech to the members of the French National Assembly, November 2, 1977, in René Lévesque, *My Quebec*, (Toronto: Methuen, 1979).

1. What prediction does René Lévesque make for North America?
2. How does Lévesque depict the United States?
3. What happened to Lévesque's dream of a homeland?

Minorities and the Majority in North America

Canadian journalist Heather Robertson wrote about her experiences travelling across the Prairies in 1965-66. In this excerpt she highlights the crises facing Native people in North America.

In the summer of 1966, when I started driving through Western Canada in search of Indians, it appeared that a civil rights movement was underway among Canada's Indians. There had been two important demonstrations in 1965: the Indians of Hay Lake, Alberta, marched on the Legislature in Edmonton, and the Kenora Indians marched on the city council. These actions by the Indians were unprecedented in western Canada and to many they were astonishing. Although both marches failed when the Indians were bought off with welfare and token concessions, many people, especially those in government, were jolted and the stereotype of the lazy, apathetic Indian was broken. Bureaucrats in the Department of Indian Affairs, accustomed to speaking of Indians as helpless, naive and politically inept, were seriously embarrassed. Indians from the most isolated areas of the country were suddenly showing initiative, intelligence and political sophistication. And as a result of these demonstrations, although Indian Affairs officials continue to speak of Indians as helpless and inept, now fewer people believe them. Most important, the Indians no longer believe them.

. . . The motives of those of us who went west to the Indians in 1965 and 1966 were similar to the impulses which sent many American college students to the South a few years earlier. I believed vaguely in liberty, democracy and the North American way of life. I believed that people were basically good, honest and well-meaning, and that skin color made no difference. I identified with the poor and oppressed, but nevertheless, I was prejudiced. I had the typical, unconscious middle class liberal inhibitions, basically a fear of losing caste. I was afraid of Indians, afraid of physical assault, of being insulted or put down, of being made a fool of, of misunderstanding. My inhibition was mainly the result of recent mythologies about Indians, reports that Indians beat up white people on impulse, that they are a silent, uncommunicative race, that they are intrinsically different. These ideas came mainly from conversations with Indian Affairs people and other Indian experts before I visited the reserves. It is common for these people to say "you have to get to know the Indians." This process, it is revealed, takes from 10 to 40 years, and is usually directly related to the length of the expert's own tenure in the Indian industry. The experts, of course, "know Indians," and frequently suggest that one has to live with Indians over an extended period of time. Many Indian agents crow loudly about their intimate knowledge of the Indian character after five years spent in government houses in the vicinity of a reserve. . . .

I was shocked by the reserves and Metis communities, shocked by the destitution, the squalor, the chaos, the brutality, the apathy. Worse, however, was the people's fear, servility and hatred, and the knowledge that these feelings were based on the color of my skin, as my fear was based on the color of theirs. I was from the outside, the other side, a stranger and a threat, irrevocably on the side of Indian Affairs, the oppressors. I realized when I became aware of the relationships between Indians and Canadian society, that I could no longer believe that society to be benevolent, nor could I believe the government to be just. Once you have stepped outside your society to look at it, you can never really get comfortably in again. You begin to understand what Indians feel like.

As I drove my car across the unmarked boundary of a reserve, I drove into a world without normal orientation, a world in which time, order, money were irrelevant. Repeated, peculiar, and different confrontations confused my responses to the situations I was experiencing: A toothless, gnome-like old man in rags and a floppy tweed hat shuffles up, plucks at my sleeve and babbles out some hilarious but incomprehensible gibberish which seems, to him, of terrible significance. A middle-aged man sits beside me on a broken kitchen chair; suddenly he turns and fixes me with a stare that goes right through. "We are human too," he says knowingly, with no connection with anything that has gone before.

Even outside reserves, the Indian industry has an air of unreality and pretense. At the annual Indian-Metis conference in Winnipeg, Indian chiefs shuffle around in rusty blue postman's suits they have been given for uniforms looking helpless and embarrassed. One after another they rise to make impassioned pleas to the government on trivial housekeeping issues while the Indian Affairs personnel, yawning behind their hands, glance at their watches and say that nothing can be done. Everyone talks in the monosyllabic language of western movies—"White man and Indian heap good friends now, eh?" Bureaucrats with university degrees talk about the nice pow-wow they're having; the Indians sometimes talk about going on the warpath or smoking the peace pipe.

. . . The trouble with the Indians has been interpreted in the light of one Canadian myth after another.

At first it was simple heathenism. One could expect little from a savage. However, a few drops of water sprinkled on the savage's head failed to bring about the expected transformation. He would have to be civilized as well as Christianized, and civilization, at the turn of the century, meant farming. The trouble with the Indian was that he had a "natural antipathy" to farming, so farming was not the solution. The trouble with the Indian was ignorance. He was too backward and illiterate to be able to learn farming and he couldn't write or read instructions from the Indian agent or do simple arithmetic. The new answer was to educate the Indian just enough for him to make a decent living on the reserve, a little of the three R's and lots of manual training like knitting and raising chickens.

This new emphasis on general learning rather than practical farming came at the end of the depression when almost every Indian, as well as a great proportion of the Canadian population, was living on relief and it was clear from the Saskatchewan dust bowl that farming was not the answer for every Canadian, Ukrainian, Scotsman or Indian. But education has not been the cure. The trouble with the Indian today is poverty. Poverty has been popular since war was declared on it in 1965. Poverty, for the Indian, is believed to result from education, or the lack of it, or the wrong kind. The Indian cannot, or will not, hold a steady job, so that his income falls to subsistence level and he goes on welfare. The solution for this current Indian problem has not been found yet, although thousands of bureaucrats, social workers and politicians are working on it. Soon the solution will be discovered, and soon it too will fail.

All these solutions are based on the premise that Indians are not people. . . .

. . . In every Indian and Metis community in Canada the same phrase is repeated over and over, perhaps not in the identical words of Hay Lake but similar: "Why don't they treat us like human beings?" "I may be an Indian but I'm just as good as any white man."

I sit on a battered wooden kitchen chair in a gloomy shack that reeks of smoke, stale cooked lard, and urine, listening to the crunch of bones and raw flesh as a cat devours some whitefish from a bucket in the corner. I try not to be frightened or sick as I continue in some aimless, circuitous conversation with which everyone is bored but too polite to say so, staring at the unkept, round-shouldered, calloused men lounging around the room and wondering how the devil I got there. A bleary-eyed, aged man with broken fingernails, hunched over in the chair beside me turns, puts his face close to mine and, staring at me out of red-rimmed eyes, his hands clenched and his body tensed to shaking like some Old Testament prophet clutching lightning bolts, says, hoarsely: "We are human too."

The word "human" is almost whispered—a word that has to be forced and may bring unforeseeable consequences. There is no anger, no hate, no bitterness, sadness or despair in the words. They are spoken in a flat, monotonous voice with a slight quizzical inflection, a half-question mark. . . .

. . . There is no word, no gesture, no right response. Only the word is needed—yes, or no. We look at each other with meaningless significance, characters in a melodrama. He turns away. The white man has failed again.

Canada's Indians are, in the eyes of other Canadians, non-people by the mere fact of being Indian. . . .

The Indians, rats in psychologists' wire cages, have been our subjects for between 100 and 350 years. They have been on the receiving end of almost every bureaucratic program, religious crusade and psychological gimmick conceived by the Canadian mind. They have been poked, prodded, berated, praised, analyzed, frightened, studied and theorized about. They have been treated like guinea pigs and supermen, like children and saints. They have been ignored, brainwashed, flattered and ridiculed. Each new wave of crusaders which has surged over the reservations, only to stagnate in sloughs and ditches, has been convinced that was going to succeed, that it was going to turn these savages, these barbarians into civilized human beings, into citizens who would be an integrated and productive part of Canada. Something has always gone wrong. The wells have been poisoned; the wave has turned into slimy backwaters breeding infection. Every day more disinfectant is needed, the walls have to be built higher, the lid is harder to keep on.

From Heather Robertson, *Reservations Are for Indians*, (Toronto: James Lorimer & Company Ltd., Publishers, 1970).

1. How was the self-concept of Canada's Native peoples changing in the mid-sixties?
2. Trace Robertson's own voyage of discovery.
3. To what extent has the situation changed for Canada's Native peoples over the last twenty-five years?

The NCAI Takes on the Whiskey Advertisers

In 1965 the National Congress of American Indians spoke out against a liquor ad that was currently appearing in American magazines. The ad and their response appear below.

the Sioux had had soft whiskey they would never have called it fire water.

The Indians didn't call whiskey "fire water" for nothing. (Why do you think they were yelping all the time?)

And basically, distilling methods haven't changed much since those days. Except for Soft Whiskey, of course.

Soft Whiskey swallows easy. It's gentle going down. You could say we've gotten rid of the evil spirits.

But don't fool yourself. Soft Whiskey isn't for old squaws. It's 86 proof. And it can do anything any other 86 proof can do. It just does it softer.

How did we put out the fire?

For one thing, we distill in small batches instead of giant ones.

The rest of the process will have to remain our secret. You see, other distillers have been trying to develop a Soft Whiskey for years. It was many many moons before we even hit upon it. 12 years to be exact. After all that work, we rather enjoy the idea of being the only Soft Whiskey.

Not to admit it would be speaking with forked tongue.

Dear Sir:

In reference to our conversation yesterday, I wish to draw some specific examples on why this advertisement is extremely detrimental to the Indian people as a whole and to the Sioux Nation and its constituent tribes in particular.

1) Why is Sioux picked out as opposed to other Indian tribes? Are the Sioux entirely different from other tribes? Are they more noted for drunkeness or for drinking? Do they yelp when they drink hard liquor? (Your initial answer yesterday was that there was no danger or malice involved as these people have been dead for 200 years.) The implication being: Indians are a funny little group from America's past and so it is safe to portray them as a funny little people and so let's just pick any tribe and talk stilted and be "sophisticated."

2) Do Indians yelp? I believe I have only heard "yelp" referred to dogs? Is the inference that Indians are dogs? (Certainly not, you are in complete sympathy with Indians, in fact the company employs Indians, you even know an Indian.) The inference that is actually behind "yelp" is that in some manner or means Indians are not really people, they are an interesting "species" found on the North American Continent. Any complaint they would have in reference to the "fire" in the water would have to be a "yelp," "bark," "growl," "whinny," "hiss," "bay," "chirp," "moo," "ugh," "snarl," but certainly couldn't be in the form of an intelligent complaint. Again we have the image that if you don't speak English you don't speak intelligently. I should remind you that many Indians have mastery of two languages. I should be most interested in your ability to speak an Indian language.

3) "We have gotten rid of the evil spirits." Do Indians live in a religious universe where they are terrified by evil spirits? Is this not a "sophisticated" way of degrading a people in terms of your own understanding of them. My 5 years in Seminary have been sufficient to inform me of the absolute terror your ancestors dwelt in. I would only remind you of the mild insanity of the Salem witch hunts to feel that your inference to "evil spirits" is much more appropriate to your group than to mine.

You also have a reference to "old squaws." Pray tell me, what is an old squaw? Do Indians have "squaws?" Do you still refer to Negro males as "bucks"? Are the Minority races still "species" for you?

. . . Now I believe that we could cooperate with you to provide some real good Indian ads that would make an impression. Let's take the massacre scene of Wounded Knee where a band of Sioux were slaughtered by U.S. Cavalry and let's show a caption "Before the Massacre we all had a shot of -----, it was smooth on us but rather hard on the Indians, but they didn't yelp for long." Or let's show a picture of the beautiful Minnesota lake country with the notation "----- helped us steal this land, ----- and a smooth talker is too hard for the Sioux to handle." You see, I believe that Indians would cooperate with your firm in good natured fun if we only had the chance. But you can also understand how the point of view makes a great deal of difference in what is fun and what is not.

You said over the phone that you generally don't check with representatives of the minority groups before portraying one of them in your ads. I would suggest that you begin a new policy in that respect in the very near future. All groups are trying to overcome an image that they did not create. There is no reason to type Mexican-Americans as "dirty," Italian-Americans as "gangsters" or American Indians as "drunken," although your people have found in 300 years that a drunken Indian is much easier to make treaties with.

. . . Your present type of sophistication shows a narrow provincial view of this country based upon inadequate knowledge of the great social concern for all people in this country.

I am enclosing some information for you on the Sioux Indians of South Dakota but would have you know that there are also Sioux tribes in Montana, Minnesota, North Dakota, Nebraska. I am also sending the Sioux tribes a copy of this letter and would suggest that your president send them all a letter of explanation of the intent of the advertisement and apology for using the use of the Sioux name without permission. I would hope that your firm would begin to lead your industry into a more constructive use of its resources for the good of all people in this country.

Sincerely yours,
Vine Deloria, Jr.
Executive Director
National Congress of American Indians

From *Indian Voices*, Tahlequah, Okla., May, 1965.

1. Summarize the offensive aspects of the ad.
2. What are the arguments put forward by the NCAI?
3. Do you think the image presented in the advertisement was the result of deliberate misrepresentation or unthinking stereotyping?

The NCAI States its Case

The following editorial appeared in The Sentinel, *the publication of the National Congress of American Indians.*

. . . We think that the time is ripe for a realistic thoughtful study of the place of the American Indian in American society and in American history and that policy be hereafter based upon this study. It is necessary for a person to stop every now and then and review his life, ponder the facts of where he has been and where he is going, and set some new and more understanding goals for himself. . . .

There is not necessarily conflict for a group of people who are different in their wants and desires from the majority of the people in their country. And we do not feel that Indians necessarily want to be different or should be different. What annoys us, confuses people wanting to help Indians, and causes untold confusion in making Indian policy, is the assumption that Indians have to be different . . . or have to be the same. The Indian is always presented with the choice: keep your beads and braids and we won't let you have any refrigerators or other modern conveniences or take all our material goods and surrender everything that is particularly Indian, beginning with your land.

Society today is moving very fast toward a new concept of itself. We shall soon be able and willing to provide a decent living for all of our citizens. Does this necessarily mean that we must all want the same things, all live in the cities and suburbs, all enjoy the same books, dances, movies, games, churches? Must we all share the same intangible values? And what will these values be?

The soul of a person is extremely complex. Even more so must be the soul of a nation. Perhaps compassion is that quality that coordinates everything in a soul to provide that humaness that we look for in people and nations. We have the compassion at present, but we lack an essential ingredient that will allow compassion to work and that is variety. We must have a variety of real values and differences so that any person has many real options for living in our society. We believe that allowing total development of Indian communities on their own basis will be a major step in providing that variety in American life which is so necessary to a healthy society. We believe that the assumption that Indians necessarily have to be like everyone else should be stricken from the books and minds of people. Likewise the idea that Indians necessarily have to be different. Give Indian tribes the economic and educational means to be what they want to be and see what happens.

From *The Sentinel*, Vol. XI, No. 1, Winter 1966.

1. Write a letter to the editor in response to this editorial.

Native Rights, 1988

In the 1960s and 1970s North America's Native peoples began to demonstrate a new militancy and determination to redress many of the economic, political, and social injustices of the past. By the late 1980s this drive had met with differing degrees of success on either side of the border.

As native peoples in Canada began to take a more prominent role in discussions pertaining to self-government and land claims, their American counterparts declined in

*political influence. In this excerpt, Kirk Makin looked at the state of the American
Indian Movement in 1988.*

Twelve years after a shootout at Pine Ridges Indian reservation, the American
Indian Movement is a scattered, near-forgotten force whose members are mostly
dead, imprisoned, or tied up in court.

But AIM hopes the well-publicized appearance of three representatives at the
Moscow summit this week presages a return to prominence of the issues it
championed in the 1970s.

Back then, things were very different. The dramatic fear tactics of the network of angry young native men and women gained much publicity for their
cause. . . .

Russel Redner . . . acknowledged in an interview that AIM's hostile rhetoric
sowed the seeds of its own destruction.

Mr. Redner, one of those in Moscow this week, said the rage took root in the
1960s as Indian youths learned how white settlers had herded their ancestors
onto meagre tracts of land with no employment or education.

Virtually every treaty ever signed with the white conquerors was broken—an
approach succinctly summed up by President Ronald Reagan this week when
he told a Russian audience: "Maybe we should not have humored them in
wanting to stay in that kind of primitive lifestyle." . . .

In its heyday, Mr. Redner estimates, AIM had several hundred members.
Their goals wre to fight the sell-off, create more employment, housing and education for Indians, and to act as an advocacy group to protect and encourage
their people.

In recent years, the goals of the movement have actually slid further away,
Mr. Redner said. "The Government tied us up. They have the resources and
the manpower and all the covert tactics. Employment[sic] is still 80-90 percent,
tribal councils are as corrupt as can be. Alcoholism is really high. The problems
remain. They are worse."

From Kirk Makin, "Radical Indian Group a Spent Force", *The Globe and Mail*, (Toronto, June 3,
1988).

*On June 1, 1988, police raided the Kahnawake Indian Reserve just south of Montreal.
In the process they impounded huge quantities of cigarettes which had been smuggled
into Canada without paying duty. In response to this violation of their rights of free
passage from nation to nation, members of the reserve blockaded one of the main bridges
into the city. Two days later,* The Globe and Mail *editorialized about the issue.*

All Canadians dedicated to more social justice and political equality for native
peoples are frustrated at the uneven pace of progress in the last 20 years. But
that does not justify suggestions that violence may be warranted, or the use of
firearms by natives to shut down public highways. Those who would condone
violence out of a sense of solidarity with native causes abuse the fabric of Canadian democracy. . . .

This week in Edmonton, Georges Erasmus was re-elected as chief of the

Assembly of First Nations and he immediately warned that violence was probable in the absence of faster political and economic progress for natives. . . .
Such statements attract wide attention; they do not contribute to practical
solutions.

Canada has had four constitutional conferences since 1983 devoted exclusively
to aboriginal rights. These conferences failed to define the right to native self-
government within Canadian society. They also failed to establish a negotiating
process by which self-government might be defined in advance of another constitutional round.

Mr. Erasmus and other aboriginal leaders justifiably complain that momentum seems to be fading on this political project. . . .

It is much less a failure of good will than a failure of political imagination
that frustrates meaningful progress on native self-government. . . .

It would be wrong, however, to paint a picture of stagnation and despair.
Important practical steps are being taken in aboriginal self-government across
Canada, from James Bay to the Northwest Territories and British Columbia.
Indian participation in education, social services, and law enforcement is
advancing strongly on many reserves. Thousands of Indian women and children
are regaining their band status and returning to reserves. The cultural revival
that appeared in the 1960s has created a native leadership of impressive quality,
well demonstrated at the last constitutional conference on aboriginal rights in
March 1987.

This is not a time for rifles and talk of rifles. This is a time to break some
logjams in a process of evolution that cannot be allowed to stall.

From *The Globe and Mail*, (Toronto, June 3, 1988).

1. Just as American Indian leaders have appeared in Moscow, Canada's Native
peoples have called upon such unlikely allies as the South African ambassador to
highlight their grievances. Write an editorial response to this approach to gaining
political and media attention for issues in Native rights.
2. Based on outside research, develop a research plan and thesis designed to answer
the question:
"To what extent have Canada's Native peoples gained a large measure of the
reforms sought by their American counterparts"?
3. Write a letter to the editor in response to either the editorial or the article
appearing in the June 3 edition of *The Globe and Mail*.

The Deportation of Japanese North Americans

*Even before war broke out in the Pacific in 1941, many Japanese-Americans suspected
that they might be subjected to some form of backlash. In the following excerpt from
his book* Concentration Camps USA: Japanese Americans and World War II, *author
Roger Daniels outlines the feelings which led up to the deportations.*

. . . If the attack on Pearl Harbor came as a devastating shock to most Americans, for those of Japanese ancestry it was like a nightmare come true.

Throughout the 1930s the Nisei generation dreaded the possibility of a war between the United States and Japan; although some in both the Japanese and American communities fostered the illusion that the emerging Nisei generation could help bridge the gap between the rival Pacific powers, most Nisei, at least, understood that this was a chimera. As early as 1937 Nisei gloom about the future predominated. One Nisei spoke prophetically about what might happen to Japanese Americans in a Pacific war. Rhetorically he asked his fellow Nisei students at the University of California:

> . . . What are we going to do if war does break out between the United States and Japan? . . . In common language we can say "we're sunk." Even if the Nisei wanted to fight for America, what chances? Not a chance! . . . Our properties would be confiscated and most likely [we would be] herded into prison camps—perhaps we would be slaughtered on the spot.

As tensions increased, so did Nisei anxieties; and in their anxiety some Nisei tried to accentuate their loyalty and Americanism by disparaging the generation of their fathers. Newspaper editor Togo Tanaka, for example, speaking to a college group in early 1941, insisted that the Nisei must face what he called "the question of loyalty" and assumed that since the Issei were "more or less tumbleweeds with one foot in America and one foot in Japan," real loyalty to America could be only found in his own generation. A Los Angeles Nisei jeweler expressed similar doubts later the same year. After explaining to a Los Angeles *Times* columnist that many if not most of the older generation were pro-Japanese rather than pro-American, he expressed his own generation's fears. "We talk of almost nothing but this great crisis. We don't know what's going to happen. Sometimes we only look for a concentration camp." . . .

It seems clear that well before the actual coming of war a considerable proportion of the American public had been conditioned not only to the probability of a Pacific war with Japan—that was, after all, a geopolitical fact of twentieth-century civilization—but also to the proposition that this war would involve an invasion of the continental United States in which Japanese residents and secret agents would provide the spearhead of the attack. After war came at Pearl Harbor and for years thereafter many Japanophobes insisted that, to use [H. G.] Wells's phrase, "the Yellow Peril was a peril after all," but this is to misunderstand completely Japan's intentions and capabilities during the Great Pacific War. The Japanese military planners never contemplated an invasion of the Continental United States, and, even had they done so, the logistical problems were obviously beyond Japan's capacity as a nation. But, often in history, what men believe to be true is more important than the truth itself because the mistaken belief becomes a basis for action. These two factors—the long racist and anti-Oriental tradition plus the widely believed "yellow peril" fantasy—when triggered by the traumatic mechanism provided by the attack on Pearl Harbor, were the necessary preconditions for America's concentration camps. But beliefs, even widely held beliefs, are not always translated into action. We must now discover how this particular set of beliefs—the inherent and genetic disloyalty of individual Japanese plus the threat of an imminent Japanese invasion—

produced public policy and action, the mass removal and incarceration of the West Coast Japanese Americans. . . .

In addition to the selective roundup of enemy aliens, the Justice Department almost immediately announced the sealing off of the Mexican and Canadian borders to "all persons of Japanese ancestry, whether citizen or alien." Thus, by December 8, that branch of the federal government particularly charged with protecting the rights of citizens was willing to single out one ethnic group for invidious treatment. Other national civilian officials discriminated in other ways. Fiorello La Guardia, an outstanding liberal who was for a time director of the Office of Civilian Defense as well as mayor of New York, pointedly omitted mention of the Japanese in two public statements calling for decent treatment for enemy aliens and suggesting that alien Germans and Italians be presumed loyal until proved otherwise. By implication, at least Japanese were to to be presumed disloyal. . . .

Even more damaging were the mendacious statements of Frank Knox, Roosevelt's Republican Secretary of the Navy. On December 15 Secretary Knox held a press conference in Los Angeles on his return from a quick inspection of the damage at Pearl Harbor. As this was the first detailed report of the damage there, his remarks were front-page news all across the nation. Knox spoke of "treachery" in Hawaii and insisted that much of the disaster was caused by "the most effective fifth column work that's come out of the war, except in Norway." The disaster at Pearl Harbor, as is now generally acknowledged, was caused largely by the unpreparedness and incompetence of the local military commanders, as Knox already knew. (The orders for the relief of Admiral Kimmel were already being drawn up.) But the secretary who, as we shall see, harbored deep-felt anti-Japanese prejudices, probably did not want the people to lose faith in their Navy, so the Japanese population in Hawaii—and indirectly all Japanese Americans—was made the scapegoat on which to hang the big lie.

From Roger Daniels, *Concentration Camps USA: Japanese Americans and World War II*, (New York: Holt, Rinehart and Winston, Inc., 1972). Reprinted by permission of Henry Holt and Company, Inc.

In Canada, the government moved quickly as well. The following notice announced the new policy.

To Male Enemy Aliens

Under date of February 2nd, 1942, the Honourable the Minister of National Defence with the concurrence of the Minister of Justice gave public notice defining an area of British Columbia, as described below, to be a protectd area after the 31st day of January, 1942; that is to say, that area of the Province of British Columbia, including all islands, west of a line described hereunder:- . . .

Pursuant to the provisions of Regulation 4 of the Defence of Canada Regulations, the Minister of Justice has, on the 5th day of February, 1942, ordered that:-

1. All male Enemy Aliens of the ages of 18 years to 45 years, inclusive, shall leave the protected area herein before referred to on or before the 1st day of April, 1942;

2. That, subject to the provisions of paragraph No. 1 of this Order, no Enemy Alien shall, after the date of this order, enter, leave or return to such protected area except with the permission of the Commissioner of the Royal Canadian Mounted Police Force, or an Officer of that Force designated by the Commissioner to act for him in this respect;

3. That no Enemy Alien shall have in his possession or use, while in such protected area, any camera, radio transmitter, radio shortwave receiving set, firearm, ammunition, or explosive.

S. T. Wood (Commissioner)
Ottawa, February 7, 1942.
Royal Canadian Mounted Police
To Be Posted In A Conspicuous Place

From The expulsion order that called for the removal of Japanese male "enemy" aliens from coastal B.C. (Public Archives of Canada)

1. Account for the irrational fear which led to the deportations in both countries.
2. Why were the Japanese and not the German and Italian North Americans affected by the policy?
3. To what extent was the treatment of Japanese-Americans and Canadians a purely racist policy?

Protection and Redress

The Canadian government has delayed considerably in redressing the wrongs of 1942; even the American government has offered a reasonable settlement to the survivors of this injustice.

In this article from the Ottawa Citizen *experts argue that the Charter of Rights is no guarantee against the abuses suffered by Japanese-Canadians on the West Coast.*

The new federal Charter of Rights does not automatically protect other minority groups from the indignities suffered by the Japanese Canadians in the 1940s, according to most constitutional experts. . . .

The notion that the Charter of Rights will somehow prevent the more severe effects of the War Measures Act is disputed in most legal circles.

The Charter's section 15, which takes effect in April, says every individual is equal before the law and cannot be discriminated against on grounds of race, national or ethnic origin, color, religion, sex, age or mental or physical disability.

However the Charter also contains an escape clause—an introductory phrase which allows for rights to be overthrown in extraordinary circumstances. All the equality rights are "subject only to such reasonable limits prescribed by law as can be demonstrably justified in a free and democratic society."

That phrase could be used to justify some future implementation of the War Measures Act, or any other emergency powers legislation. . . .

Despite the Charter, what happened to the Japanese "could happen again."

"The fact that there are potential remedies available will help, but when the crunch *comes* and there is a perceived threat to national security the courts will almost always decide in favor of the government."

Despite those reservations, and the limitations of the Charter, most civil libertarians agree that Canadians are better off with an enshrined bill of rights than without one.

From "It Could Happen Again," in *The Citizen*, Ottawa, Saturday, January 26, 1985.

The Globe and Mail *in 1985 called for a fair settlement of the Japanese question.*

Multiculturalism Minister Jack Murta has made what he says is the Conservative Government's "last best offer" to the Japanese Canadian community. How quickly atonement has turned to ultimatum. . . .

. . . The Mulroney Government continues to favor a unilateral approach. It decides arbitrarily on the value and the form of reparations, then tells the Japanese Canadians to take it or leave it. "We are not going to negotiate with anybody," the minister insists. Individual compensation is "not in the cards," he says. The $10-million will be dispensed only in the form of an educational foundation. Redress is strictly "a moral issue." Such haughtiness gives morality a bad name. . . .

The Government should accept the principle of individual compensation now and undertake an economic losses study to assess the dollar value (as did the U.S. Commission on Wartime Relocation and Internment of Civilians, established in 1980). The study's findings could then serve as the basis for negotiations between Ottawa and the NAJC.

That said, the National Association of Japanese Canadians can help, too, by defining its priorities more clearly—and realistically—when it meets this weekend in Calgary. The association has several worthy aims: in addition to negotiated compensation, these include an acknowledgement by Parliament of the injustice, pardons for those Japanese Canadians given criminal records under the War Measures Act for violating wartime relocation orders, and an offer of reinstatement for those who, despite their Canadian citizenship, emigrated under duress to Japan.

The association errs, however, when it enshrines broader political demands as a "fundamental component of any settlement." These aims include amendment of the War Measures Act and of the Charter of Rights to prevent a repeat of the internment. There is much to be said for firmer constitutional protection of minorities, but Canadians of Japanese ancestry are not the only ones entitled to say it. The Government should air this question before a parliamentary committee. Amends should not be the bearer of amendments.

From "Versions of Redress," in the *Globe and Mail*, Toronto, Saturday, February 2, 1985.

1. Account for the government's failure to redress the wrongs suffered in 1942.
2. To what extent do you agree with the contention that a similar event could happen today?
3. Write a letter to your Member of Parliament expressing your point of view on this issue.

Cultural Identity: Case for the Defence

Canadians have often defined their identity in terms of the United States. In the following three excerpts, various aspects of our cultural sovereignty are put forward.
Canadian poet Frank Scott wrote this lyric statement entitled "National Identity."

The Canadian Centenary Council
Meeting in La Reine Elizabeth
To seek those symbols
Which will explain ourselves to ourselves
Evoke unlimited responses
And prove that something called Canada
Really exists in the hearts of all
Handed out to every delegate
At the start of the proceedings
A portfolio of documents
On the cover of which appeared
In gold letters
not
A Mari Usque Ad Mare
not
E Pluribus Unum
not
Dieu et Mon Droit
not
Je me souviens
but
"Courtesy of Coca-Cola Limited"

From Hugh Innis, ed., *Americanization*, (Toronto: McGraw-Hill Ryerson, 1972).

In this 1970 article from the Toronto Star, *Howard Lentner compares the Canadian and American cultural myths.*

The people of both Canada and the United States have long been dominated by those segments of their respective societies which are derived from English patrimony. Because Canada has clung more closely than the United States to the culture of their common ancestry, there are subtle differences in class structure and deference patterns.

Both countries, however, have drawn major segments of their populations from throughout Europe, with a sprinkling of population from Asia. Although their respective myths for absorbing these non-English people differ, there appears to be no significant difference in the patterns of integration into the respective societies.

The American myth of the melting pot has concentrated on weaving non-English-speaking minorities into the fabric of the dominant culture, but there continues to be a minority language press, and one can find distinct neighborhoods which are outposts of non-English European and Asian culture. These neighborhoods continue to exist into the second and third generations.

Similar Patterns

In mythological but not practical contrast, Canada has clung to the idea of the mosaic society in which non-dominant cultures are encouraged to survive. Despite the myth, the pulls of the dominant culture are sufficient to bring about the integration of large numbers of people from these sub-cultures into the mainstream of Canadian society. Because the recent immigration into Canada is a larger proportion of society than in the United States, accents unfamiliar to the English ear are more apparent, but the pattern in Canada appears to be similar to that in the United States. . . .

There is another respect in which the two societies have different characteristics. The difference is so immense that the problem of national identity is unknown in the United States. Americans know who they are. Even the radical critiques of American society have largely been cast in terms of the failure of that society to fulfil its own aspirations and ideals. In Canada, the situation is quite different. . . .

There are many points of view in Canada on the national identity problem, but there is a virtual unanimity among those who have thought of it that there is a problem. Canadians range from those who deny that there is any need for an explication of the national identity to those who argue for the uniqueness of Canada and who find a radical tradition in Canada that differentiates it clearly from the United States. Some Canadians argue that there is no difference between the two North American cultures. Others see a difference and feel inferior because of it, while still others develop feelings of superiority because of the differences they see. In any case, there is an uncertainty in Canada about the national identity, a factor wholly lacking in the United States. . . .

From Howard Lentner, "Mosaic, Melting Pot—both myths," in the Toronto *Star*, Toronto, August 20, 1970.

During the latter part of the 1980s, many Canadians warned that free trade would mean the end of an independent Canadian culture. This same theme was espoused almost twenty years ago by Gail Dexter in her essay "Yes, Cultural Imperialism Too!"

Today, almost twenty years after its completion, the Massey Commission Report still stands as one of the sternist warnings to Canadians about the danger of the Americanization of our culture. The commissioners perceived this danger as both real and imminent, so they wrote a cultural report in which military analogies set the mood:

On this continent, as we have observed, our population stretches in a narrow and not even continuous ribbon along our frontier—fourteen millions along a five thousand mile front. In meeting influences from across the border, as pervasive as they are friendly, we have not even the advantages of what soldiers call defense in depth. . . .

Our military defenses must be made secure; but our cultural defenses equally demand attention.

One remarkable aspect of the report is that, while it detailed the dangers of American cultural imperialism (to use a term beyond the political horizons of the commissioners), to our broadcasting, scholarship, and publishing, it did not recognize the danger to our plastic arts. Indeed, the commissioners wrote of the Canadian spirit manifest in the new abstract art of the 1940s: "Canadian painting no longer seeks to express itself through the Canadian landscape but for all that, it is maintained, it is nonetheless Canadian." . . .

. . . The anti-American stance of the commissioners was not a political position. It derived from their valuation of American culture as commercialized and vulgar. Their exhortations that Canadians in broadcasting, publishing, and scholarship develop "Canadian" traditions carried the implicit assumption that these traditions were firmly planted in the aristocratic British and European past. Whereas the United States had developed a mass culture based on the imperatives of buying and selling commodities through advertising, Canadians should simply popularize ruling-class European culture—the rightful heritage of Canada's colonial elite. In promoting "Canadian" culture the commissioners were, in great part, defending their own cultural interests against the American intrusion.

Since at the time of the Massey Commission the plastic arts were hardly touched by this commercialism, they could be perceived as free from the vulgar influence of the United States. Painting, the most aristocratic of the arts, could emerge—no matter how abstract or downright meaningless it might appear—as the true repository of the Canadian spirit. This bourgeois notion of art as the objectification of some transcendent spiritual value divorced from content, style, and political consciousness has been linked to the naive assumption that paintings painted in Canada will be "Canadian." The result of this idealism is that today, twenty years after the Massey report, Canadian painting is completely absorbed into mainstream American art—an imperial art which, as I hope to show, has much more than spiritual meaning. . . .

As long as the Canadian economy is dominated by the United States, Canadian culture will be submerged and Canadian painting will bear the hallmark of the imperial style. This is surely not surprising when most of the great international styles of western culture have been the adaptation by European countries of the style innovated for the use of the ruling class in the most powerful cultural metropolis. What is perhaps remarkable about Canada's case is the singular lack of national adaptation and the recent lack of interest in the development of an art that will be meaningful to the Canadian people.

As long as Canadians define their artists as harmless if somewhat irresponsible dependants of the nation's surplus, as men whose productivity is so marginal that they are permitted to live according to the vicissitudes of the art market, our artists will never develop the political consciousness necessary to struggle against the prevailing stylistic tendencies. As long as our artists must compete in an art market and art world dominated by US interests, they can do no more than compete according to the standards established by the Americans. . . .

Questions of aesthetics in the age of imperialism are questions of politics. To take a non-political view of American art is to be dominated by it. Canadians are no longer in the happy position described twenty years ago in the Massey report when we had the choice for or against a national culture. English-speaking Canadians in particular face a situation in which our culture, especially painting, is completely submerged. It is important to understand American art because it is an imperialist art. And Canadian art, like Canadian industry, is no more than a branch plant of the American. Because American art is imperialist, Canadian art, if it is to evolve a national style, must be overtly anti-imperialist. In other words, it is my firm belief that the creation of a Canadian style of painting is nothing less than a political act. . . .

From Ian Lumsden, ed., *Close the 49th Parallel etc.: The Americanization of Canada,* (Toronto: University of Toronto Press, 1970).

1. Based upon your readings write your own analysis of the current state of the Canadian identity.

The 49th Parallel

In this excerpt from Richard Gwyn's The 49th Parallel *the author attempts to define the fundamental difference between the two North American nations.*

This Country in the Morning quiz: "Define the Canadian identity in a single, short sentence."
Winning entry: "As Canadian as possible, under the circumstances."

In the United States, it is almost impossible to buy an electric kettle. Winners of horse and dog shows are awarded blue ribbons while those in Canada receive red ones, even though we talk about "blue-ribbon" committees. Canadian beer has an alcohol content of 5 per cent as against the more genteel 3.2 per cent of much American brew. Andrew Malcolm's book *The Canadians* appeared in its American edition with a bright red, yellow, and green cover and in its Canadian edition with a pure white one. On the other hand, the title of Alison Gordon's chronicle of her years covering the Toronto Blue Jays, *Foul Balls,* appeared south of the border delicately abbreviated to *Foul Ball.*

Then there are the similarities. Almost all of the famous Winnipeg goldeye come from the Missouri River, and almost none of it from anywhere in Manitoba. Zenith 800 numbers can be used to phone from anywhere to anywhere in either country. The U.S. postal service charges the same rate for trans-border as for domestic mail, although Canada exercises its sovereignty and charges five cents more. A number of Canadian companies, such as AMCA International, quote only U.S. dollars in their annual reports.

The *Financial Post's* Washington correspondent, Fred Harrison, reports that at parties Canadians divide into two groups, one in one corner discussing cross-border similarities and the other discussing dissimilarities: "we hoard them like precious jewels." One such jewel he's observed is that Washington bureaucrats talk about "opening an account" while in Ottawa the operative phrase is "opening a file."

It's a game that anyone can play. Stereotypes about nations, no differently from those about men and women, are seldom accurate, but no other way exists to discuss the subject. In a review of Malcolm's book for the *New York Times*, Margaret Atwood warned that cross-border comparisons are "fraught with peril" and then offered some of her own: "The Canadian mind-set is skeptical-ironic, the American idealistic-optimistic. . . . Praise an American and he'll agree with you; praise a Canadian and he'll think you're trying to sell him something."

A useful way of starting the game is to consider the possibility that there are no differences between Canadians and Americans, or none that matter. The most persuasive proponent of this thesis is Joel Garreau. In his book, *The Nine Nations of North America*, Garreau sweeps aside all national boundaries, including that of Mexico, as "pale barriers, thoroughly porous to money, immigration and ideas." In their place, he identifies "regional nations," each of which "has a particular economy; each commands a certain emotional allegiance from its citizens. . . . Most important, each nation has a distinct prism through which it views the world." Among his "nations" are New England, which extends north through the Maritimes, The Foundry, which encompasses the northern industrial states and southern Ontario, the Breadbasket, which unites all the grain-growing flatlands, and Ecotopia, which extends from halfway up B.C. to halfway down California. Tex-Mex takes in the rest of California and much of Northern Mexico, "where mellow is no longer just a product of sun and surf but is being caused also by the softening influence of Spanish culture." The single existing political entity Garreau leaves untouched is Quebec: "Which properly speaking is a nation unto itself."

Garreau makes a few careless mistakes, such as writing "Ottawa" when he means "Ontario." But his observations are sharp and his anecdotage is lively. His core thesis is that nation-states are dinosaurs with shrivelled brains: "Washington doesn't work any more." At the same time, people are no longer as dependent on Washington as they once were, or on New York, because, thanks to TV, travel, and instant communications, "people less and less feel the need to move to metropolitan centres to lead complete lives."

Two conclusions can be drawn from Garreau's analysis. The first is that most North Americans are defined by their regional identity rather than by their national citizenship. Many of their values and attitudes and speech patterns are determined by regional characteristics, such as those of topography and climate, history (ancient or recent being the key dividing line), and type of economic activity—resource extraction, agriculture, smokestack manufacturing, high-tech. Clearly, there is a good deal to this: Saskatchewanians, say, and North Dakotans, have far more in common with each other than either have with New Yorkers or Ontarians; steelworkers in Hamilton and Cleveland speak a common language that condominium-dwellers in Toronto and Chicago would not understand.

The other conclusion, a more jarring one to Canadian autonomist sensibilities, is that the entire continent, including northern Mexico, is a single socio-economic unit; political boundaries still exist, but they have lost almost all meaning. . . .

Thus, to a degree, we are all regionalized North Americans. In a splendid bit of invective, Peter Brimelow, a journalist who has worked in Canada and who now is in New York, has written in a report for the Manhattan Institute: "For Canadian nationalists to have been able to raise doubts about such an obvious reality when the interaction between Canada and the U.S. is so overwhelmingly as to amount to what Goldwin Smith called "political fusion", is a classic case of ideological hegemony transcending material reality."

Yet the ideological hegemony persists. The Gallup Poll stopped asking Canadians whether they wanted to join the United States in the early 1950s when those answering "Yes" dropped to an insignificant 9 per cent. The occasional political attempts to convince Canadians to accept objective reality, such as former Saskatchewan Conservative leader Dick Cullver's Union Party, have passed quickly into oblivion through an intervening period of farce. (Cullver could never figure out an answer to those few Saskatchewanians who showed even the faintest glimmer of interest when they asked what would happen to Medicare.)

Over the years, many Canadians have voted for the U.S. with their feet. The number of footloose Canadians would increase significantly if the cross-border economic gap widened too far. But today, there is little difference in living standards. American incomes are higher and consumer prices are lower—at present because of the high value of the dollar but at all times because of the far more competitive business environment. Canadians, though, spend far less on health and hospital care; aren't required to spend, if they are middle class and have children, as much as $20 000 a year in private university tuition fees; spend little, by comparison visibly small amounts, on private security. Comparisons in international living standards are always iffy, but perhaps the best measure of the cross-border gap is that the average American family occupies 5.1 rooms while a Canadian family fills up exactly five rooms.

Canadians themselves have little doubt that they've got it made. In the winter of 1984, Decima Research asked them whether they agreed or disagreed with the proposition, "Canada is the best country in the world in which to live at the present time." Just 7 per cent disagreed; 81 per cent agreed totally or strongly, a minor decline from the 85 per cent who thought the same way in the winter of 1980, even though in the meantime Canada's economic performance had fallen well behind that of the U.S.

Over and above the cross-border regional similarities, which certainly exist and which create potent north-south interconnections, there are obviously national dissimilarities. Otherwise, Canadians would have no reason to think themselves better off than their neighbours. . . .

National differences, or at least distinctions, exist. The question is whether these are just variations on a single North American theme, comparable to the list of cultural differences that could be compiled between Californians and Georgians, say, or whether these differences derive from some quality intrinsic to Canadian society.

Of all the differences between the two societies, the most striking is the one that has been curiously overlooked by all the analysts. This is the fact that Canadians mostly live in cities while Americans, mostly, don't.

More than one in four Canadians (29 per cent) live in metropolitan areas with a population of at least one million—Toronto, Montreal, Vancouver; only one in twelve Americans (8 per cent) live in comparable urban agglomerations. More than one in two Canadians (56 per cent) live in cities or towns with a population of at least 100 000; only one in four Americans (25 per cent) live in similar-sized cities and towns.

This oversight isn't really curious. The land is Canada; Canadians are their land. Just a glance at a map to confirm that we occupy more space than any country but Russia (the Mercator projection exaggerates its extent a bit) infuses any Canadian but a dullard with a surge of pride. Only a dullard, again, could traverse the land in the comfort of an airplane and not feel small by an appreciation of the courage and stoicism of the explorers and voyageurs and sod-hut pioneers who opened it up, and not feel also, while gazing down at its immense emptiness, a sense of wonder and doubt that any nation owning all of it yet occupying so little of it could actually survive. . . .

Today, cities shape the Canadian character as much as the land once did. Because proportionately far more Canadians live in cities, they are in a certain sense more "Americanized" than are Americans. The new trends and fads of New York and California penetrate far more quickly through urban Canada than through rural America where, because of the climate and soil, proportionately so many more Americans live. Further, Canadian urban-dwellers are more urbanized than are those Americans who similarly live in cities. From Jefferson to Thoreau to Ronald Reagan, an American constant has been a suspicion of cities as effete, decadent, un-American. Rural life in Canada has never been similarly glamourized because so much of rural Canada is just too hard, too cold, too isolated to be lived in by choice; the Prairies have been depopulated, not by the banks or the CPR or other western demons but by farmers exercising their free choice to pass their winters in Regina or Edmonton, or Hawaii. In the U.S., making it means living outside a city, in Oak Forest rather than in Chicago, in Beverly Hills rather than in Los Angeles. In Canada, making it means living right downtown, in Toronto's Annex or in Montreal's Vieux Cité.

Urbanization reinforces Canada's liberalness. Urban-dwellers tend to be secular and to be more readily impressed by the benefits of an activist government, of which the advantages are harder to justify in self-contained rural communities. Tolerance comes more easily to those who live in cities because they constantly encounter people who are different from themselves.

If contemporary Canada can claim any achievement that should earn it at least a paragraph in the history books, this would be the creation of contemporary urban Canada. The nature of that achievement is summed up by the slogan about Toronto that has been used so often in American architectural and town-planning magazines: "The City That Works." Toronto, although many Canadians, being Canadians, would rather not admit it, is the urban miracle of North America. It is at one and the same time dynamic and competitive and yet is civilized and sophisticated. On the continent, only New York—possibly, although arguably, San Francisco also—surpasses Toronto in its urbanity and in its cultural variety. . . .

. . . Within North America, the difference between the two societies comes down in the end to just that: Canadians have figured out how to make their cities work for them; Americans work in their cities and live outside them.

A common perception of Canadians, by themselves as well as by outsiders, is that they are nice Americans. The nice get taken for granted. They aren't exotic enough to command attention, or troublesome enough to compel it to be paid. . . .

Last and most to the point, Americans, when they do look north, do so not just benignly but with just a trace of envy. In a certain sense, Americans seem to see in Canada the America that once was. *New Yorker* movie critic Pauline Kael once identified correctly for her readers a film made in Toronto that pretended to have been made in New York: "I spotted the infelicity immediately. Everything was too clean and everyone was too polite." Stephen Blank of MultiNational Strategies of New York comments, "Your cleanliness and orderliness are a constant of amazement." He adds, "Mind you, so are your business practices. I start calling my American clients at eight a.m.; I never call Canadian ones before nine a.m." The literary agent Nancy Colbert, an American now living in Toronto, says: "Canadians have a fixed perception that Americans think of them as the frozen north, Nelson Eddy and all that. In fact, the perception is one of openness, cleanliness, freedom."

Cleanliness and orderliness and the rest aren't the stuff out of which history is made. But they do represent a certain kind of North American history. Orderliness and civility are essentially rural virtues. They exist every bit as much in the towns and hamlets of New England as in comparable communities in Canada. Courtliness and a belief in the importance of protocol are much more a way of life in the U.S. South than they are anywhere in Canada: the southern "Y'all come back now" is at least as nicely mannered, if no more intended to be taken literally, as is the Canadian compulsion to say "Thank you" to everyone who has merely done his or her job—taxi drivers, store clerks, bank tellers, and, not inconceivably, burglars.

The Canadian particularity, the source of Canada's distinctiveness as a society within North America, is to have found a way to transplant these virtues of rural communities into its cities. Canadian cities today are confederations of communities rather than urban agglomerations. There is nothing like them— really—in the United States. Most Canadians live in them. This is why Canadians are different. To be nice Americans is no big deal: lots of Americans are every bit as nice. To be nice urban North Americans is almost a contradiction in terms, since North American cities are shaped, and are constantly being reshaped, by a relentless, ruthless imperative. Canadian society isn't anything like as dynamic and as creative as American society; but it works.

From Richard Gwyn, *The 49th Parallel: Canada in North America*, (Toronto: McClelland and Stewart, 1985). Used by permission of the Canadian Publishers, McClelland and Stewart, Toronto.

1. What superficial similarities and differences does Gwyn identify?

2. How does he account for the contrasting attitudes existing in each country?

3. Do you agree with Gwyn's closing statement about the fundamental Canadian difference? Write a paragraph in which you give your opinion.

Culture, Integration, and Identity: Analysis and Application

1. In chart form, trace the evolution of civil rights for American Blacks in the 1950s and 1960s.

2. Stage a panel discussion among George Wallace, Martin Luther King, and Malcolm X. Have each participant open with a brief position statement on the issue of forced integration and the methods needed to resist or ensure its implementation. Next open the panel up to questions from the press. Students should ask questions from the perspective of the United States in the early 1960s, being careful to avoid any foreknowledge of future events.

3. Write a newspaper account of Martin Luther King's "I Have a Dream" speech.

4. "If the Quebec referendum had been held in May 1960 rather than May 1980 the result might have been different."

Account for this statement with reference to the changing role of French Canadians within Canadian society during the period.

5. The FLQ crisis has often been called Canada's "loss of innocence." Create your own thesis in which you discuss the background of the crisis and its impact upon the separatist movement in Quebec.

6. Compare the roles of René Lévesque and Martin Luther King as leaders in the struggle for recognition of the rights of their respective cultures.

7. Contrast Lévesque's view of the place of francophones within Canada with that of his nemesis, Pierre Elliot Trudeau.

8. "North Americans responded to the increased violence of the late 1960s and early 1970s by violating the civil rights of suspected offenders." Defend or refute this thesis.

9. Identify a current issue involving cultural integration. Monitor the local and national newspapers and periodicals to create a clipping file on your issue. After following this theme for two months, analyse the issue and summarize its coverage in the press.

10. Compare the treatment of and redress offered citizens of Japanese origin who were interned during World War II in the two North American nations.

11. Based upon your study of the history of Canada and the United States over the past four centuries, create your own summative definition of the North American experience.

APPENDIX A   Canadian Charter of Rights and Freedoms

Whereas Canada is founded upon principles that recognize the supremacy of God and the rule of law:

Guarantee of Rights and Freedoms

1. The *Canadian Charter of Rights and Freedoms* guarantees the rights and freedoms set out in it subject only to such reasonable limits prescribed by law as can be demonstrably justified in a free and democratic society.

Fundamental Freedoms

2. Everyone has the following fundamental freedoms:
(*a*) freedom of conscience and religion;
(*b*) freedom of thought, belief, opinion and expression, including freedom of the press and other media of communication;
(*c*) freedom of peaceful assembly; and
(*d*) freedom of association.

Democratic Rights

3. Every citizen of Canada has the right to vote in an election of members of the House of Commons or of a legislative assembly and to be qualified for membership therein.

4. (1) No House of Commons and no legislative assembly shall continue for longer than five years from the date fixed for the return of the writs at a general election of its members.

(2) In time of real or apprehended war, invasion or insurrection, a House of Commons may be continued by Parliament and a legislative assembly may be continued by the legislature beyond five years if such continuation is not opposed by the votes of more than one-third of the members of the House of Commons or the legislative assembly, as the case may be.

5. There shall be a sitting of Parliament and of each legislature at least once every twelve months.

Mobility Rights

6. (1) Every citizen of Canada has the right to enter, remain in and leave Canada.

(2) Every citizen of Canada and every person who has the status of a permanent resident of Canada has the right
(*a*) to move to and take up residence in any province; and to pursue the gaining of a livelihood in any province.
(3) The rights specified in subsection (2) are subject to

(*a*) any laws or practices of general application in force in a province other than those that discriminate among persons primarily on the basis of province of present or previous residence; and

(*b*) any laws providing for reasonable residency requirements as a qualification for the receipt of publicly provided social services.

(4) Subsections (2) and (3) do not preclude any law, program or activity that has as its object the amelioration in a province of conditions of individuals in that province who are socially or economically disadvantaged if the rate of employment in that province is below the rate of employment in Canada.

Legal Rights

7. Everyone has the right to life, liberty and security of the person and the right not to be deprived thereof except in accordance with the principles of fundamental justice.

8. Everyone has the right to be secure against unreasonable search or seizure.

9. Everyone has the right not to be arbitrarily detained or imprisoned.

10. Everyone has the right on arrest or detention
(*a*) to be informed promptly of the reasons therefor;
(*b*) to retain and instruct counsel without delay and to be informed of that right; and
(*c*) to have the validity of the detention determined by way of *habeas corpus* and to be released if the detention is not lawful.

11. Any person charged with an offence has the right
(*a*) to be informed without unreasonable delay of the specific offence;
(*b*) to be tried within a reasonable time;
(*c*) not to be compelled to be a witness in proceedings against that person in respect of the offence;
(*d*) to be presumed innocent until proven guilty according to law in a fair and public hearing by an independent and impartial tribunal;
(*e*) not to be denied reasonable bail without just cause;
(*f*) except in the case of an offence under military law tried before a military tribunal, to the benefit of trial by jury where the maximum punishment for the offence is imprisonment for five years or a more severe punishment;
(*g*) not to be found guilty on account of any act or omission unless, at the time of the act or omission, it constituted an offence under Canadian or international law or was criminal according to the general principles of law recognized by the community of nations;
(*h*) if finally acquitted of the offence, not to be tried for it again and, if finally found guilty and punished for the offence, not to be tried or punished for it again; and
(*i*) if found guilty of the offence and if the punishment for the offence has been varied between the time of commission and the time of sentencing, to the benefit of the lesser punishment.

12. Everyone has the right not to be subjected to any cruel and unusual treatment or punishment.

13. A witness who testifies in any proceedings has the right not to have any incriminating evidence so given used to incriminate that witness in any other proceedings, except in a prosecution for perjury or for the giving of contradictory evidence.

14. A party or witness in any proceedings who does not understand or speak the language in which the proceedings are conducted or who is deaf has the right to the assistance of an interpreter.

Equality Rights

15. (1) Every individual is equal before and under the law and has the right to the equal protection and equal benefit of the law without discrimination and, in particular, without discrimination based on race, national or ethnic origin, colour, religion, sex, age or mental or physical disability.

(2) Subsection (1) does not preclude any law, program or activity that has as its object the amelioration of conditions of disadvantaged individuals or groups including those that are disadvantaged because or race, national or ethnic origin, colour, religion, sex, age or mental or physical disability.

Official Languages of Canada

16. (1) English and French are the official languages of Canada and have equality of status and equal rights and privileges as to their use in all institutions of the Parliament and government of Canada.

(2) English and French are the official languages of New Brunswick and have equality of status and equal rights and privileges as to their use in all institutions of the legislative and government of New Brunswick.

(3) Nothing in this Charter limits the authority of Parliament or a legislature to advance the equality of status or use of English and French.

17. (1) Everyone has the right to use English or French in any debates and other proceedings of Parliament.

(2) Everyone has the right to use English or French in any debates and other proceedings of the legislature of New Brunswick.

18. (1) The statutes, records, and journals of Parliament shall be printed and published in English and French and both language versions are equally authoritative.

(2) The statutes, records and journals of the legislature of New Brunswick shall be printed and published in English and French and both language versions are equally authoritative.

19. (1) Either English or French may be used by any person in, or in any pleading in or process issuing from, any court established by Parliament.

(2) Either English or French may be used by any person in, or in any pleading in or process issuing from, any court of New Brunswick.

20. (1) Any member of the public in Canada has the right to communicate with and to receive available services from, any head or central office of an institution of the Parliament or government of Canada in English or French, and has the same right with respect to any other office of any such institution where
(a) there is a significant demand for communications with and services from that office in such language; or
(b) due to the nature of the office, it is reasonable that communications with and services from that office be available in both English and French.

(2) Any member of the public in New Brunswick has the right to communicate with, and to receive available services from, any office of an institution of the legislature or government of New Brunswick in English or French.

21. Nothing in sections 16 to 20 abrogates or derogates from any right, privilege or obligation with respect to the English and French languages, or either of them, that exists or is continued by virtue of any other provision of the Constitution of Canada.

22. Nothing in sections 16 to 20 abrogates or derogates from any legal or customary right or privilege acquired or enjoyed either before or after the coming into force of this Charter with respect to any language that is not English or French.

Minority Language Educational Rights

23. (1) Citizens of Canada
(a) whose first language learned and still understood is that of the English or French linguistic minority population of the province in which they reside, or
(b) who have received their primary school instruction in Canada in English or French and reside in a province where the language in which they received that instruction is the language of the English or French linguistic minority population of the province
have the right to have their children receive primary and secondary school instruction in that language in that province.

(2) Citizens of Canada of whom any child has received or is receiving primary or secondary school instruction in English or French in Canada, have the right to have all their children receive primary or secondary school instruction in the same language.

(3) The right of citizens of Canada under subsections (1) and (2) to have their children receive primary and secondary school instruction in the language of the English or French linguistic minority population of a province

(*a*) applies wherever in the province the number of children of citizens who have such a right is sufficient to warrant the provision to them out of public funds of minority language instruction; and

(*b*) includes, where the number of those children so warrants, the right to have them receive that instruction in minority language educational facilities provided out of public funds.

Enforcement

24. (1) Anyone whose rights or freedoms, as guaranteed by this Charter, have been infringed or denied may apply to a court of competent jurisdiction to obtain such remedy as the court considers appropriate and just in the circumstances.

(2) Where, in proceedings under subsection (1), a court concludes that evidence was obtained in a manner that infringed or denied any rights or freedoms guaranteed by this Charter, the evidence shall be excluded if it is established that, having regard to all the circumstances, the admission of it in the proceedings would bring the administration of justice into disrepute.

General

25. The guarantee in this Charter of certain rights and freedoms shall not be construed so as to abrogate or derogate from any aboriginal, treaty or other rights or freedoms that pertain to the aboriginal peoples of Canada including

(*a*) any rights or freedoms that have been recognized by the Royal Proclamation of October 7, 1763; and

(*b*) any rights or freedoms that may be acquired by the aboriginal peoples of Canada by way of land claims settlement.

The guarantee in this Charter of certain rights and freedoms shall not be construed as denying the existence of any other rights or freedoms that exist in Canada.

27. This Charter shall be interpreted in a manner consistent with the preservation and enhancement of the multicultural heritage of Canadians.

28. Notwithstanding anything in this Charter, the rights and freedoms referred to in it are guaranteed equally to male and female persons.

29. Nothing in this Charter abrogates or derogates from any rights or privileges guaranteed by or under the Constitution of Canada in respect of denominational, separate or dissentient schools.

30. A reference in this Charter to a province or to the legislative assembly or legislature of a province shall be deemed to include a reference to the Yukon Territory and the Northwest Territories, or to the appropriate legislative authority thereof, as the case may be.

31. Nothing in this Charter extends the legislative powers of any body or authority.

Application of Charter

32. (1) This Charter applies

(a) to the Parliament and government of Canada in respect of all matters within the authority of Parliament including all matters relating to the Yukon Territory and Northwest Territories; and

(b) to the legislature and government of each province in respect of all matters within the authority of the legislature of each province.

(2) Notwithstanding subsection (1), section 15 shall not have effect until three years after this section comes into force.

33. (1) Parliament or the legislature of a province may expressly declare in an Act of Parliament or of the legislature, as the case may be, that the Act or a provision thereof shall operate notwithstanding a provision included in section 2 or sections 7 to 15 of this Charter.

(2) An Act or a provision of an Act in respect of which a declaration made under this section is in effect shall have such operation as it would have but for the provision of this Charter referred to in the declaration.

(3) A declaration made under subsection (1) shall cease to have effect five years after it comes into force or on such earlier date as may be specified in the declaration.

(4) Parliament or a legislature of a province may re-enact a declaration made under subsection (1).

(5) Subsection (3) applies in respect of a re-enactment made under subsection (4).

Citation

34. This Part may be cited as the *Canadian Charter of Rights and Freedoms*.

APPENDIX B   The Meech Lake Accord

The Constitution Act, 1987

Whereas first ministers, assembled in Ottawa, have arrived at a unanimous accord on constitutional amendments that would bring about the full and active participation of Quebec in Canada's constitutional evolution, would recognize the principle of equality of all the provinces, would provide new arrangements to foster greater harmony and co-operation between the Government of Canada and the governments of the provinces and would require that annual first ministers' conferences on the state of the Canadian economy and such other matters as may be appropriate be convened and that annual constitutional conferences composed of first ministers be convened commencing not later than Dec. 31, 1988;

And whereas first ministers have also reached unanimous agreement on certain additional commitments in relation to some of those amendments;

Now therefore the Prime Minister of Canada and the first ministers of the provinces commit themselves and the governments they represent to the following:

1. The Prime Minister of Canada will lay or cause to be laid before the Senate and House of Commons, and the first ministers of the provinces will lay or cause to be laid before their legislative assemblies, as soon as possible, a resolution, in the form appended hereto to authorize a proclamation to be issued by the Governor-General under the Great Seal of Canada to amend the Constitution of Canada;

2. The Government of Canada will, as soon as possible, conclude an agreement with the Government of Quebec that would:

(a) Incorporate the principles of the Cullen-Couture agreement on the selection abroad and in Canada of independent immigrants, visitors for medical treatment, students and temporary workers, and on the selection of refugees abroad and economic criteria for family reunification and assisted relatives;

(b) Guarantee that Quebec will receive a number of immigrants, including refugees, within the annual total established by the federal Government for all of Canada proportionate to its share of the population of Canada, with the right to exceed that figure by 5 per cent for demographic reasons, and;

(c) Provide an undertaking by Canada to withdraw services (except citizenship services) for the reception and integration (including linguistic and cultural) of all foreign nationals wishing to settle in Quebec where services are to be provided by Quebec, with such withdrawal to be accompanied by reasonable compensation, and the Government of Canada and the Government of Quebec will take the necessary steps to give the agreement the force of law under the proposed amendment relating to such agreements;

3. Nothing in this accord should be construed as preventing the negotiation of similar agreements with other provinces relating to immigration and the temporary admission of aliens;

4. Until the proposed amendment relating to appointments to the Senate comes into force, any person summoned to fill a vacancy in the Senate shall be chosen from among persons whose names have been submitted by the government of the

province to which the vacancy relates and must be acceptable to the Queen's Privy Council for Canada.

Amending the Constitution Act, 1982

Motion for a resolution to authorize an amendment to the Constitution of Canada:

Whereas the *Constitution Act, 1982*, came into force on April 17, 1982, following an agreement between Canada and all the provinces except Quebec;

And whereas the Government of Quebec has established a set of five proposals for constitutional change and has stated that amendments to give effect to those proposals would enable Quebec to resume a full role in the constitutional councils of Canada;

And whereas the amendment proposed in the schedule hereto sets out the basis on which Quebec's five constitutional proposals may be met;

And whereas the amendment proposed in the schedule hereto also recognizes the principle of the equality of all the provinces, provides new arrangements to foster greater harmony and co-operation between the Government of Canada and the governments of the provinces and requires that conferences be convened to consider important constitutional, economic and other issues;

And whereas certain portions of the amendment proposed in the schedule hereto relate to matters referred to in Section 41 of the *Constitution Act, 1982*;

And whereas Section 41 of the *Constitution Act, 1982*, provides that an amendment to the Constitution of Canada may be made by proclamation issued by the Governor-General under the Great Seal of Canada where so authorized by resolutions of the Senate and the House of Commons and of the legislative assembly of each province;

Now therefore the (Senate) (House of Commons) (Legislative assembly) resolves that an amendment to the Constitution of Canada be authorized to be made by proclamation issued by Her Excellency the Governor-General under the Great Seal of Canada in accordance with the schedule hereto.

Schedule

Constitution Amendment, 1987
Constitution Act, 1867

1. The *Constitution Act, 1867*, is amended by adding thereto, immediately after Section 1 thereof, the following section:

2. (1) The Constitution of Canada shall be interpreted in a manner consistent with;

(a) The recognition that the existence of French-speaking Canadians, centred in Quebec but also present elsewhere in Canada, and English-speaking Canadians, concentrated outside Quebec but also present in Quebec, constitutes a fundamental characteristic of Canada; and;

(b) The recognition that Quebec constitutes within Canada a distinct society;

(2) The role of the Parliament of Canada and the provincial legislatures to preserve the fundamental characteristic of Canada referred to in paragraph (1)(a) is affirmed;

(3) The role of the Legislature and Government of Quebec to preserve and promote the distinct identity of Quebec referred to in paragraph (1)(b) is affirmed;

(4) Nothing in this section derogates from the powers, rights or privileges of Parliament or the Government of Canada, or of the legislatures of governments of the provinces, including any powers, rights or privileges relating to language.

2. The said Act is further amended by adding thereto, immediately after Section 24 thereof, the following section:

25. (1) Where a vacancy occurs in the Senate, the government of the province to which the vacancy relates may, in relation to that vacancy, submit to the Queen's Privy Council for Canada the names of persons who may be summoned to the Senate;

(2) Until an amendment to the Constitution of Canada is made in relation to the Senate pursuant to Section 41 of the *Constitution Act, 1982*, the person summoned to fill a vacancy in the Senate shall be chosen from among persons whose names have been submitted under Subsection (1) by the government of the province to which the vacancy relates and must be acceptable to the Queen's Privy Council for Canada.

3. The said Act is further amended by adding thereto, immediately after Section 95 thereof, the following heading and sections:

Agreements on immigration and aliens

95a. The Government of Canada shall, at the request of the government of any province; negotiate with the government of that province for the purpose of concluding an agreement relating to immigration or the temporary admission of aliens into that province that is appropriate to the needs and circumstances of that province.

95b. (1) Any agreement concluded between Canada and a province in relation to immigration or the temporary admission of aliens into that province has the force of law from the time it is declared to do so in accordance with Subsection 95c(1) and shall from that time have effect notwithstanding Class 25 of Section 91 or Section 95.

(2) An agreement that has the force of law under Subsection (1) shall have effect only so long and so far as it is not repugnant to any provision of an Act of the Parliament of Canada that sets national standards and objectives relating to immigration or aliens, including any provision that establishes general classes of immigrants or relates to levels of immigration for Canada or that prescribes classes of individuals who are inadmissible into Canada.

(3) The *Canadian Charter of Rights and Freedoms* applies in respect of any agreement that has the force of law under Subsection (1) and in respect of anything done by the Parliament or Government of Canada, or the legislature or government of a province, pursuant to any such agreement.

95c. (1) A declaration that an agreement referred to in Subsection 95b(1) has the force of law may be made by proclamation issued by the Governor-General under the Great Seal of Canada only where so authorized by resolutions of the Senate and House of Commons and of the legisative assembly of the province that is a party to the agreement.

(2) An amendment to an agreement referred to in Subsection 95b(1) may be made by proclamation issued by the Governor-General under the Great Seal of Canada only where so authorized:

(a) by resolutions of the Senate and House of Commons and of the legislative assembly of the province that is a party to the agreement; or;

(b) in such other manner as is set out in the agreement.

95d. Sections 46 and 48 of the *Constitution Act, 1982*, apply, with such modifications as the circumstances require, in respect of any declaration made pursuant to Subsection 95c(1), any amendment to an agreement made pursuant to Subsection 95e.

95e. An amendment to Sections 95a to 95d or this section may be made in accordance with the procedure set out in Subsection 38(1) of the *Constitution Act, 1982*, but only if the amendment is authorized by resolutions of the legislative assemblies of all the provinces that are, at the time of the amendment, parties to an agreement that has the force of law under Subsection 95b(1).

4. The said Act is further amended by adding thereto, immediately preceding Section 96 thereof, the following heading "General".

5. The said Act is further amended by adding thereto, immediately preceding Section 101 thereof, the following heading: "Courts Established by the Parliament of Canada".

6. The said Act is further amended by adding thereto, immediately after Section 101 thereof, the following heading and sections:

Supreme Court of Canada

101a. (1) The court existing under the name of the Supreme Court of Canada is hereby continued as the general court of appeal for Canada, and as an additional court for the better administration of the laws of Canada, and shall continue to be a superior court of record.

(2) The Supreme Court of Canada shall consist of a chief justice to be called the Chief Justice of Canada and eight other judges, who shall be appointed by the Governor-General in Council by letters patent under the Great Seal.

101b. (1) Any person may be appointed a judge of the Supreme Court of Canada who, after having been admitted to the bar of any province or territory, has, for a total of at least 10 years, been a judge of any court in Canada or a member of the bar of any province or territory.

(2) At least three judges of the Supreme Court of Canada shall be appointed from among persons who, after having been admitted to the bar of Quebec, have, for a total of at least 10 years, been judges of any court of Quebec or of any court established by the Parliament of Canada, or members of the bar of Quebec.

101c. (1) Where a vacancy occurs in the Supreme Court of Canada, the government of each province may, in relation to that vacancy, submit to the Minister of Justice of Canada the names of any of the persons who have been admitted to the bar of that province and are qualified under Section 101b for appointment to that court.

(2) Where an appointment is made to the Supreme Court of Canada, the Governor-General in Council shall, except where the Chief Justice is appointed from

among members of the Court, appoint a person whose name has been submitted under Subsection (1) and who is acceptable to the Queen's Privy Council for Canada.

(3) Where an appointment is made in accordance with Subsection (2) of any of the three judges necessary to meet the requirement set out in Subsection 101b(2), the Governor-General in Council shall appoint a person whose name has been submitted by the Government of Quebec.

(4) Where an appointment is made in accordance with Subsection (2) otherwise than as required under Subsection (3), the Governor-General in Council shall appoint a person whose name has been submitted by the government of a province other than Quebec.

101d. Sections 99 and 100 apply in respect of the judges of the Supreme Court of Canada.

101e. (1) Sections 101a to 101d shall not be construed as abrogating or derogating from the powers of the Parliament of Canada to make laws under Section 101 except to the extent that such laws are inconsistent with those sections.

(2) For greater certainty, Section 101a shall not be construed as abrogating or derogating from the powers of the Parliament of Canada to make laws relating to the reference of questions of law or fact, or any other matters, to the Supreme Court of Canada.

7. The said Act is further amended by adding thereto, immediately after Section 106 thereof, the following section:

106a. (1) The Government of Canada shall provide reasonable compensation to the government of a province that chooses not to participate in a national shared-cost program that is established by the Government of Canada after the coming into force of this section in an area of exclusive provincial jurisdiction, if the province carries on a program or initiative that is compatible with the national objectives.

(2) Nothing in this section extends the legislative powers of the Parliament of Canada or of the legislatures of the provinces.

8. The said Act is further amended by adding thereto the following heading and sections:

XII—Conferences on the Economy and Other Matters

148. A conference composed of the Prime Minister of Canada and the first ministers of the provinces shall be convened by the Prime Minister of Canada at least once each year to discuss the state of the Canadian economy and such other matters as may be appropriate.

XIII—References

149. A reference to this Act shall be deemed to include a reference to any amendments thereto.

The Constitution Act, 1982

9. Sections 40 to 42 of the *Constitution Act, 1982* are repealed and the following substituted therefor:

40. Where an amendment is made under Subsection 38(1) that transfers legislative powers from provincial legislatures to Parliament, Canada shall provide reasonable compensation to any province to which the amendment does not apply.

41. An amendment to the Constitution of Canada in relation to the following matters may be made by proclamation issued by the Governor-General under the Great Seal of Canada only where authorized by resolutions of the Senate and House of Commons and of the legislative assembly of each province:

(a) The office of the Queen, the Governor-General and the Lieutenant-Governor of a province;

(b) The powers of the Senate and the method of selecting senators;

(c) The number of members by which a province is entitled to be represented in the Senate and the residence qualifications of senators;

(d) The right of a province to a number of members in the House of Commons not less than the number of senators by which the province was entitled to be represented on April 17, 1982;

(e) The principle of proportionate representation of the provinces in the House of Commons prescribed by the Constitution of Canada;

(f) Subject to Section 43, the use of the English or the French language;

(g) The Supreme Court of Canada;

(h) The extension of existing provinces into the territories;

(i) Notwithstanding any other law or practice, the establishment of new provinces; and;

(j) an amendment to this part.

10. Section 44 of the said Act is repealed and the following substituted therefor;

44. Subject to Section 41, Parliament may exclusively make laws amending the Constitution of Canada in relation to the executive government of Canada or the Senate and House of Commons.

11. Subsection 46(1) of the said Act is repealed and the following substituted therefor:

46. (1) The procedures for amendment under Sections 38, 41 and 43 may be initiated either by the Senate or the House of Commons or by the legislative assembly of a province.

12. Subsection 47(1) of the said Act is repealed and the following substituted therefor:

47. (1) An amendment to the Constitution of Canada made by proclamation under Section 38, 41 or 43 may be made without a resolution of the Senate authorizing the issue of the proclamation if, within 180 days after the adoption by the House of Commons of a resolution authorizing its issue, the Senate has not adopted such a resolution and if, at any time after the expiration of that period, the House of Commons again adopts the resolution.

13. Part VI of the said Act is repealed and the following substituted therefor:

Part VI Constitutional Conferences

50. (1). A constitutional conference composed of the Prime Minister of Canada and the first ministers of the provinces shall be convened by the Prime Minister of Canada at least once each year, commencing in 1988.

(2) The conferences convened under Subsection (1) shall have included on their agenda the following matters:

(a) Senate reform, including the role and functions of the Senate, its powers, the method of selecting senators and representation in the Senate;

(b) Roles and responsibilities in relation to fisheries; and

(c) Such other matters as are agreed upon.

14. Subsection 52(2) of the said Act is amended by striking out the word "and" at the end of paragraph (b) thereof by adding the word "and" at the end of the paragraph (c) thereof and by adding thereto the following paragraph:

"(d) any other amendment to the Constitution of Canada."

15. Section 61 of the said Act is repealed and the following substituted therefor:

61. A reference to the *Constitution Act, 1982*, or a reference to the *Constitution Acts, 1867 to 1982*, shall be deemed to include a reference to any amendments thereto.

General

16. Nothing in Section 2 of the *Constitution Act, 1867*, affects Section 25 or 27 of the *Canadian Charter of Rights and Freedoms*, Section 35 of the *Constitution Act, 1982*, or Class 24 of Section 91 of the *Constitution Act, 1867*.

Citation

17. This amendment may be cited as the Constitution Amendment, 1987.

APPENDIX C   The American Declaration of Independence

When in the course of human events it becomes necessary for one person to dissolve the political bands which have connected them with another and to assume, among the powers of the earth, the separate and equal station to which the laws of nature and of nature's God entitle them, a decent respect to the opinions of mankind requires that they should declare the causes which impel them to the separation.

We hold these truths to be self-evident, that all men are created equal; that they are endowed by their Creator with certain unalienable rights; that among these are life, liberty, and the pursuit of happiness. That, to secure these rights, governments are instituted among men, deriving their just powers from the consent of the governed; that, whenever any form of government becomes destructive of these ends, it is the right of the people to alter or to abolish it, and to institute a new government, laying its foundation on such principles, and organizing its powers in such form, as to them shall seem most likely to effect their safety and happiness. Prudence, indeed, will dictate that governments long established should not be changed for light and transient causes; and, accordingly, all experience hath shown that mankind are more disposed to suffer, while evils are sufferable, than to right themselves by abolishing the forms to which they are accustomed. But when a long train of abuses and usurpations, pursuing invariably the same object, evinces a design to reduce them under absolute despotism, it is their right, it is their duty, to throw off such government and to provide new guards for their future security. Such has been the patient sufferance of these colonies, and such is now the necessity which constrains them to alter their former systems of government. The history of the present King of Great Britain is a history of repeated injuries and usurpations, all having, in direct object, the establishment of an absolute tyranny over these States. To prove this, let facts be submitted to a candid world:

He has refused his assent to laws the most wholesome and necessary for the public good.

He has forbidden his governors to pass laws of immediate and pressing importance, unless suspended in their operation till his assent should be obtained; and, when so suspended, he has utterly neglected to attend to them.

He has refused to pass other laws for the accommodation of the large districts of people, unless those people would relinquish the right of representation in the legislature; a right inestimable to them and formidable to tyrants only.

He has called together legislative bodies at places unusual, uncomfortable, and distant from the depository of their public records, for the sole purpose of fatiguing them into compliance with his measures.

He has dissolved representative houses, repeatedly for opposing, with manly firmness, his invasions on the rights of the people.

He has refused, for a long time after such dissolutions, to cause others to be elected: whereby the legislative powers, incapable of annihilation, have returned to the people at large for their exercise; the state remaining, in the meantime, exposed to all the danger of invasion from without and convulsions within.

He has endeavored to prevent the populations of these States; for that purpose, obstructing the laws for naturalization of foreigners, refusing to pass others to encourage their migration hither, and raising the conditions of new appropriations of lands.

He has obstructed the administration of justice by refusing his assent to laws for establishing judiciary powers.

He has made judges dependent on his will alone for the tenure of their offices and the amount of payment of their salaries.

He has erected a multitude of new offices and sent hither swarms of officers to harass our people and eat out their substance.

He has kept among us, in time of peace, standing armies, without the consent of our legislatures.

He has affected to render the military independent of, and superior to, the civil power.

He has combined with others to subject us to a jurisdiction foreign to our Constitution and unacknowledged by our laws, giving his assent to their acts of pretended legislation

For quartering large bodies of armed troops among us;

For protecting them by a mock trial from punishment for any murders which they should commit on the inhabitants of these States;

For cutting off our trade with all parts of the world;

For depriving us, in many cases, of the benefit of trial by jury;

For transporting us beyond seas to be tried for pretended offences;

For abolishing the free system of English laws in a neighboring province, establishing therein an arbitrary government, and enlarging its boundaries, so as to render it at once an example and fit instrument for introducing the same absolute rule into these colonies;

For taking away our charters, abolishing our most valuable laws, and altering, fundamentally, the powers of our governments;

For suspending our own legislatures and declaring themselves invested with power to legislate for us in all cases whatsoever.

He has abdicated government here by declaring us out of his protection and waging war against us.

He has plundered our seas, ravaged our coasts, burnt our towns, and destroyed the lives of our people.

He is, at this time, transporting large armies of foreign mercenaries to complete the works of death, desolation, and tyranny already begun with circumstances of cruelty and perfidy scarcely paralleled in the most barbarous ages, and totally unworthy, the head of a civilized nation.

He has constrained our fellow citizens, taken captive on the high seas, to bear arms against their country, to become the executioners of their friends and brethren, or to fall themselves by their hands.

He has excited domestic insurrections amongst us and has endeavored to bring on the inhabitants of our frontiers, the merciless Indian savages, whose known rule of warfare is an undistinguished destruction of all ages, sexes, and conditions.

In every stage of these oppressions, we have petitioned for redress in the most humble terms; our repeated petitions have been answered only by repeated injury. A prince whose character is thus marked by every act which may define a tyrant is unfit to be the ruler of a free people.

Nor have we been wanting in attention to our British brethren. We have warned them, from time to time, of attempts made by their legislature to extend an unwarrantable jurisdiction over us. We have reminded them of the circumstances of our emigration and settlement here. We have appealed to their native justice and magnanimity, and we have conjured them, by the ties of our common kindred, to disavow these usurpations, which would inevitably interrupt our connections and correspondence. They, too, have been deaf to the voice of justice and consanguinity. We must, therefore, acquiesce in the necessity which denounces our separation and hold them, as we hold the rest of mankind, enemies in war, in peace, friends.

We, therefore, the representatives of the United States of America, in general Congress assembled, appealing to the Supreme Judge of the world for the rectitude of our intentions, do, in the name and by the authority of the good people of our colonies, solemnly publish and declare, that these united colonies are, and of right ought to be, free and independent states: that they are absolved from all allegiance to the British Crown, and that all political connection between them and the state of Great Britain is, and ought be to, totally dissolved; and that, as free and independent states, they have full power to levy war, conclude peace, contract alliances, establish commerce, and to do all other acts and things which independent states may of right do. And, for the support of this declaration, with a firm reliance on the protection of Divine Providence, we mutually pledge to each other our lives, our fortunes, and our sacred honor.

APPENDIX D   The Bill of Rights

The first ten amendments, known as the Bill of Rights, were added to the Constitution in 1791. They originally applied only to actions of the federal government. However, by virtue of the due process clause of the Fourteenth Amendment, the Supreme Court has extended many of the rights to protect individuals against action by the states.

Amendment 1   Freedoms of Religion, Speech, Press, Assembly, and Petition

Congress shall make no law respecting an establishment of religion, or prohibiting the free exercise thereof; or abridging the freedom of speech, or of the press; or the right of the people peaceably to assemble, and to petition the government for a redress of grievances.

Amendment 2   Right to Bear Arms

A well-regulated militia, being necessary to the security of a free state, the right of the people to keep and bear arms shall not be infringed.

Amendment 3   Lodging Troops in Private Homes

No soldier shall, in time of peace, be quartered in any house, without the consent of the owner; nor in time of war, but in a manner to be prescribed by law.

Amendment 4   Search and Seizure

The right of the people to be secure in their persons, houses, papers, and effects, against unreasonable searches and seizures, shall not be violated; and no warrants shall be issued but upon probable cause, supported by oath or affirmation, and particularly describing the place to be searched, and the persons or things to be seized.

Amendment 5   Rights of the Accused

No person shall be held to answer for a capital, or otherwise infamous, crime, unless on a presentment or indictment of a grand jury, except in cases arising in the land or naval forces, or in the militia, when in actual service in time of war or public danger; nor shall any person be subject for the same offense to be twice put in jeopardy of life and limb; nor shall be compelled, in any criminal case, to be a witness against himself; nor be deprived of law, liberty, or property, without due process of law: nor shall private property be taken for public use, without just compensation.

Amendment 6   Right to Speedy Trial by Jury

In all criminal prosecutions, the accused shall enjoy the right to a speedy and public trial, by an impartial jury of the state and district wherein the crime shall have been committed, which district shall have been previously ascertained by law, and to be informed of the nature and cause of the accusation; to be confronted with the witnesses against him; to have compulsory process for obtaining witnesses in his favor, and to have the assistance of counsel for his defense.

Amendment 7   Jury Trial in Civil Cases

In suits at common law, where the value in controversy shall exceed $20, the right of trial by jury shall be preserved, and no fact tried by a jury shall be otherwise re-examined in any court of the United States than according to the rules of the common law.

Amendment 8   Bail and Punishment

Excessive bail shall not be required, nor excessive fines imposed, nor cruel and unusual punishments inflicted.

Amendment 9   Powers Reserved to the People

The enumeration in the Constitution, of certain rights, shall not be construed to deny or disparage others retained by the people.

Amendment 10   Powers Reserved to the State

The powers, not delegated to the United States by the constitution, nor prohibited by it to the states, are reserved to the states respectively, or to the people.

Suggested Readings

This book contains excerpts from a wide variety of primary and secondary sources. The original texts of these resources provide an excellent starting point for detailed research. Listed below is a series of additional books to aid you in your further studies.

General Resources: The North Americans

1. Canada in a North American Perspective

Axline, W.A., et al. *Continental Community?: Independence and Integration in North America*. Toronto: McClelland and Stewart, 1974.

Bennett, Paul W., et al. *Emerging Identities: Selected Problems and Interpretations in Canadian History*. Toronto: Prentice-Hall, 1986.

Christopher, James R., and Bryan C. Vickers. *The American Challenge*. Toronto: Oxford University Press, 1987.

Clarkson, Stephen. *Canada and the Reagan Challenge: Crisis in the Canadian-American Relationship*. Toronto: James Lorimer and Company, 1982.

Finlay, J.L. *Canada in the North Atlantic Triangle*. Toronto: Oxford University Press, 1975.

Gwyn, Richard. *The Forty-Ninth Paradox*. Toronto: Prentice-Hall 1985.

Malcolm, Andrew. *The Canadians*. Toronto: Paperjacks Ltd., 1987.

Martin, Lawrence. *The Presidents and the Prime Ministers. Washington and Ottawa Face to Face: The Myth of Bilateral Bliss 1867–1982*. Toronto: Doubleday, 1982.

2. North America Before the Europeans

Dickason, Olive P. *The Myth of the Savage*. Edmonton: University of Alberta Press, 1984.

Hunt, George T. *The Wars of the Iroquois: A Study in Inter-Tribal Trade Relations*. Madison: University of Wisconsin Press, 1970.

Jaenen, Cornelius J. *Friend and Foe*. Toronto: McClelland and Stewart, 1976.

Trigger, Bruce G. *Natives and Newcomers: Canada's 'Heroic Age' Reconsidered*. Kings-

ton and Montreal: McGill-Queen's University Press, 1985.

——. *The Children of Aataentsic: A History of the Huron People to 1660*. Kingston and Montreal: McGill-Queen's University Press, 1976.

Vaughan, Alden T. *New England Frontier: Puritans and Indians, 1620–1675*. Boston: Little, Brown and Co., 1965.

Washburn, W.E. *The Indian and the White Man*. Garden City, New York: Anchor Books, 1964.

3. The Perfectible Society

Eccles, W.J. *France in America*. Toronto: Fitzhenry and Whiteside, 1972.

Jaenen, Cornelius J. *The Role of the Church in New France*. Toronto: McGraw-Hill Ryerson, 1976.

Lackford, J., and D. Reimers. *Essays on American Social History*. New York: Holt, Rinehart and Winston, 1970.

Miller, Perry. *Errand into the Wilderness*. New York: Harper and Row, 1956.

——. *The New England Mind: The Seventeenth Century*. 1939. Reprint. Boston: Beacon Press, 1961.

Miquelon, Dale. *New France 1701–1744: A Supplement to Europe*. Toronto: McClelland and Stewart, 1987.

Zoltvany, Yves F. *The Government of New France: Royal, Clerical or Class Rule?* Scarborough: Prentice-Hall, 1971.

4. Revolution and Legitimacy

Brebner, J.B. *The Neutral Yankees of Nova Scotia: A Marginal Colony during the Revolutionary Years*. Toronto: McClelland and Stewart, 1969.

Fairfield, Roy P., ed. *The Federalist Papers*. New York: Anchor Books, 1961.

Hofstadter, Richard. *American Political Tradition.* New York: Vintage Books, 1948.

McDonald, Forrest. *The Formation of the American Republic.* Baltimore: Penguin Books, 1965.

Neatby, Hilda. *Québec: the Revolutionary Age 1760–91.* Toronto: McClelland and Stewart, 1966.

Norton, Mary Beth. *The British-Americans: The Loyalist Exiles in England 1774–1789.* Boston and Toronto: Little, Brown, and Co., 1972.

Rawlyk, G.A., ed. *Revolution Rejected 1775–1776.* Scarborough: Prentice-Hall, 1968.

Tuchman, Barbara. *The March of Folly.* New York: Alfred Knopf, 1984.

5. Settlement and the Frontier

Craig, G.M. *Upper Canada: The Formative Years.* Toronto: McClelland and Stewart, 1963.

Cross, Michael S., ed. *The Frontier Thesis and the Canadas: The Debate on the Impact of the Canadian Environment.* Toronto: Copp-Clark, 1970.

Jahoda, Gloria. *The Trail of Tears.* New York: Holt, Rinehart and Winston, 1970.

Ouellet, Fernand. *Lower Canada 1792–1841.* Toronto: McClelland and Stewart, 1980.

Taylor, G.R. *The Turner Thesis.* Boston: D.C. Heath and Co., 1956.

6. Identity and Nationhood

Bergeron, Leandre. *The History of Québec: A Patriot's Handbook.* Toronto: NC Press Ltd., 1971.

Berton, Pierre. *The Invasion of Canada 1812–13.* Toronto: McClelland and Stewart, 1980.

Brant, Irving. *James Madison and American Nationalism.* Toronto: Van Nostrand, 1968.

Dangerfield, George. *The Awakening of American Nationalism.* New York: Harper and Row, 1965.

Merk, Frederick. *Manifest Destiny and Mission in American History.* New York: Vintage Books, 1966.

Russell, Peter, ed. *Nationalism in Canada.* Toronto: McGraw-Hill, 1966.

Van Alstyne, Richard. *The Rising American Empire.* New York: W.W. Norton and Co., 1974.

Zaslow, Morris, ed. *The Defended Border: Upper Canada and the War of 1812.* Toronto: Macmillan, 1964.

7. Democracy and Party

Dunham, Aileen. *Political Unrest in Upper Canada 1815–1836.* Toronto: McClelland and Stewart, 1963.

Manning, Helen Taft. *The Revolt of French Canada 1800–1835.* Toronto: Macmillan, 1962.

Read, C., and R.J. Stagg. *The Rebellion of 1837 in Upper Canada.* Toronto: Champlain Society and Carleton Library, 1985.

Rozwenc, Edwin, ed. *The Meaning of Jacksonian Democracy.* Boston: D.C. Heath and Co., 1963.

Ryerson, Stanley. *Unequal Union: Confederation and the Roots of Conflict in the Canadas.* Toronto: Progress Books, 1968.

Schlesinger, Arthur Jr. *The Age of Jackson.* New York: Mentor Books, 1945.

Tocqueville, Alexis de. *Democracy in America.* New York: Vintage Books, 1945.

8. Federalism and Confederation

Bercuson, David J., ed. *Canada and the Burden of Unity.* Toronto: Macmillan, 1977.

Fairfield, Roy, ed. *The Federalist Papers.* New York: Anchor Books, 1961.

Rozwenc, E., and F. Bauer. *Liberty and Power in the Making of the Constitution.* Boston: D.C. Heath and Co., 1963.

Waite, P.B. *The Life and Times of Confederation.* Toronto: University of Toronto, 1962.

Whitelaw, W.M. *The Maritimes and Canada before Confederation.* Toronto: Oxford University Press, 1966.

9. Response to Industrialism

Babcock, Robert. *Gompers in Canada: A Study of American Continentalism Before the First World War.* Toronto: University of Toronto Press, 1975.

Bliss, Michael. *A Living Profit: Studies in the History of Canadian Business 1883–1911.* Toronto: McClelland and Stewart, 1974.

Cross, M.S., ed. *The Working Man in the*

Nineteenth Century. Toronto: Oxford University Press, 1974.

Hofstadter, R. *The Progressive Movement*. Englewood Cliffs, New Jersey: Prentice-Hall, 1963.

Landes, David S. *The Unbound Prometheus*. Cambridge: Cambridge University Press, 1970.

Langdon, Stephen. *The Emergence of the Canadian Working Class Movement, 1845–1875*. Toronto: New Hogtown Press, 1975.

Litwack, Leon. *The American Labour Movement*. Englewood Cliffs, N.J.: Prentice-Hall, 1962.

10. Immigration and Nativism

Berton, Pierre. *The Promised Land*. Toronto: McClelland and Stewart, 1984.

McDonald, Forest, et al. *The Last Best Hope*. Reading, Massachusetts: Addison-Wesley, 1972.

Owram, Doug. *Promise of Eden: Canadian Expansion Movement and the Idea of the West 1896–1900*. Toronto: University of Toronto Press, 1980.

Potrebenko, Helen. *No Streets of Gold*. Vancouver: New Star Books, 1977.

Scott, Franklin. *The People of America: Perspectives on Immigration*. Washington: American Historical Association, 1984.

Sung, B.L. *Mountain of Gold*. New York: Macmillan, 1967.

Woodsworth, J.S. *Strangers within our Gates*. Reprint. Toronto: University of Toronto Press, 1972.

11. Imperialism and Isolation

Berger, Carl. *The Sense of Power: Studies and Ideas in Canadian Imperialism 1867–1914*. Toronto: University of Toronto Press, 1970.

Lafeber, W. *The New Empire*. Ithaca: Cornell University Press, 1963.

Plesur, Milton, ed. *Creating an American Empire*. New York: Jerome S. Ozer. 1971.

Robeson, Virginia, ed. *Debates about Canada's Future 1868–1896*. Toronto: OISE Press, 1977.

Stone, Ralph, ed. *Wilson and the League of Nations*. New York: Holt, Rinehart and Winston, 1967.

Warner, D.F. *The Idea of Continental Union*. Lexington: University of Kentucky Press, 1960.

12. The Urban Experience

Mohl, Raymond. *The New City: Urban America in the Industrial Age*. Arlington Heights, Illinois: Harlan Davidson, 1985.

Russell, V.L. *Forging a Consensus: Historical Essays on Toronto*. Toronto: University of Toronto Press, 1984.

Rutherford, P., ed. *Saving the Canadian City: The First Phase 1880–1920*. Toronto: University of Toronto Press, 1974.

————. "Tomorrow's Metropolis: The Urban Reform Movement in Canada." In *The Canadian City: Essays in Urban and Social History*. Ottawa: Carleton University Press, 1984.

Thernstrom P., and R. Sennett, eds. *Nineteenth-Century Cities: Essays in the New Urban History*. New Haven: Yale University Press, 1969.

13. A New Deal and a New Social Order

Bliss, J.M., and L.M. Grayson, eds., *The Wretched of Canada: Letters to R.B. Bennett*. Toronto: University of Toronto Press, 1971.

Horn, Michael, ed., *The Dirty Thirties: Canadians in the Great Depression*. Toronto: Copp Clark, 1972.

Irving, John. *The Social Credit Movement in Alberta*. Toronto: University of Toronto Press, 1959.

Morton, D., and T. Copp. *Working People*. Ottawa: Deneau Publishers & Co. Ltd., 1981.

Rozwenc, E., ed. *The New Deal: Revolution or Evolution?* Boston: D.C. Heath and Co., 1959.

Terkel, Studs. *Hard Times*. New York: Random House, 1986.

Young, Walter. *Democracy and Discontent*. Toronto: McGraw-Hill, 1978.

14. Foreign Policy in the Era of the Cold War

Bercuson, David J. *Canada and the Birth of Israel*. Toronto: University of Toronto Press, 1985.

Clark. J. *Competitiveness and Security: Directions for Canada's International Relations.* Ottawa: Ministry of Supply and Services, 1985.

Clarkson, Stephen. *Canada and the Reagan Challenge.* Toronto: James Lorimer and Company, 1985.

Eayrs, James. *In Defence of Canada: Growing Up Allied.* Toronto: University of Toronto Press, 1980.

Kolko, G. *Main Currents in Modern American History.* New York: Pantheon Books, 1984.

————. *The Limits of Power: The World and United States Foreign Policy 1945–54.* New York: Harper and Row, 1968.

Matusow, Allen J. *Joseph R. McCarthy.* Englewood Cliffs, N.J.: Prentice Hall, 1970.

Minifie, James M. *Peacemaker or Powermaker?* Toronto: McClelland and Stewart, 1960.

Oye, Kenneth A., and Robert J. Lieber. *Eagle Defiant: U.S. Foreign Policy in the 1980s.* Boston: Little, Brown and Co., 1983.

Payne, Anthony and Paul K. Sutton, eds. *Grenada: Revolution and Invasion.* New York: St. Martin's Press, 1984.

15. Affluence and the Consumer Society

Bothwell, R., I. Drummond, and J. English. *Canada Since 1945: Power, Politics, and Provincialism.* Toronto: University of Toronto Press, 1981.

Corwin, Norman. *Trivializing America.* Secaucus, N.J.: Lyle Stuart Inc., 1986.

Hart, J. *When the Going Was Good: American Life in the Fifties.* New York: Crown Publishers Inc., 1982.

Matusow, A.J. *The Unraveling of America: A History of Liberalism in the 1960s.* New York: Harper and Row, 1984.

McLuhan, Marshall. *Understanding Media.* New York: McGraw-Hill, 1964.

Neatby, Hilda. *So Little for the Mind: An Indictment of Canadian Education.* Toronto: Clark, Irwin and Co., 1953.

Sayers, Sohnya. *The Sixties without Apology.* Minneapolis: University of Minnesota Press, 1984.

Toffler, Alvin. *The Third Wave.* New York: William Morrow and Co., 1980.

16. The Women's Movement

Bacchi, Carol Lee. *Liberation Deferred? The Ideas of English Canadian Suffragists 1877–1918.* Toronto: University of Toronto Press, 1983.

Cook, Ramsay, and Wendy Michinson, eds. *The Proper Sphere: Women's Place in Canadian Society.* Toronto: Oxford University Press, 1976

Friedan, Betty. *The Feminine Mystique.* New York: W.W. Norton and Co., 1963.

Landsberg, Michele. *Women and Children First.* Toronto: Macmillan of Canada, 1982.

Sayers, Sohnya, ed. *The Sixties without Apology.* Minneapolis: University of Minnesota Press, 1984.

17. Culture, Integration, and Identity

Foner, P.S. *The Voice of Black America.* New York: Simon and Schuster, 1972.

Fraser, Graham. *The PQ: René Lévesque and the Parti Québécois in Power.* Toronto: Macmillan, 1984.

King, Martin Luther. *Why We Can't Wait.* New York: Signet Books, 1964.

Trofimenkoff, Susan Mann. *The Dream of a Nation: A Social and Intellectual History of Québec.* Toronto: Macmillan, 1982.

Vallières, Pierre. *White Niggers of America.* Translated by Joan Pinkham. Toronto: McClelland and Stewart, 1971.

Viorst, Milton. *Fire in the Streets: America in the 1960s.* New York: Simon and Schuster, 1979.

Wills, Gary, *Reagan's America.* New York: Penguin Books, 1988.

Credits

Documents
The publisher wishes to thank the following publishers for granting permission to reproduce excerpts from their publications as indicated with each document. The publisher regrets any omissions or errors and will be pleased to make suitable acknowledgements in future editions.

A. Coté et Cie.; Alfred A. Knopf, Inc.; American Historical Association; American Historical Documents; Anchor Press; Appleton-Century-Crofts; Avon Books; A.C. McClurg & Co.; Bantam Books Canada Inc.; Canadian Consultative Council on Multiculturalism; Canadian Political Science Association; Carleton University Press and Carleton University Libraries; Charles Scribner's Sons; Clarkson N. Potter Inc.; Clark, Irwin and Co.; Columbia University Press; Copp Clark Pitman Ltd.; Crest Books; CBC Enterprises; D. Appleton and Company; Delta Books; Dixon Ryan Fox; The Dorsey Press; Doubleday & Co. Inc.; D.C. Heath Canada Ltd.; Editions du Jour; Fitzhenry and Whiteside Ltd.; Grossman Publishers; G.P. Putnam's Sons; Harlan Davidson Inc.; Holt, Rinehart & Winston, Inc.; Houghton Mifflin Company; Institution for Contemporary Studies (San Francisco); International Publishers Co. Inc.; Irwin Dorsey Ltd.; Jackson Press; James Lewis and Samuel; James Lorimer & Company Ltd., Publishers; John Polhemus; Jonathan Elliott; Jonathan Cape Ltd.; J. Munsell; J.M. Dent & Sons; J.P. Tacher; Les Presses de l'Université Laval; Life, Stuart, Inc.; Longmans Canada Limited; Macmillan of Canada; Manitoba Free Press; Marian O. Fox, Russell & Russell Pub.; McClelland and Stewart Limited; McGraw-Hill Ryerson Ltd.; Methuen, Inc.; Ministry of Education, Ontario; Ministry of Supply and Services Canada; M. St. Clair Clarke and Peter Force; Hurtig Publishers Ltd.; Nation Associates Inc.; National Archives of Canada; National Council of Women of Canada; The New England Quarterly; New Star Books Ltd. Publishers; Northeastern University; N.S. Hardy; Oberon Press; Oxford University Press; O.I.S.E. Press; Pantheon Books Inc.; PaperJacks Ltd.; Penguin Books, Inc.; Pocket Books, Division of Simon & Schuster, Inc.; Porter and Coates; Prentice-Hall Canada Inc.; Princeton University Press; Progress Books; Putnam Publishing Group; Quadrangle Books; Random House, Inc.; Regents Press of Kansas; Richard Bently; Rowsell and Hutchinson; S. Converse; Saunders and Otley; Scott, Foresman & Co.; Signet Books; Simon and Schuster, Inc.; Smithsonian Institution, Office of American; Time-Life Books Inc.; University Press of Kentucky; University of Minnesota Press; University of Toronto Press; U.S. Government Printing Office; Van Nostrand Reinhold Company, Inc.; Vintage Books; Washington Square Press; William Morrow and Company; W.W. Norton and Company, Inc.; Yale University Press; York University Press.

Photographs
Key to abbreviations: NAC National Archives of Canada. 4 (left) Canapress; (top right, bottom right) Reprinted with permission – Toronto Star Syndicate; 32 (top) National Library of Canada Rare Book Division (NL-6643); (bottom) NAC/NMC (NMC-15661); 61 (top left, top right) The Bettmann Archive Inc.; (bottom) Old Fort Niagara; 84 (top) The Bettmann Archive, Inc.; (bottom) Alan Daniels ©

1978, The Reader's Digest Association, *Heritage of Canada*; 127 (top) NAC (C-44633); (bottom) The Bettmann Archive, Inc.; 158 (top) Library of Congress; (bottom left) NAC (C-276); (bottom right) ROM/C-955.217.15; 196 (top) NAC (C-3283); (bottom left) Canada Post; (bottom middle) The Bettmann Archive, Inc.; (bottom right) NAC (C-24937), 230 (top) Library of Congress; (bottom) Confederation Life; 265 CP Corporate Archives; 265 NAC (C-95470); 315 Provincial Archives of Alberta; 318 Information Canada; 339 Thomas Nast cartoons, reprinted by courtesy of the Harper's Magazine Foundation; 354 (top) Public Archives of Nova Scotia; (middle) Canadian War Museum, National Museums of Canada (J20642-2); (bottom) Library of Congress; 393 (top) The Bettmann Archive, Inc.; (bottom left, bottom right) Archives of the Montreal Urban Community Transit Commission; 431 (top) Winnipeg Free Press; (bottom) Library of Congress; 470 (top) Dept. of National Defence (bottom right) Canapress; (bottom left) Bettmann Newsphotos; 525 (top left, bottom) International Spectrafilm; (top right) West Edmonton Mall; 571 (top left) NAC (PA-120141); (top right, bottom left) Bettmann Newsphotos; (bottom right) Governor General's Residence.

Index